PRAISE FOR *WHAT ARE YOU DOING ABOUT IT?*

"What can I say about David Gill? (1) Have you ever been hit on the side of the head with a hard object? (2) Caught in a sudden unexpected windstorm? (3) Have you ever gotten run over by a medium-sized van? Well . . . that's what it's like getting to know David. I got to know David over six years . . . as a faculty colleague at Gordon-Conwell . . . working together in the Ockenga Institute when he was Director of the Mockler Center . . . as a fellow traveler to the other side of the world (China) . . . and most importantly as a dear and trusted friend.

I have never met anyone quite like David. So much unbridled energy . . . so much creativity . . . so eclectic! David is one of those rare people in this world with the capacity to actually start things—a true entrepreneur—but also a finisher as well. David doesn't just talk a good game, he has an unbelievable ability to follow through and manage many of his great ideas. A conversation with David begins with five ideas that he wants to try . . . some commentary on jazz and Ellul and on his wife and kids . . . some wine talk . . . and the Decalogue . . . and Donald Trump . . . and his work-out routines, not necessarily in that order. My head hurts when I talk with David . . . but my heart is filled with great admiration and gratitude for the great gift he has been to our school and to us all personally."

—DAVID HORN, former Director, Ockenga Institute, Gordon-Conwell Theological Seminary

"Few people have touched more institutions, affected more people, and simply lived more faithfully during the last fifty years of evangelical history in this country than David Gill. With long teaching stints on both right coast (Gordon-Conwell in Massachusetts), middle America (North Park University in Chicago), and left coast (St. Mary's College and his beloved New College Berkeley), no one's story intersects with more churches and parachurch organizations than Gill's. This memoir takes the reader into the inner workings of the institutions in each of which Gill has had an important role, sometimes as a founder, always as a leader. Gill humbly but directly details, analyzes, and confesses both the good and the bad of what it has meant to be a part of the educational world of one of the most interesting and diverse religious movements of the last century—the evangelical Christian church in America. A great read in every way."

—ANDREW H. TROTTER JR., senior scholar, Consortium of Christian Study Centers

"Dr. Gill was my professor and mentor at Gordon-Conwell Theological Seminary, now my dearest godfather and friend. If anybody tells me that Christians are passive, I will recommend they read this memoir. For ordinary Christians living in an ever more challenging world, Dr. Gill's life story is an inspirational resource, rich, relatable, and relevant. Changes never just happen, they start with someone somewhere, who is inspired to 'do something about it.'"

—RUQIONG TANG WALTER, former student assistant to David W. Gill

"This story of a family and a life, of a man's spiritual and intellectual commitments, helps me understand why Americans believe they live in a land of opportunities, a world where it seems that almost everybody is capable of starting again. But this is probably a misleading generalization because David Gill was endowed with an exceptional vitality and an exceptional gift for relating to other people. We (with our wives and children) have been dear friends and colleagues since we first met in Bordeaux in 1984."

—DANIEL CEREZUELLE, philosopher of technology

"One of the first things I learned about David Gill was his love for jazz—and jazz describes David to a 'T'. He has perfected his instrument, knows the notes—but has picked a variation of his own that rides beautifully on the melody of God's great song. I first knew David as a teacher when I enrolled as the world's oldest doctoral student. He was a surprise to me from the beginning. When I arrived at Logan airport for our first cohort, there was David to pick me up and ferry me to campus, twenty miles away. That servant-hearted attention to the mundane needs of his students was unprecedented in my experience. His advocacy for his students went deeper than I was aware until reading these pages. Like jazz, David is also a bit edgy, willing to let his thinking wander from the notes he might be expected to play. While agreeing theologically, I have often been surprised by our differing views on social issues that have divided our country—but never divided us. David wouldn't let that happen, and knowing him as I do, neither would I—scratch my head as a conservative Texan, yes, but never divide. The fact is I need people like David to make me think off the page of my limited perspective. To me, there's nothing marginal about David's life and commitment to Jesus, as you'll discover in these pages. He's been 'all in' in every experience I've had with him. But maybe that's the most surprising thing about David Gill—the humility of a person who has done so much—and is still doing—about what's important."

—BILL PEEL, founder, 24Seven Project

"In reading this memoir, those who already know David Gill will revisit with pleasure his generosity, warmth, and enthusiasm. Others will want to make his acquaintance. David is not just an activist, a Christian, a professor, an intellectual, an ethicist, a theologian and a specialist in the thought of Jacques Ellul, he is also the living incarnation of that most beautiful thing: friendship."

—PATRICK CHASTENET, University of Bordeaux

"David Gill did wonders and touched so many lives at Saint Mary's as MBA Faculty/Alumni liaison when we worked side-by-side from 2008 to 2010. One of his most powerful assets is his natural role as a community builder. He cares about every person he meets and he takes the time to learn about you—and he always makes a point to make you feel connected somehow, some way. He wears his heart on his sleeve—and consistently puts himself out there in a fearless way and the payoff is always huge. People who normally don't open up, open up to him. People who we normally wouldn't know are introduced to us through David. He turned himself into a hub—a central point of connection; a nucleus. His memoir tells the story."

—JACKIE YANG WILLIAMS, former director of marketing & alumni outreach, St. Mary's College Graduate School of Business

"As long as I can remember, the name of David Gill has always been attached to that of my grandfather Jacques Ellul. He has carried out a major effort to support an interdisciplinary reflection on all the fields of study opened up by Jacques Ellul. He succeeded in bringing together the necessary forces to work on translating and promoting the works of Ellul and to continue his intellectual tradition of dialectical reflection. He has carried this into the marketplace with his work on ethics and values in a society polarized by technology, efficiency, productivity, and consummation. He has understood the intellectual and rhetorical strategy of Ellul when many French thinkers failed to grasp even half of it. David Gill is not only a great professor but a true humanist philosopher, nourishing hope in a grand, united, intellectual family that crosses national borders. He has carried the triple message of freedom, faith, and hope into a society deeply distorted by excess and gigantism. His taste for the Grand Crus and the cuisine of Bordeaux is in the image of his mentor as they both sought the Beautiful, the Good, and the True! David Gill incarnates an authentic 'presence in the modern world' as my grandfather's 1948 book described it. In reading this memoir, one discovers not only a spiritual conversion but a lifelong pilgrimage consisting of adventure, travel, and above all the encounter of friends."

—JEROME ELLUL, filmmaker and Jacques Ellul archivist

"I met David when I was a student at Fuller Seminary. He was teaching a class on Ellul, of course. David was always an encourager for me. He encouraged me to go on with my studies, he encouraged me in my writing, and later, in my teaching. David didn't just encourage me, though, he also created opportunities for me to write and to teach. It was first a book review, then an article. He gave me my first teaching opportunity at New College, Berkeley. He gave me an opportunity to give my first paper at a conference. Most recently he wrote a foreword to a book I wrote. That's what friends do in David's world."

—ANTHONY J. PETROTTA, author of *God at the Improv: Humor and the Holy in Scripture*

"David Gill's memoir is a joy to read and to recall his impact on North Park University. David is a man of many gifts, a deep and vibrant faith in Christ, diverse interests, a keen sense of humor, and is kind, intelligent, and a listener. Despite the subtitle of this memoir, he is hardly marginal. Many have good ideas, but what sets David apart is he knows how to implement his ideas exceedingly well. Even more importantly, he wants the best ideas to flourish regardless of whose ideas they are, and was gracious in offering his suggestions to others who had a kernel of an idea but weren't sure where to go with it. At North Park, David developed new programs such as the faculty research group, gospel choir, and ethics-across-the-curriculum. Because of David, these programs thrived. David was a strong leader at North Park, but at the same time always had a tender-hearted and loving word of encouragement to anyone who needed it."

—SONIA BODI, North Park University

"The writer of Ecclesiastes recommends: 'Whatever your hand finds to do, do with all your might,' and David Gill's rich autobiography describes an impressive amount of doing! A welcome testament to a full life which is not 'full of itself.' By staying on the margins (which are often in the dead center of God's own presence and work in this world), Gill's life and work are marked by the hospitable space which they open up for others."

—JACOB MARQUES ROLLISON, author of *A New Reading of Jacques Ellul: Presence and Communication in the Postmodern World*

"I have known David Gill since I was writing a dissertation on the Bay Area Jesus Movement in the early 1970s. Marginal activist indeed! He never stopped engaging American Christianity and re-imagining evangelicalism. He managed a dissertation on Jacques Ellul, then a presidency of a newly created college amidst illustrious California higher education, then multiple positions in social ethics, including business ethics, all this while moving from coast to coast. He became a model and a challenge for the upward and ambitious thrust of imaginative young Christians who might have thought their calling ended at the beach, or introducing guitars to worship, or changing the venue of baptism to local lakes and streams. Let his record continue to light the way."

—DONALD HEINZ, California State University, Chico

"Pope Francis has argued the periphery will revitalize the center, and so what happens on the margins, the periphery, will be crucial for the future of the church and the world. David Gill's engaging, thoughtful, and challenging memoir indicates why seeing the world differently is already a way of beginning to change it. It shows what taking seriously our faith, our mind, and our vocation can mean as part of a desire to live faithfully in our neighborhoods, communities, states, and world."

—SCOTT M. THOMAS, University of Bath

"Here is an example of how a person from a community of narrowly defined Christians moves out and into the broader and pluralistic culture of American Christianity and then beyond that to the acquisition of an understanding and appreciation of a major French Christian intellectual and to the development of a practical philosophy of business and industry. David Gill gives the lie to the notion that evangelicals are narrow-minded ideologically free market fundamentalists and maybe racists to boot. It's people like Gill who keep me willing to be labeled an 'evangelical,' though like him I prefer 'traditional Christian,' meaning a person committed to Jesus Christ as Lord and Savior and an affirmer of the classic Christian creeds with a connection to a community of Christians whose denominational label is pretty close to unimportant."

—JIM SIRE, author of *Habits of the Mind: Intellectual Life as a Christian Calling*

"David Gill's memoir provides inspiration for anyone who is trying to live a better life. His honesty is compelling, and even though I've known David since we were ten years old, I learned many new things. David's friendship has been very important in my life. I know I can always count on him in times of need. He lends an ear, gives good advice, and in the process, makes me laugh. What more can you ask of a friend?"

—LIZ KELLAM LISMER, San Leandro classmate from fifth to twelfth grade

"A journey worth taking is what you will experience when you read David Gill's memoir. You can easily imagine being right there alongside him as he strings together the events and activities of his life. As a guest on my former Sunday Gospel Music Radio program, as my seminary ethics professor, as a guest preacher, and as the author of several books in my personal library, David is always a model of integrity and ethical excellence—personable, knowledgeable, clear, eloquent, and challenging. I am blessed to know him not just as a teacher and colleague but as a friend."

—REV. DR. SHEILA ROBINSON, associate pastor, Grace Tabernacle Community Church

"I first met David in the 1980s, drawn to his New College Berkeley office by the strong scent of pipe tobacco and Peet's coffee. Those smoke signals portended a long and durable friendship of brothers, spiritual, and intellectual. David's memoir showcases a restless but disciplined curiosity and an amazing range of projects: teaching, researching, caring for neighbors, churching, and marketplacing—with a robust moral imagination, friendship, and collegiality. As they say, this truly is a good read!"

—SCOTT D. YOUNG, president, Culture Connection

"I met David Gill as my St. Mary's College MBA and MS ethics professor. We have been friends ever since. David is not only an ethicist, activist, and professor, but also someone who devotes himself towards other people's success. He is a compassionate man with a golden heart and has been a strong supporter of Haiti On The Rise, a humanitarian organization I founded to help alleviate the sufferings of others. Knowledgeable, understanding, and supportive, deeply rooted in his Christian faith, David's memoir is a clear inspiration from a unique humanitarian."

—JACQUELINE ORISCAR LEE, found and executive director, Haiti On The Rise

"David Gill's passion for God and for life shows in his every undertaking, from entrepreneurship to teaching and writing, to business and workplace application. His *What Are You Doing about It?* memoir will inspire (and maybe also exhaust!) his readers. Enjoy the ride!"

—AL ERISMAN, Seattle Pacific University

"Dr. David Gill is a man whom I have revered as a mentor and colleague for many years. He was my ethics professor at Fuller Seminary at Gordon-Conwell. David's memoir refreshingly honest and engaging. Not only is it a delightful perusal of his life, but it served to elevate my respect for and appreciation of this distinguished 'marginal activist' all the more."

—REV. DR. GINA CASEY, acute care chaplain and AME Zion pastor

"My faculty colleague at USC, and chair of our admissions committee, walked into my office one day in the early 1970s with a sheet of paper in hand and said, 'Jack, check out this guy's Graduate Record Exam scores!' The 'guy's' name was David Gill, and he wanted admission to the School of Religion to work on a PhD in Social Ethics. We acted quickly and the rest, as they say, is history. David turned out to be a true star in the school. In classes, he absorbed complex material rapidly, made it his own, and thought of new applications, especially in the field of business. He eventually wrote a powerful PhD dissertation on Jacques Ellul's ethics under my direction. David came into our program with a dream of starting a new school of social and theological ethics pitched to working lay people. The curriculum was to be as sophisticated as that of any graduate university but designed to appeal to lay people in all walks of life. Thus was born New College Berkeley, whose story is detailed in two chapters of this memoir. David was its visionary founder, faculty recruiter and leader, curriculum writer, and all-around organizer of what became an extraordinarily successful enterprise. Hats off to you David, for your intellect, work ethic, and many contributions to the world of education. At a recent fortieth anniversary reunion David organized at USC for his cohort of 1979 PhDs, it was obvious that they love and respect him as much as I do."

—JACK CROSSLEY, University of Southern California

What Are You Doing About It?

OTHER BOOKS BY DAVID W. GILL

The Word of God in the Ethics of Jacques Ellul (1984)

Peter the Rock: Extraordinary Insights from an Ordinary Man (1986)

The Opening of the Christian Mind (1989)

Should God Get Tenure? Essays on Religion and Higher Education (editor, 1997)

Becoming Good: Building Moral Character (2000)

Doing Right: Practicing Ethical Principles (2004)

It's About Excellence: Building Ethically Healthy Organizations (2008)

Political Illusion & Reality: Engaging the Prophetic Insights of Jacques Ellul (co-editor, 2018)

Workplace Discipleship 101: A Primer (2020)

What Are You Doing About It?

The Memoir of a Marginal Activist

DAVID W. GILL

RESOURCE *Publications* • Eugene, Oregon

WHAT ARE YOU DOING ABOUT IT?
The Memoir of a Marginal Activist

Copyright © 2022 David W. Gill. All rights reserved. Except for brief quotations in critical publications or reviews, no part of this book may be reproduced in any manner without prior written permission from the publisher. Write: Permissions, Wipf and Stock Publishers, 199 W. 8th Ave., Suite 3, Eugene, OR 97401.

Resource Publications
An Imprint of Wipf and Stock Publishers
199 W. 8th Ave., Suite 3
Eugene, OR 97401

www.wipfandstock.com

PAPERBACK ISBN: 978-1-6667-5045-4
HARDCOVER ISBN: 978-1-6667-5046-1
EBOOK ISBN: 978-1-6667-5047-8

08/15/22

For J.C.

Contents

Preface	xv

PART ONE: INCUBATORS (1946–1964) — 1

1	Ground Hog Day Arrival: February 2, 1946	3
2	Tribal Roots: Gill & Hallgren	7
3	Tribal Roots: Wurz & Block	23
4	Parents: Walter Gill & Vivian Wurz	32
5	Three Sisters & Family Life	49
6	Boyhood (1951–61)	60
7	San Leandro High School (1961–64)	74

PART TWO: SHAPERS (1964–1979) — 87

8	Faith & Church	89
9	Lucia & Life Together	113
10	Fatherhood & Friendship	136
11	Cal Berkeley & SF State (1964–1971)	158
12	Christian World Liberation Front (1971–73)	178
13	Black Matters	192
14	Jacques Ellul & France (1971–)	213
15	USC Graduate School (1974–1979)	235

PART THREE: CHANNELS (1979–2016) — 249

16	New College Berkeley, Phase I (1976–85)	252
17	New College Berkeley, Phase II (1986–90)	277
18	Pastor, Preacher, Teacher	304
19	North Park & Chicago (1992–2001)	326

Contents

20	IBTE & EthixBiz Consulting (1998–2011)	347
21	St. Mary's & Adjunct Professor Life (2002–10)	372
22	Gordon-Conwell & New England (2010–16)	387
23	Postscript: Fourth Quarter (2016-)	411

Curriculum Vita	421
Acknowledgments	431
Bibliography	433

Preface

WHY DO PEOPLE WRITE their memoirs and autobiographies, their own stories? Why am I stopping my other writing projects to do this? Well, I turned 76 this year and I become more conscious of my mortality with each passing year. Old and dear friends of mine are passing on with increasing frequency. I feel their absence and treasure their memory. For me a memoir is justified for two basic reasons: First, I'm a writer and writing has always been a crucial means of clarifying my thinking, seeing my weaknesses alongside some strengths, and arriving at understanding and peace of mind. This is the time in my life to reflect on the big picture, on my lifelong pilgrimage and adventure. I love this statement in the Old Testament book of Deuteronomy (8:2–7) as the Israelite people neared the end of their forty-year pilgrimage from slavery in Egypt to the promised land:

> Remember the long way that the Lord your God has led you these forty years in the wilderness, in order to humble you, testing you to know what was in your heart, whether or not you would keep his commandments. He humbled you by letting you hunger, then by feeding you with manna . . . in order to make you understand that one does not live by bread alone, but by every word that comes from the mouth of the Lord. . . . Therefore keep the commandments of the Lord your God, by walking in his ways and by fearing him. For the Lord your God is bringing you into a good land.

This book is about my personal "remembering" the journey. Some wilderness, lots of good land.

Second, I'm writing not just for myself but for anybody else who may be interested in the issues, personalities, events, challenges, and opportunities I have faced over the years. I was raised in a small religious sect and emerged out of it as a passionate Christian—not an angry, reactionary atheist as some might have predicted. I lived, studied, and worked in the midst of tumultuous times at my alma mater Cal Berkeley, in my home town Oakland, and elsewhere. Since I am often asked to talk about these things, I am guessing others may find my writing about them helpful.

I thought about calling this memoir "Half Full"—in reference to the old saying about some people seeing things as "half empty" (and griping about what's missing) while others see the same circumstances as "half full" (grateful for what they have). I am a "half full" kind of guy, basically positive about life, finding the silver lining in most clouds that come my way. One of the keys to a satisfied life is the realization that "nobody gets it all." You can't have everything. There are inevitable trade-offs in life. When we choose one thing, it almost always means we will not get something else, maybe something we even longed for. And even when we choose something good, there are always some unexpected, unpredictable consequences. My mantra is "Do the best you can and be grateful for what you have." But as a title, "Half Full" would have put the focus more on my personal attitude than on the story itself, so that can't be the title.

For years I thought I would call this imagined book "A Marginal Life." I have had a little ten-page autobiographical text posted at my web site (www.davidwgill.org) with this title. That sounds self-deprecating to some ears but what I mean by "Marginal Life" is that I see my role, my calling—and whatever success or effectiveness I have experienced—as being on the edges, the margins. I have never been comfortable (or enjoyed being) in the center of any mainstream establishment or movement (political, cultural, economic, theological). That probably has a lot to do with my particular upbringing in a religious sect. But my "call to the margins" was also reinforced by my studies over the years, by the thinkers who influenced me. And it must be rooted in my personality as well.

It is true that at a couple points in my life (1988 above all) I reflected, initially with disappointment, on my failure to impact much the worlds of higher education and ethics that I had targeted. My books didn't sell all that much. My classes and public lectures weren't always packed. It got my attention whenever I was not invited to major conferences in areas of my expertise. But it was at precisely this point that I began to realize that it was my calling (and my gift), not to be great or famous at any one thing, not to be a major leader any particular place, but to be "pretty good" at lots of things and able to work effectively on the margins of all kinds of movements and communities. So my autobiography is largely a story of meaning and adventure on the margins. I have grown not just to accept but to love this location and this calling of mine. There are things we marginal types can do, places we can penetrate, projects we can undertake that no mainstream star could ever do. I think you will see this by the end of my story and I hope it will not just amuse you but encourage you. I like not fitting in, not being easily categorizable.

But in the end, this marginal life emphasis moved to the subtitle of my memoir. Talking about our respective and different stories a couple years ago (old men do that), I mentioned my "marginal life" idea to some friends. But I went on to talk about a lot of my projects and initiatives over the decades and said "I think this goes back to something my dad said to me whenever I was griping about anything: 'Well, what are you doing about it? We asked God for a son who would be a leader, not just a griper. Come on!'" My dad's question really challenged, provoked, and motivated me. In so many ways my life is an extended answer to that question: "What are you doing about it?" My habit, almost to a fault, is to look at something and wonder "what could be done to improve that?" I rarely look at any situation, any organization, any building, without seeing ways I think it could be better. As I gave example after example of seeing a problem or possibility and taking action, my buddies who know me well said "That's it! That's the title of your life memoir: 'What Are You Doing About It?'" Some of my favorite "slogans" align pretty closely with all of this: "Lead, follow, or get out of the way" (sounds a bit harsh but maybe you know the feeling). "You are either part of the solution or part of the problem." "It's better to light a candle than to curse the darkness." And I love St. Paul's advice to the Romans: "Do not be overcome by evil, but overcome evil with good." Another title possibility I considered was "Don't Just Stand There!"

This book is a collection of stories of my answers to my dad's challenge. I am embarrassed and apologize for writing so much in the first person. I prefer to write about "we" and "us" as you can easily see in my other nine books. But in the context of a memoir, I can't blame or speak for everyone else involved on my personal journey. So please forgive the frequent "I" language. And I certainly recognize that I owe immense debts in every direction—to God, to my parents and sisters, my friends, neighbors, and co-workers, to my teachers and the authors who have taught me so much, to my kids and grandkids, and, above all, to my companion since 1963, my wife and best friend Lucia. Whatever I have done, I had help.

I dedicate this to "J.C."—and you know who I mean. My whole marginal life and all those activist initiatives have, at bottom, been dedicated to him, to the God who I believe was made flesh in Jesus Christ. Others can put their faith in Marx, Darwin, Mohammed, Buddha, Steve Jobs or others ("let's have coffee and share our perspectives," is my reaction)—I choose Jesus. Despite my screw-ups, mediocrity, and failures, which I freely acknowledge and for which I am helplessly dependent on God's and peoples' gracious forgiveness, my life has been pretty wonderful. I have been so blessed. There have been painful struggles and losses. As I look back, however, my heart is filled with joy and gratitude.

There are dozens of my "What Are You Doing About It?" initiatives and projects I describe in this memoir. I just never could sit still for long if I saw a problem or opportunity. Some were little, some were big. Some endured, more faded away, some never got off the ground because of opposition, lack of interest, or inadequate funding. With all this project talk, I still agree with those who remind us that we are "human beings" not "human doings"! But it is a dialectic (yin/yang), not an either/or. This memoir focuses on what I did, more than what I am—but as somebody once said "by their fruits you shall know them." "Faith without works is dead," ok? Though an extreme extravert and activist, I do need, want, and love quiet time and space. I just don't stay there too long. I love my rest but the action side is my topic in this memoir.

This is my own personal recollection and interpretation. The written records and peoples' memories are not always consistent or complete. For some people and events there is a minimal record, for others a lot more—so if some get more attention than others, this is usually the reason. I don't provide a complete "family tree" because some of my relatives have not played a big role in the personal history I describe. Please don't be offended if you were left out. I have never kept a diary or journal but I do have my "week-at-a-glance" calendar books from 1973 forward—and that helps me remember or reconstruct my past, especially the timelines. I have been a very busy letter writer over my whole life and often kept copies of letters I sent as well as received. Unfortunately, I don't have many e-mail exchanges printed out since that medium replaced letter writing in the late 1990s. I have been a record-keeper of my speaking gigs, courses taught, articles, book reviews and other publications—with or without my name attached. But there are times that I got overwhelmed by how much of this there was—not to mention all my unsigned written work (mission statements, bylaws, codes of ethics, promotional statements, etc.) which was sometimes just as important and helpful as the signed stuff—I just couldn't or didn't want to keep up. I am not a famous guy but there are a few books out there that talk (usually very briefly) about my work and I will cite those when they relate to something in this book. In any case, whatever the long-term value, I have been a very busy guy all my life.

I am trying to focus on *who or what influenced me* and how. I have tried to be honest about myself and fair to all I refer to in my story (and I am doing my best to avoid naming those I criticize). I hope nobody is unfairly hurt but I can't pretend everything was smooth and flawless. I am not trying to get back at anyone but part of my story (and yours) is how we deal with betrayal, attack, and disappointment so I have to tell that part of the story too. I also am aware that most people are not writers and won't be able to counter my account with their own, so I try to be as gentle as I can. I am aiming for honesty but don't plan to do a complete personal strip tease in front of you—or bring a "guns blazing" case against anyone else. But never forget that this is just one man's personal account. It is my story of my life.

For those of you unaccustomed to the constant and intense religious/spiritual language and emphases in my story, please bear with me. Especially after I turned eighteen and went off to Cal Berkeley, what you will see is my radical, passionate Christian faith as it is lived out in a diverse, often crazy, world—not just in the church or some group of religious insiders!.

Inevitably there are many, many threads weaving through this story. I could never have plotted out a wild journey like this. Makes you believe there is a God! It is basically chronological but I follow some themes forward and then circle back to pick up others when I think that adds clarity. So I don't just describe every aspect of my life in 1964 and then the same for 1965, for example. It's complicated.

I have divided the story into three parts. First, I look at "incubators" of my youth (roughly 1946–1964). Second, I look in more depth at the major "shapers" of my life—influences that I chose and that shaped my sense of calling in life (roughly 1964–1979). Third, I then walk through the several "channels" through which my

PREFACE

calling was expressed over four or five decades (roughly 1979 to the present). I fully expect that some readers will want or need to skip over some parts of my story that are not of interest to them. No problem. Let's get started now.

Easter 2022

PART ONE
Incubators (1946–1964)

From my birth in 1946 to high school graduation in 1964 I certainly made daily decisions about my life and activities. I can't really blame anyone else for what happened. But these choices were always within a framework that I did not choose—a family, a religion, a school system, and a cultural/political context and orientation. So I think of these first eighteen years as my "incubation." My incubation was not just nine months in my mother's body, it was eighteen years in this context. After high school graduation it is true that especially my family and religious community had a continuing influence but the dominating "shapers" of my life and calling were now things, places, and people that I chose. But first my incubation.

After my brief salute to my Ground Hog Day arrival, I summarize in two chapters what I have found out about my forebears in England, Sweden, and Germany. The next two chapters describe my parents, Walter and Vivian Gill, then my three sisters and our home life growing up. My boyhood from kindergarten through junior high school comes next—not always proud of that period, as you will see. Finally, I pretty much shaped up in high school and graduated from Dave to David.

1

Ground Hog Day Arrival: February 2, 1946

I WAS BORN AT a young age. Nine months. Before that I had a couple half-lives of indeterminate length but they were completely undistinguished, especially my male side which was just one half-life sperm among thousands if not millions. But at a critical moment, sometime I guess to be around May 2, 1945, I began real life as a zygote. About ten days later I established residence in my mother's womb and stayed there for almost nine months before she kicked me out. She gave birth to me at 3:40 a.m. (Central Time, so it was 1:40 a.m. in California, my eventual long-time home—mentioned just so you know that even in California I am an authentic Ground Hog) on Saturday, February 2, 1946, in the dead of winter in Omaha, Nebraska.

I have always had a modest bulge on the top of my head which I told friends was because of extra brains (knowing it wasn't, but you can joke about your own bodily distinctives). Actually, my mother later told me I resisted ejection and maybe the head bulge is from staying in the birth canal longer than desirable. Maybe that also explains my slanted forehead (which I have long joked is my "Piltdown Man" forehead). Out of skull modesty I have avoided the shaved head look I would have enjoyed at one stage or another.

I was a fairly big baby, nine pounds, seven ounces, and twenty-and-a-half inches long (maybe that explains the slow delivery), blondish hair (what there was of it), and blue eyes. My father and Gill grandfather had full heads of hair until they died but my maternal grandpa Wurz was bald as a bowling ball in all the photos I have seen of him. I blame him for my year-by-year thinning hair these past couple decades. But I do also credit him and the Wurz/Block tribe for my big shoulders and tank-like body constitution, a farm boy or fireman kind of build. The Gills and Hallgrens on my father's side were handsome and distinguished looking but with bodies built for office work.

My big toe was longer than the second one. I have distinctive points on each ear. A weird anomaly I only noticed in my thirties were the different line patterns in my left and right palms. The left line goes straight across and is called a "simian" line or crease (I guess a lot of monkeys have these). My right palm is more conventional with two lines that do not meet. When I looked for information on line, I found that palm readers were all over the place with their interpretations (as expected). I was pleased to see that a fellow Omaha resident, Warren Buffet, has the same rare palm pattern as me. I also have always had a slightly irregular heart beat but my doctors tell me it is not a problem and I have no restrictions.

Omaha was ice cold in winter but my birth happened indoors at Omaha's Immanuel Hospital which was heated. After a quick scrub down and some kind of snip at my belly button, my mother was cuddling me close in a warm blanket. I have always loved the Ground Hog Day connection. In the dead of winter, like Punxsutawney Phil, I stuck my head out on February 2nd. I have no idea whether I saw a shadow or whether spring came early in 1946. Regarding February 2, my dad often told me growing up that three outstanding men were born on February two, twelve, and twenty-two. Putting me in the company of Lincoln and Washington and noting the "2's" we shared was typical of both my dad's love of numbers and his "positive reinforcement" parenting style with me.

Since someone started naming generations, mine has been called the "Baby Boomers"—referring to the huge number of kids born after the World War Two troops came home and got busy. Baby Boomers were those of us born between 1946 and 1964—so I was born on the 33rd day of the Baby Boom. I do feel special.

Of course, the chain of life, my life, goes back a long way before my conception and birth. This matters. It seems to me there are four primary sources and shapers of who we are. First, of course, is nature. The genetics and DNA, the nature "inside" us, inherited from our blood forbears, matter for our physical make-up, intellect, and personality. And the "nature" outside of us—food, air, water, climate, disease, and various catastrophes—also shapes us. Second, the "nurture" side of our lives may be even more formative for us. How our parents, family, and community treat us, teach us, reward and punish us—and the values and practices of the institutional, political, and social realities around us—play a huge role in what and who we become. Socialization we call it. Third, who we are depends a lot on our own decisions and choices. We are not just the playthings or victims of either nature or nurture. We are never free of nature and nurture, of course, but we do have some important choices. Fourth, and finally, I really do believe there is a spiritual reality influencing our identity and story. This is mysterious but I believe, on the positive side, that a good God has a hand in who we are, how we cope with nature and nurture, and how we make decisions. And yes, I also believe there is real evil, demonic power, in that spiritual realm. Mysterious but real.

So my "pre-history" leading up to that opening nativity and arrival story is about a German immigrant family whose daughter met and married the son of an English immigrant father and a Swedish immigrant mother. Think about the four identity-shapers: first, the genetic inheritance played a role (no male was ever taller than 5'10" in my family tree so what do you guess my eventual height would be?). Second, the nurture side of the pre-history is powerful in shaping my life, especially its religious/spiritual structure and sense of purpose. I heard this multi-generational story over and over as I grew up. Third, there were many defining moments where I made choices, including a true revolution in 1971 when I chose to walk a different religious path. And fourth, I have no doubt that God has had a gracious hand on my life the whole way.

2

Tribal Roots: Gill & Hallgren

SOME OF MY FRIENDS suggested that I put these chapters on my family history in an appendix to the book or even just eliminate them altogether. But I can't do it, partly out of respect for my ancestors but also because (maybe more than most people) I have lived my whole life with a vital awareness of my family's roots and legacy and a sense of real responsibility to carry on that legacy, especially in terms of our faith. But please feel free to jump forward to a chapter that is more relevant to your interests if you wish. For this chapter and the next I have depended on countless scribbled notes (sometimes later typed), newspaper clippings, birth, marriage, and death notices, diary entries, and a few unpublished memoirs and journals. Both of my parents and my aunt Kathryn handed on to me big files of (disorganized) documents and photos. This has been an exercise like assembling a big jigsaw puzzle.

This chapter is the story that produced my father. My mother's background will be the subject of Chapter Three and Chapter Four will be about them as my parents. The English tribe provided my family name Gill and left more photographic and biographic evidence than the Swedes or Germans. But the kid (me) is actually, ethnically and maybe culturally, half-German, a quarter Swedish, and a quarter English. Here is the English/Swedish story.

GILL & HALLGREN TRIBAL ROOTS: MY FATHER'S FOREBEARS

What does my family name "Gill" mean? Let's start with "fish breathing apparatus." As a small kid I was occasionally called "Gillfish" by some brave playground pals who thought they had enough speed to escape my wrath if necessary (I just thought it was funny, it didn't stick, and no one ever had to pay). As a verb "to gill" means to catch (in a gill net) or to "gut and clean" a fish. In Irish or Gaelic it refers to a "servant," as in "we have a lot of work to do, let's find some gills to help." In Hebrew it means "joy" or gladness. I like that. Gill also can mean "quarter of a pint," or four ounces of a liquid. Gill also, I discovered, refers to one of the radiating plates forming the undersurface of the cap of a mushroom fungus—a less pleasant association! Gill can refer to a "ravine" or small stream. And it can refer to a "sweetheart." I like that also. Despite this linguistic review, there is not much insight here about what the Gill tribe is about.

There have been a few (emphasis on *few*) famous people named Gill—and I haven't found any relational links to them. John Gill (1697–1771) was a (Calvinist) Baptist preacher and theologian based in central England, famous for writing a verse-by-verse commentary on the entire Bible and a massive systematic theology called *Body of Divinity*. Eric Rowland Gill (1882–1940) was a great sculptor, draftsman, engraver, illustrator, and radical Christian social thinker whose works have challenged me. Other random observations: the only other Gill in my high school, Robert, was part of an important Portuguese family in our town, San Leandro. I call my MBA student and friend Michael Gill "my Jewish cousin," so it is kind of fun to think I might have some Jewish relatives somewhere. There are quite a few Sikhs from India named Gill but I am hoping that is not because of the British Empire. I love all my Black friends but I confess my happiness that there aren't very many African-Americans named Gill, which would have indicated likely slave-holding back a few generations. Don't want that! So there you have it: the story of my surname, full of inconspicuous ordinariness.

After some family research on a return visit to England, my great uncle John Ruskin Gill wrote in 1938 (I paraphrase): "It has been verified that the Gill family originally came from Scotland in the days of the Claverhouse persecution,[1] and settled in the north of Ireland in the late 1600s. Later, perhaps in the mid- to late-1700s, the Gills left Ireland, one company settling on the Isle of Man, the other in Yorkshire, England. Our family is from the Yorkshire company." I take his word for it.

JOHN & HANNAH RAW GILL

Our family record of Gill forebears goes back six generations to the English Midlands (Leicester, Keighley, Yorkshire). The records are not detailed or complete and I hope you don't get lost but here is what I know. Back those six generations, Christopher Gill (b. 1783) was a well-to-do farmer—with a brother-in-law named John Raw (b. 1775), a sometimes-wealthy butter merchant.[2] Christopher Gill named one of his sons John Raw Gill (1819–1875) in honor of his brother-in-law. John Raw himself had a daughter named Hannah Raw (1826–1896). These two cousins eloped in 1843 when John Raw Gill was twenty-three and cousin Hannah Raw just sixteen. From age nineteen

---

1. John Graham of Claverhouse (ca. 1649–1689) was a Scottish military commander, known as "Bonnie Dundee" because of his good looks and "Bloody Clavers" for his persecution of Scottish Presbyterians (including my ancestors)!

2.. The Gill descendants still like butter more than two hundred years later.

onward, John Raw Gill was employed in the British Customs Office in Leicester as a tax collector. He and Hannah had ten children born between 1844 and 1869, six boys and four girls.[3] John Raw Gill died suddenly of apoplexy on a Saturday afternoon in his office in Leicester in 1875, at age fifty-six. Hannah lived on to 1896.

ALFRED GILL

The second child of John Raw Gill and wife Hannah was my great-grandfather Alfred Tindal Gill, born exactly a century before me (January 10, 1846–December 12, 1907). At age eighteen in 1864, Alfred completed a course of study at Wesley College in Sheffield and began working for the Craven Bank in the town of Keighley in Yorkshire. In February of 1871, Alfred resigned from the Keighley Bank and sailed off from Liverpool for North America. After landing in Quebec, he took a train to Boston where he lodged with his aunt Jane Raw Green, his mother Hannah's younger, widowed sister, already in America. He found a job as bookkeeper for a dry goods merchant for $10 per week which covered his $4.50 per week room and board. Just weeks later, dissatisfied with his job prospects in Boston, Alfred looked for opportunities in Des Moines, Duluth, Rochester, and elsewhere, and finally landed a position for $1000 a year in St. Paul, Minnesota, at the Union Improvement and Elevator Company. On June 1, 1871, he became the Chief Bookkeeper at the First National Bank of Minneapolis for $100 a month. Lots of changes in a brief period!

Alfred first met his future wife (my great grandmother) Eleanor Bryson (May 10, 1845–September 25, 1909) in August 1869 when he was twenty-three and she was twenty-four. He had made it clear to everyone that Keighley was too small for him. He wanted to be an adventurous man in a bigger world. Eleanor, in whom he had shown some romantic interest, told him (and continued to write him in America) that she would never be able to get serious with him unless he was a man of God, a Christian. To please her, Alfred visited several churches—and in the Spring of 1872 was born again, converted to the Christian faith. He cabled one word back to Newcastle—"Saved"—and joined Central Presbyterian Church in St. Paul. Eleanor rejoiced and accepted his long-distance proposal.

On September 4, 1872, Alfred took some vacation and went to Boston to meet Eleanor Bryson as she arrived from England (after a rough twelve-day voyage across the Atlantic chronicled in her diary) on September 10. At 9:00 in the morning, just after Eleanor cleared customs, the two were married at St. John's Church. They stayed a few days in Boston, visited New York, and then returned to Minneapolis, visiting

---

3. Six of John and Hannah Raw Gill's ten children, my great grandfather Alfred's siblings, died between the ages of two and twenty-eight with consumption and pneumonia named as causes in a couple cases. A couple of the children eventually moved to Australia. One of Alfred's siblings, Charles Edwin Gill (1865–1909) was remembered as "a very handsome and good-natured man, called 'King Edward's double,'" and known as "an inveterate golfer" (that trait skipped a couple generations before reappearing in my life).

Niagara Falls on the way. Alfred had good prospects at Minneapolis Bank but Eleanor got more and more homesick and became pregnant with their first child. So in April 1873, just seven months after their wedding, they moved back to the Bryson home town, Newcastle-on-Tyne (a city in Northumberland, in the extreme northeast of England, just south of Hadrian's Wall and the Scottish border).[4] Their first child, (my great-uncle) John Ruskin Gill, was born June 23, 1873.

Alfred and Eleanor attended the Church of England for a few years until 1879 but became restless under a new, more "modernist," rector and also wished for a simpler and more biblical approach to church. They discovered and soon joined a Plymouth Brethren meeting and stayed in that church fellowship for the rest of their lives. Alfred became a respected lay leader (more on the Plymouth Brethren in Chapter 8 below).

THE BRYSON BACKGROUND

Great grandmother Eleanor was the daughter of Thomas Bryson (1805–1867) and Elinor[5] Smith Alexander (1814–1857) "whom Thomas had long worshipped from afar." Thomas (one of eleven children born to George and Mary Bryson) and Elinor were married in 1835, aged thirty and twenty-one respectively. Thomas had left school at age fourteen to help support his widowed mother. He was employed first as a stonemason and then from 1830 onward as a foreman for construction projects in Newcastle. In 1838 Thomas slipped and fell forty feet from a scaffolding at the Exchange Building on Grey Street, being erected under his supervision. He recovered from severe injuries only because of his "healthy and vigorous constitution." In 1854 he was made Town Surveyor (city engineer) in Newcastle. He died in 1867 two days after a terrible explosion as he was supervising the burial of some cans of nitroglycerin on the Town Moor in Newcastle. His wife Elinor had died ten years earlier in 1857, only forty-three years old, as a result of a "bleeding" given by a doctor in an attempt to cure her dropsy and kidney trouble. Elinor died when her daughter Eleanor was only twelve years old. Both of my great grandmother's parents, Thomas and Elinor, were exceptional people.

Elinor Alexander Bryson was one of nine daughters. She was said to be "very attractive in girlhood" with unusual "gifts in literature, music, art, natural character and 'spiritual tastes.'" She worked for a time in London as a lady's maid and nursery governess. Here are some quotations from her teenage diary which reveal her intense Christian faith:

---

4. "Coals to Newcastle" was part of a joke related to the prominence of coal mining in the area. It was in Northumberland, near where the Tyne River emptied into the British Channel. The recent BBC detective mystery series "Vera" is based in Newcastle.

5. Most of the time her name is spelled "Elinor" and her daughter "Eleanor"—but there is inconsistency in the family records.

"Have been boating on the Thames with a gay party of young people in delightful circumstances, nevertheless uneasy in heart because my Saviour would not have been welcomed there. Query: has any follower of Christ the sanction and blessing of the Lord in such a place?"

"Attended church three times yesterday; mourned my own coldness and earthly-mindedness."

"Gloried today in the worthiness of my Redeemer, yet long to be more in his presence and service. Query: How can I serve him with my life?"

Thomas and Elinor's daughter Eleanor was a talented painter. I have a fine self-portrait and also a seaside scene from her hand. I have seen a couple still lifes she painted. The fact that Eleanor (and Alfred) named their firstborn son "John Ruskin" when a man by that name was England's most famous art and culture critic at the time tells us something about my great grandmother's cultural appreciation.[6]

ALFRED & ELEANOR GILL: FROM NEWCASTLE TO ST. PAUL

Upon their return from the USA in 1873, Alfred was hired as manager of the West Hartlepool Durham Bank. From 1873 to 1881 Alfred and Eleanor made their residence at #1 Green Terrace, Seaton Carew, a seaside town just southeast of Newcastle. Following John Ruskin Gill (1873), my own grandfather Frank Bryson Gill came along in 1876, and then daughter Edith Mary (1879). In 1881 the Gills moved back into Newcastle proper where son Alfred Edwin Gill was born (1884). On a visit to Newcastle and Seaton Carew a couple years ago I was able to find (and walk through, thanks to the gracious current owner) the modest row house in which my grandfather Frank was born. Back up in Newcastle after 1881 Alfred and Eleanor moved around from one house to another every couple years until they left the country for good in 1888.

A sweet glimpse of the marriage of my great grandparents was provided in 1884, after twelve years of marriage, when Alfred and Eleanor wrote these lines to each other (using endearing nicknames):

> Ah Ellie, my Dearest of Dears
> We've now proved God's goodness in twelve married years
> Just see our trophies looking so grand,
> Brought forth in England's well-favored land.

---

6. For more on this incredibly interesting figure see Wolfgang Kemp. *The Desire of My Eyes: The Life and Work of John Ruskin.* (New York: Farrar, Straus, and Giroux, 1990). Ruskin (1819–1900) had published *Modern Painters* in five volumes during the 1840s and followed that with books on architecture, including *The Stones of Venice* (three volumes on Venetian architecture). He lost his Evangelical Protestant faith in 1858 and turned to topics in economics, politics, and culture over the next decades until his death in 1900.

Part One: Incubators (1946–1964)

> There's Ruskin, firstborn, full of good fun;
> Then pensive Frank, a most thoughtful son;
> And Edith, the fair one, sparkling with life
> Plus winsome wee Eddie with intellect rife
>
> ———-
>
> Oh Alfie, if we only the future could tell;
> One hundred years on, will all be quite well?
> Will our Saviour capture the heart of each soul?
> What kind of offspring will make up the whole?

Why did they abandon their historic home in England? Son Frank (my grandpa) later explained that "a steadily decreasing income and the very limited opportunities for his children to obtain a reasonable salary led my father to look across the Atlantic." The 1870s and 1880s were a time of economic recession not just in England but all over Europe (my other grandparents emigrated from Sweden and Germany in that same decade of the 1880s). In 1879 there was a failed harvest. Ireland was also experiencing serious famine. The Industrial Revolution was in full swing, filling the air with pollution from burning so much coal. Newcastle was England's first coal exporting port, well-known as a coal mining center since the Middle Ages. Forests were being damaged, respiratory ailments and lung disease were rising.

In October of 1888, the Alfred Gill family sold all their furniture at an auction, packed up their china and books, sailed in November from Liverpool to Quebec, and traveled on by train through Chicago to Clinton and then Des Moines, Iowa, in search of a job. Acquaintances in their Plymouth Brethren circles welcomed and housed them until they got settled. From 1888 to 1891 they lived in Des Moines where Alfred worked as accountant/auditor for the Des Moines & Kansas City Railway. In January 1891 they moved to Kansas City where Alfred was auditor for the Kingman Packing Company (pork and beef). In 1895 they moved to St. Paul where they stayed for twelve years. Alfred worked for the Great Northern Railway in St. Paul but also was "in the Lord's work" as an itinerant traveling teacher and preacher among the Brethren.

In 1907 Alfred and Eleanor with their youngest son Edwin moved to Seattle, thinking the weather would be better and more like what they had left behind in Newcastle. John Ruskin Gill had already moved there in 1901. Daughter Edith and her husband George Gunderson relocated to Seattle in 1903. Eleanor hoped all four of her children and their families would move there. Alfred traveled back to England in 1906 but experienced serious illness of some type and wondered in letters if he would even make it home. He died in Seattle December 12, 1907 at age sixty-one. Eleanor herself died of nephritis (kidney disease) in Seattle, September 25, 1909. In 1909 son Frank decided to follow the family to the Northwest but, unable to find a good post in Seattle, he found employment with Union Pacific in Portland, Oregon, two hundred miles to the south.

FRANK BRYSON GILL

Born in Seaton Carew just outside of Newcastle on April 30, 1876, my grandfather Frank came with his family from England to America in 1888 at age twelve. Frustrated by having to repeat a couple grades because of differences in English and American school curricula, Frank talked his parents into letting him leave school in 1891 at age fifteen to try both office and manual work. From April 1891 to August 1893, he got a job at the Kingman Packing Company where his father worked, starting as a cashier and worked his way up to Assistant Auditor. In August 1893 he quit this job to spend some time traveling around the Midwest. From April 1894 to April 1895 he worked in Kansas City for Jeffrey Manufacturing. In July 1895 the whole family moved to St. Paul where both Alfred and son Frank began working for the Great Northern Railway Company. For Frank this was the beginning a forty-nine-year railroad career. Starting as an office boy, he was promoted up the ladder to Chief Clerk, a position he held from 1902 until September 1909 when he moved out to Portland, Oregon. Despite the lack of a high school diploma, his "ability with figures" made room for him.

KATIE AND THE HALLGRENS

In St. Paul, in October of 1902 at age twenty-six, Frank Gill (April 30, 1876–May 23, 1955) married a strikingly beautiful eighteen-year-old Swedish-American woman named Katie Hallgren (October 4, 1884–February 20, 1971). Katie was born in Brainerd, Minnesota, to Gustave Helmer Hallgren[7] (1858–1948) and Kate Thornburg (1856–84). Gustave had been born in 1858 to Anders and Gustava Carlson in Vadstena, on the eastern shore of Lake Vättern.[8] Gustave moved to nearby Motala in 1868 and then on to Gothenburg where at age sixteen he was converted and joined a Lutheran Church. In April 1880, at age twenty-two, Gustave emigrated to Chicago where his brother Ernst Victor Hallgren already lived and was pastor of Salem Swedish Baptist Church. Gustave found work with the Heath & Milligan Paint Company doing decorative, free-hand, ceiling painting and striping (often in very wealthy homes). He then worked at the Smith & Barnes Piano Factory doing piano finishing. He later worked for a time for the Northern Pacific Railway but after moving to Portland in 1910 had a long career as a piano refinisher and salesman. He gave a beautiful wooden pump organ to daughter Katie in 1902 when she married Frank Gill. He was also a lay preacher in Minnesota and even served as interim pastor for one year at the Swedish Baptist church in Henning. He lived in Portland from 1910 to his death in 1948.

---

7. Gustave's first name is also variously spelled as "Gustaf" and "Gustav" in family records.

8. In 1999, when a visiting professor in Sweden for the fall semester, I visited Vadstena and prowled through graveyards looking for any "Hallgrens." Nothing. But when I returned to the USA and told my aunt, she surprised me by saying "Oh no. When he lived in Sweden, he was 'Gustave Carlson.' He took the name Hallgren when he came to America!" I learned that quite a few Swedes over the last century wearied of so many last names ending in "son" and chose some alternative.

PART ONE: INCUBATORS (1946–1964)

My great grand-parents Gustave Hallgren and Kate Thornberg (1856–1884) were married March 17, 1883, in Evanston, Illinois, and then moved to Brainerd, Minnesota. Baby Katie was born October 4, 1884. Tragically, mother Kate died eight days after giving birth. With her mother passed away, my grandma spent her first five years living on Gustave's sister's farm—until in 1889 Gustave married his second wife Alfrida Larson (1858–1955) and they brought five-year-old Katie back into the family. Alfrida was by all accounts a good woman but my grandma said she always felt her step-mother favored her own two birth children, Harley (1892–1976) and Helen Hallgren (1895–1988), who I remember very fondly (though I don't doubt my grandma's story).

For fifty years my great-uncle Harley worked for the railroads, starting in 1908 at age sixteen for Great Northern in St. Paul. Harley moved to Portland in 1910 when the whole Gustave Hallgren family moved there from St. Paul (just a year after the Frank Gill family made the same move). Harley worked for the Seattle, Portland, & Spokane Railway, mostly as District Passenger Manager. After he retired, he worked another fifteen years as a travel agent until just before his death in 1976. He was a long-time lay leader at Temple Baptist Church in Portland and one of the founders of the Union Gospel Mission and Western Baptist Seminary. He was the first president of the Portland Gideons in 1926 and was superintendent of the Railroad Christian Fellowship. He served on the Board of Trustees at Multnomah School of the Bible.

Uncle Harley was proud to say he never owned a car in his life. I don't think I ever met Uncle Harley's wife Louie Tjernlund Hallgren but I have a vivid memory of having coffee with Harley in my twenties. When I marveled at how much sugar he spooned into his coffee, he explained: "There are too many sour things in life already. I believe in sweet things!" The Hallgren family remained active in the Swedish Baptist Church all their lives, while sister Katie, of course, followed Frank into the Plymouth Brethren after they married. My great-aunt Helen Marion Hallgren, a sweet lady who never married, was an active member of Temple Swedish Baptist all her life. She worked in a Christian Book Store in Portland for forty-six years.

MY GRANDPARENTS FRANK & KATIE GILL

After Frank and Katie's marriage in 1902, sons George and Arthur were born in 1904 and 1906 in St. Paul. After the September 1909 move to Portland, Oregon, sons Frank and Walter were born in 1910 and 1913, and daughter Kathryn in 1917. Soon after arriving in Portland, in November 1909, Grandpa Frank was hired as Head Clerk in the Statistical Bureau of the Oregon-Washington Railroad & Navigation Co. He was promoted to Special Accountant in the Auditor's Department. In 1916 the OWR&N became the Union Pacific Railway and Frank's title became Valuation Accountant. On July 22, 1918, the whole family of seven became naturalized citizens of the USA—I'm not sure why it took them so many years after their immigration.

In 1927, just after son George had tragically passed away, Frank was sent to work for the Interstate Commerce Commission in Washington DC until late 1929, a tough thing for him as well as the family left behind in Portland (though they were able to join him for two months in summer 1928). In 1932 Union Pacific reorganized, closed its Portland office, and transferred most of its work force to Omaha, Nebraska. Frank moved the whole family to Omaha where he worked the next twelve years as Assistant Bureau Head and Accountant in the Valuation Land and Tax Department of Union Pacific. In Portland his salary had been $325 per month. In Omaha, for the same work, he was paid $225 and this was soon cut to $200. It was tough in the Great Depression! The intense heat of summer and brutal cold of winter in Omaha were also a price to be paid for moving and keeping the job. In 1941 Frank developed arthritis which increasingly affected his mobility. He retired and Union Pacific moved him back home to Portland in 1944. He was bedridden seven years and five months, from December 1947 until he died in May 1955.

My grandpa Frank also made a name for himself as a railroad historian, mainly through a series of short, well-researched articles. Even as a young teenager Frank showed an interest and ability as a writer. In 1890 at age fourteen, Frank and a friend created a little hand-written and illustrated monthly "newspaper" they called the "Herald of the West"—with school and local news, jokes, and stories of the boys' adventures exploring on foot, and their fascination with the marvels of railroads. Frank's interest in railroad history became a lifetime pursuit, and later in life he was recognized a leading authority on railroad history, especially in the Pacific Northwest. He was given an Honorary Lifetime Membership in the Oregon Historical Society in 1953. His big collection of documents and memorabilia was donated to the archives of the Pacific Northwest Chapter of the National Railway Historical Society in 2006.

I only met my grandfather Frank Gill a few times in the early 1950s in Portland, Oregon. In 1949 our family had moved from Omaha back to Portland—where we lived until moving down to California in 1952. My bedridden grandfather's condition was a little mysterious and scary for a young kid like me. But through his writings and the recollections of others I have come to greatly admire him. As a writer myself and a history student in university, I look back at my grandpa Frank's historical efforts with warm appreciation. He was also a lay leader in the Plymouth Brethren like his father Alfred (and my father to come) and wrote an unpublished but well-circulated history and apology for the Brethren simply called "Matthew 18:20" (in reference to a famous statement by Jesus that he would be present in the midst of "two or three gathered in his name"). I have nothing but sweet memories of my grandma Katie Gill, though I only knew her as an older lady, herself hobbled (but not bedridden like her husband) by arthritis.

PART ONE: INCUBATORS (1946–1964)

FRANK GILL'S THREE SIBLINGS

Alfred and Eleanor Gill had four children, three siblings for my grandpa Frank. The eldest was John Ruskin Gill (1873–1962), born in Newcastle. He worked as a commercial artist, engraver, and amateur cartoonist.[9] He married a Swiss immigrant Emma Ramel (1872–1949) in 1896. He followed the family to the Midwest and St. Paul but moved in 1901 to Seattle for a job at an engraving company. A Seattle Brethren assembly was started in their home soon after their arrival. I briefly met my great Uncle John Ruskin in Oregon when I was a child. A bit eccentric, funny, but deadly serious about maintaining Plymouth Brethren orthodoxy: that's how I remember him. His son Sidney Gill (1906–1998) was an uncle in my life growing up in Oakland and Sid's son, Gerry Gill, an enjoyable "second cousin" whose wry sense of humor I enjoyed.

Alfred and Eleanor's daughter Edith Mary (1879–1972) and her husband George Gunderson moved to Seattle in 1903. Edith's daughter (my father's cousin) Vivian D. Gunderson (1903–1999) earned an honors BA at the University of Washington and an MEd from Western Washington State. She also did some coursework at Wheaton College, was author of many articles and books, and helped plant two churches that began from Sunday Schools she launched and led. I wish I would have known this part of the family!

A. Edwin Gill (nicknamed Teddy) (1884–1976) started working at age sixteen in 1900 in St. Paul for the Great Northern Railway in the accounting department. He moved to Seattle with his parents in 1907. After his parents' deaths in 1907 and 1909 he moved down to Portland in 1910 at the urging of brother Frank and went to work for Union Pacific as a general bookkeeper. In 1911 he married Lydia Koch (1886–1945) and, after she passed away in 1945, married Alma Burdick (1893–1980) in 1948. As an adult, Edwin left the narrow "Exclusive" Brethren to join the "Open" Brethren for whom he became a widely respected Bible teacher and preacher. He retired from Union Pacific in 1937 (age fifty-three) rather than transfer back to Omaha. From 1924 onward he was an active leader at Grace & Truth Hall and also helped produce a weekly Christian radio broadcast. Of course, his move into the "Open" Brethren separated him from the numerically dominant "Exclusive" mainstream of the Gill clan. One of my great joys was to meet him later in his life in summer 1974. What a sweet, godly man and such a shame for me, I thought, to have missed out on decades of fellowship and mutual encouragement. Thirty or so years later I had the additional joy of connecting with his daughter Jane Vogland (1919–2018) who had remained good friends with my aunt Kathryn through all the years.

---

9. I have wondered what he thought about his famous contemporary, British engraver, sculptor, and font designer Eric Gill (1882–1940)—no relation as far as we know.

THE FIVE CHILDREN OF FRANK & KATIE GILL

The first-born son to Frank and Katie Gill, my grandparents, was George Bryson Gill (1904–1927).[10] George was a very bright young man. Upon his early death, his high school Benson Polytechnic mourned the loss of "one of their best students ever." I don't doubt his potential but I have looked over a big stack of his high school grade reports and he was usually a B student (80th percentile). When he graduated in June 1921, he still needed more high school credits to qualify for University of Washington admission. At UW he was normally a B and C student and was threatened with dismissal a couple times because of borderline grades (reminds me of my own first year at Berkeley!). He was a junior majoring in engineering at the University of Washington in Seattle when he was struck down with a ruptured appendix. He was hospitalized but the medical establishment did not yet know how to manage the situation. He got sepsis and died just seven weeks later. I am still deeply moved when I see pictures of my grandma Katie sitting at his bedside in the hospital. George never married and he died long before I was born but, whenever I see his photos, I regret that I never got to know him.

Arthur Thornberg Gill (Artie) (1906–1936) was the second son. He was a business student at Oregon State University for a couple years. My dad always told me that I reminded him of his brother Art with my energy and outspokenness. He was a committed Christian and lay preacher even in his twenties. Art married Elizabeth Morrison, RN (1906–1996) in 1930 and they had one child, daughter Marjorie. Sadly, Art came down with Hodgkins Disease (leukemia) and died in 1936 while his daughter was still an infant. Marjorie grew up to marry Charles Jenner and I have been privileged to have Marjorie as a first cousin and friend over the years. Charles did a theology degree and as Presbyterians they escaped the narrowness and sectarianism of the Plymouth Brethren and have been long-time encouragers of my own work. Cousin Marjorie and Charles had two sons, Graham and techie Stuart Jenner—who has been a brilliant conversation partner of mine on matters of technology and ethics over many years now.

The third son was Frank Harley Gill (1910–2000). My uncle Frank was, I thought, the "black sheep" of the family—running off at age sixteen to join the navy (1926–31), smoking and drinking, drifting away from the Brethren, and skipping church as a young man. After the navy, Frank moved back into his parents' Omaha home in 1932. He worked as house painter and truck driver, but then decided the railroad looked

---

10. I love how my grandparents honored the otherwise-to-disappear surnames from their maternal side: Bryson was Alfred's wife Eleanor's surname; Thornberg was Frank's wife Katie's mother's surname. I have also been unaware until now of their habits of nicknaming each other. Thus, Alfred = Alfie, Eleanor = Ellie, Edwin = Teddie, Arthur = Artie, Walter = Butch, Kathryn = Cutie. Now I see why my dad liked to nickname us kids. I did NOT like his attempt to nickname me "Skeeter" or "Scooper," however. Even as a young boy I thought "Scooper of what?!!" I did call my sisters Dottie, Kitty, and Beth (but never Buffy; and Beth later requested Elizabeth, her real and beautiful name, as an adult).

better. He first worked for the Rock Island Line in Illinois, then, from 1944 to his retirement in 1972, as a Gang Foreman and freight car repairman for Union Pacific in Seattle and Portland. After getting out of the navy, Frank fell in love with Vera, a public health nurse ten years older than him who helped him get his life together. They married in 1938 and moved to Des Moines, Iowa. Frank and Vera had a daughter Ruth Marie (1940–1958) born with Down's syndrome. I may have met the family once or twice as a kid but not much more. After Vera died in 1950, Frank married Esther Imbeau in 1951, a single mother of five children from multiple fathers. My uncle Frank was looked down upon for marrying a woman with this track record. Esther died in 1995. I had no opinion growing up but was vaguely aware of the story.

Sometime in the mid-1990s I learned from my aunt Kathryn that my uncle Frank was living as a widower in a retirement home in Bellingham, north of Seattle. My aunt drove up from Seattle to visit him once a month. I learned that my uncle Frank not only married Esther but officially adopted all five of her kids and was a beloved father and grandpa to them and their kids. I also found out that he loved God and carefully studied every page of Scripture. He had a fetish about "extra" words in the text. In his Bibles (I have two of them) he used his pencil to blot out any extra words in a sentence. For example, if the verse says "Now it came to pass that Jesus entered the city . . . "—uncle Frank scribbled out "Now it came to pass"—unnecessary! Just say "Jesus entered the city." Funny. But "black sheep Uncle Frank"? No way! What a wonderful man of God with a long track record. I came home after being with my uncle Frank (and bringing a couple of his whittled balsa wood masterpieces!) and had a chat with my dad, urging him to reconnect with his brother and revise his opinion. Before long, my dad made it to Bellingham and a great reunion of brothers took place. Unfortunately, I have never had any connection to uncle Frank's adopted kids, though I would love to meet them.

My dad, the fourth son, Walter Leonard Gill was born (April 12, 1913) in Portland, Oregon. More about him in Chapter Three. He was the fourth and youngest son, joined by one younger sister who became his closest sibling and lifetime friend.

The fifth child and only daughter was Dorothy Kathryn (October 20, 1917–October 10, 2014). My sisters and I always called her "Aunt Kay" and we often heard her addressed as "Kay" but perhaps even more often just as "Kathryn," which appealed to her sense of order and resistance to familiarity. My dad and his brothers always called her "Cutie," but that privilege started and ended with her brothers. When a man in her local church called her "Cutie" one time she rebuked him instantly and informed him that she was to be addressed as Kathryn.

AUNT KAY

Next to my parents, my Aunt Kay had the biggest role in my life of any relative, and that came many years after my youth. Aunt Kathryn was incredibly pretty in the opinion of my sisters and me. I learned only later in life that she graduated with distinction and was valedictorian of her high school graduating class of 1936. I have seen her high school grade reports and they are very close to straight A's. Few people (and even fewer women) were able to attend university during the Great Depression when she graduated. She worked in Omaha from 1936 to 1944 for a real estate office and an aircraft tool manufacturer before returning to Portland with her aging parents. In Portland she took a job in 1946 as office worker, soon promoted to Office Manager, in the Mortgage Loan Department for Pacific Mutual Life insurance company. She was a much-loved and lauded pillar in the company up to her retirement in 1992 after forty-six years. My aunt lived with and helped her arthritis-handicapped parents as they got weaker and weaker. When her father Frank died in 1955, she chose to stay by her mom, my grandma Katie, supporting and caring for her to the end in 1971. After my grandma's death, she got married in 1972 to Roy Davis (1900–1993), a widower in her church, seventeen years older than her. They had a nice marriage for twenty-one years until Roy's death in 1993.

After Roy's death my aunt Kay "adopted" three elderly ladies in her church (including Francys Erisman, mother of my two lifetime "brothers," John and Al), driving them to church, on shopping trips, and for local sightseeing multiple times every week. She cooked a beef pot roast almost every Sunday and served dinner to these three widows and other guests after church. She provided the bread and wine for weekly communion and tended the flower beds around her church's building. She lived a very austere life, horrified one time when she saw the menu prices at a restaurant where I was taking her to lunch (from then on it was Arby's, Burgermaster, or nothing, if I wanted to take her to lunch). No Chinese or Mexican or other ethnic or spicy food, by the way. American meat and potatoes. And cheap. After she died, as her executor, I found out how incredibly generous she was. She had insisted on giving my parents the $7000 it took to install one of those motorized stairway chair lifts after my dad could no longer walk up and down. I found out that she had quietly given a couple thousand every month to an unemployed family in her church, over more than a year, I believe. And this is only a small sample.

My aunt never had any kids and she was fiercely independent. During the 1990s I began visiting Seattle maybe once every three months to guest lecture at Seattle Pacific University or work with my friend Al Erisman on some project. After Roy Davis died in 1993 and my aunt was alone for the first time in her life, I found it a privilege to look in on her when I came to town every two or three months. All of her life she and my dad had phoned each other once a week without fail. They were each other's confidants. But my dad was now in his eighties and slowing down so he was grateful that I was stepping in to watch out for and help his sister. Almost every visit she had some shopping we would go do, with me schlepping big bags of cat and bird food and dozens of sale-price cans of food. There were always little handyman projects and a chandelier she wanted to clean with my help.

Part One: Incubators (1946–1964)

Around 2000, my cousin Marjorie, who lived in the same Seattle suburb of Bellevue as my aunt, worried to me about whether our Aunt Kay had a doctor or any sort of emergency plan, living alone as she did, afflicted with arthritis, now in her eighties. Did she have advance health directives? A will? So I urged my dad to check into these matters with his beloved sister and confidant. Dad: "Oh no. I want you to bring up those things with her. You do it!" Uh, thanks a lot dad.[11] So I gingerly brought the matter up next time I visited her. Suddenly an outburst with angry tears: "Well, none of you will need to worry about me much longer! Leave me alone." I apologized profusely and beat a hasty retreat. Sometimes her defense was "I pray all the time and leave it in the Lord's hands." But as the months and years rolled by I gently brought it up again (and again): "Aunt Kay, I know you pray before driving but I'm worried about the other drivers who don't pray and might run into you! I don't want some police or fire emergency workers to decide on your treatment." She hadn't been to a doctor in decades. She was so independent and private but very vulnerable. She had been ripped off by a crooked roofing company recently, I knew.

Every time I visited my aunt, I would end my visit by reading her some Scripture and sharing with her what I thought it meant, usually something I had been teaching or writing about recently. It was the same Bible her Plymouth Brethren church used but I brought her a fresh way of hearing the meaning. She listened quietly and murmured approval. Then I would hold her hands or stand up and hug her as I prayed for her before heading back to Chicago or the Bay Area. She would often be softly crying and trembling a little bit when I did this. She was sometimes tough on the outside but so tender and loving on the inside.

Especially after my dad died in 2004, I started phoning her once a week like he did and kept it up until she died in 2014. By the grace of God, I was able slowly to walk with her through the will and advance directives process, then through the horribly painful process of selling her long-time home and moving (resisting every step of the way) into an assisted living residence. It was so very hard for her to grow weaker and relinquish control of her life. She sometimes raged at me and I just had to sit there quietly till she calmed down. One day when I showed up to be with her, she was crying and said "David I have been so wretched to you sometimes. I don't know why you keep coming back and helping me when I have been so awful to you." I took her hands and said 'It's because I love you, that's all it is. Just like God loves us and I know you love me. And part of how I love you is I listen to your sadness and anger. I never take it personally. We all need someone who will listen to us in our darkest hours."

My aunt Kay just loved it when I was her lunch guest at the retirement home and she could introduce me to her fellow residents. She would always say I was her nephew but I think she enjoyed it when someone walked by and guessed I was her son. As my

---

11. This will be the first of many examples of my book title: "What Are You Doing About it?" I saw a real need and wound up committing and taking action to work on a very serious challenge, rather than walk away or expect someone else to do it.

aunt got weaker and needed help from the staff, even getting a shower or combing her hair, she would get into a depressed mood and wail "why doesn't the Lord take me home? I'm no good for anything and I don't want to live anymore." Here is what I said: "Aunt Kay, the days of your life are up to God, not you or me. I think God has left you here for two reasons: first, there are a few more people here, some residents and staff people, who God wants to love and bless through you, through your smile and an encouraging word. Second, I think maybe you have one more lesson God wants you to learn before you are done. All of your life you have been the strong one who serves and helps others. You are like Peter who only wanted to wash other people's feet, not let the Lord wash his own. I think God wants you to learn how to just settle back and let others serve and help you, and then just say thank you."

I actually repeated that lesson to her more than once but the day came when I noticed the complaining had dropped off to nothing and she was so eager to introduce me: "David this is Mohammed, my helper this morning. He is originally from Nigeria. He is the sweetest kindest man to me. I so appreciate him. And Mohammed, this is my wonderful nephew David. He is a professor." She also told me she was attending the Sunday services at her Patriot's Glen retirement home and couldn't refuse communion when it was served by the Lutheran woman pastor![12] Lesson learned. Ready to go home.

Within the next year, my ninety-five-year-old aunt had a stroke and was unconscious. I flew from Boston to her bedside in Seattle where I kissed her and sang in her ear (as I had to my own mom on her last day in 2008), the sweet old Brethren song: "Praise the Savior, ye who know him, who can tell how much we owe him? Gladly let us render to him all we are and have. Soon we shall be where we would be; Then we shall be what we should be; Things which are not now nor could be, then shall be our own." The next day, after my sister Kit was able to come up from the Bay Area and say goodbye, she flew off to heaven.

Sure, when I wasn't visiting my aunt for a few hours, I was running around to meetings or classes, organizing conferences, writing books, and cooking up some scheme with Al Erisman. But my hours "off the grid," walking with my aunt through her difficult final twenty years were every bit as important, and challenging, and fulfilling to me as anything else God ever had for me to do in life. Life on the margins.

As I tell this story, I have emphasized the aspects of it—and the individuals in it—who have had the biggest impact on me. It is not an even-handed account of all the members of the tribe and I apologize to those I had to leave out.

---

12. Exclusive Brethren don't take communion with other Christians and they prohibit women from speaking in church!

3

Tribal Roots: Wurz & Block

THE OTHER SIDE OF my nature and nurture inheritance is my maternal Wurz/Block half. These are my mother's forebears. As I mentioned with the previous chapter on my Gill and Hallgren forebears, please feel free to skip over this account. I just can't skip over it because it is part of who I am and I honor it. Our family records on my mother's side are much slimmer but the heritage for me is equally rich and valued. "Wurz" is German for spice (wurzig = spicy). "Block" traditionally referred to a "block of wood" (I have wondered if it was an anglicization of the more common "Bloch" but apparently not). It also can refer to a writing pad (*Schreibblock*). As it turns out, there is some stubborn blockheadedness, a big dose of spicy liveliness, and an inclination to write a lot in the gene pool! The Gill/Hallgren heritage would remain a bit too bland and reserved without its Wurz/Block counterpart. For those interested, here is what I am talking about.

GRANDPA HERMAN WURZ

Herman Wurz (23 October 1885–August 15, 1949) was my mother's father. He was the ninth and youngest child of Johannes Wurz who had four children with his first wife Maria Elisabetha Reitz. After Maria's death in 1872 he married Eva Hoeppner and fathered five more children with her. The family emigrated in 1882 to America, voyaging from Antwerp to New York. My grandfather Herman was born in the USA. We have always speculated that the name Wurz must be associated with Wurzburg in Germany, but we don't know for sure. Darmstadt, where son Adam was born in 1874, is a city just south of Frankfort, about one hundred miles west of Wurzburg. Son John Jr. was born in 1881 in Biedenkopf, a town one hundred miles north of Darmstadt. Close but not exact enough. One other historical fact that may matter is that Johannes

Wurz's kids were baptized Lutheran, not Catholic (the dominant though not exclusive tradition in Wurzburg).

When we first meet my grandpa Herman Wurz he is a farmer outside of Wausau, Wisconsin, whose widowed mother Eva Hoeppner is living in his house. He married my grandma Erna Block (February 24, 1897–July 4, 1988) in 1918 when he was thirty-three and she was twenty-one. Soon after mother Eva died, the family sold the farm and moved into town in Wausau where their three daughters were born in 1919, 1921, and 1923. In 1926/27 Herman moved his young family from Wausau to Minneapolis where their fourth child John would be born in 1932.

Our records are scant but I believe Grandpa Herman Wurz worked as a night watchman and a city employee, maybe a custodian, in Minneapolis. From the hints we have, I think my Grandpa was a hard-headed but emotional guy who died too early (age sixty-three) from a heart attack. He was a serious, stern, dedicated, simple Christian man. He seems to have been in the Plymouth Brethren throughout his adult life. I have only the faintest memory of him when I was a very small child of two or three. I am told that at the top of the stairs in our Omaha home I wagged my two- or three-year old finger at Grandpa Wurz standing at the bottom and said "You stay right there!" Was I at risk of discipline for some reason? I don't know. Sounds like it.

GRANDMA ERNA BLOCK WURZ

My grandma Erna Block Wurz's father was August Friedrich Wilhelm Block (1864–1941), born in Breitenfelde, Pomerania ["Pommern" in German] Germany, maybe fifty miles south of the Baltic Sea Coast, twenty miles south of Lübeck and thirty miles east of Hamburg. Breitenfelde is a village in the district of Lauenburg, in Schleswig-Holstein in northern Germany. So the Block tribe was three or four hundred miles north of the Wurz tribe in Germany and would only meet later on in Wisconsin and Minnesota.

At age nineteen in November 1883, August Block came to the USA with his parents and a brother and sister and settled in Wausau, Wisconsin. His own father Ferdinand Block had fought in three wars in Germany. His mother was Louise Schulz Block. After settling in Wausau, August lived there for fifty-eight years, working twenty years for the Alexander-Stewart Lumber Company (lumber camps and saw mills) and then twenty-five years at the Cereal Mills Company plant before retiring at age sixty-two. August's wife (Erna's mother) was Marie Marquardt (1868–1949)—full name Julana Teresa Marie Marquardt. August and Marie were married in 1886 at Zion Lutheran Church in Wausau. He died at seventy-seven of heart trouble. August was active in the Brethren, "preaching everywhere he went while working daily with his hands."

Besides my grandma Erna, August and Marie Block had five other daughters: Alma, Ella, Marie, Louise, and Lydia. Of these, I got to know only Louise because she married a railroad man named Obed Weise and settled up in the town of Auburn above Sacramento, California, about one hundred miles from my house in Oakland as I was growing up. Obed could be a humorous, interesting story teller and guide to the old abandoned gold mines up near Auburn in the Sierra foothills but he was also a cranky conservative, quick to gripe and say mean, ignorant things about others. By contrast, Aunt Louise was salt-of-the-earth sweet and loving, a terrific and generous cook.

Back to my grandma Erna Block Wurz: she was tall and full of energy. She loved to work and serve others. After her husband Herman died in 1949 she remained in Minneapolis until 1955 but by then daughter Gladyce had married and moved to Canada and son John moved with his wife to Toledo—so she moved out to California for twenty years near her daughter (my mother) Vivian. During most of her time in California she worked as resident housekeeper (and companion) for a wealthy San Leandro gravel pit owning couple, the Lees. After Mrs. Lee died in 1975, Grandma Wurz moved back to Minneapolis for her final thirteen years to be near daughters Doris and Gladyce (who by then had returned to Minneapolis).

My grandma Wurz had a heart of gold but was flighty and a bit disruptive at times. For example: when we had big family dinners she would sometimes eat quickly, then stand up and start clearing the table, even grabbing saucers from under coffee cups which guests had picked up for a sip! On at least one other occasion she unloaded the dishwasher and put everything away—but it was all still unwashed. I remember once we were all in our station wagon hurtling down Highway 17 when my grandma tried to throw a ten-dollar bill for gas money from the middle seat up into the front. The wind grabbed the $10 and sucked it out the window. My grandma let out an ear-piercing shriek and scream like there was no tomorrow—at which my dad rashly veered the car across several lanes of traffic to the right shoulder of the highway, where, of course, we did not find the $10 bill. We could have all been killed but God made a clear path through the traffic. Anyway, you see what I mean. Emotional. Great hearted. Hard working servant.

THE FOUR CHILDREN OF HERMAN AND ERNA BLOCK WURZ

Grandma and Grandpa Wurz had four kids. My mom Vivian Erna Wurz was the oldest, born in 1919 in Wausau, Wisconsin, but raised in Minneapolis. More on her in the next chapter. The second daughter was Doris (1921-2004). She graduated from Washington High School in 1939, then worked for three years before suffering a nervous breakdown at age twenty-one because of an engagement that went wrong—either because the groom or her stern father called off the wedding, so the stories go. Doris, like the whole family, was high strung and deeply emotional. Sadly, the medical professionals decided to do a lobotomy on Doris's brain and, in addition to that cruelty, she wound up with an infection that damaged her so badly she had to be institutionalized for the rest of a long life. In 1943, at just age twenty-two, she was committed to Rochester State Hospital for thirty-four years—moving on to other long term care facilities after the Rochester Hospital closed, until her death. Her mom, my Grandma Wurz, visited her often throughout her sad life. The state of Minnesota acknowledged its medical errors and took responsibility for all costs. I am not sure I ever got to meet Aunt Doris. It was always a sad story.

The number three Wurz kid was my aunt Gladyce Louise (1923–1999), a tall, slim, high-energy copy of her mom. Gladyce had a tumultuous romantic and marital life in the early years. Her first husband was Saskatchewan farmer Vern Denzin she married in 1946. I remember a fun visit to their farm when I was a kid. Divorce happened after a few years—no kids, fortunately, but some kind of scandal. She returned home to Minneapolis and eventually began a long marriage to Paul Peterson. Her obituary said she had a career as a Pillsbury Company Lab Technician. I didn't see her often through the years but we always enjoyed her love and enthusiasm. She tended to irritate my dad, maybe because of her somewhat flighty, brash communication style, or maybe it was her romantic track record of which he disapproved. On one classic occasion when she was out in Oakland visiting us, my dad expressed outrage about something or other she said or did. Aunt Gladyce huffily stood up and said: "Walt, my sister Viv owns half of this house! Where is the dividing line and I'll just stay on her side if you don't like it!" She was serious.

The baby of the family was my uncle John James Wurz (1932–1999), nine years younger than his next eldest sibling Gladyce. John was a James Dean-level handsome kid who became a Minnesota high school prep football star running-back. He received several college football scholarship offers, so the story goes (and I think it is true), but his father, my stern and simple grandpa Wurz, put his foot down and told him he couldn't go. He was worried my uncle John would get carried away by fame and glory, be surrounded by bad influences, lose his faith, and be lost forever. Grandpa Wurz, died when Uncle John was just seventeen and still in high school. My sad and disappointed uncle respected his dad and didn't pursue a college or football career. Instead, he became a brick mason (in the process, I remember, ruining his skin for a while from the chemicals in the mortar). In 1957 at age twenty-five, he began a forty-year career as a New York Life Insurance agent. With his good looks, charm, and personal drive he was a huge success. He led the Toledo office in sales many times and was among the top five percent of New York Life Sales Agents in the USA, making piles of money and winning widespread honor and recognition.

John married Shirley Weaver in 1952 and they had four kids together: Sherrie (1953), Vicky (1954), Diane (1956), and John (1958). In 1953, John and Shirley moved to Toledo where her Weaver family lived. Unfortunately, the marriage didn't last. John had other marriages to Mary and then Carol. Richard Herman Wurz was his child with Mary. Because they moved to California, I got to know and love my cousins Sherrie and Vicky but otherwise I had little contact with the Wurz/Block tribe over the years. I knew there was a lot of pain and loss because of the broken relationships. Sherrie and Vicky have been joyful, positive and strong sisters despite all obstacles and I admire them for it. Their siblings, my cousins Diane and John, died as young adults without my getting to know them much.

My Uncle John was "disciplined" (excommunicated, prohibited from speaking in meetings or taking communion) because of his divorces but he never wavered from thinking there was one and only one way to do church: the Exclusive Plymouth Brethren way. He had a good heart but when I was finally able to sit down with him, later in life, I found our conversation was a bit restricted in that he already knew everything about life and theology! (I only slightly jest; he was supremely confident in his personal opinions on everything). Uncle John died at age sixty-seven of heart disease and diabetes. As wealthy as he was, I have always wished he had more thoughtfully and generously provided and cared for his California daughters.

One fun story I must share. At age ten I was tormented by a bigger kid who rode his bike into me on the playground and wanted to fight (I didn't even know this bully). I was scared but managed to say in as threatening a manner as possible: "You know my Uncle John was a boxer and a great football player and if you don't leave me alone I'm going to call him." The bully rode off quickly. I wrote a letter to my hero uncle John and told him the story and added "I didn't tell him you were back in Toledo." I still have that letter!

TRIBAL IMPACTS?

I feel some sadness that I never had very many members of my extended family (grandparents, cousins, aunts and uncles) around me during my life. Our own children, Jodie and Jonathan, always had two sets of grandparents just ten miles away during their first twenty years. They had nearby cousins, uncles and aunts as well. But in my life, the Gill/Hallgren tribe was based in Portland, Oregon, six hundred miles north of Oakland, California, while the Wurz/Block tribe was in Minneapolis and Toledo, more like two thousand miles away. Only my Grandma Wurz was close by for twenty years in Oakland (and that was great!). We did grow up with lots of old family stories from our parents so their presence, and especially the heritage of their Christian faith, was very much a living part of my upbringing.

So what does this roots story mean? What, in the end, was the impact, of the tribal heritage I have described in this chapter and the one preceding it? I am very grateful to God and my forebears, first, for a healthy body and mind. Good genes! We have some arthritis, diabetes, and heart issues in our tribe but I suspect these would be manageable enough if not for some obesity owing to bad eating habits (themselves partly explained by a tradition of frequent entertainment of guests at our tables). My mom used to giggle and say that our pudgy family was "built for famine."

Part One: Incubators (1946–1964)

It is striking to me how many of my forebears went into some kind of accounting work—and how often they were pretty much self-taught and learned through on-the-job experience. There has not been much formal education beyond high school in my tribe (both sides), even up to the present. Some of our smartest even dropped out of high school to get to work right away instead. We've had some writers but even more counters. Some worked for banks or the tax office, but it's remarkable how many worked for the railroads—mostly in railway offices but with some on the mechanical side. There were obviously some very talented women in my tribe but most of them focused on raising their children. This is not at all surprising given their traditional cultural and religious contexts. But it does pain me to think of all the gifts in our women that could not be fully developed and expressed. Almost all members of the tribe, male and female, had a terrific work ethic and did what needed to be done to provide for their families. We never became victims of our economic circumstances but worked hard wherever we could.

I am impressed by how bold and adventurous my ancestors were in leaving their families, friends, and cultures in late nineteenth century England, Sweden, and Germany for long, sometimes rough voyages and an unknown future in North America. After immigrated to the USA in the 1880s, they tended to settle in the northern states (because of familiar climates like where they came from? Because of acquaintances, distant relatives, or religious communities ready to welcome and assist them?). They settled from Omaha and Des Moines to Minneapolis/St. Paul in the Midwest, from Seattle to Portland and eventually San Francisco on the Pacific Coast. You don't see much evidence of nostalgia for the old country or its language or ways. You also don't see much political talk or interest. We have very few military veterans. The tribe seemed glad to be in the USA as a land of opportunity but it is hard to find written reflections on broader issues and trends in American life and history like Reconstruction after the Civil War, Jim Crow and racism, the Great Migrations of millions of immigrants from Europe and Asia, or the Holocaust or World Wars. It's hard to know if they liked or disliked FDR's New Deal or were bothered by the bombings of Dresden or Hiroshima.

The dominating tribal impact on me is the intense faith in God—and not just Christianity in a generic sense but in the particular thinking and traditions of the Exclusive Plymouth Brethren. For four generations, this tradition defined not just the personal faith, family life, and church reality of almost everyone in our tribe, it also structured our social life and relationships. The distinctive, idiosyncratic belief system of the PBs dictated a separatist (and often, I have to say, condescending) stance toward all other Christians—and an otherworldly spirituality that praised disinterest in "the things of this world" (political, cultural) and constantly talked and sang of the imminent second coming of Jesus Christ.

My forebears were not just members but vocal leaders and advocates for the Brethren movement and its most rigorous, narrow application. Great grandpa Alfred became over time not just a leader in his local church but a speaker and teacher at conferences and "in the Lord's work," as they say. Great uncle John Ruskin Gill was an even more vocal leader, itinerant teacher, and author of various papers and tracts urging separation from other Christians. My grandfather Frank and my father Walter were not official "laboring brethren" (men who left secular occupations to itinerate as approved teachers), but they also were not just local church but conference speakers and authors and full-on advocates for the movement. More on this in my chapter below on Faith.

Of all the things in my tribal heritage, it is this passionate faith in Jesus Christ that I value, share, and honor the most. As I will explain later, I left the Plymouth Brethren in my mid-twenties because I could no longer tolerate the contradictions between the foundational beliefs in Jesus Christ and Scripture they taught me—and the ways I came to believe they misinterpreted and misapplied them. They taught me to want to be biblical in thought and behavior. I walked away because they were not biblical enough, not for any other reason. A tradition that began (in the 1820s) so brightly and had so much to give to the whole church and world got distorted and corrupted in my view. The Gill and Wurz tribes were nurtured by this tradition in wonderful ways, but they were also captured, entangled in the complex labyrinth of "Plymouth Brethrenism," and energetically promoted it. Questioning, to say nothing of leaving, this community and tradition became as difficult as leaving the Amish, or Mormonism, or (for many) Catholicism.[1]

But before I leave the topic of my tribal and ethnic/cultural roots and heritage, let me share some random feelings about it. I have visited England a few times, including our ancestral Newcastle-on-Tyne home town (and the actual house in Seaton Carew where Grandpa Frank was born). It is a beautiful land for sure. While I have heard all the snobbish criticism of English cuisine, I like their pub food and drink—"Smithwicks and fish and chips please!" I have enjoyed visiting England—but intensely dislike the monarchy (any monarchy) and the class structure (I am not a fan of Upstairs/Downstairs and Downton Abbey). As a professor and writer, I appreciate Oxford and Cambridge and much of the British intellectual and cultural tradition—but I react against the rationalism and snobbery I find in some of their thinkers and writers. I do like Morse, Jane Tennyson, Vera and other fictional detectives I get to watch on the PBS network. I love a lot of British rock music. England is for me a very mixed picture.

We also got to live in and explore Sweden from July to December of 1999, when I had a visiting professorship in Jönköping at the foot of Lake Vättern. We traveled (and camped) all over Sweden (and Scandinavia), visiting the towns where my wife Lucia's forebears and mine came from. We find it very interesting that in the mid-19th

---

1. Remember: this is just my story. I have great respect for my family and friends who chose to remain in Brethrenism. There is a lot of love and truth in these old communities, and probably a bit more freedom as well these days. I am writing about a movement I left in the 1970s, fifty years ago. And I am under no illusion: there are no utopian alternatives outside the Brethren system. None.

century she had a great grandparent in Åmål on the western side of Lake Vänern—due west of the town of Vadstena on the east side of Lake Vättern where my great grandfather Gustave Carlson/Hallgren hailed from with his parents the Anders Carlsons. I enjoy Sweden a lot, especially its social democracy in which the wealth gap between rich and poor is not allowed to get anywhere near the obscene levels seen in the USA and other capitalist oligarchies.

But honestly, it is when I have been in Germany that my heart (truly) has skipped a beat. I feel "Heimat" and "Sehnsucht" when I enter Deutschland, as crazy as that sounds. I studied German for four years in high school, another year in college, and two summers later in Munich. My mom spoke German and shared some Germanophilia. I had to pass reading and translation exams in German for each of my graduate degrees (MA and PhD). In 1982 we visited Munich and I instantly loved the culture, the language, and the beauty. I felt at home. I have been back to Munich for two Oktoberfests (it did feel a little bit like heaven) and two summer study vacations (1985 and 1995). I love the friendliness of the casual Bayrische (Bavarian) greeting even to strangers, "grüß Gott" (God greets you!). The combination of great freedom with agreed-upon order (e.g., no speed limits on the Autobahn but strict safety traditions about lane choices when driving) appeals to me. My name is English but my soul is German. I have often said "mein Blut ist halb Deutsch" (my blood is half German) via both my mother's parents. So it was at first a bit of a shock when Ancestry.com told me my blood was in fact about twenty-five percent English and twenty-five percent Swedish—but then about twenty-five percent Norwegian and twenty-five percent German! The explanation seems to be that from the tenth to thirteenth centuries, long before our German family records begin, marauding bands of Norwegian Vikings left their DNA imprint on the German people (This, I joke, may explain my extreme fondness for salmon).

I am much more drawn to the theology of Karl Barth (Swiss German) and Dietrich Bonhoeffer than any of the British theologians (not crazy about C.S. Lewis or the Inklings). I love the German church experiences I have had and the beer gardens and brauhauses. Love to order Schweinshachsen, roasted chicken, and "ein Masz bitte"! I admire the quality automobiles like BMW. I drove Volkswagens for decades until Toyota won me over. Love the Munich opera. I could have lived there happily. Back in 1985 after seven weeks in Munich I had a very painful, difficult time just getting on the plane to come home. If I hadn't been bound for Lucia and Berkeley, I think I would have just stayed. But with all this happy talk, I have to also say that I am also always mindful of how a Dachau (Nazi concentration camp) can suddenly arise next to a Munich in our world. Today's USA better pay attention.

How often, when writing these chapters, have I wished I had asked more questions when I had the chance. In my view of the afterlife, I hope to get that chance someday.

4

Parents: Walter Gill & Vivian Wurz

FROM THE BIGGER ANCESTRAL tribe to my immediate family, in this chapter I want to talk about my parents. I actually wrote about them almost fifty years ago in Chapter One of Virginia K. Hearn's book *What They Did Right: Reflections on Parents by Their Children*.[2] My dad and mom were by no means perfect but, thank God, they knew that. As the old joke goes, they were still "way ahead of second place." I want to describe my dad, then my mom. In the following chapter I will describe my three sisters. These are all what I am calling "incubators" of my emerging "marginal" activist life. Some of you may wish to skip ahead and begin my story with the eighteen-year-old who showed up on the Berkeley campus in 1964. But this is how that eighteen-year-old was incubated and delivered into the world.

MY DAD WALTER

My dad was Walter Leonard Gill (April 12, 1913–December 11, 2004). He told us that Leonard meant "lion-hearted" and Walter meant "leader." So he was our family's "lion-hearted leader." We really did talk about the meaning of our names like this. I was told that David meant "beloved" and so as "David Walter" I was destined to be a "beloved leader." Well, I do tend to jump out and lead if need be and no one else will step up—and I do like to be loved. But "beloved leader" has never been a way I would describe myself or my life's ambition (which is to be a faithful man of God and have a positive impact on the church and the world).

My dad's nickname growing up was "Butch" and he signed some correspondence to his sister with that nickname. "Walt" is what people called him. Growing up in

---

2. Virginia K. Hearn, *What They Did Right: Reflections on Parents by Their Children*. (Wheaton, Illinois: Tyndale House, 1974).

Portland, Oregon, my dad was a newspaper delivery boy for several years (something I also did and, later still, my son Jonathan). Getting up very early every morning and working for a couple hours, rain or shine, dealing with unreliable subscribers—it's all great training for the future and a source of income. My grandparents discouraged my dad from trying out for football out of fear of injury—but he earned his varsity letter at Benson High School as student manager for the baseball team. He was also stage manager for the senior class play.

My dad's two oldest brothers were able to study at the University of Washington and Oregon State. His third brother joined the military. My dad was definitely college material when he attended Benson High School and he hoped to follow his brother George's path up to the University of Washington to study engineering. But he graduated in January 1931—just as the bottom of the economy dropped out in the Great Depression. Sorry, no college possible! In any case, in 1932, a year after high school graduation he moved with his parents and sister to Omaha, Nebraska, where Union Pacific had transferred his father's employment.

My dad's story over the next seventeen years (1932–1949) has some gaps which are best explained by (a) months of often discouraging job searching and (b) frequent road trips on the Union Pacific Railway. Because of his father's job he had a pass for free travel on the UP, and he took full advantage and got around to at least step into all of the lower forty-eight states. With college out of the realm of the possible, my dad found and completed a correspondence course in accountancy. Today's higher education has moved aggressively toward "distance learning" through the mail—and now even more online—so what seemed unusual and second best back then has now become an ordinary, normal way for many to get educated. The correspondence course gave my dad all the job skills he needed to launch his professional career as an accountant. He made up a lot for the missing humanities and liberal arts side of a college education by being an avid lifetime reader of history and of both local newspapers and national news magazines (like *Time*) covering world affairs. He missed out on (a) foreign language and, of course, (b) the give-and-take, push-and-shove, critical thinking that one usually gets in the university. He always loved thoughtful discussion but shied away from vigorous debate.

With the accounting course training, my dad got a job at J. L. Brandeis, the largest merchant in Omaha. I am guessing this was about 1934 because he says he stayed there three years and refers to some tasks in 1937. At first, he worked forty-eight hours a week for $15 (or thirty-one cents/hour) and then was "promoted" to fifty-eight hours a week for $19 (thirty-three cents/hour). I still marvel at these hours and wages. The accounting office where he worked was responsible to keep records of purchases, sales, cash register clerk deposits, and payroll for a thousand-member workforce. In 1937 he was put in charge of implementing the new requirements of the Social Security system, using a new Burroughs bookkeeping machine. My dad used his earnings to buy his mom and dad their first ever (Maytag) washing machine

PART ONE: INCUBATORS (1946–1964)

and an electric refrigerator. No more ice box! He also bought them an electric mixer and, for his own use, a moving picture camera and projector, which he used with enthusiasm for many years.

After three years, in 1938 or so, denied a raise or any prospects for advancement at Brandeis, my dad moved on to the Continental Baking Company, first as a cashier but then moving into the regular accounting department, working six days a week for forty-eight to sixty hours (now earning 37.5 cents/hour!). This was his employment for five years until 1943 when management changed. With no clear opportunities for growth or advancement, he quit to look for something else. After a brief and unsatisfying stint at his father's employer, Union Pacific, he got hired at Omar Baking in the flour mill division—but left just months later for better prospects at Farm Crops Processing Company (which produced alcohol for sales to whiskey producers—something the teetotaling Gill family wrestled with before deciding it was ok to work there. My dad was, in some important ways, a model of "faith at work," the mission of my own life). He worked there from about 1944 until May 1949 when the company was on the ropes and forced to make deep cuts in its workforce because of industry competition. Dad and mom sold their home and moved out to Portland, Oregon, to stay in my dad's parents' house and look for a new job. He had been in Omaha for seventeen years (1932–49).

Like his father Frank, who didn't even finish his high school education, my dad was naturally very gifted and a quick learner. He was so fast and accurate doing computations in his head and with pencil and paper it always amazed everyone. Later in his career he used an adding machine sometimes but he "escaped" just as computers were invading his accounting world. In Portland it took him seven weeks but he found a job as a cost accountant with Crown Zellerbach, a big paper company. He and my mom soon were able to buy a house. Then in 1952 CZ transferred him down to San Francisco where they were building a tall new corporate headquarters at #1 Bush and Market Street (now dwarfed by much taller buildings which surround it).

My dad worked for CZ until his retirement at age sixty-four in 1977 after twenty-eight years with the company. He had worked mostly in the Long-Range Planning department, crunching numbers and studying not just past performance but industry and economic trends, forecasting different scenarios for operating expenses, capital costs, sales, and so on. He analyzed the finances of specific paper mills CZ owned around the country and of the communication systems connecting the different regional operations with each other and with headquarters. He prepared financial reports for government bureaus in Washington DC that were setting price controls and regulations for the paper industry. He traveled a lot by airplane. One time in the early 1950s, he took me with him on a sleeper car train from Oakland to Portland, where he had business meetings while I played at grandma's house.

My dad was not impressed by all the MBAs coming into his department during the 1960s and 1970s, nor did he care much for the mad rush to embrace business machines and computer technology. His mind was already a fast computer and he could figure things out before the computers were even fired up. I have a similar reaction when I am trying to set up a date to meet someone: I whip out my paper "week-at-a-glance" calendar book and then have to wait patiently for the other guy to get the electronic calendar on his smart phone booted up. After he retired from Crown Zellarbach, my dad worked a few months each year for six years for H&R Block Tax Preparation Services and then another fifteen years as an independent tax preparer for a handful of family members and old clients. He was so quick and accurate all his life that it pained him greatly when the IRS rejected my tax returns two or three years in a row in the 1990s because of mistakes he had made. A minor glitch at the end of an exceptional career.

Not just his math but my dad's English was near perfect and he corrected my grammatical and spelling glitches all my life—including a few that escaped my editors and embarrassed me in print editions of my books. My dad loved doing the crossword puzzle and reading the daily newspaper and *Time* Magazine. He especially loved reading his Bible every day and studying commentaries on its meaning. He read one of the thirty-one chapters of Proverbs every morning of his adult life. Talk about staying grounded ethically! He was self-educated as a Christian teacher (standard practice for Plymouth Brethren, like his dad and grandfather) and had a bigger theology library than many seminary-trained pastors I have known, mostly, but not entirely, filled with the works of Plymouth Brethren writers. He was more open to learning from non-Brethren teachers than most of his peer leaders in the movement. We used to listen to Billy Graham's "Hour of Decision" and Charles E. Fuller's "Old Fashioned Revival Hour" on the radio and he was an early subscriber to *Christianity Today*.

My dad loved baseball above all sports and played a little golf as a teenager. I talked him into playing golf a couple times and hoped he would keep his promise of playing regularly when he retired, but he just wasn't that interested. He rode a bike as a youth but never learned how to swim. He was always chubby and never very fit or athletic—but plenty well-coordinated and strong as a home handyman! Growing up, I did play catch in the front yard with my dad with our gloves and a softball. We did share a love of watching baseball. He took me to Seals Stadium in San Francisco to watch the (Triple A) Seals baseball team, and to the old Oaks stadium in Emeryville to watch the Oakland Oaks play. When the Giants moved from New York to San Francisco we became big fans. We attended a game or two each year and often listened to the radio or watched television broadcasts of their games. We loved the Giants-Dodgers rivalry and all the great players—Willie Mays, Juan Marichal, Sandy Koufax, Don Drysdale . . . we knew all the players' names. We both loved following (and computing up to the minute) the batting averages and other statistics of our favorite players. I am sure that this helped my math scores later on.

While my dad always went to work in a business suit (never a sport coat) and tie (he took the bus from Oakland to San Francisco every day), he loved to put on his jeans and work clothes and take on some building project around the house. He plumbed in an extra bathroom, enlarged the opening between the dining and living rooms so we could accommodate bigger crowds for dinners, and did all manner of projects around the yard and in the house at 953 Alice Avenue in San Leandro where we lived for ten years (1953–1963). With only three small bedrooms inside, my dad designed and built a bedroom for me (around junior high school age) measuring about seven feet by seven feet at the back of our garage. I loved this room and could never understand why he apologized from time to time for "sticking me out in the garage." No, it was perfect, dad! When he and my mom moved to a home in the hills of Oakland in 1963, he built (with major help from my teenage son Jonathan) some incredible terraced gardens on the slope behind the house.

I learned to be a handyman from my dad—how to imagine and design projects, buy materials at the lumber yard, pour concrete, use power tools, do basic plumbing and electrical work—the whole nine yards. My own history with houses has been very much like my dad's—and my son Jonathan has carried it on in his own houses over the years. From my earliest age I was tagging along to the dump or the lumber yard, helping to carry things, crawling into smaller spaces than my dad could fit, climbing to heights he couldn't, and from about age ten or twelve onward blowing his mind with how strong I was or how I could hang out and wash the outside of a second story window.

My dad was gentle, not rough. He was strong and reliable, never weak. Stable. Calm. I never heard him curse or swear or even utter a vulgar word. Not once. He never told a dirty or risqué joke. I never heard him say a demeaning word about women (as a species; he did occasionally say harsh things about individuals whose behavior he disapproved) or other racial groups. Even in anger, he smoldered rather than exploded. My father never drank alcohol other than a sip at communion or maybe if a champagne glass was thrust at him at a wedding reception. He didn't like the taste of beer with his fish and chips or wine with anything, to say nothing of harder liquor. He had been raised to think that drinking alcohol was "worldly," a step toward addiction and a lost life, and a bad example that might stumble others with alcohol problems. He also just didn't like strong coffee or cheese or adventurous foods. He always chose vanilla when ordering ice cream! He never smoked. He didn't like loud music, jazz, or rock and roll. He liked Lawrence Welk, Victor Borge, some musical theatre (we occasionally went to Woodminster in the Oakland Hills), and, above all, Christian hymns as sung by George Beverly Shea or, most of all, as played on the piano by his wife or sung by the whole family. He didn't have a great voice but he loved to sing those hymns.

Dad was instinctively conservative in manner and outlook but he was not political. Like most Plymouth Brethren he believed in and longed for the second coming of Christ and viewed the political/cultural world as irretrievably messed up and getting worse. When World War II approached back in the late 1930s, he declared as a conscientious objector—but in the mandatory pre-draft call-up he was rejected as 4F (his draft board papers say) because of being overweight (I remember him saying it was also because of being "flat footed," whatever that is). He despised violence and war—but he would never have declined to do his civic duty in a non-violent capacity. If drafted, he would serve as a medic or something but not as a combat soldier who might have to kill an enemy. He had political opinions and stayed current with the news every day but he never voted because of his religious convictions. He liked President Eisenhower but never commented (much) on other presidents. After Watergate he was more upset with Nixon's cussing than his political crimes (though I am sure he did not approve of those either). He didn't believe Christians should engage in violence of any kind or give their primary allegiance to worldly nations like the USA.

My dad bore the scars of a fourth son who got picked on, disrespected, and ignored by three older brothers. He sometimes shared with us a dream that one day in heaven he would see his brothers again and introduce to them with pride his big family. As the little kid, and a non-athletic one at that, he grew up a bit timid and lacking in self-confidence. Birth order shapes most of us a lot and my dad was never comfortable acting like a first-born, assertive leader. Lacking a university degree also contributed to his self-doubt. He joined something called the "Toastmasters' Club" which promised to help business folk become better speakers, which I'm sure it did, though he never became a powerful, confident communicator.

One regrettable part of the saga is that sometime in the 1980s I discovered that Doug Cormack, the husband of New College Berkeley board member Jean Cormack, had worked at Crown Zellerbach and knew my dad. I also found out that Rex Morris, father of my New College student and assistant, Ken Morris, had been a long-time CZ guy who knew my dad. Both Doug and Rex were great guys and active Christians. But my dad didn't know this about them. He never participated in any company staff or holiday parties or social events. He was a much-respected, good worker and colleague. But his timidity and religious separatism kept him from enjoying what could have been years of great Christian fellowship at work.

In May of 1940 my dad fell in love and married Saramae Erisman (1914–1942). Saramae was one of the first female graduates of Wheaton College and I have always wished I knew more about her.[3] In an ironic twist of fate, her brother Maurice Erisman was the father of two guys, John and Al Erisman, who in the 1960s became close, lifetime friends and project team members of mine. Tragically, within months of the wedding, Saramae became so ill she was moved back by her parents from Omaha to her parents' home in Chicago to be closer to the best possible medical help. She died of kidney failure on January 30, 1942. My dad could never talk about his grief, out of

---

3. My good friends, John and Al Erisman, Saramae's nephews, told me that her strict Plymouth Brethren father gave her permission to attend provided she took no religion courses (which might have taught her "bad doctrine"). Most students attend Wheaton because of their solid Evangelical theology. She went in spite of it.

fear my mom might be hurt thinking he really pined for his first wife (a legitimate concern, of course). But I do think the deep suffering he felt at the tragic loss of his wife—combined with the sometimes rough and disrespectful treatment he got from his older brothers—help explain my dad's kindness, thoughtfulness, and eye for the downtrodden in spirit. He was a man of deep compassion. I think his favorite Bible passage might have been Ephesians 2:4–7 (quoted here from the King James Version, which always ruled in my father's house). "But God, who is rich in mercy, for his great love wherewith he loved us . . . hath raised us up together, and made us sit together in heavenly places in Christ Jesus, that in the ages to come he might shew the exceeding riches of his grace in his kindness toward us through Christ Jesus." Kindness. At night we were taught to kneel by our bed for a prayer that always began "Dear kind God . . ."

In June 1942 my dad bought his first car, a used 1940 Chevrolet. He took off on a solo road trip that took him through Minneapolis, where the Herman Wurzs (known through Brethren connections) invited him to lodge with them. He had known Vivian Wurz and her family before but this time she really caught his eye and heart. They corresponded. He proposed on Valentine's Day in 1943. They were married on April 26, 1943. He was just thirty, she was twenty-four. They enjoyed the next sixty-one years together.

My dad's greatest gifts to me were his kindness, patience, wisdom, and encouragement. I had endless questions about God, life, the nature of girls and women, baseball strategy, cars, money, church. He patiently listened and then gave what to me were convincing explanations. It was only after I left home at twenty-one that I realized that he didn't know everything and wasn't perfect! Our question-and-answer sessions could go until 1:00 or 2:00 a.m. when I was in junior and senior high school, even though he always got up the next morning at 6:00 a.m.. My dad did spank me a few times as a young child—and reproved and disciplined me when I needed it. But he was always gentle and kind, if firm and strict. He led by challenging me to live higher, to rise up and be what God intended and gifted me to be.

One time when he was called into Bancroft Junior High, the principal described my disruptive behavior. My dad was a little gloomy and ashamed of my behavior. But here is what he said: "Mr. Larsen, my son David is a young man of God and this behavior is beneath him and he knows it. This is not who he is and I am confident that from now on he will rise up and be the great young man God made him to be." Of course, I was embarrassed to death to have my dad called in like this and prevented from getting to work on time. But you can see how this positive reinforcement could be so much more effective than shaming and cursing me out in front of the principal. My dad kept telling me, every once in a while, "we prayed that God would give us a beloved leader for a son and that's you." Of course, this kind of parenting could put a crushing expectation on some kids—but I think my dad (and mom) could see how this approach drew the best out of me. I wanted badly to live up to their hopes and confidence.

I always wanted to make my dad proud of his son. His encouragement, love, and kindness as I grew up were powerful life-shaping forces for me. My dad never talked about my (or his) hopes for my college or career unless I brought it up. He didn't try to motivate me to get good grades or admitted to a great university, never suggested one career track or another. What mattered to him was my faith and character. He was not given to complimenting me much about my eventual academic or literary achievements. I very rarely heard him say "great speech" or "great idea" or "great book" my whole adult life. He did like to introduce me to his friends as "My son "DOCTOR David Gill" and that was nice, I guess, but it was about a formality, an honorific title, not about a substantive project or idea of mine. When he wrote a fifty-page story of his own life I got one page, exactly the same as each of my sisters. He said nothing about my faith or career. I know he loved my wife and admired our home and family and often said so but I'm not sure he understood much the world and the work to which I was called when I left our home and church.

On three occasions I was able to surprise my dad with an unusual gift. First of all, somehow I got a call from born again Watergate burglar Chuck Colson who was a new Christian and wanted to ask me about Jacques Ellul. We spent an hour or two at a San Francisco Hotel in discussion. Colson was smoking his pipe when I arrived so I got mine out and joined him. As we finished up I asked Chuck if we could take a photo together with our pipes in the grand tradition of C.S. Lewis and Karl Barth. ("OK David but don't let this get out and harm the weaker brethren"). Then we took another photo together without pipes and I asked Chuck to autograph it (when it got printed) to my dad and say something like "Great job on David. Happy Father's Day, Chuck"—which Colson was happy to do. I gave it to my dad the next Father's Day. I knew this would be a kick because my dad had just read about Colson's conversion and been delighted.

My dad also read the magazine *Christianity Today* regularly. I had recruited CT's legendary founding editor Carl F. H. Henry out to teach in one of our summer programs at New College Berkeley in the early 1980s. Henry was about my dad's age. So I had my parents over for dinner with Carl Henry and a few other luminaries—and sat my dad next to Carl Henry. I loved being able to set this up. Two wise and faithful old men I loved were feasting and fellowshipping together. Finally, in the late 1980s and early 1990s I was working out most early mornings at Berkeley's Gold's Gym with retired baseball star Reggie Jackson. Very intentionally I never asked Reggie for autographs, tickets, or anything else. But one year when Reggie again invited me to come over to the ballpark for an A's game sometime (he was a batting coach at this stage), I asked if he could get tickets for my dad and me to a game on the Friday before Fathers' Day—and if I could introduce my dad to him (remember my dad was a lifelong baseball fan). Reggie left us tickets to two field level seats behind the A's dugout on the third base side. We got there during batting practice just before the game. Reggie was out on the field in uniform and saw us make our way to our seats. He called us down to the field and walked us out to short left field where he chatted with my dad and then autographed a baseball to him. We returned to our seats and everyone around us was saying 'hey who are you guys? How do you know Reggie?" Fun!

After my nine years in Chicago (1992–2001) we moved back home to Oakland. I was now living close enough and had enough flexibility in my working hours to be able to help my mom and sisters care for my dad in what turned out to be the final three years leading up to his death in 2004 at age ninety-one. I did a huge amount of work clearing out his big house and getting it ready for sale. We spent hours and hours side-by-side in his home office going through boxes and drawers full of old papers, financial records, correspondence. I helped him get rid of two-thirds of the paper and organize the rest, which had all fallen into disarray over the most recent decade. I was careful not to throw anything out without his review and agreement—so, in effect, we were reviewing much of his life. Lots of hours side-by-side with my dad. I organized the sale of the family house, the review of the estate and will, and much of the move into the in-law unit at my sister Kit's house. Of course, everybody pitched in to the best of their availability but providentially I was back home in Oakland and free to make this big transition my main job for a few weeks.

As my dad got closer to the end, he asked me to lead his memorial service to which I agreed. I have seen so many memorial services led by "professionals" who could not possibly capture the life or faith and legacy of the person deceased. No matter what the state of my own grief, I wanted my dad honored. The hilarious thing is that, just after my dad died, in a family meeting we discovered that he had at some point also asked my nephew John Iwawaki and my brother-in-law Ron Faria to lead his memorial! Each time he forgot. So in the end my dad had three mini-sermons at his memorial service! It was all joy and so appropriate.

One other memorable moment on dad's last day or two of life on earth was when he was resting at the hospital in a semi-conscious state and we were gathered around to love, sing, and pray him from this life to the next. During his final night, our sister Elizabeth was by his bedside and heard him suddenly say, "But what about Viv? I don't want to go without her." My mom's response when she came in and heard about this was "Walt, I will join you soon but I'm not ready yet." And my dad sailed away with the angels.

MY MOM VIVIAN

Vivian Erna Wurz Gill was my mom (January 15, 1919–April 18, 2008). Her name is related to words like "vital" and "vivacious." And she was all of that. My dad was quiet, conflict-averse, sometimes brooding. My mom was full of energy and dreams. Unrealistic at times. Illogical at times. Emotionally on the edge of breakdown sometimes. Always sacrificial and serving. Sunday after church we almost always had guests over for a big meal. My mom was bouncing around cooking and serving and directing her kids (and sometimes Grandma Wurz) as we got ready.

My mom was born in Wausau, Wisconsin, January 24, 1919, but raised in Minneapolis, Minnesota. Her parents, Herman and Erna (Block) Wurz, were simple, hard-working, pious children of German immigrants. As with many families with non-English backgrounds, German was not spoken in the home as the family tried to become as American as possible. But my mom took German courses in high school and always kept some affection for the language and her family's national roots. In 1980 she was finally able to visit Germany for a few days on a European trip with my dad. I got a kick out of writing her postcards in German several times when I was in Germany.

Mom attended the University of Minnesota for just one year after high school,1937–38. After this she worked five years as a librarian until her 1943 marriage to my dad. When I visited the University of Minnesota to give a talk to a student group in the 1990s, I bought my mom a big UM sweatshirt which she proudly wore a few times. She was always very proud of that one university year. None of her other family members attended college. She was always a bit regretful not to have had an outside-the-family career of some sort. When we kids were in high school she briefly got a part-time job bookkeeping for a gas station and then was an enthusiastic Avon lady for many years.

My mom used to reminisce about ice skating on Lake Harriet in Minneapolis in the winter and swimming in the summer. My dad never learned how to swim or ice skate but I remember my mom taking us all for skating at Iceland in Berkeley and swimming in Fleishhacker Pool in San Francisco—out near the zoo and the ocean. My dad could ride a bike but not my mom. My mom learned how to play the piano as a child. She could read music but was most impressive in being able to sit down and "play by ear" almost anything she heard. She had a real feel for it. She and her sisters sang in three-part harmony growing up. It was a handsome family with the three beautiful Wurz sisters and their cute little brother John.

MARRIAGE & PARENTING

My parents met through the network of Plymouth Brethren churches ("meetings" or "assemblies"). Annual three-day Bible conferences in Chicago and Des Moines helped midwestern Brethren stay in touch (and look for potential mates!). My dad, then based in Omaha, and my mom from Minneapolis had to be aware of each other. Herman Wurz had to approve of the serious young Brethren man, Walter Gill. I asked my dad and mom how World War II and the Holocaust affected their thinking and living in the Forties. They said that of course they were aware of the news and concerned about it. But the Brethren had an other-worldly theology and perspective, praying and hoping for the imminent return of Jesus Christ. They were, as St Paul says, "citizens of heaven," pilgrims and strangers in the world. There was some real anti-German sentiment at times during the war against the German Nazis, but I don't recall my mom saying she experienced it in the heavily-German upper Midwest.

My parents spent the first six years of their marriage based in Omaha. Their first three children were born there in 1945, 1946, and 1948. In 1949 they packed up and moved west to Portland, Oregon, in search of better employment prospects for my dad. For a few months our family of five lived in the upstairs of my grandparents' home. After my dad found work with Crown Zellerbach they were able to buy their first home. In 1950 our little sister Elizabeth was born. In 1952 Crown Zellerbach moved us down to Oakland, California, so my dad could work in CZ's new corporate headquarters at #1 Bush Street in San Francisco.

For one year we rented a house on Outlook Avenue in Oakland and then moved just across the Oakland city limit into San Leandro in 1953. Our home from 1953 to 1963 was at 953 Alice Avenue, a block off MacArthur Boulevard, near Jerry's Beefburgers. My parents paid about $10,000 for it and sold it for about $20,000 in 1963 when they moved a half-mile to 3318 Revere Avenue in Sheffield Village in East Oakland. They paid about $32,000 for the Revere house in 1963 and kept it until 2003 when it became too much to take care of, and sold it for about $450,000. This was actually lower than one would have expected but a serious earthquake fault had shifted and twisted the house a few inches over the years and some extensive hill reinforcement would be needed. It was my mom who found the Revere house for sale and pushed hard for its purchase. My financially-conservative dad was worried about getting over-extended and initially opposed the move. But my mom prevailed and for the next forty years they both loved this big house with its great entertainment spaces, four bedrooms, great Bay view, and fertile soil for their terraced garden in back.

Wherever the Gill home was, my mother was a whirlwind of child care, home decoration, and entertainment. Almost every Sunday—unless we were going over to Spenger's Restaurant in Berkeley (where I learned to love clam chowder and halibut Florentine by copying my dad's regular order!), or maybe for a longer jaunt up to the Union Hotel's abundant feast in Occidental, or to some other Brethren household as guests—we had dinner guests. We usually followed my dad's English family tradition of having a big pot roast, potatoes and gravy, overcooked green vegetables, and some apple crisp or other homemade pie for dessert. It was comfort-food extraordinaire and we loved it. All of us kids took turns (my sisters insist they did it more often than me) setting the table (just right: knife facing inward on right side of plate with spoon next; forks on left side; cloth napkin folded just right). We helped serve, refill the water glasses, clear the table, and wash and dry the dishes. Of course, my mom was the whirlwind making it happen. But my dad would often go out and help wash and dry the dishes, a great example for his son. Once in a while my dad would cook. I remember his corn chowder and cinnamon rolls. But my mom was the kitchen star.

When dinner was ready, we would all stand behind our chairs and never sit down until the "queen" took her seat at the opposite end of the table from my dad. My dad insisted on that. There would be a lot of conversation around the table. We kids learned to be quiet participants and defer if there were adult guests. Lots of stories and laughter. We did not leave the table except to serve. (No mobile phones in those days!). We all stayed at the table until everyone finished eating and a request to be excused was granted. After dessert we often passed around a box of cards with Bible verses written on one side. We would go around the table with each person reading the card they had picked. Then we would all guess the reference (book and verse in the Bible). Great training for a Jeopardy category in the future! Younger kids got help from their neighbor in sounding out the words as they read (King James English of course).

We all kept our Sunday clothes on all day. Dresses for the girls—suits, white shirts, and neckties for the males. OK, we did take off our suit coats and loosen the ties. The women and girls could take off their church hats. I did go out in the street in front of the house and heave a football back and forth with anybody my age I could get interested. Maybe we'd play some board games like Monopoly or Checkers (but no playing cards allowed because of their association with gambling). School work was frowned upon—it's the Lord's Day (our preference to "sabbath" terminology). Many times we would all gather around the piano and sing hymns and Christian songs in amateur three-part harmony. As we got older and learned other musical instruments, we would sometimes add a guitar, clarinet, accordion (my mom could play), or violin as part of the experience. No television except maybe a Dodgers/Giants game and then only if there were no guests in the house. Re-gather at the table around four or five p.m., then back to church for the Sunday evening Gospel meeting.

We often had overnight guests: Brethren families passing through, itinerant Bible teachers in town for a few days of special midweek evening talks. Of course, to make all this happen my mom became a shopper extraordinaire, always looking for the best food prices, sometimes taking us out to farmer's markets or to berry farms where we could all help pick some baskets to take home. When her four kids were grown up, and especially when grandkids started showing up, my mom could never resist buying extra bags and boxes of food and household goods at Costco or elsewhere and bringing them to our houses.

Having four kids so close in age created a lot of stress on my mom when arguments, complaining, whining, fighting, and resistance to chores persisted. I remember a few scary times when she went into the bathroom and raised a pitiful wailing, crying sound that scared us to death. Once at least she called my dad at work in San Francisco and begged him to come home right away before she put her head in our gas oven! Horrible, but remember that her whole Wurz family lived on that emotional edge. There was also so much deep longing and satisfaction and joy in her personality. I could see and feel my mother's soul when she sang and played, when she listened to

Part One: Incubators (1946–1964)

Mahalia Jackson, when she was watching her grandchildren, and when she looked in my eyes with such deep love (I could cry even now as I remember and write this).

My mom didn't just "keep house"—she was a "home maker." My dad always insisted on that language. He was a traditionalist and thought women should (mostly) be homemakers—but did he ever honor that vocation! Home makers, in his view, were no less honorable than doctors or lawyers or professors. My mom would do anything for us kids. My best buddies growing up —Julius and Wally—could always come over to our house, stay for dinner, get a ride somewhere. My mom absolutely adored the fifteen-year-old Lucia Paulson I brought home to meet her in fall 1963. My mom was just made out of love.

Mom would come to all of my football games in high school. When I was a sophomore, she and Tom Vargas's mom would be the only people in a big grandstand which would be jammed the next day for the varsity game. Of course, she later came to all my varsity games but it was those earlier times when she came and no one else did that really showed her heart. She was there at the Alameda County Fair when my Snurd Brothers folk group (Julius, Wally, Jim Hyde and I) performed (and my sister Kit's Motown cover group was on the same program). She was always there for her kids and our friends.

My mom thought (and told me) I was the handsomest, smartest, most athletic, wonderful son on the face of the earth. Of course, she wasn't right. I had my disruptive side and raised hell for some of my teachers until I got to high school and changed my ways. But here is a sort of typical episode: Julius, Wally, and I (and others) were particularly disruptive in our seventh-grade teacher Mr. Braine's class. Finally, the school principal called my mom in for an appointment. "Mrs. Gill, Mr. Braine's seventh grade class is in chaos and we think your son David is the ring leader." My mom: "Mrs. Johnson, my son David is a wonderful boy and I just can't imagine that this would be his fault! Now do you have a two-way intercom system so you could listen in on Mr. Braine's class right now? My David has been home all week in bed with pneumonia and is not in class this week." Mrs. Johnson: "Why yes, we could just turn this on and listen." When she turned on the intercom a wall of noise came through. Mom: "You can see Mrs. Johnson that my David has nothing to do with it." Mrs. Johnson: "I am sorry to have troubled you Mrs. Gill." (Actually, I was a problem in that class, just not the only one!).

My parents, especially my dad, tried to treat my three sisters and me as equals when it came to chores, time to speak at the table, or receiving compliments. One time, however, I got special treatment from my mom that really ticked off my sisters. It was during a hot August in high school when our football team was having two-a-day workouts (nine to noon and two to five). One noon I came home and my mom cooked up a big steak for me (not sure that is recommended nutrition anymore). My sisters had their lunch sandwiches while I munched on my steak. Sisters: "why does David get a steak and we just get sandwiches, mom?" I paid for it for the rest of my life!

My mom was so proud of me and my wife (who she adored like her own daughter and in whom she saw so many of her own dreams and values) and our kids and the house and home we created. She was crushed, devastated, in 1971 when I was excommunicated from our family church and we were no longer part of the church life so central to our whole being. She did not like my beard and longish hair in the 1970s. But as the years rolled by, she often would semi-tearfully hug me and say "We miss you so much in our meeting (church) but I see how God has been using you and your gifts in ways that never would have been possible with us."

After I moved to Chicago in 1992 to begin a nine-year teaching stint at North Park, I tried to phone my parents once a week, and I came back home two or three times each year to visit them, check on our property (rented out), visit our kids in San Diego and Santa Barbara, and do the occasional visiting teaching or preaching gig. After I moved back home to Oakland in 2001, and especially after my dad died in 2004, I phoned my mom even more often, visited her, took her to lunch, and was able to take her with me to a few of my speaking gigs and study groups so she could see and experience my world—and get a lot of attention as my honored mom. At a Sunday evening talk I was giving at Tiburon Baptist Church, my friend, Pastor John Shouse, moderated a discussion with the congregation and surprised us all by saying at the end "Let's have the final comment tonight be from Dr. Gill's mom who is with us tonight!" Applause. My mom stood up and said something insightful about the topic (Plymouth Brethren women don't speak in church!). Fun. People adored her and loved her at every stop.

She died at age eighty-nine in 2004. I organized and led her memorial service, (as in my father's case four years earlier) putting aside my own grief again to be sure she was remembered and celebrated as she deserved.[4] I did a talk showing how she could tick off all the boxes in the famous Proverbs 31 description of the "virtuous woman" who not only cares for her family and makes her husband proud but does all sorts of other things in business and for the poor. Mom I still miss you so much.

In April 1993 we had a big 50th anniversary celebration of our parents' marriage. We brought together close to a hundred of their relatives and old friends. I got my guitar out of the closet and sang with my three sisters. We showed slides, reminisced, and feasted. Each of us four kids gave a brief tribute to our parents which we typed up for a memory book. Here is what I wrote (and said) at the party on April 25, 1993 (two days after their actual anniversary date). This pretty well sums up how I feel about my parents:

> Dear Mom & Dad
> What can a son say to his parents on the occasion of their 50th anniversary?

---

4. The Brethren tradition of funerals was to give little attention to the deceased but warn the living attendees of the imminence of death and their destiny in the fires of hell if they did not repent. I couldn't have stood for this for either my father or mother (or later for my aunt Kay when she died).

"Congratulations" is certainly one of the appropriate words. Your marriage has not just been a story of survival—but one of victory and joy. And you complicated the task by inviting four other souls into your household for many of those fifty years. So hearty "congratulations" to you both, first of all. Congratulations for never allowing anyone or anything to put asunder what God has joined together.

But "thank you" is the word that is even more appropriate.

Thank you Mom and Dad for inviting a seventh person into your marriage and our family and for keeping this person, Jesus Christ, at the center of your life for all these years. Maintaining the presence of Jesus Christ at the center of your marriage is your greatest accomplishment and your greatest gift to me.

Thank you for having a marriage in which you submitted your goals, ambitions and plans to the Lordship of Jesus Christ instead of pursuing your own self-interest. Thank you for attempting to live for Christ instead of for mammon or other false gods.

Thank you for practicing as well as preaching the importance of forgiveness in life's relationships, for showing how peace results when confession is met with mercy and justice is accompanied by grace.

Thank you for reading the Bible, for writing the Word of God on your doorposts, and for thousands of hours of exciting family discussions of its life-giving, life-guiding wisdom.

Thank you for making prayer a regular conversation with the living God and not just an exercise in formal piety.

Thank you for building a marriage and home that were open and generous in service and hospitality to friend and stranger alike. Thank you for a table that groaned with good food and was even richer in fellowship with brothers, sisters, and neighbors.

Thank you mom for the vivacious energy, wild creativity, and undaunted hope you have given to your marriage and family. Thank you for your laughter as well as your tears, for entering with full feeling into the heights and depths of human experience. Thank you for never failing to have a burst of creative ideas, for teaching us to reach for the stars, believing that God could take us there. Thank you for never giving up hope, never losing faith, never ceasing to love God, your husband or your kids with passionate loyalty and service.

Thank you dad for the seriousness and depth of your commitment to the things of the Lord. Thank you for your listening ear and your wise, compassionate counsel in your marriage and home. Thank you for knowing how to set limits and boundaries in a world that suffers greatly from their absence. Thank you for keeping the anchor firm while maintaining an exhilarating breadth of vision. Thank you for modeling and teaching the importance of growth during all the stages of life. Thank you for loving my mother as Christ loved the church and gave himself for it.

Thank you both for giving me three sisters and for loving my wife and children as your own. Thank you for continuing to care for me in the twenty-five-and-a-half years since I left your nest.

Your marriage has blessed me with the blessing of God. And while you have been tested with most of the tensions and trials that are common to man, you have yourselves been blessed a hundredfold for your humble efforts to live for Christ. It is hard to believe that the best is yet to come but that is our confident hope. May God shower you with his goodness in the years to come and when it is time—but not before—may the next phase begin with you hearing the words "Well done thou good and faithful servants! Enter into the joy of your Lord"

Love always from your son
David Walter Gill

5

Three Sisters & Family Life

I GREW UP WITH not just my mom and dad but three sisters, all of us kids pretty close in age. My dad was a kind and thoughtful husband and father and I was raised to show respect to women. There is no denying that it was a patriarchal even sexist culture in profound ways and I will comment on that below. But my dad, even more than my mom, insisted, loudly and often, that all four of us were equally important, valuable, and loved by them as gifts from God. The older I have gotten and the more time I have spent with my sisters in recent years, the more I have realized how very different their experiences were from mine. While I wanted to write in a somewhat more detailed way about each of them—because their presence was and remains a significant part of my own story—I have decided it is best to leave it to them to tell their own stories as they may choose. As I will try to explain, birth order and gender are major factors in the formation of children—alongside all the other incubators of our early lives.

DOROTHY ANNE GILL WEISE

My older sister Dorothy was born January 15, 1945. We always called her Dottie or even just Dot. Physically, she looked the most like our mom. I was born just one year and two weeks after her so we were the older pair in the foursome. Birth order is not quite fate or determinative but it is deeply influential. So from the day that I, Dottie's little brother, was born she heard constant messages about watching out and caring for her baby brother. She got to be the primary focus for just one year, then it was my turn for two years until my little sister Kitty came along—who got her two years until Elizabeth came along and forever became the baby of the family with all the benefits and privileges as well as the costs and burdens of that role! Dottie grew up with constant messages to set a good example, show leadership, protect, and care for her younger siblings. This is understandable and these are good messages but it puts a lot of pressure on the firstborn's whole life. They just don't get "babied," cuddled, and coddled much like the younger, smaller siblings. They are criticized from early on if they somehow fail in that protective, leadership task.

I always loved my older sister and yet I also felt sorry for the pressure she must have felt, which I could see taking its toll during adolescence and after. She was super-bright. I remember even in elementary school we took these things called "achievement tests"—standardized, national tests of knowledge and intelligence (of a certain type, I came to realize much later). I have pretty vivid memories of how both Dottie and I brought home every year scores in reading, mathematics, and other areas that placed us in the 97th to 99th percentiles of all test takers. Our grades were not straight A's but the raw potential was always super-high for both of us. I was no smarter than she was. The social and physical challenges of growing up were hardest on her as the firstborn. Boys like me had sports as an identity-shaper growing up; girls, for the most part, did not.

Dottie had a beautiful singing voice. She always had an interest in health care and was a volunteer "candy striper" at Fairmont Hospital during high school. After high school she took classes at Chabot College (our local community/junior college). She worked for a year as a counselor at the California School for the Deaf in Berkeley and then for decades as a medical assistant and transcriptionist, converting doctors' notes and scribbles into legible, permanent, and safe records. She always knew more than the rest of us about medical and health care topics in family conversations. She learned sign language so she could communicate with the deaf. She also became a blazing fast typist and in later years would help me by transcribing interviews I had recorded on tape.

In her medical records work, she was outstanding, reliable, and beloved by her doctors and employers. Sometime in her sixties, she and the other medical records transcriptionists were laid off in a corporate cost-cutting measure—and then rehired as temp workers at lower wages with no benefits. (An example of the kind of corporate greed that has enraged her brother all his life; more profits for the shareholders, bigger salaries and bonuses for the hospital executives, but exploit the employees at the bottom). Dottie did not spend much time griping about this injustice; she carried on. She even had to overcome carpal tunnel syndrome and surgery, a direct result of the constant wear and tear of working on a keyboard.

On May 9, 1970, Dottie married William Weise (1940–2000), who served in the Air Force for twenty years. They had one child, a son, Billy (b. 1973) nicknamed "Bear." In retirement she decided to move away from the expensive and noisy city up into the Sierra foothills to Paradise (near Chico), California, where she found a great deal on a big wooded lot with an old double-wide trailer (permanently anchored) and a broken-down building or two. Joined by son Billy and a shifting collection of six to twelve "guests," she became the presiding "mom" to an interesting, often needy and challenging "family." Whatever hardships and difficulties she has endured in life, she emerged as what I can only call a "saint." Housing and caring for her big "family" was not a "side gig" but a real ministry and calling. Few would be capable of doing what she has done. The downtrodden, hurting, lost and struggling found acceptance, support, compassion at what I called "Chateau Dottie" for several years until she finally "retired" to a simpler, quieter life.

KATHLEEN ANNE GILL FARIA

Two years after I was born, my sister Kathleen Anne arrived on May 13, 1948. We always called her Kitty or Kit. She didn't have the kind of "first born" pressure that Dottie had. After our youngest sister Elizabeth was born and became the permanent "little kid" in the family, Kitty was the permanent middle kid. I think that meant at least two things. First, she learned to be a mediator, the conciliator in the family. Second, she was often ignored, overlooked, or (more positively) able to move around beneath the radar! I was always aware of my older sister Dottie one year ahead of me in school but she didn't make many waves so we were not well-known as siblings as we moved through our school years. By contrast, Kitty was two years behind me in school and, especially in high school, our lives had some fun connections. Most importantly, my girlfriend and future wife was her classmate and friend. Kitty loved having a football player as her brother when she was a sophomore and I was a senior. We each had a singing group of high school friends that performed at the Alameda Country Fair and at a downtown San Leandro Music Fest.

I think we only had one clash or disagreement in our whole life and that was quickly enough resolved. All of our lives, no matter where we have lived, we have stayed in touch. She is the sister who never failed to send me a birthday card. She always told me how much she loved me and appreciated me. She was always proud of being my sister and wanted to meet my friends and hang out together. Of course, the fact that I married one of her school friends also enlarged and cemented our bond. We have a temperament and personality combination that works. But again, a primary factor in our close relationship is our birth order. My youngest sister Elizabeth was never in the same school with me and that, unfortunately, left some distance between us.

After high school Kit attended Chabot College for a while but got disrupted by a serious auto accident at the beginning of her sophomore year. She got married at nineteen to a guy who turned out to be a physically abusive, relationally unfaithful, bad dude. Our home church did not have any formal pre-marital counseling—or family crisis counseling if things got bad. Kitty had to struggle on her own and suffered greatly, physically and emotionally. But in an incredible story, Kitty met and married Ron Faria in 1979 and they have enjoyed a wonderful life together for more than 40 years. Kitty's daughters, Christy and Denise, could not have had a more wonderful dad and mom. Kitty spent seven years as a clerical worker at Moore Business Forms but then, after a couple intermediate moves, became Executive Assistant to the President of Citibank, Western Division, first in Oakland then in San Francisco, serving eleven different Citibank CEO/Presidents. Her skills in organization, communication, and team building were highly valued. I got to attend her Citibank retirement party and see the love and admiration she had earned.

Kitty and Ron love people and have been generous hosts of endless guests over the years. They have traveled the world, loving to explore God's creation and meet the people and cultures of the world. They have been "aunt and uncle" or unofficial parents to many who have come across their path. They hosted me uncountable times when business trips called me back to the Bay Area from Chicago or Boston. When our parents could no longer take care of their long-time home, they moved in 2004 into a wonderful in-law unit in Ron and Kitty's new home in Hercules—where our dad died just a few months later at age ninety-one, and our mom four years later in 2008 at age eighty-nine. Ron and Kitty gave so much love and care to our parents in those final years when doctor's appointments, weakness, and immobility made especially our dad dependent on extra care every day. Ron and Kitty have also stayed faithful to the little Plymouth Brethren church in Oakland where we all grew up. Their lay leadership is a huge factor in its survival as a joyful little fellowship through the years. When I describe in a later chapter my negative experiences with that little church, I am talking about something fifty years ago that bears little or no resemblance to that fellowship today, still less to what Kit and Ron believe and live.

ELIZABETH ANNE GILL

Our youngest sibling is Elizabeth Anne, born December 12, 1950 in Portland, Oregon. All three of my sisters were given the same middle name "Anne" which has Hebrew roots meaning "grace." We always called our sister "Beth" or sometimes "Buffy." Old habits are hard to break but Elizabeth announced to us one day as an adult that she didn't want to be called "Beth" but "Elizabeth" from now on. "Beth" was the Hebrew word for "house," not a great name for a person, she pointed out! I instantly admired her for making this change and she has been "Elizabeth" or "E" to me ever since.

Elizabeth was little and quiet and the youngest. Therefore, she was coddled and cuddled as the baby in the family—but also underappreciated and ignored, drowned out in family conversations (though our dad tried hard to give everyone time to express an opinion or report on the day's activities). She was always the last one to get old enough to try something (e.g., go out alone, get a driver's license, etc.). During pretty much all of their upbringing a youngest sibling is told "you are too young/small to do that." And they don't have any younger siblings over whom to be the leader and care giver. Elizabeth had leadership instincts but not much of a leadership pathway, not much mentoring or encouragement in that direction. As she came up through the ranks in school she might be asked if she was any relation to me (who had passed through four years earlier). This was not helpful, she assured me, and it did nothing for her own growing sense of who she was, her own gifts and abilities.

My parents really wanted to treat all four of us as equals in the eyes of God and themselves. But we attended a church and lived in a culture with what we now call "male privilege" or paternalism and sexism. Women were valued but the expectation was that their primary, likely role in life was to become a wife and mother. Of course, I was expected to become a husband and father, but I was also expected to have another vocation or work calling besides husband and father; my sisters were not, at least not to the same degree. And in church, the central institution of our life beyond family, I was expected to be a leader, maybe even a lay preacher or teacher. My sisters were expected to contribute to church potlucks, keep a nice home, be good cooks and gracious hosts, and maybe teach some Sunday School to young children.

The impact of all this, as I see it, was to repress and frustrate my sisters' giftedness and ambition. It wasn't just church. School and society didn't offer much relief. Girls took "homemaking" classes; boys took "shop." Boys had lots of sports teams available to work off their adolescent energy and competitiveness. Girls sports were very limited if they existed at all. So my sisters were pressured towards early (and, in my opinion, unwise) marriages. I'm not sure what my parents said on the subject but the cultural and churchly pressure and expectation was clear. Like her older sisters (and her brother), Elizabeth was married very early—to one of our church friends, Stan Iwawaki. They soon had a son John and then a daughter Jackie. John became an award-winning high school science teacher in Richmond, California. I was incredibly proud of my niece Jackie for graduating from Cal with her degree in history, just like I had done a couple decades earlier.

From early on, Elizabeth wanted to carve out a life and career distinctive from her older siblings. As a high school senior, she was able to enroll in a Fashion Design program at Laney College rather than being confined to the high school campus and curriculum. Without enough funding to continue the program a second year she took a full-time job at a bank. Then came marriage and motherhood. While her kids were young, Elizabeth had some great success as an Avon salesperson, a Special Education teacher, and grammar school PTA president. When the kids were nine and eleven years old, Elizabeth began to work in sales with New York Life Insurance (for whom her husband also worked at the time). She was soon breaking sales records and hosting national symposia for agents on both coasts.

After some frustrating times in the late 1990s looking for the next right job opportunity, Elizabeth started working in the early 2000s as executive assistant to a famous medical researcher at Stanford University where all of her leadership and organizational gifts could flourish. As we four have gotten to "retirement age," Elizabeth has been the prime mover building up our sibling community by hosting a monthly ninety-minute zoom gathering in which we share our lives with each other. Overlooked no more, our little sister is a leader and star in our family. I feel bad that I was often either unavailable, ignorant, or critical when she could have used a strong brotherly shoulder to lean on, but that was then and this is now!

One funny story I have shared many times with audiences when talking about my books: I would often give copies of my books to my sisters over the years. One time I asked my sister Elizabeth if she had read a book I sent her recently. "No, I haven't but I keep it by my bed and whenever I can't get to sleep, I read a little bit of your book." Oh, thanks a lot! She always felt part of her calling was to keep me humble. When I gave her a copy of the book I mentioned earlier, Virginia Hearn's collection *What They Did Right: Reflections by Children on their Parents,* to which I contributed a chapter, she spoke up in a family gathering and referred to my essay as "What they did right so I turned out so perfect." Another funny thing Elizabeth told me: her married name was the Japanese "Iwawaki"—but with her European appearance she got called Mrs. "Iwawaski" by some who must have thought it more likely (from her appearance) that she was Polish.

LIFE TOGETHER AT THE GILL HOME

Our family had clear boundaries as we all grew up. Some of this will only become clear in the chapter on my Christian faith but let me try to describe life in the family of Walter and Vivian Gill. Our dad got up very early and sat in the kitchen drinking his coffee and eating some cereal while he read the morning newspaper. Then he walked off in his business suit with his briefcase to catch the bus to San Francisco where he worked until 5:00 pm and took the bus back home by 6:00 pm or so. We always sat together at the dining room table for evening supper made by my mom. After supper, we assembled in the living room to read the Bible together. We each had a copy of the King James translation of the Bible. We went around the room and each read two verses till the chapter was done. Those too young to read tried anyway and the older siblings or parents helped them sound out the words. We are talking about two-year-olds getting started on this. Yes, we all killed the reading tests when we entered school already good readers (of Shakespearian English, no less). After our reading we all knelt on the floor by our chairs and my dad offered a brief prayer. Then for a couple kids it was their turn to wash the dishes, for all of us it was homework time, then off to bed, where one more time we kneeled and said a personal prayer for grandparents and anything else on our minds (e.g., "Forgive me God for being mean to my sister," etc.).

We didn't have a television until maybe the late 1950s. My suspicion is that the arrival of the San Francisco Giants and their appearances on tv were the main reason we decided to finally get a set. Television was frowned upon if not banned by our church because it brought Hollywood and worldly entertainment into the home. I remember a small tract with the title "TV: Turn your eyes away from beholding Vanity"—a reference to a line in Ecclesiastes. Eventually the prohibitions relaxed and I remember watching Bonanza, Leave It to Beaver, Andy Griffith, and a few other programs. We never went to movie theatres, never to bars. There was never any alcohol in our lives. We did not dance. We were not permitted to go to school parties (where there might be dancing and only God knows what other temptations). When Elvis and rock n' roll came along in the late 1950s we somewhat furtively listened to it on small radios in our bedrooms or when dad was off at work. Our mom was more tolerant.

We did have good friends from school growing up and they would sometimes come to our house to play after school or (less often) we might go to play at their houses. We would maybe go to see the Ice Folies or Ice Capades once a year. We might go down to the Santa Cruz beach and boardwalk once a year. I would go to a couple baseball games with my dad each year. On Saturdays I often went to the dump or the lumber yard with my dad to help him on some home repair or handyman project. I mowed the lawn and washed the car. All of us kids had domestic chores to do, from emptying the garbage to making our beds (daily) to helping in the kitchen, vacuuming the rugs, dusting the furniture, washing windows, etc. I don't recall getting much, if any, allowance but there must have been something.

My dad had only two or three weeks vacation each year so our usual routine was to pack up the station wagon and head to a Bible conference of Plymouth Brethren either in Los Angeles (around Christmas time) or in Walla Walla in eastern Washington (summertime). We would usually stay for four or five nights at old friends' houses and attend the meetings day and evening. There were some youth-oriented Sunday-school type events but most of the time we were expected just to sit quietly and listen or read something (or day-dream). We kids ran around the aisles in between the conference sessions. There was often a big picnic or beach event (in modest swimwear of course) the day after a conference. On the way to or from a conference like this our family might stop and camp at a lake. This was always fun but since my parents and sisters were not athletic, this was not about vigorous mountain hikes, swimming, skiing, or the like. But I have only fond memories of these vacation/study trips.

I had vast energy as a kid and I remember driving through northern California and Oregon a few times when we stopped to get the gas tank refilled and my dad told me just to start running down the side of the highway and they would pick me up. Fifteen minutes later I would be as far down the road as I could run before they caught up with me. I remember one time when I was about fourteen that my dad let me get behind the wheel as the family was heading north. I remember so vividly looking at the center line whizzing by and jerking the car a bit from side to side. My dad said "No, look at the line further down the road and you will drive more smoothly." Ever since then I have thought that is a good metaphor for leadership: look farther down the road where you are headed, don't just react to what is under your nose.

We always called Sunday "the Lord's Day" (not "the Sabbath") and went to church for an hour of Sunday School followed by an hour or more of worship. Then we returned Sunday evening for the "Gospel meeting"—a sermon by one of the brothers. We always went back to church on Wednesday evening for an hour and a quarter of prayer and Bible study. It did not matter a whit whether we had school assignments due on Monday or Thursday morning. We never ever skipped church on Sunday or Wednesday evenings. I have joked that if Sunday was the "Lord's Day" we might as well have called Wednesday evening "the Lord's evening." We had a lot of fun and fellowship with other families in our church. Family picnics, Sunday evenings at Fenton's Creamery after church. This was not just our faith or religious world; it was our social world, the center of our lives.

At home, I participated in all the domestic chores (kitchen, room cleanup, etc.)—though my sisters insist I did not share in those equally with them. They do acknowledge that I did more of the yard care and car washing duties. I saw my dad's joyful participation in dishwashing and even in some limited cooking, so I never thought of these things just as "women's work." But I loved to go off to the playground with my neighborhood buddies whenever possible. So when I got up on Saturday morning I hustled around and completed all my list of chores and, if my dad didn't need me, I got permission to run off to play with the guys. I learned early on that it is better to jump on a task and get it done than to procrastinate or argue why someone else should do it.

I feel so privileged to have been raised in a family as I have described it here. My parents were so loving and caring. They taught us our core values and things like kindness, caring, and honesty were at the top of the list. We knew all human beings including ourselves were failing sinners at times. But we were encouraged to face up to our mistakes, take responsibility, and apologize. Then we were forgiven. Tears maybe but then a fresh start. It was emotional, honest, painful sometimes, but forgiving and reconciling as I experienced it. Our parents taught it constantly and then lived it out. No hypocrisy. As I have said often, I have no excuses! I lived in this family until the day I got married at age twenty-one.

THE IMPACT OF MY SISTERS

Being raised with a kind father in a house full of women impacted me. For one thing I have always enjoyed women and been comfortable around them. I was surrounded. It was one of my middle sister Kitty's school friends who I noticed and courted and married. I never saw my dad treat my mom or sisters with disrespect or a lack of attention, kindness, and encouragement. I came much later to realize that my dad as well as mom were sometimes harsh with my sisters—but as I say, I didn't see or hear it growing up. I now realize (from talking with my sisters) how critical and negative my mom was toward them—such a contrast to how she treated me. But in my experience, mean talk around the house was not tolerated. Apologies and behavioral improvements followed any possible violations. I did not really recognize my "male privilege" for what it was in my family and church until I was married and in a different environment. I have more than once apologized to my adult sisters for the religious, family, educational, and societal culture that encouraged me to be a leader, grow, and reach out—but which pointed them toward marriage and domestic service at best. What a waste of talent and repressive box.

My sisters and I grew up to inhabit very different worlds after we left home. We moved into very different religious, educational, vocational and social circles. Often in different cities. We were all occupied with raising our own families and working hard on our very different tasks and challenges. I tried to keep contact with my sisters over the years by way of annual birthday cards and lunches when possible, and in bigger family gatherings at Thanksgiving, first at our parents' house, then at our house, but then split up at our individual domiciles when the total tribe got too big to fit anywhere. Our employment scattered us across the country. Between 1973 and 2016 I lived and worked a total of twenty years (in that forty-three-year period) in Los Angeles, Bordeaux, Chicago, and Boston. All three of my sisters lived for periods of time in other cities like Houston, Cincinnati, Newark, and Victorville—so we can't be too hard on each other for diminished contact during many of these decades. Today's email, social media, cell phones, and zoom have made staying in touch much easier. I still, of course, have some regrets about years that passed when we were not very close.

MY BIG ATTEMPT TO BRING US TOGETHER

As our parents' 50th anniversary loomed, I took the initiative to bring us back together. We had not spent even one night under the same roof for the twenty-five years since September 8, 1967, the night before I got married. For May 15–16, 1992, I organized an overnight "original six" family reunion in Bodega Bay as a kind of "prequel" to a 50th anniversary party we wanted to organize for 1993.[1] Through the 1980s I had gone on writing retreats once or twice each year to a rustic little three-bedroom place up on the coast just above Bodega Bay. I had also arranged annual overnights for my weekly men's "posse" and once or twice for the New College Berkeley faculty at this place. So I suggested that just the six of us have an overnight retreat up there—no spouses or kids, just the original six, now ages seventy-nine, seventy-three, forty-seven, forty-six, forty-four, and forty-two years old.

Part of my motivation was my awareness that my sisters sometimes expressed that they didn't feel known or recognized for who they had become, who they were today, not just in our parents' eyes but in each others' eyes. I hadn't realized how traumatic this might feel for some of us. There was a lot of hurt in a couple of my sisters, scars from hard times, unrealized hopes, criticism. There was some real suspense about whether all six would show up until the last minute. We divided up the cooking duties. I assigned myself the big Friday evening feast, Kitty took Saturday morning breakfast, and Dottie and Elizabeth were responsible for the lunches on Friday and Saturday.

---

1. A "What Are You Doing About It" initiative. No copyright on this. I would urge everyone to think about doing something like this with parents and siblings.

We did two hour-long Bible studies on texts chosen by each of our parents—no assigned teacher, just read and comment as you wish. The main events were for each of the six of us to take a full hour to share about "This is My Life"—"tell us all who you are right now, what really matters to you. Where have you been these past twenty-five years? Where are you now and where are you going? What do you think God is teaching you that you could share with the rest of us? Do you have things to share that we could celebrate with you? How can we best pray for you and support you? Think about this in advance, make a few notes maybe. We need to find a deeper level than a superficial "ain't life grand"—but not so deep that we can't get back up after an hour." We drew names out of a hat to decide what order to go in. After each person shared and we quietly listened (no interruptions allowed!), we asked a few questions or made some encouraging comments. Then we gathered around the person and laid hands on them and prayed for them.

As I said, some of it was very emotional. "You never understood . . . you said or did this hurtful thing . . . etc. etc." It was by no means all negative but it was open and honest and painful. What amazed me was how both my mom and dad listened so fully, carefully, and thoughtfully—and asked for forgiveness. They did not make excuses or seek to justify themselves, even though some of the criticisms they heard were overstated and must have been very hard to listen to. But their attitude was amazingly gracious and humble and loving. It was an amazing, unrepeatable gathering. We wept, we sang, we feasted, we celebrated and thanked God.

Actually, this gathering was more of a beginning than a resolution of the issues raised. Many of the hurts that were described could not be resolved during just one retreat like that. We could have used quite a few more sessions in the months and years to come but we scattered back across the country for much of the twelve years that followed until our dad's death in 2004. It is really only since our retirements from full-time jobs that we have been able to more fully and intentionally approach some of these issues of our upbringing and find some real peace and understanding.

In the end, even though after I left home at twenty-one I lived in a very different world from those of my sisters, I am very grateful to God for my sisters' roles in my life. I am very blessed to have these three strong women still in my life, now in retirement more than ever. I am proud of them and grateful for their love.

6

Boyhood (1951–61)

IN THIS CHAPTER AND the next I want to describe my life growing up, my boyhood, from my earliest recollections through high school, from age five to eighteen. There may be some fun stories in here but there are also things that I regret and am ashamed of. You could say that they were just harmless kid things. You could also say "You outrageous, faithless little thieving, disruptive brat!" And I would say "Yeah, sorry, I know, please forgive me—and kids, don't do this yourself." In my chapter on "Faith" I will reflect on the contradiction between my espoused faith and the bad behavior described in this chapter.

Starting from the beginning, I have just one memory from my first three years (1946–49) at what I called the "green step house" (2463 N. 47th Ave, Omaha, Nebraska). I remember growing up in a big, tall house with green steps leading up to the front porch. In 1992, when moving back to Chicago, we got off the highway and drove into Omaha to find the house. Surprise! The steps were no longer green. Even more surprising, it was a small two-story bungalow. My memory of the house had been created when I was two and three years old, when each of those steps came up to my waist!

In Portland (1949–52) I have fond memories of my Grandma Gill's house, snow fall, Sugar Crest Donuts, driving through beautiful Reed College, visiting Multnomah Falls, and the Sester's family farm and swimming hole out in Gresham. I attended kindergarten at Llewelyn Elementary School. My only memory there was being sent to the office for discipline by the principal, Mr. Bow. I stood facing the reception counter which was taller than my eye-level. I don't know what I had said or done but it was the beginning of my life of school offenses.

In 1952 we moved down to Oakland and for the first year rented an interesting house on Outlook Avenue. My only memory of first grade at Burbank School was chasing a girl named Geraldine around the playground and never catching her despite my speed. In 1953 we moved to a little house in San Leandro, 953 Alice Avenue, near MacArthur and Foothill Boulevards, near Jerry's Beefburgers. This was our home for ten years until 1963 when we moved a half-mile to Sheffield Village in Oakland. It is the home I think of when asked where I grew up. Jerry's Beefburgers was *the* burger joint in those days, always busy but every few months they would have a ten-cent sale—all the burgers you want for ten cents apiece. The eight or ten ordering windows would have lines of customers all the way out to the sidewalk.

We lived just a block or two from busy MacArthur Boulevard. It was a neighborhood of small, nondescript stuccoed, one-story, twelve hundred or so square foot houses. In my youth our street was lined with trees, two big camphor in front of our house. It was a modest, post-war, middle-class neighborhood. Our corner of San Leandro was just a few blocks from the Oakland city line. I didn't think much about or understand why there were no Black people in my school or neighborhood, while not far away there was a large Black population in Oakland. Maybe late in high school I heard for the first time about deliberate housing discrimination and red-lining to keep Blacks from buying or renting property—something that outraged me when I learned more about it while a student at Berkeley. I will say a lot more on this topic in an upcoming chapter.

Our house had just a small back yard so most of my running and playing happened in the street and around the neighborhood. There were always lots of kids in my neighborhood and we would play baseball (softball) or football in the street, scurrying out of the way whenever a car wanted to pass through. Just two blocks away was our public grammar school, Roosevelt Elementary. Roosevelt offered grades kindergarten through seven. I started there in second grade. Roosevelt had what (to us little kids) was a big lawn in front of the building and an even bigger dirt field behind our classrooms, where both organized and impromptu play happened.

Beginning in the sixth grade, my two best friends were Julius ("Family Jewels") Chernak and Walter ("Wally Bear") Paroczai. Julius lived the other side of my block on Helen Avenue and Wally lived at the end of my street, Alice Avenue, less than two blocks away. We were in the same school room all day and essentially inseparable after school. Julius's and Wally's moms were like second moms to me. Julius's mom would be scooping out some ice cream for us and laughing at our antics through her cigarette smoke. I loved this lady all my life. Wally's mom would bring us popcorn and orange juice while we lay on the floor of their front room and laughed hysterically at the Three Stooges or Little Rascals on tv. We were also big fans of Red Skelton, McHale's Navy, and Leave it to Beaver.

Julius's dad was a chef down at Jack London Square at the Bow n' Bell Restaurant owned by Jackie Jensen, a baseball star for the Boston Red Sox (the San Francisco Seals were Boston's Triple-A farm team so we were Red Sox fans until the Giants and A's arrived). From his dad Julius learned to love fishing. In those days our beautiful nearby reservoir, Lake Chabot, was closed off to any visitors. No trespassing. But we snuck in one day to see what we could catch. We hiked through thick bushes and underbrush until we got to a place where we could throw our lines in the water. We caught ten or fifteen little Bluegills (no relation) and were almost back out to escape over the fence when the loud gruff voice of a park ranger stopped us. He confiscated our fish, warned us, and deposited us outside the chain link fence. We sat mournfully on the swings in the park right next to the reservoir entrance. Pretty soon we saw smoke coming out of the ranger shack and could smell some tantalizing fried fish being prepared! This was not our only punishment. The next day Julius and Wally were covered with poison oak! Misery. I had none. Then and ever since I do not seem to be allergic to poison oak.

We rode our bicycles and walked everywhere. We sometimes put up a tent in Wally's big back yard and camped out overnight. We sometimes paid the twenty-five-cent fare and rode the bus all the way to Lake Merritt in downtown Oakland, rented a row boat, and chased ducks for a while. It all seems so innocent and safe now looking back on it. A simpler, safer time.

THIEVES

Somewhere around age eleven in the 6th grade we became thieves. I think this ended by the 8th grade. We even jokingly called ourselves "the Robbin' Hoods." We fashioned a small net on the end of an eight-foot pole, with two razor blades positioned over the net to facilitate reaching over Julius's back fence and harvesting apples from his neighbor's tree. We stole from merchants—never individuals or houses—we were shoplifters, not robbers. We would go into stores and put stuff in our pockets or down our pants or under a baggy sweatshirt and walk out. We accumulated significant rock'n'roll record collections, not just little forty-fives but big LPs. We had a tradition that whoever had a birthday had to invite the other two guys over for a birthday dinner. We did this for years. At those birthdays, whoever's birthday it was was sure to get a beautifully wrapped up stack of LPs (like ten or so)—records we didn't like and wanted to get rid of. The same collection would be given as a gift to the next guy when his birthday happened. Our mothers would say "What sweet boys you are to be giving each other gifts like this!"

We also added to our hobby collections—plastic model airplane kits, stamps and coins, and fish for our aquariums (I didn't have an aquarium but I helped with the heists). Scooping out a colorful fish and putting it in a plastic baggy with some water before storing in a pants pocket took some skill. I remember we wanted a new football one year. We took turns sitting on a football in the Capwell's's athletic gear department until it was flat enough to get out of the store. We also appropriated a lot of food. We were especially fond of high-quality steaks. Julius was the expert because of his dad's work as a chef. T-bones, filet mignons, and other fine cuts walked out of the store with us. We would fire up a Weber barbecue and grill ourselves a feast while our moms would be watching us out the window and saying "what wonderful boys, to have an interest in cooking rather than gang activity."

I don't remember Julius's day of reckoning but we would often leave a store one by one and wait by our bikes for the other guys. One day Wally took forever until he came out with his head down after being caught with several LPs down his pants. My final theft was at George's Drugstore on Bancroft at Dutton Avenue. I had already put some sun tan lotion in my pocket and was just about to swipe a new pair of sunglasses when a male voice rang out "Do you want to put those back on the shelf or should I call the police?" I quickly put the glasses back on the shelf and exited the store. Julius and Wally were still impressed with the Coppertone in my pocket (yeah, I know: why does a seventh-grade boy need Coppertone?). But that was it. I did not want to get caught and have to face my parents for my life of crime. I never stole anything again. If I even found some property or money, at any time in my life, I would look for its owner, never just take it for myself. I knew stealing was wrong but for the three of us it was just a kind of game we fell into. Of course, I renounce it. I don't think I ever cheated on a test or plagiarized anybody else's work. But somehow, I fell into the petty theft adventure for a couple years with my two best buddies.

While I am in a confessional mood, I should also admit to learning how to cuss a blue streak in my age eleven to fourteen period. I never "took the Lord's name in vain"—never could stand it when people said "Jesus Christ" or variations on that theme. And I didn't even like it when people used "God" or "Lord" in a casual way. But I learned how to say damn and hell, not just darn and heck. I learned all the vocabulary for human (and bull) excrement and applied the label wherever it seemed appropriate. I never liked the f-word because it was a vulgar reference to sex—something even as a kid I knew was intended to be an expression of love—but now being used to refer to something violent or at least very messed up. I never used antisemitic or racial slurs. My dad, as I said earlier, never said a bad or questionable word and prohibited even the slang "minced oaths" like darn, gosh, and heck. Anyway, may God and my readers and relatives forgive me for my youthful transgressions.

WORK

I mentioned in an earlier chapter how my sisters and I were expected to clean our own rooms and take our turns doing household chores like setting and clearing the table, washing dishes, vacuuming the floors, and dusting the furniture. And I mentioned how I was also expected to wash the station wagon and mow the lawn.[1] I also decided to make some money by mowing lawns and washing cars for neighbors. A quarter here, a quarter there. My kids Jodie and Jonathan did the same thing around our neighborhood when they were little kids.

---

1. Can you tell I am trying to mitigate just a little the charge that "David got treated better"?

Part One: Incubators (1946–1964)

When I was ten years old, I qualified to get a newspaper carrier's route. I did this from July of 1956 to September of 1960 (from age ten to fourteen). My dad kept careful records of my career. I averaged delivering seventy papers each day and made $25 to $35 per month. I always delivered a morning paper because the afternoon papers would get in the way of after school sports. First, I delivered the *San Leandro Morning News* for a couple years, then the bigger and more profitable *San Francisco Chronicle*. It was hard but good discipline to have to set my alarm and roll out of bed at 6:00 a.m. each morning. My dad would already be up, rolling and rubber banding some of the papers while he drank his morning coffee and read the paper. He had been a paper boy himself as a kid and he loved helping me out. I packed the papers into a canvas delivery bag that fit over my bike handlebars and I was off to throw the papers on customer porches (without banging them on the door and aggravating the customer!). On Sundays, when the papers were twice as big, a parent and maybe even a sister, would help drive me around the route. Good exercise, good skills. The hazards were unleashed dogs running after me (I remember one morning jumping from one side of my bike to the other several times while a German shepherd tried to get at me; he finally got tired and walked away) and irresponsible customers who wouldn't pay up at the end of the month when I came by to collect, making me return several times.

We were also encouraged to go to houses that were not subscribers and try to sell them a subscription. I sold enough subscriptions one year to earn a free trip to Disneyland: my first airplane ride. On another occasion the *Morning News* made us deliver a complimentary paper to every house on the streets serviced by my route to try to win over new subscribers. We were not paid anything for a huge extra amount of work—delivering two hundred instead of seventy papers or something like that. I rebelled the second or third time this happened and dumped the extra papers in an empty lot a block away from my house. Wouldn't you know: my mom somehow found the pile and figured out the culprit. She made me retrieve the pile and go deliver them.

SPORTS & ACTIVITIES

Cub Scouts and Boy Scouts were not allowed (they seemed like a paramilitary group like the Nazi Youth with all that saluting and uniform wearing). Outside of the classroom it was sports that got my constant attention. I was a big fan of the San Leandro High School football teams during Junior High School and even earlier. I loved the 1958 Cal football team with quarterback Joe Kapp that went to the Rose Bowl (and lost to Iowa) and I have been a (long-suffering) Cal Bear football fan, sometime season ticket holder, ever since. In 1959 the Cal basketball team defeated West Virginia for the national title. In 1960 they made it to the finals where they lost to Ohio State. In 1958 the New York Giants baseball team moved to San Francisco and I loved rooting for them with stars like Willie Mays, Willie McCovey, and Orlando Cepeda. In 1968 the baseball Athletics moved to Oakland from Kansas City and my primary allegiance shifted to the home team.

I was a huge fan of the San Francisco 49ers football team during the 1950s but became a Raider fanatic when that team was formed in 1960. The Raiders were an exciting team for twenty years, selling out every game they ever played in the Oakland Coliseum but in 1982 they moved to Los Angeles for twelve years and became for me the "Traitors" led by "Al Devious" (real name Davis). They came back to Oakland in 1995 after talking the city and county into an expensive addition of luxury boxes and an upper deck to the stadium. We citizens are still paying extra taxes for it even though the team was lousy and never sold out games anymore. The Raiders ran out of town to Las Vegas leaving Oakland residents to pay millions for their 1995 stadium renovations. Good riddance. In the 1980s and 1990s the 49ers became the best team in football, winning five Super Bowls. I am still a big fan though I don't like how they built a stadium in Santa Clara instead of San Francisco's Hunters Point. The NBA Warriors moved to the Bay Area in 1962. I followed them closely when they won the NBA championship in 1975 but not much before or after that until Steph Curry arrived in 2009. As you can see, being a pro sports fan in the Bay Area has been fun throughout my life, beginning when I was ten years old.

As for my own sports activities, I was running and jumping over obstacles from my earliest days. I loved throwing balls back and forth. We played four-square, dodgeball, and kickball. I loved playing baseball from second or third grade onward. We played tag and hide-and-seek in our neighborhood. I remember hiding under a bush successfully until some bird pooped on my shoulder and my reaction revealed my location. After a rain, a lot of us neighborhood boys would go to an empty lot with tall grass and have dirt clod fights, firing wet clumps of grass with dirt clods on the end at anyone who stuck their head up. We all got hit in the face once in a while. Our mothers expressed shock at how filthy we were when we returned home!

Sometime around fifth grade there began an organized after-school and vacation-break activity program run by the City Recreation Department. We had a terrific guy named Randy Grimes as our Roosevelt School playground supervisor. I learned to play tennis in his summer classes. We had regular track competitions at Roosevelt and then in San Leandro citywide competition. By the seventh grade I could run the fifty-yard dash regularly in 5.9 seconds in my tennis shoes or just my socks—tying Rodney Jackson for fastest kid in the school. Only Jefferson School's Jim Donnelly at 5.6 was faster in San Leandro. By seventh grade I was the only kid at our school who could hit a softball over the left field fence. I was the Babe Ruth or Barry Bonds of Roosevelt. I also won the City of San Leandro "Pigskin Pete" Punt, Pass, & Kick contest in 1958 at age twelve.

Randy organized and coached our Roosevelt flag football team that played other schools on Saturday. (There was no Pop Warner, no tackle football for us until High School). Barrett Pullman and I were the ends (pass receivers) for whom Randy designed some great plays and our team was the best in the city. Our quarterback, Jerry Gaustad or Corky Barrett, would hit me or Barrett Pullman with a pass in a crossing pattern over the middle and we would hand off to the other guy crossing underneath and he would be off to the races. We also had homeroom teams. In the seventh grade there were three different classes taught by Severson, Hutcherson, and our teacher, Raymond Braine. Severson actually had most of our school's best athletes. The Severson and Hutcherson classes predictably called their teams something like the Lions and the Bears.

Our team decided to call ourselves "Braine's Baked Beans"—in an act of youthful psychological warfare. The reference of course was to flatulence. We each made a team shirt with brown baked beans and our number painted on. Craig Reynolds would play quarterback, Rodney Jackson halfback, Julius Chernak at end, Wally played center. The girls in our class led by Elizabeth Kellam would cheer for the Baked Beans. We designed trick plays where, for example, Wally would snap the ball through Craig's legs to me at tail back, everyone ran right, I ran left into the end zone. Championship for Braine! We really did win our 7th grade championships in both football and baseball.

I learned how to swim at Farrelly Pool next to Roosevelt School. I think we had a week of required swimming lessons every year all though grammar school. I was ok but never became a really strong or enthusiastic swimmer, probably because my dad didn't swim and my sisters weren't really into it. The excuse I haul out when necessary is that "I am a land animal"—though I do enjoy the occasional snorkeling expedition and floating on my back in the water after a day of demanding exercise.

I really loved it in 1959 and 1960 when our local Cal basketball team won the NCAA championship one year and then came in second the next year. I listened to their exciting games on the radio but never attended a game. I played basketball into junior high but was never great at it. By the ninth or tenth grade I could touch the rim if I jumped but I was not a good shot and just not a big fan like I was of football. I loved playing softball and was a star at it in my grade school. Hard ball was another story. I hit a lot of home runs but struck out a lot. I pitched regularly and struck out a lot of hitters with my fast ball but I walked a lot more and hit a lot of batters also. Opposing batters did not "dig in" if Gill was pitching! After the 9th grade I stopped playing basketball and baseball to focus on football and track.

More on my high school football experience in the next chapter but I have thought a lot about my athletic "career." Why was I such an exceptional athlete with my name frequently in the paper until about age sixteen and then just "above average" from then on? I think it is because I was given a muscular, strong-boned, well-coordinated body by God and my forebears and my body went through adolescence earlier than most of the other guys. By seventh grade I was 5'6" tall. By the start of 8th grade in October 1959, age thirteen, I was 5'7–1/2" and 155 pounds. By October 1960, the start of 9th grade, at age fourteen I was 5'10" and 175 pounds, my full-grown body. I was one of the taller, bigger kids during those years—but I was on the way to 5'10" not 6'5." For that reason, I didn't go through a gangly or gawky stage like many guys endured on their way to much taller destinations. My speed, strength, and coordination were fairly exceptional for someone aged eleven to fourteen but after that, as my contemporaries all caught up or even passed me, I was a good but not great athlete. Too bad for any sports dreams I might have had!

ROOSEVELT GRAMMAR SCHOOL

My sisters and I attended Roosevelt elementary school, just two blocks from our house. I still have no idea whether the school was named after Teddy, Franklin, or Eleanor (I admire them all, especially Eleanor). Every morning we stood and put our hand over our heart and said the pledge of allegiance. We never had any prayer in school. We would have been automatically suspicious and negative about any bureaucratic, state-organized prayer. Pray at home, in church, and in your own heart, we believed. No Bible study or religious indoctrination either. I knew my classes included Jewish fellow students as well as non-believers. Peoples' religious orientations were just not a factor in what we studied or how we related to each other. I heard no anti-semitic remarks (that doesn't mean my Jewish fellow-students never heard any insults but that I never heard anything like that from teachers or fellow-students). I also always had Asian-American fellow-students in my classes and never thought that was anything but normal. It was only later that I found out that my classmate Connie Korematsu was the niece of Fred Korematsu, the heroic American civil rights activist who objected to the internment of Japanese Americans during World War Two.

We had fire drills where we marched outside of the school buildings and air raid drills where we crouched under our desks until given the all-clear signal. We were cautioned about a possible nuclear attack from Russia. We were assigned to classes of about 30 to 35 students, boys and girls together, and we were together from 8:45 to 3:15 five days a week. The teacher organized our time so we had math for an hour, reading for another, and so on. A music or art teacher might come in once in a while. My education also came via the tiny little branch library on Dutton Avenue near Bancroft. Maybe as early as 4th grade I discovered the value of a library card. I read every Black Stallion novel Walter Farley wrote and dozens of other sports and western fiction books—as well as doing some youthful research for school essays. Later on, I used the San Leandro Main Library for research. I remember doing a term paper on the transistor and another one on airplanes.

I was a really smart kid as measured by the annual "achievement" tests—nationally standardized tests of reading comprehension, grammar, spelling, mathematics, and maybe other subjects. I always scored in the 97th to 99th percentile on all these tests and the tests said my IQ was 134, in the top 2% nationally, so my parents and teachers were told.[2] As a result, I was always tracked into the highest academic level and lived under the pressure as well as the benefit of high expectations. This was my story all the way through high school. I'm not asking for sympathy, just making the point that high expectations have a downside as well as upside. I know people who have been destroyed by them.

Anyway, my actual performance all the way from elementary school through high school was around "B" level. From my second through seventh grade report cards I once counted up 90 Excellents, 353 Goods, 222 Satisfactories and 12 Unsatisfactories. If those grades are converted to the conventional A through F system, my gpa for elementary school would be 2.8 (a B- average). My high school and undergraduate college gpas were not much higher. I have always joked that somebody in the honors program had to get a B. That was me. My favorite part of the curriculum was always recess! Once in a while I concentrated and got a great grade but most of the time my head and heart were elsewhere and I did something less than excellent. It was only in my senior year at Cal Berkeley that I finally found my way as a student. I share this here to encourage any other "late bloomers." Keep trying!

SCHOOL MISBEHAVIOR

What really got the attention of my teachers and parents besides my academic potential was my behavior. From second grade onward (actually kindergarten, if you remember my Mr. Bow story) I got regularly written up on my report cards for "Needs to improve on self-control" and "Needs to improve on citizenship and being courteous and considerate of others." I feel embarrassed as I look back at this nonstop bad behavior. Why did I get in trouble? Why couldn't I stop trying to be funny or goofing off in class with Julius or other friends? Often I had to stay after school and sit in "detention" or write a hundred times "I will be a better boy" or "keep my mouth shut" or something to that effect. Sometimes I was sent to the principal's office. Sometimes my mom or dad was phoned or called in for a conference.

Once at least I remember a male vice-principal who grabbed my shoulders and banged me back against a wall a few times to get the point across (no real damage to me or wall). I just couldn't seem to grow out of this immature behavior. I was not a mean kid. I didn't hate my teachers. I was bigger and stronger than most kids my age but always a defender of others. I can remember a few times (successfully) threatening someone who was trying to bully a girl or smaller kid. They always backed down. But I couldn't seem to keep my mouth shut or settle down and work hard in class. Looking back at pictures of my classmates from second grade onward (through high

---

2. These (and any other) tests are valid measures of only one kind of intelligence. There are many kinds of thinking, reasoning, and intelligence and our educational strategies should be better customized to these variations. I am under no illusions that I am actually any smarter than anyone else. In any case, performance is what counts, not some abstract "potential."

school)—like Mark Ehrlich, Lonna Miller, Barbara Bond, Corky Barrett, Steve Lones, Margo Stern, and Mimi Gersten—I wonder how they could stand my ridiculous, disruptive behavior (my wife Lucia says she would have requested a transfer to another class—and my response is "I wouldn't blame you!").

At Roosevelt it all came to an inglorious head in the seventh grade. Raymond Braine was just out of college and assigned to be the teacher of our high potential, advanced ability student group. Mr. Braine's first mistake, of course, was his name. We were endlessly amused to be in "Braine's" class. He had traveled widely and was a well-meaning, good man, but he was socially/relationally naive and slow to pick up on what was happening. But this was no ordinary group of students. This was Dennis the Menace, Eddie Haskel, or Ferris Buehler times thirty. It was chaos and noise from day one. "Everybody drop your ruler at 9:43." Rubber bands flying through the air constantly. When Mr. Braine showed a slide of his wife standing next to an elephant in Egypt and pointed at the woman and said "this is my wife"—whoever was running the projector moved it so he was pointing at the elephant, to uproarious laughter. When someone was kept after class for a little detention, Wally or Craig might be in the closet muttering "Boo for Braine" and causing the disciplined student to laugh.

Yes, I was one of the ring leaders but only one of many. Digging through my old files I recently discovered that I was actually Roosevelt Student Body President and Sports Editor for our School Newspaper during the 7th grade. But I was the opposite of a good leader at that time of my adolescence. It was interesting that around 2004 it occurred to those of us on our high school reunion committee that most of us on the reunion committee were Braine alumni! In my account of my mom earlier I described the episode where she was called into the principal's office and they listened to the roar of noise from the class over the two-way intercom—while I was home in bed! One of my naughtiest moments was when I looked out the window of the classroom across the big lawn and saw some stranger walking down the sidewalk. I said out loud "Oh that's my dad!" Mr. Braine suddenly said "Oh I want to talk to him!" and ran out to this guy across the lawn. After meeting this stranger, Mr. Braine turned around and slunk back into the room. I hadn't intended to embarrass Mt. Braine. I was just being stupid and had no idea he would run out there.

Mr. Braine was fired during Spring vacation that year and Mr. Hutcherson came in to take his place. Hutcherson was a short, compact, tough-talking military vet kind of guy. After some general threats to our class, he got us quietly working on some assignment. That's when he came by my desk, smashed a long ruler on my desk, and leaned over to whisper in my ear with his teeth clenched: "Gill, I know who you are and if you get out of line I'm going to kill you." I was a well-behaved boy for the final six weeks of the school year.

Mr. Braine went back to graduate school and five years later I saw his picture in the newspaper with the headline "Dr. Braine Bound for Liberia Job." He had completed his PhD dissertation at UC Berkeley, the story said, on "Problems of School and

College Operations." He was hired by the U.S. Agency for International Development to work with a team developing schools and colleges in Liberia, West Africa.

There are two postscripts to this story of my seventh-grade sins. You could entitle them "There is a God and he sees what you're doing." Fast forward to 1969 when I was looking for a high school teaching job. No high schools in our urban area were hiring (the Baby Boom was over in 1964 and student enrollments were declining) so I took a job at John Muir Junior High teaching 8th graders. I was assigned a two-hour daily class with the twenty worst behaving, lowest performing students in the school. I loved the kids (mostly) and they loved me (mostly) but three years managing the adolescent behavior of these "boygills" was all I could take. I did have some great students at John Muir in my other "regular" classes, including Mary Girard who became a successful high school dean in Hawaii, still my Facebook friend fifty years later.

Fast forward again to 2002 when I was teaching a Christian ethics class of forty Fuller Seminary students in Menlo Park. When I called the roll and said "Andrew Braine" and a young man answered "here," I said "Oh my seventh grade teacher was named Raymond Braine." Andrew: "Oh, that's my dad!" I then said "Andrew, I was a horrible student in your father's class so you have complete permission and freedom to disrupt this class for the rest of the term. No penalties of any kind." I explained a bit of the story to the class. After class I found out that Raymond Braine was alive and well and I urged Andrew to bring his elderly dad to class, which he did the following week.

The next week I welcomed Mr. Braine to my class and publicly apologized and asked him to say a few words about his life and career. He stood up and said he never had anything against me and was only surprised to find me a professor of Christian ethics instead of a star baseball player for the Giants. It was a sweet reunion. But Mr. Braine rambled on at some length before he sat down. Later during the three-hour class I called on him and asked for his take on some ethical issue I thought he could address wisely. Again, he stood up and rambled for ten or fifteen minutes. No big deal but my class and I could see why he could have been taken advantage of because of his difficulty in reading even this audience of adult students. I had a couple more contacts with Mr. Braine and in 2009 I attempted to invite him to come to a lunch with several of his former students from that 7th grade class, all of whom wanted to apologize and show him some love. But he had just recently died. We truly mourned.

BANCROFT JUNIOR HIGH

Then we all moved up into the 8th grade at Bancroft Junior High. Now we all picked our electives and rotated through six different courses every day. Our class of four hundred fifty or so was drawn from six or eight elementary schools in San Leandro. Eighty or ninety came from Roosevelt (including the thirty from Mr. Braine's class). Julius and Wally and I were still in the "advanced" classes. After school sports were still roughly the same. I played as a mediocre starting center on the basketball team.

One new thing was that I got involved in the drama program taught by a fun guy named Mr. Bond. I had a small part in a school play called "Tiger House" in which I played a villain whose only line was "If you don't do what I say, by God I'll leave you here to starve to death." My dad was mortified that I took (as he saw it) God's name in vain. That was his only comment. I also discovered in my late dad's files a letter in which he vigorously protested to the Bancroft principal an assignment I had completed by watching the famous Greek tragedy Medea (by Euripedes) on television. The play is full of love, marriage, and children—then betrayal, divorce and murder. The principal wrote back to explain to my dad that studying the play was not an endorsement of the behavior of its characters but a way of getting us students to grapple with the moral dimensions of life. My dad did not understand how a liberal arts education works (or is supposed to work). Drama was the only class in which I earned A grades all year.

In junior high we were propagandized that since Russia had recently launched Sputnik it was critical for us to be a brilliant new generation of math and science students. That was a big emphasis in our studies. I really enjoyed my courses in wood and metal shop (and still have a c-clamp, domino, and chisel I made in metal shop)—and I think it is terrible that today's students (female as well as male) aren't required to study these subjects (as well as the cooking and homemaking classes only girls took in those days). But I put up no resistance to high demand math and science courses, foreign language (I began German in 9th grade and continued through high school with one more year at college level).

My English courses required a lot of reading and a lot of writing. The writing emphasis in my schooling actually began in elementary school when at least one substantial term paper had to be produced every year. This accelerated through high school and I had a tall stack of papers I had written by the time I got out of high school. Without any doubt all these writing assignments turned out to be great preparation for my career as a writer.

Julius and Wally and I continued to be classroom and school jerks at Bancroft, shooting off our mouth, trying to be funny, and disrupting class. We managed to get appointed to "Campus Control" which patrolled the hallways during lunch—which entitled us to get out of class twenty minutes early so we could eat. One of those lunch times we saw across the cafeteria a tray of kool-aid in paper cups, ready to be picked up and sold for some fund-raiser in the school yard during the lunch time. I don't know who started it but we found it a challenge to use our forks and spoons to propel chunks of jello across the room maybe eighty feet and watch them make a splash. The air was filled with jello until the bell rang and we went to our Campus Control posts. Before too much time passed Julius and I (why us?) were in Vice-Principal Thomas "the Buzzard" Cruza's office (pronounced "kruze—aye"). Would you believe it? He made us pay for the entire tray of kool-aid drinks (and told us to collect from our campus control colleagues their various shares in the damages).

Part One: Incubators (1946–1964)

Another time, old Cruza came walking out on the stage at a school assembly holding his arm out straight in what looked to us like a Nazi salute. Julius and I leaped to our feet (I guess I must have been first) and answered with a Nazi salute of our own, and several other students joined us. Mr. Deutsch, our English teacher (with the German name), quickly grabbed me and marched me to the principal's office. My mother was called in and Mr. Deutsch passionately warned her "Mrs. Gill your son will be the next George Lincoln Rockwell if he keeps this up!" Rockwell was the leader of the American Nazi Party at the time. In reviewing my report cards I noticed this comment to my parents (he apparently forgot he had already made the point in a parental visit to the principal's office): "If Dave has not made you privy to the 'sieg heil' incident, I think he should. It has not been written off from a school district standpoint." Mr. Deutsch used to take time in his English class to update us on the saga of adding a swimming pool to his home. One day he told us how some vendor had tried to install a pool cover that was the wrong size and he had told him "if you don't bring back the right size cover for my pool I will beat the crap out of you." At this point I lost control and let out from the back of the room a disbelieving, loud "Oh yeah!" He exploded and marched me to the office again. This might be the time I described in an earlier chapter, when my dad had to stay home from work and come in for a meeting with the principal.

We were just immature idiots, that's all. Too much energy. Hormones exploding. Actually, I didn't start the year in Deutsch's class. I was in Miss Webb's class with Julius and other Braine alumni. One day Julius and I gave a joint report on George Washington Carver, the famous scientist and inventor. Carver had found three hundred uses for the peanut. As we went through a long list one by one, something struck us as funny. We said something like "soap" and giggled slightly. "Rubber" and laughed. "Shampoo" and laughed. Pretty soon the whole class was uncontrollably shrieking with laughter. With this roaring continuing for many minutes, Miss Webb was apoplectic and marched us both to the principal's office. Julius was already in trouble with her because a couple weeks earlier in an after-class moment he had asked the tiny but curvaceous Miss Webb if she would mind telling us her bust size. "NO" she indignantly threw back at him. We sort of admired his display of boldness.

I'm not sure what I learned in Junior High. My math teacher Mrs. Phillips, my geography teacher Mr Stevens, my drama teacher Mr. Bond, and my English teacher Mrs. Williams thought I was pretty great and dismissed my behavior as adolescent nonsense, not to be taken too seriously. But it really was pretty dumb and even shameful. I was never cruel but plenty thoughtless and irresponsible, a child's mind in a young man's body. But there was one dream pulling me forward to a newer, more mature stage.

Every other Friday afternoon or evening we walked up to San Leandro High School to watch the powerhouse football team play. I wanted nothing in life more than to put on that uniform and play. When I graduated from Bancroft Junior High I decided to stop being an immature idiot and grow up.

7

San Leandro High School (1961–64)

In fall 1961, at age fifteen-and-a-half, I started the 10th grade at San Leandro High School. Our high school had only three grades, ten through twelve. There were about four hundred fifty people in my graduating class, maybe fourteen hundred total in our school. It really did feel like I was a big boy now and I should put away the foolishness of my behavior up to that point. I was never sent to the office, never got in any trouble for my high school behavior. That was over. One thing I still had to overcome in my private and home life was an occasional but intense outburst of anger. I was basically an upbeat guy, energetic but gentle. But I remember one time slamming my fist down on our coffee table in frustration at not being able to go off on some adventure or other. I then had to buy a big piece of plate glass to replace what I shattered! Another time I put my fist through the wall of my bedroom—I have been forever grateful that I hit through a section of half-inch sheet rock and didn't break my hand on an underlying stud! Most of my youthful aggression had a regular relief on the sports field (today's youths need the same opportunities!).

I will describe my religious and church life in the next chapter but, of course, that was still the major force in my life and identity as I went through high school. One thing that must be mentioned here, though, is that my separatist church did not allow me to hang out with the SLHS Young Life group or any other religious organization. My "candle" was deliberately "hidden under a bushel basket" by church policy. The church's rationale was that I might be exposed to bad doctrine or unapproved practice. My schoolmates may have wondered why I never went to movies, parties, or dances but I was a busy guy and it was a big school so only my closest friends were aware of those restrictions on my activities. Of course, in the years since high school and in part because of the public exposure of Facebook, my radical Christian position has become visible. It has been fun to discover many other Christians in my high school class. I just wish we could have shared the faith together back then.

SAN LEANDRO HIGH SCHOOL (1961-64)

SPORTS

The next most powerful high school "incubator" of the man I would become (after my faith and religion) was sports. We were the mighty San Leandro Pirates. We had three football teams. The first was a sophomore team, then junior varsity, then varsity. No sophomores played on the varsity team in my era. We had our own practices and our games were on Thursdays, not Fridays. We finished 6-1-1 in fall 1961, my sophomore year. As a junior I played in the jayvee games on Thursday (we went 7-1) but also suited up and played (as a second-string substitute) in enough varsity games in our 4-5 season to earn my block S letter. We had a powerful team that finished 7-1-1 when I was a senior in fall 1963. I "lettered" in football two years and track (as a shot putter) two years. I joined the wrestling team in the winter of my junior year but quit after an accident in practice gave me a shoulder separation that took a couple months to heal. I didn't want to risk missing football or track.

Toward the end of ninth grade at Bancroft the San Leandro High football coaching staff showed up to conduct tryouts for the coming fall sophomore squad. Half the boys in the school tried out! I always thought it was amusing that James Bull and Charles Bear (actually spelled "Bare") got cut early—two guys with fierce names! I went over with the throngs to try out with the ends, the receivers, my usual position in football up to that point. I was still one of the fastest guys my age in the city. But the coaching staff walked by all of us, looked us over, and pointed at me and said "you go over with the tackles." I was a big 9th grader at 5'10" and 175 pounds and the coaches probably imagined me growing to 6'3 and 220 pounds but that was not in the genes. A huge number of the guys were assigned to move from the "glamour" positions to others, just based on what their physiques looked like. As soon as I got to the tackles group though, I asked if I could join the centers. My wish was granted and center became my position for the next three years.

What I liked about playing center was I got to handle the ball, I organized the huddle, and it was up to me to call out the blocking schemes on every play during the game, based on the way the defense lined up in front of me. The center becomes the quarterback's protector and therefore best friend. I was already good buddies with our two quarterbacks, both from Roosevelt, Jerry Gaustad and Corky Barrett. I was also our best place-kicker and always kicked off but was never able to kick extra points and field goals because our back-up center blew the snap every time he tried and the coach gave up. We just ran or passed for the extra points and never attempted field goals. Funny sophomore story: I say I scored the first points against our team when we were sophomores. We had shut out our first two opponents and won by big scores. But against our third opponent I snapped the ball over our punter's head. Instead of him falling on it, he circled back and was eventually tackled in the endzone for a safety. Final score 14-2 San Leandro. Those two points were my fault.

Part One: Incubators (1946–1964)

What I learned from playing football was to work inconspicuously in the blocking trenches on behalf of a team win. I had always been a star before; now I was working in the trenches. I learned about team. We became a powerful offense, especially in the running game which depended on our blocking up front. Sometimes after the snap I pulled and sprinted around the end ahead to block for a running back. Sometimes I had to snap the ball and drive straight ahead to take out a linebacker. The left guard next to me was Manuel (Mick) Abascal who became an all-state honoree with a football scholarship to Cal. The camaraderie and team spirit were an amazing thing to be part of and several of us maintain our friendship fifty years later. In my sophomore year I was one of the bigger guys on the line. By our senior year Ron Hart and I were the smallest guys on our line. We played against many high schools (like Berkeley and Alameda) with three thousand or more students and four-year football programs. In our senior year we (fourteen-hundred student San Leandro High) won all of our games except for a tie with Alameda High School and a 12–6 loss to Berkeley High, even though we significantly outgained both teams in total yardage when we played them. Frustrating! We won all of our other games, usually by huge margins, like our 35–7 win over Orinda/Moraga's Miramonte High School, the champions of their league over the hill.

We had a great coach, John "Biff" Crawley, and several great assistants like Cas Munoz. We were among the first high school football teams to lift weights to muscle up in the off season. Biff used to have us all take a knee before a game and he would pray in his heavy Louisiana accent: "God help us play our best possible ball." That short prayer was it. He was a tough taskmaster. When I was painfully racked up in a practice, his response was "Rub a little grass on it, Gill, and get back out there!" I was clearly the heir apparent to be starting center my senior year but when I showed up for our first practice in August I saw my name on the second string list and Sonny Aranaydo listed as first string. Before our first game I was named the starter but when I asked Coach Crawley why this had happened he said: "Some players need a 'medicine man' to bring out the best in them. Gill you needed Aranaydo as your medicine man—to motivate you to play harder and better."

By the time I was a senior, though, as great as our team was, it was clear to me that I didn't have a future in college ball, especially at the major level like Cal and Stanford, the two local universities we thought most about attending. The local press voted me third team all-league (coaches around the league told coach Crawley I should have been first-team based on my performance). But no major college football team was going to have a 5'10" center weighing 185 pounds. I hadn't grown an inch in three years. But I wasn't much disappointed by this. (I have, however, sometimes wished I would have played rugby on Cal's year-after-year championship teams. My body and mind were built for rugby—though the permanent reorientation of rugby players' noses, teeth, and ears might have been the cost of a rugby career!). The reality was that we SLHS football players were amply rewarded by all the attention we got from our friends and teachers at school—as we cruised the campus wearing our letterman sweaters—or wore our football jackets while our girlfriends wore our sweaters!

I also joined the track team. My Roosevelt school mate Craig Reynolds became a very close buddy in high school because of track. He was an outstanding distance runner. I was the same 50-yard 5.9 second runner in high school as I was in the 7th grade but that no longer won races in high school so I tried out the shot put. I won a lot of points for our track teams all three years. As a sophomore my best was 38'11." As a junior I improved to 45'11" which was second best for my grade in our Alameda County Athletic League. But I slacked off my workouts after my senior football season and only improved to 48'7"—enough to help us win track meets but not achieving the 55' plus I should have. After the football season I had also leaned out from 188 to 170 pounds and that might have limited me a little. But I have often said that football taught me about sacrificing for the team—and track taught me about individual discipline. Powerful lessons.

Beyond football and track, I was a very active and athletic kid. I became a decent ice skater at Berkeley Iceland as a result of church outings there. I tried to play golf a couple times in high school with my church friend Steve Imbeau. I remember my first ever game at Tilden Park around 1962. It took me 154 strokes to finish 18 holes! I played very little until after college in 1972 when I could start playing weekly at Oakland's Lake Chabot municipal golf course. (Best score ever: a 78 at Lake Chabot in 1992; usual scores in the 80s; today in the 90s on a good day). I played tennis once in a while at an intermediate level with Jim Hyde in junior and senior high school but only got really active after Lucia got interested from 1975 onward (our tennis careers ended with Lucia's knee injury in 2000 but we were fanatics from 1975 to 1999). Julius was still a fishing enthusiast in high school so at least once we drove down to catch a fishing boat from Half Moon Bay way before dawn and returned that afternoon with a gunnysack full of ling cod, red snapper and other varieties we had caught. In high school I started working out with weights at Gene's Health Studio and have been pretty much a lifetime gym rat since then. After high school I started jogging a lot and ran in many Bay-to-Breakers events (usually around 60 minutes for the 12k) during the 1980s—I also ran the Dipsea once and one half-marathon when we lived in Bordeaux in 1985. So much for my athletic career!

SCHOOL

Football and track taught me some important lessons. Their impact was perhaps most important on my sense of self. In high school I no longer spoke out like an idiot. I still liked being witty or funny in and out of class but I no longer pushed it or aggravated my teachers. Not much, anyway. I wasn't whispering in the back of the class and being disruptive.

Part One: Incubators (1946-1964)

I have often said I was a product of "mass counseling techniques" in high school. Every bright kid was steered toward a Russia-beating engineering career. From 9th grade at Bancroft through my senior year at San Leandro High I took four years of math, four years of science (full years of biology, chemistry, and physics), four years of social studies (culminating in a veritable classics seminar led by our professorial August Vaz), four years of German, and four years of English literature and composition. I always had 6th period physical education like the other varsity athletes so our team practices could begin at 2:15 instead of 3:15. It was a heavy academic study program and most of my classes were designated "honors" tracks for the best students in the school. As I said earlier, I was the B student in the honors program, not for lack of intelligence but because of distraction and lack of effort.

Miss Avo Sims, my math teacher as a junior and senior was called Sargent Sims behind her back. We speculated that a scar on her chest was a bullet hole from her past (It wasn't). She was tough and even mean at times. She sneered at me and the class and told us nobody was smart enough to get an A. So one semester I busted it so she would have to give me an A (she did). Then I promptly relaxed and took my B minuses and Cs the rest of the way.

Julius and I were lab partners in biology as sophomores. For our Spring semester project we decided to prepare a rabbit skeleton. Mr. Everingham approved our research plan and we had actually gone out to UC Berkeley to study rabbit skeleton literature. We went to a rabbit slaughterhouse near our high school and purchased a live rabbit. We got permission to skip our other classes and work in the biology lab all day. We anesthetized (with ether, I think) the unlucky victim and then dissected and studied its organs as we worked our way down to its skeleton. Incredibly fascinating and more complex than frogs. Julius and I, being who we were, were covered in blood in our formerly white lab coats so, naturally, when we noticed the hallways were filled with students going from one class to another we walked out into the hallway in our full bloody gore, freaking out a considerable number of students walking by and shrieking at their bloody classmates, Drs. Julius and David Frankenstein. We soaked the skeleton in some kind of acid or lye overnight and then assembled it, using a coat hanger up its spine to hold it together. Two final problems: there were a lot of tiny foot bones left in the bucket, impossible to assemble properly so we simply sprinkled them on some glue in the general location of the feet, hoping Mr. Everingham wouldn't mark us down for this (he didn't). The other problem was that as we presented our skeleton project to the class the coat hanger came apart and "Bugs's" head detached from his body and waved back and forth during our presentation. I think we still got an A.

I still took those achievement tests every year in high school and killed them all but my grades were never consistently high. I graduated 58th in a class of 447 with an official 2.95 (B) gpa. I had applied for admission to UC Berkeley in the spring of my Junior year and had solid enough grades in all the core college prep courses they required for admission. I knew I was admitted to Berkeley just as my senior year in high school got started. It was the only college I applied to (or had any interest in). Of course, this early admission undercut my motivation to work hard as a senior. I never had to take the SAT test because of the tough classes I completed with B or better grades.

When I look back at my formal education up through high school, I feel generally good about what I studied (including the shop classes in junior high). My future grad school and writing career no doubt benefitted immensely from the loads of essays and term papers I was assigned. By the time I graduated from high school I had a two-foot high stack of my schoolboy essays and papers. I value my four years of German but wish I had a couple years of Latin as well. The four years of math were good, especially algebra and advanced algebra which train the mind to figure out "unknowns"—x or y or z or some combination—based on what you do know. I liked those "word problems" where we assigned variables to what we wanted to know and set up formulas to move from the known to the unknown. I have used algebra all my life but beyond the math, the logic helps in all fields.

Two of my regrets about my high school program are, first, that I never took a typing class. Who could have known that I would not be an engineer but the author of ten books and hundreds of essays and reviews? All of my writings I have typed with just my right index finger (which has been typing-tested at thirty-five words per minute!). Yeah, I know. Stupid. I have sometimes closed my office door to avoid embarrassment if anyone looks in and laughs at old "one finger Gill."

My other regret was not being able to act and sing in the musicals the drama department put on. I actually tried out and got a part in "South Pacific" but then had to give it up because of our team practice or game schedule. That really hurt because I loved music and singing. I had been given a year of piano lessons by Miss Mann when I was six or seven. I remember I could play some of the opening of Beethoven's Moonlight Sonata. I quit because I wasn't disciplined enough to practice and I didn't care for Miss Mann. (Our daughter Jodie became a stellar pianist in high school and then did her Bachelors and Masters degrees in piano performance and pedagogy at UC Santa Barbara and Northwestern University. She has always had droves of adoring students and parents begging her to teach their kids. If only I had had a teacher like her!).

Instead of piano, I bought a cheap guitar and took lessons for a few years beginning around age ten from Mr. Bob Richards who lived down the street from me and ran Richards Guitar Studio nearby on MacArthur Boulevard. I washed his car and mowed his lawn in return for lessons and credit toward a guitar. I got to be a decent rhythm guitarist but never learned how to play great solos as a lead guitarist. I inherited my mother's good musical ear and could usually hear something and figure out how to play it on my guitar (or maybe on the piano in the key of C!). But I was impatient with reading music. Lots of my friends also had guitars in this rock'n'roll era. Julius, Wally, Jim Hyde and I formed the "Snurd Brothers" with our four voices and acoustic guitars and performed in downtown San Leandro's city music festival, at the Alameda County Fair, and in a memorable student assembly in front of the whole student body. Our two-song repertoire was "Wolverton Mountain" and "Some Fool Made a Soldier of Me." In three-part harmony!

Then came the Beatles in our senior year! We loved the new sound and look. I got an electric guitar and organized a foursome with Steve Paulson on drums (my future brother-in-law), Mike Warman, and Jim Hyde. We got a spot on an all-school talent assembly. I persuaded Liz Kellam to get a bunch of our female classmates to scream and rush the stage when they announced us as "The Beatles!" The curtain parted, and there we were with our hair combed down over our foreheads like the Beatles and broke into a decent amateur cover of the Beatles' "She Loves You" (yeah, yeah, yeah).

I could not be involved in the social activities of my fellow students because of my religious restrictions but student government (like sports) was ok. I ran for student body vice-president in the Spring semester of my senior year. Jim Hyde and I were a ticket trying to unseat the fall government. We flipped a coin and made Jim our candidate for president and me for vice-president. Unfortunately, Jim lost, though I won and served my final high school semester as vice-president. Then I wished I had run for the top spot! Oh well. The returning president Bob Johnsen was also a friend and football teammate. As a senior I was also President of our "Block S" letterman's club.

JOBS

As soon as I hit fifteen-and-a-half years old I got my driving learner's permit and at sixteen my driver's license. At fifteen-and-a-half I could also get a work permit. I had dropped the paper route job at age fourteen. At age sixteen in 1962 I got a part-time job which lasted six months at Wadler's Milk Depot which paid the $1.50/hour minimum wage. I took care of customers coming in to buy milk and ice cream at their non-union cut rates. A young man who had been working there much longer than I told me it was ok to stand in the refrigerated room behind the shelves of milk where we could keep an eye on any entering customers—while eating as much ice cream as we wished. Nice perk. Unfortunately, Wadler's had a second store in a rougher part of town and I was assigned to work there. But at one point a quick-handed customer short-changed me and I was fired for a missing $10 the next day.

Then I got a job in 1963 at Donuts Unlimited on Victoria Circle at Bancroft Avenue. I had to get there at 3:00 a.m. to help the owner make dozens of donuts in the morning. He told me to go ahead and eat all I wanted. I did—but remember I was a nonstop athlete and bundle of growing energy in those days! At maybe 6:00 or 7:00 the owner would take off for a couple hours to deliver boxes of donuts around town. But he also began to have some add-on special "deliveries" now and then and one day his wife called and asked if he was there. I told her he was out on a special delivery. She had figured out he was having an affair while I watched the store. He fired me when he got back to the store. I had only lasted two months.

Then my friend from Roosevelt, SLHS quarterback Jerry Gaustad, got me hired in early summer 1963 at a gas station on the corner of San Leandro Boulevard and Davis Street. It was one of those huge places with several "islands" of gas pumps. In those days customers expected to have someone run out and fill up their tank, wash their windshield, and check their oil and tire pressures, if they asked for it. I was hired but given no training and no help. Multiple cars came in and I was running from one island to another and not keeping up very well. I was the only employee on duty. The owner was just standing in a small office looking out through a one-way mirror and drinking booze from his flask. He fired me after just two weekends. But by then Jerry had landed a job at Lynch's Shell on MacArthur next door to Jerry's Beefburgers. He got me hired at Lynch's and that became a terrific job during the twelve months till I graduated. Still $1.50/hour.

At Lynch's Shell we were all SLHS football players except for John Lynch and his adult son who both really liked us guys. We could put our own cars up on the rack and tune them or change the oil if business was slow in the evenings. But we kept really busy running out to serve our customers. Since it was next door to Jerry's, an endless stream of cute girls and high school friends came through, either with their parents or maybe driving themselves. It was easy to walk next door and pick up a burger, fries and a shake for dinner. I think I averaged ten or twelve hours per week when classes were in session, more during school breaks.

Some crazy folk also came through Lynch's Shell. One night a clearly drunk guy asked me to check his oil. I did and showed him he was down a couple quarts. He slurred out to me "Fill it up with water." I argued with him that that would ruin his engine and told him I couldn't do it. He angrily got out of his car, grabbed the water hose and filed the oil receptacle with water to the brim and drove off down the street. I don't know how far he got. Lynch's Shell was on a point where two busy streets came together, Foothill and MacArthur. Once in a while some impatient driver would cut through our station from Foothill to MacArthur rather than waiting at the traffic stop at the point. As they drove over the ringers we would jump up thinking we had a customer only to see them exit the other driveway. One evening some malefactor drove through our lot and directly across MacArthur to the cheap discount gas station. What an insult! I said to Jerry and the guys, "that really ticks me off. I'm going to go let that guy know he'd better not do that again." I marched across the street and knocked on the driver's window. A huge dude about 6'6," probably named Boris, got out of the car and said "What's on your mind, punk?" I was a very fit football guy but had no interest tangling with this big goon towering over me. So I said "Sir, I just wanted to say, go ahead and drive through our Shell station lot whenever you want!"—and I walked back across MacArthur to Lynch's. Hoots and jeers.

Speaking of cars, like most guys my age I desperately wanted my own. When I was a sophomore, it was no longer cool to ride a bike so I walked a couple miles each way to school every day (and to my jobs). As a junior in 1962 I bought a 1954 Ford sedan for $260, paid for the insurance through my parents' Allstate agent —but then sold it three months later for $240. I just couldn't make the finances work. I bummed a lot of rides from Jerry Gaustad. My parents were ok with my buying a car as long as I paid all the costs including the insurance. A year later in fall 1963 of my senior year, I was ready. I bought a very cool 1956 Chevy sedan for $375. Now we were talking. I got it repainted a beautiful forest green and loved driving it around. I did blow a couple engines over the next three years and traded it in for a cheaper VW Karman Ghia two-seat car in 1967.

THE END OF THE INNOCENCE

As my senior year wound down to its end, we had been shocked by the assassination of President Kennedy in November. The Cold War was pretty hot. Civil Rights and social protest were in the news. But our lives were still safe, fun, innocent, and full of hopes and dreams. I was going to Cal to enter the College of Engineering in the fall along with my football buddy Roger Zolldan. In November of my senior year I had started dating and going steady with a cute sophomore named Lucia Paulson which did wonders for my happiness (more on her in a later chapter). The youth group at my church was alive and healthy and I spent no time envying my SLHS classmates' social lives.

I had not gone to a dance in my life but there was no way I would miss my Senior Ball. I persuaded my parents it was primarily a big banquet (it was that). I didn't tell them Lucia was teaching me some dance steps in her basement. Her mom made her a spectacular ball gown. I rented a tuxedo and drove us in my Chevy with my buddy Craig Reynolds and his date Janice Field to a glorious evening. The graduation exercises a few days later were fun. We signed each other's yearbooks, wished each other good luck, and promised to keep in touch. Then we unloaded our lockers and departed. It really was the end of an era of innocence in 1964.

Of course, I made all kinds of choices up to that point but the basic institutions and forces, even the basic philosophy of life, were chosen for me by others. Now it was all going to change and I would be the one choosing the shapers of my life that would prepare me for my life calling. I was about to embark on an exciting, tumultuous, unexpected set of adventures that would guide me and equip me for a lifelong calling that became clear by 1979.

The epilogue to high school is that many of us in the Class of 1964 are better connected today than ever before. Every five years since 1964 we have had a class reunion. I started attending these with the ten-year reunion in 1974. I even joined the reunion planning committee and helped organize the 2004 (forty-year) and 2009 (forty-five-year) reunions. I kept in relatively close touch with Julius, Wally, Craig, and Liz Kellam over the years. I had a couple football team reunion dinners at my house with ten or twelve of the guys. I hung out a lot with my old teammate Manuel Abascal for several years. Largely because of those class reunions but also assisted by Facebook connections and networking, many of us in our high school class are closer than ever to each other. In some cases, classmates I barely knew in high school have become close friends over the decades since 1964.

Liz Kellam was a good friend beginning in the fifth grade at Roosevelt. She became a French and Spanish high school teacher back at SLHS. She and her husband Pete hung out with us whenever we could—wine-tasting, dancing, dinners, jazz. I didn't know Darien Speight Chandler more than to say hello in high school but we and our spouses have become great friends. I barely knew Kendall Mau in high school but we reconnected around the 2004 reunion and he became a close friend and guest lecturer in my business ethics courses because of his banking and microenterprise development work in Honduras and elsewhere. I reconnected with my brainy classmate John Merrill just as he retired from a distinguished career as Professor of Geography at the University of Rhode Island. John and I may be the only PhD career professors in our class. My football teammate Ron Hart turned out to have a special interest in "faith at work" issues, much like my own calling. And I could go on. Our post-high school careers and family stories have been all over the map but you never get the slightest sense of competitiveness, just love and acceptance. Many years have passed since high school, with plenty of sadness and tragedy, but the reality is that we enjoy getting together more than ever. The mutual affection and care is real and I love to see my classmates from back in that age of innocence.

I'm a very sentimental, nostalgic guy by nature. I hate to say goodbye to people I care about. I get a little emotional whenever I revisit places where I taught or lived. It takes some effort but I love to keep reweaving those threads of my early life into today's tapestry. It all gave birth to the young man who walked on to the Cal campus in fall 1964 just as a revolution began—around me and eventually in me. Good-by Dave. Hello David.

GROWING UP GILL

Before I leave this account of my youth, let me give a few summary reflections, for what they may be worth. The period from 1946 to 1964 was relatively stable, safe, and positive, at least for a white boy like me. I see my advantages growing up then—how women and ethnic minorities bore much greater challenges of sexism and racism—and how the whole culture got more challenging when my own kids were growing up—and the even more extreme challenges for my grandchildren today. But consider this:

1: I grew up in a stable, loving, middle-class but economically-secure, two-parent family—with three sisters. Not being an only child meant learning to share and get along. Having two parents meant they could help each other in the hardest job in the world, raising kids. I see my privilege—and urge today's mothers and fathers to stay together and parent together.

2: I had a few, but only a few, relatives active in my life but I grew up very aware that I and my family were part of a multi-generational story that was God's gift and my legacy to carry on. I was born and raised with a story. This was and is so important to the formation of one's identity. Discover, create, and tell your story. "Adopt" some older folk as your "godparents."

3: We rarely ever went out to restaurants, almost never to what became "fast food" joints, but there was always good, tasty, healthy food on the table.

4: My family was not very athletic and expensive sports like skiing, or athletic club memberships, were never in the picture. But I was always encouraged to participate in playground and organized school sports. I matured physically a bit in advance of most of my peers and had a lot of success and recognition for my athletics—a huge part of my positive identity, a huge contributor to my health, and an investment of time that left little room for just hanging out and maybe getting into trouble. My school friends Julius, Wally, Craig, and Liz, were a constant, hilarious part of my daily life all through my youth.

5: From age two or three onward, reading was a daily part of my family life. Reading the Bible every day as a family built my reading skills and my moral/intellectual/spiritual character. We revered the Bible as the Word of God but could always question and discuss its meaning and application. We also were a book, magazine, and newspaper reading and discussing household. Television was severely limited and we did not suffer the curse of smart phones.

6: I grew up expected to do my share of the daily chores around the house. There were no housemaids but us. I learned basic kitchen skills alongside my sisters—and lots of handyman skills alongside my dad. I always cleaned my own room and made my own bed.

7: And I learned the joys and burdens of outside work, first by hiring myself out to neighbors for lawn mowing and car washing, then four years of early morning newspaper delivery, and a series of part-time jobs through high school. I developed a ferocious work ethic and enjoyed the results/products of my work as well as the minimum wage pay—which I learned to tithe to my church and other charities, save for the future, and use to buy my clothes, my car and insurance, and dates with my girlfriend.

8: From age six onward I was personally committed to the Christian faith and life. More and more each year I tried to understand biblical faith and life more fully. My parents modeled and encouraged me in a loving, joyful version of Christian discipleship. We did not expect the culture around us (its schools or government or entertainment) to buy into or support our faith. We did not want or expect our schools or government to pretend to be "Christian" and serve up some wimpy, official version of our faith. We just wanted the freedom to live as Christians in a pluralistic world. I learned how to be (and love to be) a bold follower of Jesus in that pluralistic culture.

9: We were always (three times every week at least) part of a little local church (maybe 125–150 people of all ages) in Oakland. It was a quiet but confident fellowship, strict and narrow in faith and values, but warm and family-like in relationships. My dozen or more fellow "young people" were my primary social group with lots of fun activities and tons of music (including my guitar). This (along with my sports activities) made up for the religious and familial restrictions when it came to parties, movies, and dancing. I rarely felt sorry for myself.

So I have often said that "I have no excuses" to screw up in my life (I have—but I knew it was my responsibility and was taught to admit my failings, seek and accept forgiveness, and do better). I tried to provide these nine supports to my own two kids growing up, even though the world was changing and getting more difficult for them. I do not hold myself up as any kind of model or standard—but I do urge today's parents to try to bless their children with something like the kind of upbringing I received.

PART TWO

Shapers (1964–1979)

FROM 1964, WHEN I enrolled as a freshman at Cal Berkeley, until 1979, when I graduated with my PhD from the University of Southern California, I was on a search to find my voice, my calling, vocation, and purpose in life. Certainly, my schooling at Cal, SF State, and USC was a huge part of that process. But there were other forces, events, and shapers just as important as formal schooling. Some of these, of course, were unbidden, out of my control—both positive and negative, often a mix of both. But to a great extent all of this was because of choices I made. I invited these shapers into my adventure. These were unforgettable, exciting, challenging years of adventure. Some of it was incredibly painful not just to me but to my wife and others. Some of the pain I caused, some of it was inflicted by others. Most of it was an inevitable cost of taking on big challenges with limited resources and experience. Growing pains. Here is part two of my story. I hope my fifteen-year search to find my voice and calling is an encouragement to readers for whom those answers are slow in coming. The shapers I describe did not stop influencing me after 1979, of course, but this was the decisive beginning.

First in time and importance is my pretty deep and steady faith commitment to Jesus Christ as Lord of my life—and my sometimes tumultuous experience of church, which took me (after four generations in my family) out of a separatist sect into the broader Christian church. Barely less important is the love of my life, my companion every step of the way, Lucia Lynn (Paulson) Gill. She gets her own chapter even though she (like God) is present every step of the way in this memoir from 1963 on. My kids, grandkids, and friends are next. My life and studies at Cal Berkeley (BA) and SF State (MA) get a chapter and then comes a transformative two years with Berkeley's Christian World Liberation Front. I give whole chapters to two gigantic shapers of my life: (1) the Black church and community and (2) the French sociologist and ethicist, Jacques Ellul. The final shaper is the University of Southern California where I did my PhD.

8

Faith & Church

Advance Double-Warning to Readers: First, for some, this chapter might be way "too much information," getting lost "deep in the weeds!" It could be like being led into a deep and unfamiliar cave or labyrinth. Feel free to speed read or even skip over this chapter if you wish. For others, this chapter may raise more questions than it answers and call out for longer, fuller discussion. Some may feel I am too harsh and negative in places—that these days (fifty years later) my former church and tradition are really not so bad. But I have to tell it like it was. I'm not saying that this is everybody's story, just that it is mine. This is the story of (a) my personal faith as it developed from my childhood onward—and (b) my church experience in the "Exclusive Plymouth Brethren," a small Protestant sect (I will often just call them the "PBs"). I am grateful for my religious background and upbringing and harbor no ill feelings (though radically disagreeing with much of that church tradition). My faith story is part of everything in my life story, often explicitly so, other times implicitly and just beneath the surface.

For many of my friends it seems like "Gill is a very religious guy." Others (fewer) might say "Gill is a very spiritual person." It all depends on what you mean by these terms but I would never describe myself as especially religious or spiritual (even if it is true in some definitions). "God-centered" is more how I would like to be described. I also really like the term "disciple"—meaning an adherent, a learner, a follower. I am above all a follower of Jesus—far from perfect, but a pretty loyal and serious disciple throughout my life. I have always taken very seriously Jesus' statement that his followers are sent *into* the world. Christians are supposed to be "in" but "not of" the world (i.e., bringing a distinctive, alternative reality into a lost and hurting world). There is no justification for withdrawal into some holy huddle of the pure and like-minded. I am a passionate and committed follower of Jesus who is "out there" in our crazy, beautiful, hurting world. Here is the basic story.

Part Two: Shapers (1964–1979)

When I was just six years old, I began my self-consciously Christian life. Of course, I had attended church, lots of it, from soon after the day I was born. And my family had daily Bible reading and prayer. But the emphasis was on every individual's responsibility to choose to believe in Jesus Christ. Your parents could not do it for you. I was not baptized as an infant. The motivation to declare yourself as a believer in Jesus was mostly negative: you have sinned and will burn in hell forever if you do not personally repent of your sin, turn to Jesus Christ and accept him as your Savior. Once you make that transaction you are forgiven, saved, born again, headed for heaven at the end of your life. One Sunday evening at age six I had trouble sleeping after the Sunday evening Gospel preacher put the fear of hell in me. I got out of bed and asked my mom to kneel beside me as I prayed simply to accept Jesus Christ as my Savior.

I never doubted for the rest of my life that I was (and wanted to be) a Christian, a believer, a child of God. I never changed my mind or had a second conversion experience. Our church believed in "eternal security"—once you become a Christian you can never lose your salvation, no matter what, even if you renounce it. No one can ever "pluck you out of God's hand" Jesus assured his followers. So that was that. At age ten I asked to be baptized (done by immersion, dipping you under water)—an "outward witness" to my "inward faith," a symbolic burial of the old life and assumption of new resurrected life. Baptized believers would not be perfect, we knew, but the ritual testified to a real public commitment. Like my initial "conversion" experience at six, my baptism was a once-in-a-lifetime thing. Then at age twelve I asked to become a full, participating member of the fellowship—to begin taking weekly communion. I was interviewed by some of the leaders and welcomed in.

In many church traditions something like this happens all at once around adolescence (age twelve or thirteen). Kids are taught the basics of the faith for several months (catechism or confirmation classes), then questioned at the end if they understand and want to be "confirmed" in the faith. If they wish, they then publicly profess that faith, get baptized if it didn't happen as an infant, and are welcomed in as full members of the church. Often this is when they first take communion (mass, the Eucharist, the Lord's Supper). This is roughly parallel to the bar or bat mitzvah process in the Jewish tradition.

In my family (and most others in our church, I am sure) there were nightly family "devotions" (Bible reading and prayer). But there was also great emphasis on the daily reading of the Bible (and prayer) as an individual. No later than age twelve I began this practice and have rarely missed a day since. I was given my own leather-bound copy of the King James Version and encouraged to read actively with a pen in hand to underline or otherwise mark up the text as I sought to understand and remember it. The Bible was the "written Word of God," our insight and authority for all of life. It was viewed as second-best if you used any kind of annotated Bible with explanatory notes; better just to stick with the text. I was fairly compulsive about all this. Sometimes when I would get to my bed late at night and exhausted, I kept my streak alive by quickly reading just one verse, leaping into bed, and falling immediately asleep. But more and more as I went through high school and then off to college, I did read the Bible and underline and circle and make notes as I found favorite statements and began to see intriguing patterns in the text.

This is where you ask: "how is this all happening during that age eleven to thirteen period when you were shoplifting and disrupting your school classes with Julius and Wally?" I was ashamed of myself at times—especially when my parents were called in. At other times I just didn't think about it. I drifted along with a sort of compartmentalized life. We boys were never cruel but we were foolish and immature. What we did and said just seemed funny or inconsequential to us. And a final explanation: I grew up in a very strict church but a very kind family—and my view of God was (and remains) of a gracious, patient, forgiving Creator and Redeemer. I was taking God and his patience and forgiveness for granted.

There was a lot of Bible reading in our church services, often enough with someone trying to explain its meaning and maybe its application to our faith and practice. We had Sunday school classes every week with lessons about Bible stories. From roughly kindergarten to junior high we were assigned a Bible verse to memorize and stand up and repeat on Sunday. It was embarrassing if you stood up and didn't know it! We also memorized the names of the sixty-six books of the Bible (in order). Once a year for a special celebration we would memorize and recite a whole chapter of the Bible, like Psalm 23.[1]

As I got into high school and even more so university, I began reading commentaries on the Bible that explained the history and meaning of texts. I read a few biographies of missionaries and histories of Christianity. I was especially interested in "apologetics"—the intellectual and historical defense of the faith. The main concerns of these books were to defend divine creation (against evolution), the historicity of miraculous things like Noah's flood, Jonah's "whale" story, the miracles and resurrection of Jesus, and the inerrancy of the Bible.[2]

YOUTH LEADERSHIP

I had nothing but warm feelings toward the other kids in my church growing up. We often played together at each other's houses or at church picnics. Sometime beginning around junior high school there were occasional "young peoples' meetings" at somebody's house on a Friday or Saturday evening. The music and singing were uninspired

---

1. I love the Bible and consider it God's Word but I don't worship it. I worship God, not the Bible.

2. I have an open mind about miraculous things. I believe in a supernatural God capable of anything good. But I also think the point of (for example) the Genesis creation stories is to tell us the truth about *who* created the world and *why*—not about how long it took or in what precise manner the Creator did it. I don't see God's power and glory diminished in the slightest if it turns out he took a billion years of art and construction work to get the job done.

and the message from some elder in the congregation was okay. But I remember being irritated by the snarky, superior, detached attitude of some of the guys just a few years older than me. They sat in the back at meetings and stood together out on the sidewalk after church services and maybe made a wisecrack at me or another younger person. I remember griping to my dad about it. His answer to me: "Well, ok, but what are you doing about it?" That is where the title of this memoir comes from.

In my late teens I traded my electric guitar (remember our cover of the Beatles' "She Loves You" in high school?) for a twelve-string acoustic guitar and pushed forward as a song leader in our meetings. Other young people might add a guitar or violin or keyboard. Tim Clarke created an old-fashioned "gut bucket" which served as a bass. We upgraded the song selection and eventually printed our own song book. The snarky guys stayed snarky but we definitely took over and changed the culture. An older man named Clarence Mayo mentored me and often spoke to our fellowship. Clarence had been a Baptist minister in his younger days but converted over to the Plymouth Brethren—who have no pastors and look down on the whole idea. He was undervalued in our church because of his Baptist preaching style and was considered somewhat tainted as a formerly-ordained minister, but he was a gift of God to me and our whole youth group in high school and college.

For several years (until 1975) I played guitar and led music at various church events, summer camps, youth retreats, and other gatherings. I couldn't stand boring music, disinterested, passive audiences, or egocentric wanna-be-a-star song leaders. I was all into finding simple music with good words and a groove and then firing the people up to sing with some spirit. I traded my twelve-string in for a Martin D-18 after seeing Joan Baez do her magic with one at Cal's Greek Theatre. Somewhere along the way I was invited to share a brief message (mini-sermon, homily) for a weekly church service at the long-term rehab hospital across the street from our own church building. I think I was about eighteen. I spoke on John 14:6 where Jesus says "I am the way, the truth, and the life; no one comes to the Father but through me." That was the beginning of a lifetime of such requests.

It can't be stressed enough how "all in" I was in my church and its tradition. I trusted my father's (and mother's) opinion that this was the one and only right way to do church. I felt the weight of being the fourth generation in the Plymouth Brethren and keeping the historical line going. I listened and learned, studied and served. I dragged my friends Julius, Wally, and Craig to my church once in a while. I brought my high school girl friend Lucia there when she was fifteen and I was seventeen and joyfully watched her commit to the Christian faith and before long be baptized and join the church. After our Saturday afternoon wedding and reception in 1967, a few years later, we drove four hours to Eureka for the first two nights of our honeymoon (then returned south to Carmel). No matter how exhausted, we wouldn't miss even one Sunday communion service at an (approved) assembly of PBs. When I had a very painful operation to remove a pilonidal cyst from my tail bone, I brought a special pillow to church and sat in misery through the services. I was "all in.

As I moved into my twenties I was invited to preach now and then not just at my home church but when I visited similar PB churches in other towns. I was always ready with a sermon if called upon. I was not a wave-maker but a cheer-leader for our church and the movement. I played a significant role in encouraging people on the margins of our church to actually join. Roy Akagi and Stan Iwawaki are just two of my contemporaries who I drew into active membership like that. At some point in my early twenties I played a major role in organizing an "Appreciation Dinner" for the adults in our church. We high school and college students prepared and served an elegant feast and delivered a musical concert, the likes of which none of them had ever experienced in our PB tradition. It was like (the movie) "Babette's Feast" without the wine.

OUTREACH LEADER

One thing that began to agitate me around age twenty was our lack of outreach to the neighborhood around our building on 40th Street in Oakland. We rarely ever had any visitors to our services and yet there were periodic reminders by our leaders and teachers about the "Great Commission" where the resurrected Jesus tells his followers to share his message and make converts around the world. Our church thought that by distributing little leaflets (Gospel Tracts) they were obeying that commission (and certainly they were). Of course, some individuals did speak up to non-Christian folk and suggest they become believers, sometimes successfully. All the same, we had maybe one or two visitors per year on average. I griped to my dad. "If we claim to have all this Gospel truth, why aren't we sharing it?" He said "Well, what are you doing about it?" He got me again.

The first thing I did was to drive out to the Alameda County Juvenile Hall on 150th Avenue, a mile south of my house. I went on Saturday of Labor Day weekend in 1966. As I drove out there, I really felt like the Devil was on one of my shoulders saying "Who do you think you are? You are nobody, with no credentials, no chance of getting into that jail with your big ideas. And it's Labor Day weekend you fool! Nobody will be in their office. Go home!" But an angel was on my other shoulder saying "Don't listen to him. Keep going. Don't give up." I pulled up, parked, took a guess, and knocked on a door that said "Boys Receiving." I couldn't see any other office. A huge warden answered in a gruff voice "What do you want?" My answer (knees literally shaking) "I was just wondering if there was any chance I could come here and lead a Bible study or something like that?" Warden: "Here is the phone number of Chaplain Hilton Schlecht. You have to call him to find out." Victory already just in overcoming my fears. Friends who have met me over the years tend to think I am

Part Two: Shapers (1964–1979)

some exceptionally bold, fearless guy—but I too have had to overcome occasional fears and low confidence.

Hilton Schlecht was a Lutheran minister working there full-time. The Juvenile Hall had hundreds of boys and girls up to age eighteen, incarcerated for various offenses. When I called him, he quizzed me about my faith and life (I was beginning my junior year at Cal)—and then said "Could you come out and preach at our chapel next Sunday?" "Yes," I answered. The next Sunday (September 11, 1966) I preached a twenty-minute sermon to about seventy girls at 9:00 a.m. and to a hundred and eighty or so boys at 10:00 a.m. before rushing back for worship at my Oakland church at 11:00 a.m.. That was the beginning of a five-year ministry for me. Chaplain Schlecht quickly decided to totally trust me and my leadership. I gathered a small team of seven or eight of my peers from our PB church and we would lead singing at these services as well as share a message. Over five years we led the services ninety-three times—about once every three weeks. I preached about half of those times and my friends Tim Clarke and Stan Iwawaki handled the others. By the beginning of the second year, the chaplain asked us also to take over the weekly Sunday School program for about seventy-five children of all ages in protective custody at Alameda County's Snediger Cottage. Now our commitment was weekly and all seven or eight of us got involved in loving and teaching these kids. This ministry continued for many years after I had gone in 1971, led by my friend Roy Akagi.

I started a Bible study for late teen guys on Tuesday evenings at the Senior Boys Ranch. It was the first time I had been part of a Bible study where the room was filled with thick cigarette smoke start to finish, where comments might include some vulgarity and cussing as we wrestled with one text or another. I announced ground rules that anyone could say anything they wanted so long as we always circled back to the biblical text and asked "what is God's opinion on this topic?" I loved it, loved these young men, and learned a ton.

I wanted to give these kids New Testaments and found a good deal on paperback copies (twenty cents each!) from the American Bible Society. The first time we gave out the King James Version but ever after it was the Revised Standard Version with its modern English. We gave out twelve hundred of these New Testaments over the five years. My dad and mom gave me $25 or so once in a while to help pay for them. My team and I paid the rest. Our home church contributed zero over the five years (and I don't recall them ever mentioning our outreach effort, or encouraging or praying for us in church. Pathetic, I have to say).

We also wanted to give them something to read outside of the formal services. I checked out the youth material from Gospel Light and David C. Cook—the two leading publishers of Sunday School and Christian youth education materials at the time. But literally everything was illustrated with pictures of white people and paintings of an imagined European Jesus (e.g., the Sallman "Portrait" of Jesus). No way on earth was I going to use that stuff with my majority Black Juvenile Hall kids.[3] So I bought a used mimeograph machine for $80.00—an old technology for making cheap copies by typing on a stencil and rotating a hand-crank that printed out copies. For four years I wrote, printed, and distributed every other week a one-to-four page paper I called "Straight To You" (one hundred issues over forty-four months, usually two hundred fifty copies). I wrote articles about Jesus, happiness, life, peace, justice, etc.—but also about Malcolm X, Frantz Fanon, Tom Skinner, Nicky Cruz, and Edwin Hawkins.

When I was a "student teacher" at Castlemont High School in 1968–69 I had fun a couple times when an ex-Juvy guy would see me on campus and give me a warm greeting. Indirectly, this Juvenile Hall ministry led to my excommunication in 1971 but I will get back to that later. This was an incredible experience for me and my colleagues. I cannot thank enough my Stanford brother Tim Clarke and my Berkeley-based brothers Roy Akagi and Stan Iwawaki, as well as my girlfriend Lucia Paulson and sisters Kitty and Dottie, for their partnership. Chaplain Schlecht eventually officiated at my marriage to Lucia in 1967. When Plymouth Brethren came through Oakland from other parts of the country they often begged me to come along so they could see what had to be one of the most (if not the only) exciting, edgy outreaches going on in our PB church world. For me personally, I often say this was my "seminary education"—studying the Bible in a community of young Black brothers during the Civil Rights and Black Power movement days. Any of my cultural naivete and white assumptions got stripped away in a hurry and we got down to wrestle with what the biblical text actually said to us right now, where we were.

When Lucia and I got married in 1967 we rented an apartment one block from our 40th Street church building. Lots of our contemporaries, not just in our church, were fleeing to the suburbs. We wanted to move closer into the city and be more integral to the neighborhood around the church. I used my mimeograph machine to create hundreds of half-page leaflets inviting neighbors to visit our Sunday evening services, ostensibly geared for inquirers and visitors. Very few ever came but boy did we try! I got permission from the elders to construct a big four-foot by eight-foot sign next to our building on 40th Street where a four-lane road meant a lot of traffic passing by. "Come Hear the Gospel. Sunday evenings at 7:00 p.m. All welcome," it said boldly. Stan and I got the redwood four-by-four's and concrete from the lumber yard and built a solid frame. I paid to have the sign painted. Few people ever attended our church as a result but we were trying, not just watching and waiting for others to act.

Maybe ten years after I was kicked out of the church I happened to drive past and noticed the sign had fallen out of the frame and was lying on the ground. I alerted someone about the fallen sign but it was never reinstalled (my niece Jackie made an attempt!) and for decades that empty frame served me as a powerful symbol of a church turned in on itself. There was no acceptable excuse for their almost total failure

---

3. Plymouth Brethren did not believe in paintings or images of Jesus so my mind was already half-way there.

to share the biblical heritage God gave into their possession. I tried hard to do something about it. I don't remember my home church and its leaders ever encouraging or publicly praying for, to say nothing of helping to fund, any of these initiatives and activities I mentioned here. They actually just didn't care—but that didn't matter to me. I hardly noticed it then because I wasn't doing it to get their praise or approval. I was "all in" and on "a mission from God" (as the Blues Brothers would have described it).

EXCLUSIVE PLYMOUTH BRETHREN

The church tradition and system I was born into came to be known as the Plymouth Brethren, "PBs" for short, as I mentioned earlier.[4] A small group of young men began meeting in the 1820s in Dublin, Ireland, some of them connected to Trinity College, to study their Bibles and discuss the teaching and practice of the New Testament church. They were in reaction to what they saw was the spiritual coldness and the captivity of not just the Church of England but all the denominations to non-biblical tradition and doctrine. They craved a return to the simplicity and vitality of the New Testament, especially as developed in the writings of St. Paul. The brilliant young scholar John Nelson Darby became the most prominent and influential leader. In some places this movement came to be known as the Darbyites, though he would be appalled to hear this. They preferred to call themselves "brethren"—brothers and sisters, "gathered only in the name of Jesus Christ." The adjective "Plymouth" was attached by others because many of their early writings were published out of Plymouth, England. This is why PBs have tended grudgingly to admit "we are the so-called Plymouth Brethren." They preferred saying they were just simple "saints gathered in the name of Jesus Christ"—not claiming to be more saintly than others but believing this was biblical terminology for those separated out and made holy by God. PBs never put the label "church" on their buildings but preferred "chapel" or still better "hall" or "meeting room." "Church" is the people, not a building.

---

4. There is a great deal of information online about the Plymouth Brethren. British Open PB leader F. Roy Coad provided a fairly detailed account in *A History of the Brethren Movement* (Grand Rapids: Eerdmans, 1968). More recently my friend and colleague Robert Baylis wrote *My People: The History of those Christians Sometimes Called Plymouth Brethren* (Carol Stream, Illinois: Harold Shaw, 1995). Just to give you some idea of who is (or was—most of these folks are former PBs) in this mostly invisible movement: probably the best-known public figure who grew up Exclusive Brethren was Garrison Keillor of Prairie Home Companion fame. (My mother knew his mother back in Minnesota). Keillor describes the PBs in a chapter called "The Sanctified Brethren" in his *Lake Wobegon Days* (New York: Penguin, 1985). Poet Luci Shaw is the grand-daughter of prolific early Brethren hymn-writer J. G. Deck. In the theological world, Manchester University New Testament scholar F. F. Bruce was the most famous PB scholar in recent decades. Al Erisman, Katherine Hayhoe, Tom Skinner, Bill Pannell, Sharon Gallagher, Dale Ryan, Don Tinder, Jim Wallis, Paul White and Stacy Woods (among the founders of Inter-Varsity Christian Fellowship) were PBs, as were Jim Houston, Ward and Laurel Gasque, Carl Armerding, Paul Stevens and other founders and leaders of Regent College in Vancouver BC, Canada. Without an ordained clergy to join, most PBs called to theological vocations go into academia or parachurch ministries.

This movement grew rapidly, not least because of the nonstop travels and advocacy of Darby. Darby remained single all of his life, wrote voluminously, was fluent in French and German, and translated the Bible into English, French, German, and Italian from the original Hebrew and Greek. He was by all accounts a man who lived in a modest even sacrificial manner. One story is that his clothes were so worn out he was mistaken for a beggar and offered a donation. His personal spirituality and charisma were irresistible to many.

Darby was the ingenious creator of a way of interpreting the Bible called "dispensationalism." In this system, God relates to the world and to his people in different ways during seven epochs including "innocence" in the Garden of Eden," "law" from Moses until Jesus, "grace" from Pentecost until the Rapture, followed by a thousand-year millennium and eternity. He believed the Bible itself presented this system. This way of interpreting Scripture, however, drives an extreme wedge between the Law and the Gospel and between this present age and the age to come, among other things. Not all Plymouth Brethren agreed with Darby on this but it had a huge impact even beyond Brethren circles. In America, the Fundamentalist Movement, the Scofield Reference Bible, and Dallas Theological Seminary were major guardians and promoters of dispensationalism. The dispensationalist interpretation of prophecy and the "end times" that people like Hal Lindsey (*The Late, Great Planet Earth*) and Tim LaHaye (*Left Behind*) promoted at a popular level all goes back to Darby.

The Plymouth Brethren are a small and declining movement in recent decades. Part of this is because many or most non-PB churches today now agree with their rediscovered emphasis on lay ministry (not just professional clergy) and many voices promote John Darby's systematic theology called dispensationalism and its ways of talking about prophecy and the second coming of Christ. In at least these ways PBs have, in effect, lost their distinctive reasons to exist over against other church traditions. They could view this as a victory.

In the mid-1840s a major split ruptured the movement, dividing it into "Open Brethren" and "Exclusive" or "Closed" Brethren. The Open Brethren were *congregational*, leaving doctrinal and practical issues to be decided congregation by congregation, though they remained unified by common concerns, views of church, and shared missionary and publishing projects. The Exclusive Brethren are *denominationally* organized so that a decision about doctrine or practice in one congregation is binding on all congregations in their circle of fellowship. If some teacher is disciplined or silenced in one of their congregations, he may not teach in any of the others in the network. This loss of congregational freedom has led to frequent splits among the Exclusives into ever smaller sects that refuse fellowship with each other. A dispute over whether the "sealing of the Spirit" occurred at the moment of conversion or happened in the decision of God in eternity past divided the Grant Brethren from the Natural History Hall Brethren. A dispute over whether to endorse a congregation's discipline of a brother who was raising issues of possible child abuse back East, split the Natural

History Hall brethren across the continent, including my home church in the Bay Area a few years after I left.

On top of that, most of the Exclusive Brethren refuse any kind of "amalgamation" or reunion of formerly divided Exclusive PB groups, insisting that any "restoration" must be one by one, not congregation by congregation. The famous London preacher Charles Spurgeon once said the Brethren "rightly divide the truth of Scripture but wrongly divide themselves." Easy to criticize, judge, and divide—almost impossible to ever (re-)unite. I was raised (the fourth generation) in these Exclusive PBs. It's like not just being an Anabaptist/Mennonite but an Amish, not just Jewish but Hasidic—the most separatist and intransigent version.

CHURCH LIFE

My home church, like all PBs, believed the central act of a local church (usually called "the assembly" or "the meeting") was the breaking of bread on Sunday mornings at 11:00 a.m.. We (maybe a hundred thirty folk in our Oakland congregation) all sat in a circle or square for this, with a simple table in the center with a loaf of (leavened) bread and a goblet of wine (no grape juice!) upon it. As in traditional Quaker meetings, there was no written order of service.[5] The only talk before the service might be someone standing and reading a "letter of commendation" from another approved congregation, introducing a visitor and assuring us of their good standing back home. We sat in silence, just like traditional Quakers (a movement that began in England two hundred years before the Brethren). At some point a brother might say "Let us sing together number 104."[6] Once in a while we might be asked to stand but most of the time we sit while singing. Some brother sings out to start the song and we do the best we can a capella. No musical instruments are allowed.

More silence for meditation as we wait for some other brother to stand and pray, read a Scripture about the sufferings of Christ, or suggest another hymn. Maybe thirty or forty minutes in, some brother will say "Let us break the bread" and walk up to the table, say a prayer of thanksgiving, break the loaf in two (no pre-cutting or individualized crackers allowed) and start passing it around with each official member pinching off and eating a small piece. Having one (initially unbroken) loaf symbolizes the one

---

5. It didn't need to be written down. It was a fixed pattern as predictable and unchangeable as any detailed, written liturgy. Their hope and confidence was that the Holy Spirit would lead the meeting. As I mention below, they don't believe the Holy Spirit is powerful enough to lead any advance planning (I jest but it's true, just as true as the converse: some pastors and churches just repeat written prayers and liturgies of the past, failing, it seems, to believe God's Spirit might lead in an extemporaneous fashion!).

6. The proposed hymn can only come from the "Little Flock"—a collection of words-only-hymns edited by John Darby—containing some classic material like "When I Survey the Wondrous Cross" but also a lot of hymns written by Darby and other early Brethren. Classic hymn lyrics were slightly re-worded to conform to PB doctrine.

body of Jesus Christ which was broken and sacrificed for us. After the bread makes its way around to everyone, being careful to skip anyone not in good standing, the same brother once again approaches the table to say a prayer of remembrance and thanksgiving for the shed blood of Christ which has bought our redemption. The wine cup is passed around. We all take a sip from the cup (not worrying at all about passing any germs to each other).

Then a collection box is passed around (but in silence; nobody ever urges donations). The money will be used for building expenses (congregations sometimes rent but often own their buildings) and contributions to our publishing arm "Bible Truth Publishers" or to those on the approved list of "laboring brothers." These are itinerant teachers. There are no professional pastors of individual congregations but there are a dozen or more of these teachers who have been "commended to the Lord's work" by their local congregations—some with admirable teaching gifts, others clearly not so gifted. Visitors are not served communion and they are not invited to donate anything to the collection box. Some brother is likely then to stand up and offer a brief homily or teaching message, probably urging everyone to stay faithful to PB truth in this "day of small things," and to the "place of his presence and choosing" (i.e., the PB Meeting). Maybe another hymn and a prayer and we are done. By the way, the prayers better be in the "thee" and "thou" language of the King James Version—"out of respect for God," they remind us.

The midweek Bible study (preferably called a "reading meeting") and prayer meeting begins by everyone physically kneeling at their chair for maybe a half hour of spontaneous prayers, mostly for the sick and for missionary activity (there are 'laboring brethren" working in other countries). When extended silence suggests we are finished, we rise to our seats and someone announces the biblical text where the meeting ended a week earlier. After the text (maybe a chapter long) is read, various brothers make comments on it. No one gives a comprehensive overview so it is pretty much a set of random comments, some more edifying than others. The introductory (and authoritative) statement "Mr. Darby says . . . " may be heard from time to time.

An approved "laboring brother" (itinerant PB teacher) may come to town for special two or three-evening (or Sunday afternoon) meetings. It may be a series of talks on a specific biblical book—or some explanation of biblical prophecy charts—or an exposition of the symbolism of the Tabernacle in the Old Testament. For the regular Sunday evening preaching (Gospel) service or other teaching meetings, the older brothers huddle just before the meeting and, after a prayer, sit in silence until someone asks "Does anyone have a word for tonight?" Or lacking a quick response they might turn to someone and ask, for example, "Brother David, do you have a word for us tonight?" Or, rarely, they might say "Could our young brothers David and Tim share the word tonight?"—meaning we each take twenty or thirty minutes. By the time I was in my early twenties I usually joined these pre-meeting sessions and, believe me, I always had a sermon or two in my hip pocket. And I wasn't playing any games; I studied my

Bible regularly wanting not just to learn for myself but be ready to pass on some great stuff I learned. With this training, I have always been the guy who could jump in at the last minute if a speaker got sick or didn't show up!

There was no specific education or training requirement before teaching or preaching or even becoming a missionary or itinerant "laboring brother." Everyone was self-educated: no Bible school, no denominational training program, no credentialing/ordination process, no essay exams. And it often shows. Study the Bible and pray. Read old, approved PB publications. Test out your thoughts on PB congregations and see if they approve. Do you affirm their main doctrinal concerns? Can you use PB cliches and formulas with genuineness and appropriateness? Your ministry may not be helpful enough to get invited back to some congregations. Full-time laboring brothers and missionaries have no salaries and completely depend on benevolent donations sent their way. They are not accountable to anyone for how they budget their income. I do not think Exclusive PBs support many non-PB benevolences so their Laboring Brethren may be well-supported.

SIX GREAT GIFTS TO ME

What do I still truly value from my experience and my four-generation heritage in this sect? First, I learned not just to follow but to love Jesus Christ as my Lord, Savior, and God. Jesus is the center of not just our worship (many churches forget this) but all of life. Jesus is Lord of all, all the time, including our family, relationships, work, politics, finances . . . everything. Second, I learned to love the Bible and its guidance for all of life. In Acts 17:11 the text says: "Now the Berean Jews were of more noble character than those in Thessalonica, for they received the message with great eagerness and examined the Scriptures every day to see if what Paul said was true." I got this drilled into me. The PBs always insisted that the Bible ruled over all of our doctrine and practice. I took this very seriously. Third, within the confines of the fellowship and its boundary conditions, this was usually a warm and caring extended family to grow up in. Fourth, I really appreciated the mission to get back to the simplicity of New Testament Christianity, especially in doing church. Fifth, I have never waivered in agreeing that all Christians, all "members of the Body of Christ"—not just a priestly or pastoral class—have individual gifts and are called to exercise these gifts and abilities in and beyond the church.

And sixth, in an ironic twist, I am so glad I grew up in a church that pushed us out into the secular academic and working world where I learned to be "in the world but not of the world." Because of their suspicion of the doctrine (teaching, ideas) and practice of all other non-PB Christians, we did not attend Christian schools or participate in Christian fellowships like Young Life and InterVarsity. We all went to public schools and then if we were going on to university it would be Cal, Stanford, or some other secular school. We did not trust the theology of any Christian school, not even the premiere Christian college, Wheaton. As a result, I learned over time to be comfortable as a passionate follower of Jesus in the middle of a challenging, diverse, often chaotic world.[7] I have no idea what it would be like to be in a protected, "safe," school for indoctrination (except that I would probably rebel).

Of course, none of those six "gifts" were perfect or robustly developed in either theory or practice. While the point was made that Jesus was Lord of all, all the time, for example, there was next to no help exploring what that actually means in the academy or workplace. While the Bible was said to be our only rule of faith and practice, it actually wasn't. There were other assumptions and authorities, including dispensationalism, that undermined biblical authority. I love the emphasis on the ministry of the laity but reject the male-centered way this was applied. When your laity-emphasis means that pastoral care will be taken care of by everybody, it sometimes means it gets taken care of by nobody. I am so glad I went to secular schools all the way through but regret not being part of Christian fellowship groups when I matriculated. Still—remember my point—I emerged from this separatist sect as a committed follower of Christ. Most of that is because of the PBs. Some of it is despite the PBs.

CRISIS

I didn't question the basic doctrines of the PBs, at least not until I was almost out. But I did question more and more of the practices, not by speaking up and stirring up our church or leadership but with questioning in my mind and in discussions with three or four close friends. As I mentioned earlier, how could we constantly be told that our church was the one true place where Jesus would be present in our worship—and then not try to invite other Christians to join us? Why didn't we reach out with the Gospel to our city? Why didn't we help the poor? How could we sing (as we often did) the dirge "Happy people, happy though despised and poor"—and then get into expensive cars and drive home to expensive houses?[8] It was said that musical instruments were not acceptable because they were not required by the New Testament churches who were instructed just to "sing and make melody in our hearts to the Lord." Well, first, that sounds like we should not make any sound at all but just sing in our hearts! Second, if only what is commanded is permitted, where are chairs (or clocks or heaters) mentioned in the New Testament churches any more than musical instruments?

As I alluded to earlier, if we insist on letting the Spirit be our guide, why do we think God's Spirit can only lead in an extemporaneous manner—rather than through

---

7. Of course, other PBs might have just learned to be quiet about their faith and "keep your head down."

8. This is not about any particular person. My point is about fooling ourselves by singing how despised and poor we are—but doing next to nothing to help the real poor around us, and seeing no hypocrisy in living a very comfortable lifestyle. Yeah, it's uncomfortable to admit it, to whatever extent it is true in our lives.

some advance planning (teaching, liturgy, etc.). Isn't this tying the hands of God, minimizing God's power to lead? How can we insist on using Shakespearean English in our prayers (thee and thou) and Bible (the King James version) when the New Testament itself was written in a common Greek idiom rather than the more formal classical Greek alternative? Why can't people meet and hear God in their ordinary language? And why must men be clean shaven and wear suits and neckties, conforming to today's business world look, when the early PBs were mostly bearded and it was God who created facial hair on men? This is the kind of stuff that bothered me.

The reality was also that Darby and his dispensationalism were the unstated, unquestioned authority, not just Jesus and Scripture. Jesus said he "did not come to abolish the law but to fulfill it." Dispensationalism insisted on effectively abolishing it, clueless about how both Jesus and Paul encourage its interpretation, relevance, and application. All of the fascination with the Last Days and the second coming of Christ was reduced to clock watching and calendar speculation (waiting, watching and escaping)—totally ignoring the way virtually all biblical references to this topic have prominent "therefore live this way" conclusions. PB theology as I heard it over and over, was often "theology by cliché" not by careful biblical exposition. It was self-justifying and beyond criticism. It didn't rise up with truth in love, it cowered and hid in what was called the "day of small things." It imposed a historical interpretation on the letters to the seven churches in Revelation 2 and 3 to justify itself as the Church of Philadelphia, uniquely praised for its faithfulness in weakness. These contradictions in practice and unbiblical viewpoints began to really bother me.

More serious still: Exclusive PBs disrespected the Body of Christ and its head. In First Corinthians chapter twelve Paul teaches that all members of the Body of Christ are necessary and must never say "I have no need of you" to any other member—or "I am not worthy" about yourself (and thus unneeded by others). Paul points out that Christ is the head of this Body and has placed each of its members exactly where he wants them. It is not up to us. If he placed them in a Baptist or Catholic church, who are we to criticize and reject them? The Exclusive PBs were fond of the warning to the Corinthians that "whoever eats and drinks the Lord's supper in an unworthy manner, eats and drinks judgment to himself." They claimed to be faithfully guarding the communion table from the unworthy and defective in doctrine and life. But wait a minute. Paul says that anyone like this "eats and drinks judgment to himself"—not to the others at the table (I Corinthians 11:26–31). Paul's teaching point is for Christians (PBs as well as others) to do some self-examination—not to set ourselves up as the judges of others. It is the Lord's Table—not the PB table. Stop trying to take over as Lord of the table, I thought.

Despite their ferocious commitment to what they thought was "Paul's doctrine" of the church for this dispensation of grace, their most often quoted verse was from Jesus in Matthew 18:20: "Where two or three are gathered together in my name, there

I am in the midst."⁹ The PBs claim that they alone are meeting this way. If St. Paul came to Oakland (or if Jesus himself showed up) it would only be in the little 40th Street PB meeting. Everybody else, it was said, is meeting in the name of Luther, Roman Catholicism or whatever. But this is just not true. The Jesus People I got to know back in the 1970s were just as radical and simple. And "in my name" is not just a magical formula that you repeat. "In my name" means "in my character, in my ways, in my truth, in my authority."

I have often talked about the "tyranny of the unstated assumption." The Exclusive PBs meet in the name of John Darby (as well as that of Jesus) even though they won't admit it. Alongside their legitimate biblical convictions, they are committed to all sorts of traditions and processes and ideas that have no explicit biblical justification. Now I don't want to be unduly harsh. No individual and no church is pure or perfect in this. The PBs certainly want to be faithful to Jesus Christ, but so do Methodists and Pentecostals. A dose of humility and some sound biblical exposition would help a lot here.

One more point: the Matthew 18:20 text is *not* about forming worshipping communities. It is about ethical decision-making. Where there is a challenging problem, Jesus is saying, two or three of you should meet as Christian brothers and sisters to discern the best thing to do. "What you bind on earth is bound in heaven"—i.e., "I will respect your decision-making—because, remember, where two or three of you gather together in my name (i.e., consciously trying to be faithful) I will be there with you." Two or three meeting in the name of Plato or Aristotle or St. Paul or Moses won't bring the insight and authority that resides in the name of Jesus. This is not an isolated passage but a recurring message about Jesus-centered, koinonia (community-based) ethics and discipleship (vs. individualistic approaches). It is not about organizing a church.

I didn't bring up all these troubling points in public back then, but I did talk about them with my closest friends and confidants and with my dad, who seemed weary at this stage, unable to do more than invoke the faithful example and tradition of his own father. But I thought PB reform was possible. I was a bit stunned when one of the leading itinerant laboring brothers, Clifford H. Brown, wrote and distributed a little essay on the Blood of Christ, to settle a dispute with a former missionary who had said that the blood from Jesus' feet and hands had accomplished redemption so that he could genuinely say "It is finished"—even before the subsequent outrage of piercing the side of his corpse with a sword. It was dumb to make an issue of this, of course. But Mr. Brown helped discipline if not excommunicate the old missionary because, he argued, our old hymn says it was the blood flowing from his side that cleansed us. I wrote to Mr. Brown and questioned him (nicely): "I thought that Scripture, not a hymn, decided such issues?" Mr. Brown wrote me back a one-line letter: "Rebuke not an elder!" OK Mr. Brown, I thought, I see where you are coming from. But don't give

---

9. Dispensationalists usually don't seriously embrace the teachings of Jesus like the Sermon on the Mount because they are supposedly only relevant in the coming Millennium. So why is this Matthew 18:20 text an exception?

me this stuff about the Bible alone being your authority. Can you see why my church world was beginning to deteriorate?

In 1968–69 I started thinking about the need for a publication addressed to our PB students and young adults. Our only PB publications were a weekly Sunday School paper for children called *Messages of the Love of God* and a little journal called *Christian Truth for the Household of Faith*—whose content was almost entirely just reprints of 19th century PB writings.[10] My friends John and Al Erisman and I were all loyal, thoughtful (3rd and 4th generation!) PBs in our twenties and we imagined a bimonthly magazine we would call *The Seeker*—which would have some interesting stories from PB history, some articles on faithful Christian discipleship in our tumultuous times, some Bible studies, and so on. We felt our peers in the PBs could really use a resource like this. To allay any fears among our leaders, we recruited an editorial board of eight respected older brothers who would review our issues before they were published.

But even with all this caution, when we got near our start date, several fearful and controlling elder-types raised a huge objection to our project and insisted we not go forward.[11] Half of our editorial review board bailed out on us and wouldn't support us going forward. We were disappointed but yielded to the authority of our elders. This is an important point in my story: when it came to my initiatives and involvement in the internal life of our church, I yielded to the leadership and judgment of our elders, even if I thought they were unwise or wrong, as in the case of *The Seeker*.

LIBERATION

The Exclusive PBs were suspicious of any Christian teachers or writers from outside their circle. I heard people speculate on whether Billy Graham was actually a Christian ("probably so" they concluded, but he was harshly criticized for including Catholics and more liberal Protestants on the platforms and in the choirs at his "Crusades"). My family was just a tad more open. We would never have broken break bread or taken communion with Billy Graham or Charles E. Fuller but we would listen on the radio and be grateful and positive. Some of the apologetics we read were from non-PB writers. My dad was an early subscriber to *Christianity Today*, a thoughtful journal that began in 1956. He also became a fan (for a while anyway) of Bill Gothard.[12]

---

10. In the 1850s there were a dozen or so Brethren magazines and journals with circulations of forty or fifty thousand in several cases! I thought it was a very "Brethren" thing to do to start up a magazine or journal. The editors of these journals were often young.

11. A "What Are You Doing About It" initiative that never got off the ground. This happens!

12. I was kind of shocked at how so many PBs embraced traveling non-PB guru Bill Gothard and his "Institute of Basic Youth Conflicts" not long after my exodus. More on my encounter with him later but this embrace put the lie to the alleged concern about us young Turks and fears that we might not be "separate" enough. No, the real reason was fear of change, fear of truth, and cultural conservatism of a toxic sort.

When I entered Cal as a freshman in 1964 I still thought about faith and culture (education, work) mostly in terms of promoting and defending the faith. I instinctively supported (as a cheering bystander, not a participating demonstrator) the Free Speech Movement that erupted right after the school year began. Just a few years later, in 1972, my friends Walt and Ginny Hearn pointed me to John Milton's famous "Areopagitica" speech (1644) which voiced my opinion on free speech then and ever since:

"I cannot praise a fugitive and cloistered virtue, unexercised and unbreathed, that never sallies out and sees her adversary, but slinks out of the race where that immortal garland is to be run for, not without dust and heat." "Though all the winds of doctrine were let loose to play upon the earth, so Truth be in the field, we do injuriously, by licensing and prohibiting, to misdoubt her strength. Let her and Falsehood grapple; who ever knew Truth put to the worse, in a free and open encounter?"

I was initially drawn to historical arguments for the persuasiveness of Christian truth claims. Books by John Warwick Montgomery (about whom I wrote a chapter in my MA thesis at SF State) and Clark Pinnock (e.g., *Set Forth Your Case: An Examination of Christianity's Credentials*) were important in my thinking at that stage. More recently this kind of historical argument is well-summarized by Lee Strobel in *The Case for Christ: A Journalist's Personal Investigation of the Evidence for Jesus*. In 1968 I discovered Francis A. Schaeffer's books, beginning with *The God Who Is There: Speaking Historic Christianity into the Twentieth Century*. Schaeffer's work was not so much about historical evidence and arguments but about a grand philosophy/theology of life, a worldview that tried to interpret and make sense of all of life: art and music, philosophy and religion, history, social change, pain and evil, and the search for meaning. I became a big fan, read all of his next ten or so books, exchanged a few letters with him, and urged him to start a branch of his Swiss "L'Abri" study center in Berkeley.[13]

More recently, it is the work of Leslie Newbegin that best represents my thinking about promoting and defending the Christian faith. *Foolishness to the Greeks: The Gospel and Western Culture* and *The Gospel in a Pluralist Society* argue for a humble but confident articulation of Christian faith as a "plausibility structure" that best and most comprehensibly accounts for life and the world as we know and experience it. It is in many respects similar to Thomas Kuhn's description of "paradigms" in *The Structure of Scientific Revolutions*. Timothy Keller's *The Reason for God: Belief in an Age of Scepticism* argues in a similar fashion. It is like a metaphor I once heard: "theories and facts are like shoes and feet; it is not just how the shoe looks but whether you can comfortably walk in it over varying terrain." For me, Christianity is a worldview and philosophy of life that doesn't resolve all problems but is the best, most comprehensive and livable account of life as I see and experience it. It is a "shoe" that I can

---

13. I never got to visit L'Abri but met Schaeffer in person when he spent a day with us Berkeley fans around 1972. I ceased being a big fan of his as I discovered many errors and weaknesses in his work and then as he was captured by a divisive Fundamentalism and an angry Right Wing politics. It is a sad story but his basic project was admirable and inspired a whole generation of us back in the Sixties and Seventies.

walk in comfortably over all terrain. For example, I don't like pain and suffering and injustice in the world—but I would rather grapple with them as a Christian than as, for example, an evolutionary, survival-of-the-fittest, atheist.

This was my developing "Christian mind" while an undergraduate, still deeply committed to the PBs. It continued after my BA at Cal with an MA in history at San Francisco State (1971) completed over three summers while I was teaching junior high school. My 130-page MA thesis was entitled "Contemporary Christian Philosophies of History: The Problem of God's Role in Human History." I wrote chapters on six different thinkers who had written on this problem since the Holocaust. I didn't want any cheap answers. My thesis committee was composed of three secular historians on the faculty. I passed with rave reviews. This only made me feistier than ever about relating our Christian faith and values to what we studied and then how we lived and worked. I was not interested in "hiding my candle under a bushel basket" (something Jesus commanded his followers not to do in his Sermon on the Mount). But I had been squelched in my effort to create a PB magazine called *The Seeker*.

In the Spring of 1971, we were living two blocks north of the UC Berkeley campus. I happened to see a flyer stapled to a telephone pole inviting people to a meeting to hear Os Guinness (yes, a descendent of the stout folk) give a lecture. I jumped at the chance because I knew Os was a close associate of Francis Schaeffer at L'Abri. I went to the meeting and loved Os's lecture on contemporary culture. It was the beginning of a lifetime friendship with him. But what really blew me away was the group that sponsored Os: the "Christian World Liberation Front." More on them in Chapter Twelve. When I arrived, I saw two or three guys smoking cigarettes outside. Only in my Juvenile Hall Bible study group had I seen this and to me it symbolized freedom for these folks to come as they were. Smoking (like overeating) might be unhealthy but it was not something banned by Scripture. Then the meeting began with some boisterous a capella singing led by a long-haired guy nicknamed "Zeus." Most of the words we sung were direct quotations from the King James version of the Psalms, the Gospels, and Galatians! This was "more Brethren than the Brethren," I thought. The intensity of interest in biblical faith, growth, and cultural witness put to shame the shallow, passive, lackadaisical spirit I lived with at the Meeting.

After the meeting I met Jack Sparks, the founder and leader of CWLF. What a kind, gentle brother this bearded man in overalls was, I thought. I had seen around Berkeley a copy or two of the CWLF tabloid *Right On* (intended as a counterpart to the *Berkeley Barb*) and now picked up and browsed a copy more carefully after the meeting. "Hey Jack, I have been writing some brief articles for a little rag called "Straight to You" that I created for the Alameda County Juvenile Hall. Would you like to see a couple samples? I'd be happy if you could use them in *Right On*." "Sure brother David, send me some of your stuff." I did. *Right On* was distributed for free (about 40,000 copies each month) around Berkeley and other campuses and countercultural sites like the Haight-Ashbury. Just a month or so later I saw the new issue of *Right On* which included a couple of my articles. So I picked up and distributed three hundred copies at the Juvenile Hall later that month when I preached there.

It happened that a supportive PB friend, Ken Brimlow, was visiting Oakland that weekend and asked if he could come along to the Juvenile Hall. "Sure," I said. Later on, after church, Ken was lunching at a PB elder's house where he pulled out the issue of *Right On* and shared his excitement. But my name on an article in *Right On* was enough to fire up this elder's purity/separation sensors. He then organized clandestine meetings of the elders (pointedly leaving my dad out of the loop). They decided to show up (six of them as I recall) at our tiny apartment in Berkeley on a Saturday afternoon where they presented their edict: I must agree to have nothing to do with these people (CWLF) or *Right On*. Without actually knowing anything about them, my inquisitors banned any contact with these brothers and sisters.

I pointed out that I was paid no money, signed no contract, joined no organization, and did not share communion with anyone outside the Meeting. One member of the visiting excommunication team, taught at a Catholic School. I asked how his being on "the Pope's payroll" was okay but my donating an article was not? I read them the Corinthian passages about saying "I have no need of you" to other Christians. Finally, one of the old elders slammed his big Bible down on the table and said "Stop confusing the issue by bringing up those Scriptures." Uh, what are you saying? I proposed a hypothetical: "are you saying that I can never publish an article in an outside channel—even, say, to call on other Christians to abandon their denominations and seek to worship as we do? Never? It would be okay for me to write secular material or advertising copy for Levi Strauss jeans but not Christian material?" "That is our position," they told me and left.

A week or so later I wrote them a letter and said "I cannot comply with your request. I was willing to submit to your judgment when it concerned the internal affairs of the Meeting but this is different. Someday I expect to stand before God and give an account of my life. I don't want God to say to me 'Why did you let those men act as Lord of the writing gifts I gave you?' Like Martin Luther said, 'Here I stand, I can do no other.'" Within a week or two a letter was sent to me and Lucia and to every Brethren assembly in the western USA announcing my formal excommunication. No one from the church ever followed up with us to try to persuade us to come back. Not a word. My dad protested and was "silenced" for a year.

Of course, this was a shocking and intensely painful transition. I had been an activist, a passionate participant and supporter of the Brethren system. They had heard me preach and teach, watched my leadership, noted my fidelity week-by-week for years. I was the fourth generation PB in my family. I was not a trouble-maker. None of that mattered. I was formally excommunicated, and I quote, for "defiling association with the camp (Christian World Liberation Front and *Right On* magazine)." "Camp" was "Brethren-ese" for "other Christians" (based on a dispensationalist spin of Hebrews 13:13).

Part Two: Shapers (1964–1979)

I handed off the five-year-old Juvenile Hall ministry to my associates, some components of which ended immediately, while others faded away over time. But this was not just my religious but my social world that we were being cast out of. One of the providential ironies was that even while that inquisition was happening in our apartment, Bill and Cathy Squires from CWLF phoned to invite us over to their home in Berkeley! What a wonderful message, definitely a "God-thing." My parents were devastated by my excommunication, of course, but they never blamed me because they thought I was wronged. It didn't take long for Lucia and me to embrace it as our day of liberation from an authoritarian sect. "Free at last, free at last, thank God almighty, we were free at last." Looking back on these events I do see unfairness in the way I was treated. But I also see a genuine, well-intended effort by PB leaders to faithfully maintain their tradition and protect it from threat. I don't really believe they had anything personal against me. They saw a threat and acted as heroic prophets within their system to remove that threat. For me, though, it had become not just a matter of practices, it was about basic biblical truth and principle. My departure from this sect had become inevitable.

FORWARD & OUTWARD

I was officially excommunicated from the Exclusive Plymouth Brethren in summer 1971, fifty years ago. I then spent the next four years in a couple of "Open Brethren" contexts before finding my way to the Evangelical Covenant Church (which has been my main church home for fifty years now—more on that later). Initially we visited Berkeley Friends church (a Quaker fellowship) and enjoyed it to a great extent but could not live with the Quaker rejection of the celebration of the Lord's Supper and baptism. The "Jesus People" of the Christian World Liberation Front provided us with some great worship, teaching, and fellowship but with our infant daughter we felt we needed a somewhat more organized, diverse, and family-oriented fellowship.

We decided to visit Fairhaven Bible Chapel, a vigorous Open Brethren congregation in the San Leandro neighborhood bordering Oakland where I had grown up. We were overwhelmed with the warmth of the welcome not just to us but to a lot of counter-cultural youth we saw. There was solid teaching and a commitment to Brethren-style worship centered on the weekly celebration of the Lord's Supper. I felt like I walked into heaven in a lot of ways. For the next two years this was our church home and several friendships were formed that continue to this day. One day I found out that in the months before we arrived there had been a big scandal in which two of their elders had left their wives and married two women from other marriages in the church. Four families had been radically disrupted and injured. Under the shock of this, the entire church had come together to kneel and pray for healing from this devastating wound. Everyone in the church—everyone—was humbled. We had walked into a fellowship of the humble and broken without knowing it. It was clear that this was the major reason the church was so kind and welcoming. After two years we moved to Los Angeles for graduate school. Sadly, four years later when we returned home to Oakland, Fairhaven had reverted to a legalistic culture dominated by authoritarian leaders. Sad story. But we did enjoy a little heaven from 1971 to 1973.

From 1973 to 1975 we were part of an Open Brethren start-up church related to a Bible school in the Los Angeles area where I was invited to teach. There were good days and bad, ideals and realities. I learned a lot about my own strengths and weaknesses as a leader. I began to see how much the "we are the only way" Exclusive PB thinking and culture was also part of the Open Brethren. Our perfectionism was sometimes paralyzing. In 1975 we moved to Pasadena for my final two years of PhD study at USC. There were no viable PB options in Pasadena so we joined Pasadena Covenant Church, part of the original Swedish Mission Covenant renewal movement of the late 19th century. This denomination became our primary church fellowship for the rest of our life. I have often chafed over some of the Covenant practices (such as monthly instead of weekly communion) but, on balance, it has been a fellowship I am glad to call home. More on them in later chapters.

MY FAITH AND MY CHURCH AFFILIATION

On my understanding of church, it has been my Bible studies over the years that have been the biggest influences by far. I'd like to be biblical. I have also read a lot of church history over the years. I have been especially interested in "free church" history: the recurring movements to renew tired old church traditions and practices and get back closer to New Testament teaching and practice. "Free" church means free of state sponsorship and control—with members who were not born into fellowship but freely chose to join. Reading this history in my early twenties helped me see that the Plymouth Brethren were not, as they claimed, the first such renewal movement since the first century. They were only (in the 19th century) the latest. There were many common features, common successes, and common outcomes over the centuries—including the fact that all these free churches also often evolved into rigid institutions and systems, undermined by dissent and schism.

The most helpful book I read (in the very month I was excommunicated!) was Donald F. Durnbaugh's *The Believers' Church: The History and Character of Radical Protestantism* which included a section on the Plymouth Brethren part of the story.[14] It was an appreciative history by a careful historian who knew the tradition from the inside but could be honest about the weaknesses alongside the strengths. During my visiting professorship at Juniata College in Pennsylvania in 1994–95 I was able to meet Professor Durnbaugh and thank him for his work which had been so personally helpful to me. I am happy to see myself as still part of that movement. I am closer

---

14. Donald F. Durnbaugh, *The Believers' Church: The History and Character of Radical Protestantism* (New York: Macmillan, 1968).

to the Anabaptist/Mennonite tradition than any other free church (but grateful that my Covenant Church denomination embraces or shares most of their emphases on discipleship).

As for my personal faith, I am happy to affirm the Apostles' Creed with Christians around the world and throughout history: "I believe in God the Father Almighty, maker of heaven and earth. And in Jesus Christ, his only Son, our Lord; who was conceived by the Holy Spirit, born of the Virgin Mary, suffered under Pontius Pilate, was crucified, dead and buried; he descended into hell; the third day he rose again from the dead; he ascended into heaven and sits on the right hand of God the Father Almighty; from thence he shall come to judge the living and the dead. I believe in the Holy Spirit, the holy catholic church, the communion of saints, the forgiveness of sins, the resurrection of the body, and the life everlasting. Amen."

Of course, there is more to my faith and belief than this ancient summary of trinitarian theology. Not least for me, I believe that "faith without works is dead" (as James writes in the New Testament) and Christians are called not just to faith but to hope and to love God and our neighbors near and far in a daily adventure of following Jesus as Lord. That's why ethics became my primary field of study and teaching my whole career. For me, biblical Christian faith is the sure foundation for a robust worldview, philosophy of life, mission and purpose, and set of core values for a meaningful life—even with all the mysteries, unknowns, and difficulties that remain. And at the living center of it all stands the person of Jesus Christ, who I am convinced really was "God made flesh" in our history, I love his teaching and example. I love him and want to faithfully follow him till I die.

My religious upbringing might strike some readers as unusual and maybe it was. But many people throughout history have been raised in such tightly controlled religious communities, sometimes even in what we call the cults. It is easy to find stories of Catholics, Mormons, Amish, Muslims and others who struggled for freedom as they become adults (or even in midlife). Two novels I love about growing up in Orthodox Judaism are Chaim Potok's *The Chosen* and *The Promise*. I could relate! But I am so grateful that the basic teachings about Jesus Christ and the Bible stayed part of my core even while I had to get free from the Plymouth Brethren tradition. I have long struggled with religious "perfectionism"—the quest to find the one perfect model of church. It doesn't exist however, and while we never want to cease trying to improve, we must not fail to be grateful for what we have, to appreciate the glass half-full.

When the PBs suffered their huge split into Exclusive and Open Brethren, John Darby got a letter from Open brother Anthony Norris Groves that said "As any system is in its provision narrower or wider than the truth, I either stop short or go beyond its provisions, but I would infinitely rather bear with all their evils than separate from their good." Rather than practicing a faith or ecclesiology defined by what it is against, I want to be defined by what I am for.

I used to have a recurring nightmare after I left the PBs: I was clinging to the steep hillside behind and below our (1952–53) house on Outlook Avenue in Oakland. Our house was being consumed in a raging fire. My parents were inside and I was tortured wishing I could go up and save them—but knowing with the raging fire I couldn't. My nightmares only ended when I awoke from sleep, not in a successful rescue. In my real, non-nightmare life, I never tried or expected to influence my PB family and friends to identify with my experience or follow me out of the movement. I respect all who stayed in the movement and I laud their desire to be faithful to God in the process. For many years, I have tried to focus my prayers one day of the week on my church. I often begin by thanking God and praying for God's blessing on the little 40th Street meeting in which I was raised. Then I work through the list of all my subsequent churches and end with my current church, First Covenant of Oakland.

9

Lucia & Life Together

NEXT TO GOD HIMSELF, my partner Lucia has been (and remains) the most powerful shaper of my life—since our first date November 1, 1963. With God and Lucia as my constant companions and the twin anchors of my life, I have been liberated and empowered to take on any challenge, enter any territory, and pursue any dream before me. I can remember several times in my life when unattached women asked me "why are all the good men married?" (or, more flatteringly, "do you have any brothers?"). My answer: to the extent we are good men it's because of God's grace and our marriages; our wives have civilized us and saved us from the barbarian life. Anyway, that is how I see it.

My parents loved and adored Lucia from the day they met her when she was fifteen. From about my forties onward, it became a recurring joke Lucia and I laughed at, that whenever my parents complimented me they would add the phrase "because of Lucia." "David, we are so proud of what a good dad you have become . . . because of Lucia." "It's wonderful how you learned how to cook . . . because of Lucia." "You have accomplished so much in your career . . . because of Lucia." It really was pretty constant. And to a huge extent, they were right.

Lucia Paulson was a fifteen-year old sophomore at San Leandro High School when I saw her class photo in my sister Kit's collection. I was instantly stunned by her beauty (I know, not very spiritual) and desperately wanted to meet her. I had a different lunch period than Kit and Lucia but my German class was on ground level with windows opening up to the cafeteria patio. I asked Kit if she could stroll by those windows with her friend Lucia so I could see the real, living goddess. I must have been hanging one arm out the window in anticipation because as the two girls got closer, Lucia spotted the over-eager guy hanging partway out the window, abruptly turned around and retreated from sight. She would not then (or ever) be paraded in front of anyone, admirers or otherwise!

PART TWO: SHAPERS (1964-1979)

Next attempt: I arranged an introduction by another mutual friend, Sharon Mayo, to take place in the school library just before school began in the morning. Lucia was in a driver training class that met before first period and I must have freaked her out when I peered through the tiny window of her classroom door. When the bell rang I hoped to meet her but she darted out of the room and right across the hall into the girl's bathroom, I waited. Suddenly she bombed out of the restroom and headed into the library. I followed with determination. She disappeared behind the stacks but I found her back in the corner. Sharon Mayo introduced us. I soon invited her to attend the traditional Big Game Concert out at Cal on Friday night, November 1, 1963 (with a then-famous folk group called The Weavers). I think Julius and his date went with us. I went to her house ahead of time so her parents could check out the senior guy pursuing their cute little sophomore. They approved and life began.

BL (BEFORE LUCIA)

I always liked the female species, starting with my mom and sisters of course. I mentioned earlier that my only first grade memory is chasing a girl named Geraldine around the playground but she was too fast to catch. In the second grade I still remember I was kind of smitten with Ann Barr. In third grade I was so overcome by Mimi Gersten's hula performance in class that I broached the subject of marriage. She told me it would be impossible because I wasn't Jewish. I can think of several other school girls I found attractive every year—but no dates, no parties, no dances were options because of my church's prohibitions. I sublimated all that energy into my sports activities!

Until my senior year in high school began! Joanne Martinelli was a super-smart Italian-German only child who was, I think, in every one of my classes except shop and physical education from 8th through 12th grades (German every year, math, science, English, the whole thing). She and her friends Beth and Paula were as quick-witted and impish as Julius, Wally, and me. They knew how to ignore us, irritate us, whatever. There was no particular boy/girl attraction—we were just constantly part of the same school scene. In my junior year I somehow wound up as Joanne's chemistry lab partner in the fall—but switched to Julius in spring semester to escape her. But at the beginning of my senior year in English class I was sitting behind her and suddenly fell head-over-heels in love (I guess that's what you call it) with Joanne. Honestly, I felt dizzy.

I persuaded my parents to let me use the station wagon to take Joanne over to San Francisco to see the amazing new blockbuster film, Lawrence of Arabia (I assured my parents it was basically a historical sort of documentary with no romance or women in it, just thousands of guys racing around the desert on camels and horses). We had a great time and afterward I gave Joanne my Block S letterman's sweater to wear (it was a big deal to have your girlfriend wearing your sweater). Maybe she wore it a few times but one day (this is all within a time frame of a month or less) she walked into class wearing Neil Peck's letter sweater (Neil was my friend and our left tackle). She thought it was great to have both of us pursuing her. I was not happy (too insecure to share her, I guess). I retrieved my sweater and immediately fell out of love. Dizziness gone in a flash.

Then just a month later I met Lucia and I was a goner for life. And she wore only my letter sweater, nobody else's. We "went steady" for four years and got married September 9, 1967, when she was nineteen and I was twenty-one. We were ready. She finished high school while I did my first two years of college, then for one great year she was a freshman at Cal while I was a junior. We both lived at our parents' homes (but spent as much time as possible together) until we got married because (a) it was free, (b) our college jobs were near our family homes, (c) Berkeley was in tear-gassed chaos most of the time, and (d) our houses were just two blocks from each other. Convenient! I used to park my '56 Chevy pointed downhill on Revere Avenue (my parents moved there in 1963 from Alice Avenue on the flatlands a mile away)—and then just release the parking brake and roll down the hill to park in front of the Paulson's house on Marlow. (I had to replicate this legendary maneuver first for my kids, then my grandkids, when they came along; it still worked for them but with power steering I had to have the motor turned on). Within a year after we met, Lucia committed to the Christian faith (her family was unchurched) and joined my PB church, weird as it must have seemed in some ways. My family and church would have come down strong on me if I was going with a non-Christian (or a Christian going to a non-PB church).

Lucia Lynn Paulson was the youngest child of a German-American mother, Lucia Marie Thelen, and a Swedish-American father, Harold Hamilton Paulson. Her oldest sibling (nine years older) is her sister Kathryn (Paulson) Arbuckle. Her older brother is Steve—who was in my high school class, though a year younger and not in my academic program. I didn't know Steve well but he played drums as part of our high school "Beatles" performance of "She Loves You." Steve did four years in the U.S. Army (stationed in Germany) and then had a long career in the Oakland Police Department as well as in real estate investment and management. Steve married Marilyn Erickson, also a member of our SLHS Class of '64.

LUCIA'S THELEN ROOTS

Lucia's mom, Lucia Marie Thelen (1906–1995) was born in Armour, South Dakota, the ninth of thirteen children in a big Iowa Catholic farming family (not sure how or why she got to South Dakota to be born). Her father (Lucia's grandpa) Michael Thelen (1866–1931) and mother Catherine Lehnen (1871–1961) were married in 1889 in Breda, Iowa. Lucia's grandma Catherine was born in Dubuque, Iowa, to Mathias Lehnen (1822–1910) a wagon-maker born in Luxemburg who emigrated to the USA in 1861, and Maria Anna Brumenshenkel (1835–1915) also born in Luxemburg.[1]

---

1. Mathias and Anna Lehnen came from Luxemburg in Europe right around the time the town of Luxemburg, Iowa, was created near Dubuque, Iowa, so five of their six kids were born in the Iowa version.

PART TWO: SHAPERS (1964–1979)

Lucia's grandfather Michael Thelen (born 1866 in Mills County, Iowa) was the son of John Thelen (1837–1913) and Anna Koll (1842–1899). John Thelen emigrated from Prussia to the USA sometime in the 1850s. Anna Koll was born in Germany in 1842 and came to the USA in 1849 at age seven. John and Anna bought some farmland near Breda in 1872 and added small tracts up to 1890. Between 1862 and 1875 John and Anna had five sons (including Michael) plus a daughter who died in infancy. The sons all lived and farmed on land adjacent to their parents' farm. Around 1910 Michael and Catherine Thelen moved from Iowa to Minnesota. Michael Thelen died on November 25, 1931, of injuries suffered from a charging bull (crushed chest and abdomen, broken bones, severe lacerations, internal hemorrhage). Catherine lived until 1961 (age ninety).

Mother Lucia Paulson was a tiny little woman about five feet tall. She left home at age sixteen for St. Paul where she put herself through nursing school and began a long career as an RN. In 1931, at age twenty-five, she married Harold Paulson. After eight years in St. Paul they moved to Oakland, California. She loved to play bridge. She had a low raspy voice from a lifetime of cigarette smoking (a nurse!). She read novels by the dozen. When we recommended that she visit Venice, Paris, London or other amazing places we had been, she would insist that her novels had already taken her there! She was raised Catholic but married a Protestant and didn't feel a need for church but she often surprised me by asking me to offer a prayer before meals. On very hot days when we were all sweating and there was no air conditioning, others might gripe but she would always say "mind over matter." I still repeat her on that. She drank strong coffee (always fully caffeinated) day or night with no impact on her sleep. She was a great mother-in-law who accepted me as her own (as soon as she knew I would love and protect her youngest daughter!). She loved her grandchildren and they loved her. Once in a while she would attend church with us if one of her grandchildren was playing a special musical piece. On one such occasion, the preacher was describing the trials of Job, at which point she turned to Lucia and said in a loud, raspy whisper "Wow that guy is having a helluva time." I loved this little lady. She lived until 1995.

LUCIA'S PAULSON ROOTS

Lucia's dad, Harold Hamilton Paulson (1906–1985) was the youngest of eight children born to John Paulson and Emma Sophia Halvorson. John Paulson was born in Virestad, Småland, Sweden, in 1855 to Jon Persson (1809–1859) and initially went by the name Johan Jonsson in the Swedish tradition. But his father died in 1859 when he was only four years old—and his mother Anna Andersdotter had already died when he was only age two in 1857. My guess is that his grandfather Per Palsson (1783–?) assumed the role of "father" at that point, even at age seventy-six, leading to the kids' family name change from Jonsson to Palsson (then anglicized to "Paulson" on immigration to the USA?). In Virestad, Småland, southern Sweden, the Paulsons shared a farm with another family that had ten children. The 1850s to 1880s were economically and agriculturally difficult times and emigration was in full swing. There was not enough farm land (and what there was was not productive enough) to support a growing population.[2] In 1868, 13-year-old John emigrated alone to Minnesota! The whole family must have followed by the early 1870s because we have records of his brother Andrew being married in New York in 1874 and his sister Caroline dying in Minnesota in 1883. The grandfather, Per Palsson, who I am guessing raised the kids after the 1859 death of his son and his son's wife, was born in 1783 so by 1859 he was already seventy-six years old and if he passed away in the 1860s, the grandchildren had another reason to emigrate. John Paulson left the farming life behind in Sweden and worked for the railroad until his 1944 death at age eighty-nine in St. Paul.

Harold's mother, Emma Sophia Halvorson, was born in 1861 in Halden (then called Frederickshald—Norway, on the border with Sweden) and died in 1951 in St. Paul at age ninety. Emma's father Per Halvorson (1828–1920) was a tailor in Åmål, Sweden on the western edge of Lake Vänern. Her mother was Christina Jonsdotter (1830–1917), born in Vermland, Sweden. By the late 1850s Per and Christina were married and living in Halden, where Emma, the first of their four daughters, was born in 1861. Their long- time home in Halden was #3 Skippergata. The family story is that Per and Christina walked the fifty miles when they moved from Åmål to Halden. In addition to their tailor business, they acquired the Skippergata property which served as a lodging house for sixteen renter/borders, including fishermen, sea captains, and other workers. In fall 1999 when I was a visiting professor in Jönköping, we were able to visit the house at #3 Skippergata in Halden.

Emma Sophia Halvorson emigrated to America in 1881. Her parents stayed behind and died later in Halden in 1917 and 1920 from the great flu pandemic that swept over Europe and America. Emma met John Paulson in St. Paul and married him in Ramsey, Minnesota, in November 1883 when he was twenty-eight and she was twenty-two. Together they had eight children. Lucia's dad Harold was the eighth, born February 8, 1906. Harold began playing the violin in 1917 when he was eleven. In 1921 at age fifteen he was baptized at the Swedish Baptist Church in St. Paul. He graduated from Mechanics Arts High School in St. Paul. He told us old stories and shared memories of hanging out with his friends on Rice Street. He attended the University of Minnesota from 1923 to 1928, focusing on business. management, economics, and accounting. He married Lucia Marie Thelen (Lucia's mom) in Anoka, Minnesota, on December 23, 1931. In 1939 Harold and Lucia moved to California. In 1941 he began a twenty-five-year career as an IRS agent and that same year the Paulsons purchased their lifetime home, 160 Marlow Drive, Sheffield Village, in Oakland, California. He

---

2. Vilhelm Moberg's four-part historical novel *The Emigrants* (St. Paul, Minnesota: Borealis, 1949–1959) vividly portrays the struggles that led many Swedish farmers to emigrate to America. The fictional Karl-Oskar Nilsson and his wife, Kristina Johansdotter moved from Småland to Minnesota in 1850.

was an active Mason for forty-five years and part of the SIRS retirement group (lots of bowling with the boys) for eighteen years. He died suddenly of a stroke (at the bowling alley!) at age seventy-nine in 1985.

Mr. Paulson was a wonderful father-in-law to me as well as dad to my wife Lucia, his youngest daughter, on whom he doted. At his memorial service I praised him for (1) humility—an unpretentious, regular guy, (2) simplicity and contentment, (3) acceptance of others, (4) curiosity and eagerness to grow, (5) reliability, and (6) family—his care and nurture of a wonderful home and family.

GROWING UP LUCIA

To hear Lucia describe her life as a child in the Paulson family is to feel transported back to Ward and June Cleaver's neighborhood or the Cosby home. Their small but comfy home on Marlow Drive was in a modest but Norman Rockwall-cute community named Sheffield Village in east Oakland. Lots of neighborhood kids played in each other's yards and in the street. The Village had its own public elementary school they almost all attended. Only for seventh grade and higher did they trek over to join us at my school, Roosevelt, and then on to our junior and senior high schools. (My parents bought a house just up the hill from the Paulson's soon after I met Lucia; great timing, eh!).

Mrs. Paulson worked as a Registered Nurse mostly in downtown Oakland (Merritt and Providence hospitals) but sometimes as a private duty nurse. She often worked evening swing shifts so both parents would not be gone at the same time. It was a peaceful, stable family routine. Mr. Paulson got home every evening at the same time. Dinner together (spaghetti and meatloaf were two specialties I enjoyed when I entered the scene). Mr. and Mrs. Paulson loved to go out dancing whenever possible. Weekends often included car rides out into the surrounding towns and countryside.

Lucia learned to help her family by cooking, house cleaning, and some yardwork early on. Every month her dad would bring home his pay in cash, spread it out on his bed and allocate it to whatever monthly bills they had—and then pay Lucia and her brother and sister their allowances based on the chores they had done. The three kids all learned to swim at nearby Farrelly Pool and loved every opportunity to get in a lake, pool, or ocean, especially on annual vacation trips. All three Paulson kids took music lessons. Mr. Paulson still got out his violin and played a little. Kathryn worked on violin. Steve focused on the drums. Little Lucia took up the clarinet at around age eight. She practiced diligently and got better and better so that she not only played in the San Leandro High School orchestra but an all-star prep band. I still feel horrible and guilty for persuading her to stay home near me rather than go on a road trip to Montreal for this all-star band to play an important gig. She remembers her dad sitting with her and listening to her while she practiced. As she grew up Lucia also learned how to sew and created some of her own beautiful clothes as well as some for our kids when they were little.

Lucia was a diligent student who always did her homework well and on time. Good grades all the way from elementary school onward. She graduated in the top ten per cent of her high school class. Her dad shelled out a financial reward for each good grade she could show him whenever report cards came out. She applied only to the University of California at Berkeley and was admitted in Fall 1966. In high school, Lucia won the competition to be San Leandro High School's designated retail sales employee at Capwell's Department Store (each regional high school had one slot for a female student). She was a terrific employee and soon entrusted with extra responsibilities like closing up the department at the end of the day when she was at work. One night, however, she mistakenly set the timer on the safe to re-open the next morning two hours after the store opened! Horrified at her mistake, she called her boss right away to let him know. Naturally, her boss (who figured out how to improvise the next morning) thought more highly of her integrity than ever. Lucia never caused her parents or teachers any trouble. They were always positive and encouraging to her. Neither Kathryn or Steve went on to a college degree so Lucia really was the academic star of her family when she graduated from Berkeley with her BA in French.

The Paulsons were a huge part of our lives all through our marriage and family life from 1967 to 1995. They lived just ten miles from our house and regularly spent time with Lucia, our kids, and me. Lucia would go out to lunch and for walks with both her mom and dad—before and after our kids came along. They were always good for attendance at our kids' music recitals and soccer games. We usually celebrated Thanksgiving Day with my Gill tribe—and Christmas with Lucia's Paulson tribe.

THE LIGHT ENTERS MY LIFE

You know that "Lucia" means light, right? Honestly, when I met her in October 1963, I thought she was both the prettiest and the purest thing I had ever seen or met. I often thank God for giving me such a beautiful wife. Whenever I look at pictures of her from the past fifty years, I am honestly dazzled. When her brown hair turned brilliantly white at a certain age, I was dazzled again. I have often had the experience of being on some stage speaking to a crowd and seeing her walk into the back of the auditorium and been smitten with love and desire. Crazy, isn't it. I think I have told her almost every day of her life how beautiful she is. She has cute dimples, the face of a model, and a beautiful, healthy, athletic, feminine physique. She has always stayed fit and healthy and in shape. She buys and wears beautiful clothing and jewelry (purchased at reasonable prices!). She is so attractive but never slutty or suggestive or distracting. And when I say "pure" I mean that she has no bad habits, is innocent, and unpretentious. And she has a very hard time believing what I or others tell her about how beautiful she is. That is called modesty.

I was so proud of her as my girlfriend in high school. I loved every second we were together. She was shy and soft-spoken in those first few years together (she got a lot bolder and tougher later on!). We both worked hard and then spent as much time together as possible. Church activities, of courses, but also lunches, dinners, music concerts, and sports events were part of our lives.

Our first date was November 1, 1963. (Fifty years later, November 1, 2013, we flew to Paris for a week of celebration of that first life-changing event). From November 1963 to September 1967 we dated, attended church together, talked and prayed a lot, and really got to know and love each other over almost four years. Even though we were really young, ages twenty-one and nineteen, we were ready to tie the knot and make it permanent. It was time to "fish or cut bait" as the old saying goes. The year 1967 was called the "Summer of Love" in Berkeley, San Francisco and up and down the Pacific Coast. This usually included hippie music, hallucinogenic drugs, anti-war peace activism, and the so-called "free-love" scene. I loved a lot of the music and shared the anti-war concerns. We didn't believe in drugs or even have a glass of beer or wine until we were twenty-one. We were already high on life, love, music, and God so no drugs were needed or wanted. And when it came to sex, we were interested and eager as you might expect but our Christian philosophy was "no total intimacy until there is total commitment," i.e., marriage. The culture around us believed in an experimental intimacy which might or might not lead to commitment to one or another extent. We believed the opposite: commitment first, then intimacy.

TOGETHER FOREVER

We got married on September 9, 1967.[3] September 9 is the anniversary of California joining the USA, called "Admission Day." In 1967 it was our day of "admission to (our) union." Getting married was like liberation day. Now we were free to create our own home and family and future, free to travel together. Later on, having children was like suddenly dropping anchor. Marriage was being set free. We rented an apartment on 41st Street, a block from our church and just two miles south of the Berkeley campus where we were both enrolled. Lucia was beginning her sophomore year and I would be a senior. Before I officially proposed to Lucia I took her dad out for lunch at Rod's Hickory Pit and laid out the financial plan in front of him to convince him (old school thought) to assent to my marrying his daughter. He was positive, the ribs were good, and we began planning the wedding for the following year.

Unfortunately, during our first year of marriage, Lucia and I realized that our savings and income were not going to be enough. As a draft-age male, I had been called up the previous year (1966) for a "pre-induction" physical. At the time I had a

---

3. My birthday is 2/2 and our anniversary 9/9. I totally forgot to make a big deal about my 02.02.02 birthday but at 09.09 on the morning of 09.09.09 we shared a champaign toast in the wine country with our friends Dave and Marty Stewart, also married on September 9th (but five years after us).

serious case of skin eczema on my hands and arms from all the petroleum solvents used in my factory jobs every summer and school vacation. Unexpectedly I was given a temporary physical deferment, 1-Y status. I was very anti-war and especially anti-Vietnam war (after studying the history of the conflict and hearing Senator Mark Hatfield unpack its origins and misguided purposes) so we briefly thought about escaping to Canada if need be. But I was also feeling the pressure to stay in school and stay up with my class (i.e., graduate in no more than four years). Maybe being married also made me less draftable. I never heard from the draft board again but we did feel anxious for those few years while the Vietnam War continued.

But with me absolutely needing to stay up with my class full-time, I really couldn't cut back on classes to work more. Lucia made the sacrifice, cutting way back on her education from 1968 to 1975 when it could resume. She worked briefly in an expanded role at Capwell's Department Store but then got hired to work full-time in the front office of Cal Berkeley's business school. She did this for three years until our first baby came along in 1971, by which time I had a full-time job teaching junior high school. In those days the business school was in Barrows Hall, directly behind Sproul Hall and Sproul Plaza where all the campus and political movements staged their rallies and demonstrations, sometimes with big clashes with the police and sheriff's department. She has lots of stories of the building shutting down and having to scurry across campus through clouds of tear gas to our apartment.

One providential development was that after one year renting our Oakland apartment, we got invited to replace a graduating Cal history PhD student as caretakers of a beautiful fifteen-unit building two blocks north of campus (corner of Virginia and LeRoy). In return for our daily chores picking up garbage and otherwise assisting the mostly elderly tenants, we got free rent in a tiny downstairs unit. This living arrangement continued from fall 1968 until spring 1972 with our baby Jodie and with Jonathan on the way. Needing more room, we rented a larger apartment for three months and then we bought our old house on 62nd Street in Oakland.

But other than a class here and there, Lucia was focused on her Cal Berkeley job, then on having and caring for our children until 1975. In that year we moved to Pasadena for the final two years of my PhD program at USC. That is when Lucia began taking French courses at Pasadena City College, whose academic challenge and excellence matched any university's first two years. The fact that I was trying to master French for my studies of Jacques Ellul is probably what got her interested in French rather than Spanish (which she studied four years in high school and another year at Cal). Over those two years (1975–77) She got all A's. When we moved back home to Oakland in 1977 she completed her BA in French and graduated from Cal Berkeley in 1981. She accomplished this as a half-time university student but full-time mom (our kids were born in 1971 and 1972). She was close to a straight-A student. When our kids were not in a school session but she had a class, she took them with her to

Cal and had them sit quietly and read or otherwise entertain themselves in the back of the classroom.

Later on, during my 1984–85 sabbatical study leave in Bordeaux, France, Lucia completed the coursework for a master's level diploma at the University of Bordeaux. I encouraged her to pursue a graduate degree or a teaching credential if she wished. I was willing to try to cut back on my own work and watch the kids more but she didn't feel that call. She did tutor some graduate students preparing for language exams. And, of course, she became my indispensable French-expert fellow-worker for the rest of our lives—translating when I needed it, correcting my grammar when I wrote a speech or essay or letter that needed to be perfect. Early on, I had memorized a thousand French words and could eke out rough translations but I was terrible at speaking, or understanding speech, and horrible at constructing sentences. Eventually (during that 1984–85 sabbatical in Bordeaux) I took a lot of French courses and became bold and fluent (though never inerrant!).

Funny story: Lucia *did* try to coach me and tutor me in French from time to time. But whenever the kids were in school and we sat at the table to begin my lessons, I kid you not, hearing her speaking French created a raging romantic feeling in me for her and I couldn't help but express it in a way that completely disrupted our lessons. She gave up at that point but she went on to translate extemporaneously for Jacques Ellul and me in our conversations and interviews in 1982. She coached our kids through the incredible challenges of French public school during 1984–1985 (Jodie in 8th grade, Jonathan in 7th). Both kids ended the year totally fluent and believing they could meet any challenge! Lucia used her French to assist her bosses at times during her work life. We still today read the Bible together out loud in French every morning and often find ourselves speaking to each other or to other folk in French.

Lucia's parents were forty-two years old when she was born so they weren't active in her growing up activities to anything like the extent twenty-three-year old mom Lucia could be. Our kids had endless fun growing up with Lucia as their mom. Swimming: they were like three porpoises whenever they got the chance. Excursions, hiking, running, playing Canasta after school. She knew how to get the kids involved in helping her shop, do chores, and clean house. She helped Jonathan with his paper routes and Jodie with her piano lessons (funded by Grandma Paulson). She made clothes for herself and the kids when little. She was involved in their public schools and in our home church—teaching Sunday School, organizing hospitality events, playing her clarinet, co-teaching confirmation, and serving as an elder for a term.

I always have remembered my mom as a great cook, and she was, both in quantity and quality. But I married a true culinary star. This is actually one of my lifelong problems ever since marriage: the food in my house is just too good, too tempting to me to overindulge. Our daughter Jodie and I used to audibly groan, almost weep with pleasure, tasting her version of moussaka or her stuffed chicken. We became dizzy, our minds swirling in ecstasy, when eating her cheese-cake bars. I'm not exaggerating.

Over the decades I cannot begin to calculate the hundreds (thousands?) of relatives, students, colleagues, neighbors, church members, and other guests for whom she has cooked. I started trying to carry half the cooking load after our kids were out of the house and Lucia was full-time in the banking world. I learned a huge amount by asking her questions and just by watching how she works. I remember when I was invited to dinner at the Paulson house when we were in high school. The fifteen or sixteen-year-old Lucia often was the cook. You could tell already about this girl.

Lucia chose to prioritize caring for our kids and being home when they got back from school each day. They thank her to this day for being there, whether they came home alone or brought some friends. She protected and loved and assisted them every day. When the kids were at the end of high school, athletic Lucia asked her rental-property-owning brother Steve if he would be willing to pay her to do some of his rehab apartment unit painting in between tenants. She did enough of this to pay for our first ever vacation in Hawaii. Amazing.

FINANCE OFFICE AT CITIBANK

In 1988 Lucia asked my sister Kit Faria if there might be some temp employment opportunities in the Citicorp executive offices where Kit worked. Yes. Before much time had passed, she was asked to help an incoming executive in charge of Citi's real estate business in the western USA. As a final task she was to help him set up a search for his Executive Assistant—but he said he didn't need to search, he wanted Lucia in that job! That began a twenty-year career in Oakland, then Chicago, then San Francisco, working as executive assistant to a variety of top finance executives—organizing their team meetings, arranging her boss's flight and hotel travel, turning monthly financial data into power point diagrams and notes, making her bosses look good when reporting back to Citi-headquarters in New York. She learned her bosses' routines and needs and when they might remind her that they needed to start getting the monthly report ready, she already had it half done, just waiting for final data from the field to come in. She showed special care for her bosses' spouses, patching through their messages to the boss, suggesting restaurants, jazz clubs, museums, and Broadway shows to them if they could join their husbands on a business trip. (She knew so much from her own world travels, and knew how to look up information on anything else). She always was on time, worked late if a crisis demanded, always spoke and looked classy and professional. She took all the free in-house courses she could and became the staff member to whom everyone on the floor came for help mastering PowerPoint, Excel, or whatever.

When after her first four years at Citi I got an offer I couldn't refuse to teach at North Park University in Chicago, word was passed to Citi executive leaders in Chicago that "Lucia Gill is available." Within two days, she had two offers from Citibank leaders. She took the job working for Mark McKenzie, President of Citi's Global Finance and

Part Two: Shapers (1964–1979)

Electronic Payments operations. Here is how much he and his colleagues loved her: after just two years at North Park I was committed to a one-year visiting professorship in Pennsylvania. Mark McKenzie agreed to use job temps in her place if she promised to come back after the year. Then four years later I earned a one-year sabbatical in Sweden and France. Once again, her boss agreed to hold her job for the year if she promised to come back. The cruelest blow came when we returned from France in fall 2000 and announced we would be moving back home to Oakland in 2001.

Back in the Bay Area, there were no executive assistant job openings at first so Lucia spent a year trying to help Westminster House's campus housing and student ministry at Cal. The mismanagement and chaos almost drove her over the edge at times but she was saved when at last a new executive in San Francisco Citi headquarters needed an assistant in the finance department. She thrived again, taking the twenty-minute BART ride each day to her office in the SF financial district. In 2008, however, the national economic meltdown was a Wall Street banking disaster. Citi had to reorganize and lay off almost all personnel in her department. Of course, she could have moved on to another banking or business post but as she was discerning next steps, I got an offer I couldn't refuse to join the faculty of Gordon-Conwell Seminary in the Boston area. We had recently vacationed back there and said to each other "Wouldn't it have been great if we could have lived here for a while?" So we did for the next few years.

CHATEAU GILL

Not until the mid-1990s did we get anywhere near financial stability and comfort. So we have always been very hands-on wherever we lived. We laugh when someone groans to us about how rough it is remodeling their kitchen, repainting, or whatever—when they really mean "when workers we hire are doing it." When Lucia and I say our house is being painted, our car is being washed, or our living room is being wallpapered, we mean *we* are doing it! And we have loved doing it—planting and tending our gardens, painting, whatever. I learned a ton about power tools, building, plumbing, and electrical work from my dad. I love to impress my bride by fixing something that she just can't seem to do and then saying (as dramatically as possible) "Aren't you glad you're married to a handy man?"

In 1972, living in our tiny apartment with our one-year-old and another baby on on the way, we had to find more spacious housing. We had saved up $3000 for a down payment if we could find the right house. We looked and looked but couldn't find the right place. We wanted to be in Oakland, not the suburbs, with maybe a big enough place to rent out a room or two. We hoped for a reduced price "fixer-upper." We got so discouraged we spent $1000 of our $3000 savings on a used VW bus to accommodate better our growing brood than our old bug could do. One day driving home from Tilden Park I stopped the van in front of Rockridge Realty on College

Avenue. My pitch: "We are looking for a fixer-upper around here with potential for rental space if possible. We have $2000 to put down and a steady income ($12,000/year) as a school teacher. Do you by chance have anything like that?" "No, sorry," they said and I headed for the door. "Wait a minute!" some other voice called out. The sales agent went into a back room and pulled out a sheet describing 363—62nd Street. It was very broken-down with a hippie commune living there. The hippies tore any "for sale" signs down and were hostile to any visitors. The HUD housing project across the street was a sore spot on the block because of the noise and accumulated trash. The house was painted all pink on the outside all green on the inside. Trash everywhere. A couple broken windows.

When we walked through the place it was a mess. My fastidious wife was a bit put off and doubtful. But I could see the beamed ceilings, the intricate hardwood flooring design, the proximity to Cal Berkeley (one-and-a-half miles)—and the two two-bedroom rental units at the back of the property, filthy but redeemable. Our offer was accepted by the desperate seller who had fled the city to Nevada. The bank would only lend us 80% of the $40,000 sale price for a twenty-five-year mortgage. We only had $2000 instead of the $8000 we needed to put down. The eager owner loaned us a $3000 second mortgage for five years, plus $2000 for a three-year personal note, and two of the realtors each kicked in $500 and gave us a year to pay them back. We were in. Desperate seller. Marginal neighborhood. High potential fixer-upper. We have remodeled, enlarged, and improved our house and gardens in many projects and stages over the past fifty years. When we lived away in Los Angeles, Bordeaux, Chicago, or Boston we always just rented it out and then returned when the time came.

During our time in Chicago (1992–2001) we bought a little house two blocks from the North Park campus where I taught—and then sold it and reinvested the equity growth in our Oakland house when we returned—earthquake retrofitting and a big upstairs expansion. During my teaching gig in New England (2010–16) we bought a condo in Gloucester, on the coast north of Boston. Same deal, we sold it and moved back into our Oakland home. There is not a square inch of our Oakland home that we have not personally painted, built, remodeled, cleaned or otherwise put our touch on. Lucia and I have worked side-by-side on all of it. I have sometimes said that our housing story was God's joke on financial realism. We, who were "downwardly mobile" and idealistic in an initially depressed and declining neighborhood, now live in a fabulous house and neighborhood. I love that our street is in what is sometimes called "Lower Rockridge"—west of Broadway and even College Avenue. We are not "Upper Rockridge" people.

A STRONG COMMON LIFE

Lucia and I have been together so long: fifty-nine years since our first date, fifty-five years since we got married. How did you do it? (the astonished crowds ask). Well, what I sometimes say is this: "Before we make any important decision we talk it over and each give our opinion. Then we do it her way. No problem!" This is when Lucia lets out an "Oh yeah! Don't let him fool you!" Of course, it's just a joke. (Humor is an important factor in a long-term relationship!).

The key to a long and good marriage, in our case, is the determination from day one to build a common, shared life together, to become best friends. Lucia and I might have a furious argument about something but I always wake up the next morning next to my best friend, the one person in the world I most want to be with to do almost anything. We never agree to lead any marriage seminars or classes because we just can't present ourselves as "experts" on marriage. We are not any better than anyone else. Our siblings and friends who have been divorced are not fundamentally any different than us and we don't at all look down on them. We just feel lucky, blessed, and determined to keep on going and growing. Of course, we are very fond of each other; we really like and enjoy each other. We are not just altruistically dying for each other as an act of sacrificial love. But fondness and attraction alone are never enough of a foundation for a healthy, long-term marriage.

The first common thing in our life is our faith and commitment to God, more specifically to Jesus Christ. We are not our own (or each other's) ultimate authority. Each of us has always felt accountable to—and sustained by—God. We have always prayed alone and together. It is unimaginable to us to go through life married to someone with a fundamentally different faith or philosophy of life. On our own and together, more now in our retirement years than ever, this life of prayer, Bible reading, worship (attending the same church each week), and attempting to serve God and our neighbors—this is the powerful, durable foundation of our long marriage.

Next is our (extended) family and network of close friends. They give us strength. The way we look at it, a divorce would not just be with each other but with our band of shared friends, our family. No more united holiday gatherings. We don't want to let our friends down and lose our fun times together. The replacement spouses just wouldn't be the same! Both of our sets of parents had long marriages and set us a good example. All five of our siblings got divorced (for good reasons!) and, while we don't think this makes us any better than the others, we did not want to grieve our parents by breaking up. Let's hang in there!

I sometimes hear warnings against "early marriage" (like our ages twenty-one and nineteen). "You need to wait until you discover who you really are," they say. I certainly do not believe people should rush into marriage but the truth is, first, that many people in their late twenties or thirties are just as lost as they were at eighteen. Second, if your aesthetic tastes, financial practices, and life-style have clarified by, say, your thirties, you have radically narrowed down the field of compatible prospects. There is something to be said for early marriage before all your tastes and preferences have clarified. A young married couple can make the commitment to craft a life together.

Lucia and I knew we loved God, loved each other, and wanted to live together forever. We didn't know that after our kids were born we would buy bicycles, at first with kid seats, and take a fun ride almost every week for the rest of our lives! We didn't know that lack of money would push us to get into inexpensive, public court tennis by 1975, beginning a twenty-five-year period of regular, fun, intermediate competitive matches between us. When we began, I was a low intermediate and she a beginner at tennis. By the end of the first year of playing together, she could hold her own (actually I think she won two-thirds of our games over the next decades) even when I served and played at my maximum. We didn't know we would both get into jogging and run the Bay-to-Breakers race across San Francisco multiple times.[4] I suppose after our wedding I could have still gone "off with the boys" and played soccer or whatever. But Lucia was athletic and I much preferred developing our sports life together.

We didn't know that we would together develop a taste for strong dark-roast coffee from Peet's. But we did and it is our morning treat. We had no idea about good beer or wine when we got married but over time we both got to love the same kind of dark, hearty beers—and the same kinds of dark red, big, dry wines like zinfandel and petite sirah. Wine tasting in the Sonoma Valley. Sharing great wine over a meal with friends, we both grew into loving the same entertainment and culinary style. We knew nothing about these matters when we got married.

When we got married we headed over to Cost-Plus imports and bought some inexpensive beads to hang in a doorway, some wicker chairs, and a few other items. We grew to share the same general ideas about how we like our homes decorated, how our gardens might look, and how we like to clean and care for everything. We are both neatniks—though I never feel like I quite meet her high standards (I always used to tell people that at any given impromptu moment, day or night, *Sunset* or *Better Homes and Gardens* could drop in for a photo shoot at our place).

We danced at my senior ball and then off-and-on at rock concerts in the early years of our marriage. We always loved a lot of classical music, blues, and rock'n'roll. But who could have predicted that fifteen years in (1982) we would accidentally discover the dance music of the Roaring Twenties being played on local station KJAZ. It was a group still active today: Don Neely's Royal Society Jazz Orchestra. When we saw in the paper that they were playing at the Great American Music Hall in San Francisco, we went and were blown away by the energy, the flapper dress, and the swirling joy of it all. We had no idea how to dance together in an up-tempo Fox Trot or Waltz. We took four other couples back with us to another show and they too were mesmerized. Together with these couples we hired a dance instructor for five or six group lessons. The other couples did not much continue because one or other in the couple didn't enjoy dancing. For Lucia and me it was the beginning of many more lessons and

---

4. We didn't do everything together. Lucia loves to swim and for many years swam a full hour before work each day; I am a land animal. I love to lift weights at the gym and play golf whenever I can. She finds golf "boring" (see, I'm not saying she is perfect).

a lifetime of ballroom dancing (especially if we can find that Twenties and Thirties stuff!). Lucia is a fabulous dance partner, better than anyone I have ever danced with. I can be totally upset with something she did and when I take her in my arms and hit the dance floor, I immediately fall head over heels in love with her. Riding her bike had a similar impact on Lucia, I found. All hell can be breaking loose around her but if I can get her in the fresh air on her bike, her mood is transformed.

Starting with that Twenties Big Band jazz around 1982, we gradually became more interested in American jazz. Our good friends Jay and Susan Boone encouraged us by taking us out to hear flutist Herbie Mann and pianists Ellis Marsalis and Marcus Roberts. Our friends John and Marj Erisman introduced us to more jazz. Our New College Berkeley Business Manager (and sax player) Amy Brannon Keltner got us to an extraordinary concert by Ella Fitzgerald. By 1990, we turned the car radio dial from KRQR (Classic Rock) to KJAZ (or WDCB when in Chicago). After we moved to Chicago in 1992, my New College student and friend John Ephland, a writer for *Downbeat Magazine*, introduced us to the amazing jazz scene at the Jazz Showcase, the Green Mill, Ravinia, and elsewhere. Jazz became the soundtrack to our lives. Wherever we have traveled in North America or Europe, either Lucia or I will have researched the jazz club and concert possibilities.

And finally, I have to talk about French. I studied German for four years of high school and an additional year as an undergrad. Lucia did the same with Spanish. But four years into our marriage I discovered a French sociologist (and lay theologian) at the University of Bordeaux in France. I became consumed with his ideas, wrote reviews of his books, and got deeper and deeper all through a PhD program. As this developed, I wanted and needed to learn French. Lucia did not feel any passion for continuing in Spanish and was intrigued by French, not least because that was the direction I was going. To make a long story short, she became an expert in French and I got the job done also learning the language. She could have stuck with Spanish but chose our common commitment to French. The rest of the story is frequently visiting Bordeaux and France, living in Bordeaux the full year 1984–85 and the first half of 2000. We love French food and wine, organize French soirees wherever we live, read and speak a lot in French, and love our many friends living in France. Who would have predicted this when we got married?[5]

So I have said to Lucia "God forbid the thought, but if you were to die before me I could never get married again because nobody but you is that combination essential to my happiness: a faithful Christian, extremely beautiful, great at ballroom dancing, a neatnik, fabulous cook, lover of dark beer, strong French Roast coffee, and hearty dry red wines, French speaker and francophile, compassionate political progressive, jazz lover, and bike rider." "Hah!" she responds, "you wouldn't be alone for a minute.

---

5. Grandma Lucia has taken five of our six grandchildren, one at a time, for ten-day personal tours of Paris, usually around age fourteen. Many adults tell her they wish she would adopt them as her grandchildren!

I know you." Me: "well, ok, I might date a little but I could never possibly get married to anyone but you." She: "Hah!"

IT'S NOT ALL A BED OF ROSES, OF COURSE

So far, it all looks pretty perfect. A storybook romance and relationship for fifty-nine years! And all that I have described is true. But nothing and nobody and no relationship is perfect or without pain, and that includes us. I think a long-term relationship requires a strong and growing common life and even common perspective on things. But *difference* is also an important strength. Lucia and I are very different in several ways, usually strengthening each other, but sometimes creating pain. With the following examples just remember, these are habits and tendencies, not ironclad differences. Sometimes we trade these habits and behaviors.

Simple example to start with: she has a great sense of direction; I do not. If I can just keep my mouth shut, we always arrive where we wanted to go. Alas, not always possible. Next: I am quick, she is more deliberate. In the larger picture, I do think, reflect, pray, and study a lot—but I am typically like a quarterback in a game situation in that I step up to the line and call the play. At restaurants I look through the menu and choose something. I respond and speak quickly (sometimes too quickly of course). In general, Lucia prefers to take more time before speaking or making a decision. I incline to be very optimistic (unrealistic, she might say) about both people and situations. I am a fiercely convinced leader who often inspires people to pursue a challenging goal. She is much more cautious. If it wasn't for me, we might have missed out on buying our house—or some other adventures in life. If it wasn't for her, I might have jumped at some opportunities that wouldn't had ended well. I tend to want to give away more charitable contributions; I view "tithing" as a minimum. She is very generous in her own right but sometimes cautions me not to just give away my services when those who invite or host me could easily pay me something. I do think about preparing for a rainy day, but if it wasn't for her, we wouldn't have saved up enough to retire or to travel so much. Differences!

I rarely assume people have bad motives toward me personally or otherwise (I just view their hurtful words or actions as a mistake—clumsy or stupid, but not intentionally cruel). She might say I am naïve, that people's hurtful behavior must come out of some negativity directed at her (or me). I have rarely ever thought any woman's friendliness or attention masked a flirtatious interest in me. Lucia might see or sense flirtation immediately. They say women can detect each other's "game" while their men walk right into it, whether knowingly or naively, like an ox to the slaughter. Sometimes I think she has been right, other times wrong, but I've learned to respect and honor her judgment. Her realism and caution about people probably saved me from some naivete and gullibility. My way of spinning things positively and not speculating about bad motives might have saved us from cynicism, negativity, and pain at times.

We are not big fans of diagnostic personality tests but somehow we both took the Meyers-Briggs Type Indicator a few different times. I always test out as a hardcore extravert. To be sure, I need and enjoy some quiet, alone time—but when forced to make a choice, give me people, lots of them. Lucia, early in our marriage, came out as a modestly introverted person. She did seem shy and sometimes wearied by too many people and too-long gatherings. But over the years she has become more and more extraverted. I always want more guests over, more dinner parties, more people. She also is a generous, people-loving hostess, but reaches her limit before I do. I am addicted to staying in touch with friends, students, neighbors, and colleagues from over the years. I love speaking to (or celebrating with) big crowds, meeting lots of new people as well as old friends. I leave more energized than exhausted. That is the extravert/introvert distinction.

The other interesting category on the Meyers-Briggs scale is about "judging" or "perceiving." Lucia is a hardcore "J" on this scale. What this refers to is one's instinct to organize, order, and control life. I am a softer "J" and sometimes in my life tested as a slight "P" ("go with the flow") personality. When? Whenever I worked for or with hardcore "J's" I reacted by wanting things opened and loosened up a bit. When I worked for a free form "P" I tended to become a "J" getting things organized. You can see how there is potential for some conflict. We are both organizers, bordering on control freaks at times. What gets done around the house, by whom, and when, sometimes flared up in controversy. I am eager to do my share of the domestic chores but I want to schedule my tasks, not be scheduled by someone else. Let's discuss the tasks and divide them up and decide on a completion date—then let me determine my best times to do my tasks. Please don't interfere. We both are temperamentally and professionally ready and even eager to take control of situations and manage them to a good outcome. That's usually a good thing but it can go bad.

Our little church had no pre-marital or marital counseling. We learned and grew as we went along. We read some books about marriage. Later on, I especially liked Walter Wangerin's *As For Me and My House: Crafting Your Marriage to Last*. In the early 1980s, we met a couple at a church where I was speaking who were both PhDs and marriage counselors. They seemed like nice, bright, wise people so we decided to have a kind of "twenty-year" marriage tune up. We groaned but paid the money for eight counseling sessions and got started. I learned one thing: when Lucia is describing her feelings or her understanding of something, I should not interrupt or try to correct her even if I think she is mistaken. Let her completely finish, then say "What I hear you saying is . . . " And then, "Did I hear you correctly?" Pretty good advice.

Anyway, another couple around our age happened to ask if we knew of a marriage counselor. We gave them our counselor's name. This led them to develop a counseling relationship over many years. When back in town I would sometimes ask them: "By the way, how are our marriage counselor and her marriage counselor-husband doing?" Usual answer: "Great." But after several years this was the answer: "Oh it is so sad. She and he are getting a divorce." Me: "Oh that is terrible—our double-PhD Christian marriage counselors couldn't make it work?" My friend: "Yes, and it was her third marriage." Made me wonder how much I would be offering myself as an ethics professor and consultant if I had three ethics scandals on my resume. We are certainly not anti-counseling! But our experience taught us that counselors are not perfect and they don't have all the answers.

The worst thing that ever happened in our long marriage was when I got too close to a female student at a little Bible school (freshman college level) where I taught ethics and history courses while beginning my doctoral studies at USC. We had been married seven years and had two darling little pre-school kids. Lucia was as beautiful as ever and I had absolutely no complaints about her, our marriage, or our family life. But I listened to my student share her painful story of a bad relationship. I sympathized. I felt her pain. Then I did something very stupid. I said something like this: "I can't understand how someone could treat you like that. If it was me, I would have been crazy about you and protected you." *That*, unfortunately, was an invitation for her to confess her feelings for me and it opened the door to a two-week period of mixed up feelings, going off together for lunch, kissing her in my office . . . and guilt. After two weeks of this, we both agreed it was wrong, it must end now, and we are so sorry it ever got this far. If we stopped it now and got back on the right side of the line maybe we could be friends forever. It did stop immediately and totally. But just one month later, I got called in and fired for my inappropriate relationship with a student. It was very harsh but I agree with their decision. I was wrong and out of line. Just stopping it was an insufficient price to pay. I needed to be fired.

At no time did I then (or ever) not want to be married to Lucia and Lucia alone. It may be possible to love more than one person at the same time (just like more than one kid)—but no marriage can endure a third party, romantic competitor. Why and how did this happen I often asked myself afterward? First of all, I was alienated from my faculty colleagues at this school who were unhappy about (threatened by?) my USC PhD program. So I tended to socialize with my students, many of them just a couple years younger than I was at the time. Second, I did not think this kind of thing was possible for me. I thought I was invulnerable and above temptation. But my heart was tender and caring and I failed to guard it and my feelings. Third, I know it is a lame excuse but my dating and romantic experience was confined to Lucia and I just didn't recognize or manage my feelings—for two weeks—until I did, but then it was too late. It became a public scandal, humiliating and deeply wounding my poor, innocent, trusting wife (and incidentally trashing my reputation among people eager to imagine something far worse than what actually happened). Lessons: Guard your heart. Don't let your compassion, caring, and emotion overwhelm your reason and will. Be sure you always have a functioning, supportive, accountability group around you as you go through life—don't get isolated. I had no one to talk to when this hit me.

Liberated from the strict PB culture I was raised in, it took me a while to learn how to love my women friends in the biblical senses of *agape* and *philia*—and not be flirtatious. A relationship may be completely innocent to start with but it can go wrong and lead to serious harm. I really believe in monogamy and fidelity in marriage. It is not just about survival but about trust and flourishing together. I'm sure it would have been fun to "play the field," date a lot, and chase other beautiful women. But going that route means you cannot enjoy the lifelong love of your one true soul-mate and companion. I have never doubted that I made the right choice in committing myself to Lucia forever. And I deeply regret when my flirtatiousness and caring too much for another woman wound up hurting her so deeply.

There were times when the shoe was on the other foot. I never doubted Lucia's loyalty to me but I can recall five different guys over the years who started spending huge amounts of time with her (tennis, skiing, etc.). I began to notice and get a little peeved at times. Three of the wives actually phoned me concerned about their husbands' interest in Lucia. I threatened a couple of the guys but all the situations eventually resolved themselves. My point is that our male/female chemistry is often subtle and we can live in denial, with painful consequences. It's not just a "man lesson."

THREE PHASES

On reflection, I have thought that our marriage has gone through three phases. From 1967 to 1988 (twenty-one years), was the *age of spontaneity and innocence*. We didn't really know what to expect of marriage or of each other. We followed our passion and instinct. Of course, we had some basic expectations and dreams but we were young and growing and could easily change our thinking on most matters. I admit that I had initial hopes that she would enjoy deep philosophical discussions, co-teaching a group with me, and playing golf. Nope! Partly through the influential example of some feminist friends, I realized how this amounted to creating an "image" of her—rather than loving and accepting her for who she was and supporting her pursuit of her own agenda. For her part, she might have struggled with an expectation that I would come to love swimming and have a work schedule more like her dad and most other husbands in the world (and not be so much up front in public events instead of sitting by her, or so busy writing at night instead of watching television with the family). My point is that we all probably project some expectations on our mates (and later our kids) but in these early years of marriage there is a lot of fluidity and spontaneity possible.

Phase two went from 1988 to 2000: the *age of expectation and demand*. Most of the innocence, spontaneity, and fluidity is gone. I mean expectation and demand of ourself as well as our mate. By 1988 Lucia had become a strong, powerful woman.

I think this had a lot to do with her new outside-the-home work, with its income, independence, and respect. Now that the kids were gone, she had her job and I had mine. She was bold in her own way of thinking about herself, her husband, and everything else in life. She was a strong, independent woman and I loved it (usually). Sort of funny story: around 1989 or 1990 her boss gave her a stellar performance review—and then a pitiful raise of one or two percent. A day later she went in to protest and make her case. She got the raise but she told me afterward that she could tell her boss was trying to intimidate her a bit when she asked for the well-deserved raise. "And I realized I have you to thank. After being married to you for all these years, I realized nobody can intimidate me!" Uh, thank you sweetie. I don't mean to suggest that the 1990s had no fun or spontaneity but with the kids out of the house and our two-career life, I felt some frustration over what I expected of myself and our marriage and what I thought my mate expected of me. Just so you know, though, we still had fabulous times through the 1990s at Chicago jazz clubs, with bike rides and a dip in Lake Michigan many summer Saturdays, one-year study leaves in Pennsylvania and Europe, a twenty-five-year anniversary trip to Quebec, and a thirty-year anniversary at the Drake Hotel downtown in Chicago.

The third phase of our marriage began in 2001: the *age of acceptance and no expectations*. I started out 2001 very depressed and upset and hired my own very first ever counselor, Dick Matthews. Meeting with him really helped me to basically "give up" all the (unrealistic, unsatisfiable) expectations I had (personally, professionally)—and give up trying to satisfy other people's expectations. Time to chill out, be grateful for what I have, and give up on what I used to wish for or expect of others. Give it up to God! You can't have everything. There are trade-offs and limits. It is wrong to expect your mate to give you everything you need and want—and wrong to think that you could ever be everything your spouse or others need and want. Give up, chill out, be grateful, celebrate! I think I really did turn a corner twenty years ago with this counsel. I love my wife (and my life) for all the blessings I receive, all the joy I experience. But I am just not going to fret about what I don't have or what I never achieved or what I could never perfectly do for others.

MARRIAGE GUY

As I said above, I (we) do not teach marriage seminars. We don't want to jinx ourselves or hold ourselves up as experts or any kind of standard. But I have been called upon maybe a dozen times to officiate at the weddings of relatives, students, or friends. Long ago I learned that everyone (including the bride and groom) forgets the little message or homily at their wedding. So I figured out how to summarize the essentials of a good marriage in an acrostic that spells "Christ."

> C. Communicate honestly and freely, but always with
> H. Honor and
> R. Respect for your partner.
> I. "I love you," "I was wrong," and "I forgive you": the three critical "I" statements in a good marriage.
> S. Serve God, each other, and the world. No selfishness.
> T. Together. Build your common life every chance you get.

This pretty fairly describes what we have tried to do in our marriage over these five decades. And I am still as insanely in love with her as at any moment in my life.

When a guy has a solid, durable, loving marriage, he is no longer in the market for romance with anyone else. One thing this means is a generally increased comfort-level in relating to other women. Anybody who knows me or has been anywhere near my classes knows that I proudly and easily talk about my wife and family. I am always "David Gill, married guy who loves Lucia." There has never been any doubt about it. Women don't need to fear that I am "on the hunt" or will "come on" to them. My mother, wife, daughter, and sisters have all been strong women so I love to be around similarly strong women. My theology and philosophy of life is that both men and women are equally made in the image and likeness of God, both equally gifted, talented, and interesting, both deserving of honor and respect in attitude, word, and deed. I am horrified and outraged by sexism, harassment, discrimination, misogyny, unfairness, and disrespect.

In the chapters to come you will meet some of the great women I have worked for and with. My whole life and career have been enriched immeasurably by a long list of gifted and talented women. And the greatest of them all, my steadfast partner for nearly six decades, is Lucia.

10

Fatherhood & Friendship

IF GETTING MARRIED WAS like being set free, becoming a father was like suddenly dropping anchor. Suddenly someone else is in charge and sets the priorities. Lucia and I started going together in November 1963. We married in September 1967. On March 29, 1971, our daughter Jodie Lynn was born. Eighteen months later our son Jonathan Christopher was born on September 14, 1972. Twenty-five years later the next generation began to appear. In 1997 our first two grandsons were born, cousins, just nine days apart: Dreyke Jonathan Gill and Elijah David Hoffman. In 1999, our first granddaughter was born, Sophia Lucia Hoffman. In 2001 granddaughter number two, Natalya Lynn Hoffman was born, followed just three days later by cousin Kaden Zachary Gill. In 2003, grandson number four Gabriel Leonard Hoffman was born, completing our tribe of twelve, which includes our son-in-law Andrew Hoffman and daughter-in-law Carrie Gill.

In this chapter I will introduce you to our daughter Jodie and then our son Jonathan. I will try to describe our family life together as they grew up and I tried to be a good dad. Then I will introduce you to our six grandchildren who, as I write, are becoming independent young adults. Finally, a few comments on my friends and neighbors, an invaluable part of my informal "family."

JODIE LYNN GILL

We were so excited when Lucia first got pregnant. We took Lamaze classes, multiple sessions to learn about labor and birth, in which the husband helps assist his wife through labor with breathing exercises and a couple massage techniques ("counter back pressure," I remember). When the due date arrived, we felt eager and ready but then had to wait a few more days for serious labor. Nearing midnight on March 28, we rushed over to Alta Bates Hospital in Berkeley. Next morning at 8:00 a.m. on March

29 Jodie Lynn was born a healthy, beautiful baby girl. Funny coincidence: when we showed up at the hospital we chatted with a young Black couple at the same point in their labor. Next morning I met the husband in the hallway. "Hey, how'd it go? What did you guys have?" "A little boy! You?" "A little girl! What did you name him?" "Jody! How about you?" "Jodie."

I was really happy that our first-born was a girl (and equally happy that number two was a son). This was because of my observation about birth order. A first-born child is raised, as soon as a second child arrives, with messages to lead and protect. But in our male-privileged society, a son, even if second-born, will already get those kinds of messages. I felt that daughter first, son second would provide more balance and I think it did. Jodie was very expressive, creative, and independent from day one. She was born and raised to lead. I bought a box of twenty-four cigars saying "It's a Girl" but wound up smoking most of them myself, wondering what happened to that tradition (and repeated the cigar celebration when Jonathan was born!).

Jodie's first public school experience was being bussed across town to kindergarten in Pasadena (famous for its commitment to desegregation) in the fall of 1976. We put her on the school bus the first day and drove alongside the bus all the way to her school so she could see us and feel safe. Back home in Oakland in the fall of 1977 she enrolled in the innovative Peralta Year-round Elementary school three blocks from our house. She continued in the Oakland Public Schools until high school when she got a transfer into Berkeley High to take advantage of a much better French language curriculum.

During 1984–85, when I had a sabbatical in Bordeaux, France, Jodie was enrolled in College Francisco Goya (the quatrieme level, equal to our 8th grade). She knew almost no French at the start of the school year but with Lucia's coaching, a fierce will to succeed, and a band of supportive schoolmates, she was passing some of her classes by the end of December, and at the top of a couple of them by June. In a French public school system where it is common for students to have to repeat a grade, Jodie was promoted. When she spent a couple weeks at a youth sailing camp at the end of that year, her fellow campers asked her what part of France she came from! Jodie did take four more years of high school French, more still at UC Santa Barbara, and has returned to France for a few extended immersions in the language and culture.

PIANO TEACHER EXTRAORDINAIRE

When she was six, Jodie began taking piano lessons. Her grandma Paulson was her piano lesson benefactor all the way through high school. Jodie was always good for her age and she played the occasional offertory solo at church or even at one of my New College Berkeley events. But she sometimes resisted practicing (as well as playing for our house guests). By the time she was thirteen, we just said, let's take the whole next year off while we are in France (there would be no piano in the house we rented).

Part Two: Shapers (1964–1979)

When we returned home the following year, she started up again with her teacher but soon insisted on a change of teachers so she could study jazz piano. Fine. But the practicing commitment did not improve, so we said, let's just take a longer break until you really want to commit yourself to it.

Months passed. But one day she announced to us that she wanted to start up again but go back to a classical teacher. She wanted a new teacher, preferably a female. She found Susan Waterfall who taught in her home up in the Berkeley hills. The next thing we knew, Jodie announced that our old upright piano was not good enough. It was very old and even the best piano tuner couldn't help it as much as it needed. But we told her that given her history we just couldn't invest the four grand needed for a decent new piano. That's when she decided to ask if our church, Berkeley Covenant, would let her practice after school on their beautiful grand piano. We drove Jodie to and from her weekly piano lesson but it was never certain in our minds the extent to which she was practicing, since it wasn't at home anymore.

One day, after maybe a year, Susan Waterfall came out to the car when I was picking Jodie up and invited us to a recital of her students. She told me "I think you will see Jodie has made a lot of progress." We had not heard Jodie practice for almost a year. We hoped she was diligently practicing at the church but didn't really know how serious she was. Honestly, Lucia and I had tears in our eyes as we sat there at the recital watching this beautiful, poised young lady sit down and play with such feeling and command, and as she smiled and took a bow at the end. This was not about her parents guiding her any more. On her own, Jodie had determined to take over her own musical path. There's a lesson there! We then invested the $4000 in a new Yamaha piano! After high school she did her bachelor's degree in music at UC Santa Barbara and then a master of music in piano pedagogy and performance at Northwestern University in Evanston, Illinois. Her teacher on the UCSB faculty became a close mentor and had Jodie housesit for her whenever she had to be out of town. She even gave her the keys to her sports car to drive around town when she was gone!

At Northwestern Jodie took her skills to an even higher level. She was pregnant with her first child during her final year in the program and performed her "senior" concert with a huge baby bump between her and the piano. A couple weeks later she walked through graduation commencement exercises carrying little Elijah in her arms and the Dean conferred the master's degree on "Jodie Lynn Hoffman and Elijah Hoffman." Fun story: not very long into Elijah's life we visited Jodie at her apartment and Elijah was fussing a bit. Jodie told us, "Watch this, mom and dad." She went to her piano and with Elijah curled in her lap facing the keyboard she began playing one of the pieces from her master's program. Elijah immediately calmed down. All of his nine months in the womb she had been playing the piano many hours each day. He was hearing it. We joked that when he was born he must have looked around and wondered "where were those sounds coming from?"

Jodie's degree was not just in performance but pedagogy. She was a natural born teacher. During her undergraduate days in Santa Barbara she already had many young piano students. When she moved to Evanston, she very soon had twenty or thirty students. When her Northwestern professor advised her class that it was time to find a student on whom they could practice teaching the piano, she already had twenty or thirty! Parents would call her to ask if she could possibly take on their kids as her students because "Mrs. Smith has been telling us how her kids love their teacher and want to practice for her." Jodie is a magical teacher who loves her students and inspires them to love the piano. Twenty-five years later she still is a busy and successful piano teacher. She has always tried to schedule her student piano recitals in retirement homes where the senior citizens are very appreciative audiences. At one such recital in Evanston a little old lady in the audience asked Jodie if she could use a baby grand piano she had put in storage after moving from her former home into the retirement home. She had been admiring "that young lady" who brought her students to present their recitals. Amazing daughter.

WORKER & ATHLETE

At least by the time she was six, Jodie would visit some friendly neighbors and ask if they would like to hire her to rake up some leaves for twenty-five cents per bag. Lots of business generated. When she offered to mow their lawn or wash their car, the neighbors might hire her but then help her on the job which actually was too much for her size and strength. She also developed a baby-sitting business which carried on until she left for college. Many of our neighbors and their grown-up kids even today sing her praises to us. I remember one family gave her the keys to their Mercedes in case she wanted or needed to run an errand while watching their kids! She has always loved children and they love her back. She has always had a terrific work ethic and been characterized by creativity, responsibility, determination, and a quest for excellence.

From her earliest years she became a strong swimmer (and courageous diver!), thanks to her mother (who, if I believed in reincarnation, may have been a dolphin in another life). When she was a high school sophomore we cajoled her into running the Bay to Breakers 12k race across San Francisco with us. She was not enthusiastic, to say the least; it was our record slowest time. But at Berkeley High School, to our surprise, she went out for cross-country and track. I used to jog three or four miles almost every day and was a pretty fit dad. I took her with me to Dallas when I was speaking at a nurse's conference and suggested we go for a jog in the morning. I could not keep up with her! I loved attending her track meets and cross-country races when I could. I loved watching how her track teammates (many of them champion sprinters) cheered on their little white teammate through the final stretches of her distance races. That distance running really is a great metaphor for her life: Long-term determination, fighting off pain and exhaustion.

She was always an avid reader and decent student but in high school she decided to get really serious about her academic work. At one point she announced she wanted to participate in a public affairs debate organization. The first event was an overnight conference in San Francisco. We were a little wary of the potential distractions (and danger) lurking in the city since we didn't know much about the organization or the Berkeley High kids she would be with. But it went fine. Next big thing was a two-week civic affairs program in Washington DC. But she raised the money and had a great learning experience. Her intellectual, social, and spiritual growth was more visible all the time.

I have often told the story of her faith and feistiness as a Berkeley High School sophomore or junior when she was in a required "Social Living" course on sexuality, taught by some airhead (excuse me). As the class began the teacher said something like this: "Our class will be about open discussion of these issues. Your grade is based entirely on your participation. No one's views or feelings will be criticized or rejected." Then in one of the next class meetings the teacher said "We won't be talking about traditional monogamy, sexual relations, and marriage because nobody believes in that anymore." At that, Jodie raised her hand and said, "Well I still believe in that and I think others do as well." The teacher pushed back: "why do you believe that?" Jodie told me "Dad, I couldn't just quote Jesus or the Bible, so I gave her the basic underlying reason: we believe that it is relationally, physically, and emotionally very risky to engage in total intimacy without total commitment." At the end of the semester my sweet daughter was given a D in the class, despite her fulfillment of the "class participation" standard. Her only D in school ever. Total discrimination and injustice. I told her "Jodie, I am going to brag about your D for the rest of my life wherever I go."

Funny story: on that Dallas trip when she left me in the dust jogging together, I suggested we attend First Baptist Church on Sunday morning. We sat up near the front of this packed 3000-member congregation. Their famous pastor W A. Criswell preached a spell-binding sermon entitled "God Loves Extravagance"—emphasizing over and over how God chose to create extravagantly beautiful birds, not just some common brown things, same for flowers, and nature and people. He reported that in his pre-marital counseling he told a young man of modest means: "Go out and buy the biggest diamond ring you can find to give to your fiancée. . . because God loves extravagance!" Noting the extravagantly dressed, coiffed, and bejeweled Dallas ladies sitting all around us, Jodie leaned over and whispered to me "Dad, I don't think these people need to hear this sermon!" All of her life Jodie has lobbied and worked to serve and empower the poor, notably in Haiti as well as in her home town.

UC SANTA BARBARA

Growing up in Oakland and Berkeley, Jodie decided instead of her parents' alma mater to go to the University of California in Santa Barbara and experience a very different

California culture. She learned a lot. After a year in university housing, she joined a sorority her sophomore year but soon was repelled by the excessive drinking as well as sleazy ways they willingly played into a frat boy culture that demeaned women. She got out and shared apartments with other university women friends.

I was very eager for her to get involved in the UCSB InterVarsity Christian Fellowship which would strengthen her faith and build friendships with a great group of people (the campus minister was a friend of mine). After a few weeks in her freshman year, I asked her if she had made it to the big Tuesday night IVCF meeting yet. "No, dad, I haven't been able to do that because that's the night the Gospel Choir practices." Now *that* was a surprise to hear! A Gospel Choir at a predominantly white, secular state university? Jodie insisted that we should drive down for the fall concert in December, which I did. She insisted that I spend the night in her room—which I agreed to do only after her three female roommates in the suite said it would be just fine. Around eleven p.m. I needed some sleep and hit the sack on her bed—she would sleep on a sleeping bag on the floor next to me. As I gradually fell asleep, I heard her in the hallway asking the noisy bunch of male residents drinking and running around in her hallway to "please keep it quiet—my dad is trying to sleep." They piped down immediately!

The next day as we walked around campus, she was regularly interrupted to say hello and sometimes stop for a brief chat with students she passed. She always introduced me with pride to her friends but then if her conversation went on I would pull out my book and read a few minutes on a nearby bench till she was ready to move on. Far from irritating me, this made me so proud of her joyful ability to already be so connected to so many people. Later in the day she invited me to sit in on the Gospel Choir's practice/rehearsal for the program to come the next night. The choir room was jammed with the two hundred or so choir members and the only place for me to sit was on a folding chair in the front, on the side but facing the choir. Lots of chattering until a tall African-American woman named Diane White stood in front and lifted up her arms. Immediate silence. Then the piano accompanist played a chord and I swear I almost fell out of my chair as I heard the sweetest and most powerful sound (both!) as they sang "Jesus" and stopped for a beat, then "how excellent is thy name" . . . and onward in a soul-full, worshipful Gospel anthem. Then they rocked it Gospel-style. It was incredible. I told Jodie afterward that I, too, would be in the choir rather than the IVCF group if I had to make a choice. It was like a little bit of heaven.

Black Gospel music had been a significant part of our family from before Jodie and Jonathan were born. The Edwin Hawkins Singers and Helen Stephens's Voices of Christ Choir were two of the groups whose concerts we frequented. Our house rang out with Gospel Music every Sunday morning as we got ready for church listening to Sheila Robinson's program on KSOL-FM, the Bay Area's premier soul music station. Our Gospel record (and later CD) and tape collection was often the sound track to our lives at home and on the road. No surprise that Jodie got so deeply into it.

The concert the next night sold out a six-hundred-person theatre on campus. Ten bucks a ticket. Every academic quarter for the next four years had the same story and Lucia and I often drove down to attend. I met the choir director and learned that Black graduate students in the music program had insisted that the great musical legacy of the African-American church should be represented in the official curriculum. The university and music faculty agreed. Many secular and state-sponsored universities (Cal Berkeley included) now have the same kind of program. The choir class is for credit and is open to all students, as it should be. I know there is some real anti-religion bias and sometimes persecution on campuses. But it would be wrong for all Christians to abandon our universities. There are all kinds of ways, official as well as unofficial, to be present and visible and positive.

ENTER ANDREW HOFFMAN

As a senior, Jodie had already experienced some male student suitors, for better and worse. One guy was really broken-hearted when she broke off the relationship because he just couldn't share the faith at her core. But not too long after this, she started telling us about a fellow-student in her music program named Andrew Hoffman, a classical guitar and comparative literature major. This, she said, was so great—to have a solid Christian guy friend with whom she could talk without any romantic angle to have to deal with. But a few months later she surprised us by announcing that they were in love and wanted to get married around Valentine's Day in a couple months! "Hold on! Just a minute now! This is too fast. Could we come out (now from Chicago where we had moved in 1992) and meet him?"

Jodie and Andrew invited Andrew's parents to come up from San Diego and meet with them. Lucia and I had a long phone call with Charles and Sharon Hoffman. Great people. He was long-time pastor of a United Methodist Church. Sharon was a piano teacher and photographer. We all liked each other and approved of our kids' relationship but agreed we needed to slow this way down. At the close of a lovely, leisurely dinner together in Santa Barbara, I suggested we take a vote. "All those in favor of Jodie and Andrew's engagement, raise your hand." Six hands went up. "All those in favor of delaying the marriage until October (ten months later), please raise your hand." Four of the six hands went up. "Well, it looks like the marriage has been approved by a six-to-zero margin. And the delay till next October has been approved four-to-two." I remember that I said "I don't believe too much in early marriage but if I ever had to pick out a husband for my daughter, I would pick someone exactly like Andrew." Jodie and Andrew yielded and planned the wedding for the next fall.

Lucia and I privately gulped. We had just finished supporting Jodie's five years of university—and suddenly had the cost of a wedding coming up. On October 9, 1994, Charles Hoffman officiated at their wedding. Lucia and I stood together and "gave her in marriage." Jodie insisted on an expensive wedding dress but made her own (fabulous) wedding cake(s). We feasted and danced (to a taped set chosen by Jodie and Andrew), and celebrated like never before. And they were off. Jodie and Andrew spent their first year together in Santa Barbara and then moved in 1995 to the Chicago area near us, so Andrew could begin seminary studies at Trinity Evangelical Divinity School[1] and Jodie could enroll in the graduate school of music at Northwestern. Their firstborn son, Elijah David Hoffman was born in Evanston in 1997. Lucia got to be in the delivery room. I nervously paced in the hospital lobby. About the same time Andrew accepted a one-year ministry practicum at First Presbyterian Church of Evanston, Lucia and I transferred our membership there for the rest of our time in Chicagoland.

In 1998 they moved to Hershey, Pennsylvania, where newly-minted Evangelical Free Church minister Andrew, with his MDiv (and later an MA in New Testament), had accepted an invitation to a special one-year internship at the giant Hershey Free Church. At the end of that one-year program the church asked Andrew to stay on and create a ministry to young adults, a demographic the church was failing to reach. His creative initiative thrived in both numbers and quality. One year in Hershey turned into four before they moved out to Oakland in 2002. Daughters Sophia Lucia and Natalya Lynn were born in Hershey in 1999 and 2001.

During those years Jodie and Andrew were in Hershey we often wished that someday we could all live in the same town and be closer together as a family. Lucia and I decided to go home to Oakland in 2001. Jodie and Andrew moved there in 2002, one year later. Andrew's church in Hershey was very reluctant to let him go but family called. Andrew's parents and our son Jonathan and his family were in San Diego. Andrew's brother Mike and his family were in Oakland like us. After Hershey, Andrew had a deep desire to plant a new church. Oakland Free Church, with the strong backing of its pastor Dan Lahl, welcomed Andrew as Associate Pastor and with an agreement to "hive off" another congregation in two years if all went well. Sure enough, the Oakland Church grew significantly in those two years and a group of about fifteen of their members, after a year of praying and seeking God's guidance, planted a new congregation, Solano Community Church, in Albany, California, just north of Berkeley, and yards from Cal Berkeley's University Village housing enclave. We tried to be as supportive and involved as we could be for the next several years—while continuing my teaching commitments at First Presbyterian Church of Berkeley—and then spending 2010–16 in Massachusetts at Gordon-Conwell Seminary.[2]

---

1. Personal regret; Andrew also applied to North Park Theological Seminary in the Covenant denomination I called home (and part of North Park University where I taught). He had been recruited and accepted not just by Trinity but Garrett Evangelical Seminary at Northwestern and the University of Chicago Divinity School (in both cases with a full scholarship; at Trinity he would have to pay). But despite my personal pleas to the North Park Seminary leaders to pay attention to this extraordinarily gifted young man, they totally bumbled his application and lost him.

2. In 2010, we moved back to the Boston area for a newly endowed professorship invitation I couldn't refuse (2010–2016). After my retirement and return to Oakland in 2016, with Solano

PART TWO: SHAPERS (1964-1979)

THE ENERGIZER

Son Gabriel Leonard was born in 2003 in Berkeley. Jodie's piano teaching and her decision to home-school all four of the kids would be enough to exhaust anyone. But she also became extremely active in Solano Community Church. She loves people and exudes joy and care, drawing people by the dozen toward Christian faith and toward Solano Community Church. Everybody living on her street, baristas at Peet's Coffee, employees at Trader Joe's, young mothers with their babies in the park, the mail delivery people, restaurant workers, people walking their dogs, trainers and workout people at the gym, anybody she overhears speaking in French . . . everybody knows Jodie and Jodie reaches out to all of them. Literally hundreds pass through her home and eat at her table every year. She is a magnet. It's not just a surface gregariousness, either. She spends hours with people, especially young women, some of them hurting and confused.

Jodie and Andrew alike have a real passion to see people come to know Jesus Christ and the fellowship of other Christians—what we call "evangelism," sharing the good news with people. She is a strong pro-life advocate, loving children even when they are in utero, wanting to protect all people from abuse, neglect, violence, and exploitation. She (with Andrew and Solano Community Church) reaches out to the homeless and poor in the community with time as well as material support. She is a lifelong activist for racial reconciliation and the dignity and value of all people.

Not surprisingly, on the Meyers-Briggs framework she is a strong "E" (extravert) and a strong "J" (organizer). As in the case of her parents, those characteristics are both assets and (potential) liabilities. The quantity of relationships can sometimes reduce the quality time and attention given to anyone in particular, even those closest to you. Some are more understanding about this than others. And a strong, take-charge "J" organizer can overreach and become a domineering "control freak" in some situations. I know it because I have struggled at times to stay balanced—and see my brilliant daughter doing the same. But she is our pride and joy (equaled only by her brother Jonathan!).

JONATHAN CHRISTOPHER GILL

By early 1972, when Jodie was just under a year old, we discovered that Lucia was pregnant with our second child. A lot was going on with our fixer-upper house purchase in April of 1972 and my decision to leave my junior high school job to work with the Christian World Liberation Front full time starting that summer. I was in my handyman overalls working on a new fence around the front yard when Lucia

---

Community Church booming (five hundred now attending and with a strong cadre of both staff and lay leadership), we felt called back to our long-time denominational home in First Covenant Church of Oakland.

told me around 11:00 a.m. that we needed to get to the hospital in a hurry! We rushed down to Kaiser hospital a couple miles away and found their new maternity wing. Remembering Jodie's birth after eight hours of labor, I sat in the delivery room and got out the book I planned to read as the doctors and nurses rushed around trying to find their gear. Boom, all the sudden Jonathan was on the table by 2:00 p.m. on September 14, 1972. A boy! Now we would have a son as well as a daughter. We named him Jonathan, after David's best friend back in the Old Testament, and Christopher, meaning "Christ bearer"—a life that brings Christ to others. I was happy that he had a "Wurz" body—big shoulders and athletic looking (ok, I was projecting a bit!). He was a blond tow-head just like Jodie. When Lucia (a brunette) was out in public with our little blondies, she was asked sometimes if they were her kids! Cuteness got them a lot of attention when they were small.

Jonathan attended Peralta year-round elementary school and then Claremont Middle School, our Oakland neighborhood schools. He did the equivalent of 7th grade in the Bordeaux, France, public schools—starting with almost no French in the fall of 1984 but then achieving fluency by the next June. Back in the USA, he spent his first two years of high school at the College Prep School, a high-powered private school close to our home. He never cared for the (expensive!) experience, though, and transferred to Berkeley High School for his final two years. After high school he was determined to go down to San Diego State—where the weather would be warm all year round. San Diego has been his home ever since. Jonathan completed a year or two of college but began a career even in his teens as a personal trainer and fitness expert that did not require a formal degree. Most of his expertise has been acquired by personal study of health, nutrition, anatomy, and kinesiology. He has found, over nearly thirty years, that even job applicants with degrees in kinesiology and fitness (from San Diego State and elsewhere) rarely know the human body or fitness and nutrition basics as you would think they should. More on his fitness business below.

GROWING UP JONATHAN

Jonathan was a peaceful, joyful, loving kid growing up. Jodie might stir things up in our family, Jonathan calmed us down. Cooperative and positive, he was. He was (like his sister) a great reader and very smart. A memorable example of this was his year in France at age twelve. Jodie, Lucia, and I worked incredibly hard at acquiring and improving our French. Jonathan just seemed to naturally absorb it. It always seemed to me that he had the most natural French accent in the family. And even though he has not taken language classes or been French-immersed for thirty years, he still can flip the switch and speak French with us and read or listen to French material with great comprehension.

When we lived in France, I decided to teach him how to play chess. He quickly understood the rules and I suggested we have a fifty-game tournament. I took it easy on him and won maybe seven of our first ten games, having to play more carefully every game. But from game eleven to game fifty he must have won at least thirty-five of the forty! I would take a lot of time figuring out my moves. More and more he was just dancing around in his chair and would make his moves in a flash. The whole family was witness that I would often go to bed replaying our matches in my head. Sometimes I got out of bed in the middle of the night and went into the living room to study the chess board and try to figure out some better strategy and moves! I lost big but was incredibly proud to have a son like this.[3] There is something about the capacity to see the whole board and think three or four moves ahead of the game. You can see Jonathan's mind working like this in his business career as well.

From his earliest years you could see Jonathan was an exceptional athlete. Like his mom he became a powerful swimmer from childhood and worked some as a lifeguard. Youth soccer was the most popular organized sport as he grew up. He never got interested in playing baseball, basketball, football or track, the popular sports of my generation, but he started playing youth soccer at age five or six. I used to take him to his midweek practices and Saturday games. He was always one of the two or three best players on his (usually winning) teams. I took a coaching class and became an assistant coach for some of his teams—and loved scrimmaging with the boys. On our eight-week camping trip through Europe in summer 1982, Jonathan and I often kicked the ball around. We had contests to see how many times we could juggle the ball without it hitting the ground—usually ten to twenty. Then one day I suddenly juggled it fifty-two times, a huge and sudden increase. Then Jonathan took his turn and juggled it fifty-five times! Dad's big record stood for about ten minutes!

In Bordeaux during 1984–85 we loved rooting for the professional Girondins de Bordeaux, one of the best soccer teams in France (and Europe) in those days. Jonathan tried out for (and made) Le Coq Rouge, one of the best youth soccer teams in the region. He did as well playing for his Bordeaux team as he did for his USA teams. It was a great experience—with one exception. When Le Coq Rouge was invited to play an exhibition game in the city stadium before the big pro team's match, Jonathan was left off the roster so only French boys could play, a painful injustice and prejudice. Back home Jonathan played for Berkeley High School and qualified for a regional all-star team that played in the Netherlands and Scandinavia.

But his interest was shifting to weight-lifting and fitness. When he was just 15, we wrestled on the floor in front of the New College faculty, staff and families at a Pt. Reyes retreat—and he managed to pin me on my back, despite my best defensive efforts, to the cheers of his mother and everybody else! About that time, I stopped working out at the YMCA and created a workout set-up in my study, with barbells and dumbbells, an inclined bench and a "lat machine" we built in the corner of the room. We worked out together at home until we really craved a better set-up. In 1988 Gold's

---

3. Jonathan's sons Dreyke and Kaden have also taken immense pleasure in wiping out grandpa in chess!

Gym opened up in downtown Berkeley and we both joined. He was now a junior in high school and soon was lifting almost as heavy weights as I was. By his senior year, he was able to bench press three hundred pounds, when I always topped out around two-eighty-five. Jonathan was also noticing the personal trainers working with clients in the gym and the seeds of his future calling were planted.

Jonathan always had a terrific work ethic. As a little guy he helped me with my building and remodeling projects (as I had helped my own dad when I was growing up). He got stronger and stronger and helped me schlep lumber and concrete to our home—and debris to the dump. Along with Lucia, he helped me paint not just our house but New College hallways, offices, and classrooms. When New College moved to another campus building with more space, he was my helper dragging heavy furniture and file cabinets from the ground floor up to our new second floor faculty offices (my faculty colleagues did not feel the call to help and probably didn't have the necessary muscle—except for my assistant Ken Morris, as hard a worker as I ever met in my life). Jonathan had a great attitude and a hilarious sense of humor so our toil was accompanied by lots of laughter. An especially memorable home project was when we moved the wall of our living room out to the former edge of a long porch running across the front of our house, adding ten more feet to the living room. It was a huge project but made an amazing improvement to our house, giving us a big gathering space. He was just an incredible helper to me whenever I needed him (often!).

ENTREPRENEUR, MANAGER, DAD

As a kid, Jonathan went out into the neighborhood and sold his lawn mowing and car washing services as Jodie had done. When he was ten he got a San Francisco Chronicle newspaper delivery route which he kept into his early teens. He worked for several businesses during the rest of his high school days, including a donut shop, a pizza business, Noah's Bagels, a video rental store, and as security at a night club. He even got a gig modeling leather jackets (handsome guy he was). The kid kept busy! He also observed at first hand a lot of bad management (and employee) behavior and practices—an education that shaped his own business and management practices in the future in a much more exemplary direction.

After high school, Jonathan began working in San Diego as a personal trainer. He realized that the buff and beautiful young people near the coast had little money and their gyms were crawling with wannabe personal trainers. So he moved a bit inland and found great success as a personal trainer and salesman for a gym. The owner loved him and promised him commissions on the dozens of new clients he signed up. But the owner reneged on paying the commissions and was arrested for selling steroids and other illegal activity. So at age twenty, Jonathan and his Berkeley buddy John Sims (also working as a personal trainer) decided to branch out on their own and start a personal training business. They signed on to rent a small space in a shopping mall, maxed out their credit cards to buy some basic equipment and install some wall mirrors. They passed out advertising flyers and drew in some clients, including a cute woman named Carrie Gonzales who worked at a photo shop in the mall. Some of those early clients are still with Jonathan almost thirty years later.

Carrrie and Jonathan were married (I got to officiate) on October 24, 1993. He was twenty-one, the same age that I got married. Carrie's Hawaiian father Anthony was an expert in shoeing horses. Her mother Robyn got into real estate, buying, rehabbing, renting, and selling properties in San Diego and Hawaii. Carrie was herself very athletic and was a champion roller skater in her youth. For many years she helped Jonathan develop his Gill's Fitness business but in recent years moved into the food and hospitality business—waitressing, bartending, managing both the front and back ends of some great restaurants in San Diego. She became a much sought-after food and hospitality organizer not just in San Diego but Las Vegas, San Francisco and elsewhere for big conventions for tech industry giants and other industries. She is an amazing, gifted woman.

Jonathan learned early that eccentric (pronounced "e-centric") training was the best way to build muscle and strength (often called "negatives"—where you resist a heavy weight as, for example, you slowly let the weight pull your arms down in your curls, or resist a barbell slowly lowering to your chest, or resist a heavily loaded leg press machine as it slides down toward your contracted legs). The fastest way to bench press three hundred is not to gradually add weight but to load it up with more than you can press and slowly lower it to your chest. He had tremendous success, not least with older clients who had been told they would never ski or do other sports again. But e-centric training requires a strong and well-trained "spotter" to help lift the weights into position and then protect you from injury. This remains a key feature of Gill's Fitness—hands-on training tailored to each client's strength and needs.

So Jonathan had a brilliant idea: to design (and patent) a leg press machine and a shoulder press "Smith" machine with electric motors and clutches where users can push a button to pull the weight back off and then resist it when coming down on them. A client might resist 700 pounds on the way down but be incapable of leg pressing it back up without a spotter—or Gill's machine! Great muscle growth and strength are the payoff. He invested a lot of money and effort into this product development but it came at the expense of developing his paying customer base. Business was tough. Cash flow was barely enough. But just then, in the late 1990s, a fitness columnist at the San Diego Union-Tribune devoted his monthly column to the story of a San Diego attorney who had rebounded from injury and not just regained but vastly improved his health and fitness—by training with Jonathan Gill and his methods (the first of several stories about Gill's Fitness over the coming years). The phone began to ring off the hook (or buzz incessantly!) from interested clients and the rest is history.

Soon there was an enlarged workout space in Mission Valley, a staff of six or seven trainers, themselves taught the eccentric techniques by Jonathan. The studio was always immaculate, the trainers dressed neatly, and clients were cared for in best practice ways. Word of mouth by satisfied clients was the main recruiting tool, but Jonathan also gave (not "sold") his clients high quality "Gill's Fitness"-branded hats, golf shirts, workout bags, umbrellas, folding chairs, and the like. In the neighborhoods and on the golf courses of San Diego, satisfied clients were walking advertisements for the business, regularly provoking inquiries "What is Gill's Fitness?"—and then new customer sign-ups. He paid his staff well-above-normal personal trainer wages. You will not be surprised that I dedicated my book *It's About Excellence: Building Ethically Healthy Organizations* to "Jonathan Gill, Founder and proprietor of Gill's Fitness, consistent exemplar of both ethics and excellence, beloved and admired son." Watching him as he interacts with his clients, manages and cares for his staff, and has contributed to the community and those with special needs warms our hearts and makes us so proud.

Jonathan's interests go beyond fitness training. He was becoming a competitive mixed martial artist and fighter, though he backed off from competition after injuries risked threatening his own health. Though he didn't show much interest in American football growing up, he supported and often coached his two sons through fun Pop Warner and school-based football seasons. His handyman and building skills have left a positive mark wherever he has lived. While he dropped out of San Diego State to run his own business, he is an inveterate and wide reader, the match of any college graduate in the breadth of his learning and interests, always recommending books and podcasts we should read or hear. He has a deep interest in geological and ancient history, not least, in the almost inexplicable building achievements of Machu Pichu, the pyramids, and other construction wonders of the world. He tweaked his diet toward healthier and healthier levels and has been a vegan for many years (and a knowledgeable wine connoisseur). He has drafted some fantasy fiction that might someday be published.

Jonathan is an amazing guy. We only get down to see him in San Diego (five hundred miles away) a couple times each year but, almost always at his initiative, we have an hour on the phone once or twice each week. We thank God for our son.

GILL FAMILY LIFE ON 62ND STREET

Our family life was a swirl of activity over the years. My days usually started with running off to the gym for a one-hour workout. Lucia got the kids ready and off to school. Lucia and I tried through the years to play tennis or otherwise hang out together one morning a week after the kids were at school. After school there were soccer practices and games, piano lessons, and sometimes visits with grandparents. We watched some television, like the Cosby Show and Family Ties. Lots of homework—for Lucia until her graduation from Cal in 1981 and for both kids until they left home in 1989 and 1990. We always sat around the table and had dinner together in the evening, and often read the Bible together after the meal. Sometimes we played games like boggle, scrabble, or canasta (Lucia also played these a lot with the kids when they got home from school in the afternoon). I worked long hours and was out at some speaking gig, meeting, or class maybe two or three nights a week—but my office was just a mile from home and I had the flexibility to skip out and watch the kids at a soccer game or piano recital. I often hung out with the family all evening and then worked on my computer organizing and writing projects from 11:00 to 2:00 while everyone else went to bed. I feel like I was pretty reliably present in family life despite my super-busy work life.

We had lots of family and friends to our place for dinners and sometimes were invited out by others. Lucia cooked up a storm for dinners with my students and colleagues and for neighbors and church friends. Her cooking was legendary. I only got busier with cooking, kitchen chores, and doing my own laundry after Lucia took a full-time job outside the home in 1988. Our kids were expected to help with household chores, especially by keeping their rooms clean. Our house was filled with music, some of it "live," some recorded (classical, gospel, blues, rock, and jazz). For three or four years, between 1972 and 1990, we rented a room in our house to a friend or a visiting scholar. We eventually decided this was too disruptive to our family privacy and routines. That extra room became just our guest room. Undoubtedly the most memorable renter was Ingeborg Goethel, a (very loyal) East German visiting professor at Cal Berkeley. When the Berlin Wall came down in 1989 she watched it on tv with us but paced around the room muttering and totally upset that the communist system, in which she was among the privileged minority, disintegrated before our eyes seven thousand miles away.

After Jodie was born our VW bug was too small so we traded it in on a used VW bus which we repainted blue and gold (Cal colors) and drove for ten years not just locally but on camping trips up and down the Pacific Coast. In the summer of 1982, we made our first trip to Europe. From 1971 to 1981 my interaction with Bordeaux sociologist and theologian Jacques Ellul was limited to exchanging letters. But thanks to the efforts of my boss at New College Berkeley, Ward Gasque, we were able to spend two months traveling around Europe in summer 1982—including a two-week stay in Bordeaux. I did not want to leave my wife and kids out of my experience discovering Europe so I waited until we could all go together. We sold our old VW bus and bought the new version VW Vanagon, which we picked up in Frankfurt on arrival. First stop was at a camping sore to buy a couple little tents, sleeping bags, pillows, a cooler, and a few other basic items.

We had purchased a big guidebook to all the campgrounds of Europe and we were off—all over France, Germany, Switzerland, a little bit of Italy, Spain, and England—and all costing an average of $6 per night for a camping spot. We loved all the international diversity in the campgrounds and had daily opportunities (sometimes necessities) to use our French and German. The VW purchase plan was called "European delivery." We actually bought it new through an American dealer, then intercepted it in Germany and used it in Europe before returning it to VW in Europe to ship to our California home. Two years later, for our sabbatical 1984–85, we did the same thing again. And when Lucia and I spent 1999–2000 in Sweden and France, we did the European delivery routine again with a Volvo S80 (intercepted in Gothenberg). It has always been a great deal, saving dollars and facilitating our travel in Europe.

I think our kids grew a lot in poise, confidence, and people skills just by being part of a home with lots of people, young and old, diverse in every imaginable way, passing through. They got very comfortable expressing themselves and meeting new people. Being an active part of Berkeley Covenant Church was also a significant part of our family life. God and God-talk were central to our family. Jodie embraced it all and has continued our long family tradition of personal faith and active church membership. Jonathan went through confirmation class and was baptized as a young teenager (by me in San Francisco Bay where our church met for the occasion) but he never seemed to personally come alive as an enthusiastic Christian. He has rarely visited a church over the past thirty years. This doesn't mean he is anti-Christian and he is certainly an exemplary character with high ethics and he respects our faith. But I learned that parents have to let their children go, leave it to God and to them as independent adults to navigate their own path—not just religiously but educationally, vocationally, and geographically. No matter what parents may dream or hope, we need to let them go and just encourage and pray for them, no matter how painful some aspects of that might be (e.g., moving far away).

I feel so very grateful that our kids have always loved us and wanted to be together. The fact that they both chose to get married in their early twenties (and have made it work for twenty-five years or so since then) I take as an affirmation of sorts. They watched our marriage and then took the plunge themselves. Funny story: Lucia and I did have some big arguments (I can't remember what about!) and I can remember a couple times when one or the other teenager told us to sit down with them at the dining room table and calmly articulate our perspectives without interrupting each other. Our kids as our marriage counselors! They certainly saw us hugging and kissing and helping and dancing with each other a lot, so I think our example was positive. We may have had big disagreements (all four of us) and hurt each other—but I think we learned how to acknowledge our various sins and failures, take responsibility, and both ask for and deliver forgiveness. Not perfectly of course!

When I took Jodie down to UC Santa Barbara to begin her university days, I cried as I drove away. When Jonathan moved to San Diego and left home, I didn't cry (Lucia probably did) but I had an aching sadness at losing him from our daily life. Jodie and I are temperamentally similar and Jonathan and Lucia are similar in temperament. Of course, these are generalizations and there are important ways that Jonathan and I are alike—same for Jodie and Lucia. But I think those cross-gender relationships are especially important for the kid's future relationships with the opposite sex. If a daughter knows that her dad adores her, thinks she is beautiful, talented, and strong, she will be less vulnerable to domineering, controlling guys. She will be looking for a *partner*, not a father figure she never had. Same for a son who has a great mom: he will not be looking for someone to be his mother but for an equal partner.

There is also an identity issue. A son grows up realizing he is a male like his dad. He will inevitably feel some pressure to measure up to his dad. He is not female like his mom so feels no pressure to fit into her pattern. As the boy becomes a man he needs to differentiate himself from his dad (and the dad needs to let go and encourage the son to be free and be all that God has created him to be). The same dynamic applies to daughters and their moms. The daughter needs to differentiate herself from her mother, so there could be some clashes. The daughter is safe from the same expectations with regard to her dad. As the years go by, however, I think those needs to differentiate from the same-gender parent recede as the kids become independent and confident in who they are (and as the parents finally back off and let go!). We probably looked great as a fun-loving family with a daughter and son living in a cute house with a white picket fence back in the 1970s and 1980s. We had struggles and conflicts and made mistakes just like every other family. We were by no means perfect. But I loved being dad and husband in this family and often thank God for the experience.

SIX GRANDS RICH

With Jodie and Jonathan we were already blessed far more than we deserve but we thank God for the next generation that came into our lives. We are blessed with six wonderful grandchildren. Let me briefly introduce them, in the order of their birth.

Dreyke Jonathan Gill was born in San Diego May 31, 1997. Dreyke (pronounced "drake") has been the sweetest, kindest young man imaginable since he was born, an incredibly loyal grandson who still phones us off and on. He was always an athlete, a great swimmer, and a soccer and football player growing up. He is very smart (and funny) but, like his dad, decided (so far) to enter the job market rather than go on to college. He has assisted his dad as a trainer at Gill's Fitness and moved into the restaurant business, following his mom. As a young child he scared us all to death when he leaned on a window screen that fell out of the second story window of their apartment and fell maybe twenty feet—fortunately onto some bushes that saved him from serious injury. Even as a small kid his fitness and athleticism probably helped save him as well.

Elijah David Hoffman was born in Evanston June 9, 1997, just nine days after his cousin. He became a strong swimmer from his earliest years and in high school added mountain hiking and skiing to his athletic life. Starting at age two he learned the violin with Suzuki method lessons (emphasizing hearing over reading music). By his teens he was an accomplished violinist, sometimes even playing for public events. All these years his mom also taught him piano and he picked up the electric bass which he often played in the band at church. He has perfect pitch and huge natural talent though he has been disinclined to pursue it all since high school. Elijah has done some college but not found his passion there (yet?). He has explored several jobs including retail sales at REI, pizza delivery, and working for a moving company (in Boise, Idaho).

Sophia Lucia Hoffman was born in Hershey, Pennsylvania, August 4, 1999. She reminds us that she plans to live in three centuries before she is done. Like Elijah, she also became a superb violinist who played and swayed with deep feeling—and also showed some impressive talent improvising on the piano. She was active in ballet for several years in her youth. We loved watching her in her youth ballet and violin performances. Sophia also became a strong swimmer. Since high school she has blown us away with her incredible balance slack-lining! Sophia has always loved children and been a high demand child care-giver (sometimes teaching violin along with it). She has done the first two years of college and is interested in child development.

Natalya Lynn Hoffman was born in Hershey, Pennsylvania, August 23, 2001. Natalya like her siblings, became an excellent swimmer and musician. She participated in ballet with Sophia in her youth. She has become an excellent cello player (complementing her older siblings' violins), singer, and song writer. She is learning guitar as well (her dad was a classical guitar major at UCSB). During high school Natalya tried out for and joined a youth chorale called Voena, sometimes called on to sing solos or accompany with her cello. Voena's performance schedule took her to Dubai, Cuba, and other exciting venues. After spending her first year of university in Paris she was a sophomore at Diablo Valley College and is now working on a music degree at the Berklee School of Music in Boston. She is quiet but with an impish sense of humor. When she was just learning to say a few words as an infant I happened to babysit her for an evening when nobody else was around. She would occasionally say "grandma"—and I would say back "grandpa, say grandpa." Her response was always "grandma." When Jodie came to pick her up and asked me how it went, I said "it was great, we had a good time. But when I tried to get her to say grandpa she could only say grandma—at which point Natalya chimed in from the blanket where she was lying 'grandpa.'" She was teasing me the whole time. People used to say Natalya was my favorite but what happened was that whenever she was near me she would climb up into my lap for a long stay. Another time I was headed to a Cal football game and whoever had been planning to go with me backed out at the last minute. I wondered out loud about taking Natalya but we all thought that taking a five-year-old to a noisy three-hour event would probably be too much (and I knew I wouldn't want to leave early). Natalya suddenly had the saddest little face I have ever seen and asked if she could go with me. We had a wonderful three hours together (she, sitting on my lap most of the time!). (I did take the other grands to Cal football and Oakland A's games with me at one time or another—one time impressing Elijah when I caught a foul ball with my one bare hand!).

Kaden Zachary Gill was born August 26, 2001, (three days after his cousin Natalya). Kaden played soccer as a kid and then really got interested in football. He became a star running back and defensive back in Pop Warner and then at Point Loma High School. His broken field running, sure-handed pass catching, and reliable, tough tackling as a defensive back, often competing against much bigger players, earned him lots of recognition and acclaim in the prep football world. I have flown down to San Diego to watch him play every fall—and flown him up to watch a Cal Bears' game with me in Berkeley. His senior year performance was outstanding until he suffered a broken leg in a game late in the season. Kaden has been an outstanding student in the classroom and is now beginning his college studies and the possibility of some college ball.

Gabriel Leonard Hoffman was born in Berkeley November 23, 2003. He was the youngest and smallest in the family until his last year or two of high school when he sprouted upward, started serious weight training and became a tall muscular powerhouse. Gabriel also took violin lessons and with his older three siblings would set up on the sidewalk in front of Peet's Coffee or at a shopping mall or next to Union Square in San Francisco. Crowds of people would stop to listen to this cute little classical string ensemble (while all the old and young hippies with guitars down the block had no audience). They left a violin case open for donations (in the hundreds of dollars) which paid for their lessons and instrument purchases. Sometimes they raised the money for homeless ministries and other good causes. Lucia and I often went to watch and listen. I remember one time some San Francisco beat cops voluntarily did some crowd management to protect the kids and help the foot traffic get around their impromptu street audience. Gabriel has been a Boy Scout and worked his way up to the edge of becoming an Eagle Scout. He is working some as a life guard and is a surfer. He is beginning college, thinking about possibly studying kinesiology and physical education.

When any of the six grands had sleepovers with us growing up, I had to replicate my pattern from when Jodie and Jonathan were young, get my guitar out of the closet, and pull up a chair in the little alcove looking into our kids' old bedrooms where the grands were going to sleep. I played the old songs we used to sing together at night as Jodie and Jonathan lay in their beds in the dark. I told the grands the same wild adventure stories I invented to tell their parents when they were little—especially one about a "Green Monster" that escaped from a lab at Disneyland and another about a wild ride on a deer's back through the Oakland hills. Then we prayed together and they flew off to dreamland. And yes, I had to drive them by our old houses where we grew up in Sheffield Village and replicate the ride from my parents' house on Revere down the hill to Lucia's on Marlow Drive.

Grandma Lucia was an even more memorable part of their growing up, always providing tasty snacks she would have ready for them when they got to our house, taking them to the zoo and to animal shelters and pet stores to pet the little puppies and kittens and look at all the colorful birds. On August 8, 2008 (08.08.08), she took the Hoffman four to eight different parks around town to play. She taught them all to love playing canasta. As each one turned around fourteen, she took them on a special, one-on-one, "Grandma and me" ten-day tour of Paris (which Lucia knows extremely well after many visits there over the years). Small wonder that almost everyone (adults!) who hears about this asks Lucia, "could I be your grandchild?"

These days it is harder than ever to get the whole tribe together because of busy work and school schedules but individually and together Lucia and I have flown or driven to San Diego as often as possible—and gotten together with the Hoffmans (who live five miles from us) individually or together as often as possible. We are trying to have a monthly "Big Family Dinner" but sometimes none of the grands can come. Phone calls, e-mails, text messages, and instagram communications happen a lot. There was a time when we could all gather in our house for Thanksgiving or Christmas. Four times we also rented vacation homes near the Russian River, at Lake Tahoe, and in central California for a wonderful week together, rafting, water skiing, playing games and having fun together.

We are a tribe of outspoken individuals, pretty diverse in faith, philosophy, political leanings, and lifestyle. We have had serious (and trivial) disagreements and conflicts at times. I keep hoping someone in the tribe will eventually want my big library—but no prospects of that yet. We enjoy eating together even though half the tribe is now vegan (fortunately all of us omnivores also like to eat plants). We all really enjoy good coffee and the fruit of the vine. We dream of spending another week all together when possible. But in the meantime, we all would say we love our family, our tribe, and are so grateful for our history together, our present blessings, and our hopes for the future.

FRIENDS AND NEIGHBORS

I have been so blessed by my parents, sisters, wife, in-laws, children and grandchildren. Their love, support, and counsel have been amazing. But I can't leave this chapter without a brief word about the "non-relative family" that has accompanied me in my "marginal" life. Friendship means everything to me. When it is reciprocated, it lasts my whole life. That starts with my elementary and high school friends—some of whom I mentioned in chapters six and seven and who continue to be a treasured part of my life. Several of my best friends have been part of my history in the Plymouth Brethren and since. I mentioned Al and Nancy Erisman and John and Marj Erisman in chapter eight. Al and John are my "brothers from another mother." Many of my friends are from the churches I have called home over the years. In many churches it has been traditional to use the biblical language and call each other brothers and sisters—and refer to the older members as "uncles and aunts." Facebook, phone calls, e-mails, and zoom meetings help us stay connected and, when possible, meet face-to-face.

Things were so crazy during my BA and MA experiences at Berkeley and SF State (see next chapter) and I didn't stay connected to classmates or professors from

Part Two: Shapers (1964–1979)

those universities. Much different was my experience as a PhD student at USC. I organized an in-person forty-year reunion of our PhD class of 1979 on the USC campus with fifteen of my fellow-students and professors from those years together (and a zoom follow-up since then). Heidi Hadsell is just one of those wonderful comrades, conveniently retired a mile from our house these days. In coming chapters, you will meet some precious friends from the other "channels" where I have lived and worked. Lifelong friendship is so important to me. I often used to tell my students that I would be their "professor-for-life" if they wanted to stay in touch. Many do.

Lucia and I really believe in neighborhood as well. We have been active organizers of block meetings and street parties on 62nd Street. We have helped build trust, community, and solidarity on a street that once was troubled by racial conflict and misunderstanding. We have worked with our neighbors to prepare for possible fires, earthquakes, and other problems from parking to noise to trash. We have had many of our neighbors into our home for dinners. We have helped map out our block so we know everyone's contact and emergency info, the locations of every gas, water, and electric shutoff (in case of emergency), every pet, child, and disabled person who might need attention in a crisis. We have two exterior sheds on the block with emergency supplies and most of us have taken city-sponsored training in disaster-preparedness. We have been meeting monthly for several years with three other couples in an "oenology" (wine-tasting) group. When we were leaving in 2010 for my teaching gig in Boston, the neighbors threw a farewell party out in the street to wish us well and make us swear to return home. One of the neighbors piped up and praised the diversity on our block, ending by saying "we even have Evangelicals on our block—and we like them!" My guess is that on any Sunday morning it is only Lucia and I, along with our African-American neighbors, who drive off to church. Our neighborhood is by no means great just because of Lucia and me; we have several other long-term community builders and leaders. But when I think about family, I have to also thank God for our "family" on the block.

11

Cal Berkeley & SF State (1964–1971)

THE ONLY UNIVERSITY I even thought about attending was the University of California at Berkeley. Private university tuition (like at Stanford across the Bay) was completely out of the question. Those were not my people anyway. I had grown up a fan of Cal sports teams like the national champion basketball team coached by Pete Newell in 1959 (runner-up in 1960)—and the 1959 Rose Bowl football team led by quarterback Joe Kapp. One of my favorite elders in my home church was Stephen Wilhelm, Professor of Plant Pathology at Berkeley (whose son Paul was one of my best friends in those days growing up). My good friend in school, Wally Paroczai, had an older brother at Cal and I envied him the leather-sleeved Cal jacket he used to wear all the time. I was proud that there were more Nobel Prize-winning faculty at Cal than any other university in the world. It was certainly not just for Cal's sports reputation that I wanted to go there, not just because it was inexpensive and twelve miles from my home. I wanted to go to what I thought was, by any measure, the greatest university in the world..

As a high school junior I applied for admission and got a letter of acceptance just before my senior year began. I was admitted based on the core required subjects I had already taken and in which I earned at least B grades: science, math, history, English, German, and social studies. I didn't have to take the SAT or other admission tests. When my high school football teammate, Roger Zolldan, and I commuted together to the Cal campus in September 1964, we sat outside of McLaughlin Hall with several hundred other incoming engineering majors and heard the engineering dean say: "Welcome to Cal engineering. This is an elite program and I have to alert you to the fact that only one out of four of you will actually graduate from this program." I remember looking around at the crowd and wondering, "who are the other three?" Hah! One of the three of four to drop out of engineering would be me within a year.[1]

---

1. The irony is that my eventual applied ethics interests came to include a major emphasis on technology, including engineering, of course.

I earned my BA degree in four years and spent a required fifth year enrolled in the School of Education to get my "Standard Secondary Teaching Credential." I then taught junior high school for three years (1969–72) while I also earned my MA in history at San Francisco State University (1968–71). In this chapter I want to describe my educational, intellectual, and vocational pilgrimage and the social and cultural impacts on me during this time period. But let me begin by describing my work and other contextual circumstances that were an important part of those days.

COLLEGE JOBS

In chapter 8 I described my church-related activities that loomed large through this whole time period (ending with my excommunication in 1971). I was an active force in the youth and other activities of my church and, from 1966–71, very busy with the weekly ministry I had started at the Alameda County Juvenile Hall. After high school, organized sports were over for me. I needed to make some money to pay my college expenses. Tuition was unthinkably low: $98 per semester when I began at Cal. But my parents, caring for four young adults on one income, couldn't help pay for my school expenses (books, commuting, etc.) or my car maintenance, gas, insurance, clothing, and other things. I was just grateful to my parents for free housing and meals of course!

My high school job at Lynch's Shell paid only minimum wages—$1.50 per hour. So as soon as I graduated, I started looking for better paying employment. I got a job working at Continental Can where I operated a machine on the line that made metal oil cans. It was incredibly noisy and I wrecked my hands (eczema) with all the solvents I had to work with, but it paid just under $3.00 per hour, a huge improvement from minimum wage. Continental Can went on strike after a couple months but I soon got hired at Crown Zellarbach's Flexible Packaging factory on Williams Street in San Leandro.[2] That became my main employer until I graduated from Cal in 1968. I worked from forty to seventy hours per week during my summers and Christmas breaks. One month in summer 1966 I worked two hundred eighty hours in four weeks—basically four seventy-hour weeks of six twelve (or ten)-hour days. Swing and graveyard shifts and overtime hours (e.g., Saturdays and anything over eight hours in a day) earned time-and-a-half or even double-time pay. When Crown Zellarbach employees went on strike in 1967, I shifted over to a grimy, depressing Owens-Illinois factory out in Richmond for a miserable six weeks until the CZ strike ended.

The first summer at Crown Zellarbach I worked at the end of a production line of packaging material, like the wrappers that would enclose loaves of bread sold in grocery stores. Giant rolls of this paper would be cut down by the "splitter" machine into sixty or seventy-pound smaller rolls. Four of these smaller rolls would come rolling toward me every few minutes. I would pound a metal core into each end, wrap up and

---

2. My father worked for this company in its San Francisco headquarters but, other than being a fun coincidence, it had nothing to do with my getting hired.

tape these smaller rolls and stack them on a pallet behind me. A forklift driver would move the pallets away when they were stacked with twenty or so rolls. We got a fifteen-minute coffee and bathroom break every two hours and a thirty-minute lunch break. Otherwise, it was non-stop, not-for-the-weak, hard labor. From my second summer onward, I moved to an oil can production line and operated a "seamer" which put lids on one end of oil cans racing through the line. I spent all day lifting boxes of lids, refilling my machine, and clearing up line stoppages caused by occasionally defective cans that jammed up the line.

One summer the company brought in some time and motion technocrats (enthusiasts for Frederick Taylor's "scientific management") who stood around with stop watches and clocked our movements. Their recommendation was that CZ could eliminate some workers from the production line to save money. For a few days they had me not just tending my seamer machine but jogging over to tend another machine a few yards away that cut long tubes down into oil can size and sent them on to my seamer. This led not just to exhaustion for us workers but chaos, breakdowns, more line jam-ups and costly waste. The inept efficiency experts took their stop watches and big consultation earnings and were invited to leave. Later on in my career as a technology critic and organizational consultant I was speaking not just from an ivory tower but some significant in-the-trenches experience.

I actually enjoyed my factory work. It was noisy (we wore earplugs) and we were too busy to talk with our fellow-workers during our on-line hours but during breaks we got to know and appreciate each other. I was welcomed back whenever I was free to work. I especially liked a Filipino martial artist who ran the machine before mine and an older German guy (who loved to converse in German with me) who worked the machine down the line from my seamer. They worked hard and reliably for the company and took personal pride in their work. The company had a suggestion box that offered rewards for any employee suggestion that was adopted. I got $25 one time for suggesting they install a big wall clock visible to all of us where we worked so we wouldn't have to leave our machines (risky!) and run around the corner to see if it was our break time. Another time I suggested a modification to the assembly line to install a sensor and automatic shut-off when any defective cans came off the machine that cut the tubes down to can size. This had been the main source of line jam-ups that cost time (and money from waste and lost production) to clear up. I was paid $50—though I later thought that was pretty small for a suggestion that saved them thousands of dollars. Even in those early days I couldn't keep still when I saw ways of improving things.

The benefits of this labor experience were, first of all, the money I earned.[3] Second, I got to experience the life of a hard-working factory laborer. I learned to work safely around powerful machines (I got a few cuts and finger injuries, and suffered the

---

3. I averaged about $2.85/hour for my factory wages during these four years. I felt that being a reliable, hard-working team member was part of my "faith at work" but I didn't yet think about the products themselves as ministry and service to God. That came later.

eczema on my hands, though I never missed an hour of work). I learned the stories of my fellow workers, including some of their personal and professional struggles and dreams. In all the noise and repetition of my tasks I was free to dream a bit and had some of my deepest spiritual and intellectual moments (if you can believe it) even while I worked. I also realized that I was essentially free to choose this work and could move on to my vocation as a teacher someday—whereas my fellow workers were stuck for the long haul in these jobs. I recognized my privilege.

The downside to all of this was that I never really had a vacation longer than a weekend, and often worked evenings, nights, and Saturdays as well. I was not one of those college kids who could tramp around Europe in the summer! I can remember briefly stopping by Lucia's home in the evening on my way home, grimy and exhausted, just to see my love for a few minutes of conversation before I showered and crashed in my own bed up the hill. And I would typically start my summer job on swing or graveyard shift during Spring semester finals week, when I had just a couple exam sessions but no regular classes on my schedule. In the Fall I would move to graveyard shift and keep working two or three weeks into the new semester before quitting, putting me already behind in my coursework. My Christmas vacations were similar: start up during finals week and quit a couple weeks into the January term. I thought I could do this with minimal impact on my grades, but I was wrong. I didn't become a consistently good student until after I got out of Cal. But I did have plenty of gas money and could pay my bills and take my girlfriend out to dinner once in a while at Fisherman's Grotto Number 9 or even the Tonga Room at the Fairmont Hotel in San Francisco (though Straw Hat Pizza, Kip's, or Larry Blake's were more likely destinations!).

CAL ACADEMIC PILGRIMAGE FROM ENGINEERING TO HISTORY

I started at Cal thinking I would be a civil engineer. I was a product of "mass counseling techniques" that steered bright boys into science and engineering. Something about Sputnik and Cold War competition I think. I didn't care about beating the Russians at anything but I did always love watching building and construction projects (and helping my dad with our home projects). So there I was in Cal Engineering as an eighteen-year old. I did great in my classes for the first half of the fall semester but then, partly distracted by my outside jobs and by the massive Free Speech protest on campus, I slacked off and wound up with all C's but one D in calculus. That was enough to put me on academic probation (this was well before the era of grade inflation).[4] In the spring semester I got a B in Intro to Social Science and a C in Calculus this time, but a D in Chemistry.

---

4. Not to belabor the point but the generations that followed us into Cal had much higher high school grade point averages—and much lower test scores. When I was admitted to Cal, maybe 10% of incoming Freshman failed the Subject A English composition exam and had to take the non-credit "bonehead English" course. Within a couple decades more like 70% of incoming freshmen, despite their sterling high school grades, failed the same exam. You get my point?

This rise to C average did not make up for my D in the fall so I was dismissed from the university! The one fun thing I had done was take gymnastics for physical education, got super-fit, and earned a B and an A over the two semesters, but these were not enough in academic credit to make a difference[5] Of course I felt ashamed, disgraced, and frustrated by my performance but I didn't let it keep me down. It motivated me.

Part of my problem was that I was kind of alone in those struggles to keep up. My calculus courses had about four hundred students meeting in Dwinelle Hall. Intro to Social Science had five or six hundred each semester with famed professor Nathan Glazer leading the lecture team in Wheeler Auditorium. The Chemistry lectures were by a brilliant and entertaining lecturer with a class of nearly one thousand. There were assigned discussion or lab sections led by graduate students, still with twenty-five to thirty in one's section. I don't recall having a faculty advisor to go to for help. UC Berkeley at the time had 28,000 students. I just got behind and distracted and lost my way. During that Spring semester, around Easter, I was walking up the hill toward my physics course lab session and suddenly thought "I don't want to do this! I don't want to measure waves in a tank or work with an oscilloscope!" I walked instead to the registrar's office and dropped the course (a requirement for an engineering degree). My high school teammate and Cal commuter buddy, Roger Zolldan, suffered the same fate.

As sophomores Roger and I enrolled at Chabot College, a fairly new community college with an academic program that matched up with that at Cal. I got my act together and had a B average that year at Chabot, including a year of advanced German, even writing a term paper in German on Heinrich von Kleist's *Das Erdbeben in Chili* (*The Earthquake in Chile*). I enjoyed intro classes in psychology, logic, American history, and English composition. Despite my difficulty with first year calculus at Cal I passed second year calculus at Chabot. I had decided that my calling was to be a teacher, not an engineer, but probably a high school math teacher. I wanted a career working with people, not civil engineering projects.

My application for readmission to Cal was accepted so in the fall of 1966, I returned as a junior, this time accompanied by my girlfriend Lucia Paulson, entering as a freshman. Cal also shifted in 1966 from (two) fifteen-week semesters to (three) ten-week academic quarters, an academic calendar I much preferred then and throughout my career as a professor. A minor bump in the road that fall of 1966 was a two-week bout of mononucleosis, a blood condition where one's white blood cell count gets dangerously out of control. One day when climbing a big stairway on my way to class I could hardly make it and knew something was wrong. I went to the campus hospital and took a blood test which confirmed my condition. I was ordered to avoid any contact sports and to sleep as much as possible—which I did and mostly recovered two weeks later. My long hours and late nights working in the factory were the precipitating cause and it had to stop.

---

5. Then and many times since, Cal has had a nationally ranked gymnastics team. I loved working on the still rings and parallel bars (at a very introductory level!).

In the fall quarter I experienced another 'aha" moment in my education. The first part of this was a course in Abstract Algebra. The massively rotund Professor Lubkin got the attention of our forty-member class by wearing the same white shirt the entire ten weeks. Every week there were additional food spots (easy to see even from the back row). It was a spectacular, entertaining, eccentric mess by the end of term. More significantly he would write all over the chalkboards on all four sides of the room to prove that one equals one, part of the identity principle in math. I thought to myself, "I already believed that one equals one and am not interested in spending my life in this labyrinth of abstract mathematical proofs." I only needed two more math courses to qualify as a "minor" field I could teach in high school, so I suffered through courses in statistics and in the history of math in later terms.[6]

But what should I major in to prepare for a high school teaching career? As a junior I had to declare a major and I found that the physical education department would accept me so one of the courses I took in that fall term of 1966 was called "Community Recreation." I was beginning to think a lot about "how do my Christian faith, worldview, and values relate to what I am studying? I can't live in two unconnected worlds. Biblical Christianity is about every aspect of life, not just church and personal matters." So in that Recreation class, I wrote a term paper on "Recreation in the Bible." I got a B- in the course but I am glad I lost that (mediocre) paper. After I finished it, I realized how simplistic it was but it really was the beginning of a fifty-five-year mission to integrate faith and learning.

I not only wanted to *work with people* (as a teacher) I now wanted to *study people*. I thought about sociology, psychology, and English but decided history (more concrete and fact-oriented, less speculative) was the field for me. The history department (one of the largest majors at Cal in those days) accepted me as a major and I was off and running. In order to complete the history major and graduate in four years, fully thirteen of the next fifteen courses I took over five quarters were in history. This meant a massive amount of reading and writing. But what field of history? In the winter quarter of my junior year, I took a course in the history of the Roman Empire from a young professor named Erich Gruen. Professor Gruen was a brilliant scholar and lecturer and became my academic advisor through to my graduation. He smoked his pipe while he lectured, which (along with the similar examples of C.S. Lewis, Karl Barth, Helmut Thielicke, and my USC prof Jack Crossley a few years later) became my enjoyable habit as well. I loved studying the history of the Roman Empire not least because all the issues of early Christianity and its spread and interaction with Roman politics and culture were on the table (though not the focus of the courses).

I took other courses in the Age of Cicero (Gruen brilliant again), the history of modern Europe and the United States, the Renaissance, the Ottoman Empire, and American Folklore. My course on the Reformation was taught by Luther expert John

---

6. One of the historical ironies was that at this very time (unknown to me) the future Unabomber, Ted Kaszinski, was teaching in the Berkeley math department.

Dillenberger, who would ten years later become a friend and colleague in the Graduate Theological Union next door to Cal. Teaching about Luther to what he thought were all secular Berkeley students, he dismissed the importance of the key theological motivator of the Reformation, "salvation by faith alone," saying he wouldn't spend time on theological matters because "nobody is interested in those anymore." I tracked him down after class to let him know that I (probably with others) was actually very interested in those ideas. He was surprised and, I think, pleased to hear that.

In my senior year, like all history majors, I had to take a research proseminar. I chose one led by Prof. Rafael Seeley (who did not smoke but dipped snuff during classes) on 5th century B.C. Greece. Then the capstone course for history majors was a two-quarter "Introduction to Historical Method." I chose a Roman history section and produced a long research paper on "Racial Prejudice in the Roman Empire"—focused on the Roman Senate's rejection of an application for membership by a delegation of Gauls (modern France). The research involved detective work comparing the summary by Tacitus of Emperor Claudius's speech to the Senate (against Gaul membership) and a more literal but partial record of the speech on a two-column stone inscription of which the top was broken off (so both the opening and middle of the speech were lost). I got an A and some strong affirmation that when I could choose my subject and do independent research my academic potential and performance were vastly higher than when I was confined to timed exams writing essays in Blue Books. It had been a grind but I managed to graduate from Berkeley within the four-year time frame. In Memorial Stadium, June of 1968, I was one of seven thousand students graduating in the centennial class (UC Berkeley was founded in 1868). So personal!

During my fifth year at Cal, while enrolled in the School of Education, I took more U.S. History in anticipation of that being my main subject in high school teaching. I got to take the first ever two-quarter sequence on African-American History at Cal—a curriculum addition directly resulting from massive student demonstrations demanding "Third World" studies and attention to ethnic minorities. These were extraordinary courses taught by two leaders in the field, Winthrop Jordan and Leon Litwack. They plunged me into extensive readings in African history, slave narratives, and the major voices of W.E.B. DuBois, Booker T. Washington, the Harlem Renaissance, Ralph Ellison, Richard Wright, Claude Brown, Martin Luther King, Jr., and Malcolm X among many others. The education/pedagogy courses I had to take in that fifth year, however, win the prize as the most worthless waste of educational time in my life.

SAN FRANCISCO STATE: ELEVATING AND FOCUSING MY GAME

During the summers of 1968, 1969, and 1970, I took courses toward an MA in History at San Francisco State University.[7] One motivation: high school teachers get higher

---

7. I love my Berkeley education and pedigree (while seeing clearly its challenges and weaknesses as well as strengths) but my great experiences at Chabot College and SF State convinced me that

pay for completing post-baccalaureate courses and degrees. I was also wanting to strengthen my expertise in American history. In that first summer of 1968 at SF State, I took two courses including a seminar in American Intellectual History led by Professor John Diggins, a highly-regarded expert in the field. Diggins called me in and rejected my first draft of a long paper on Walter Lippmann. I was a bit shocked but he explained that I was too heavily relying on secondary sources, and not digging down enough into the primary sources. I had just done that properly in my senior seminar at Cal but I needed Diggins's "rejection" to once and for all teach me how to do good research.

In the summers of 1969 and 1970 I took other courses in American Intellectual History (the history of ideas, values, etc.) and two courses on the history of immigrant and minority groups in America from one of the world's experts, Moses Rischin. Starting at Berkeley and continuing at SF State I was developing my focus not on the history of conflict and warfare or of the ruling classes, presidents, kings, and queens, but on the history of *people* of all social and economic classes, of all national and ethnic origins. I was interested in their ideas, their thinking, values, and their lived experiences. I still consider myself a social and intellectual historian, though the primary focus changed to ethics and values as a doctoral student. History was the "outside field" in my PhD studies at USC.

In 1970, my final summer at SF State, I took a course on "History as a Field of Study" with Professor Donald Lowe, a Chinese-American. It was a small seminar on historiography. Professor Lowe's having us all to his apartment for discussion over wine, cheese, and French bread, was as influential on my future professorial style as Professor Gruen's pipe! During my more than forty years as a professor, Lucia and I hosted droves of students for discussions over great food and beverages (appropriate to the ages of the students of course!). Now the coursework was done, my German exam was passed, and it was time to write an MA thesis, which I did in my evenings and on weekends through the academic year 1970–71. SF State offered a traditional Master of Arts degree: thirty semester hours of graduate course work following a BA in the field, passage of an exam demonstrating reading and translation competence in a foreign language appropriate to your field, preparation and oral defense of a thesis (usually 100–150 pages) presenting original research in your field. No short-cuts.

I graduated with the MA in summer 1971. My thesis topic was "Contemporary Christian Philosophies of History: The Problem of God's Role in Human History." I was not writing this for a theologically-sympathetic faculty at a seminary but for a secular one. I was not interested in winning the academic approval of (just) a band of fellow-believers. I wanted to study this problem in the public academy. I chose six

---

(probably) for most college students it may be a good idea to do the first two years at a quality community college before transferring a big university. Lucia's experience studying for two years at Pasadena City College before returning to Cal were also a high-powered, satisfying (and inexpensive) academic experience. And many state universities, like SF State, San Jose State, and Sonoma State, provide an excellent education. Another factor for me was that SF State, unlike Cal, accepted part-time MA students.

different thinkers who had each written books on God and history *since the Holocaust*. "God's Role in Human History" during the holocaust is as tough a problem as you could find. Where was our good God and what was he doing? I wrote chapters on hyper-Calvinist Gordon Clark, existentialist theologian Rudolph Bultmann, British historian Herbert Butterfield, American social ethicist Reinhold Niebuhr, political philosopher Eric Voegelin, and evangelical apologist John Warwick Montgomery—representing a very wide spectrum of opinion. I created an analytical framework to analyze and compare their views.

There was no clear, definitive, or shared answer to my big thematic question. There are insights and some help understanding the nature of God, history, human nature, collective responsibility, and the (*kairos*) moment amid the (*chronos*) trajectory of time and eternity—but it all ends in mystery, lament, and a will to fight against evil in the name and power of a good God. My director Professor Lowe and the other two faculty on my committee really liked my 130-page thesis, while distancing themselves from my faith stance. I never thought about publishing my thesis—but I should have. This successful experience made me feistier than ever about Christians entering the academy and actively representing a Christian perspective on all fields of study. I don't believe in an unbridgeable secular/sacred divide.[8] By the way, one thing I learned and have often shared with others: better to "piggyback" on other respected thinkers who have addressed your subject than to just write on your own limited authority, especially when what you are studying might challenge your professors! My master's work trying to bridge the sacred/secular divide was far from perfect but I remembered my dad's question "what are you doing about It?" And I was by no means done trying to answer that question.

SOCIAL AND CULTURAL ADVENTURES

Now I need to back up to 1964 and reflect briefly on seven events/movements that deeply affected the society and culture around me during my university days. My education didn't just happen in the classroom.[9]

Free Speech.

Within two weeks of the beginning of my freshman year at Cal, in fall 1964, the whole campus was rocked by what came to be known as the Free Speech Movement.

---

8. I do believe in a separation of church and state and at the same time am happy to recognize and value other non-state institutions (and their ideas and values) whether ideologically secular or religiously non-Christian. I am not in favor of coercion or uniformity but of meaningful, fruitful conversation and advocacy. I favor a "thick" pluralism where people can bring their whole mind and self to the table.

9. Two excellent introductions to Sixties history and culture are Todd Gitlin, *The Sixties: Years of Hope, Days of Rage* (New York: Bantam, 1987) and Mark Kurlansky, *1968: The Year That Rocked the World* (New York: Random House, 2004).

I thought I was going to be "Joe College" and get to watch the highly-rated Golden Bears football team (with quarterback Craig Morton) go to the Rose Bowl. Not a chance. Police arrested a student who violated campus regulations by sitting at a table on Sproul Plaza, trying to recruit people and raise money for an off-campus activist group. He was placed in a police car—which was rapidly surrounded by dozens, then hundreds of students and supporters calling for an end to this suppression of free speech on campus. The situation escalated with more police called in, students sitting on top of the police car, and eventually a huge sit-in in the Sproul Hall administration building. It was a non-violent protest with tactics some of the student leaders had learned when participating in Civil Rights campaigns in the American South. But it brought the university to a stop.

I was a somewhat confused, surprised, but supportive bystander of the Free Speech Movement. I believed in free speech and advocacy. I believed it was far better to invite diverse and conflicting views and values into our universities for debate, than to force such disagreements out into the political arena or into conflicts on the street. Where better than a university to host the freest speech and debate possible? As a Christian, I liked the proposal of Jewish leader Gamaliel in the New Testament book of Acts (5:34–39) who counseled would-be suppressors of the young Christian advocates to leave them be and trust that time would tell whether what they were advocating was true or not. And I liked how St. Paul in Acts 17 engaged people in public debate at the Areopagus. In chapter eight (above) I mentioned the speech against censorship by the famous Puritan John Milton—"let truth and falsehood grapple."

I am a true free speech advocate. Those who pathologically lie and, in effect, cry "fire" in a crowded theatre must be answered and sometimes silenced. But disagreement should ordinarily be welcomed. I disliked Dow Chemical's profiteering from manufacturing napalm to drop on the Vietnamese and would support actions like demonstrations and perhaps even sit-ins to oppose their practices—but I did not like the efforts at Berkeley to just shout them down and physically drive them off campus. I am not an ROTC or war guy but I did not like the attempt to drive ROTC off campus. I am concerned about harmful language that demeans, ridicules, disrespects, and misrepresents individuals and groups. But I oppose the excesses of political correctness, "trigger word" oversensitivity, and what is called "cancel culture." Too often when the minority demanding free speech gets into power they lose their way and become the new censors. Through history Christians have often been guilty of this flip from oppressed to oppressor. The Free Speech Movement at Berkeley in the 1960s benefitted and opened doors for Christian witness and advocacy as much as any other movement (as the next chapter on the Christian World Liberation Front will attest).

PART TWO: SHAPERS (1964–1979)

Civil Rights.

The movement for civil rights for Black Americans led by Martin Luther King, Jr., was in full swing during my university years. MLK was assassinated April 4, 1968, in my senior year. The struggle for voting and educational rights, and against racism, discrimination, violence, and Jim Crow segregation laws and practices was in the news all the time and widely supported on campus. It certainly awakened my consciousness and affected my politics. Growing up, I had several Black sports and music heroes but had attended schools and lived in neighborhoods where somehow I was oblivious to the depths of the problem. At Berkeley that was impossible. Awakened by what was going on in Berkeley, including in some of my classes, I could never turn back on the quest for civil and human rights. It might surprise you but I was actually much more moved by Malcolm X than by Martin Luther King, Jr., in those years. His brilliant and uncompromising speeches were the strong medicine our culture needed to hear.

Environmental Care.

The Sixties also saw the surge, if not the very beginnings, of environmental, ecological concern. Rachel Carson's *Silent Spring* was published in 1962. Three women (including UC President Clark Kerr's wife Kay) organized the "Save the Bay" movement starting in 1961 to stop the pollution and filling in of San Francisco Bay. Real estate developers, with the support of politicians, were hell bent on filling in more and more of the Bay for residential and industrial development. The Bay itself was filthy from untreated industrial and residential sewage discharges. It was impossible to swim or eat any fish caught in the Bay. Today their campaign to clean up and save the Bay is a huge success though pollution, waste, and failure to protect God's creation continue in many other domains. The environmental movement awakened in me a deep commitment to be a good steward, a sustainer and caretaker for God's creation for the health of both people and planet. This is a core mandate of biblical faith, not just a politically-correct viewpoint.

The Women's Movement.

Betty Friedan's book *The Feminine Mystique* came out in 1963 sparking a new wave and awareness of women's rights and concerns. I didn't read this book or much of the literature on feminism or the women's movement until the Seventies but from the beginning of my time in Berkeley I couldn't help but be increasingly aware of the unfair treatment of women in the home, the workplace, the university, and society. I had been raised to respect and love women but not to see the deeper sexist structures and practices in our society. I did not think (yet) about the structural inequities that meant that virtually all my professors at Berkeley were men. I am grateful for the help to wake up to women's issues and concerns beginning in the Berkeley of the Sixties. I am not in agreement with every idea or trend in feminism (or any other movement), but my understanding of biblical teaching leads me to affirm women's value and to a lifelong fight for women's rights, respect, and equal treatment in society and the workplace. I am all for the Equal Rights Amendment still shamefully stuck in Congress.

Vietnam War.

From 1966 onward, the biggest upheavals on campus (and beyond) concerned the war in Vietnam. The war could not be ignored because of the compulsory military draft. I was called in for a pre-induction physical (which resulted in a temporary deferment because of the factory-work-caused eczema on my hands). I am so thankful that I was not raised in a war-hawking, nationalistic family or church. We were grateful to be Americans but had no illusions confusing the United States with the global kingdom of God. We did not believe Christians should be coercive and violent—rather than persuasive and peaceful.

In the fall of 1966 there were rallies and demonstrations against the draft and against the war. I was fundamentally a pacifist, admiring Ghandi, Martin Luther King. Jr, and the Quaker tradition—though I felt then (and now) that there might arise extreme and exceptional situations when a Hitler must be confronted with violence. But the peace emphasis of Jesus and the New Testament was strong and central. "Blessed are the peacemakers for they will be called the children of God." Jesus is the "Prince of Peace" who famously said "Those who live by the sword shall die by the sword." St. Paul counseled "As much as it depends on you, live peaceably with all people." The broader free church tradition, of which my Plymouth Brethren were a part, the Quakers, Mennonites, and others, were pretty consistently pacifist and non-violent.

Vietnam was also not just a "generic" case of war. Mark Hatfield gave a speech on Vietnam at Berkeley that fall. I managed to get a seat in a packed auditorium and shook his hand and thanked him afterward. A Republican Senator from Oregon, Hatfield had served in the Navy in southeast Asia and was an expert on Vietnamese history. He pointed out that the Vietnamese people had a long history of fighting against colonial invaders from the Chinese to the French and now the United States. When Ho Chi Minh wrote their post-WWII declaration of independence from France, he used the words of the American Declaration of Independence! For sure he was a socialist or communist, but his main objective was to free Vietnam from colonial power, whether Chinese, French, or American. Over-reacting out of Cold War fear, the USA wanted to "stop the spread of communism" and so stepped in to support a series of corrupt anti-communist regimes in the south. I read a lot of the history of Vietnam and concluded that this war was not only unjust but unwinnable. Fifty-eight thousand American deaths (and millions more Vietnamese deaths) later, the war finally ended.

I participated in some anti-war demonstrations and protest marches but this whole episode reinforced my commitment to things like the peace corps, constructive diplomatic engagement, and people-level educational and economic assistance around the world as partners to receptive countries, and not as domineering, insensitive invaders. The subsequent U.S. experiences with Iraq, Iran, Afghanistan, Nicaragua and other countries bear this out. I am radically opposed to providing powerful weapons of war to Israel, Saudi Arabia, and others. I was happy when Richard Nixon opened up political and economic relations with China. I wish we would do the same with Cuba. Mind you, there are no perfect strategies or actions in these matters but violent, warlike interventions rarely have much upside and the downside is a series of catastrophes. My Bordeaux mentor Jacques Ellul often urged the example of the ancient Hebrew "watchman on the wall"—trying to see coming threats when situations are still distant and fluid and wise responses still possible. Bully rhetoric and threats are not the answer, not any more than violent military actions.

Third World Studies.

In 1967 and 1968 maybe the biggest campus movement, besides anti-war, was led by the "Third World Liberation Front." Huge rallies demanded that the university include courses on cultures other than the standard white, European one. "Dead white men" from the European and American tradition should not be the only voices. The rationalistic Modernism of the Enlightenment was not the only avenue to knowledge. It was not about disvaluing or ignoring the classic mainstream but about expansion and inclusion. As a Christian who truly believed that all people are made in the image and likeness of God and have extraordinary value, that all are the objects of God's providential and redemptive love and justice, I was all-in. As I mentioned earlier, this movement was the direct cause of my being able to enroll in the first-ever, two-quarter course in African-American history. It went right along with the courses in Immigrant and Minority History that I got to take at San Francisco State. I am all for an open, inclusive university where as many voices as possible are heard and their histories and cultures respected. For me it is not just a curricular and social necessity but a Christian mandate.[10]

Here's Life Berkeley.

In 1966–67 a big furor on campus was caused by Campus Crusade for Christ's project to evangelize the Berkeley campus. Berkeley was targeted for an obvious reason: it was the epicenter of the student movement and counter-culture. At the time, the other

---

10. A parallel development was the introduction of a course at Cal on the History of Christianity led by Prof. William Bouwsma—which started after I left Berkeley but became a highly-enrolled course option for decades to come. Free speech and curricular inclusion at Berkeley!

national college student ministry, Inter-Varsity Christian Fellowship, was, at Berkeley, a small, quiet, headier presence (in the late 1970s and since, Cal IVCF grew to often have three hundred or more students involved). Campus Crusade (more recently re-branded as "Cru" since the bloody European crusades proved an alienating reference) had simplified and summarized the Christian message as the "Four Spiritual Laws" and viewed their task as to present that four-fold message to everyone possible.

Crusade put on a series of campus events through the academic year including a "magic" show accompanied by a Christian talk, a concert by their well-scrubbed (and talented) folk group, talks by Crusade staff members brought in from their headquarters in Arrowhead Springs, southern California, and culminating in a talk by Billy Graham himself at UC's ten-thousand-seat Greek Theatre. Lucia and I attended those major events and enjoyed Billy Graham's usual eloquent, winsome talk (I ran down and got to shake his hand afterward, the only time I ever met him). By contrast, we were totally turned off by Crusade leader Jon Braun's glib talk about a "slick God" we could know. But the worst aspect of this campaign was Crusade's determination to share the "Four Spiritual Laws" with every person on the Berkeley campus. Their message had some traction in the fraternities and sororities (Crusade targeted sports stars and fraternity leaders on college campuses, thinking they were leaders)—but the Greek scene was in radical decline at the time. Many in the campus population got button-holed by Crusade folk as they walked across campus. To be sure everyone got the message, Crusade folk began phoning everybody. Some of these calls had to be late at night toward the end of the campaign to be sure literally everyone was presented with the Four Spiritual Laws. Many were aggravating, unwelcome intrusions. Result: maybe a few conversions (I don't know the statistics) but a widespread anger at these aggressive, simplistic crusaders and a negative impression of evangelical Christianity for years to come.

Berkeley has always been a sort of "target" not just for Christian evangelists but for all other religious groups and movements, East and West. When Cal was founded in 1868 its leaders committed to a secular university but welcomed the seminaries clustered around the campus, especially on the northside "holy hill." Anglicans, Dominicans, Franciscans, Jesuits, Unitarians, Methodists, Presbyterians, and Baptists formed the Graduate Theological Union (today with Mormons and Muslims also part of the neighborhood). The GTU created a magnificent joint theological library and some joint-programs with UC Berkeley in Near Eastern Studies and other fields. Churches of all denominations also clustered around the campus. In particular, First Presbyterian Church of Berkeley became a bright light for thousands who came through (or stayed in) the university community, with sometimes three hundred Cal students in their college fellowship.

There were also some street preachers who came to campus, the most famous of whom was "Holy Hubert" Lindsey who almost daily showed up in Sproul Plaza to preach an old-time, simple message of "Turn or Burn" because you are headed to hell otherwise. Hubert was famous for saying to his heckling crowd "God bless your dirty heart!" And heckle they did. His antagonists would surround him and get up in his face with outrageous disruptive tactics. Sometimes with their own portable mike and speaker. "Hey Hubert, how do you like your women? Big breasts or what?" It was relentless and cruel but the raspy-voiced little man was tough and never stopped. Once in a while a Christian would get involved and try to give some support but it remained a sort of circus atmosphere (thinking of the ancient Roman circuses!).

One day Hubert was preaching and under severe attack when a thirtyish man jumped into the conversation and managed to get everyone's attention (twenty or thirty people) and then delivered a powerful, eloquent fifteen-minute speech defending the Christian Gospel. When he finished and walked away I went up and thanked him. I asked him what church he belonged to and he said the Latter-Day Saints (Mormons). I was surprised, to say the least. What he had said to the crowd was a straight-on Billy Graham-style message, no Mormon add-ons. He insisted to me that this is what Mormons believe. I still can't accept the Book of Mormon or the LDS church but the experience showed me that God can use all people for truth and good. (By the way, I did not spend all my days listening to Hubert but he was an unavoidable presence most afternoons I happened to walk through Sproul Plaza!).

Let me say also that I applaud the boldness of Campus Crusade. The Berkeley "Here's Life" campaign may have backfired but these are good, well-meaning, courageous people I have come to respect over the years. They put to shame the passive, comfortable Christians who just hide in their enclaves. But for me, there are better ways to represent Jesus Christ in the academy. In coming chapters I will describe some of the initiatives my friends and I pursued—and all of them were also imperfect!

Thoughtful Counterculture.

One of the major buzzwords of the time was "counterculture." Theodore Roszak (on the Cal State Hayward faculty) wrote *The Making of a Counterculture: Reflections on the Technocratic Society and Its Youthful Opposition.*[11] Roszak described not just the university student revolution which began in Berkeley but the hippie culture associated with the Haight-Ashbury neighborhood in San Francisco and beyond. To the intellectual, social, and political concerns expressed by Berkeley folk were added changes in dress, hair styles, music, sexual behavior, living arrangements (communes and "pads"), and the use of drugs. It was a revolt against the "system" and the conservative values and ways of the older generation.

In Berkeley the impact of the counterculture was partly in housing patterns— fraternity row lost its popularity and university dorm housing lost in numbers as many preferred to create their own lifestyle in group-rented and shared houses or

---

11. Theodore Roszak, *The Making of A Counterculture:Reflections on the Technocratic Society and Its Youthful Opposition* (Garden City, New York: Anchor, 1969).

apartments. Just south of the Berkeley campus students and local residents took over a big vacant, university-owned lot and worked together to landscape and cultivate it. When the university ordered them all to leave and fenced it off, announcing plans for a university building project in 1969, People's Park became a cause celebre. Police were called in to guard the park and hundreds, then thousands, of protestors showed up day after day to try to tear down the fence and reoccupy the park. In the end violence erupted and one guy was shot and killed, another blinded, and Telegraph Avenue storefronts again trashed. Ever since (fifty years now!) People's Park has lain fallow, occupied by otherwise homeless folk with their tents.

One of my favorite biblical texts is Romans 12:2 where Christians are told "Do not be conformed to this world (Greek: *aeon*, age, era) but be transformed by the renewing of your mind so that you may prove what the will of God is, that which is good, pleasing, and perfect." Mindless conformity to the world around us is a besetting sin among Christians through history. Searching for the good, pleasing and perfect will of the *God who created and loves every man, woman, and child* is the mandate for Christians. I don't believe in simple-mindedly, uncritically conforming to any establishment—or any counterculture. The will of God is often counter to the culture(s) around us. New Testament Christian teaching shaped me to be reflexively questioning of the world around me (the Berkeley world as much as Wall Street or the suburbs). I love the bumper sticker slogan "Question Authority." I am inspired by the Berean questioners in the Book of Acts. Berkeley helped me see more of what was at stake. I emerged sharing many (but not all) of the passions and concerns of Berkeley and the counterculture of the 1960s and 1970s. I always remain critical and always want to discover the countercultural difference Jesus would make. We are supposed to be the salt of the earth and the light of the world, not just more earth, more world. My goal is to be part of a thoughtful, biblical counterculture in the heart of the world.

CASTLEMONT HIGH SCHOOL AND JOHN MUIR JUNIOR HIGH

For the first half of my university days my outside work was in factories (1964–1968). The second half was in junior and senior high school teaching (1968–1972). During 1968–69 I was enrolled in the School of Education working toward the California State Secondary Teaching Credential, necessary for a job in the public schools. Part of the work was called "student teaching"—supervised, practice teaching. In the fall I managed to get assigned to teach an 8th grade math course at my own old school Bancroft Junior High in San Leandro. The head teacher, Mrs. Phillips, who I assisted, was my own teacher in 8th and 9th grade. She always had loved me as a kid and now again as a young adult. The fall quarter with her went well. The only negative experience was when I arrived on campus the first day of the term and, seeing me down the hall, the Vice-Principal, my old nemesis, Thomas "the Buzzard" Cruza, curled his nose and sneered at me: "I can see you are the same guy, Gill!" That was my only interaction with him during my time there. "What an ignorant fool," I thought, but did not say.

January to June of 1969 I applied for an assignment to teach American history at Castlemont High School in Oakland. Castlemont's principal had been shot and killed a few months before I arrived so things were tense. My class was twenty-nine Black kids and just one white kid (so much for desegregated schools!). It took me less than a week to realize that the little old guy teaching the course didn't know how to teach and hated his job. But he had a secure, tenured position and had no skills to look for a career change. He saw that I could handle the classroom teaching right away (remember that I had been teaching kids at the Juvenile Hall for three years by then—in fact, I ran into some of my Juvy kids at Castlemont, always with pleasure). Anyway, the teacher was happy to disappear for the rest of the year and let me take over.

The first thing I did was throw out the standard American History curriculum. Of course, we studied the basics and classics of US History but I also brought in some interesting documentary films. We studied the Native American side to the story and listened to recordings of Indian chants and songs. We read great passages from Black authors, watched and listened to speeches by Malcolm X and Martin Luther King, Jr., and unpacked the "hidden" U.S. history of Black folk and immigrants. I loved the class and tried hard to get a longer-term job at Castlemont or another Oakland high school but there were city budget problems and a hiring freeze. The Oakland Public School District had just increased its downtown administrative budget by 85% and couldn't afford more teachers.[12] The school population was also declining now that the Baby Boomer population had topped out (after 1964 the birth rate started to decline).

I really wanted a high school job but I did not want to move out to the suburbs to get one. So I took a job at John Muir Junior High School in San Leandro, the cross-town rival to my Bancroft Junior High. A quarter of my classes were in math. In fact I probably got the job because math teachers were rare while history and social studies grads were a dime a dozen. My experience teaching junior high math made me think that I would have been ready to do it after finishing my high school at age eighteen. All the calculus and advanced math just distanced me from what my students needed to learn. Being twenty-two instead of eighteen did not help me relate better to my thirteen-year-olds. The social studies experience was even worse. The twenty worst students and biggest behavior problems in the school had been rejected by the language department. This group was designated "double R" (below remedial) and I heard more than once references in the faculty lounge to my students as the "retardo-rejectos." Shame!

So the school assigned this group to young Mr. Gill for a two-hour daily course called "History and Communications." As it turned out, I also had this group for another hour each day for math! Three hours per day, with a new group each of my three

---

12. Too typical! I would rather deeply slash administrative jobs and salaries, hire more teachers and increase their pay, and turn the schools over to parents and teachers to run!

years on the faculty. I tried hard to make it an interesting history course but much of the time I was just trying to keep some order. ("Don, please stop jabbing Juanita with your pencil," etc.). Typically, there were eighteen boys and two girls each year in the class. Student attendance was irregular, pencils and books rarely brought to class, homework almost never done no matter how easy, and parental support almost non-existent. I often said that I should have majored in adolescent psychology rather than history.

Sometimes when the behavior got too rowdy (or the fidgeting just became unbearable for them stuck at their desks) I would walk my class over to the neighboring park and play football with the boys. I know it wasn't accepted protocol but I sometimes knocked the bullies on their butts during our games to discipline them and establish my authority. (I would never really hurt them of course and it was just part of our football game (heh heh)). The school told me I could apply for a school bus for (just) one trip each semester. That was ridiculous. Most of these kids had rarely been outside their lower middle-class neighborhoods. Their home and family situations must have been bad. I decided to work on getting them to think bigger and dream of various job possibilities. Since there were no official school bus options, I would pack the fifteen (of twenty) students who showed up on a given day in my VW bus and take them on field trips to tour some local working establishments—including the Oakland Airport, the sewage treatment plant by the bay, a pizza place, and so on. I'm sure it was totally against accepted protocols (and insurance policies!) but I had to do something. I loved these kids and they came to love me, though I am not sure whether I had any lasting impact.

Of course, I did also have one or two sections of "regular students" in math or social studies and enjoyed being their teacher. I have only kept in touch with one of them who found me on Facebook. Mary Girard always sat eagerly in the front row, did her work and behaved perfectly—a teacher's dream (much like I know my Lucia was in school). Mary went on to great success as a student, then teacher, and now Dean of a High School in Hawaii. We have had some brief exchanges in recent years but I would love to meet her and her husband one of these days.

My career was about to change pretty dramatically. I tried and failed every year to get transferred to the high school but there were no openings. As I finished my MA degree, I began thinking I would probably not be satisfied teaching high school, after all, and was better suited to teach college age and adults. I also was pretty dismayed during my time on the John Muir faculty to find that maybe one-third of my fellow-teachers were really exceptional at their job and loved their students—but another one-third seemed to just put in their hours without enthusiasm. The bottom third of the faculty seemed to actually hate their job, and sometimes the kids as well—but they had tenure and were effectively trapped in their job.[13] Growing up, my parents always

---

13. I have been a teacher/professor for fifty years. I am opposed to life-time tenure and much prefer other ways of protecting teachers from arbitrary dismissal. Tenure usually protects mediocrity,

insisted my teachers were fair and impartial and had my best education in mind. My experience at John Muir (and in several higher education faculty contexts) is that this is sadly not true. A (usually small) part of the faculty hates their job and a slightly bigger group is unenthusiastic, uninspired, and just passing their time with minimal effort till they can get to vacation or retirement. Few deans seem able to detect this and help these teachers regain job satisfaction and meaning.

Still, my junior high teaching career was far from a mistake. All of our experiences are part of what makes us who we are. I learned a lot about adolescents, faculties, and educational institutions. It paid our bills while I finished my MA, became a father of two children, and acquired the house that has been home since 1972.[14] And I finally, once and for all, paid the cosmic price for my own terrible behavior in junior high school years earlier!

I am often asked what it was like to be at Berkeley in the Sixties. I have often joked that I have trouble studying if I can't smell tear gas—because the two were so closely associated in my university days. I also have fun reminding audiences of the time Bill Clinton (same age as me) was asked if he had ever smoked a joint back in his college years. "Not exactly," he replied. "I did smoke a joint once—but I didn't inhale." By contrast, my experience was that "I never smoked a joint—but I inhaled all the time!" You couldn't walk very far on the campus before encountering a cloud of marijuana fumes!

In so many ways this period was a powerful shaping force in my life. My faith got deepened, enriched, and toughened up. I became both humbler about my faith claims and bolder in asserting the relevance and power of Jesus and his Gospel. I was cranking out popular level writings at the Juvenile Hall while writing over five hundred pages of research papers at Cal and SF State. Same thing for my speaking/teaching: many dozens of talks, classes, and sermons at a popular level at the Juvenile Hall and in teaching junior high school—but a significant beginning in creating, presenting, discussing, and defending research papers, especially in my senior year at Berkeley and my MA program at SF State. For the rest of my life, I would (a) both write and speak, (b) work at both a popular and scholarly level, and (c) teach and learn with both religious and non-religious communities. These are the years that initial shaping took place.

---

not excellence or edginess.

14. According to my records, my public school salary was $623/month in 1969–70 my first year, $743/month my second year, and $873/month my final year, 1971–72. Big money!

12

Christian World Liberation Front (1971–73)

THINGS HAPPENED FAST IN 1971, a landmark year for us. Our first child (daughter Jodie) was born in March. I was excommunicated from my family's church in July. I graduated from San Francisco State University with my MA in history in August. I got deeply involved in something called the "Christian World Liberation Front" (CWLF) in Berkeley by fall 1971. I discovered the work of French sociologist Jacques Ellul. The pace continued through 1972 when we bought what would become our long-time home on 62nd Street in North Oakland, I quit my Junior High teaching job after three years to work full-time for CWLF, and our second child was born in September (son Jonathan).

In general, a "liberation front" is "an insurgency movement fighting for freedom" against an oppressive regime. Movements have used this language in Yugoslavia, Namibia, Algeria, Eritrea, Korea, Sri Lanka, Cambodia, Poland and elsewhere. The language connotes militancy and a fight for freedom, often (but not always) using violence. Like the term "revolution," "liberation front" has been used (co-opted?) by non-political interest groups promoting ideas, activities, reforms, even commercial products. In 1969, the "Christian World Liberation Front" was organized in Berkeley. This sometimes-appropriate, sometimes-embarrassing, cliché was not retired until six years later and replaced by "Berkeley Christian Coalition." At the time, though, it was an exciting flag to march under!

At both UC Berkeley and San Francisco State, "Third World Liberation Fronts" were organized in 1968 to demand the addition of ethnic studies programs in the curriculum. There was a conscious identification with decolonization and liberation movements in the "Third World" (countries not aligned with either the Western or Communist worlds). Student-led demonstrations and strikes (sometimes with violent clashes with police) led to the creation of ethnic studies programs at both SF State and Cal Berkeley by mid-1969 (with both faculty and administrative support). It was with this background that a "Christian World Liberation Front" (CWLF) was formed at Berkeley in July 1969.

CWLF was, at least in part, interested in "liberating" the *Christian world* (churches, institutions, and individuals) from its traditionalism, lethargy, negativity, legalism, narrowness, and timidity. CWLF broke the mold in many ways. But even more profoundly, CWLF was interested in seeing Jesus Christ and the radical message of the Bible *liberate the world*, including the academy and the counterculture. It was about not just watching the chaos of the Sixties safely (and judgmentally) from the sidelines but moving into the center of the action with a message of hope and freedom. CWLF organized a chapter on the Cal Berkeley campus with student leaders like Doug Stevens and Glen Bayly—and an off-campus non-profit organization. The primary founder and leader for the next six years was Jack Sparks who had gotten involved in Campus Crusade for Christ as a professor of statistics and research design at Penn State. Part of Jack's motivation come from witnessing a violent conflict in Goleta near UC Santa Barbara and wanting to bring the transformative message of Jesus Christ into the heart of the student movement and counterculture. That could only mean Berkeley. Jack and his wife Esther along with two other Campus Crusade staff leaders moved to the Bay Area to innovate a new style of Christian witness to both campus and counterculture.

Campus Crusade's sponsorship ended within a few months as CWLF diverged too much from the standard Crusade model of outreach and witness. I, like many others who got involved in CWLF over the next months and years, was not aware of that early connection to Campus Crusade and might not have joined it if I knew (remembering the 1966–67 "Here's Life" episode). Jack and Esther Sparks (and Bill Squires, another Crusade staff member who came to Berkeley for CWLF) moved into the heart of the Oakland-Berkeley urban and campus culture. When Jack came to Berkeley, he left behind the conservative, traditional ways and formulas of the American Evangelical establishment in order to be fully, radically, and simply present in the culture as a disciple of Jesus. He took St. Paul quite literally about "becoming all things to all people in order to win them." Bearded and bib-overalled, Jack blended into the campus and counter culture very quickly.

Jack Sparks was, without doubt, one of the greatest leaders I ever met or worked with. He brought a passionate faith in Jesus Christ and a bold, militant commitment to be present and bear witness absolutely anywhere and everywhere possible. He was a loving, creative, wise "Daddy Jack" to many people. He never abused his power or position. Unfortunately (from my point of view), three or four of the other Crusade guys who came to Berkeley, lived safely in the suburbs and were mostly not integral to CWLF's operations. Sometimes they would get in the way by objecting to some essay we planned to publish in our newspaper *Right On* (just a little too edgy and critical of either the Evangelical or conservative political establishments). Happily, these guys were more sideline critics than core leaders. They meant well but just didn't fit in.

Part Two: Shapers (1964–1979)

As I have said at various points in earlier chapters, this is my personal story, not a comprehensive or balanced account of any organization (like CWLF) or individual. I don't question the personal faith or good intentions of anyone.

Jack sometimes gave a talk on "creative evangelism" and pointed out not just Jesus' use of parables and his piggybacking of insightful messages on actions bringing food, healing, justice, and reconciliation to people, but stories from the Jewish prophets like Jeremiah and Ezekiel with their dramatic public "theatre." Here were some of Jack's examples:

- Jeremiah buys a new loincloth and after wearing it awhile hides it in the cleft of a rock near the river; sometime later he retrieves it and uses the ruined loincloth to represent the rot in a disobedient, unfaithful people (Jeremiah 13).

- Jeremiah buys an earthen jug, and after reproving the elders of the people throws it to the ground and smashes it to represent the coming disaster owing to their misbehavior (Jeremiah 19).

- Jeremiah makes a "yoke of straps" and puts it around his neck to represent the oppression about to be endured—and then has another prophet come and take it off of his neck to represent God's promise of deliverance (Jeremiah 27–28).

- Seraiah is told by Jeremiah to read aloud from a scroll detailing the disasters coming on Babylon and when he is finished to tie a rock around it and heave it into the Euphrates River while the people watch in shock, to show that "thus shall Babylon sink and rise no more" (Jeremiah 51).

- Ezekiel is told to build a little model city on a brick and set it up (in full view of city leaders) with toy siege works, walls, ramps, and battering ramps—then lie next to it on his left side for some days, then turn over and lie on his right side. And this is just the beginning of Ezekiel's prophetic theatre! (Ezekiel 4).

You can imagine the impact this had on CWLF creativity and boldness!

Jack attracted colleagues to CWLF whose own creativity knew no bounds. His usual response to good creative ideas was "Why not?" Let's do it!" rather than "Be careful! We never did that before!" Staff leaders like Bill Squires, Arnie Bernstein, Howard "Lono" Criss, and Ken "Koala Bear" Winkle oversaw several CWLF urban residence houses and the rural "Rising Son Ranch" which provided housing and caring relationships. Hundreds of hippies, "flower children," dope users, and counter cultural drop outs found acceptance, care, redemption and new life through the loving outreach of Jack and his CWLF "Forever Family" colleagues. The Bible studies, often at the regular Monday Night Meeting, were open, honest, free and exhilarating, attended by Cal students as well as hippies and political activists. The music growing out of the experience was catchy, singable, inspiring, and often amazingly deep. CWLF also held rallies on Sproul Steps at Cal, baptisms in Strawberry Creek or Ludwig's Fountain on campus, Christian rock concerts, food giveaways, picketing and protesting against war and for the gospel in Golden Gate Park or on city streets, demonstrating against the exploitation of women and for the gospel outside North Beach strip joints, and rattling the cages of wannabe religious gurus and frauds, complacent liberal Protestants, and fearful, backward looking fundamentalists and evangelicals. CWLF's Street Theatre troupe could always draw a crowd when they performed on Sproul Plaza or elsewhere. Moishe Rosen got some of his inspiration for starting "Jews for Jesus" from Jack Sparks and CWLF. CWLF folk spoke or performed in churches, on other college campuses, and on tours not just around Berkeley but across the United States.

CWLF was informally (and distinctively) also part of the broader "Jesus People" movement across the continent and beyond.[1] Like other Jesus People, CWLF was committed to evangelism, conversion, and the spiritual renewal of searching individuals—numberless throngs of people exploring (and often getting lost in) meditation, mysticism, Eastern religions, hallucinogenic drugs, sexual freedom, and alternative lifestyles. CWLF offered the way of Jesus Christ as Lord, as a life-giving alternative. Many responded to the truth, love, and hope they saw and heard.

CWLF was also politically and socially thoughtful and engaged. Especially in the earliest days, there were a few political and social conservatives who wished for CWLF to fight what they saw as a threatening counter culture and help the country (not just the church) return to a safer, more traditional past—but this conservative impulse did not define or dominate the movement. CWLF shared much in common with the early Post-American/Sojourners movement in Chicago and then Washington DC and with the Anabaptist/Mennonite approach of John Howard Yoder, Ron Sider, and others. CWLF's concerns about poverty, homelessness, environmental care, sexism, racism, warfare (Vietnam was usually the focus) and violence were genuine and often led to concrete actions and participation in larger debates, demonstrations, and even the political party conventions of 1972 (see below). Some of this participation was witness *with* others concerned about the issues, but it was also witness *to* these movements about a deeper perspective rooted in Jesus Christ. Peace in the world was related to peace among neighbors and peace with God. Walt and Ginny Hearn inspired many to pursue "simple living" less wedded to a culture of consumption, waste, conflict, and indulgence.

---

1. For some history of CWLF in the context of the Jesus Movement see Larry Eskridge, *God's Forever Family: The Jesus People Movement in America* (New York: Oxford, 2013), Robert S. Ellwood, Jr., *One Way: The Jesus Movement and Its Meaning*, (Englewood Cliffs, New Jersey: Prentice-Hall, 1973), Ronald M. Enroth, Edward E. Ericson, Jr., & C. Breckenridge Peters, *The Jesus People: Old Time Religion in the Age of Aquarius* (Grand Rapids: Eerdmans, 1972), Richard Quebedeaux, *The Young Evangelicals*, (New York: Harper & Row, 1974), Jack Sparks, *God's Forever Family*, (Grand Rapids: Zondervan, 1974), and David Swartz, *Moral Minority: The Evangelical Left in an Age of Conservatism*, (Philadelphia: University of Pennsylvania, 2012).

PART TWO: SHAPERS (1964–1979)

RIGHT ON/RADIX MAGAZINE

My own involvement with CWLF began in April of 1971. From 1968 onward I was living on the quieter northside of the campus and was occupied with commuting to my practice/student teaching assignments out in East Oakland and San Leandro, my MA work over at SF State, my Juvenile Hall ministry, and our new baby. I wasn't often hanging out or crossing Sproul Plaza where most of the action was. I had heard of CWLF and seen copies of their tabloid *Right On*, but that was it. As I described in the earlier chapter on my faith, what got my attention was a flyer on a telephone pole inviting people to a meeting where Os Guinness would be speaking. I went because I had been reading books by Os's colleague Francis Schaeffer at L'Abri in Switzerland. I loved Os's talk but loved even more the amazing group that sponsored him: CWLF. The music, the freedom, the diversity, the warm welcome, the enthusiastic discussion of the Gospel and culture: it was amazing.

Out of this meeting and my conversation with Jack Sparks, I began contributing some brief book reviews and essays to *Right On*—and got to know some of the people also working on the paper. Jack had launched *Right On* in 1969 as an alternative to the "Berkeley Barb"—the local "underground" or alternative press which promoted all things and events counterculture, hippy, and radical but whose paid advertising also included sex industry entertainment we felt exploited women (and their customers). There had to be a better way. *Right On* for its first eighteen months appeared irregularly (though frequently—more than once each month). The art and illustration were creative but inconsistent. Content was also eye catching and creative but often thin and of intermittent quality. It was no *Rolling Stone!* Most of all, it lacked editorial vision, planning, and quality control. Often *Right On* printed and gave away as many as 50,000 copies of its usually four-to-eight-page tabloid. Jesus People in other cities often got copies in bulk and distributed them.

Jack called a meeting of several of us *Right On* contributors in late summer 1971. I was now finished with my MA and had been excommunicated from the sectarian church I belonged to (which would otherwise have banned my participation). We all shared our thoughts and dreams and then Jack turned to me and asked in front of everyone if I would be willing to serve as Editor of *Right On*. Yes, I said, I would be happy to do this—but only if Sharon Gallagher and I were appointed together as Co-Editors. Sharon and Jack and everyone else agreed and the die was cast! We worked together for the next two years until I moved to Los Angeles in Fall 1973 to begin work on my PhD—at which point I insisted that Sharon should become sole Editor and I would continue as columnist and Contributing Editor.

Sharon Gallagher was twenty-three, two years younger than I. She also came from a Plymouth Brethren background, but the "Open" brand rather than my "Exclusive" type. After getting her BA in Sociology at Westmont College in Santa Barbara she spent time at the L'Abri community in Switzerland and then came to Berkeley in late

1970 to spend time with CWLF. Sharon began contributing film reviews and essays to *Right On* and was a superb, creative writer, interviewer, and editor. To me, and then everyone else, it was clear that she was as qualified as I was to become Co-editor. Our partnership was one of the greatest and most satisfying leadership and work experiences of my life. We were just a great team. Our gifts and personalities complemented each other. Sharon became a dear life-time friend of both Lucia and me.

She was strong but I felt a little protective of her, as if she was my sister. In year two of our working together a creepy guy up in Oregon started calling the office and writing Sharon to say that God had told him he was meant to marry her. She politely but firmly declined over some months, asking him to stop writing and calling her. "Weird Guy" then wrote to say he was coming to Berkeley to meet her. She told him not to come. But one day he showed up at our office door, where I met him. I told him to get lost, Sharon is not interested. I guess I must have threatened him. To which Weird Guy replied: "David, I have read your columns for months and I know you are a pacifist, so your threats don't bother me!" At which I said to him: "Weird Guy, it's true that I am a pacifist, but sometimes I fall into sin." He left and didn't bother Sharon again.

We both had to raise money (tax-deductible contributions) to pay our pathetic little salaries and help fund the paper (a few churches and individuals donated to CWLF to help fund its operations, including *Right On*; the CWLF newsletter built and motivated a growing constituency of churches, campus groups, and generous individuals). Much of our *Right On* readership got the paper for free but we started also building a paid subscription list and bulk orders to campus organizations and bookstores. At one point a local foundation gave us money to buy and install about ten street vending machines, though that sales channel never really took off.

Right away when we were appointed co-editors, Sharon and I organized our staff. Some incredibly talented graphic artists like Keith Criss, Kit Van Buskirk, Karen Hoyt, and Larry Hatfield took on significant roles. Photographers Steve Sparks and Keith Criss took (and developed in a dark room) some memorable photos. We regularized a monthly publication schedule, and redesigned the masthead and look of the publication. We expanded the tabloid paper to twelve or sixteen pages with regular book and film reviews, and thematic essays and commentaries on current topics. Sharon wrote about film, culture, and feminism. I started writing a regular column called "The Radical Christian" which I continued for seven years. We began doing regular joint interviews of musicians like Edwin Hawkins ("O Happy Day") and Sonny Terry and Brownie McGhee, Black Panther leaders Bobby Seale and Elaine Brown, and pop prophecy author Hal Lindsey (*Late Great Planet Earth*).

On her own, Sharon interviewed many others including Bob Dylan, Eldridge Cleaver, and Maria Muldauer. Brooks Alexander, David Fetcho, Jerry Exel and others wrote about contemporary eastern religions, gurus, and cults, and with Bill Squires created the "Spiritual Counterfeits Project" which produced a trove of quality research, often facing strong opposition from the groups they exposed. Walt and Ginny

Hearn wrote about simple living. Walt served as "Poetry Rejection Editor" and also wrote about science (he had been professor of biochemistry at Iowa State before coming to Berkeley). Ginny eventually served as Copy Editor. Jack Sparks contributed thought pieces. Jack Buckley came on as Book Review Editor. Many other guest writers and reviewers contributed. In short order *Right On* made a lot of waves and got a lot of attention around Berkeley and even across the country. Sharon was invited to participate in a path-breaking 1973 national conference on "Evangelicals for Social Concern" led by Ron Sider and Jim Wallis (I was not invited, they told me, because they already had too many white guys on the invite list!).

We started choosing major themes for each issue. In the fall of 1971, we decided to do an issue on the city. What insights did biblical Christianity have for urbanization? My task was to find any books where Christians had reflected on the topic. There wasn't much to choose from but I found and reviewed *The Meaning of the City* by French sociologist and lay theologian Jacques Ellul, my first real encounter with his work. Then in early 1972 Jack proposed that CWLF should be present in Miami Beach that summer for the July Democratic Convention and the August Republican Convention. Typical Jack. I would go in July to the Democratic Convention (where George McGovern would become the nominee) and Sharon in August to the Republican meeting (where Richard Nixon was renominated, soon to be undone by his Watergate scandal).

I immediately wrote to Democratic Party National Headquarters to apply for a press pass—which, frankly, surprised us when it came through![2] In preparation, I read and reviewed, among other things, four more of Jacques Ellul's books: *The Political Illusion, The Politics of God & the Politics of Man, Presence of the Kingdom,* and *False Presence of the Kingdom.* (Later in the fall of 1972 I sent those reviews and an essay "The Messiahs of Miami Beach" reflecting on the convention to Professor Ellul at the University of Bordeaux; more about his response in a chapter below). Jack Sparks, Bob Guio, Carl Gallivan and I flew to Miami Beach a day or two before the convention week began. We slept outdoors in Miami Beach's Flamingo Park near the convention center, with just a sleeping bag under us in the hot and humid summer weather. Sometimes late in the evening we would walk to the nearby beach and take a dip to cool off at the end of the day. Flamingo Park was packed with hundreds of members of the Southern Christian Leadership Conference led by Ralph Abernathy, Benjamin Spock's "People's Party" supporters, something else called the "People's Pot Party," and several other interesting activist groups. A friendly local let us set up our operation in their apartment. We created and distributed widely a "bust card" with phone numbers for legal help, medical help, and information on Jesus and his way. We leafleted the park with invitations to the "Flamingo Park People's Church" (it was

---

2. The DNC itself issued a press release bragging that for the first time the radical, underground press was credentialled. The release specifically mentioned *Right On, The Great Speckled Bird,* and one other publication!

just us) complete with some good guitar music, singing, talks by Jack and me standing on a car in order to be seen and heard, and a food giveaway we organized with a supportive local church.

Meanwhile, I was going into the convention itself every day with my press pass and a tape recorder, not just paying journalistic attention to the platform speakers but walking the convention floor and getting short interviews with various representatives, delegates, and attendees. Every night all week I wrote up a one-page press release and brought a stack into the big auditorium to articulate a radical Christian perspective on the issues being discussed at the convention—war, poverty, civil rights, and so on. Who knows if it had much impact but I did get a thank-you letter after the convention from Florida Governor Ruben Askew who had seen our stuff. This was the convention that nominated anti-war Christian candidate George McGovern (who then lost in a landslide to Nixon—who, in turn, was soon forced to resign because of Watergate!). On the last night of the convention, as McGovern was giving his acceptance speech, my three colleagues managed to get into the convention by retrieving convention passes from people leaving early. Together up in the balcony the four of us unfurled a huge bedsheet sign we had painted saying "Serve the Lord, Serve the People!" Christian witness, CWLF style.

Whoever bought our airline tickets had booked us through Kingston, Jamaica, for a two-night stay on the way home, knowing our team would sleep little during convention week. We stayed in a modest hotel in the city of Kingston, not in a Montego Bay resort, and got to sleep and recover as well as have a brief taste of Kingston urban life.

In 1976 the name was changed (I think on my suggestion but others may also make a claim), from the worn-out cliché *Right On,* to *Radix*—the Latin word for root and the linguistic root of "radical." The tabloid format yielded to a magazine look, a paid subscription list, a reduced frequency of publication, but an ever-robust quality. Sharon only retired from the editorship in 2020 after an incredible run of fifty years (just the first two with me as co-editor). There was nothing quite like it over those five decades. After 1973 I was no longer part of the leadership. After 1979 I was no longer a regular columnist (I wrote fifty-six of my "Radical Christian" columns for *Right On/ Radix*) but I continued to contribute articles from time to time. I resigned from being a Contributing Editor after 1992 when I left Berkeley for Chicago.

THE CRUCIBLE STUDY CENTER

During my first year with CWLF and *Right On* (1971–72) I was also full-time employed as a teacher at John Muir Junior High. But in year two (1972–73), I quit that job, my MA degree (1968–71) was finished, and my Juvenile Hall Ministry (1966–71) ended—so I had the time and energy to really throw myself into the new challenges. This second year with CWLF was an undistracted blur of activity with the overall movement, with *Right On,* and with a new educational initiative we called "The Crucible: A Forum for Radical Christian Studies."[3]

CWLF was distinctive from both the Jesus Movement and the Evangelical political activists like Sojourners in its educational orientation. Jack Sparks had been a Penn State University professor and was intensely committed to interaction with Berkeley as a university community—to the combat of ideas, not just the saving of individual souls from drug addiction or for the afterlife. Jack's passion for learning attracted many other Christians influenced by Francis Schaeffer's L'Abri movement and Regent College's new presence at the University of British Columbia (from 1969 onward). We were not just Jesus Freaks getting "high on Jesus."

During 1971–72, my first year with CWLF, I watched Ronald Roper, a very bright Christian intellectual try to get something off the ground called (ever so modestly) the "Christian Liberation University of Berkeley." Some liked the acronym CLUB! A few classes or study sessions took place but didn't get much traction and Ron returned to his Michigan home in summer 1972. Ron's model was the brainy intellectual Institute for Christian Studies in Toronto, inspired by Dutch Reformed thinkers like Herman Dooyeweerd and Abraham Kuyper. The approach was theologically rich, philosophically deep, and academically rigorous but without a community of financial support, a qualified faculty, and an eager student body, it could not really get off the ground.

So the CWLF leadership turned to me to spearhead an educational initiative. I thought the right model was a study center, something like the L'Abri fellowship in Switzerland, though not as dominantly "Reformed" in theological orientation and situated at the university rather than at a distant mountain retreat. I sketched out some ideas on paper and brought together a discussion group that included my *Right On* colleague Sharon Gallagher (who had been to L'Abri), a Quaker intellectual friend of mine, Carmoreau Hatie, former biochemistry prof Walt Hearn, book editor Virginia Hearn, former statistics prof Jack Sparks (of course!), and three or four others. We discussed and fine-tuned the plan, which included a quick start-up program of non-credit short courses.

Everyone was enthusiastic and on board . . . but what to call it?! We kicked around all sorts of ideas and suggestions for a name, without coming up with anything. We decided "Quaker-style" to go silent for some meditation and prayer. After a few long minutes Walt Hearn suddenly piped up "The Crucible." We were all sold instantly. A crucible is a vessel for the refinement of a metal or other material. Metaphorically, it was "a situation of severe trial, in which different elements interact, leading to the creation of something new." Our Crucible study center would be a setting for the trial and refinement of our Christian thought. We launched as "The Crucible: A Center for Radical Christian Studies."

---

3. See Charles E. Cotherman, *To Think Christianly: A History of L'Abri, Regent College, and the Christian Study Center Movement* (Downers Grove, Illinois: InterVarsity, 2020) for the story of The Crucible.

I offered a course on the "History of Radical Christianity." Sharon Gallagher offered courses giving Christian perspectives on "The Movies" and "Feminism." Walt Hearn taught on "Christianity and Science," Ginny Hearn offered a "Journal-keeping Workshop," and together Walt and Ginny taught on "Simple Living." Brooks Alexander taught on "Contemporary Cults and New Religions." Others offered short courses on the Bible and Christian beliefs. Ethics and politics were on the table. It was ambitious, exciting stuff, taught and studied for no charge. All of our teachers were volunteer and part-time. We taught our courses in churches, in campus classrooms, and at our building called "Dwight House," just up the street from People's Park. We began building up a library of hundreds, then thousands of books. We had enrollments from five to forty in our classes.

But even while I was leading the Crucible, I was beginning to doubt its potential for significant impact on the university and its graduates. An unaccredited institution relying on a self-appointed (sometimes mostly self-educated—though always capable; you had to be good) faculty was not going to win much of a hearing in the academy. No matter how great they were, our students were from a limited demographic. Furthermore, our theological profile skewed left and Anabaptist—great, often ignored, but not big and inclusive enough for impact. Meanwhile, another, more ambitious, model was rising in Vancouver BC, Canada: Regent College. Regent was a graduate school of theology for laypeople, not for clergy training. It was multi-denominational. Regent achieved course cross-registration with the University of British Columbia as well as with the Vancouver School of Theology. Their faculty were graduates of great doctoral programs. They sponsored amazing summer schools with hundreds of summer students coming from around the world for classes with the world's leading scholars (visiting for a week or two or three). They acquired a campus on the edge of UBC. Regent faculty created and nurtured a UBC faculty Christian fellowship of forty or fifty.

Earlier, in the late Sixties and early Seventies, I had exchanged letters with Francis Schaeffer, the leader of L'Abri, urging him to start of branch of his L'Abri Fellowship in Berkeley. Schaeffer agreed with me that Berkeley deserved something like this but said it was not a project they could take on. Now, in 1972–73 I wrote to Clark Pinnock and some other scholars I admired and urged them to come to Berkeley to create a kind of "Regent College." They all agreed that this would be great and Berkeley was THE place—but they declined to come, saying they just could not lead such an effort. So I began to think it might have to be me to lead such an effort. But to found a graduate school I would need the education—and the credentialling—of a PhD. I was so wrapped up in leadership responsibilities and distractions in Berkeley that I knew I would have to pursue a PhD out of town. The opportunity came for me to move my little family of four to Los Angeles and do a PhD. This story will be told in chapter fifteen below. But once again I saw a big need and opportunity and, failing to get someone else to rise up, I remembered my dad's question "What are you doing about it?" It was very painful to leave these colleagues I loved but both *Right On* and The

Crucible were in good hands and I was embarking on a "mission from God!" I had every intention of returning.

I turned the Crucible leadership over to Donald Heinz who had joined our Crucible board and was just finishing his own PhD at the Graduate Theological Union with a big dissertation on CWLF, "Jesus in Berkeley."[4] Following Don Heinz, Bernard Adeney came to Berkeley and provided great leadership to the Crucible for the next four of five years until the Crucible was folded into the emerging New College Berkeley graduate school project in 1978. Bernie himself then went on to do a PhD in ethics at the Graduate Theological Union and join the New College faculty in the early 1980s.

CWLF continued for two years (1973–75) after I moved to Southern California. I was in close touch with Sharon and other leaders, contributing regularly to *Right On*, and promoting it at bookstores and schools in the LA area. The various ministries of CWLF became stronger and more independent as the years had passed. It was a complex organization. During my two years on site (1971–73), we didn't have Sunday morning CWLF activities and many if not most of our people participated in local churches of many denominations. In 1974 or so a decision was made to form a CWLF church, not that everyone had to attend it but that it would provide a church home for those who wished. But by 1975 Jack Sparks had decided it should be re-organized as an Eastern Orthodox church. Jack had been meeting with several of his old former Crusade staff colleagues across the USA. This group decided they were chosen by God to be a band of Apostles leading a new denomination.

This was a shocking change from the relaxed, non-domineering leader Jack had always been. And only a few in CWLF were willing to submit to this strange, unknown group of self-appointed "Apostles." In 1975, Jack left with about one-third of CWLF, including Arnie Bernstein, to create a new "Evangelical Orthodox Church." After a few years of working on their independent denomination Jack and his friends were able to merge into the Orthodox denominational mainstream (a very healthy move, in my view).[5] Meanwhile with leadership from Bill Squires, Bernie Adeney, Sharon Gallagher, and others, CWLF in 1975 become the "Berkeley Christian Coalition" still operating the Spiritual Counterfeits Project, *Radix*, the Crucible, Street Theatre, and the hospitality houses. Gradually each of these ministries became fully independent of the others although *Radix* stuck fairly close by the Crucible (and later New College Berkeley). You can imagine the pain and confusion of this family split.

In 2002 Bill Squires organized a big CWLF Reunion, attended by nearly a hundred people. Several of those who had left to join the Orthodox movement came to the

---

4. I enjoyed the irony that I was (with other CWLF folk) the subject of a doctoral dissertation before I wrote my own.

5. Odd story: soon after Jack arrived Berkeley in 1969 his eyeglasses fell and broke. He did not need glasses to see or read during the six years of CWLF 1969–75 but as soon as he left to work on his apostle job, he needed to get glasses again to see. Explanations?

reunion, including Jack Sparks. The separation twenty-seven years earlier had been very painful and many had felt like Jack had turned his back on the CWLF community and its work. But in one of the reunion sessions in the living room of our house, I asked Jack directly if in retrospect he viewed the wildly free CWLF as a mistake. His strong "No" and his loving affirmation and embrace of CWLF for those six years brought tears of relief to many eyes and healing to many hearts. Jack died February 8, 2010. I still thank God for what he meant in my life.

In 2019 I organized a fifty-year reunion (CWLF started in 1969). Fifty of us attended a wonderful day together. We sang the old songs from our CWLF days. We looked at a huge collection of pictures from CWLF days. We read the names and mourned a long list of our departed old CWLF friends. We had special reports from six of our old leaders: Kenneth "Koala Bear" Winkle, Bill Squires, Sharon Gallagher, Brooks Alexander, Charlie Lehman, and me. We feasted and laughed together. We had an hour of two-minute shares that allowed everyone in the room to speak, reminisce, and update us briefly. I was asked to give a brief message and I talked about my favorite text in the Bible, Romans 14:17–18: "The kingdom of God is not eating and drinking but righteousness/justice, peace, and joy in the Holy Spirit. Whoever serves Christ in this way is well-pleasing to God and approved by the people." It was an absolutely unforgettable day, remembering our amazing past together, getting past the hurts, loving each other, and worshipping Jesus together again like we used to do. You had to be there.

FINDING MY VOICE, FINDING MY VOCATION

This chapter is about one of the key "shapers" of my "marginal life." CWLF had a life-changing, powerful impact on me. To be sure, I had been a sort of pioneer, innovator, and leader in various ways since high school. But for the first time, during 1971–73 with CWLF, I was surrounded, encouraged, and joined by equally passionate pioneers and innovators willing to go where no one had gone before and express faith and creativity to the max. I learned more about being bold in my dreaming and strategic in my planning, to build teams, to take on any challenge. I loved the famous motto of missionary William Carey, "Attempt great things for God, expect great things from God." I was working and worshipping with people as biblical and missional as my earliest Plymouth Brethren forebears must have been. We never looked at a barrier or obstacle that we didn't say "there must be a way around, over, under, or through it. The God who can raise a body from the dead can do anything."

During my two years with CWLF I published about thirty articles, reviews, and interviews in *Right On* (in addition to my "Radical Christian" columns which continued to 1979), and got a tremendous experience in both the publishing and editing side of the newspaper/magazine. I worked on budgets and financing and dealt with all the conflicts and controversies an editor will get! I learned a lot working with a boss like

Jack Sparks and a colleague like Sharon Gallagher. My CWLF experiences speaking to crowds on campus, arguing for the faith in debate settings, speaking at our Monday Night meetings, and teaching Crucible courses were incredible. Innovating, organizing, and leading The Crucible study center was another amazing learning experience, another "What Are You Doing About It?" project.

By summer 1973 my vocation and calling were becoming clearer but I was not there yet. I had discovered and developed some gifts and abilities but the process wasn't complete yet. I was still finding my own voice. Looking back on my earliest Christian writings I sounded a bit like the pietists of the Plymouth Brethren, sometimes falling back into their cliches. After immersing in the books of Francis Schaeffer I think I sounded sometimes like the eccentric way he wrote. And with CWLF I sometimes fell into the hip (and pseudo-hip) jargon of the counterculture ("right on, man!"). I wrote and spoke a lot. I think I had a lot to say, but I still was in process of finding my own, authentic, distinctive voice.

13

Black Matters

THIS PART TWO OF *What Are You Doing About It?* is about the major "shapers" of my life—my mission, values, worldview, and concerns. I have described how my wife and family, my universities, my faith and church, my different jobs, and the Berkeley environment (Christian and otherwise) impacted me. In this chapter I want to talk about race and, in particular, how African-Americans have shaped my life and calling. In passing I will also write about some of my experiences with other ethnic and cultural groups, diversity, inclusivity, respect, and faculty searches. Most teachers and writers in my field of ethics have particular issues and arenas that get their special attention, whether that is bioethics, end-of-life issues, the environment, politics or something else. Most of my attention in applied ethics has had to do with business, work, and technology. But if I had to name just one moral and social challenge that has haunted and moved me more than anything else over the past fifty years it would be racism and the wretched, unacceptable, unjust, sinful mistreatment of Black folk, especially in the USA.

Just to be clear, I am not writing this to signal any virtue on my part. Rather it is the story of a deepening awakening, a story of my debts to others I will name, and then a story of my responses to my dad's big question to me: "what are you doing about it?" And this story, this pilgrimage, goes on even today at the tail end of my career.

As you know by now, I am a blue-eyed, blond son of people who came to the USA from England, Sweden, and Germany in the 1880s and settled in Omaha, Minneapolis, Portland, and Oakland. I didn't know the word for it until recent decades but I was "privileged" by my stable, middle-class, two-parent family, by being male in a male-dominated society and culture, by being a native English-speaker in an anglophone culture, and by being white in a frankly racist nation. I didn't choose these privileges but I benefitted from them. With privilege like this comes responsibility. Ignorance is no excuse; knowledge plus opportunity brings responsibility to act.

My family and my church taught me from my earliest days that all humans beings throughout history and throughout the world are equally created in the image and likeness of God, equally the objects of God's redemptive love, and equally given gifts and abilities from God to teach, serve, and lead. I was taught to be grateful to be an American but never to think the USA (or any other nation of the world) deserves the patriotism due only to the transnational, transhistorical kingdom of God. I get no chills singing the war-like "Star Spangled Banner" and I applaud athletes who take a knee to remind us of how far we have yet to go. As children we often sang "Red and yellow, black and white, all are precious in his sight. Jesus loves the little children of the world." I liked that.

JEWS, JAPANESE, & BEYOND

We were Gentiles but loved the Hebrew Bible (Old Testament) and believed the promise to Abraham that his descendants and Israel were chosen by God to be a "blessing to all the nations of the earth" and a special channel of God's guidance and truth. We knew that our Lord, Jesus of Nazareth, was Jewish, as were all the early Christians who gave us the New Testament—and often their lives along with it. We knew that official Judaism mostly rejected Jesus as Messiah and participated in his crucifixion—but no more or less than Pontius Pilate, the Roman occupiers, and 'the crowd." I never heard (in my family or church) any anti-Semitic talk or references to Jews as "Christ-killers." I know that wasn't the experience of every Christian but it was mine.

During my twenties I rejected Dispensationalist theology (described in my earlier chapter on Faith and my Plymouth Brethren upbringing) in large part for its relegation of the Old Testament Law and Prophets to a kind of second-class status. That approach seemed to me very counter to the ways Jesus and the New Testament writers wrote in appreciative continuity with their Hebrew roots. I grew to think that Christianity after the New Testament was much too influenced by Greco-Roman thinking and that it was urgent to think much more Hebraically to get our theology right. I came to think that anti-Semitism was one of the greatest of sins and must be strenuously opposed. I loved finding out that when the greatest theologian of the 20th century, Karl Barth, was part of a religious leadership gathering in Basel he insisted "shouldn't we invite the brothers of our Lord to join us?" I have learned a ton from Jewish thinkers such as Abraham Heschel and from dozens of Jewish experts on the Ten Commandments such as Andre Chouraqui, who I quote extensively in my book *Doing Right: Practicing Ethical Principles*.[1]

In my public school experience growing up, I knew that several of my friends such as Mark Ehrlich and Madelyn Bruser were Jewish but never felt or saw anything negative attached to that distinction. Portuguese-origin families with names like

---

1. Gill, *Doing Right*.

Part Two: Shapers (1964-1979)

Cruz, Ferreira, and Vargas had the biggest representation in my San Leandro schools but diversity was all-good as we saw it. Barbara Shimizu and Connie Korematsu were among the Japanese kids in my class. Only later did I learn of the heroic leadership of Connie's uncle Fred Korematsu during the appalling internment of California's Japanese citizens during World War Two.

My little home church (until I was age twenty-five) had several Japanese families, including the Akagis and Iwawakis. A much-loved elderly Plymouth Brethren itinerant minister, Mr. Togasaki from Japan, sometimes paid a visit to guest teach in our church. My contemporaries Roy Akagi and Stan Iwawaki joined me as valued co-leaders of the Juvenile Hall ministry I ran from 1966 to 1971. Keiko and Reiko Akagi were a core part of our exciting youth group. I was appalled to learn from Stan that he was born in a Utah internment camp! There were several marriages of Japanese and Anglos in our church which we celebrated with enthusiasm—including that of my youngest sister Elizabeth to Stan Iwawaki. I don't recall any Latino members in our Oakland church but I do remember vividly our family driving our station wagon down to visit respected Mexican Brethren leader and teacher Ramon Alarcon outside of Ensenada—and getting to sample the delicious products of the bakery he operated! All of this is to say that, growing up, I heard nothing of "white supremacy" (it would be unthinkable)—but I also unthinkingly, unknowingly lived with our society's "white privilege."

BLACK FOLK: FIRST ENCOUNTERS

There were no Black folk in my church, my schools, or my neighborhoods. Only in high school did I become aware of the deliberate "red-lining" conspiracy of political leaders and real estate agents—prompted by racist ideas, prejudice, and greed—to keep Black folk from buying houses in San Leandro (and in the Sheffield Village enclave of East Oakland on the edge of San Leandro). Our high school teams (I played football and was on the track team) competed in the Alameda County Athletic League and I remember wishing we had some of the great Black athletes who played for Berkeley High School and our other high school rivals (Jerry Williams of Berkeley High School ran a national high school record 9.3 seconds in the hundred-yard dash!). Black music stars like Chuck Berry, Fats Domino, and several Motown groups were part of the soundtrack to our daily lives. Television was not much a part of my home life so I only saw American Bandstand and Soul Train a couple times—I was more impressed with the fact that the Soul Train folk were much better dancers than the people on Bandstand and didn't stop to think much about the racial segregation on display.

I think our little Oakland church would have welcomed Black members but we did nothing to reach out to them (or anyone else, I have to say). I do remember vividly a point about America's slave experience made in our church's weekly Wednesday evening Bible study. It must have been during my high school days. Stephen Wilhelm, a Cal professor who had our special respect as a highly-educated scientist, commented on the passage in James 5:1–3 that reads: "Come now you rich, weep and howl for your miseries which are coming upon you. Your riches have rotted and your garments have become moth-eaten. Your gold and your silver have rusted and their rust will be a witness against you and will consume your flesh like fire." Wilhelm said that, in nature, gold and silver do not rust (like iron). Those who profiteered from slavery thought their gold and silver would never rust—but in time and in the judgment of God it did. Today's USA is experiencing (in its civil unrest and racial conflict) the rust and corruption of its unjust, sinful, ill-gotten gold and silver from the backs of Black slaves. Powerful and courageous lesson—no dissent to be heard!

Of course, at the Ballinger Lumber Yard and some other businesses I encountered Black workers and customers when accompanying my dad to get supplies for our home building projects. Always positive. And as a child of eight or nine attending a big Bible conference in Los Angeles I was so impressed with the work of the Black food service workers that I went into the kitchen and got the autographs of about ten big Black men (I still have that piece of paper with their autographs!). Another important experience I had was attending concerts by Mahalia Jackson at the Oakland auditorium. My mother loved Mahalia (in her final months and even as she was dying, I brought my boom box and some Mahalia CDs to her room to let Mahalia sing her on her way to glory). This was the beginning of my life-long love of Black Gospel music—and my first experience of being white in a sea of Black brothers and sisters.

I had lots of sports heroes growing up but the greatest of them all was the "Say Hey Kid" Willie Mays, the Hall of Fame outfielder on the San Francisco Giants. When the Giants moved from New York to San Francisco I was ecstatic. The morning of November 14, 1957, as an eleven-year-old boy, I read on the front page of the *San Francisco Chronicle* I was delivering in those days, that neighbors in a posh part of San Francisco banded together to stop Mays from buying a house in their white neighborhood. I said to my dad, "How can this be? There is no one on earth I would rather have as my next-door neighbor than Willie Mays!" My dad's response: "It is just not right but some people have racial prejudice toward Black people." I had learned in school about America's history of Black slavery but this was probably my first moment of beginning to wake up to the reality of Jim Crow and ongoing racism. I knew the basics of Jackie Robinson and Larry Doby as the first to break the "color barrier" in baseball and I already had Black football heroes like "Alley Oop" R.C. Owens and Joe "the Jet" Perry on the football 49ers but I was just not aware of the depths of racism that affected them and all other Black folk. The awakening was gradual but the Willie Mays story was a decisive moment.

LEARNING TO SEE AND LISTEN, 1964–1977

My first years of college got me out of the San Leandro cocoon and into a larger, more ethnically diverse world. The Civil Rights Movement was in full swing and I thought it was an overdue and great thing. I admired the sit-ins, boycotts, and marches, but hated the vicious, racist white resistance and mourned the fires that burned in the cities. But all this was still something distant from my daily life. I wasn't hanging out in the parts of Oakland where the conflict was most intense. I was preoccupied with academic survival and confusion and working long hours in my factory job. In 1966, though, at the beginning of my junior year at Cal, I initiated a five-year ministry at the Alameda County Juvenile Hall (described earlier in chapter eight on my faith experience). I will only remind you of what I said earlier: this was kind of like a seminary education for me (the practicum part). Due in large part to the unfairness of a police system that picked on young Black kids more than white kids for possession of marijuana and juvenile hijinks, a large majority of the kids were Black. My sermons and lessons kept it simple and stuck tightly to biblical texts. I had no interest in promoting American culture or conservatism.

As I mentioned in chapter eight, I wanted to hand out some reading material to the kids but refused to use the white-Jesus-illustrated Sunday School stuff from publishers Gospel Light and David C. Cook. So I bought a mimeograph machine and started cranking out my own publication I called "Straight To You"—with stories about former gang leader Tom Skinner (who had a weekly radio program I listened to and loved), Malcolm X, and others (alongside the stories of various biblical characters). I quoted Malcolm's statements in his *Autobiography* about why he rejected a racist Christianity—and added "if what Malcolm described was really what the Gospel was about, I also would reject that faith! But he is talking about a false Gospel he has encountered, not the true message of Jesus Christ." At my Tuesday night Bible studies with a dozen or two older teenagers at the Senior Boys Ranch we would read a chapter together and then throw it open for discussion: "what is it saying? And how does it apply today? What does the Bible say and mean for us today in Oakland?" I learned as much from these freewheeling studies as my guys did!

In the fall of 1967 Lucia and I got married and rented our first apartment on 41st Street just east of Broadway. It seemed like our contemporaries often moved out to Walnut Creek or Pleasanton when they could. We wanted to do the opposite and move deeper into the city, to the neighborhood of our church on 40th Street off Broadway. Oakland was finally being forced to face up to its often horrible treatment of its Black citizens. In 1966 Bobby Seale and Huey P. Newton formed the Black Panther Party, first of all to monitor and confront the racist behavior of Oakland police. While they were at first known mostly for openly carrying weapons (it was legal then), they also organized major programs to provide free breakfasts to school kids and free health clinics. I understood but didn't like the resort to weapons and threats of violence—but I did like the militancy of the demands for reform. I believed then and now in community-based policing. I loved how just a few years later the yard duty supervisors at our kids' Peralta Elementary School were often pastors from store-front churches in our part of Oakland—not armed Oakland police officers.

As I mentioned in an earlier chapter, I began reading a lot of Black history and literature like Richard Wright's *Black Boy* and *Native Son,* Claude Brown's *Manchild in the Promised Land,* Ralph Ellison's *Invisible Man,* Frantz Fanon's *Wretched of the Earth* and *Black Skin, White Masks,* Martin Luther King Jr.'s *Why We Can't Wait* and "Letter from Birmingham Jail." In 1968–69, I was able to take the first ever African-American History two-course sequence at Cal which got me into Basil Davidson's histories of Africa and the slave trade, W.E.B Dubois, Booker T. Washington, and the Harlem Renaissance. I not only devoured Malcolm X's *Autobiography* but dozens of his pamphlets and recordings of his speeches. All of this played large in my "revisionist" approach to teaching American history at Castlemont High School in fall 1968.

In late 1968 I was driving toward the Cal campus on Telegraph Avenue when a song came on KSAN-FM, the top hard rock station in the Bay Area. Totally out of character for this station, it was the Edwin Hawkins Singers' "Oh Happy Day." A huge choir of more than one hundred singers, mostly drawn from the Ephesian Church of God in Christ on Alcatraz Avenue a half mile from my house, delivered a song so powerful I literally pulled over to the curb to stop and take it in. The next Spring, the Hawkins Singers were the main attraction at the sold-out UC Jazz Festival's Gospel Concert, featuring not just the Hawkins Singers but James Cleveland and his choir from southern California, and the massive "Voices of Christ" directed by Helen Stephens. I was hooked for life! I got Edwin Hawkins to donate fifty tickets and Alameda County to provide two big school buses so we could take fifty of our Juvenile Hall and Snediger Cottage kids to their big concert at the Oakland Auditorium. There were some happy kids with me that day!

Lucia and I often attended Gospel concerts at local Black churches or auditoriums, taking our two babies with us when they came along. At one point I learned how to play the piano background to the Hawkins arrangement of "I Heard the Voice of Jesus Say, Come Unto Me and Rest" and got a few singers to do it for an offertory at Berkeley Covenant Church—an expression of my love for the music, certainly not my limited talent! Our family always got ready for church on Sunday mornings through the 1980s listening to Sheila Robinson's award-winning Gospel program on KSOL-FM radio. Much later, in 2003, I was delighted to find Sheila herself enrolled in a Christian Ethics class I taught for Fuller Seminary in Menlo Park. I was an occasional guest on her Gospel music show and, beyond the music, we have become life-time friends. She even came to Allen Temple Baptist Church in 2010 to participate in my ordination. Our daughter Jodie sang in the mighty UCSB Gospel Choir for four years during her college days. More on the story of my love for Gospel music below.

From 1971 to 1973 I left my junior high school teaching job to work with Berkeley's Christian World Liberation Front. Our heart was in the right place, when it came to racial inclusion and our support for Black liberation and respect, but a good attitude and welcoming stance were not enough. We failed to attract much Black participation in our activities. Sharon Gallagher and I, as co-editors of *Right On,* did feature lengthy interviews with Bobby Seale and Elaine Brown of the Black Panthers, Eldridge Cleaver, and musicians Edwin Hawkins, Sonny Terry, and Brownie McGhee. Our essays and reviews also paid attention and valued Black ideas and issues. But we didn't reach out or listen enough and we failed to get to know and include Black leadership from the inception of our programs. We were, in effect, just inviting our Black brothers and sisters onto our mostly white turf.

During my graduate school years in Los Angeles, 1973 to 1977, I was part of our USC School of Religion welcoming committee to have Jesse Jackson pay us a visit and lead a seminar. I got to know and become lifetime friends (and sometime golf partners) with Bill Pannell, a professor at Fuller Seminary and author of *My Friend, the Enemy*—a powerful little book I loved. Bill actually had some Plymouth Brethren background in Detroit and had led the Tom Skinner organization before coming to LA (Skinner also had some PB connections). When my thirtieth birthday approached (February 2, 1976) Lucia asked Bill if he could get me out of the house (so she could prepare a surprise party for me). So on my birthday Bill brought my white self to a big meeting of Black church leaders with Tom Skinner, in town for a visit. (Yes, I kept quiet and listened!). What a fabulous experience (and the big party Lucia organized that evening was also pretty awesome).

STRUGGLING TO MAKE A DIFFERENCE (1977–1990)

From 1977 to 1990 I was deep into founding, then leading—as initial Project Director and Board Chair, then as Dean and finally as President—New College Berkeley. We tried hard to recruit Black students and Board leadership but with only limited success. For our first ever Summer School in 1978, Bill Pannell came up as Visiting Professor for a three-week course—we especially had fun sharing jazz interests since he stayed in our house those three weeks (we owe him for introducing us to Stephane Grapelli and the Hot Club of Paris). John Perkins came later as a visiting professor and guest lecturer. New Testament scholar Clarice Martin spent a year on our faculty but left when we couldn't begin to match the financial offer she got from another seminary. The Rev. Dr. J. Alfred Smith, Sr., pastor of Allen Temple Baptist Church was guest lecturer and commencement speaker, and became a lifetime friend and mentor to me.[2]

My own courses in Christian ethics addressed issues of racial justice and included readings from Martin Luther King, Jr., and other Black writers, but this was by no means enough. New College Berkeley was always strapped for cash, barely hanging on, and had not developed the networks—or the institutional commitment—that could have realized our dreams for a more Black-inclusive community of learning.

2. J. Alfred Smith Sr., *On the Jericho Road: A Memoir of Racial Justice, Social Action, and Prophetic Ministry*, (Downers Grove, Illinois: InterVarsity, 2004) is a wonderful introduction to this great brother and mentor of mine.

We always had Black folk as neighbors on 62nd Street but I got really lucky when Albert and Kathy Raboteau bought the house next door. Our kids grew up playing together. Al, raised Catholic in New Orleans, was Professor of History and African-American Studies at Cal and the author of books such as *Slave Religion: The "Invisible Institution" in the Antebellum South*. Another lucky break was meeting Hall of Fame baseball star Reggie Jackson in 1988. I had joined the new Gold's Gym in downtown Berkeley and was working out early one morning and noticed Reggie working out with a friend. After a little chit chat over a couple weeks, Reggie invited me to work out with him and his friend Curt. This continued for three or four years. I was relatively buff for a forty-two-year-old professor and long-time gym rat but no competition for a Hall of Fame slugger (both of us born in 1946). I always loved doing inclined dumbbell presses but had to drop out after a set with the 95-pound dbs. Reggie and Curt kept going up to the 130s!

I made it a policy never to ask Reggie for autographs or tickets to the A's for whom he worked as a batting coach—and I always asked him about his life and opinions. One morning he asked me "David, you are always asking me about my life and thinking—but what about you? What do you do?" "Well Reggie, I am a Professor of Christian Ethics here at New College Berkeley," I responded. Reggie: "I am not surprised. I thought you must be a minister or something like that because you always care about me and never ask me for anything." A few weeks later, Reggie and I began to meet at my house or his for a little Bible study, prayer, and sharing time whenever he was in town (he traveled a lot with the baseball team). A couple years later he signed a copy of his newly-released autobiography to me, thanking me for "making him a better Christian man." What a privilege.

Hanging out with Reggie from time to time, I got to see how he was treated in public. He could not hide. People recognized him everywhere and called out "Hey Reggie!" "Hey Mister October!" Reggie told me he couldn't attend church because he disrupted the service just by being seen—so he really valued our Bible studies. I remember how comfortable he was when in a Black barber shop—but I saw so many instances of people on the streets or in stores begging for his autograph, but then rudely walking away without saying thank-you. When we visited his ailing mom in a hospital or walked through an airport together, everybody, I mean everybody, recognized him and called out "Hey Reggie" to him. So it was pretty funny when one time we were walking toward the gate at an airport and a dazzlingly beautiful flight attendant came from the opposite direction and called out "Hey David, how are you doing?" Hah! Reggie looked at me, wondering what this was about! She didn't seem to recognize Reggie but wanted to tell me she had heard me preach and loved it whenever she had been home to Davis and attended University Covenant Church with her parents.

In October 1991 a horrible fire raged through the Berkeley and Oakland hills. It came to within a half-mile of our house but it had totally consumed Reggie's place (and all his memorabilia) in Hiller Highlands near us. Reggie had suffered watching the blaze on television while he was in New York City with the team. When he got back home, he came in shock over to our house where we could mourn together. Soon after this, Reggie left the A's to join the New York Yankees organization and our contact slowed and eventually ended. I moved on the Chicago for the next nine years and we lost touch with each other. But I learned a lot from Reggie, getting an inside look at not just the life of a famous Black sports star, but that of a great Black brother.

WHEN BEING A WHITE GUY DID NOT PAY

As I neared the end of my fourteen years with New College Berkeley, I had almost no time to look for my next academic home. But my friend, Fuller Seminary Provost Rich Mouw knew that I would soon be "on the market" and called to ask if I might be interested in being a candidate to succeed their venerable and much-loved retiring professor of Christian Ethics, Lewis Smedes. I had thought that I would never want to live in the LA area again (northern Californians often feel this way). But this was a great possibility. Lew Smedes had actually been the one to invite me to teach a course at Fuller in 1976 as I was finishing up at USC—my first grad school teaching experience, and it had been great. So I agreed to be a candidate. Like Smedes, I was a dedicated churchman (I would have brought a Covenant Church connection to Fuller), and navigated between scholarship and practical communication with the laity in my teaching and writing.

As the search proceeded Rich called me every couple months to update me and make sure I was still interested: "we have narrowed our search to twenty and you are in the mix, are you still interested?" Yes. Then it was ten, etc.. Finally, I got a call from Rich to say that he had just become the president of Fuller and was handing the search leadership to Prof. Jim Bradley—who would soon be in touch with me. Then Bradley called to tell me they had settled on a finalist group of six—and they had me rated as the number four candidate. He asked if I would like to have an interview but warned me that it was unlikely numbers one to three would all be passed over. I said "Yes, I would like to be interviewed just to see how you do it. But, by the way, can you tell me anything about these three candidates you have rated over me? Did Stanley Hauerwas apply?" I knew pretty much all the leaders in my field and was a bit surprised that they had three ranked above me for this particular position the way it had been advertised. Bradley: "Well our faculty decided to preserve the top three spots for women and minorities. That is why you are number four."

Later on, I found out that one of those candidates had not yet finished her PhD, another was a freshly-minted PhD with no publications or deep church connection, and the third a Korean man who was professor of philosophy (not ethics) in Hong Kong. They offered him the job, he accepted, then had to withdraw at the last second to help his Hong Kong school through a crisis. Smedes then delayed his retirement a couple more years before Fuller hired Glen Stassen, who went on to a long and distinguished career. So I was actually the most qualified candidate (on paper) but lost out to an affirmative action strategy. How did I feel about it? Great! The Fuller faculty was too white and male and needed to diversify. I would have done the same thing if I was the dean.

In 1997–98 I had a similar experience with Seattle Pacific University. I was the only candidate brought to campus to interview for a new position teaching ethics in the School of Business. The interview went well. Lucia and I checked out property around Green Lake. The dean told me I was great, the faculty was agreed, and I would hear from him soon. Months passed with no word until the dean sheepishly phoned to say that another candidate had emerged and they offered him the job. His MBA and forthcoming business ethics textbook sort of balanced with my publications and experience—but he was also Chinese-American, available to integrate the white faculty. Yup, I thought. Sad for me, but good for you.

I said then and since: we white guys have been the beneficiaries of affirmative action and preferential treatment forever. It is past time to start making strong efforts to have our faculties represent the whole Body of Christ, not just the white male parts of it. For any faculty search that happened during the time I was leading New College Berkeley (1976–90) we would have hundreds of applications. Any Black, Hispanic, or female applicants were automatically forwarded to the second round for a closer look. If you were a white guy, your PhD from a reputable school better be in hand and you would need to have some publications or other distinguishing accomplishments to make you stand out from the crowd. We were not against white guys but believed that other voices, experiences, and perspectives were missing. Still, we could have done better by broadening the terrain where we searched.

CHICAGO PROGRESS (1992–2001)

From 1990 to 1992 I was pretty much cocooned in, mostly white, Davis, California, as Interim Pastor of University Covenant Church. But in 1992 I accepted a call to serve as the inaugural Carl I. Lindberg Professor of Applied Ethics at North Park College in Chicago. I will leave the full story to a later chapter, but I was surprised and dismayed to find only one African-American on the faculty, Dean of Students Edward Eddy. There was also just one Black professor on the next-door faculty of North Park Theological Seminary. Maybe ten percent of our students were Black—many of them there mainly for the chance to play basketball or football. I began asking around how this could happen? Chicago was roughly half Black and half white and North Park claimed to be there to serve the city and the church. Dean Eddy appreciated and shared my discontent.

I credit the campus chaplain Jodi Mullen Fondell with bringing the Rev. Jeremiah Wright, pastor of Trinity United Church of Christ on the southside, to preach in our chapel. His sermon, "Salvation Without Suffering," was the best and most biblically faithful I heard in my nine years at North Park, challenging the too-common message of the "Best Life Now" prosperity gurus. Later on, Wright's harsh (but I think faithful) rebuke of American racism caused trouble and misunderstanding for TUCC-member and presidential candidate Barack Obama. But I remain a big fan of Pastor Wright and his long witness to the Gospel.

My first move on arrival at North Park was to get to know and encourage my Black students. Maybe the word spread that "Professor Gill loves athletes"—because I soon had many of the Black athletes in my courses. All of my career I have begun my courses by telling my students I believed in their capabilities and expected their success. I would say to all my classes "I am your coach and you are my players and I want to help you succeed and win. We are not on opposite teams!" So often students feel on trial and even disrespected from day one. Not in my classes if I can help it! But I heard plenty of stories of racist remarks by students, administrators, and teachers. Mostly subtle, but always harmful.

My second move was when Dean Ebner sent around a list of faculty committees and asked all faculty members to check off their top three preferences for assignment. That first year and for the next four or so, I wrote a note on the sign-up sheet: "Dean Ebner, would you be willing to let me create and lead a new committee on "Minority Faculty and Student Recruitment and Retention." Every year my request was denied. How sad and unthinking. President David Horner insisted to me that the college wanted to do a better job on this. (And eventually they succeeded—North Park University in the 2020s has a much healthier and more diverse faculty and student body. I am so thankful and impressed).

But I got busy informally and made it my mission to find and recruit strong Black faculty candidates. I found a great professor of nursing (NPU then hired) at a national ethics conference I attended. I strongly encouraged and recruited a Black professor of communications who joined us. I became close friends with History Professor Theodora Ayot from Kenya—I didn't find or recruit her but I certainly contributed to her welcome into the core of our faculty. When a Center for Africana Studies was added alongside our centers for Scandinavian and Korean Studies I made sure to befriend and support Director Dr. Rupe Sims. While several of my white colleagues had actually marched with MLK in the south, they were institutionally conservative and rather unwelcoming to our new, more politically-progressive colleagues. The greatest of all faculty additions was music Professor Rollo Dilworth, brought in because of the growth of our Gospel Choir (see below). I kept my eyes and ears open for good prospects and then provided warm collegiality and support from a senior colleague—simple things but so important.

My third move was to join Oakdale Covenant Church, the largest Covenant Church in Illinois, at 95th and South Vincennes, thirty miles south of North Park. The congregation of one thousand was 99% Black. Lucia and I were not the only white members but we may have been the only white couple. I was totally blown away by the loving welcome we experienced—and by the music and worship experience. If we didn't get there a few minutes before 11:00 we probably wouldn't find a seat. The services always began with the seventy-member adult choir and thirty-member youth choir up front, led by Farnell Jenkins. "The Lord is in his holy temple" the choir burst out . . . "Let all the earth keep silent, keep silent before him." I almost tremble even now remembering that magnificent call to worship. Then the Hammond B-3 slowly started cooking and pretty soon everyone was on their feet clapping and singing out "we've come to praise the Lord, we've come to magnify his name . . ." The place was rocking with praise to God for several minutes. When we sat down a young pastoral associate or intern bounded to the podium to lead a heartfelt prayer welcoming God into our temple of praise. The service was always two or more hours long with short "devotionals" from one of those associate or assistant pastors, three or four amazing gospel solos and choir numbers from the adult choir and one from the youth choir, then a long heartfelt sermon from Pastor Willie Jemison.

When I went down for a visit with Pastor Jemison I asked him about North Park. Almost every graduating senior at Oakdale attended a Historic Black College or University. Each of those students had an assigned sponsor and mentor from the congregation. All the seniors went on a long bus ride to visit a series of those HBCUs. Pastor Jemison told me stories of racist treatment of his young people when they went to North Park and the refusal of the administration to take adequate action to change the culture. He gave up. He told me "until North Park has at least ten Black faculty that culture will not be safe for my students and we won't send anyone there." I was so sad to hear this and motivated to work for change on campus and on the faculty.

I have always urged my white colleagues and friends to put themselves in places where they are not part of an ethnic (or linguistic) majority. Get the experience of being different, standing out by that difference in color or culture. Experience being a minority. Even learn a second language and go live among people where you have to struggle to understand or speak the language (as Lucia and I and our kids did in France). We could never attend Oakdale without standing out as "people of no color" (I always chuckle about this when I hear about "people of color"—as though my pale pinkish tan is not a color). If I had been on the road two or three weeks, it was not unusual for Pastor Jemison to see this white couple in short "centerfield" in the sanctuary and say "It's good to see Dr. Gill and his wife back here this morning" (as Lucia shriveled up in her seat next to me). After a few years, we moved up to First Presbyterian Church in Evanston to be with our daughter now enrolled at Northwestern, but the Oakdale experience was amazing. Ed and Kitty Coleman and Larry Griffin became special friends of ours when they came up from Oakdale for seminary at North Park (and Ed earned his DMin under my supervision later at Gordon-Conwell).

My fourth move was to start a Gospel choir at North Park. I thought it was actually a scandal not to have one. Our daughter was part of a huge Gospel Choir at UC Santa Barbara, a secular, mostly white university! Here we were a Christian college in Chicago, a city which was a center for great Gospel music. I mentioned this to my Black students in conversations in my office. I urged Dean Eddy to get something started. He insisted that I should take the initiative. "What Are You Doing About It?" my dad had challenged me as a young man. My students Vernard Jones, Ishmael McGhee, and Fadil Lee were all in. "Come on Dr. Gill, let's do it." OK, I said. I will create a little flyer inviting "anyone interested in singing the great Gospel music of the African-American church tradition to come together in the basement of Sohlberg Hall at 9:00 p.m. on Wednesday." We had to meet at 9:00 so the basketball players could attend after practice.

I brought my boom box and a tape of the UCSB choir to the meeting so they would know that this white prof was not thinking of Bill Gaither-style Southern White Gospel (good stuff but not our goal). Only Vernard was in the room at 9:00 but he had heard positively from several other students so he ran around campus to remind them and we soon had a dozen Black students in the room and maybe one Hispanic and one white student. I shared with them three reasons why North Park needed a Gospel choir: first, we needed spiritual renewal on campus and this choir could have a powerful impact. Second, we prided ourselves on our great music department but it just wasn't broad enough in its curriculum and needed to include music from more than European and white roots. I pointed out that were lots of great classical musicians like Wynton Marsalis who crossed over to jazz, and great jazz artists like Cyrus Chestnut who played Gospel, and the UC Santa Barbara faculty which included not just classical piano but Black gospel for my music-major daughter to study. Third, I said, we have lots of "white things" we ask our Black students to do on campus, we need to add some "Black things" that our white and Asian students could try to do. I got quoted a lot on that third point by my Black students around campus.

Each person got a chance to share their thoughts and experiences with Gospel music. Everybody at our meeting was totally sold on the idea. So I said, "ok let's go for it. We need a director and a keyboard player and then we can get started." At this point, Vernard said "let's not delay. Michele Thomas here is a freshman who already leads the youth choir at her Chicago church!" Michele agreed! "And who can play keyboards? How about Louis Hansard who graduated last year? He might come back and he is a fine Gospel pianist." I agreed to approach the music department to get a practice room for 9:00 p.m. the next week. Vernard agreed to contact Louis (he agreed to come back). And everybody spread the word.

The next week we had twenty recruits, several of them our Black men athletes. Maybe a couple more Hispanics and a couple whites, including a white ethics professor singing tenor and bass in the back row. Michele began teaching us two songs in beautiful three-part Gospel style. We practiced every week at 9:00 p.m. on Wednesdays. I was the faculty defender and sponsor of this unofficial activity. My faculty friends in the music department objected pretty strenuously, viewing Gospel as less-than-professional "folk" music not worthy of inclusion in their "serious" North Park music program. I stood strong (these were well-meaning music faculty but narrow and elitist in their perspective). I gave them all my arguments from Wynton Marsalis to UC Santa Barbara. They grudgingly gave us the keys to a practice room. North Park Chaplain Jodi Fondell caught wind of our Gospel choir start-up and asked if we could sing in Chapel soon? I asked for the last pre-Christmas chapel date in the fall of 1993.

When the chapel date came, we twenty marched in slowly to the piano and drum intro by Louis and our drummer and got to the front where we performed the only two songs in our repertoire. Huge applause! Afterward, faculty and others were running up to thank all the singers and me saying "This is the greatest thing ever to happen at North Park! How did you guys do it?" Black students did not often attend the (culturally) white chapel services. When we came back from Christmas vacation *forty* kids (Black and white and everything in between) showed up for the choir practices at 9:00 on Wednesday nights. I suggested that we learn enough songs for a full concert on Mother's Day in May and charge $10 to raise money to benefit a homeless shelter in downtown Chicago. Now we had a guitar and bass along with Louis on the piano. I arranged for Farnell Jenkins from Oakdale to come up and lead a Saturday Gospel workshop which was attended by fifty or so. Michele Thomas did a fabulous job. We sold out our six-hundred-seat Chapel on Mother's Day. A new chapter began at North Park.

That next year I had a long-standing commitment to be visiting professor at a college in Pennsylvania. But in September *seventy* kids showed up! Unfortunately, my replacement as faculty sponsor, a newly-hired director of our Africana Study Center, was well-meaning, I'm sure, but did not have any pastoral or relational skills with the Black men who in that first year had been the heart and soul of our leadership. They began to drift away. The choir practices were moved to an earlier evening hour—but this ruled out the Black athletes who had basketball practice until 9:00. This is an example of how structural/institutional choices can have prejudicial consequences. But the choir continued to grow under Michele Thomas's direction for the next four years until there were typically a hundred seventy singers, racially-integrated and with Black leadership but now with mostly white kids in the choir. In the late 1990s North Park hired Dr. Rollo Dilworth as full-time music faculty and director of the choir. Rollo was a nationally-recognized composer and choir director (not just Gospel but classical). The choir thrived under his leadership and ever since has often gone on tour, often asked to sing at big national Covenant Church events. It is still the most popular student activity at North Park and by far the most racially-integrated.

I returned to North Park in 2003 for a tenth anniversary celebration and concert at which Rollo recognized me as the faculty founder, along with Michele, Louis, Vernard, Fadil, and Ishmael, my original posse. Oh man do I love and admire those young people. In 2018 I returned once again to campus to give a couple ethics lectures and met the current choir directors. I asked if I could just attend a practice to watch and listen. I couldn't help but tear up a bit listening to their heavenly sound. The current director introduced me and asked me to tell this story of how it all began. Starting the NPU Gospel Choir was the best thing I ever did at North Park during my nine years there!

CALLING ON THE COVENANT DENOMINATION

During my time at North Park (1992–2001) I was still a licensed (not fully ordained) minister in the Evangelical Covenant Church which had been my denominational home since 1975. I still attended the annual meetings of the thousand-member ministerium. In February 1995 I was asked to serve on the "Commission on Christian Action" and draft a "Resolution on Racial Reconciliation"—which was adopted by the conference and published in the denominational magazine the *Covenant Companion*. This is what it said, to give you an example of the thinking I was trying to promote in our Evangelical Covenant denomination.

> Whereas the Word of God teaches us that
>
> (1) God is the great Reconciler; in the cross and resurrection of our Lord Jesus Christ, God has graciously reconciled us to himself and he has reconciled male and female, slave and free, Jew, Gentile, barbarian, and Scythian into the one body of Christ, the Church, the koinonia, in which there is but one faith, one Lord, one baptism, one Holy Spirit, and one head, Jesus Christ (Rom. 5:10; 2 Cor. 5:20; Gal. 3:26–28; Eph. 2:16; 4:4–6; Col. 1:20–21; 3:11);
>
> (2) God has given us the ministry of reconciliation in the world, as his ambassadors; he has commissioned us to preach the Gospel of reconciliation to himself; and he has called us to bear witness to his reconciling power by our love for one another, by our community with "saints from every tribe and language and people and nation" (John 17:20–21; 2 Cor. 5:16–20; Rev. 5:9–10).
>
> Whereas God has been at work in the Evangelical Covenant Church
>
> (1) gathering us into a global fellowship of believers in the United States, Sweden, Zaire, Mexico, and other parts of the world, and into an American fellowship of believers from black and white, Hispanic, Asian, and other ethnic and national backgrounds;
>
> (2) leading us to express repeatedly, in these Annual Meetings and elsewhere, our anguish and disapproval of racism, racial injustice, prejudice, discrimination, and division, and our commitment to racial justice, understanding, reconciliation, and harmony;
>
> And whereas our churches, our neighborhoods, our cities, our nation, and our world continue to be troubled, even plagued, by the sins of racist attitudes, words, and deeds, of racial fear, animosity, misunderstanding, discrimination, division, and even violence;
>
> Therefore, be it resolved, that the 1995 Annual Meeting of the Evangelical Covenant Church issues a call to
>
> (1) condemnation of racism as a grievous sin against God, whether in attitude, word, or deed, in personal or public life; let us examine ourselves

and repent of any and all vestiges of sinful racism in our lives and communities; and let us pray for forgiveness, healing, and renewal, for an unwavering, militant, commitment to God's great purposes of uniting our diversity into one glorious kingdom of justice and love in Jesus Christ;

(2) vigorous proclamation of the Gospel of reconciliation to God through faith in Jesus Christ, with its attendant good news of reconciliation and fellowship among those formerly divided by sex, race, class, and nationality; and faithful education in our households, churches, and beyond, concerning God's judgment against the sin of racism and, still more profoundly, God's promise of a new and better way in the fellowship of saints from all ethnic backgrounds;

(3) action in our personal lives by initiating and nurturing at least one meaningful, ongoing, caring friendship with someone of another ethnic background;

(4) action in our local parish churches by initiating and nurturing a meaningful, ongoing, mutually-beneficial, "sister"-relationship with a congregation predominantly of another racial or ethnic membership than our own;

(5) active support (prayer, financial, spiritual, material) of individuals and ministries directly addressing the injuries of racial injustice and the challenges of racial reconciliation and harmony in church and in society at large;

(6) action in our businesses, schools, community organizations, and political life, to overcome any policies and practices which perpetuate racial discrimination, injustice, and ignorance, and to take all available steps to facilitate racial understanding, justice, and harmony in these arenas; let us reject the pessimism and indifference which argue that nothing can be done, and insist on the brash hope of the cross and the empty tomb, that what is humanly impossible, is possible with God, that in Jesus Christ we shall overcome someday.

I don't know the impact this resolution had on our ministers and churches but over the next decades there were huge changes and improvements in the denomination and leadership. I was truly stunned and delighted in 2018 when I returned (after twenty years) to the Midwinter Conference of Covenant pastors. The voices and leadership of Black Covenanters in that meeting were powerful, omnipresent, and inspiring. It was and is a new day in the Evangelical Covenant Church.

BACK HOME IN OAKLAND 2001–2010

In 2001 I left the North Park Faculty and returned home to our Oakland neighborhood. When we got back to 62nd Street we found some racial conflict had been brewing on our block. The five-unit HUD apartment building across the street from our house had occasionally been a source of noise and minor neighborhood conflicts over the years (parking, kids running through back yards, (unfounded) suspicions about car break-ins, etc.). The neighborhood had slightly gentrified over the years though our street was still anchored by lots of long-term residents like us. But a bullet had been fired through the window of a house next door to the HUD building, no one was maintaining the grounds around the building, and a couple disagreements and complaints were getting loud.

Somehow a neighborhood meeting was scheduled at a nearby church, to be chaired by Oakland Housing Authority police and administrators. It was a tense environment as we all sat around in a big circle. The OHA official started the meeting by saying something like "we are here to discuss the complaints and problems relating to the OHA building on your street. Who would like to make the first comment?" Being me, I held my hand up and said "I just want to say that my wife and I have lived directly across the street from the OHA building since 1972 and I want to say that these are good neighbors who we love having on our block. Sure, there have been problems at times but no more than with other residences on the block. I think whatever has happened recently can easily be settled. We have a wonderful block." The head honcho looked surprised and said "Well, we don't often hear a statement like that. Thank you." The tension in the room was basically gone.

I proposed that we recognize a "triumvirate" to lead our block meetings and I nominated Kathy Smith, a Black, long-time resident of the OHA building, with whom I always got along great because she was a Christian and loved sharing the faith with me. The third person I nominated was the next-door neighbor who had experienced the bullet in her window and had some issues with smoke and noise from the HUD building. She was also my friend, studying for her PhD with a professor friend of mine at Cal. The three of us then began to organize and lead our semi-annual block meetings and annual block parties. Peace reigned. I tell this story not because I think I am anything special—but to illustrate how simple, positive, creative interventions can defuse tense misunderstandings and contribute to racial reconciliation. There are no surefire formulas and nothing is permanent, of course.

ALLEN TEMPLE BAPTIST CHURCH & ORDINATION

During the next nine years back home (while I was teaching MBAs at St. Mary's College and doing business ethics consulting in the Bay Area) I also was able finally to get more involved at Allen Temple Baptist Church, the most influential Black church (actually I would say of "any" church in my Oakland home town) over recent decades. Pastor J. Alfred Smith, Sr. was an associate of MLK and part of the Progressive National Baptist Convention that broke away from the National Baptist Convention when it wouldn't support MLK's social justice and civil rights actions. As I mentioned earlier, Pastor Smith was an occasional lecturer and commencement speaker in the 1980s for our New College Berkeley. I had often listened to his sermons on the radio and was always moved and enlightened.

After my return to Oakland in 2001, I started worshipping at Allen Temple from time to time (but was also needing to fulfill my teaching commitments to First

Presbyterian Church of Berkeley and Solano Community Church of Albany). One of my highest honors was being invited to preach at Allen Temple August 24, 2008. One of my best friends was Reggie Mastin, a deacon at Allen Temple, and my main thought and discussion partner as we dreamed of creating an entrepreneurship program for Oakland churches and neighborhoods. Reggie was always hustling, building the network, finding places for me to speak on business ethics, and attending business conferences together with me. It was no small tragedy when Reggie suddenly died in 2013. To this day I grieve his loss.

When I was surprised in 2010 by an "offer-I-couldn't-refuse" from Gordon-Conwell Seminary in Boston, I was about to join an actual theological seminary (my posts at New College Berkeley and North Park were not for teaching seminary students, though I had guest-taught many courses for seminarians at Fuller, Regent College, and elsewhere over the years). I really wanted to go to Gordon-Conwell not as a freelancer but examined, ordained, and sent by the church in Oakland. Allen Temple Baptist represented the theology, ethics, social concern, and ecclesiology closest to my own identity. Baptist churches ordain by congregation, not by denomination, a simpler, more direct process. So I asked Dr. J. Alfred Smith, Sr., if I could possibly be put through the ordination process and ordained by Allen Temple. Obviously, I was an unusual candidate at my age (age sixty-four) and with all my publications and experience. But I told Pastor Smith and the Allen Temple Board that I didn't want any special treatment. I would write all the essays on theology and go through the oral and written examination process. Everything went smoothly and I passed! On one of the greatest days of my life, with my friends Rev. Sheila Robinson and Rev. Randy Roth joining Rev. J. Alfred Smith and the Allen Temple elders, I knelt on May 9, 2010, to receive their laying on of hands and ordination to the ministry of the Gospel before I went off to Gordon-Conwell in fall 2010.

BLACK SEMINARIANS MATTER

More on my Gordon-Conwell experience (2010–2016) in a later chapter but one condition I gave the seminary before agreeing to come was that I could teach at least one of my annual courses at their urban Boston campus in Roxbury. They agreed. The student body at the main campus in Hamilton, Massachusetts, twenty miles north of Boston was ethnically fairly diverse, for which I was glad. The faculty was less so. One of my closest associates and friends was Prof. Patrick Smith in our theology and ethics department (Patrick is now on the faculty at Duke). At an early faculty meeting when we were discussing a couple faculty openings, I reminded the faculty that we must overcome the structural racism of recruiting only through the academic channels that found us, the current faculty. We needed to broaden our search through our Black pastors and churches and through the historically Black colleges, universities, and seminaries. Patrick thanked me afterward for not leaving it up to him to make this point! All of my own courses included required readings from the works of Martin Luther King, Jr., John Perkins, and other Black voices. The students noticed and appreciated it. These are such small and obvious things but so often ignored in seminary training. Their absence leads to pastorates occupied by only the partially-educated, prepared to perpetuate the past.

At an early gathering of the downtown Gordon-Conwell Advisory Council I met African-American pastor Larry Ward. During the meeting, Larry mentioned his entrepreneurship training for young folk near his church. This began a friendship that led a couple years later to our co-leadership of a Gordon-Conwell course called "Entrepreneurship in Church and Community." Over three years, Larry and I helped mostly inner-city folk create forty-five new small businesses (fifteen each Spring; more details in chapter 22 below). It was a demonstration that people in our churches and neighborhoods who need jobs can often create them with the help of Christians who know how to assist and accompany them. We were mounting a redemptive, creative response to the jobs crisis in our urban areas where the pain is so often born by our Black communities.

Another part of my Professor of Workplace Theology and Ethics position was running a Doctor of Ministry track in workplace theology. With a fairly free hand I redesigned the program away from its tendency to focus on white business executives so that it would instead relate to the whole people of God and their working lives. My students were half pastors and half laity. I made a special effort to recruit Black students, including those with African and Haitian backgrounds. More than one of my Black students over the four years I led this program told me how unusual it was and how much they appreciated being not just a "token" Black in the course but being part of a visible quarter or third of the group. I privately raised thousands of dollars to be sure no willing student was denied admission because of its cost.

Finally, I organized the first "Summit Conference" of Faith at Work leaders and organizations in North America. Again, so many of these ministries were focused on (white) business executives—"CEOs for Christ," Christian Businessmen's Committee, etc.. I made sure that we had significant Black voices on our program, which was sold out with 280 participants in October 2014. At a big follow-up conference in 2016, I chided the movement for still being "too pale and too male"—which got quoted long after the conference. Simple steps. Why are so many conference programs almost totally dominated by white guy speaker rosters? It is ridiculous.

BLACK WORKING LIVES MATTER (2016 ONWARD)

In 2016 I retired at age seventy and moved back home to Oakland, terribly missing my Boston colleagues and projects but knowing it was time to go home. After some quiet months of discernment, we joined First Covenant Church of Oakland, not least because of its commitment to include, hear, serve, and bless the whole people of

Oakland, including our Black brothers and sisters—in leadership and all other roles. I found my "lane" in teaching and writing about "Workplace Discipleship" and started a non-profit called "Workplace 313." Four of our founding eleven board members are African-American and we are determined that our leadership and programs listen to and serve the whole people of God. One of our first Workplace Forums was on "Black Lives Matter in the Workplace" led by the Rev. Dr. Gina Casey, an AME Zion pastor and former Intel executive. Despite the long interruption of face-to-face meetings by the Covid-19 pandemic, we are all committed to supporting Black working lives every bit as much as any others.

The Black Lives Matter movement, sparked by the too-frequent episodes of police brutality and even killing of Black folk, is a gift from God. It is about time. I love how people of all colors and backgrounds around the world have taken to the streets to insist that Black lives matter. Of course, we need police reform (better training, more community-based policing, less weapons-oriented responses, more accountability and discipline of wrong-doers). But we also need a focus on jobs, workplace fairness and development, and economic flourishing for all. Marching for "Black Lives Matter" does not entail or imply support for a Marxist worldview or attacks on traditional marriage any more than for the occasional vandalism perpetrated by anarchists and opportunistic fellow-travelers. Those are excuses, not reasons. Black lives (including Black working lives) matter because God and Scripture say so! We must stand up and say so and behave accordingly.

On a structural-institutional level we must acknowledge and confront the racism, prejudice, and injustice that have long infected our society, including our businesses, schools, seminaries, and churches. Repentance and new redemptive approaches are our mandate in the workplaces of our time. On an individual level, we all need to read much more history and biography and educate ourselves about the sins of the past and the best way forward. We need to act creatively, redemptively, wisely, and personally to overcome racism and build the Beloved Community MLK and Jesus call us to. Our tables—in our homes, churches, businesses, and neighborhoods—must become places where quite literally people are welcomed from east and west, north and south. That is what God promises for the future in the kingdom of God—and it is our mandate for now.

I have described a lengthy personal adventure in trying to answer my father's question "What Are You Doing About It?" My actions were never perfect and my learning continues. I am so grateful for the Black brothers and sisters who have patiently accompanied and taught me over the decades—including Bill Pannell, J. Alfred Smith, Sr., Sheila Robinson, Gina Casey, Larry Ward, Patrick Smith, Reggie Mastin, Reggie Jackson, and Ray Hammond. What I have done is nothing heroic or requiring exceptional talent. I want to inspire others to not be bystanders but do the right thing in the eyes of the God who created and loves everybody, including Black folk.

14

Jacques Ellul & France (1971-)

CERTAINLY ONE OF THE greatest shapers of my thinking and calling was French sociologist and theologian Jacques Ellul. I have sometimes said that my children learned how to say "Jacques Ellul" before they could say "Donald Duck." He and his name have been a constant presence for me and my family. Related to Ellul's influence on me, of course, is that of his country France. Here is how it happened. As I described above in my chapter on CWLF, Sharon Gallagher and I decided to devote an issue of *Right On* magazine in early fall 1971 to the theme of "the city." My assignment was to find and review anything that Christian thinkers had written about urbanization, its challenges and opportunities. I didn't find much help. Harvard theologian Harvey Cox's *Secular City* was popular but was more about celebrating the triumph of secularization than about the city per se. But I did find a new book, just published in 1970, called *The Meaning of the City*, by a French thinker named Jacques Ellul. I had barely heard of him but now read one of his books.

In *The Meaning of the City* Ellul studied the way the Bible treats cities from Genesis to Revelation.[1] I had written my pathetic paper on "Recreation and the Bible" in 1966 and then a (not so pathetic) MA thesis on "God and History" in 1971. I was not just interested in the Bible's take on "religious topics" like prayer, worship, and church. What might it have to say about law, work, money, art, and topics like that? I found Ellul's book on the city inspiring. He showed how God's original plan was for a garden, not a city. Plan B was for Cain to be a wanderer, a migrant (under God's protection). But Cain, and even more his son Enoch, decided to do their own thing, settle in one place, and build a walled city—trying to secure their own protection instead of relying on God. Ellul tracked the biblical cities through the Tower of Babel, to the slave cities

---

1. Jacques Ellul, T*he Meaning of the City* (Grand Rapids: Eerdmans, 1970).

of Egypt, to Babylon, Ninevah, and Rome, to the apocalyptic horror of Babylon the Great in the Revelation.

Meanwhile another track proceeded from Melchizedek's Salem, to the "cities of refuge," to Jerusalem, and finally to the eschatological New Jerusalem, the ultimate creation of God, the counterpart to Babylon. The end of history is not a new Garden of Eden but a new city, the New Jerusalem (with a beautiful garden at its heart). What began in rebellion, God graciously adopted, purified, and redeemed. In the meantime, God warned about the seductive power and corruption of the city as one of the potential abodes of the "principalities and powers." And yet the prophet Jeremiah called on the people of God not to abandon the city but to live and work in it, raise families, and actively seek its welfare and blessing. What Jeremiah called for, Daniel and others actually did, along with the early church, which was largely an urban movement. I thought Ellul was a little too pessimistic but very insightful. In my view, the basic (theological, anthropological) roots of the city are in our social nature created by God—people want and need to live and work together. Cain, Enoch, Lamech and the city of war are an aberration, not an essence. But what a marvelous, stimulating challenge Ellul had provided.

Just a couple months later I wanted to find some theological reflections on politics as I prepared to go cover the 1972 Democratic Convention with my press pass. I remembered some political titles from the cover jacket of *Meaning of the City*. I quickly found and read Ellul's sociology of politics and the state called *The Political Illusion*—in which he argued that, underneath all the ideological and rhetorical arguments between communists and socialists on one side and democrats and capitalists on the other, the common and decisive feature was the growth and bureaucratization of the state apparatus.[2] East and West, the state was growing and taking over more and more aspects of human life—and all of it was being subjected to the judgment of technological rationality and efficiency. I could really see what Ellul meant about the illusion of participation and control—though it still seemed to me that some differences of foreign and domestic policy were pretty important and not illusory (e.g., for the Vietnamese people).

Then came *The Politics of God and the Politics of Man*—Ellul's strictly biblical study of what he called "the most political book in the Bible," Second Kings.[3] This study was unyieldingly pessimistic about "ordinary politics." But what appeared useless and weak (prayer and faithful witness) could and did have decisive consequences. The next book I read was called *The Presence of the Kingdom*.[4] This little 150-page book had been written in 1948 just after the horrors of World War Two and Ellul's disappointments with the political reconstruction efforts in France. The church's stance

---

2. Jacques Ellul, *The Political Illusion* (New York: Knopf, 1967).

3. Jacques Ellul, *The Politics of God and the Politics of Man* (Grand Rapids: Eerdmans, 1972).

4. Jacques Ellul, *The Presence of the Kingdom* (New York: Seabury, 1967). A new translation by Lisa Richmond has been published as *Presence in the Modern World* (Eugene: Wipf & Stock, 2016).

was up for grabs. Ellul's first two chapters provided a brilliant call to a radically biblical, revolutionary Christianity which sought and exhibited the difference God could bring to our lost world. Christians should be the light of the world, the salt of the earth, and sheep in a world of wolves.

Ellul added a third chapter on "the End and the Means" to argue that the contemporary world worshipped endlessly proliferating "means" but lost sight of any worthy "ends." In fact, the (technological) means had become ends in themselves. If it can be done, it will be done. A fourth chapter discussed the problem of communication when we are assaulted and buried by bits of information and people are prone to take refuge in "explanatory myths"—conspiracy theories, rigid ideologies, or self-serving fantasies. In his final chapter, Ellul challenged Christians to be fully present in the heart of the world but with a fierce loyalty to the kingdom of God and a revolutionary life-style as faithful ambassadors of that kingdom. Finally, I read Ellul's *False Presence of the Kingdom*—a warning not to politicize the church in a way that its spiritual essence gets captured by secular politics.[5]

To say I was captivated by Ellul's thinking would be a massive understatement. Ellul expressed perfectly what I had come to see as biblical discipleship in politics and culture. I have read and re-read *Presence* several times, assigned it in every Christian ethics course I taught over the next five decades, and funded a new (more accurate) translation with an "Afterword" from me. After attending the Democratic Convention in 1972, I wrote a piece on the experience for *Right On* called "The Messiahs of Miami Beach." Then I took a chance and put my article and a couple book reviews in an envelope simply addressed to "Professor Jacques Ellul, Faculty of Law and Economic Sciences, University of Bordeaux, Bordeaux, France."

A couple months later I received a handwritten letter from Ellul himself (dated 14 September 1972). I couldn't yet read French so I walked over to Logos Bookstore on Telegraph Avenue to ask my friend Joan Terpstra Anderson to help me with a translation. Here it is:

> "Dear sir—How can I tell you of my joy in receiving your letter and reading Right On. It is excellent and full of Christian humor! Your summaries of my work are very good and I have rarely encountered as good an understanding of what I tried to say . . .
> Sincerely, Jacques Ellul"

Talk about an encouraging affirmation! Ellul went on in the letter to give his reactions to Jean Francois Revel (negative), Wolfhart Pannenberg (positive), John Warwick Montgomery (never heard of him), and Francis Schaeffer (never heard of him)—I had asked him about each one in my earlier letter. Over the next two years I read another fifteen of Ellul's books that were in English translation and also started researching, collecting and reading his journal articles which had been published in

---

5. Jacques Ellul, *False Presence of the Kingdom* (New York: Seabury, 1972).

PART TWO: SHAPERS (1964–1979)

English. My correspondence with Ellul continued for the next ten years until I finally met him in the summer of 1982. After 1982 we had personal visits in Bordeaux as well as correspondence until his death in 1994.

WHO WAS JACQUES ELLUL? (1912–1994)[6]

Who was this thinker and writer who acquired such a central place in my own thought? A sociologist, historian and Christian ethicist, Jacques Ellul was born (January 6, 1912) and raised in Bordeaux near the Atlantic Coast in southwestern France. He was the only child of Joseph and Marthe Ellul. His father, Joseph, of Italian and aristocratic Serbian origin, lived in Trieste and Malta before coming to France. He had a British passport because of his time in Malta. He had been raised Greek Orthodox but was personally a Voltairian agnostic. He had been ruined financially before son Jacques was born in 1912. Jacques's mother, Marthe (Mendes), was of French and Portuguese background, a Protestant believer but not a church attender out of respect for her agnostic husband. She painted until age eighty-two and a portrait of Jacques as a boy hung on the wall of his living room when I visited.

Ellul was thus raised in a relatively poor family. He spent his youth hanging out among the dock workers at the Bordeaux port on the Garonne River. He began earning his own living by age fifteen and continued to be self-supporting through his university years—by tutoring students in Latin, Greek, German, and French. He says he had only a "very remote knowledge of Christianity" in his childhood. Ellul graduated from Lycee Michel Montaigne in 1928 and began his studies at the University of Bordeaux where he earned his Licence (basically, a bachelor's degree) in Law in 1931 and then the Doctor of Law degree in 1936 (with a thesis on the Roman institution of the "Mancipium," a process for handling ownership transfers, including those of slaves).

Around 1931, Ellul read Marx's *Das Kapital* and said it seemed to answer all the questions he had been asking about what was happening in the world. He carefully and appreciatively read Marx's writings but never joined the Communist Party because it seemed so far from what Marx was actually advocating. About the same time Ellul also began a struggle with Christianity which intensified until around 1934 when he was converted to Christ with "a certain brutality." Ellul mentions three important factors (1) reading the eighth chapter of St. Paul's Romans, (2) translating Goethe's Faust, and (3) an almost mystical experience of the presence of God in his life.

The challenge for Ellul then was whether one could be both Marxist and Christian. By the late 1930s, he says, he "chose decisively for faith in Christ"—while retaining

---

6. The best introduction to Jacques Elul's life and work is *Jacques Ellul on Politics, Technology, and Christianity: Conversations With Patrick Troude-Chastenet* (Eugene: Wipf & Stock, 2005). Chastenet was Ellul's graduate assistant at the University of Bordeaux. More on him below. Another good introduction based on interviews is Jacques Ellul, *In Season, Out of Season* (based on interviews with Madeleine Garrigou-LaGrange). Introduction to the American Edition by David W. Gill (San Francisco: Harper & Row, 1982).

216

a deep appreciation for Marx's sociological method and insights. He believed Marx's economic analysis was especially insightful for the nineteenth century but that in the twentieth century *technique* (technological rationality and the quest for quantitative efficiency) was the key. In 1935 Ellul wrote his first article on *la technique*: "Since 1935 I have been convinced that on the sociological plane, technique was by far the most important phenomenon, and that it was necessary to start from there to understand everything else."[7] Ellul was a sociologist in the European tradition of Max Weber, Emile Durkheim, and Karl Marx, which draws together immense social historical data, creates an explanatory model, and puts it out there for examination, debate, and testing. This is not the obsessively quantitative and statistically-oriented American sociology which tries to imitate the physical sciences.

From 1933 to 1938 he and lifelong friend Bernard Charbonneau were associated with Emmanuel Mounier and the Personalist Movement and their journal *Esprit*. They eventually left the movement because they thought it was (a) drifting toward ordinary socialism, (b) too uncompromisingly Catholic, (c) too centralized as a movement, and (d) sociologically and theologically superficial. France had been devastated by World War One and was now hard hit by the Great Depression which reached its lowest point in France in 1935–36. People were nervous about the rise of National Socialism in Germany. The political tide turned left and Leon Blum's Popular Front coalition led the government from 1936–38. Ellul and his friends also supported the Spanish Civil War opposition to future dictator Franco.

After receiving his doctorate in 1936, Ellul taught law for a year at the University of Montpellier (1937), then transferred to Strasbourg in 1938. In 1937 he married Yvette Lensveldt (born in Holland to a Dutch Protestant father and a Belgian Catholic mother). They had first met at the University of Bordeaux. In 1939 Germany declared war on France and Ellul's Strasbourg faculty retreated south to Clermont-Ferrand. Paris fell on June 14, 1940, and the collaborationist Vichy government of Marshal Petain took power over defeated, occupied France (which included Bordeaux). Charles DeGaulle led a government-in-exile in England.

Ellul was fired from his university post in 1940 by the Vichy government for openly opposing Petain. From 1940 to 1944 he and Yvette retreated to a small farm at Martres, forty kilometers from Bordeaux. Ellul's father, Joseph, was arrested and sent to a detention camp in Besançon near Grenoble and the Swiss border in the east. Ill health led the Red Cross to intervene and get Joseph released after eighteen months and sent home at age seventy only to die a year later in 1942. During the Nazi occupation, Ellul worked with the French Resistance, engaging in espionage, sabotage, and protection of Jews (many from Bordeaux were sent to death camps). After the end of the War Ellul was among those honored for their efforts to protect Jews from the Nazis.

---

7. "Foreword" by Jacques Ellul to James Holloway, editor, *Introducing Jacques Ellul* (Grand Rapids: Eerdmans, 1970), 6.

During the occupation, Ellul studied theology with the Strasbourg faculty (Protestant) which had been exiled to Clermont-Ferrand. He completed all the coursework before the Liberation except the final thesis—so he never received the actual theological degree. He was always technically a layman—but a seminary-educated layman at that who became a frequent preacher and church leader in the French Reformed Church.

As a participant and leader in the Resistance, Ellul was briefly part of the Bordeaux city government after the Liberation in 1944. His responsibilities were for public works and commerce. He tried to insist on integrity in government—refusing bribery and favoritism in giving contracts for city public works projects. But all his hopes for a revolutionary new order were dashed by DeGaulle's insistence on returning French politics and administration to its prewar pattern. Bordeaux Mayor Jacques Chaban-Delmas was on the fast track to becoming a millionaire from his political power and connections. The departmental chiefs below Ellul were in cahoots with those who bid on contracts. From both above and below, Ellul found reform efforts were thwarted and he gave up ever again trying to bring about political change through ordinary participation. He even abstained from voting, thinking it was a useless exercise.

ACADEMIC CAREER

In 1944, after the war was over, Ellul was appointed Professor of the History and Sociology of Institutions in the Faculty of Law and Economic Sciences at the University of Bordeaux, where he worked without a break until he retired in 1980. He also taught regularly in the Institute of Political Studies. Ellul taught courses on the history of legal, political, and economic institutions, on the history and sociology of technique/technology, and on its impacts on politics, propaganda, and other areas. He regularly taught courses on Karl Marx and his successors. As a professor he read his lectures in class and welcomed student questions at the end of his written sections. He never had a sabbatical or any secretarial support—but also told me he had no committee assignments to distract him.

Typically, he read and did research through the academic year and then finished writing his books during his summers. As a French university professor, he told me, his manuscripts were almost automatically published without much editorial review or correction. In our conversations, Ellul marveled at all the editorial hoops I had to jump through to get published. He never used a typewriter but rather wrote in longhand (almost indecipherably!). He gave his manuscripts to a hired typist (the same woman for many years), then made additional notes and corrections, got them retyped, and submitted them to the publisher. He was pretty much a single-minded and undistracted scholar year after year but he did courageously stand up as a student advocate and arbiter during the massive student protests of 1968. Ellul was awarded honorary doctorates from the universities of Aberdeen and Amsterdam, the latter on the same occasion as Martin Luther King, Jr., in October 1965.

THE SOCIOLOGICAL ANALYSIS

I have to give you a summary of the massive authorship that forever influenced me. First the sociology, then the theology. Ellul published some sixty (there are still unpublished manuscripts, hence "some sixty") books and more than a thousand articles, essays, and reviews—for professional journals within and beyond France, popular channels like *Le Monde, Ouest-France*, and *Le Quotidien de Paris*, and religious journals like *Foi et Vie* and *Reforme*. Ellul was a regular contributor to the local and regional newspapers, *Sud-Ouest* and *Ouest-France*. The literary production is monumental in scope and in quality.

Ellul is known best for *The Technological Society*.[8] It was Aldous Huxley who recommended the translation and publication of this book in English, saying that it made precisely the point he was trying to get across in *Brave New World*. "Technique" (the method of rationalistic, quantitative analysis in search of measurably efficient means) is the increasingly dominant mode of thought and source of value not just in science and technology but in the politics, economics, pedagogy, art, religion, communications, and the popular culture of the modern world. Two other major studies he wrote explored how "technique" had invaded and transformed politics into the *Political Illusion* and communications into *Propaganda: The Formation of Men's Attitudes*.[9] Among Ellul's other sociological books are *The Technological System, The Technological Bluff*, and *The Autopsy of Revolution*. His sociology of religion, *The New Demons*, argues that the state and technique have become today's locus of the sacred in what amounts to new "secular" religions, complete with saints, worship, and ritual.[10] His *Humiliation of the Word* argues that our culture has suffered the loss of truth by its preference for visual images over the oral and written word.[11]

Jacques Ellul is regarded by all scholars in the history of technology studies as one of the most important pioneers in the field which includes Max Weber, Herbert Marcuse, Martin Heidegger, Aldous Huxley, Lewis Mumford, and, more recently, Neil Postman and Albert Borgmann. Ellul is often criticized for being too pessimistic and even fatalistic about the growth and dominance of technology but two responses must be made. First, he often wrote that he was describing things as they would unfold if human beings did not rise up decisively to resist. And secondly, it is hard to deny the actual scope and power of what he preferred to call "*la technique*" in today's world.

"Technique" includes, of course, all of the tools, machines, and devices which dominate our lives, and the networks which connect our fate and amplify both our

---

8. Jacques Ellul, *The Technological Society* (New York: Knopf, 1964). Original French edition, *La Technique, ou l'enjeu du siècle* (literally: "technique, the stake of the century' or "what is at stake this century") (Paris: Armand Colin, 1954).

9 Jacques Ellul, *Political Illusion* (New York: Knopf, 1967) and *Propaganda: The Formation of Men's Attitudes* (New York: Knopf, 1965).

10 Jacques Ellul, *The New Demons* (New York: Seabury, 1975).

11. Jacques Ellul, *The Humiliation of the Word* (Grand Rapids: Eerdmans, 1985).

opportunities and dangers. But even more profoundly, Technique (he advised using a capital "T" to emphasize that he wasn't just talking about one specific technology or another but the whole) refers ultimately to a method and an ensemble of methods centered on rationality, artificiality, efficiency, power, speed, standardization, and replicability which is taken for granted and welcomed into every corner of the globe and every aspect of human existence. The dominant reality of our culture is the increasingly networked "technological system"—expressed concretely and visibly in our built environment, machines, and devices but even more profoundly as the (almost) unchallenged spirit of our civilization. Quantifiable, rational efficiency is the supreme value. But a method that is often good and appropriate in addressing a specific challenge to meet a human need, when untethered from human purposes, becomes both dehumanizing to people and devastating to the natural environment.

Modern technology critics like Neil Postman (*Technopoly: The Surrender of Culture to Technology*), Albert Borgmann (*Technology and the Character of Contemporary Life*), Carl Mitcham (*Thinking Through Technology: The Path Between Engineering and Philosophy*), Langdon Winner (*Autonomous Technology*), David Lovekin (*Technique, Discourse and* Consciousness), Evgeny Morozov (*The Net Delusion* and *To Save Everything, Click Here*), Sherry Turkle (*Life on the Screen: Identity in the Age of the Internet*), Nicholas Carr (*The Shallows: What the Internet is Doing to Our* Brains), Richard Stivers (*Technology as Magic*), and Martin Ford (*The Rise of the Robots: Technology and the Threat of a Jobless Future*) are among those exploring and extending the critique that goes back to Ellul and his generation of pioneers.

Of course, the cheerleaders for technological development are even more numerous, with bigger platforms, utopian promises, vast financial resources and opportunities for wealth, power, and influence. Technological problems are always answered with technological solutions—almost never with boundaries or agreements on "enough." Nothing is sacred except Technique which continues to invade personal and religious life as much as any other domains. Ellul articulated a massive, powerful critique of our civilization, starting many decades ago. My Ellulian colleagues and I think it is more important than ever. How to respond? Much of Ellul's suggested response is in the phrase he coined in the 1930s: "Think globally, Act locally" (penser globalement, agir localement).

ELLUL'S THEOLOGICAL RESPONSE

Ellul became almost equally famous for his creative and insightful theological writings, parallel to his study of the sociological (and spiritual) reality of technique/technology. Some of his readers seem to know only one side or the other of his writings but he insisted they is a kind of dialectic between his sociological study of reality and his theological study of what is true. Only the "Wholly Other" transcendent God can possibly leverage fundamental change in our technological civilization closing in on itself. To see where he was coming from, consider this: in the secularized nation of France, Ellul was a believer. In a country dominated religiously by the Roman Catholic Church, Ellul was a Reformed thinker. Even within the Reformed Church of France (heirs of the French Huguenots), Ellul was a distinctive voice, nurtured by his immersion in the Bible, by his special friendships with Jewish scholars like Andre Chouraqui, by his Reformed pastor Jean Bosc, by the existentialist (anti-Modern) Christianity of Soren Kierkegaard, and by the neo-Reformed theology of Karl Barth. For Ellul, the "Wholly Other" God spoke and acted in the Hebrew prophets and then decisively and uniquely in the incarnation of Jesus of Nazareth, in whom the transcendent God became flesh in our here-and-now.[12]

Jacques and Yvette Ellul formed a small house church in their living room/salon. Blue collar workers gathered alongside professional types. Men as well as women became heavily involved and the growth in numbers required a larger meeting space so the Elluls donated a parcel on the edge of their property and a modest chapel was built by the hands-on labor of church members. However, Ellul told me, as the house church became a bit more formal and "church-like" they lost many of the original participants, especially the men. Ellul continued to provide pastoral care, teaching, and worship leadership until his death forty years later. He also was a frequent guest preacher and conference speaker, especially for Reformed congregations, all of his life.

From 1951 to 1970, Ellul served on the National Council of the French Reformed Church and worked on several of its committees. In those years the Reformed Church, the biggest and oldest Protestant denomination in France, had maybe 300,000 members but was declining year-by-year in attendance. In the 1980s when I visited Ellul in Bordeaux, there were still at least a dozen Reformed parishes in the region—but today there remains only one in downtown Bordeaux, populated mostly by the elderly. I loved attending not just the Pessac chapel next to his house (and his weekly Bible studies on Ecclesiastes in 1984–85) but his guest sermons at other parishes and at a conference of university students for the GBU (French InterVarsity). I was also inspired by Ellul's stories of efforts in the 1950s and 1960s to form "Associations of Protestant Professionals" for reflection on the implications of Christian faith for medicine, law, business, art, and other fields. He told me that our New College Berkeley project (described later in this memoir) was an even better attempt to achieve the goals of those Associations.

For the national French Reformed leadership, Ellul helped form a Commission on Strategy in 1957–58 to help the church improve its organization, its relation to society, and its approach to evangelization. The ten-member commission worked out a good plan but after six years of frustration it ended in failure, defeated by a ponderous bureaucracy, tradition, apathy, and indifference. Ellul also set up a six-member

---

12. Even the non-religious among Ellul's followers like his emphasis on incarnation. Truth must not remain abstract but be incarnated in daily life and reality.

commission to study the problem of hermeneutics (biblical interpretation) but the liberals and Calvinists dropped out until only the three Barthians, including Ellul, were left.

Finally, Ellul worked on the reform of theological education. His commission proposed a year of basic theological study open to laity as well as prospective clergy, something I have always advocated. Then those interested in the pastorate were to spend a year or two as interns and apprentices in actual parishes—after which they could return for a year or two of study in the specific tasks of preaching, pastoral care, worship leadership and the like. This approach was intended to prepare a much stronger, more theologically-integrated lay presence in the world as well as a more carefully tested and "called" clergy. Again, the plan went essentially nowhere in the face of institutional conservatism and ineffective implementation. Based on these experiences, Ellul decided the institutional church was incapable of reforming itself. Dialogue and communication were as difficult inside the church as outside in society.

Backing up a bit, Ellul also participated in various commissions of the newly-founded World Council of Churches from 1947 onward. As a member of the WCC Committee on Work he felt a growing dissatisfaction which "came out in the open in 1966 at the Conference on Church and Society"—because (a) the WCC was becoming an enormous bureaucratic machine obeying sociological law instead of the promptings of the Holy Spirit; (b) the old theological differences were being overcome only because theology was unimportant!—and new political lines of cleavage appeared which were even more ominous; (c) failure to perceive and deal with the real problems of society—inadequate social research and failure to engage in careful theological research—instead taking rash, irrelevant, foolish positions; and (d) a tendency to minimize the tension between church and world. Faith in the Wholly Other, Ellul always argued, should lead to specific, unique positions and an ability to see ahead and in depth like the "watchman on the wall" in Ezekiel 33.

Ultimately much more theologically impactful than his organizational efforts, was Ellul the writer. Not least was his work as Editor from 1969 to 1986 of *Foi et Vie*, the leading protestant theological journal. He wrote many volumes of theological and biblical studies promoting a radical Christian way of freedom, holiness and love for individuals who refuse to bow to the "principalities and powers" of our era, i.e., nationalism, technique, rationalism, quantification, and efficiency. His theological works included *The Meaning of the City, Prayer and Modern Man, Money and Power, Living Faith, Hope In Time of Abandonment, Genesis, Apocalypse: the Book of Revelation, the Judgment of Jonah, the Politics of God and the Politics of Man, The Theological Foundation of Law, Reason for Being* (on *Ecclesiastes*, his favorite book of the Bible), *If You Are the Son of God: Sufferings and Temptations of Jesus*, and *Violence: Reflections from a Christian Perspective*.

Specifically in my field of ethics, in addition to the 1948 masterpiece, *The Presence of the Kingdom*, he produced a superb introduction to Christian ethics, *To Will and To Do: An Ethical Research for Christians* and *The Ethics of Freedom*.[13] His massive, thousand-page *Ethics of Holiness* is still in process of publication after many delays getting his hand-written manuscript ready. His *Subversion of Christianity* was a brilliant review of ways Christian theology and witness have been compromised over the centuries by the Crusades and other influences. *What I Believe* summarized his key theological ideas and convictions.[14] Since his death in 1994 several other unpublished works have appeared, including *Islam and Judeo-Christianity* and transcriptions of his Bible study tape-recordings and lecture notes on John. James, and other biblical texts. Two small volumes of Ellul's poetry have been published, *Silences* and *Oratorio: Les Quatre Cavaliers de l'Apocalypse*.[15] It all amounts to an incredible collection of theological reflection, always grounded in Jesus Christ and Scripture but ground-breaking in creative insight and application.

AND MORE

Ellul traveled to North Africa, Israel, and throughout Europe but never on an airplane, and never to the Western Hemisphere, despite my and many other's invitations and efforts. When he expressed concerns about his health on such a long trip, I offered to arrange for his physician to accompany him but he still declined. I told him that appreciative American audiences would flock to hear and meet him even if the French were taking him for granted much of the time! After moving fourteen times during their first ten years of marriage, the Elluls settled (by 1952) in an unostentatious, sprawling, one-story "chartreuse" in Pessac (29, avenue A. Danglade), called La Marriere. They also maintained a modest summer house in Le Canon on the Bay of Arcachon near the Atlantic Coast. Beginning in 1948, Yvette led a monthly book discussion group for a dozen women—some of her studies were written up and published in *Foi et Vie*. Yvette drove their car (aggressively—I am witness!) but Jacques never got his license. A pet boxer dog named "Pearl" totally ruled the household from what I could see.

The Elluls had four children. The oldest, Jean (b. 1940), earned a doctorate in anthropology specializing in Cambodia and was married to two Cambodian sisters (not at the same time!). They had four children: Wim, Eric, Jerome, and Veronique. The Ellul's second-born son Simon (1941–47) was tragically killed by a speeding car at age six. Yves (b. 1945) was first an architect but then became a French Reformed pastor in Toulouse, raising four children with his theologian wife Danielle. Finally, daughter Dominique (b. 1949) was long married to a French Reformed pastor and has one son,

---

13. Jacques Ellul, *To Will and To Do: An Ethical Research for Christians* (Philadelphia: Pilgrim, 1969) and *The Ethics of Freedom* (Grand Rapids: Eerdmans, 1976).

14. Jacques Ellul, *The Humiliation of the Word* (Grand Rapids: Eerdmans, 1985) and *What I Believe* (Grand Rapids: Eerdmans, 1989).

15. Visit www.ellul.org and www.jacques-ellul.org for a comprehensive bibliography of Ellul's books.

Part Two: Shapers (1964–1979)

Rafael. Especially after their father's death in 1994, Jean, Yves, and Dominique have all been active in seeing their father's unpublished works brought to press and kept in print. Of the grandchildren, Jerome has taken the strongest lead in promoting his grandfather's work, liaising with us North Americans, and working on a film on Ellul's life, including many clips from his broadcast talks and interviews.

Jacques Ellul also led a film discussion group in Bordeaux from 1945–55. In 1958 he founded (with Yves Charrier) one of the first French clubs for the prevention of juvenile delinquency, a sort of "drop-in center," and spent time with street kids and gangs, even helping them with representation in court cases. His books include a critique of society's usual definition and stigmatization of "deviant" behavior. Beginning in 1968 he got involved in the environmental movement, especially with the "Committee for Defense of the Aquitaine Coast" (against the plans of developers and energy companies).

STUDYING ELLUL (1974–79)

After my informal beginnings in 1971–73, as a graduate student at the University of Southern California (1974–79) I did a deep dive into Ellul's writings. I took a crash course in "French Reading and Translation" so I could understand his untranslated writings. I took copious notes on what I read and also exchanged several letters with Ellul. I did major seminar research and writing projects on his three primary intellectual sources: Karl Marx, Soren Kierkegaard, and Karl Barth, and also studied biblical, theological, and social ethics, and the history of the American intellectual response to the rise of industrialization and technology. My USC doctoral mentor Jack Crossley was an expert on Kierkegaard and Barth. One of those years I was privileged to study with Visiting Professor John Coleman Bennett, an icon in the social ethics field (and colleague and contemporary of Reinhold Niebuhr). Bennett pressed hard against Ellul's theology and ethics from his Christian Realist perspective. We had a wonderful year debating each other in and out of class. After passing my comprehensive/qualifying exams in these subfields I embarked on a doctoral dissertation on "The Word of God in the Ethics of Jacques Ellul."[16]

My dissertation investigated how the ancient Scriptures and the figure of Jesus (two representations of the "Word of God") could possibly provide form and content for an ethics for our time, two thousand years later in a vastly different cultural milieu. I explored how Ellul bridged that gap and compared his approach to the viewpoints of other Christian social ethicists. During the fall of 1976 Professor Lewis Smedes invited me to teach a one-quarter course on Jacques Ellul at Fuller Theological Seminary in Pasadena (where I lived). Every week I prepared my lectures and engaged a "sold out" class of thirty great students. Teaching this course forced me to complete

---

16. Later published as David W. Gill, *The Word of God in the Ethics of Jacques Ellul* (Metuchen, New Jersey: Scarecrow Press, 1984).

a broad, synoptic understanding of Ellul while my dissertation project took me deep into the core issues. Several of those Fuller students, including Anthony Petrotta, Robert Mayer, and David Fraser, went on to distinguished academic careers and became lifetime friends.

I was publishing some occasional book reviews of Ellul and, through my research into the secondary literature and participation in ethics conferences, getting connected to other Ellul scholars. One of my primary conversation partners became Professor Vernard Eller of LaVerne University just east of Pasadena. Eller had written some interesting essays on Ellul and exchanged a few letters with him so we had a lot to share. One day Eller told me about a proposed book of essays by Ellul scholars to better introduce Ellul to American scholars.[17] He showed me the bibliography of Ellul's writings that was proposed as part of the book. It was hopelessly incomplete so I wrote to the book editor Professor Cliff Christians and offered him a much more comprehensive and accurate version, which then appeared in the book. Over a lunch together, Eller showed me his essay on Kierkegaard and Ellul which had been rejected by the editors! On a napkin at the restaurant (followed up in a letter) I outlined six or seven clear and distinct parallels and echoes of SK in Ellul's work. I was shocked when the book appeared a few months later and Eller's essay followed my outline exactly—with no mention that I was the source! Of course, I couldn't believe that Vernard intentionally stole my ideas; he just forgot! But it was a strong lesson to me that I would always be sure to give public credit to anyone whoever helped me along the way![18]

During and after my PhD studies I was frequently invited to give lectures on Ellul's thought. I taught a six-week course on Ellul for our first ever summer school in 1978 at New College Berkeley and gave a series of lectures at Westmont College in Santa Barbara. I was also publishing reviews of Ellul's books not just in *Radix* but in *Eternity, Christianity Today, the Reformed Journal* and elsewhere. In the American Academy of Religion and the Society of Christian Ethics I presented research papers and began working with other Ellul scholars like Darrell Fasching to get a hearing for his work.

BORDEAUX AT LAST

I often thought about making a pilgrimage to Bordeaux to meet Ellul face-to-face during my doctoral studies, but we didn't have the money and I had sufficient access to his writings in French as well as English. I could always write to him with my questions. I also really didn't want to leave my wife and kids out of the great adventure of visiting

---

17. Published as *Jacques Ellul: Interpretative Essays*, edited by Clifford Christians and Jay Van Hook (University of Illinois, 1981). My bibliography is pp. 309–328.

18. My article "Jacques Ellul: The Prophet as Theologian" in *Themelios* (7.1 September 1981: 4–14) describes Ellul's relationship to the ideas of Kierkegaard and Barth.

Part Two: Shapers (1964–1979)

Europe for the first time. We were finally able to go as a family to Europe for two months in the summer of 1982. Ward Gasque, the president of New College Berkeley, and his wife Laurel were world-travelers and insisted we needed to get over to France. They raised a couple thousand dollars to help us buy the tickets. Finally, in June 1982, we sold our old VW bus with two hundred thousand miles on it and ordered a new one to be picked up on our arrival in Frankfurt. From the airport we drove directly to a camping equipment store and bought two little tents, four sleeping bags, and some basic camping equipment. We drove off from Frankfurt with a couple good maps and a detailed four hundred-page directory of campgrounds all over Europe. We figured out later that our housing cost averaged $6 per night over two months for the four of us as we camped around Germany, France, Switzerland, and England. We mostly bought our food at grocery stores and ate in the campgrounds. We loved meeting and chatting with fellow-campers from all over Europe, with endless opportunities (often necessities) to speak German (me) or French (Lucia). We visited a lot of cathedrals and museums and bribed our ten- and eleven-year old kids to be patient on those visits: if they would be patient, we would stop for a swim at the very next river or beach we saw when we departed!

We finally got to Bordeaux in July 1982 to meet and interview Ellul. For that two weeks, we stayed at the downtown flat of Joyce Hanks, who was in Bordeaux for a year-long sabbatical from the University of Costa Rica where Joyce was Professor of French. Joyce had committed herself (at my instigation!) to the detailed detective work of preparing an accurate, comprehensive bibliography of Ellul's writings, an enormous task which eventually resulted in several published volumes that became essential for all Ellul researchers. Joyce went on also to prepare excellent English translations of three or four of Ellul's books. In 1982 Joyce not only hosted us in Bordeaux but agreed to go with us to meet with Ellul in his home and translate during the interview (Lucia also helped with the translation, especially later back in Berkeley as we prepared the recorded interviews for publication).

Meeting Jacques and Yvette Ellul in their home was my dream come true. They were both exceedingly kind, offering us tea, and Yvette making sure our kids were happy (partly with their dog Pearl's help). Neither of the Elluls spoke English with us. I could not yet speak much French so I spoke in English and Ellul answered in French. He spoke so clearly and, by this time, I understood his thought and conceptual framework so well that I didn't need a translation about a third of the time. Later that fall I published translations of our interviews in *Christianity Today* and *Radix*. Joyce had cautioned me that Ellul had no interest in being a celebrity and I should not try to take a lot of photographs. As a result I have only one decent photograph together with him in his back yard. I snapped a couple others of the Elluls with my wife and kids. On the Sunday in between our two weeks in Bordeaux we planned to attend the church where Ellul was preaching and I urged Joyce to let us all invite the Elluls to Sunday lunch at the Hanks apartment. She was very hesitant but I prevailed, the Elluls agreed, and brought two bottles of great Bordeaux wine to our mid-day feast. We passed a joyful and wonderful Sunday afternoon together.

BORDEAUX SABBATICAL 1984-85

Before we parted at the end of our two-week visit, I asked Ellul if I could spend my upcoming 1984–85 sabbatical study leave in Bordeaux and meet with him. He agreed! I wanted to be able to interview him about his work but also more generally discuss Christian and technological ethics with him—and I told him I would like to be of help to him in any way during our time together. He said he would love some help discerning what were the most important American voices in contemporary Christian ethics. During that sabbatical year I met with him in his home every other Friday afternoon. He read and commented on my book on the New Testament figure of Peter (a commentary in the Ellulian style was my goal) and we engaged a lot in discussions of the Decalogue (I was beginning some research that eventually led to my 2004 book *Doing Right: Practicing Ethical Principles*) and of education, work, and other topics. I prepared for him fairly thorough introductions and reviews of the work of James Gustafson, John Howard Yoder, Stanley Hauerwas, and other American Christian ethicists. I often accompanied him to his guest preaching gigs and once to a weekend retreat of university students sponsored by the Group Biblique Universitaire (like the American InterVarsity). I attended his evening series of studies on Ecclesiastes which he eventually published as *Reason for Being*. We did have the Elluls to our Bordeaux home for an evening dinner and conversation.

To help fund our year in Bordeaux (since my monthly sabbatical pay would be fifty percent of normal for the year) we rented out our Oakland house for about $2000 per month while in less expensive Bordeaux we rented a spacious old flat for only $1000 per month. Ellul himself helped us by calling on his old friend Henri Cerezuelle who had a vacant place at 6, rue St. Joseph, in the old Chartrons neighborhood near the Jardin Public where Ellul had grown up, just blocks from the docks of the Garonne River. That was our home for twelve months. We repeated our Volkswagon bus strategy again for the sabbatical year, selling what we had in America and picking up a new one in Frankfurt. With no street parking, we rented a space in a garage a block from our flat. We were totally immersed in French language and culture, rarely hearing English except in our own family.

We got to know our neighbors and the nearby shops where we bought our provisions. We often drove out into the wine country of the Medoc and St. Emilion to explore our Lord's favorite beverage. Jonathan and I ventured out early every morning to a great boulangerie for a fresh loaf of pain de compagne ("country bread") still warm from the oven (augmented by croissants fairly regularly!). I joined a nearby gym where I could lift weights and also ran a lot of miles in the Parc Bordelais. Toward the end of the year I ran the Bordeaux half-marathon (twenty-one kilometers) in one

Part Two: Shapers (1964–1979)

hour and forty minutes. We visited the beach at Arcachon from time to time. During school breaks we visited Italy, Spain, Holland, and Belgium as well as several regions of France. We attended a nearby Eglise Evangelique Libre and often invited these new friends to Sunday dinner after church at our house—or were invited to church friends' homes.

When we arrived in Bordeaux in summer 1984, I enrolled at the University of Bordeaux's Center for the Study of French for Foreigners. I did an intensive daily language course during four weeks of July, then had a week off, followed by another four weeks in August. While I had a pretty big reading vocabulary I couldn't really speak or listen with understanding and didn't know the grammar or how to construct a sentence. I was tested and assigned to the most elementary level: A-1. No one else spoke English in a class full of Germans, Italians, Turks, Chinese and other internationals. It was French or nothing! After finishing the second intensive in August, I bought Ellul's latest book and made a vocabulary card for every word I didn't recognize—six hundred more to add to the box of one thousand basic French words I had been working on for several years. Every day I would smoke my pipe and review those cards. By the end of September I was ready to start meeting with Ellul every other Friday!

At this point I was on my own. Ellul asked me to speak French and I agreed but urged him to correct me. At one of our first meetings at his house, I greeted him with "Comment vous appelez vous?" I had meant to say "Comment allez vous?"—"how are you?"—not "what is your name?" He laughed and said "Jacques Ellul" and I was horrified at my gaff. Lucia was now busily enrolled in an advanced master's level French program all year at the university—and finished all the coursework but not the final project or thesis for the degree. We enrolled our kids (ages twelve and thirteen now) in regular French public schools. They knew almost nothing at the beginning of the school year but, with Lucia's coaching every evening, their own dogged determination, and some sweet encouraging friendships with French school mates, they were both fluent by the end of the school year (and remain so today). Jonathan played soccer all year with Le Coq Rouge, a local boys soccer team. We all loved walking around beautiful old Bordeaux and most aspects of living there. The noisy motorcycles and daily garbage collection trucks during down our street, the dog poop everywhere on the streets, the drivers who never stopped for pedestrians, and occasional rudeness irritated us but the overall impression was wonderful.

Learning a language is tough. When we started attending our nearby church, I could introduce myself in two or three coherent sentences but soon was exhausted and went out in the street with Jonathan to wait for fluent Lucia and adventurous Jodie to finish their longer conversations. I remember saying to her on our walk home: "You know what they are saying back there at the church: 'What a lovely lady that Lucia is from California. Too bad she had to bring her dull-witted husband along with her!'" I got a lot better as time went on, of course. Another big gaff was when I returned for that second month-long intensive in the first summer. I had been assigned to level A-3 but really wanted to be in level A-2 because of a great teacher Mr. Roussille. I marched into the registration office to ask for a change and explained "Mais je desire Mr. Roussille!" The five women in the office shrieked with laughter. I thought I was saying "I want Mr. Roussille" but they told me what I actually said was "I have sexual desire for Mr. Roussille." Oops. My Canadian friend in Bordeaux, Jennifer Adams, later told me about an American student who was asked to speak at a graduation ceremony and began "Quand j'observe mon derriere, il tombe en deux partie," at which point there was hysterical laughter. She thought she was saying "When I look at my past (what lies behind me) I see it falls into two parts," but what she actually said was "When I look at my rear end, I see it falls in two parts."

It was an amazing year, full of challenges but of incredible learning and joy. I have thought about the progression a lot. For the first four months or so I was dazzled by everything we experienced and thought life in France was next to perfect. Then I struggled a bit for three or four months with some of the aggravations. And in the final four months I found an equilibrium where I realized I was really an American in so many ways but loved France as a true second home. I have often said that if we had just stayed there for six months, we might have left with a sense of some failure. Not just me, our kids didn't fully hit their stride until the second half of the year. A lesson for others I think.

I returned to Bordeaux to be with Ellul for a month in summer 1988 and two weeks in 1991. Lucia and I returned again for a month in summer 1995 but Yvette had died in 1991 and Jacques in 1994. The world felt like an emptier place for me when they passed on. Henri Cerezuelle, who had been our proprietor in 1984–85, became a good friend during the years and visited us in both Oakland and Chicago. He loved American jazz and accompanied us to some blissful clubs and concerts. He had plenty to share about Bordeaux and his friend Ellul and their common interests. Henri also drove me in his car into the foothills of the Pyrenees below Bordeaux to spend a day with Bernard Charbonneau, Ellul's best friend and a leading French intellectual and author in his own right. Henri's son Daniel and wife Anita Cerezuelle became dear friends from 1984 onward. I often stayed with them on my Bordeaux visits and we again rented 6, rue St. Joseph for six months at the beginning of 2000. They had renovated the old place and made it their home. I love returning to them, the old neighborhood, and the shopkeepers we got to know. "The Americans are back" they would greet us, "welcome home!"

Through Daniel and Anita, we got to know many other Ellul scholars and friends over the years, such as Simon Charbonneau (son of Bernard), Franck Brugerolle (Ellul's doctor and the recorder of some two hundred fifty cassette tapes of Ellul's Bible studies—a set of which he prepared for me and for American scholars, now digitized in the Ellul Collection at Wheaton College), and Prof. Jean-Francois and Burney Medard. When people ask me to describe my favorite experiences in Europe I always describe a Sunday afternoon picnic lunch on the big lawn in front of Jean-Francois and

Burney Medard's summer house on the banks of the Dordogne River. Children are running around and a dozen family and friends enjoy great Bordeaux wine, a veritable feast at a long picnic table, and long hours of conversation about every topic imaginable. Heaven. I also got to know Ellul's adult children Jean, Yves, and Dominique after Ellul's death in 1994, most of his grand-children, and the leading Ellul scholar in the world, Patrick Chastenet, and his wife Chantal Demongin. The Cerezuelles and Chastenets have visited us in the USA and been part of our Ellul conferences.

PROMOTING AND ORGANIZING

In the 1980s with Ellul scholars like Joyce Hanks, Carl Mitcham, Cliff Christians, and Darrel Fasching I helped organize discussions and scholarly meetings on Ellul's thought at the American Academy of Religion (the largest professional association of religion and theology professors in the world) and the Society of Christian Ethics. In 1988 I was part of the founding board of the *Ellul Forum for the Critique of Technological Civilization* edited for the next twelve years by Professor Darrell Fasching of the University of South Florida. In 2001 Cliff Christians, Professor of Communications at the University of Illinois, succeeded Darrell as editor and I began serving as publisher, sharpening up our look, strengthening our content, and improving our subscription service and financing. I continued that until 2013, our 25th anniversary and publication of our 50th issue. Since then, we have added a great online presence and our editor Dr. Lisa Richmond took the *Ellul Forum* to new levels of quality and impact. I also worked hard to assist Lisa Richmond and others in building up large archives of Ellul's works at Wheaton College (and later at Regent College).

After my visit to Bordeaux in 1995, the year after Ellul's death, I tried hard to launch a project to buy his very large house and property to be the base for a "Jacques Ellul Center for Sociological and Theological Studies," housing his immense personal library, hosting visiting scholars and academic conferences, and financing operations by renting housing to graduate students from the nearby University of Bordeaux. I drafted a plan and approached fifty North American Ellul scholars and "fans" in search of funding and leadership. There was a great deal of enthusiasm but little funding and few who could join in the leadership. I simply could not afford to leave my own academic post at North Park University. My French colleagues were also eager to do something with this very strategic property but the adult children of Ellul preferred to sell the property to realize their inheritance (understandable!). The property has since been redeveloped as retail housing. Sad. One of my "What Are You Doing About It?" projects that failed to get off the ground!

I returned to France several times for conferences on Ellul's thought and from 1995 onward became close friends and colleagues with Patrick Troude Chastenet. Patrick had been Ellul's graduate assistant when doing his own doctorate at the University of Bordeaux. After serving as "Maitre de Conferences" at Bordeaux's Institute for Political Science, Patrick was named Professor of Political Science at Reims (2000), then Poitiers (2002), and finally at Ellul's old Faculty of Law and Political Science at the University of Bordeaux (2010). He is the author of several books about Ellul and the best, most complete, interviews with Ellul. When I spent the first six months of 2000 in Bordeaux, Patrick and I often met to discuss the future of Ellul studies. Many of Ellul's books were going out of print and his influence was waning. I proposed that we do something parallel to what the students of Dietrich Bonhoeffer had done (in German and English): start two sister societies, a French-language Association Internationale Jacques Ellul (AIJE) and an English-language International Jacques Ellul Society (IJES).

The burgeoning internet was full of misinformation about Ellul, referring to him as a "dour Catholic," author of fifteen books (not fifty!), and the like. By contrast, the Bonhoeffer web sites had accurate bibliographies, biographies, and networks of scholars. I invited Jean Ellul, then Dominique Ellul, to our house in Bordeaux for dinner and showed them the Bonhoeffer internet sites—and then the appalling results when one searched for "Jacques Ellul." Their initial resistance to using internet technology disappeared and they gave us their blessing. Yves came up from Toulouse to Bordeaux to meet with Patrick and me and was soon on board as well. We recruited boards of directors, formed non-profit organizations, and launched our groups in the fall of 2000. We began with one web site at www.ellul.org but later hived off a French counterpart at www.jacques-ellul.org. Both have been developed over the years into amazing resources for students of Ellul's thought. Patrick launched a series of thematic journals called *Cahiers Jacques Ellul*. In 2000 the IJES adopted the *Ellul Forum* as its semi-annual journal.

There have been several Ellul conferences in France (and other countries of Europe and beyond) over the years. Others have taken place in North America—sometimes as significant sections of larger conferences on communications, science, technology and society, Christian ethics, and the like. For the IJES, I organized a big centennial conference at Wheaton College in 2012 (Ellul was born 1912) and raised funds to help several French scholars join us. Professor Randal Marlin organized a 2014 conference on propaganda and communications at Carlton College in Ontario. In 2016 our conference was on "Political Illusion and Reality" at my (and Langdon Winner's) alma mater, UC Berkeley. In 2018, with Jeff Greenman, I organized the IJES conference on "Ellul and the Bible" at Regent College in Vancouver BC. Our joint 2020 IJES/AIJE conference in Strasbourg was delayed by the Covid-19 pandemic. Our 2022 conference in Montreal in 2022 is on "Ellul and the Arts," and in 2024 we plan to meet in Chicago to study modern digital technology and celebrate the 70th anniversary of the 1954 publication of Ellul's *la Technique*. The papers from the Berkeley and Vancouver conferences were gathered and published as books.[19]

---

19. David W. Gill and David Lovekin, editors, *Political Illusion and Reality: Engaging the Prophetic Insights of Jacques Ellul* (Wipf & Stock, 2018). Jacob Marques Rollison, editor, *Jacques Ellul and the*

Part Two: Shapers (1964–1979)

Over the years, beginning in the 1980s, I worked hard to get Ellul's books translated and published in English, with Harper & Row, InterVarsity, and other presses. Many of these English editions have my introductions or promotional cover blurbs. With the leadership of Ted Lewis, Wipf & Stock Publishers in Eugene, Oregon, has reprinted dozens of Ellul's books as well as publishing several new translations of Ellul material previously available only in French. Ted has become the Executive Director of the IJES and done amazing work on upgrading our web site as well as expanding the Ellul Series with Wipf & Stock. My New College Berkeley student Ken Morris, an attorney, has served the IJES from its beginnings giving us legal counsel as well as being our Secretary-Treasurer. I am still a board member of the French AIJE and the President and Chairman of the Board of the IJES but we now have a wonderful group of younger scholars and leaders getting involved and I can finally visualize my retirement from the leadership.

LEGACY

I have been a very lucky and blessed man to have Jacques Ellul as my main mentor not just through his writings but in a personal relationship. He autographed a copy of his *La Technique* to me saying "with a profound sharing/harmony of our thinking." He wrote a strong reference letter to the NCB search committee when it considered me for president in 1986. I have been deeply and broadly enriched and challenged by his work. Ellul often said and wrote that he was never seeking disciples but rather wanting to provide others with the means to think through for themselves the meaning of the world and their existence. Mutual friends told me that he enjoyed working and talking with me because I knew and appreciated his ideas but challenged him with my own thinking. I disagreed with his theology of work and calling and his interpretation of Genesis. I disagreed with his differentiation of the kingdom of heaven from the kingdom of God and his differentiation of Satan and the Devil. I didn't buy his inclination to believe in universal salvation because I thought it trumped his view of individual freedom. I agreed with most of his political perspective but not his abstention from voting and dismissal of any significant difference in political parties and leadership. He loved debating me in his living room about these and other topics. And no matter how hard I pushed, he always seemed to have another level deeper at which to see these discussions. He was hands down the most brilliant, learned man I ever met.

Several of my Ellulian friends have urged me to collect my Ellul interviews, essays, and reviews into a book. I have published dozens of scholarly and popular essays on Ellul's ethics, his views of education, technology, politics, violence, the theological virtues, work and business, history, and Christian discipleship. I have no idea the number of book introductions, book reviews, *Ellul Forum* editorials, and interviews

---

Bible: Towards a Hermeneutic of Freedom (Wipf & Stock, 2020).

people have done with me about Ellul. I always envisioned writing a book called "Jacques Ellul: Prophet in the Technological Wilderness." To me, that was his role and calling: not to be a systematic teacher but a prophet who challenges our comfortable assumptions and helps us see more clearly and deeply, and hear a truthful Word from God. And I have to add, a "prophet to the intellectuals or the thinkers"—not always easily comprehensible to the ordinary reader. Ellul sometimes also said that he had "not written forty books but one book with forty chapters." Without seeing the whole picture it is hard to understand the parts in isolation. And I would add that without seeing and knowing Jacques Ellul the man, it is hard to fully appreciate his writings.

I have often urged younger students and scholars to become expert on one or two great thinkers—but not to become unqualified disciples or restrict their work to that person (I certainly have not). But that anchor (whether Augustine, Aquinas, Luther, Ghandi, Marx, Lincoln, Dorothy Day, Adam Smith, John Locke, Martin Luther King, Jr., Toni Morrison, or someone else) will provide endless opportunities to develop creative ideas, opportunities, and relationships. But choose carefully so it can last your whole lifetime! And (I joke a little) ask yourself "where might this special interest require me to travel?" Although I knew nothing about wine or France when I first got interested in Ellul, I have been "forced" to learn French and to spend significant time in Bordeaux (and its vineyards). Like I say, I have been blessed. I am not a famous guy at all, not an author of best-sellers, just a marginal thinker and activist. But if I am known for anything in the twilight of my career, it is probably for my work with Jacques Ellul.

15

USC Graduate School (1974–1979)

WITH ALL THAT I experienced through 1973, my vocational preparation was still not complete. I was getting closer but still had not truly found my voice. We had a very challenging year financially in 1972–73 when I left my junior high teaching job to be totally dependent on "missionary" support from the Christian World Liberation Front and a few friendly financial donors (at a modest level!). We eked out a pretty simple existence for the next almost twenty years until in 1992 both Lucia and I had full-time "regular" salaries and benefits and both of our kids were out of the family nest. Lucia was a terrific shopper for food, clothing, and other necessities. She prepared true "feasts" for hundreds of students, friends, and even strangers over these years, on a shoestring budget. She even got us qualified for food stamps during the depths of our graduate student days living in Pasadena when my USC teaching assistant salary was $375 per month and $235 of that went to the rent for our tiny house. Most of those years our trusty old VW bus served us well for 200,000 miles of driving around town, up and down California, and on our camping trip vacations. We jogged on city streets, played hours of tennis on free courts around town, and rode our bikes with kid seats on the back when they were little. Our kids went to free public schools. We avoided restaurants and costly entertainment. We struggled to keep our credit card balances under control.

But my educational initiatives with the Crucible Study Center in Berkeley and my busy schedule of lecturing and preaching gigs for churches and student groups were just not enough to fulfil my mission to promote radical Christian discipleship and impact the academic and working worlds. I felt that it was now on me to complete my formal education with a PhD and step forward to lead something more ambitious, probably a graduate level program next to my alma mater, the University of California in Berkeley. There was no way I could do this kind of graduate-level study while living in Berkeley or Oakland. I had to find a program that would detach me from the network of tasks, expectations, and obligations in which I was inextricably tangled in the Bay Area. I took the Graduate Record Exam which ranked me in the 97th percentile of all college grads seeking admission to advanced degree programs—on both the quantitative and verbal sides of the exam.[1] I think I did so well partly because I had all that math and science in my high school and early university days—and because, along with my broad humanities and social science education at Cal and SF State, I was always a voracious reader, not least, during the two years between my MA and now my taking of the exam.

Into my lap came an invitation to teach at the Plymouth Brethren Culver City Bible School next to Los Angeles. I had met and become friends with a member of the CCBS faculty, Nathan "Skip" Smith, who recruited me to join him and three other teachers for their "one-year-for-life" study program. I would teach their church history, Christian ethics, and evangelism and apologetics courses to a student body of about forty men and women taking a year off from their undergraduate studies to become biblically literate and develop a Christian worldview to serve them for life. More on that experience at the end of this chapter but, along with a (very) small monthly stipend, we would have free use of a house for our family. I would continue to appeal for financial support from the people who had donated to our "mission" during my work with CWLF in Berkeley.[2]

So we rented out our Oakland house and moved down to LA. The rent we collected over the next four years (barely) paid the mortgage, taxes, and insurance on our 62nd Street house. It was tough going and we almost sold the house halfway through our time in LA—but, thank God, did not do so. Property values were rising and we might never have been able again to afford a house on our block in Oakland. God's providence saved us from what would have been a terrible loss.

UCLA admitted me to its PhD program in history. Claus-Peter Clasen on the UCLA history faculty was the author of *Anabaptism: A Social History, 1525–1618* and I would be working with him. What attracted me was the chance to study how the Anabaptist/Mennonite movement approached politics, economics, and social life. These were my people historically, theologically, and ethically. But I was just one of one hundred newly-accepted doctoral students in the UCLA history department and it soon became clear that I would be part of a big impersonal department. Meanwhile, one of the board members of CCBS was Clarke Howatt, a professor of engineering at

---

1. I mention my test scores not to brag but to remind readers of the simultaneous existence of my spotty academic performance from grammar and high school through my undergraduate days. I was admitted "provisionally" to both my MA and PhD programs, i.e., on trial until I proved myself in a couple initial courses. Lesson: Don't give up! You are probably as gifted as any other student but all intelligence and gifting is not identical. It comes in many varieties. I was never "dumb" but I was "lost" and distracted at times. I have often said the PhD is not so much an intelligence test as an endurance test.

2. I was never very good or very enthusiastic about raising money for our personal support. I had a lot more enthusiasm and success raising money for the movements, programs, and schools I got involved in after grad school.

USC GRADUATE SCHOOL (1974-1979)

USC. Clarke urged me to investigate USC and not just default to the state university for its inexpensive tuition. I told him that I could never afford USC tuition but he told me not to give up because "70% of USC students receive financial aid at one level or another."

THE UNIVERSITY OF SOUTHERN CALIFORNIA

So I visited the beautiful USC campus about six miles from our house in Culver City. USC was founded in Los Angeles in 1880 and was the largest private university in the country with over twenty thousand students. It was perhaps most famous for its football teams (and you already know I love football). USC was founded by Methodists and I loved its annual game with Catholic Notre Dame! While at USC I had season tickets in the student rooting section for three years, 1974-76. We loved watching the Rose Parade in Pasadena and then the USC Trojans defeat Ohio State 18-17 in the January 1, 1975, Rose Bowl. Trailing 16-17 late in the game, even after a touchdown, coach John McKay called for a risky attempt at a two-point conversion—which succeeded right in front of where our seats were. Earlier in the season on November 24, 1974, I saw the greatest game of my life when Notre Dame came to town. Just before half-time the Trojans finally scored to cut Notre Dame's lead to 24-7. We were getting wiped out all during the first half and the visiting Irish fans were going crazy. But our star running back Anthony Davis ran the second half kickoff back a hundred yards for a touchdown. Two or three plays after the following kickoff to Notre Dame, our defensive back intercepted a pass and ran it in for a touchdown. It was madness in the stadium as USC scored fifty-five points in a seventeen-minute period (counting that last minute before half-time). Lucia's parents happened to be down for a visit that weekend and I was able to upgrade to four tickets to witness the greatest game ever. I am still a big USC Trojan fan and always root for them—unless my Cal Bears are playing them. Berkeley Blue is in my blood.

USC's professional schools in law, medicine, business, and the arts were highly rated and influential. People joke that USC is the "University of Spoiled Children" but that gibe is no more appropriate than dismissing Berkeley as "Berserkeley" or Stanford as a "Junior University" or UCLA as our "Los Angeles extension campus." I was about to have an extraordinary educational experience. The USC history department was a disappointment, given my interests in social and intellectual history, not comparable to the one at UCLA. But somehow—I don't remember how—I discovered and visited the USC School of Religion, all of whose doctoral students and graduate faculty focused on Social Ethics. Until 1956, USC had a Divinity School on campus training Methodist pastors but that program moved off to become Claremont School of Theology. What remained in place was an academic program in religious studies whose undergraduate menu covered all the basic fields—biblical studies, world religions, sociology of religion, the history of religion, and so on.

Part Two: Shapers (1964–1979)

At the graduate school level, the USC School of Religion faculty was completely focused on Social Ethics. Each year they accepted ten new PhD students into the Social Ethics program. Here was a chance for me to slide over from Social History to Social Ethics. I spent an hour with Professor John Orr, the Director of the Program, rehearsing my academic and activist background and talking about my interests in Jacques Ellul and in innovative graduate theological and ethical education for laity of all denominations. Professor Orr followed up by writing to tell me what an "interesting bird" I was and to urge me to apply. I was soon admitted with full financial support.

Since I was moving fields from history to religion/social ethics I was admitted as a "provisional" student subject to getting B grades in my first two classes in summer 1974.[3] I loved the courses and knocked out two A's and the adventure began. The faculty even voted me a small (but significant to us) $500 stipend beyond tuition that first summer, knowing I had a family of four to support. From day one, the USC faculty leaders kept in close and caring touch with me. During the first full year (there would be two years of seminar courses) I was given a full scholarship. No tuition charges. During year two, I was Professor Jack Crossley's teaching assistant in his undergrad courses, often giving lectures to his huge classes, grading papers, leading discussion sections, and helping undergrad students. Teaching assistants got full tuition remission plus $375 per month. During my third year I was John Orr's Research Assistant which kept the $375 per month going until I moved back to Oakland in 1977. The department also had a "slush fund" that allowed us grad students to borrow $500 at a time to meet our emergency financial needs—with no interest or repayment due until six months after we graduated. I borrowed $4000 total during my PhD days.

The School of Religion was physically based in a space in old Founders Hall. A huge room had been lined with maybe eight small faculty offices around the sides. Their office walls only went up about seven feet and were open at the top but still felt relatively private. Only Director John Orr's walls went up to the ceiling for complete privacy. The Teaching Assistants shared one of those offices and another had copy equipment and supplies. All of the offices opened up to a reception area with couches and coffee tables and, separated by a room divider, the two or three receptionists and administrative support staff. What this meant was that all of us, faculty and students, came out of our offices into a congenial (if low-budget) conversation and gathering space. Just that configuration by itself contributed to a lively and constant sense of camaraderie and community. Several years after I graduated, a gift of some millions of dollars led to a total remodel of the space in which individual offices were now lovely new wood paneled private havens—but all of them led out into hallways that took people away from each other! Feng shui matters. A physical space is embedded with

---

3. Having served on many admission committees I would encourage applicants to bring not just a record of classroom success but of significant "outside-the-classroom" activities and have an intellectual and vocational mission more precise and robust than just vaguely liking school and thinking you would like to be a professor (especially in fields that are glutted with graduates, like history, theology, and ethics).

values—promoting equality or hierarchy, supporting community or individuality. The old departmental sense of community was radically undermined.

At USC I got to know and study with some great scholars and teachers. John Orr was an expert on the sociology of religion and a great guide into the thought of Max Weber and Emile Durkheim. He and Henry Clark had studied with Reinhold and Richard Niebuhr, icons in the social ethics tradition. Robert Ellwood was an expert in world religions and had also just written a book about the Jesus Movement. Ronald Hock was a New Testament expert with whom I studied the "Social Teaching of the Acts of the Apostles." Don Miller was a young professor of the sociology of (especially American) religion and a great teacher. Bill May was also a great teacher and applied social ethics scholar in health care and business. John Coleman Bennett and his wife Anne McGrew Bennett were visiting professors during my second year of coursework, 1975–76. He had started the magazine *Christianity and Crisis* with Reinhold Niebuhr and was one of the last of the great founders of the social ethics tradition at Union Seminary and beyond. In his course, as I mentioned in the previous chapter, I debated with him the contrasts and similarities of his and Niebuhr's Christian Realism with Jacques Ellul's approach. The Bennetts were living in the Pilgrim Place retirement community out in Claremont to the east of LA. Lucia and I enjoyed visiting them in their home a couple times. Gracious people.

My main teacher was Jack Crossley who had written his own doctoral dissertation on Soren Kierkegaard and Karl Barth years earlier—exactly the two most influential sources of Ellul's thought. He was now working mostly on Friedrich Schleiermacher, a major Protestant father of Liberal Theology. So Jack had leaned Liberal in the years since his Neo-Orthodox younger days but he was a superb guide to SK and Barth as well as knowing Marx's thought very well (also an important source for Ellul). Jack was one of the very best teachers and seminar leaders I have ever studied under. He was an articulate gold mine of information. He was also a great editor who really helped me become a better writer. Jack did not publish a great deal so he was not famous outside of USC but he was a giant to his students. Jack took a great personal interest in me and his other students. One of his counsels that I never forgot was to make sure I always read widely, outside of my usual sources and influences.

The PhD program was demanding. Two years of coursework were the foundation, typically ten courses. We usually took two seminars each semester and worked as teaching or research assistants (or outside employment of some kind). Only a few could handle three courses in a semester. Over the fifteen weeks, the seminar would meet for one four-hour session each week. Maybe half the class time the professor would give a lecture. The other two hours were focused on student research papers—presentation and discussion. The condition of one's research paper varied depending on how early you got scheduled; later papers were closer to final form. My research papers for each course ranged from thirty to fifty pages in length with copious footnotes. Seminar participants were expected to be prepared to discuss and critique each other's work. It was an exciting, sometimes intimidating, lively, learning environment. There were a few written exams in some courses but often the research paper and discussion was the only graded work. For the first time in my academic life, I was a straight A student.

Not only were my professors superb, so were my fellow students. About a dozen of us were often in the same seminars (a couple dozen others were ahead of us in their qualifying exam or dissertation writing phase of the doctoral program). Ken Overberg was a Jesuit priest, later with a long career on the faculty of Xavier University. Chris Joachim went on to a long career as Professor of Comparative Religious Studies and Director of the Center for Asian Studies at San Jose State University. Pete Lowentrout went on to the Religious Studies faculty at Cal State University, Long Beach, where he specialized in Religion and Modern Culture. My fellow Cal alum Heidi Hadsell taught in Brazil, worked with the World Council of Churches, served as Professor of Social Ethics and Dean of McCormick Seminary in Chicago, and then became President of the Hartford Seminary in Connecticut. Frida Kerner Fuhrman brought a rich Jewish perspective and went on to a long and distinguished career on the faculty of DePaul University in Chicago. Michael O'Sullivan went on to a career as an award-winning journalist and West Coast Bureau Chief for the Voice of America. Anne-Janine Morey moved between Religious Studies, Ethics, and Literature during a long and distinguished career at Southern Illinois University and then James Madison University. Marvin Erisman joined the faculty of Azusa Pacific University where he taught psychology and business courses and also developed a consultancy in organizational leadership. Paul Seldon became an executive leader of homeless housing projects for both New York City and the City of Chicago. Many of these colleagues published fine books and were active in our professional, scholarly associations (where we often had USC reunion evening get-togethers).

Other students were in and out of my classes bringing their own unique contributions. During the second half of my time at USC I commuted from Pasadena with professors Don Miller and Robert Ellwood and with fellow-student Patricia Reed. Patricia didn't finish the program as her interests took her another direction but I remember how wicked smart she was in our seminar discussions. After I got to know her, I asked her out of curiosity one day about her GRE scores. They were very ordinary, as it turned out, and it made me realize again that intelligence comes in many different forms and styles and no single test can ever capture it. We were a lively and diverse community. Ken Overberg, Ed Sanderson, Marvin Erisman and I were among the actively engaged church folk, others were "decline to state," "other" or no personal faith, or were strictly interested in religion as a research subject. We were, after all, an academic program, not a confessional community of religious practice! Anne-Janine and I organized a regular monthly lunch-time graduate student symposium with a different one of us leading a subject of personal interest at each session. I led a session on the history of Fundamentalism and Evangelicalism to try to help my colleagues gain an accurate background, thinking they might need it for teaching in the future. We brought in guests once in while including a Catholic Worker leader and civil rights leader Jesse Jackson. Our faculty sometimes joined us.

In addition to the coursework, all of us had to pass exams showing we had a basic, workable ability for reading and translating two foreign languages appropriate to our research area. There were formal exams one could take to demonstrate this—or you could do as I did: have designated German and French professors send you into a room for two hours with just a dictionary of the language and a surprise text in your field to prepare a translation and have it checked by the language professor. When the language exams and two years of coursework were completed, the next step was to prepare for what are called Comprehensive or Qualifying Exams. Each student formed a committee of five professors, one of them from an outside field. You negotiated a long bibliography for your major, minor, and (proposed) dissertation fields, and for your outside field (I chose American intellectual history, specifically the response of American thinkers to the rise of industrialization and technology since the Civil War).

After a year (or sometimes more!), when you feel you are ready, you take four half-day written exams and one full-day exam, spread out over two weeks any way you like. I wrote the full-day exam on Monday and two half-day exams on both Wednesday and Friday of my chosen week. Each morning I picked up the essay exam questions and took them with just my typewriter, paper, thermoses of black coffee, and plenty of pipe tobacco into an empty room in the building. I must have written well over a hundred pages total by the time I finished. After a couple months' time for my committee to read what I wrote, I was brought in for a two-hour oral exam before the five committee members. They first asked me if there was anything I would like to add or change. I said that there was only one thing—a comment on one of the more obscure figures in my exam on American intellectual history. I had blanked on this person while writing the exam. With that correction made, the oral exam proceeded amicably and positively and they voted to advance me to "candidacy." It was only correct to say you were a "Candidate for the PhD" after passing the qualifying/comprehensive exams.

Admission to the PhD program was pretty selective to begin with: ten out of a hundred were admitted to my program each year. Two or three of the ten admits typically drop out or fail to complete the coursework over the next couple years. It could be grueling. Two or three more typically don't get past the comprehensive exams which require tremendous discipline and determination over a lengthy period of solo study. But doctoral students probably have a greater command of their field when taking those exams than at any other point in their career. Your brain is bursting with information. The final process of writing a dissertation also typically eliminates still another couple candidates because they can never finish their project. The PhD dissertation is a book-length piece of research that is an original contribution to one's field. Students can sometimes run out of money or be derailed by their employment.

Sometimes they have chosen to work on a topic that is too broadly or poorly defined. Often I have found that students don't make it because they lack a supportive and good director of their research (or a tolerant and supportive spouse and family. All hail to my Lucia, Jodie, and Jonathan!). I have known several doctoral students who received little or no help, sometimes even opposition, from the professor in charge of their work! This can be especially perilous when working under a famous scholar with too many dissertation students to direct well.

My director was Jack Crossley, a superb overseer of my work. I passed my comprehensives in early 1977 before I moved back up to Oakland and Berkeley. I had taught the course on Jacques Ellul at Fuller in fall 1976 and knew exactly what I wanted to write about. But in my first year back in Berkeley I only got one chapter finished out of the projected five. My project to start a graduate school (described in the next chapter) exploded into a massive time-investment and I was barely hanging on in terms of my writing. But as I was feeling desperate with our college launch date scheduled for fall 1979, some dear friends, Bill and Barbara Moore, urged me to get away from the Bay Area up to their vacant vacation condo at Lake Tahoe.

I took a small commuter plane from Oakland up to Tahoe, hauling my typewriter and paper, a couple big boxes of my books and notes, and a big box of food Lucia prepared. I took a taxi from the Tahoe airport to their snowed-in place. The first day I spread out and organized my notes and ate half the food, nervously distracted by all the work I left behind, and paced the floor a lot. By day two I could type a couple sentences and start focusing a little on my writing project. By day three I wrote a couple paragraphs. And so it went, more productive and inspired each day until the last day when I wrote all night in a blaze of productivity. Then I packed up, flew home, and didn't touch it for the next three weeks of entrepreneurial madness. Then back up for another week with the same experience, writing all night the last day. And again, three more times—and a three-hundred-page manuscript was done.

I made a photocopy of my manuscript and mailed it down to Jack Crossley with an apologetic cover letter noting seventeen ways (yes, I listed seventeen) it was inadequate and needed more work. A couple weeks later, Jack wrote me to say: "David this is great stuff! You can write your magnum opus later. This is a very worthy and defensible dissertation. Clean it up, submit it, and come down for your oral defense." What an unexpected outcome and relief! I managed to submit it within a month and go down to USC for a successful defense a month after that. My committee of three professors led by Jack, greeted me by saying it was a quality piece of work and it was accepted without revision. But they told me, they disagreed with my and Ellul's approach to ethics and now wanted to debate it! This we did for two hours and I was almost home free.

The university had strict rules about format, typing, paper quality, and deadlines for graduation in June. I hired two blazing fast typist friends Linda Coleman and Linda Duddy to retype it almost day and night to get the final document ready. They finished on a Thursday before the Friday deadline. I called the USC thesis editor's office to ask if I could deliver it to them Monday morning the moment the office opened rather than Friday before 5:00 p.m. closing. She said, "No way. It is due tomorrow or you can't graduate in June." So the next day, Friday, I took a flight from Oakland down to LAX and then a bus across town to USC, handed in the document, and immediately bussed back to LAX. During that afternoon the flight attendants had gone on strike and my flight home was delayed for several hours! Among the hundreds of stranded, irritated passengers in the terminal I happened to see a neighbor lady from my block in Oakland. She joined me in a couple celebratory beers to mark the day of my PhD completion. I don't even remember her name.

My dissertation was called *The Word of God in the Ethics of Jacques Ellul*. The organizing issue was "how can contemporary ethicists draw on sources from an individual and a collection of documents two thousand (and more) years earlier—and situated in vastly different cultural contexts." My first chapter reviewed the literature, especially the current debates on how Jesus and Scripture influenced or guided ethics, what the critical issues and challenges were. I described Ellul's basic understanding of ethics and his views of Jesus and Scripture. I then wrote major chapters on his writings on "urban-technological civilization" and "politics and the nation-state"—testing out his approach on concrete problems. I concluded with "Through and Beyond Ellul's Ethics"—my take on his strengths, weaknesses, and the potential of his approach. My dissertation was one of the first four or five doctoral studies of Jacques Ellul (many dozens have followed) and it really did plow new territory in the field. I was being deliberately provocative by using the phrase "Word of God" in my title and enjoyed hearing the Dean read out my title as he bestowed my degree. It was also funny a couple times later on to hear people introduce me, shortening my book title to save time: "Our speaker tonight is Dr. David Gill, author of 'the Word of God.'" Uh, not quite.

On June 7, 1979, I walked through the graduation exercises at USC in front of the old library. LA Mayor Tom Bradley was our speaker. In those safer, pre-terrorist days, Lucia was able to get up to the top floor of the library and shoot some pictures of the whole crowd seated down below. After the all-university pomp and circumstance, all USC PhDs convened at the faculty club to walk across the stage and be recognized one-by-one before being feted with champagne and strawberries. All of us Religion/Social Ethics folk then went to the home of our professor Bill (and Sherry) May for a wonderful celebration through the evening. One of the greatest days of my life.

When I got back home to Berkeley, a joyous celebration was awaiting me with my old Berkeley friends who were really invested in my journey to that mountaintop over the years. Walt Hearn read a fun little poem he wrote for the occasion. Then our old friends Bill and Barbara Moore had us up to their Lake Tahoe place where I had conquered my dissertation writing challenge. With our combined group of four kids we water-skied and celebrated for a few days. Back at USC my professors had nominated my dissertation for publication in the distinguished American Theological

Library Association monograph series. While I was invited to publish it right away I (mistakenly) dragged my feet for four years, thinking I first needed to significantly improve it. Only after being told by my colleagues that I was crazy to delay an offer to publish did I do some minor edits and see it to print in 1984.

My USC PhD experience was a wonderful capstone to my formal education. My approach to ethics was vastly deepened, broadened, and enriched. My writing and teaching skills had been significantly improved. I was prepared for a career as a professor of ethics at a graduate level. Over the following years and decades, I remained in good contact with my doctor father Jack Crossley and several of my fellow students, especially in annual professional meetings like the American Academy of Religion and Society of Christian Ethics. When Heidi Hadsell retired back to Berkeley from Hartford and I from Boston, we decided to organize a forty-year reunion of a dozen of our classmates in November 2019, meeting on campus at USC. Our old rapport was recovered in an instant and for three days we shared our memories and our experiences over the forty years since we had all been together as students. An extraordinary time with an extraordinary group of friends.

ANOTHER GRADUATION: PB TO COVENANT

Nineteen seventy-nine also marked another kind of graduation process, this time in my church affiliation. In 1971 I had been excommunicated from the "Exclusive" Plymouth Brethren of my first twenty-five years, the church tradition of my parents, grandparents, and great grand-parents. I moved into the "Open" Plymouth Brethren for the next four years—two years at Fairhaven Bible Chapel in San Leandro and then two years (1973–75) at Culver City Bible School and the Culver City Neighborhood Church founded by the five faculty members, including me. I really loved my students at CCBS and many of them—including especially Lynn and (the late) Andy Cole, Dennis and Ann Holden, Billy Batstone, and Rod and Kathy Hanson—are my friends to this day. I brought all my unleashed energy and creativity from CWLF to CCBS in my teaching and my supervision of their required "practical Christian work" projects. I was especially proud of a few of my guys who did their projects by moving into the LA Mission downtown for a couple weeks of living with and assisting the homeless and downtrodden.

For the CCBS itself, I upgraded the look and content of the school brochures and the regular newsletter sent to constituents and supporters. I created what we called the "Anthony Norris Groves lectures" and brought famous Peninsula Bible Church pastor Ray Stedman down as our first lecturer. I loved playing my guitar with my friend Mike Henderson on violin and first-rate guitarist, composer, singer, and (before long) recording artist Billy Batstone (who played with the Richie Furray Band at one point). We sang a lot of Eagles and Love Song tunes (Love Song was, in my view, the best of the Jesus Movement bands, coming from Calvary Chapel). Lucia and I started a

"Neighborhood Kids Club" meeting one afternoon a week and soon had forty young kids attending. I taught courses in Christian Ethics, Church History, and Evangelism (appropriately sharing your faith with others) and Apologetics (sharing good reasons for that faith). What CCBS was trying to offer in its "One Year for Life" study program was much the same as what both Regent and New College Berkeley did at a graduate level, similar also to various programs like the Gotham Fellows or Cascade Fellows in New York and Seattle. Lay Christians are mostly uneducated theologically and these were and are valiant efforts to correct that.

But clouds were gathering from soon after I arrived. Dick Matthews, one of the professors, told me in later years that my coming was like plugging a 220 volt appliance into a 110 circuit. He felt overwhelmed by my energy and ambition to make things happen. My world was Berkeley and the Christian World Liberation Front. CCBS was a progressive but calm and safe PB sanctuary. My faculty colleagues were ten years old than me. My students were often closer to my age than the faculty and, more and more, I tended to socialize with them because of our common musical and other interests. My studies at USC for the PhD were also a bit threatening I believe. My closest colleague Nate Smith had a ThM but the other faculty members had no graduate theological education. They were great guys for sure but we grew apart. I got called in and reprimanded for being seen by a CCBS board member at a USC game drinking a beer. As I mentioned in chapter eight, for two weeks I got too close to a woman student and, though we cut it off, a month later I was fired, just at the end of my second year. It was inappropriate and I acknowledged and repented of it. But it was the straw that broke the camel's back and I was done.

One of my more interesting discoveries on arrival at CCBS was that once a year they suspended classes and sent their forty or so students to attend traveling guru Bill Gothard's "Institute in Basic Youth Conflicts." Gothard's seminars were attracting thousands around the country; I had yielded to pressure and attended one of his weeklong lectures (all communication was one direction: from the oracle's lips to the thousands who packed the Coliseum Arena in Oakland). Gothard had a few good insights but I found it mostly to be pious, authoritarian rhetoric with little or no basis in Scripture despite the hundreds of "proof-text" references. At CCBS I attended again, along with our students while my colleagues took the week off. After the final session I sat through a meeting of adoring pastors with Gothard. After all of the others had left, I (ever so gently) asked Gothard: "Do you have a group of leaders, peers, and advisors on whom you test out your ideas? Maybe biblical exegetes and experts on counseling?" Gothard got furious and asked me if my father approved of the length of my hair? (I was short-haired and just mustached after leaving Berkeley for LA). I told him: "Mr. Gothard that response exactly illustrates the problem I see with your teaching: you concoct these 'fifteen steps to being a rebellious son' or some such formula—which then gives you your format for pigeonholing me at step six or whatever on your ladder. But your whole project is an invention in your mind and will not withstand biblical critique from your peers. Your views of music are absurd, unhistorical, and unbiblical as just one example. Actually, sir, my father does approve of the length of my hair." Happily, I got CCBS to cancel this annual student pilgrimage. Providentially, Gothard's theological mistakes and personal hypocrisies came to public light before long and he was dethroned.

FROM PASADENA TO BERKELEY COVENANT CHURCH

We moved across town to Pasadena in search of cheaper housing for my last two years at USC. There actually were no Brethren assemblies that would work for us and our young kids in that town so we visited Pasadena Covenant Church on the recommendation of my friend Richard Quebedeaux. We were drawn in and that became our church home for two years until we returned to Oakland in 1977. The preaching of Pastor Mel White, the wonderful, worshipful music led by Roland Tabell, and the programs for our pre-school children were very important. We also were drawn in by the embrace of several young couples our age, including Steve and Joyce Smith, Dick and Diana Trautwein, and Paul and Tonia Fletcher. My first day visiting the church I was greeted by Joyce Smith and somehow mentioned "Jacques Ellul." She showed interest and I blabbered on for a few minutes until she could get a word in to tell me not she but her husband Steve was interested in Ellul.

Steve Smith was finishing a PhD in theology at Claremont and he and I quickly became close friends encouraging each other through the demands of our programs and enjoying hours of discussions about our common interests. We both taught adult education courses at the church to enthusiastic groups. When Mel White, who was also a film maker, asked us to be a panel of respondents to a screening of Francis Shaeffer's "How Should We Then Live" film series (which he was editing and producing), we shared on stage both our approval and disapproval of various aspects of Shaeffer's message. Not too many years later, in a tough job market, I connected Steve to a faculty search at Trinity Episcopal School for Ministry near Pittsburgh, Pennsylvania, where Steve then thrived over a long career. I had been a visiting lecturer at the school and was in a position to help them find a perfect match for their needs: Steve Smith.

But even while we were pretty fully engaged with Pasadena Covenant Church my "perfectionist" tendencies chafed and I found a group of a dozen young Mennonites from Fuller Seminary with whom we met weekly during that two years. When we returned to the Bay Area in 1977 Fairhaven Bible Chapel had regressed to a more separatist, authoritarian culture. A leading elder there, Jean Gibson, took me out to lunch to tell me (I hadn't asked) ten reasons why Fairhaven would have nothing to do with the New College Berkeley project I was leading. Two of the reasons I recall were that we were not dispensationalist in our theology and we allowed women to teach. Our old friends Bill and Barbara Moore had moved from Fairhaven to Oakland First Covenant so we followed them there. I taught a long adult education course on Peter's

Life and Letters (which would in 1986 become one of my books). But I was unhappy with the lack of a strong "vertical" dimension in the preaching and worship and a bit put off by the Lawrence Welkish-musical groups and conservative white cultural vibe. So for most of 1978–79 we were part of the Berkeley House Church, mainly comprised of former CWLF friends. The endless church meetings to hammer out questions of leadership and vision wore me out. I was about done with my search for the perfect New Testament Church.

Meanwhile I had gotten involved some at Berkeley's big First Presbyterian Church. The pastor Earl Palmer loved Karl Barth as I did and was a positive, joyful preacher and leader. Earl was my closest colleague in supporting my leadership of the New College Berkeley project (see next chapter). He had me preach at First Pres and I began teaching some for the various adult education fellowships. First Pres had a robust university student ministry, a dozen Cal faculty, and an eager learning congregation of two thousand. I loved being part of it, though I was not at home in Presbyterian bureaucracy and church government. I loved how Earl would say he would rather be known for what he was for, than (as many churches) what he was against. That was how I felt. I began to say that we should try to keep our "sects" within the church, rather than organize them outside the larger, more inclusive, "body of Christ."

We ended up joining Berkeley Covenant Church in 1979 and raising our family there until 1992 when we moved to Chicago to join the Covenant denomination's North Park College. The Covenant Church's theological and ecclesiastical tradition was closer to my commitments than the Presbyterians. In addition, I felt that it would be better for New College Berkeley to have its two best known leaders, Earl and I, not part of the same local church and the same denomination. We were trying to build an interdenominational school. The pastor of Berkeley Covenant Church, Craig Anderson, was a dear friend, a founding member, and for three years chair of our New College Berkeley Board. That was also an important factor.

So in 1979 I graduated from USC with what is called a "terminal" degree in my field of ethics. And I finally graduated from my Brethren and sectarian church life to fully embrace the broader church, represented by the Evangelical Covenant Church, as my ecclesiastical and theological home. My calling to the life of a professor of Christian and workplace ethics was now clear, certain, and strong. My voice was now my own, imperfect and still learning of course, with my own message and style. Time to get busy. I was thirty-three.

PART THREE

Channels (1979–2016)

PART THREE OF MY story is about the channels through which I carried out my calling from 1979 to my retirement in 2016. I actually started working in the first channel, New College Berkeley (and taught a course at Fuller Seminary), in 1976, so I was a professor for forty years. I had started regularly teaching earlier in 1966 (Juvenile Hall) so I have been a teacher for fifty years! The first big channel project was New College Berkeley to which I gave fourteen years (1976–1990). At the time, I envisioned NCB as my "channel" for the rest of my life—but God had other plans and, looking back, I wouldn't have it any other way.

While all those "shapers" I described in Part Two continued to influence me during the following decades, by 1979 my calling was pretty clear and consistent: to study, teach, and write about ethics for two audiences and contexts: (1) Christians committed to Jesus and Scripture and (2) workers in a diverse workplace and marketplace where no single religion, philosophy, or set of values reigns. It was all an incredible adventure as a "What Are You Doing About It?" educational entrepreneur, organizer, and community builder. Looking back, I see lots of energy, vision, and initiative, plenty courage, persistence, pain, and joy, and amazing and wonderful people—my story is fundamentally very positive. But I wouldn't be telling the truth if I papered over the mistakes and difficulties, whether caused by economics, ignorance, or evildoing. My own judgment and performance were not perfect, but I gave it everything I had to give.

The first channel was the most ambitious: founding and leading New College Berkeley. Next was my work as an Interim Senior Pastor at University Covenant Church (and a later pastoral gig at Trinitarian Congregational in Massachusetts). That was followed by a nine-year run at North Park University in Chicago, then work as a business and technology writer and consultant with the Institute of Business, Technology, and Ethics and with Harris & Associates and other firms. Another long faculty

Part Three: Channels (1979–2016)

stint followed, teaching ethics to MBAs at St. Mary's College. My final channel was on the faculty of Gordon-Conwell Seminary in the Boston area. Actually, it's more complicated than this list. But I lived to tell about it and write about it. It was rough going at times and I've got the scars to prove it. I regret to say I must have inflicted a few scars as well. At least it demonstrates an energetic answer to my dad's challenge "What Are You Doing About It?" Only God can judge how well I did but I thank God for an exciting, gratifying ride all the way. In these pages I will be providing lots of specific examples and even lists to show you what happened.

16

New College Berkeley, Phase I (1976–85)

ONE MEMORABLE AFTERNOON IN September 1979, I found myself walking down Telegraph Avenue in Berkeley—probably heading over to pick up a treat at Yogurt Park on Durant Avenue—when I remember being overwhelmed by a feeling of joy and contentment and saying to myself "This is what I was born for; this is what God called me and prepared me to do with my life." I was thirty-three years old. Classes had begun that week at New College Berkeley. We had a beautiful campus building, a distinguished faculty, an exciting curriculum, and classes of thirty or so in our core subjects, including my Christian Ethics course. We were officially up and running as a California non-profit corporation for educational purposes. We were a graduate school of theology for lay folk (not a seminary for future pastors)—the only such school in the USA, modeled on Regent College in Vancouver, Canada. We were welcomed by faculty and leaders in the Graduate Theological Union (a consortium of nine Catholic and Protestant seminaries based in Berkeley) as well as several UC Berkeley faculty and dozens of local churches of many denominations. Our project had even attracted some attention and encouragement from Christian leaders across the USA and Canada. It was a heady beginning.

New College Berkeley was the biggest and most ambitious "What Are You Doing About It?" endeavor of my life. I have sometimes said that, like Joseph in Egypt, I experienced seven "fat years" and seven "lean years" during my fourteen years with NCB—though the fat and lean times were mostly jumbled together, not consecutive. In this chapter I will describe the project from its inception in 1976 to my sabbatical year away, 1984–85, and in chapter seventeen I will describe it from the fall of 1985 to my departure in 1990 and add some comments on NCB in the decades since my departure. I will try to step back, explain, and evaluate the story as much as I can.

I won't repeat all the details of the back story covered in my earlier chapters but the outline goes like this: I grew up with a view of Christianity that Jesus was Lord of the whole of life, including our studies and our work—not just our personal and church life. A critical moment for me was in 1966 when, as a junior at Berkeley, I began to wonder how my theological understanding of God and human *history* related to my "secular" university study of history—and then how Jesus' model of *teaching* related to the university's preparation of future public school teachers like me. While exploring these kinds of connections was not on the agenda of the churches and seminaries, or on the minds of most Christians, I knew I was not alone. And even if it wasn't a "felt need" by all Christians, it was a clear and repeated mandate of Scripture to be "transformed by the renewing of your mind" (Romans 12:1–2) rather than just thoughtlessly conforming to the thinking and behavior of the culture around us. But where could those of us on this quest to integrate faith and learning get any help?

There was a small but growing literature by Harry Blamires, C.S. Lewis, John Stott, and others that promoted the development of a "Christian mind." Of biggest impact was the work of Francis Schaeffer and his Swiss-based L'Abri Fellowship arguing for an all-encompassing Christian worldview. I had friends back then and since who complained (justly, I think) that, after spending decades in church and Christian education classes, they ought to have accumulated an MDiv-level of theological knowledge—but instead had only a random, grade school theology to stand alongside their university and graduate professional education. We could do a lot through individual study but couldn't there be something more?

Individual congregations could do a lot better job with university and adult education, especially if they had hundreds or thousands of members and a committed, informed, pastoral leadership. But most churches were smaller, with only one or two hundred members and without the financial or teaching resources to offer a robust program at the level of their members' professional educations. I tried and failed to persuade Francis Schaeffer to launch a satellite L'Abri study center in Berkeley next to our university. Described above in my chapter on CWLF, with my friends I pioneered "The Crucible: A Center for Radical Christian Studies" in 1972. It had some success but soon showed that it would forever remain marginal in its impact. It needed a broader ecclesiastical and theological profile than our (mostly) Anabaptist radical orientation and a higher, more academically credible, faculty and educational profile.

Regent College had been founded in 1969 as a graduate school of Christian studies for laity. They created their own Diploma and Masters-level study programs and developed official relationships with the next-door University of British Columbia, Vancouver School of Theology, and Carey School for Baptist theological training. Regent defined itself as "trans-denominational" (not just "nondenominational") and not only had its own small but distinguished full-time faculty but was offering summer school courses taught by the very best theological scholars from around the world, drawing hundreds of part-time summer students.

Regent became the model for my dream of a similar project in Berkeley. I had no illusions thinking I was qualified by education or experience to be the founder or leader of a credible graduate school. But after several failures to convince others to come lead such a project in Berkeley, I became convinced that I should go back to school and earn a PhD to at least gain some minimal qualification to work on graduate education. As I described in chapter 15, I enrolled in the PhD program in religion/social ethics at the University of Southern California and got both a wonderful, rigorous education and my "union card"—the doctorate. During all those years, I periodically floated my "Regent in Berkeley" dream to my old friends like Sharon Gallagher and Walt and Ginny Hearn. While they encouraged me, I'm sure they wondered whether I would actually come back. As I finished my coursework, my little family (two pre-school kids and a longsuffering wife) were barely getting by "on a shoestring" and I was faced with invitations to teach at a couple Cal State University campuses. Should I opt for immediate job and financial security? It was tempting—but "No!" or at least "Not yet."

INSTITUTIONAL OBSTETRICS: THE BIRTH OF NEW COLLEGE BERKELEY[1]

In early 1976 I wrote a letter to Earl Palmer, the Senior Pastor at First Presbyterian Church in Berkeley from 1970 to 1990. I didn't know Earl personally and I had never attended First Pres. But First Pres had a couple thousand members and was for decades the strongest university church in Berkeley, with many Cal students and faculty in attendance. First Pres and Earl had a solid reputation for a broad and positive evangelical faith. In my letter I introduced myself ("you probably don't know me but here is my Berkeley and Christian background" etc.). And I wrote "I am wondering what you think about the idea of founding a new graduate school of Christian studies, like Regent College, in Berkeley. If it were to happen, I think it must have the support of First Pres and other local churches." Earl wrote me back ("yes, David, I know of your work in Berkeley and have read your essays in *Radix Magazine*") with an enthusiastic agreement, saying he was actually scheduled to teach in Regent's next summer school. He loved the idea and we began to talk and exchange letters about how to move the idea forward. When Earl came down to Pasadena (where I lived) to give some lectures at Fuller Seminary, he spent an evening over dinner at our little house and we were off and running.

The next step was my writing up a one-page "Proposal for a New College in Berkeley" which Earl thought was great as is. We decided to host two informational discussions in October of 1976, one at First Pres Berkeley and the other at Menlo Park Presbyterian Church near Stanford. Fifty people showed up at our first meeting in Berkeley, half were my friends and contacts and half were Earl's. Across the Bay at Menlo Park Pres, Associate Pastor Kent Meads helped us gather about twenty people for our meeting. At each of those meetings, I passed out and reviewed the one-page

---

1. Charles Cotherman, *To Think Christianly* (InterVarsity Press, 2020) devotes a chapter to the story of The Crucible and New College Berkeley.

proposal and Earl gave his enthusiastic endorsement. We handed out a questionnaire for the attendees to fill out with their contact info if they wanted to be kept posted (they all did, so now we had a starting mailing list of seventy!)—and a question: "Would you be willing to work on a feasibility study committee to pursue this idea further?" Ten of those present at the two gatherings signed on to work with our committee once a month starting in January 1977.

Beginning with those October meetings in 1976, I drove up to Berkeley from Pasadena once a month or so to meet with Earl Palmer and connect with others interested. The Men's Breakfast Fellowship at First Pres gave me $20 for gas money—the first donation to New College Berkeley! I expanded the one-page proposal into four pages and detailed out a possible start-up plan and task list. Beginning in January 1977, First Pres member and attorney Minor Schmid gave us some essential legal counsel about how we could launch a 501(c)3 non-profit and reviewed the Articles and Bylaws I drafted. In addition to Minor, Earl, and me, our Feasibility Study Committee included Sharon Gallagher, Walt and Ginny Hearn, Bev Schmidt, Bob Schoon, Cal Farnham, Kent Meads, Bob Baylis, and Craig Anderson.

I contacted Regent College and their president Jim Houston, and my friends Ward Gasque and Carl Armerding on their faculty (who together played the start-up organizing roles at Regent that I was now doing in Berkeley). The Regent guys sent me a four-page mimeographed document describing "The Founding of Regent College" and gave me strong encouragement for the project. We had our own unique founding history in Berkeley but one key thing we copied from Regent was their decision to run two summer schools before launching a full-time program—to demonstrate the kind of education we proposed and to build credibility and constituency. We decided to have summer schools in 1978 and 1979 and begin full-time operation in fall 1979. The summer schools would put us on the map as we got started.

How does a relatively unknown graduate student found a new graduate school—with no money? Each time I came up to the Bay Area in 1976–77 I hustled around meeting pastors and interested laity and building our network. I sent out our expanded proposal not just to our list of a hundred Bay Area folk but to about fifty national Christian leaders, most of whom I did not know personally but whose opinion I valued. Carl Henry, Os Guinness, and the others to whom I wrote were all enthusiastic about the idea and liked the proposal—which encouraged us locals. I also shared the proposal with my USC professors Jack Crossley, John Orr, Bill May, and Henry Clark. They all encouraged me to forge ahead: "You are young and should go for it. Forget the Cal State positions. If you get locked into that career track you may never have this chance again. If anyone can do it, you can! We will do what we can to introduce you to the Graduate Theological Union leadership up there." Encouraging!

I also shared the NCB proposal with our distinguished USC visiting professor John Coleman Bennett, who had had a long career not just at Union Seminary in New York with Reinhold Niebuhr but with a stint leading the GTU. He was very supportive, feeling the GTU needed both an evangelical presence and a lay theology presence. Our study committee had followed Regent's example and simply adopted the Statement of Faith of the International Fellowship of Evangelical Students (and InterVarsity Christian Fellowship), a post-Fundamentalist affirmation of basic doctrines about Jesus, Scripture, sin, salvation, and the like. When John Coleman Bennett read the NCB proposal he affirmed it all but said to me: "David, I don't think this statement of faith adequately captures what you believe and are all about. It is just about theological doctrines with nothing about discipleship and ethics!" He was right.

So I went back to the drawing board and crafted a simple but powerful statement that described us as (1) "Biblical"—committed to the Scriptures of the Old and New Testaments as God's Word and our guide for all of our faith and practice, (2) "Evangelical"—defined by us as being committed to Jesus Christ as our Savior, Lord, and God, for all of life, (3) "Ecumenical"—defined by us as being committed to learning from and serving the whole Church—and on this threefold basis—(4) Committed to exploring and living out our faith and values in all aspects of our thought, life, and work. Our committee especially loved using both terms "Evangelical" and "Ecumenical" as we defined them and not as brands for usually opposing theological camps.

One challenge we faced was deciding on a name for our school. All the early documents were simply entitled "Proposal for a New College in Berkeley." We wrestled with "college" which in the British and Canadian world could refer to a graduate school but in the USA usually meant undergraduate school. We considered using the name "James" or "St. James" because of the Apostle James's emphasis on showing our faith in our work—but thought it could sound high church with the "Saint" or could connote William James without it. We thought about "Berkeley Institute" but it sounded too cold. Some (not me) liked "C.S. Lewis College" but there were lots of other C.S. Lewis projects. In the end, Earl and I suggested we just stick with "New College" and add the tag line "for Advanced Christian Studies" to give a clear sense that we were graduate-level ("advanced") and theological ("Christian Studies").

I suggested that we adopt as our motto *"novitate vitae ambulemis"*—Latin for "let us walk in newness of life" from Romans 6:4, which put the emphasis on "walking" not just believing or talking the faith. And I pointed out that New College Oxford was founded in 1379. If they could still call themselves "New," so could we for decades to come. As it turned out, the short form "New College Berkeley" or "NCB" became our commonly used name. Just after we were founded, a financial sandal hit the front pages of the newspaper: a San Francisco-based "New College of California" was in deep trouble for selling honorary doctorates for $25,000 donations! It looked like this school was finished—but it did survive (and reform). By using our "Berkeley" name (and working with completely different constituencies) we avoided much (though not quite all) confusion with this other New College in the years to come.

By the time we got to April 1977, after a year of prayer and study, after three months of intense working sessions by our Study Committee, we decided unanimously that it was time to make our move. Ginny Hearn and I drove in the Hearn VW bug up to Sacramento on April 7, 1977, and filed our incorporation papers, walking them through the various departments in the capitol building. New College Berkeley was founded. Every year since, I think about NCB on April 7.

PROJECT DIRECTOR (1977-79)

Our official founding was on April 7, 1977. My family moved back into our Oakland home (just a mile south of NCB and Cal Berkeley) in June of 1977 and I was hired as Project Director for $700 per month to work two-thirds time on NCB (and leave the other third to work on finishing my PhD dissertation). Of course, I had really started putting in some long hours from March 1976 onward but my role became official in April 1977 and compensated in June 1977. I was also the initial, founding chair of the board for 1977 (our study committee members all agreed to serve on the board except for attorney Minor Schmid who had too many other commitments). For 1978, Earl succeeded me as chair for one year with our plan to find another chair in 1979—we did not want NCB to be seen as either the "David Gill Project" or "Earl Palmer Project." I still did all the organizational and legwork for our meetings but Earl did a great job as our enthusiastic and wise chair. Harper and Row editor Roy Carlisle served as board chair in 1979 and Berkeley Covenant Pastor Craig Anderson came on as chair for three years, 1980–82.

It is impossible for me to adequately praise Earl Palmer for his support and leadership. He had a level of popularity and respect among both pastors and lay Christians that I could never have. His sermons and First Pres services were broadcast every Sunday morning on KGO-radio, the most popular station in Northern California. He was one of the best preachers I have ever heard, always working from some biblical text to a profound, practical, positive application in life. He gladly announced and promoted New College Berkeley study programs from his pulpit. He had me as a First Pres guest preacher several times. His stream of published books helped thousands. He taught a course for New College Berkeley every year with big enrollments (from 1979 to the present!). For many people, New College Berkeley had credibility and was attractive because of Earl's presence. For me personally, he was a sounding board, encourager, and wise counselor. He convinced First Pres to put us in their missions support budget year after year for a thousand or two dollars.

It was tempting for me to join First Pres as my home church but I felt the NCB project would be stronger if I was a member of another church in another denomination, so I maintained my Evangelical Covenant Church affiliation and raised my family at Berkeley Covenant Church, whose pastor Craig Anderson was a founding board member of NCB and a superb chair of our board for three years. As it turned out, NCB was able to be a truly interdenominational project with leaders, faculty, and students from not just Presbyterian and Covenant circles but Brethren, Assembly of God, Baptist, Quaker, Mennonite, Episcopal, Methodist, even Catholic, Orthodox, and many other traditions.

My own profile also helped us build a positive relationship with the Graduate Theological Union. Earl Palmer and First Pres were viewed with suspicion and jealousy by the local Presbyterian Seminary, San Francisco Theological Seminary, partly because Earl was a Princeton graduate, served on its board, and directed Presbyterian seminary students there instead of to SFTS. I was viewed much differently by the GTU because of my USC pedigree and the letters of support and introduction my USC profs John Coleman Bennett, Jack Crossley (an SFTS grad himself), and John Orr wrote to GTU president Claude Welch, Pacific School of Religion president Neely McCarter, and others. Not long after my arrival in Berkeley I was invited by James McClendon, professor at the Episcopal Church Divinity School of the Pacific in the GTU, to join the Pacific Coast Theological Society, an invitation-only group of faculty from GTU schools and other institutions up and down the coast. I was active in this fellowship all through the 1980s and served a three-year term as PCTS co-chair with Claude Welch and Prof. Clare Fisher from Starr King Unitarian School of Ministry. NCB's connections to, and relations with, the Graduate Theological Union were organic and positive from day one.

Back home in the Bay Area in June 1977, I worked out of my home study for six months through the end of the year. I immediately created a professional looking brochure "Introducing New College Berkeley" and a quarterly eleven by seventeen newsletter starting in Fall 1977. I began a routine of what amounted to fifty to eighty speaking engagements per year during my whole fourteen years with NCB—sermons, classes, seminars, professional gatherings, university and seminary visits—anywhere I could find an audience. At every gig I passed out NCB brochures and took names and addresses for our growing mailing list, which numbered 10,000 by the late 1980s. I created an NCB "bulletin insert" which was used at churches where I preached. Every chance Earl Palmer got, he was also building our constituency and interest in our project. Our board member donations and some financial support from First Pres and Berkeley Covenant provided us with $1000 per month in 1977 and double that in 1978.

By December 1977, after six months, I was buried in correspondence and organizational tasks and needed some assistance. I was able to hire as a half-time assistant Debra Sands Miller, a Cal grad looking for a good job after quitting a terrible one in protest against its unethical practices. First Pres loaned us the weekday use of a Sunday School room, into which we moved a couple desks and file cabinets, and installed a carpet, drapes, and our own phone line. Debra was a wonderful colleague and worked with me for eighteen months until her first baby was about to arrive, just as we transitioned to full-time operation at our nearby campus. In 1978 she was paid $700/month and I was upped to $1000/month. At that stage we still had no health care or other benefits but we got by!

NEW COLLEGE BERKELEY, PHASE I (1976-85)

FIRST ACADEMIC PROGRAMS

In addition to all my organizational, publicity, and promotion tasks, I began planning for our first program, a six-week summer school in 1978. Directly because of Earl's Princeton connection and friendship, Bruce Metzger agreed to come and teach a three-week course on "Letters of Faith, Hope and Love: Galatians, I Peter, and I John." Metzger was a wonderful teacher, world-renowned NT scholar, and lead translator of the New Revised Standard Version New Testament. Because of my and Sharon Gallagher's radical Christian roots and connections, John Howard Yoder and Donald and Lucille Sider Dayton agreed to come. My friendship with African-American theologian and social ethicist William Pannell at Fuller convinced him to join us for that first summer school. Old Testament Professor Carl Armerding came down from Regent College to join us. York University Professor Mary Stewart Van Leeuwen joined us to teach a course on "Gender and Grace"—probably drawn by confidence in our Evangelical feminist board members Sharon Gallagher and Virginia Hearn.

Thus, we had three brilliant scholar/teachers during each of our two three-week sessions and I taught a six-week evening course on Jacques Ellul. We arranged for housing in the Cal Berkeley dorms for those who needed it. Visiting professor Bill Pannell lived at my house for three weeks and John Howard Yoder stayed with his wife Annie and several of their kids in the house next door to mine (Cal Professor Al and Kathy Raboteau's place, while they were away on vacation). We offered our classes in First Pres buildings. Logos Bookstore on Telegraph Avenue, whose proprietor Bob Baylis was on our board, stocked our books. Every Thursday evening one of our visiting profs gave a free, highly-attended public lecture in a different nearby church. We had a chapel service daily to which most students came. On July 4 we rented Cal's recreation center and pool in Strawberry Canyon for a wonderful afternoon and evening. Ninety-eight students enrolled in our courses and gave us rave reviews of their experiences both in and out of class. While I sat in on a class or two, I remember feeling some sadness that I just couldn't attend more classes because I needed to hustle constantly on the non-stop organizational details. I consoled myself knowing the great experience I was helping make happen for everyone else.

In early 1978 I was also organizing a slate of part-time evening courses for the Fall, Winter, and Spring Quarters of 1978–79, held not just at First Pres Berkeley but Menlo Park Pres. And we were lining up a great group of visiting professors for our second summer school in 1979: OT Prof Elmer Martens from Mennonite Brethren Seminary in Fresno, Seattle Pacific anthropologist Miriam Adeney, C.S. Lewis scholar Kathryn Lindskoog, Westmont sociologist Ronald Enroth, Fuller NT prof Ralph Martin, theologian Clark Pinnock, Professors Alice and Kenneth Hamilton in Literature, and social ethicist Ron Sider. It would be a stellar visiting faculty for our second go-round.

PART THREE: CHANNELS (1979–2016)

RECRUITING A PRESIDENT AND FACULTY

Also in 1978, we began our search for a President and faculty in time for our full-time launch in Fall 1979. I rejected all talk of my being a candidate for president. We created a presidential job description and began looking. We settled on three major candidates: retiring Oregon Senator Mark Hatfield, Regent College OT Professor Carl Armerding, and Regent NT Professor Ward Gasque. Hatfield graciously wrote to say he thought and prayed about it but decided God wanted him to return to Oregon. Carl Armerding was then called in 1978 to be president of Regent College. But Ward Gasque agreed to come to Berkeley as our first President in fall 1979. More on Ward Gasque below. In Spring 1979 Donald Tinder agreed to leave his post as a member of the editorial team at *Christianity Today* to join us as Professor of Church History in the fall 1979. Don had earned his PhD at Yale University under the dean of American Church Historians, Sydney Ahlstrom. He and Ward Gasque had been long time friends and fellow students at Fuller Seminary. Veteran missionary to China David H. Adeney was appointed Chaplain and Professor-at-Large. Australian OT scholar Francis I. Andersen agreed to spend the 1979–80 year as Visiting Professor of Old Testament and British theologian H. D. MacDonald agreed to come as Visiting Professor of Theology. As local adjunct professors, Stanford's Richard Bube and former Iowa State professor Walt Hearn agreed to teach courses on Christianity and Science. Burlingame Presbyterian pastor Tom Gillespie, with a PhD in NT would also teach for us, along with Laurel Gasque in Christianity and the Arts, Virginia Hearn in communications, Sharon Gallagher in film and media, and, not least, Earl Palmer in biblical and theological studies. For our little start-up, we were loaded with great and accomplished scholars and teachers.

FINDING A CAMPUS

Another big challenge was facilities. I dropped in to visit President Doward McBain who had recently come to the American Baptist Seminary of the West. ABSW was located on the south side of the Berkeley campus (most other GTU schools were clustered just north of the Cal campus). It was just across the street from Berkeley's famous "Peoples Park." ABSW owned a cluster of buildings that had the look and feel of a classic place like Oxford. Several of their buildings were rented out to other non-profits since their student body could be accommodated in just two or three of their buildings. When I visited with President McBain and described our project he got visibly excited. "David, I love this vision and I will do whatever I can to help you succeed."

We looked at some possible facilities at northside GTU schools but the ground floor of Johnston Hall on the ABSW campus was being vacated by its renters and was available. It had been one of the original campus seminary buildings and was a classic, beautiful place that would accommodate our needs for offices and a classroom for forty students. I asked President McBain if I could get a "poor peoples' discount" and rent the facilities for $750 per month the first year, 1979–80, and $950 per month for the second year, 1980–81. He agreed! We could only thank him and thank God for this amazing, beautiful, affordable beginning.

We also had no furniture—but I found out that ABSW had a basement warehousing old desks, file cabinets, and wooden arm chairs with old-fashioned writing tablets attached. I bought forty of them for $5 each! We were in business, almost. ABSW had a beautiful little chapel building which we could use for our biweekly chapels and other gatherings and Karpe Hall, their bigger auditorium and adjoining kitchen, would host our occasional conferences and banquets. The Crucible merged into New College Berkeley in 1979 and added a couple thousand books to the several thousand Don Tinder donated from his years as book review editor at *Christianity Today*. The massive GTU library could be accessed by any of our faculty or students for a modest fee.

GETTING THE WORD OUT AND RECRUITING STUDENTS

E-mail and the internet did not exist until the mid-1990s so our publicity was old-school. We ran a few paid one-sixth page ads for our summer schools and upcoming degree programs in *Christianity Today, Eternity,* and other magazines but this was expensive. Our quarterly newsletter kept our growing mailing list (hundreds now after our summer schools) informed and announced upcoming programs (along with faculty additions, regular financial reports, and funding appeals). Our local artist and designer friends like Keith Criss created interesting posters for local churches to display and inserts for church bulletins. We visited InterVarsity campus fellowships and local churches to preach, teach, and promote our programs. I spent untold hours writing letters and telephoning potential students. Later, in December of 1981, 1984, and 1987 we had display tables at InterVarsity's big Urbana conventions to get our message out to their 18,000 attendees. I also spoke and recruited at Nurses Christian Fellowship conferences and Pittsburgh's amazing Jubilee Convention in those early years.

In early 1978 we hosted our first big NCB banquet attended by hundreds. Our banquet speaker was Homar Goddard, the founder of Fuller Seminary's extension programs. Fuller operated a robust extension program in Menlo Park and some of their leaders like Ray Anderson were clearly threatened by a potential rival in the Bay Area—until we convinced them that we were not recruiting seminary students (like they served) but laity. I had met with Goddard while I was still living in Pasadena in 1976–77 and received his counsel and blessing—so it was a great affirmation for him to come as our first big banquet speaker. For our second big banquet in early 1979 our speaker was Jim Houston, Principal of Regent College—another affirmation that mattered a lot as we got started. In the years to come, John Stott became a great friend to NCB (and to Lucia and me), teaching three times in our summer schools and speaking at one of our big banquets. Tony Campolo also taught and guest spoke for NCB. Having the endorsement and on campus contribution of leaders like Stott and Campolo was a huge gift.

For part-time students who enrolled for credit or audit in our summer and evening programs, it was a pretty straightforward deal. Course quality was all that mattered. But for those considering joining us as full-time students in fall 1979, it was a real leap of faith coming to a brand new, unproven school. I spent a lot of my time working with those prospects and helping them see that NCB was for real and in it for the long haul. Many who tasted the experience in our summer schools were convinced and a talented group of pioneers came from across the USA to join us in fall 1979.

DESIGNING A CURRICULUM

With our Academic Affairs Committee, and input from Ward Gasque and Don Tinder before their arrival, we designed a basic first year curriculum that would earn a "Diploma in Christian Studies" and second year options that could lead to either a Master of Christian Studies or Master of Arts degree. The MA allowed specialization in Biblical Studies, Church History, Christian Ethics, Theology, or Interdisciplinary Studies. Our MA required a foreign language and thesis like other traditional MAs. The basic first year program for all students included required courses in Old and New Testament Theology—we wanted the primary focus to be on the ideas of the Bible, not on critical textual matters. Our course in Church History was primarily focused on the history of the people, not on just the leaders and their institutional controversies. We had a course on Systematic Theology. My Christian Ethics course was not (like so many) on "Enlightenment-moral-philosophy-plus-Bible-verses" or on "the ten hottest ethical controversies of today" but on the basic framework of the ways the Bible deals with matters of right and wrong, good and evil, and how to build healthy ethical character and community, as well as how to make wise ethical decisions. Organically biblical and practical ethics for layfolk was my aim.

Our foundational course, designed and led by Don Tinder and Doug Anderson, was on the "Ministry of the Laity"—what does the Bible teach about the role and ministry of the people of God—all of them, male and female, old and young? Our eye was on the academy and the workplace. The capstone course was on "Integrative Studies" in which every student did a project to integrate faith, learning, and vocation. Unlike a seminary, our capstone was not about how to preach, pastor, and lead a Christian congregation. Of course, we also had, in both summer and academic year programs, a host of elective courses and workshops on thinkers like C.S. Lewis and Jacques Ellul, topics like Christianity and Health Care, Art, Law, Science, Violence, Poetry, Prayer, and Journal-keeping. For our advanced students we offered seminars in all of our subject areas. We had a talented faculty of full-time resident and visiting faculty each year complemented by fifteen or twenty superb local adjunct faculty. From early on, PhD candidates Doug Anderson (Church History) and Bernard Adeney (Social Ethics) played essential and growing roles on our faculty. Later on, Frances Adeney (Ethics) and Susan Phillips (Sociology) became integral to our teaching community after finishing their doctorates.

CONFERENCES AND SPECIAL EVENTS

In addition to our classes and courses for full- and part-time students, we were committed to organizing shorter seminars, workshops, and conferences on different topics. When we had a great theologian in town like John Stott, Helmut Thielicke, Markus Barth, or Carl Henry we often hosted a special "Pastors' Breakfast," e.g., Stott on expository preaching. Anywhere from one hundred to three hundred pastors would attend. I think the first interdisciplinary conference we organized (in 1980 or 1981) was called "Health Care Professionals as Christ's Servants." My first step was to get the co-sponsorship of the regional leaders of the Nurses Christian Fellowship and the Christian Medical Society. NCF leader Lynn Ellis was all in from the start. CMS leader Joe Ludders was agreeable but told us that he worried that doctors might not participate in a conference with nurses and other health care professionals just because of a traditional professional distance (and feeling of superiority?). I (of course) could not accept this "class" attitude! I asked Joe what was the largest group of MDs ever to meet in a Bay Area CMS gathering? "Six or eight" he replied. Me: "Joe, I already have ten Christian MD friends who I am certain will come so we're going to set a new record for CMS no matter what! And let's recruit hard in our local medical schools to find a new generation of MDs with more of a team attitude!" Joe, Lynn, and I went to work and we drew three hundred twenty-five attendees: twenty-five MDs plus twenty-five medical students, over a hundred nurses and nursing students, another fifty dentists and other health care workers, and the rest pastors and laity interested in the topic. It was a huge success. Dr. Charles Beal, Dr. Rebecca Klint (along with our MD students Phil Stillman and Bob McGrew), Doctor of Dentistry Bill Patterson, and many others became long-time NCB friends and supporters.

We followed up with a conference on "Law and Justice in Biblical Perspective," co-sponsored with the Christian Legal Society, with plenary lectures by distinguished Cal Law School profs John Noonan and Phil Johnson and by Regent Professor Klaus Bockmuhl. Conferences on Business, the Arts, and other fields followed.

THE CAL BERKELEY CONNECTION

As a theological school we cultivated relationships with the Graduate Theological Union. But at least as important was our neighboring University of California. The GTU had built an institutional and programmatic bridge to the University and we hoped eventually to take advantage of course cross-registration (it came in the late 1980s). From the beginning, many of the core leaders at NCB were Berkeley alumni. By the time of my presidency (1986–90), our chair of the board Fred Vann was a Cal graduate in engineering from the 1930s, Board member Prof. David Cole graduated from Cal in the 1940s, Earl Palmer in the 1950s, I in the 1960s, Marty Stewart (alumni director) in the 1970s, and business manager Amy Brannon Keltner in the 1980s. Six decades of Berkeley grads in our leadership! Cal professors David Cole (Biochemistry), Richard Benner (Business), Clay Radke (Chemistry), Robert Bellah (Sociology), Stephen Knapp (English), William Bouwsma (History) and others were among our official and unofficial participants and encouragers. (Remember also that our board member and adjunct professor Walt Hearn had retired from Iowa State University and Stanford University Materials Science professor Richard Bube (a national leader in the American Scientific Affiliation) added heft to our university-level culture of learning).

I had learned early on that Regent College faculty, especially Ward Gasque, had reached out to University of British Columbia Christian faculty and helped them begin gathering (as many as forty!) for discussion of their mission and vocation. With Professor David Cole I began networking around the Cal faculty and we soon had as many as twenty for periodic meetings at the Faculty Club (no one could remember more than six or eight Christian Cal faculty gathering before that). Later on, in 1989, one of my favorite days was when the chair of my old Cal history department organized a gathering to hear me present my new book *The Opening of the Christian Mind* (InterVarsity, 1989) in which I described my 1966 experience as a junior history major, wondering how my faith related to the study of history.

In the mid-1980s, the biggest foray onto the Cal campus was a conference I organized called "Thinking Christianly in Today's University." Over three hundred students and faculty gathered on campus to hear plenary lectures by Os Guinness and break up into academic disciplinary discussion groups led by thirty university professors in the various fields (mostly Cal faculty). Our efforts through the 1980s to work with Cal students were less successful because the campus IVCF director at the time did not share our concerns for the development of the Christian mind and insisted IVCF confine its focus to traditional Bible study, prayer, evangelism and fellowship. This was especially disappointing since our NCB resident and visiting faculty was flush with InterVarsity Press authors and I and others were regularly speaking to IVCF chapters on other university campuses around the country. Oh well. Not everything goes as planned or dreamed.

BUILDING A COMMUNITY

From day one, NCB was not just about the classroom. We held biweekly chapel services with great music and teaching, not just from our faculty but some of our students. Not a few of our students told me that these chapel services nourished their souls more than their home churches (though we always strongly encouraged active local church membership and participation). We often went to lunch or coffee with our students and visiting faculty—our campus neighborhood was a mecca of restaurants and coffee shops. Our faculty homes and tables welcomed the NCB community. No one was ever left out if we could help it. We created an in-house newsletter we called "News Collage" (the imagination never stopped). We had monthly faculty feasts and endless dinners and gatherings in faculty homes. During our summer schools we organized dinners, receptions, and conversations with our visiting faculty. I recall a summer in which Lucia and I invited all interested to our house to hear old veteran Carl F. H. Henry tell the story of his life over two afternoons, from baseball writer through his two doctorates and the founding of *Christianity Today* to the present. Some sixty people crammed our living room and hung out the windows listening to this amazing man.

After we began full-time operation, I announced that I was also "Athletic Director" for our team called (with a dig at the Fighting Irish of Notre Dame) the "Fighting Doves." We had some tennis tournaments. Lucia and were sort of intermediate level players like our colleague Bernie Adeney and we often played together. But I was severely humbled by our students such as Shannon Thwaite. One of our students, Ann, had been the number two player on the women's team at Stanford. She preferred to concentrate on her studies but finally relented and agreed to play with me one day. While in those days I was pretty fit and fast and at the top of my game, I was exhausted just warming up with her. Every ball came back across the net from her. When we played two sets, I swear I played the best tennis of my life and lost 6–0, 6–0. I won maybe one point per game only when I crushed a return down the line or got a great serve in. But my percentage on making shots like that was only 25%—the rest of the time she throttled me and I knew my place! If I needed any more tennis schooling, former tennis pro Chip Fisher patiently wiped me out 6–0, 6–0 also!

In May 1980 I organized about twenty or thirty of us to run in the famous, annual, "Bay-to-Breakers" 12k race across San Francisco. We opened training season on St. Patrick's Day by feasting on corned beef and cabbage and drinking green beer at our place. Eight weeks later we carpooled to San Francisco and ran (in our NCB tee shirts). Lucia and I would clock in between 60 and 65 minutes, far behind our board member and attorney Jim Barringer in the low 50s. (The actual race winner was usually in the mid-30s). A big picnic in Golden Gate Park was our final act where we awarded first prize to whoever accumulated the most minutes (usually in the high 80s) on the Christian principle that "the last shall be first." Our "Fighting Doves" ran in the Bay-to-Breakers for several years through the 1980s. NCB was a fun place to be—at the same it was so stimulating intellectually and spiritually.

Part Three: Channels (1979–2016)

LAUNCHING FULL-TIME OPERATIONS IN FALL 1979

Going back to fall 1979, Ward and Laurel Gasque moved from Vancouver BC down to their new home in the Berkeley hills. Don and Edie Tinder moved from Chicago to Albany, California. Our visiting faculty members Francis and Lois Andersen from Australia and H.D. McDonald from England moved into the rental cottages at the Berkeley Presbyterian Missionary Homes. (In the years to come, Robert K. Johnston, Peter Davids, Stephen McCray Smith, Robert Banks, Clarice Martin, Francis and Lois Andersen (again), and others spent years in that visiting role). I had worked hard to get our offices and classroom set up but I was blown away our first week when Laurel Gasque pulled up in her station wagon packed with green plants she had just purchased at a local nursery and brought in to grace and beautify our campus. Laurel, then and always, brought beauty and "class" into what would have otherwise remained a more utilitarian environment.

Ward Gasque was the perfect choice for our first president. At a robust 6' 7" our small college suddenly had the biggest president around in Ward. His warmth and vision were as grand as his stature. He was an endless source of ideas and optimism. He would sometimes emphatically say to me "possibility thinking, brother David, possibility thinking!" We hit it off immediately and became lifetime friends. While I am a pretty big-thinking visionary myself, I am also a detail-obsessive administrator who could give Ward the kind of partnership and support he needed. Ward was a gregarious people-lover who seemed to know everybody. He was a graduate of Wheaton College and Fuller Theological Seminary. He had done his PhD in New Testament under the great F.F. Bruce at Manchester University in England. He had played the pioneering organizational role for Regent College (with Carl Armerding) that I had played at NCB. At the end of my work as Project Director getting NCB to its full-time launch, I did not feel qualified to be the Dean (much less President). I was a freshly-minted PhD and now wanted just to be an Assistant Professor and earn my spurs in that role. But Ward told me he wouldn't come unless I would be his dean. So I agreed but insisted I be called the more modest "Acting Dean." (After two years I agreed with him that the "Acting" modifier could go).

Ward and I usually were in complete accord—but we occasionally disagreed. I remember one (rare) time when he was loudly yelling at me about something in his office and when we came out, our Registrar Joan Anderson was looking a bit shaken by all the noise and yelling! We assured her it was not a big deal as we buddies went off to lunch on Telegraph Avenue. I just loved working with this big guy. Like Earl Palmer, Ward was a big vision, unthreatened, totally honest and forthright partner and older brother under whom and with whom I thrived.

Ward took a huge pay cut to come from Regent to NCB. I think he was only paid $24,000 the first year and I was paid $22,000. Don Tinder had to exist on that same low salary. We also were able to provide Kaiser-Permanente health care coverage but there was no retirement contribution (all the years I was at NCB). In September of 1979 we had a big celebration of the dedication of New College Berkeley in the sanctuary of First Pres, with Earl Palmer giving the major address. It was our first academic convocation in full regalia with appropriate pomp and circumstance.

When my great administrative assistant Debra Sands Miller left NCB, about to deliver her first child. I managed to recruit Polly Odom from the office of the Berkeley Christian Coalition to be our office manager and Joan Terpstra Anderson from Logos Bookstore to be our Registrar. Polly served NCB for several years before returning to her native New Orleans. Joan was an anchor of NCB for almost the whole decade of the 1980s. She was an extraordinary detail manager as well as a wise and warm leader. She did not hesitate to exhort me if she thought I needed it! She was a godly, quiet spiritual presence. We sent her up to Regent College for a week to study their registration and student records systems and come back to NCB and create our systems. She is definitely one of the greatest people I ever worked with, She had a significant pastoral impact on our students and staff (and me).

Ward and I did most of our own "secretarial support" during the first academic year 1979–80 but we were soon drowning in those tasks. In the fall of 1980 Ward hired Dottie Anderson (wife of our board chair Craig) as his Administrative Assistant, a supremely competent, reliable help in his presidential tasks and a joyful, humorous part of our community. I ran a search and hired Chris Carlisle (later Sillerud) after she type-tested at ninety-five words per minute compared to the fifty scored by three or four other applicants. Chris was a joyful, hard-working, reliable, smart, upbeat colleague who I loved working with in good times and bad. During these years I dictated countless letters onto a cassette tape recorder and Chris typed them out for me to sign. We had long application forms to fill out for state board of education and accreditation agency purposes. I would walk around the office inventing and dictating the "bureaucrat-ese" paragraphs as she typed them and we often roared with laughter at the required rhetoric. No matter what she was up against outside the office as a single mom or what our little start-up grad school was facing, she always brought a smile, a laugh, and a ferocious work ethic to my office. One of my worst personnel decisions ever was letting my successor dean keep her as his assistant when I became president in 1986!

During those first years we had some marvelous students, only a few of whom I can mention as examples. Lauri Strayer Stott joined us after graduating from UCLA and did her MA with us on the way to being a teacher of Spanish and English as a Second Language. Scott Thomas came from the American University and did an NCB MA before his PhD at the London School of Economics and a long, distinguished career on the faculty of the University of Bath in the UK. Marty Stewart, a Cal grad, did her master's degree with us and then went on to a masters in Marriage and Family Therapy and a long career as a therapist. She also helped us begin an NCB alumni organization. Phil Stillman and Robert McGrew were both recent MD grads who did master's degrees with us before embarking on long careers as physicians. Phil has long served on the New College board, including a term as Chair. Mimi Haddad graduated from NCB, then from Gordon-Conwell Seminary and a PhD from the University of Durham. She has been the long-time president of the Council for Biblical Equality. Cynthia Hall was an RN and active leader in Nurses Christian Fellowship. Paul Tokunaga, Bobby Gross, and Jay Sivits went on to have long careers as InterVarsity Regional Directors. John Ephland has been a jazz writer and reviewer for *DownBeat* magazine. Robert Hudson went on to become a professor at the University of Illinois. Donna Symington was a dancer and dance teacher after graduating from NCB.

Two of my all-time favorite students were Betty DeMont and her eighty-year old mother Esther Ware who were a constant presence for three or four years. One day Esther looked me in the eye and told me she was concerned by how exhausted I looked. Would I be interested in getting away for a few days at her usually-vacant, rustic home up on the coast at Bodega Bay, where she had lived with her husband Jim before he died? Sweet and caring lady. That Bodega Bay place became a writing retreat for me for the next several years—and the location for occasional faculty retreats. What a gift. When Esther died, she wanted her memorial service to be at the NCB chapel because it had meant so much to her. Earl Palmer and I led the service.

STRENGTHENING OUR FUNDING AND LEADERSHIP

We collected tuition from students in our classes but were always dependent even more on charitable donations. We tried to keep our tuition levels as reasonable as possible and had deep discounts for auditors. None of our founding board members were wealthy but we all kicked in what we could every year. First Pres Berkeley, Berkeley Covenant, and a few other local churches put us in their annual missions budgets but usually for "solidarity gifts" in the hundreds rather than thousands of dollars. We did not raise much if any foundation grant money. We operated pretty much hand-to-mouth, constantly having our faith tested. We always paid our bills and our payroll but Ward and I sometimes had to wait a couple weeks on our pay so we could provide the modest salaries we promised to our people on time. I recall at least one time when our bank account was down to just $10—and I insisted to Ward that he and I go over to Larry Blake's Rathskellar on Telegraph and each have a $5 beer to celebrate our confidence that God would come through (and God did).

The core of our financial support was always our growing, faithful band of supporters who donated $50 to $500 per year. In Spring of 1978 when we were recruiting students for our upcoming, first summer school, a young attorney who was an expert on international oil drilling rights and contracts, Jay Boone, somehow found our little second or third floor NCB office at First Pres and wanted to sign up for a couple classes. Before he left, he asked "How can I make a donation to the school? How do I make out a check?" After he left, we were overjoyed to find our first ever donation for

$500! Jay and his wife Susan became regular supporters and big fans of NCB for the next decade. In a short time Jay joined our Board of Trustees, donated $25k and also became my longtime golf partner and faithful, wise, confidant of both Ward and me.

Techie Steve Phillips and his wife Susan (our future professor and then Executive Director from 1994–2021) enrolled in our classes almost from day one. Steve donated an IBM computer we nicknamed 'Phil" in his honor—on which we managed our financial and enrollment data for the first years—and soon joined our Board of Trustees, serving as Chair during my final year, 1990. My friend Mark Kvamme was just finishing his BA at Berkeley and was already Apple Computer's sales director for France. In 1984 when the Mac personal computer came on the scene, Mark donated six or eight Macs to NCB and helped us set up an internal network at NCB. UC Berkeley Professor of Biochemistry David Cole came on to our Board in those early days and did an amazing job strengthening our academic systems and processes to a "Berkeley-level." David and Thelma Cole also became generous not just in time and effort but in financial support. They donated the first $20k to the endowment fund I initiated after I became president in 1986.

A tall, handsome, retired businessman and C.S. Lewis fan, Fred Vann, enrolled in our first summer school and went on to complete our MCS degree. Fred Vann got deeply involved not just as a student but as a board member. He had built up an amazing business, Vann Engineering, which installed the air conditioning in many skyscrapers in San Francisco. Fred was the major donor to NCB year in, year out. He purchased for NCB the twelve-bedroom student residence we called "Dwight House" in the mid-1980s and later gave $100k to our endowment fund. Lucia and I played tennis and golf with Fred and visited him and his wife Betty in their Mendocino home and later in Rossmoor. Fred often stayed with us when he came down for NCB meetings and events.

PRESIDENTIAL TRANSITION TO BILL DYRNESS (1982–86)

One of the biggest challenges in academic administration is finding people who have the academic pedigree and background to provide wise leadership and understanding of the academic vocation. Hiring a non-academic business leader is often a mistake, in my experience and observation, as financial matters begin to crowd out the concerns for research and teaching. Basically, all academics love ideas and research. Many (not all) also love students and teaching. But very few (ten percent?) also have administrative gifts and passions. Most academics who become presidents and deans suffer and even carry some guilt about the vast amount of time and energy they take from their research and teaching to do administrative work. That was certainly a constant factor for me at NCB and in much of my career.

While Ward Gasque was a great president for NCB and we all wanted him to stay on, he decided he must return to his research and teaching, especially a promised major work on the Book of Acts, and return to Regent College after three years at NCB. The funnest (and funniest) night in the history of NCB was our farewell banquet for Ward, which included my dying my hair and beard dark brown, borrowing (and padding up) one of Ward's big suits, building some wooden "stilts" that made me nine inches taller, writing and singing a song about him called the "Florence Blues" with a student blues band, along with a cover of the Beach Boys' "Be True to Your School." I heard that we offended one donor but everybody else in a huge crowd laughs about it to this day. But we were so sad to see him and Laurel go.

One of Ward's final acts was to raise a couple thousand dollars to fund my (and my family's) first ever trip to Europe (and to see Jacques Ellul) in summer 1982. My spoken French was appallingly weak but Lucia helped that summer with translation (and I conquered basic French two years later on my sabbatical). But I have to mention my indebtedness to what I call the "Laurel Gasque School of Language Acquisition." Whenever Laurel was about to travel or encounter someone speaking a language new to her, she would get a phrase book, memorize some basics, and then boldly forge ahead speaking as best she could! I was with her in several contexts like this. She inspired me to be similarly bold and not hesitate to (sometimes apologetically) engage people with what little I had. Thank-you Laurel!

Several of our NCB board members and community members pressed me to succeed Ward as president but I declined because I still had not experienced the life and vocation of a scholar and teacher to the extent I dreamed and wanted. So a presidential search took place and NCB called William Dyrness to succeed Ward. Bill was a first-rate theologian (always, I should say, eager to push back at my Barthian, Ellulian, and Anabaptist leanings) with special strengths in Old Testament theology and Christianity and the arts and culture. He was also a wonderful classroom teacher, mentor to students, and faculty community-builder. In recent years, with more time to read, I have come to appreciate his scholarship more than ever, especially his rich theology of the arts. Bill and his wife Grace gave their all during his four years as president (1982–86) and then continuing as professor of theology another four years (1986–90) before moving on to Fuller Seminary.

I initially tried to resign as dean but Bill insisted I must continue (because of my core leadership role, fund-raising, promotional work and networking up to that point). I agreed to stay on for one year. Then, as my sabbatical year approached, he told me I could only have the sabbatical if I stayed on as dean for one more year until I left. Finally, he told me if I took the sabbatical I must agree to come back for a year after my sabbatical as dean. I wanted that sabbatical big time! But I always felt bad about my performance working for Bill. We were temperamental opposites (unlike Ward and I—or Earl and I). We all took the Meyers-Briggs test and he was a clear introvert to my hardcore extravert personality He was a go-with-the-flow "perceiver" to my get-organized "judger" in the Meyers-Briggs categories. We drove each other nuts I think. It was like yoking together two incompatible horses and expecting them to pull the wagon well.

We did have some real success during Bill's presidency: quality students and faculty, a growing reputation and respect across the country (and world). There were certainly many who preferred Bill's style to the louder, bolder style of Ward and me. I worked my tail off (with the help of Chris Carlisle and Joan Terpstra Anderson) to move us toward stronger relations with the GTU and not just California State approval of our degrees but initial steps toward accreditation by the Western Association of Schools and Colleges (a long and costly bureaucratic process). We still were holding summer schools with outstanding visiting faculty. But our fund-raising was always weak, our student body did not grow, our publicity did not strengthen, our debts were growing. After Craig Anderson left our board (for Chicago), the new chair was Richard Benner, an assistant dean at Cal's Business School. Benner was totally committed to the New College vision and mission and served as board chair through 1986. I had stepped off the Board during both Ward's and Bill's presidencies because I didn't want any confusion about their being the leaders of NCB. Unfortunately though, board membership, organization, and morale were slowly declining—though not for lack of commitment, hard work, and good will.

I hadn't been focusing much on fundraising during either Ward's or Bill's presidency but we were always stressed and stretched. Early in Bill's and Richard's terms as president and board chair, they called me into Bill's office to beseech me to help out. I offered to raise $50,000 from new sources (with God's help!). I made a list of a hundred people (or more) who I could ask for $500. I went back and got most of those names from people who had attended the conferences we had sponsored and were not on our donor list but probably capable of writing a check for $500. I wrote them each a personal letter of appeal and told them I would follow up with a phone call in the coming weeks. It was successful and they contributed over $50,000.

In one amazing case, I approached a woman (I will call Sarah) who had attended our conference on "Health Professionals as Christ's Servants." When I phoned to follow up, she said she was so sorry but they were not in a position to donate because her husband (I will call Bud) had just been laid off from his banking position. "Oh no!" I sympathized. "Please don't worry about it. May God help you guys to get through this trial." "David, Bud is a little depressed. He is sitting right here, could you talk to him?" Bud and I chatted a while and I tried to encourage him and prayed for him before hanging up. A week later we were surprised to receive a check for $1000 from Sarah and Bud. I called to thank her, a little worried about their finances based on what she had told me. "No David, your phone call was such an encouragement to Bud that we decided just to fling ourselves on the Lord and send you this check, trusting God to help us through." That was not the end of the story.

A year or so later I got a note from Sarah and a check for $75,000. "David, a distant relative died leaving us a big inheritance and we wanted to make our first donation to NCB." Thank you, so much, Sarah and Bud! In the next year Sarah and Bud gave another $300,000 or so to pay NCB's entry fees to become the tenth member of the GTU Library. I flew off to France in fall 1984 for my year-long sabbatical. Halfway through that fall I received a sad letter from Sarah. "David, Bud and I just had a very upsetting experience. We were coming up to Berkeley and asked if we could sit in on the NCB Board meeting just to be with this little school we have come to love. But no one so much as introduced us to the board members or welcomed and recognized our investment of faith in NCB. This had been the biggest step of faith in our life and we were so disappointed." I hate to be critical, but that would never have happened if Ward or I had been in the room. Fund-raising is first of all "friend-raising." The loss of Sarah and Bud's passion and support was a huge blow—and should have been a leadership lesson learned.

1984–85 SABBATICAL: BORDEAUX AND MUNICH

In 1984–85 I was awarded a one-year (at half-pay) sabbatical study leave in Bordeaux, France, to study with Jacques Ellul (I described this year in my earlier chapter on Jacques Ellul). I was exhausted after eight years of non-stop work on NCB, starting in 1976. I had been promoted from Assistant to Associate Professor after three years and now from Associate to full Professor after six years. I taught a full course load every year with good to great student reviews. My first published book appeared in 1984, a revised, updated version of my PhD dissertation *The Word of God in the Ethics of Jacques Ellul*. I had published dozens of essays and reviews in the scholarly journals and other publications and been an active participant in the American Academy of Religion, Society of Christian Ethics, and the American Historical Association among others. In typical graduate school fashion, my teaching counted for 50%, my research and publication was 25% and my school and community service was 25%. My school and community service required several pages to describe. An academic review committee chaired by Cal Professor David Cole evaluated my performance and recommended me for promotion to full professor in 1984, the end of my sixth year as an NCB professor.

During my sabbatical year in Bordeaux I mastered enough French to be able to read and write, converse, and even give (imperfect!) sermons and academic presentations over the coming years. My *Peter the Rock: Extraordinary Insights from an Ordinary Man* was written in Bordeaux and later published in 1986.[2] It was a study of the New Testament Peter from his appearance in all four Gospels, the Acts, Paul's Letters, and the two NT Letters bearing his name. I was drawn to this project because (1) so very few books were about Peter compared to Paul and Jesus, (2) Peter's story runs across the New Testament, start to finish, like no one else's, and (3) Peter's experiences, victories and defeats, run the range of Christian experience like no one else in the New Testament.

2. David W. Gill, *Peter the Rock: Extraordinary Insights from an Ordinary Man* (Downers Grove, Illinois: InterVarsity, 1986).

My Peter book had chapters on (1) the meaning of conversion, drawing from Peter's own conversion stories, then his speeches in Acts and his Letters, (2) the content of discipleship, three basic tasks Peter carried out, (3) a chapter focusing on Peter's many questions—and Jesus' questions for him, (4) his view and experience of the church, (5) his denial of Christ in the clutch, (6) his amazing recovery, (7) his evangelism and apologetics, and (8) the basic message of his two letters. I was, of course, inspired by Jacques Ellul's way of writing about biblical material, inviting it to teach us as God's Word to us. It is the closest thing to a kind of "systematic theology" I wanted to write. Ellul read my drafts and gave me his encouragement and comments through the year. I also rough drafted a manuscript on "Evangelical Ethics: Foundations" but continued working on that project for another two decades before finally publishing *Becoming Good: Building Moral Character* and *Doing Right: Practicing Ethical Principles*.[3]

While in Bordeaux, I was, of course, struck by the difficulty of learning French. In late September 1984, after four months immersed in French, I traveled to Munich, Germany, to stay with my friends Carol and John Adeney and check out the summer language programs at the University of Munich (I also made sure to take in the annual Oktoberfest, which essentially blew my mind because of the food, beverages, music, and celebration!). I decided that before returning to Berkeley in fall 1985 I would spend seven weeks enrolled in language courses at the University of Munich to try to bring back my German (remember I had four years of high school and another year of college German).

In June 1985 I headed to Munich where I rented a room from Ulf Kliesch, a Munich professor who preferred to speak only German with me. Helpful! I took my language classes every morning for seven weeks, and also found I could sit in on world-renowned theology Professor Wolfhart Pannenberg's lectures on eschatology and Professor Trutz Rendtorf's lectures on Christian ethics. After my classes I worked out at a gym and also ran a lot of miles—getting fitter than any time in my life since my twenties. Then I would sunbathe in Englischer Garten while reviewing my vocabulary cards and doing my homework before returning to the apartment. Every evening I also made time to draft a manifesto for NCB-style education which was later published in 1989 as *The Opening of the Christian Mind*.[4]

Many evenings I would go to a biergarten or brauhaus and find a seat by a bunch of old German guys, often in Lederhosen, who would engage me in (German) conversation. Over and over, I had to explain where I was from, what I was studying and teaching, and discuss world affairs with these groups of guys. I was able to attend Mozart's Zauberflöte (Magic Flute) in Munich's famous opera house and bike and play clay court tennis with John Adeney. John and his son Keith took me on a hike up into the Alps on a rugged trail marked out by Nazi Youth four or five decades earlier. At the

---

3. David W. Gill, *Becoming Good: Building Moral Character* (Downers Grove, Illinois: InterVarsity, 2000) and *Doing Right: Practicing Ethical Principles* (Downers Grove, Illinois: InterVarsity, 2004).

4. David W. Gill, *The Opening of the Christian Mind* (Downers Grove, Illinois: InterVarsity, 1989).

summit of the mountain, we drank schnaps and beer and ate Erbsensuppe (pea soup), listening to locals sing and play folk songs on their accordions, before making the long descent as darkness fell. Every Sunday I attended a wonderful 700-member Evangelische Kirkliche Gemeinde (church) on Holzstrasze in the town center. I loved the music and worship, the thoughtful sermons, and the warm welcome. On my first visit, the pastor invited me to his home for great theological conversation over wonderful German beverages and food. Another Sunday Helmut and Angelika Kunik-Sauder invited me to their home for lunch and then a dip in a nearby lake.

I loved every minute of my time in Munich and my immersion in Bavarian culture. I loved the combination of order and freedom, for example on the Autobahn (freeway) where there is no speed limit but strict rules about always driving to the right and passing on the left. I loved the beer and the Schweinshachsen and roasted chickens. I sometimes had supper at the Klassisches Musik restaurant where I sat under the trees and dined to the accompaniment of stringed quartets. In the middle of my study visit, on her July 22 birthday, Lucia flew over to join me for a few days from Paris where she was having her own study visit (Jonathan had flown back to Berkeley early and Jodie was at a summer camp). I gave her the complete tour, including a night at the Opera House for a great ballet performance, the university, the gym and sauna, the sunbathing in the park (though she did not embrace the total approach the rest of us in the park engaged), some clay court tennis and biking, and the Hofbrauhaus evenings. When she got off the plane she said she almost didn't recognize her superfit husband! The Munich lifestyle was good for me!

I returned to Munich for two weeks in the summer of 1988 and a full month with Lucia in 1995 (when we both studied German at the Goethe Institute and enjoyed the German experience). We visited the Munich Oktoberfest again (heavenly again) a few years later. As I described in an earlier chapter, I love France (and Bordeaux in particular) and would love to spend more months or years there. But culturally and in my heart, I am Bavarian and would love to have lived there for an extended period of time. My French is stronger than my German but my accent is much better in German. Mein Blut und mein Herz sind Deutsch. When I had to board the plane leaving Munich at the end of summer 1985, I had a real ache in my heart. If Lucia and the kids and Berkeley were not at the end of my flight, I wonder if I would have boarded.

Final story: I loved the Schweinshachsen (pork knuckle/roast) at the restaurant Hachsenbauer and elsewhere. Before leaving Germany I tried to freeze a couple, then wrap them tightly in foil and paper and smuggle them in my luggage coming home. It worked once. The second time (1988) my luggage never made it and I have always wondered if some security dogs smelled it and tore apart my suitcase before it got thrown away. Unfortunately, that suitcase also carried several documents Jacques Ellul had given me when with him in Bordeaux in earlier weeks. No more Schweinshachsen smuggling for me.

SABBATICAL BENEFITS AND COSTS

I returned to Oakland in the fall of 1985 fit, rested, with two book drafts, an amazing year of interaction with my mentor Jacques Ellul, my German reborn, and my French now a viable second language. My NCB colleagues and our board members were delighted to read my three-page sabbatical report. A sabbatical is not a vacation but a study leave with a very different rhythm to life and work. In academia it is traditionally an option every seventh academic term or every seventh year (going back to the ancient Israelite practice of the sabbatical year when farmers abstained from ordinary planting and harvesting). It is not automatic: a faculty member must submit a strong study plan to be approved by the administration. Results worthy of the approved plan and objectives are required afterward. It is usually at half-salary for a full academic year or full salary for a half year—so full year sabbaticals require one to find funding for the other half of one's income needs (I did this by taking my sabbatical in a place where my housing costs ($1000/month) were half what I could rent my California house for ($2000/month). A professor's sabbatical work is intended to benefit the school and one's academic field through your research and publications and enhanced ability to contribute as a teacher. Financially, my cost to NCB was my half salary (about $18,000). My dean's and professor's tasks were covered while I was gone by our existing faculty, so no extra financial costs there (I helped cover for others when they were on sabbatical).

But in hindsight, a wise business friend of mine, knowing the history of NCB, recently challenged me. Does it really make sense for a founder and leader of a start-up organization to be gone for a whole year—and, for that matter, to have two-month study leaves every other summer, no matter how many books one may write? In retrospect I think he has a point. But NCB was committed to a vision of a distinguished faculty whose publications (and teaching) were enriched by research requiring periods of intense, undistracted study. Why did people come (at least initially) to NCB (or Regent or Fuller)? Because of the reputations of faculty scholars and writers. All of us, especially on our faculty but also those on our board, believed in this model. After I returned, Bill Dyrness and Bernie Adeney also spent full-year sabbaticals off campus and brought back added scholarly and teaching gifts to our students and faculty. We missed their on-campus presence but believed their sabbatical work was an asset to NCB. Yes, I see how my absence was a significant cost to our administrative leadership—even if I can point to my huge administrative impact in the times I was on campus (i.e., most of my NCB time). Eventually this traditional faculty model proved unsustainable for NCB. Apart from the school's benefits and costs, for me, personally, I don't think I would have survived, emotionally or professionally, without these study breaks. But I do get the validity of this organizational critique.

17

New College Berkeley, Phase II (1986–90)

As I acknowledged at the end of the previous chapter, especially on a small faculty, the absence of a faculty member and core administrator for a whole year is a significant immediate cost to the operations of the school. First of all, for my post at New College Berkeley, this meant summer school leadership. I had been the on-site, ever-present dean and community-builder for our summer schools in 1978, 1979, 1981, and 1983. I was absent during the summers of 1980, 1982, and now 1984 and 1985. Our first president, Ward Gasque, and I had agreed that we would alternate summer school leadership to allow the other guy to get away for a few weeks of summer study leave every other year. I still recruited visiting faculty and students for all summer programs but it was a matter of not being there for on-site presence, direction, and hospitality. I stepped back in to lead the summer schools in 1986, 1987, and 1989. Nineteen-eighty-eight would be a traumatic time of back-up leadership betrayal by my dean while I was scheduled to be away in Bordeaux. I left NCB permanently just before summer school in 1990. So I was absent from day-to-day summer school leadership during five summer schools, present for seven.

NCB summer school was always cash-flow positive even with reduced tuition charges for the many auditors who attended. Our summer schools kept us on the map, and were a great gift to the church, especially in Northern California. We brought the best and the brightest in Christian scholarship and teaching to Berkeley. Along with our visiting stars, our summer schools rotated our own resident faculty through our core courses so students could return each summer and gradually complete their basic academic programs. Many did during those years. After the first two or three summer schools, we decided to have fewer three-week courses and more and more one- and two-week study experiences—to make it easier for more summer students to attend. With a long list of great writers and scholars teaching for us, our summer schools usually enrolled a total of two to four hundred students. John Stott taught for three of our summer schools, usually drawing hundreds of students; John Howard Yoder also came out three times. Madeleine L'Engle, Luci Shaw, Kathryn Lindskoog, Burton Nelson, John Perkins, Clark Pinnock, Carl Henry, Richard Mouw, and many others, whose names you would recognize, were part of our visiting faculty.

So summer school on-site leadership took a hit while I was on sabbatical. Even more challenging was the absence of a teaching faculty member for a whole year (as I was in 1984–85, Bill Dyrness in 1988–89, and Bernie Adeney in 1989–90). During my sabbatical in 1984–85 our newest faculty addition Bernie Adeney, fresh from his PhD in Ethics at the GTU, stepped in to teach my Christian ethics courses and serve as Acting Dean in my absence, with Chris Carlisle holding things together as our veteran administrative assistant. Bernie was a brilliant scholar and great colleague. He had been director of the Crucible Study Center (which I founded in 1972–73) from 1974–79 and was one of our adjunct professors while completing his PhD. He was well-known and respected in our community. Bernie and Fran lived in a huge home we all called "the Ark," where their many guests and renters comprised a fun community in itself.

After our New Testament scholar Ward Gasque left in 1982, Peter Davids came for a year as Visiting Professor of New Testament. While we were very interested in Peter continuing on and even joining us full-time for the long haul, he decided to pursue another direction. Our search for a New Testament scholar then resulted in our hiring Lincoln Hurst. But UC Davis was also pursuing Lincoln and he ended up living in Davis and teaching half-time for each school. Eventually UC Davis upped the offer to full-time and we lost him. During my sabbatical, NCB caried out another search and hired Joel Green, a young Methodist NT scholar who arrived just as I returned from sabbatical in the fall of 1985. Joel was an excellent, productive scholar and writer and a solid classroom teacher. He remained with NCB until joining the American Baptist Seminary of the West faculty next door to NCB and then moving on to another seminary before winding up at Fuller Theological Seminary.

THE COSTS OF THE GTU CALENDAR AND LIBRARY

In addition to these costs related to our commitment to sabbaticals and study leaves, we were dealing, in the late 1980s and beyond, with two major costs of our commitment to full accreditation and membership in the Graduate Theological Union: a big academic calendar change and a huge library cost. When I was an undergraduate at Cal Berkeley, my first two years (1964–66) were on the fifteen-week semester system. In 1966, my junior year, they switched to the academic quarter system, dividing the academic year into three ten-week sessions in Fall, Winter, and Spring (plus typically a ten-week summer session as well). But in the mid-1980s UC decided to go back to the semester plan with two fifteen-week academic sessions. To avoid the older calendar, in which the fall semester finished with the final three or four weeks in January, the new "early semester" approach meant starting up in late August to finish before Christmas break. The Spring semester would then start up in mid-January and finish in early May rather than in June. This was a tough and I still feel very unwise move—but part of our vision was to become the tenth full member of the GTU (which was following Cal Berkeley's calendar change).

The first downside was that the early semester calendar interrupted end-of-summer travel and work experiences for families and individuals. Much better to start up after Labor Day. And it ended in May before kids are out of school, reducing vacation options for families at both ends of the summer. Even more importantly, it meant that full-time students typically enrolled in four courses per semester instead of three per quarter—having to juggle four different learning tracks at a time instead of three. In my view (and much experience as a student and professor), the few subjects needing more than ten weeks attention (research seminars, sometimes) can be accommodated over two successive quarters. It was further claimed that the registration process is simplified by dealing with two instead of three academic enrollment periods—but most semester institutions add intensive January-term options and a lot of half-semester mini-courses—hardly a move toward simplification. With computers and good management, quarter system registration is no problem. The biggest downside for New College, with so many part-time and evening students, was asking for fifteen-week course commitments, a big additional burden. I think our enrollment suffered as a result, not to mention the huge amount of work it took to restructure our curriculum and catalog.

From the very beginning, NCB was committed to achieving full accreditation by the Western Association of Schools and Colleges (WASC) and full membership in the Graduate Theological Union (with its academic bridge to UC Berkeley). We were not interested in accreditation by the Association of Theological Schools (ATS) which was for clergy-focused seminaries—but might in retrospect have made more sense if they would accept NCB as a "seminary for the laity." The process was a long one. When we began full-time operation in 1979, we had first achieved State of California permission to operate the school. Then came a ton more bureaucracy and a committee visit to achieve California state "Approval of Degrees." Got it—but then the next step was to apply to be a "Candidate for Accreditation" with WASC. In addition to vast amounts of paper work, we needed to demonstrate that (1) our faculty were academically qualified (not a problem, although we were probably pushing the limit of courses taught by visiting and adjunct faculty), (2) our degree-seeking students were qualified for graduate work with at least an earned bachelor's degree from an accredited school. That was not much of a problem but we were heavy on auditors present in our classes (WASC-types think that dilutes the academic rigor of classroom study; we thought their presence enriched our discussions; the vast majority of our auditors had at least a bachelor's degree).

We also needed (3) to have an adequate library for our students if there was to be any chance at accreditation. This meant one thing: we needed to join the GTU

Common Library. We were required to liquidate our own house library to "force" our students to use the GTU Common Library on the other, north side of the Berkeley campus. Inconvenient, to say the least! We had needed more space than Johnston Hall provided so after just three years we had moved next door to the grand old Hobart Hall ABSW campus building, taking over the first two floors. That building had a big library room with shelves for our ten thousand or so books from Don Tinder and the Crucible. This was a more than adequate library for our purposes (most of our students and faculty purchased the books they needed for our intro courses) but we didn't have a purchasing program to strengthen it and it didn't cover all of our teaching fields adequately. Under pressure, we bit the bullet and sold off these books at a deep discount to our students, faculty, and all takers. Tragic, as it turned out! How I wish we had moved that collection into a house library at our student residence Dwight House.

The GTU welcomed us officially as the tenth member of the Common Library (though not yet as the tenth theological school in the consortium). The GTU charged us something like $300,000 as an entry fee because, unlike the other nine schools, we had not been an original book donor to the Common Library. That initial cost was a severe challenge by itself, but the GTU also computed an annual dues fee for each of the ten Common Library member schools based on their student full-time equivalent (FTE) enrollment. This formula came to haunt our budget because summer enrollment and audit students had to be included in our FTE count. This added hundreds of class attendees who never needed or used the GTU library but were still part of our FTE count. Only a dozen or two of these summer and part-time students were pursuing diplomas and degrees so only they (out of hundreds) availed themselves of our GTU Library access. We were paying (in effect) at least double, maybe even triple, for the library services NCB used.

Finally, (4) accreditation evaluators looked at our finances. We owned our student residence Dwight House up the street and had a modest amount of office furniture and equipment but otherwise rented our facilities. We had no endowment whatsoever until I raised an initial $125,000 as president. From 1979 to 1986, we were habitually in some debt, holding invoices until we had money to pay. NCB always looked too weak financially to be fully accredited, even after we got out of debt.

The other cost of the pursuit of accreditation was the countless hours of work that had to be devoted to the process by a small staff. In retrospect, of course, I regret these GTU-related changes we made. After our graduate faculty and degree programs ended in 1994, Executive Director Susan Phillips built an official relationship of NCB to the GTU as a "Study Center." How I wish we would have done that in the late-1980s and figured out an alternative path to degrees for our small degree-seeking student population.

So my happy return to NCB in fall 1985 was seriously muted by facing these problems of finances, accreditation, and GTU affiliation. Our overall enrollment was also down slightly from the early-1980s, despite our strong reputation and ever-growing constituency, our well-published and tireless faculty, a solid support staff, a beautiful campus, and our nearby student residence. What was going on? In addition to the less-accessible fifteen-week course schedule we offered, the growing cost of living, especially housing, in the San Francisco Bay Area had an impact. Many families needed two incomes to survive, without enough time or money to enroll in educational programs that, frankly, would not promise job advancements.

The culture was also changing. A famous national survey of college students indicated that, in 1967, 82% of college students rated "developing a meaningful philosophy of life" as a "very important goal"—while 40% (some overlap of course) indicated "being well-off financially." By 1987, those numbers reversed! Now 80% wanted to be "well-off financially"—and only 38% listed "developing a meaningful philosophy of life." When did the lines cross? 1977, the year NCB was founded. I have sometimes said that NCB was founded by the children of the Sixties (for whom meaning was everything, at least back then)—but we "ran out" of children of the Sixties by the late Eighties. In any case, the recruiting and care of students by the mid-Eighties was a growing challenge. NCB looked like a luxury, desirable but difficult to actually get involved in.

MOVE UP OR MOVE OUT?

Bernie Adeney had done a good job as acting dean but even there I had a massive job to organize and get caught back up on the dean's work. President Bill Dyrness and our support staff were giving their all, admirably and even heroically leading NCB. I returned in fall 1985 still as passionate about our mission and vision as ever and I loved my students and colleagues as much as ever. That hadn't changed. I could not accept any thought that we should change course on our pursuit of an accredited graduate school affiliated with Cal and the GTU. No one at NCB felt any different.

But I really struggled to fit back into the administration when I came back that fall. Overall morale was down, mostly, I think, because of disappointing enrollment and financial shortfalls. Staff let me know that things were not going well and they were unhappy. To save money our literature was looking shabby and cheap. Our advertising and recruiting had fallen down. Fund-raising had not been successful since the big gifts I mentioned in the last chapter. Board membership and meeting attendance had fallen. Student inquiries and registrations had fallen slightly. We were still awarding twenty or so diplomas and degrees each June but enrollment in my core, required ethics course was down significantly, a real tipoff to our growing challenge. Midway through the fall of 1985 I informed our president that maybe my NCB time was up, at least in the dean role. We needed change and I didn't want to be a disruptive part of the administration. I wanted to play a stronger than ever role as a faculty member only.

At this stage some of my colleagues and members of the board began to think it was time for a change of presidents. I (tended to agree but) made no such suggestions, but people began lobbying me privately to consider being a candidate if our president decided to leave with all the pressure he and the school were under. In the spring of 1986, he decided he would step down from the presidency by June and continue just as a faculty member. As we did with Ward Gasque on his retirement in 1982, we commissioned in 1986 a big painting of our retiring second president to hang in our hallways, and celebrated his tenure with a great banquet. Bill Dyrness was a wonderful community-builder and teacher, a widely-admired scholar and writer, and had given us four years of his hard work and leadership in a very challenging time. Bill devoted himself fully to his role as professor of theology for the next four years.

This time, the third time now, I agreed to be a candidate for president and, if called, prioritize leading NCB over my scholarly writing and teaching calling. I came to feel (and was told repeatedly by others after the search began) that I *must* be a candidate. I prepared my dossier and mobilized my references (including Jacques Ellul himself!) to be ready to write letters or be telephoned. The Search Committee and the Board called me to be president starting in summer 1986. One of the "conditions" the board imposed on me in calling me to be president was that I must have an academic dean to help lead the school—and they picked the person from our existing faculty.

In hindsight, mistakes were made and the transition was far more challenging than it needed to be. First of all, it was a difficult for us to keep Bill on as a faculty member for the next four years—not at all because he wasn't a great colleague and faculty member (far from it!) but because it tied our hands financially and I couldn't hire my own dean. Second, related to this, the board should not have picked my dean for me. I should have balked at this. It turned out that the board's choice of dean was completely incompatible with me in terms of leadership, teamwork, and (most importantly) ethical values. Third, I made a terrible mistake by (generously) letting my talented, trusted assistant Chris Carlisle stay in the dean's office instead of moving to the president's office with me. At the moment I desperately needed an assistant like her, I then suffered through the next year with a well-meaning but distracted old friend who, it turned out, really didn't like the work as she had thought she would.

Finally, in retrospect, it had been a mistake for our faculty review committee to have basically pushed professor Don Tinder to leave our faculty not long before I became president. Don was and is a terrific colleague and teacher but we had a clear and firm requirement that our faculty do research and publish. Don was a great colleague, productive and effective as a teacher and but not as a publishing scholar and we were hell-bent on measuring up as an accredited graduate school faculty. With twenty-twenty hindsight, I deeply wish we had kept his library and the man himself and de-emphasized that publication standard. I also don't think our faculty culture would have degraded as it did over the next four years if Don had been present. After Don left NCB he taught at Biola University and then more than two decades for theological schools in the Netherlands and Belgium—drawing students from around the world, often from countries hostile to Christianity. Since "retiring" back to the Bay Area, Don has become a core faculty member at Olivet University.

Not just Don's departure but all of these mistakes just made the hill I had to climb that much steeper as I became president in fall 1986. My business colleague, who I mentioned at the end of the previous chapter, challenged me recently after reading a draft of this chapter, "why did you go along with these things" when you became president? The short answer is that I was inexperienced, got bad counsel, and wanted to be positive and respect the board's decisions. And I also confess what I felt then was a virtue: I simply believed that, with God's help, I could handle anything, any challenge. Starting a college with no money and little experience? We can do it! No capacity to select faculty or my dean? No problem! Wrong. Was it arrogance, naivete—or deep faith? Maybe some of each as I look back.

TWO YEARS OF GETTING THE PLANE OFF THE GROUND AGAIN, 1986–88

In September of 1986 I was inaugurated as the third President of NCB. UC Berkeley Professor of Sociology and author of *Habits of the Heart,* Robert Bellah, gave the inaugural talk on "The Bible in American Life" to a big crowd gathered at First Pres Berkeley. Bellah had been an encouraging friend on the Berkeley faculty and spent a wonderful dinner and evening in our home with his wife Melanie. GTU President, Michael Blecker, and presidents or representatives from several other seminaries and colleges (including my "doctor-father," Jack Crossley from USC) marched in our academic ceremony. I was given "charges" from our board, faculty, students, and from my teenage son Jonathan. It was a great day.

One of the first things I did in fall 1986 was to get a local artist friend to redesign our look and our literature. We soon looked sharp and professional again, with good-looking and informative advertising, brochures, posters, and newsletters. My predecessor had our president's and dean's offices up on the second floor. As soon as I could, I moved my office to the ground floor next to our reception area and registrar's office in order to be fully present and available and create a welcoming vibe for all visitors and students (the extravert in me could do no less). I also immediately raised (50% or so) all the salaries of our office staff to minimal living wage levels, then increased our pay to part-time adjunct professors. Soon would come our pay to Assistant profs, then the Associates, finally the full professors. I refused any raise until the lowest paid were helped out—and I never took a salary more than double the lowest paid (and I probably was working double their hours and with double their stress, if my salary needed any justification). I report this not to signal my virtue but to challenge conventional practices. I (like the other veterans) had bought my house at 1970s prices, a real advantage over late 1980s purchasers or renters on our payroll.

In my second year as president, I hired Carrie Heffner Smalley, a joyful, gregarious, hard-working, upbeat people-person, as my administrative assistant. Carrie worked with me for two years until marriage took her out of town. For my final year, I hired Bonnie Johnston away from Earl Palmer's office at First Pres—one of the greatest people I ever worked with: godly, responsible, multi-talented, sacrificial, warm, and encouraging to all. Paul Fleck worked part-time to get our finances back in order. What a gift he was. Joan Anderson continued to anchor our Registrar's office and whole staff with her unrelenting excellence. Cheryl Garlick and volunteer Ruth Newell brought warmth and competence to our front desk.

I hired our MA student Ken Morris as manager of our student residence Dwight House and frequent assistant at our events and projects. I never knew a harder, more effective, loyal co-worker (since 2000, attorney Ken has served our International Jacques Ellul Society as Secretary-Treasurer). Finally, in our search for a full-time Business Manager, we hired Amy Brannon Keltner right out of Cal with her business degree. Amy was an amazing colleague who we loved. Her work was meticulous, her spirit joyful. She led a bunch of us to a San Francisco Symphony Summer Pops concert by Ella Fitzgerald—a night we will never forget. Bottom line, after that first depressing year, my next and final three as president I was surrounded and supported by the best staff on earth. They carried me and NCB to whatever heights we reached—and through the depths we intermittently faced. I will never forget them.

We continued to have many great students, though I was teaching less and less because of the administrative and fund-raising demands. Mark Baker studied at NCB on his way to major impact as a scholar and professor at the Mennonite Brethren Seminary in Fresno. Elizabeth Sendek became professor and then president at the Colombia Theological Seminary in Bogota. Allen Flemming went from NCB to Fuller and then a career as proprietor of Present Body fitness and as biographer of Christian rocker Larry Norman and others. Other graduates were strengthened in their callings to child care and to effective Christian education roles in local churches. Some went on to complete seminary degrees and callings to work with local churches as pastors or as bi-vocational missionaries at home and abroad. Poets, artists, nurses, dancers and many other vocations were represented in our student body.

Our summer schools soon boomed back up to record enrollments. Earl Palmer invited NCB to co-sponsor First Pres's annual Berkeley Lectures. Among the distinguished speakers were Helmut Thielicke and Markus Barth (son of Karl). Celebrating the birth of Karl Barth, Earl and I each gave plenary lectures on Barth's thought (my talk was on Barth's ethics). We had these luminaries also speak at pastor's breakfasts as we had done in the earlier years with John Stott and Carl Henry. Funny story: when the tall German Thielicke finished one of his lectures in the First Pres sanctuary to the seven hundred attendees, he lit up a big cigar as we strolled together to a reception in Westminster Hall (people don't smoke at church events or on church premises). I had my usual pipe in my coat pocket and sneaked Earl a peek and softly asked him "don't you think I should smoke my pipe just to make him feel more comfortable?" Earl (snickering but firm): "No." I was actually joking and expected that answer.

Meanwhile I was speaking and teaching anywhere and everywhere there was a receptive audience. On a typical road trip, I gave a lecture on Jacques Ellul and technology criticism for Arizona State University's sociology department, then spoke at the InterVarsity chapters of ASU, the University of Arizona in Tucson, Northern Arizona University in Flagstaff, and the University of Nevada at Las Vegas. As I mentioned in the previous chapter, I ranged from fifty to eighty off campus speaking gigs like this every year. I have felt exhausted reviewing my calendars from those years as I wrote this memoir. Our mailing list grew to around ten thousand.

STILL A WRITER

In 1986 my book *Peter the Rock: Extraordinary Insights from an Ordinary Man* was published. I was still writing and presenting scholarly and more popular articles (many of them listed in the curriculum vita at the end of this memoir). I burned a lot of midnight oil working on these projects after my wife and kids went to bed. In 1989, my *Opening of the Christian Mind,* drafted in Munich in summer 1985, was finally published.[1] I was adding my take on what it meant to "be transformed by the renewing of your mind" (Romans 12:2) and "take every thought captive" to Christ "in whom are hidden all the treasures of wisdom and understanding." Of course, I had been influenced by the writings of Francis Schaeffer, Arthur Holmes, John Stott, Charles Malik, and others. An Englishman, Harry Blamires, had written the standard text on the topic, *The Christian Mind,* but I thought there was a better way to describe it.

Blamires thought the great cultural challenge of our time was secularism. While I didn't fully disagree, I argued that it was technological rationality (as described by Ellul) and pluralism/diversity. In place of his list of four or five characteristics of a Christian mind I proposed that a Christian mind must be (1) Open—to God and the supernatural, not just the material world. A best-selling book at the time was called *The Closing of the American Mind* and my book was a positive Christian alternative (not just a return to Western modernity and tradition). I explained that the Christian mind was not "empty"—"open at both ends"—but centered on God's incarnation in Jesus Christ and, from there, open to critical learning from Scripture (above all), nature, and our neighbors of all kinds; (2) Historical—with a broad perspective on the past and the future; (3) Humanistic—in the sense of valuing and caring for people, all people, learning from and serving them; (4) Truthful—committed to a search for the truth; (5) Ethical—concerned for the good and the right; and (6) Aesthetic—concerned for beauty, not just utility.

---

1. David W. Gill, *The Opening of the Christian Mind* (Downers Grove, Illinois: InterVarsity, 1989).

I added chapters on (1) the strengths and weaknesses of today's university, in which so many of us have studied, (2) the application of the renewed Christian mind to the workplace (which developed into my main focus over the next decades), (3) the "environment" of a healthy mind—our prayer and worship, rest and play, family and friends, and so on, (4) a basic "curriculum" or study plan, and (5) suggested strategies for working on that Christian mind curriculum. *The Opening of the Christian Mind* became my best-selling book at about twelve or thirteen thousand copies—hardly a best-seller but something that I know helped and inspired many. It really was a "manifesto" for an NCB education.

REBUILDING THE BOARD (AND LIVING WITH SABOTAGE)

When I took office as president, I found a Board of Trustees that was, in my view, weak and poorly functioning. Not enough had been done during the previous four years to build up the size and strength of the board. Absenteeism at board meetings and low morale and performance were obvious to me. I want to stress that I am not blaming anyone for lack of good faith. It was about networking and community development. One of my first trips in fall 1986 took me to Princeton Seminary where I met with President Tom Gillespie, former pastor of Burlingame Presbyterian Church in the Bay Area. I described NCB's challenges to Tom and asked his counsel. He told me my very first and most important task was to find a fresh, new board chair and begin strengthening our board. NCB had no major endowment or foundations undergirding its operations. We badly needed a bigger, stronger board of trustees as our foundation.

When I returned to campus, I had confidential talks with Fred Vann, Jay Boone, Earl Palmer, David Cole and a couple trustees I knew well, to discuss how we could strengthen our board and its leadership. Our current chairman resisted our suggestions that he retire from the chair (out of love and commitment, to be sure). He insisted he wanted to continue until we achieved accreditation but we made it plain that we needed to make a change. We persuaded Fred Vann to stand for election as our next chair, despite his reticence to take on that role. Fred was a close friend, long-time business executive, major donor, NCB graduate, relationally warm, gifted man, completely devoted to NCB. He agreed and was elected our new chair. Over the next months Fred and I recruited several new board members and invested hours visiting with all of our trustees, awakening or re-awakening their passion, hope, and vision for NCB.

During my predecessor's presidency I had dropped off the board because I didn't want in any way to disrupt or threaten his leadership by having board members turn to me during meetings rather than to him. It was partly about personality and even more about my profile as founder and a major leader from day one. But now when I became the president, I wanted my staff, especially my dean, to be present at board meetings to strengthen our leadership, community, and communication. I had no fear of anyone on my team threatening my leadership.

Unfortunately, at the first big meeting of our newly expanded board, we met for dinner and a meeting at a beautiful conference room in the GTU Library. Everything went beautifully until right after the opening prayer, introductions, and approval of minutes and agenda, trustee Kelli Burrill interrupted our brand new chairman Fred Vann to ask for an "executive session"—meaning that the board would meet without any school employees present. So I, my dean, and our new alumni association director Marty Stewart were sent out the room. I was shocked and totally mystified but complied. The three of us sat out in another room for thirty, then sixty, then ninety minutes wondering "what the hell is going on?" When we were called back in, chairman Vann somberly said "we have been discussing the big conflict between our president and dean and what to do about it." "What conflict is that?" I asked. "The dean assured me that he totally supported the academic plan we developed together and brought to this meeting." Fred: "Well that is not what we understand." Because of the late hour we hurried through the rest of the agenda and adjourned.

The next day I called the dean into my office to ask how this had happened. The dean pleaded innocent. But I soon found out that, sitting next to trustee Kelli Burrill during dinner, he had filled her ear with complaints and griping about me. In all of our previous meetings together he had given me a big smile and said he totally supported our plan. It was news to me that he had any problems with it or me or the process. I told him: "Dean (I will withhold his name), you need to be completely honest with me if you disagree about anything. You can come into my office and cuss me up one wall and down the other (I really said this) and you know what I will say? 'Thank you Dean, for your honesty!' But don't you ever again give me a big smile and tell me you support something and then go behind my back and criticize or reject it." Later that week, one new trustee I had recruited told me he couldn't follow through on the $25k he had earlier promised to me—because of this confidence-shattering incident.

This was first of a series of episodes where Mr. Dean agreed on something to my face after hours of meeting together—and then griped or bad-mouthed it to others (trustees, faculty, students) behind my back. I asked Bill Dyrness to sit in as a mediator after another episode and pray for us. Things didn't change. I recall that both Bill and I had some tears during this meeting; no tears (ever) from Mr. Dean. After dealing with two or three more of these episodes of lying and sabotage, I asked Earl Palmer if I should just fire this guy. "Yes," Earl said, "you have every reason and right to do so." But when I met with our board chairman, my beloved old brother Fred Vann, he said "David, you are the older brother here and we are a Christian institution. I think you should rise above it and help your younger brother and colleague to grow." Mr. Dean was, in fact, a great detail administrator, solid classroom teacher, and a budding scholar with a genial smile—so I let him get away with it with additional (unheeded) warnings and pleas. Over and over, I heard surface agreement and a smile—then lying, betrayal and sabotage. He never apologized, never admitted any wrong doing, never played the role I had wished for of a close, trusted confidant, to say nothing of an advocate, partner, and protector. Judas, not Jonathan, for this David!

Why did I put up with this behavior by the guy supposed to be my closest associate leader? We were a small, close community and had no margin for dismissing a core member and operating short-staffed. I also got bad advice from our board chair, my beloved older brother. And, finally, as I mentioned earlier, I actually believed (wrongly, overconfidently) that I could handle any challenge and forge ahead even with his unreliability and backstabbing. I was a kind, forgiving guy. Not firing this guy after the second infraction was the worst mistake I ever made in my fifty-year leadership history. Especially while I was out on the road raising money for (his and the others') salaries, he was sowing discord back on my team. At one point I asked a therapist friend of mine (from outside NCB) about this man's inability to look me in the face and tell me the truth and he suggested that sometimes people like him just stuff everything inside rather than openly, vulnerably expressing themselves. This explanation made a lot of sense. What I had to deal with during my four years as president was not just outside challenges and threats but inside betrayal and (what I can only call) sabotage from (what I can only call) a pathological liar. It was a psychological and moral pathology way beyond my capacity to fix or heal. I blew it as a leader. Entrepreneurs and leaders: please don't make the same mistake!

FINANCIAL CHALLENGE & STUDENT RECRUITING: REACHING THE SUMMIT

Meanwhile, we faced a huge financial challenge when I took office in fall 1986. During our start-up phase (1976–79) we always paid our bills on time and operated in the black, even if on a smaller budget. Beginning in Fall 1979, we were always running deficits, sometimes paying our bills late. We never actually defaulted on any debts but reimbursements (and our presidential and dean salaries in those early days) were slow. To my wife's great chagrin, I sometimes carried $5000 or more in NCB expenses on our personal Visa card for weeks or even months. I hated this situation but how else could we get through?

To an outside observer, NCB was looking a bit stronger by early 1987 but our finances were still depressing. We carried forward $40,000 or $50,000 in debt when I took office (some of it, I have to say, wasted on an ineffective financial development consultant—all talk, no action). We needed execution, not more talk, when it came to fund-raising. In early 1987, I decided to try to put together a $100,000 matching grant challenge. I hoped I could find maybe four or five donors to put up a total of $100,000 to be paid if we could find $100k in matching donations from our constituency. I approached everyone I knew who might possibly be able to put up funds like that but my list wasn't very long. The two or three biggest donors to NCB were already maxed out.

My colleague Bernie Adeney had passed on to me a business story about three guys who had started a remarkable company, Chicago Research and Trading. CRT had come out of nowhere to an industry leadership position in commodity futures trading. Their progressive, humane way of treating their employees and their charitable giving were as impressive as their mathematical, computerized, trading genius. I contacted Gary Ginter, one of the three CRT principals, and, when I visited Chicago that winter, I met with him and toured his company trading floor and cafeteria. Gary was already living and breathing the NCB faith at work vision and mission. I told him all about NCB and our challenges and my hope to put together the $100k challenge grant. Over the next two or three months we talked on the phone a few times.

On April 7, 1987, we celebrated the tenth anniversary of the founding of NCB in our chapel. We had much to celebrate but, honestly, our spirit was a bit down because of our ongoing financial peril and struggle. When I got back to my office after chapel my phone rang and it was Gary. "David, how is the proposed campaign shaping up? Have you found the $100k challenge grant yet?" "No Gary, I am still looking, still praying and hoping." Gary: "Well David, Joanna and I have been praying about it and we decided to put up the whole $100k for you." "Hallelujah! A more cynical board member on campus for our tenth anniversary chapel responded, "Do we have it writing?"—but the rest of us either cried or danced or both for a few minutes, and lifted our voices to thank God.

With Gary, I decided to make September 1 the deadline for matching gifts, giving ourselves just under five months. I challenged our whole constituency—trustees, faculty and staff, students, alumni, pastors, former donors, and prospective donors to help us meet the challenge. There were no major gifts given but amounts from $25 to maybe $3000 came in. In August, with just one month to go, still $20k short of the goal, I made a pilgrimage with Lucia to visit Sarah and Bud (who had been alienated from NCB in that board visit episode I mentioned earlier). They mercifully and graciously gave $10k. Finally, we drove up to visit Irene Alonso in her retirement home in Sparks, Nevada. She had followed the development of NCB with interest and was a great fan of Earl Palmer. She gave the final $10k and we were home free. We drove back to the Bay Area that night but I swear I felt like we were flying above the road. A couple weeks later we had a faculty, staff, and family retreat up at the Pt. Reyes Lighthouse retreat center with a joyful, grateful theme as we prepared for our fall 1987 semester. We were out of debt for the first time in eight years and could now afford to move ahead with some cash in our account. Morale was at a peak.

In December of 1987, I took a team of our six best, most articulate representatives back to a recruiting booth at IVCF's big Urbana conference (18,000 college students). Believe me, we worked the crowd around our exhibit. We also made huge efforts with our mailing list, area churches, our alumni, and everywhere we could possibly recruit students for the coming academic year. As a result, during the Spring of 1988 we had far more inquiries about study at NCB than ever in our history. We had achieved so many of our goals in making NCB as attractive a place as possible for lay studies at a graduate level. As I mentioned earlier, our faculty was well-known and well-published. Our public visibility and reputation had never been higher. Hundreds of alumni and visiting faculty sang our praises and recommended our programs. We had a great student residence two blocks from our campus. Our campus itself was a beautiful old building (though being across the street from Peoples Park with its casual drug use and somewhat intimidating population was decidedly not an asset, especially for evening students). Doug Anderson and Bernie Adeney had finished their PhDs and were strong additions to our faculty. Joan Terpstra Anderson anchored a competent staff. Carrie Smalley and Ken Morris were as wonderful as any assistants I ever had. Our dean had done some good and promising work on our application for "candidacy" for WASC accreditation. The coming fall would tell the story for us: would our enrollment final bump upwards significantly? If it didn't, it would be time for a thorough review and refocus. But we never had more hope and positive expectation.

TURNING POINT: 1988

The ongoing thorn in my flesh (and a mostly-hidden virus in the NCB operation) was my dean who continued to gripe about his contract, lie to me and others, and sow discord among our faculty and trustees. To justify extra financial help to younger faculty (meaning our dean), I had pushed our board to create a special "housing supplement" line in our budget. It got to the point that I just gave him a blank piece of paper and said "Look Mr. Dean, why don't you just write down the contract you desire on this blank sheet of paper and I will take it to the board for approval." (My business friend, in reading this recently, was shocked that I would do this). He did so and in the late Spring of 1988 I brought it to the board which basically agreed to it, with my support. Despite giving him what he asked for, just before graduation exercises, the dean handed me his resignation.

Unbelievable. To add insult to injury, his resignation was immediate. He refused to manage our 1988 summer school (as I had done to cover his absence the year before, in our long-standing president/dean alternating pattern). I was up against the wall because I had already bought my plane tickets and was scheduled to be in Bordeaux for six weeks—exhausted after three years of my nonstop running hard. (My business friend also has questioned how NCB could afford to have me away like this for even six weeks). I successfully begged Bill Dyrness to delay departure on his own 1988–89 sabbatical and lead the summer school, and I managed to fly over to France for my study leave.

Lucia had decided not to go with me to Bordeaux, not least because I was such an exhausted, burned-out wreck, and not much fun to be with (I guess). I had a good time meeting with Ellul and my old contacts in Bordeaux but also a lot of alone time by myself with God for reflection and prayer. I had been driving hard on NCB for twelve years and was now forty-two years old. I often have described the summer of 1988 as the time when I finally gave up. What I mean by that is that I "gave it up to God," realizing I just couldn't meet my goals through my hard work. I "gave up," first, on my son, Jonathan, entering his junior year in high school. I was unhappy with some of the choices and directions he had taken but I finally gave him up to God and decided I should stop expecting him to follow the academic and faith directions for which I thought he was so gifted and enabled (good move, as his life and work have demonstrated ever since!).

Secondly, I "gave up" on my career as an ethicist. What I mean is that as I reflected on my teaching and writing, it just didn't have the impact I had hoped for. I was not a best-selling author or high-demand guest lecturer. My ideas and convictions remained "marginal" and the mainstream ethics guild carried on as usual. Thirdly, and most significant for this chapter, I gave up on "my baby," New College Berkeley. I accepted, finally and fully, that this project belonged first to God and, in a secondary sense, to the church. It didn't belong to me (I would never have said it did but I felt and acted otherwise). I would continue to work as hard as I could, but only God could give the "increase" and decide if it flourished or failed. I prayed, I struggled, I wept, I gave it all up to God.

When I came home at the end of summer 1988, our registrar Joan Anderson and I decided to try to cover the dean's office tasks together since Mr. Dean had resigned at the last minute but stayed on the faculty. We had no financial capacity to recruit a replacement. Unfortunately, despite our massive recruiting efforts, when fall registration arrived, we did not see any increases in enrollment. It was time for a major reassessment.

In the fall of 1988, I initiated a self-study we called "Focusing the Mission of NCB for the Nineties." We surveyed and interviewed our current students and alumni to get their input. We interviewed and met with dozens of Bay Area pastors and business and professional folk. "Do you know about NCB? How do you view it? Have you ever taken any courses or attended any events? What are the biggest obstacles to your attendance? What would be a format that would enable you to attend? How could we be of service to you and your church?" We found that NCB was, in fact, well-known and highly-respected—but many (most!) prospective students just couldn't make our schedule or location work for them. Several of our respondents said they wished they could listen to our teaching while commuting to and from work. Achievement of a graduate degree was not nearly as desired as the education itself, we were told. My conclusion was that our traditional graduate school format was not working and not sustainable. Trying to keep the core of our operations a set of graduate-level courses and seminars with full-time master's degree students was doomed.

Part Three: Channels (1979–2016)

FINAL DAYS: 1989-90

In early Spring 1989 I submitted my letter of resignation (effective June 1990) from the administration and faculty of NCB to give the school 18 months to find my successor. Staying on as a professor was unthinkable to me when the school desperately needed salary space to hire a new leader—something that had really handicapped me when our former president and my rebel dean had each resigned as administrators but stayed on as professors. I had given my all, done everything I possibly could. In retrospect, though, my timing was a mistake. I should have left in June 1989 because I immediately became a "lame duck" leader and the faculty began to think and plan ahead without keeping me in the conversation, as I wished and thought they would.

For my first three years as President, I was on the road so much of the time trying to raise funds that the faculty led by my rebel Dean often met without me. It just got worse for my fourth and final year. The $200k I had raised in 1988 was running out. The GTU library fees were killing us. The new president of our landlord ABSW, dealing with their own financial and enrollment downturns, doubled our rent overnight to $40,000 per year (remember that we started at $9000, then $11,000 annual rent our first two years, 1979–81, and then moved up to $20,000 by the mid-1980s). I made another huge mistake by supporting rather than aborting a faculty addition that had been in the works for years: Frank and Lois Andersen had sold their home in Australia to join NCB full-time in 1989–90 and so they did—even though it was clear by summer 1989 that NCB was in desperate financial straits. I didn't have the guts to tell them they couldn't come after selling their home. The financial noose was tightening.

That 1988–89 year was administratively peaceful without Mr. Dean but I was devastated in June 1989 when my assistant Carrie Smalley and alumni director Marty Stewart both came in to resign on the same day (to pursue other personal and professional goals, which made sense of course)—and when Joan Terpstra Anderson also decided to leave the Registrar's post after a decade as our staff anchor. Fortunately, Bonnie Johnston came on to provide great assistance and I still had Ken Morris and Amy Brannon Keltner on my staff. My closest faculty colleague, Bernie Adeney, was off to Indonesia on sabbatical for my final year, 1989–90. With Joan gone, Bernie on sabbatical, and my retirement looming nine months ahead I followed Board Chair Fred Vann's suggestion, held my breath, and asked my toxic former dean to assume that role once more. Yes, stupid decision but I was over a barrel and on the way out.

Meanwhile, Steve Phillips succeeded Fred Vann as chair of our board in January 1990. Steve was a long-time, generous NCB friend and board member. Rookie chairman Steve's ears were filled with negative messages from our toxic-dean-led faculty. I was on the road about 80% of my final five months, trying to raise money to keep the lights on and pay our faculty and staff salaries. I rarely taught a class or attended a faculty meeting in those final months. As you can imagine, this lack of personal contact left me incredibly weak in "social" and "communication" capital." If ever there was a time I needed a trusted dean to be my liaison . . .

Our primary challenges, besides cashflow, were finding a successor to me as president, and clarifying where we needed to go as an institution. The presidential search was essentially impossible until we decided what my successor would be presiding over. The latter challenge revolved around how to interpret the results of our "Focusing the Mission of NCB for the Nineties" study caried out through the first half of 1989. My closest friend on our Board, attorney Jay Boone, and I took a shot at interpreting the results of our data (all of our faculty and board were invited to submit their interpretations and proposals).

Jay and I proposed leaving ABSW's now-expensive buildings and moving our administrative offices into the (to be remodeled) garages running across the face of our student residence on Dwight Way. No cars ever used those garages (which stored who-knows-what). The core faculty all lived within a couple miles and could study in home offices. The dean's home was a little smaller so we proposed renting him an office at ABSW. We would expand the large Dwight House living room out onto its porch (as I had done at my own house) and build a deck off the dining room—all to create a congenial space for classes to meet maybe fifteen to twenty hours per week during academic sessions—and for fifteen resident students to use all the rest of the time. We would close off the stairways with locked French doors to keep the upstairs and downstairs residences private and secure.

Jay and I proposed a "Three Pillars of NCB" revamping of our curriculum and approach, based on our three basic constituencies. First, we would serve those mostly interested in the workplace by offering short courses and events (a) in downtown San Francisco on business leadership, (b) in Silicon Valley on technology and entrepreneurship, and (c) in Oakland on small-scale entrepreneurship and job development. Second, we would serve those mostly interested in strengthening Christian education programs by offering Bible, theology, and discipleship courses—based in five or ten partner churches we would formally link up with. Third, we would partner with InterVarsity, World Vision, and other "mission" groups to provide their required staff training in theology, Bible, and cross-cultural studies.

We would pull out of the GTU Library and end the quest for free-standing accreditation, instead directing our master's degree-seeking students into GTU-sponsored programs. We would seek appointment of our core faculty to GTU Adjunct Professor status so we could continue to teach and mentor our handful of degree-seekers. We would continue to sponsor our big summer schools with great visiting faculty and organize quarterly conferences of the kind we had done over the years. We could think about partnering more closely with *Radix* Magazine or publishing our own modest journal to broaden our impact. It was a great plan—and some of its major pieces actually characterize the NCB Study Center led by Susan Phillips after the graduate school program ended in 1994.

Mr. Dean led the faculty to come up with its own interpretation of the "Focusing the Mission for the Nineties" research project: mostly just "keep on keepin' on and NCB will one day turn the corner and become financially viable." They didn't say it but it is true that professors (me included) love to teach only daytime hours, mostly small seminars with advanced students. They do not like teaching evenings or weekends or (these days) online. They don't like commuting to extension sites. They typically do not understand budgets or know much about fund-raising or student recruitment. It was no surprise that our faculty just wanted to move in a traditional direction. When word got out of my proposal to move offices into the Dwight House garages and offer some courses in their big living room, my dean rallied the student residents to sign a letter to the board begging them not to approve "President Gill's proposal," because it would "destroy their community experience." I warned the students that our situation was getting dire and there might not long be any Dwight House community at all. Deaf ears.

With the hand-writing on the wall, "your days are numbered and you are found wanting," I initiated serious conversations during my final year with both Regent College and Fuller Seminary in hopes they might adopt us as their extension programs—but both schools were scared off by our precarious financial condition. In any case, when our board met to consider our future, we took an unofficial straw poll of our trustees and the vote was thirteen to one in favor of the proposal Jay Boone and I wrote. Only our former board chair Richard Benner supported the "stay the course" faculty preference.

But the board was paralyzed because I was definitely headed out the door and the dean and core faculty resolutely opposed any substantive change. Our NCB mission—our "End"—had always been to provide graduate-level education to laity wanting to integrate their faith with their vocation. Our chosen "Means" was a degree-granting graduate school. I fought like heck from 1976 to 1988 to achieve our End by the graduate school Means. Now Jay and I proposed a way to maintain the End—the mission—but radically modify the Means—the organization and strategy—in pursuit of that unchanged End. The core faculty insisted on sticking with our old means. The means, for them, became the end, rather than serving the end. I certainly understand the faculty love of old-style graduate education. I share that love. But staying the course would not work.

By January of 1990, I was a wreck, physically, emotionally, and spiritually. I was really as close to a nervous breakdown as I ever came. Lucia was exhausted by my sad tales and occupied with her own great new full-time work at Citibank. Our daughter Jodie, always such a light in my life, was down at UC Santa Barbara. I remember sitting on the ground near my car at the back of our house uncontrollably weeping. I would return from another road trip to Chicago, LA, Pittsburgh, or Seattle trying to raise money, only to get hit by some new griping, criticism, lying, or sabotage. The whole faculty and the new board chair were meeting and communicating together but not, in my judgment, facing up to our extreme challenges. I can't recall what provoked it, but I intemperately offended their sensitive ears with some colorful language at some meeting or other. I did regret it, apologize, and ask their forgiveness (I had an explanation but no justification!). The hostility of the faculty reached the point where they persuaded chairman Phillips and the board to try to put me on a leave of absence for the final semester, Spring 1990. I pushed back and insisted on finishing out my term but relinquished all future planning involvement for the final two or three months until I left. It was the worst, most painful few months of my entire life. I would have completely died had it not been for my loyal staff, my friendships with Jay Boone and my workout partner Reggie Jackson, and my weekly men's group (Bill Squires, Gary Gates, Max Lopez-Cepero, and David Adeney).

As we neared my departure date and the presidential search was stalled, it was I who made the motion to the board to invite Richard Benner to serve as "Interim President." Richard had been that single vote to support the faculty's "stay the course" interpretation of our "Focus the Mission of NCB" project—versus the thirteen votes favoring the restructuring proposal Jay Boone and I presented. I just could see no other option for the school. Motion passed, invitation happily accepted by incoming President Benner. Richard was an assistant dean at Cal's business school and had been on the NCB board for almost a decade, serving four years as chair. He was a nice, dedicated man, our only hope. Maybe, just maybe, the faculty and broader community would rally behind him and the NCB grad school could be saved. So we prayed.

I have rarely suffered as miserable an evening as the farewell dinner I had to attend as my NCB time came to an end. Of course, I loved and appreciated the hundreds of NCB supporters and former students who came out (knowing little of what I had been through). My wonderful staff, Bonnie, Amy, and Ken, did an incredible job, trying to honor and thank me (to this day I have on my wall a wonderful cartoon/caricature Bob Keltner drew of me in my academic robe opened up to show a Gold's Gym tee shirt underneath, and signed by all three to "The Best Boss"). But the hypocrisy of my faculty colleagues that evening led me to throw their calligraphied plaque in the trash when I got home that night. Metaphorically, relationally, psychologically, and spiritually I was bleeding for months to come from all the wounds in my back. The scars are still there though the pain is mostly gone.

I gave fourteen years of my life to New College Berkeley. I often say there were seven fat years and seven lean years (intermittent rather than strictly sequential). That's actually too negative and pessimistic because there were far more great days than bad ones over the fourteen years. I made plenty of mistakes, sometimes out of ignorance and inexperience, sometimes because I just thought with God's help I could handle (and even forgive or redeem) any challenge. I had been great at rallying people to the mission and to courageously take on and often conquer any challenge or obstacle. But I eventually met my match.

Part Three: Channels (1979–2016)

Most people I have been around for the past sixty or so years have said that I am a strong and effective leader. Most people who have worked for me or alongside of me would say they loved my leadership. But I am by no means perfect. I made some costly mistakes, especially during my NCB presidency, and I am happy to admit them. But even without my mistakes and weaknesses, even without the serious personnel issues I had to deal with, I don't think NCB as an independent, free-standing, tuition-driven, degree-granting graduate school could have been saved (unless Bill Gates gave us two or three million dollars). It needed to be restructured along the lines Jay Boone and I proposed, along the lines Susan Phillips led it for twenty-seven years since 1994, along the lines of today's forty or more Christian Study Centers at major universities across North America.

As I look back, I do feel some pride and a lot of gratitude that I was able to conceive and lead this "big, hairy, audacious" project (remembering Collins and Porras's phrase in their *Built to Last*). It was exciting. I learned so much about entrepreneurship, administration, leadership, movement and institution building. I learned a lot about teaching and writing. In addition to my work on and with Jacques Ellul (finally getting my dissertation published, *The Word of God in the Ethics of Jacques Ellul*, along with several journal articles, chapters, interviews, and reviews), I published *Peter the Rock* as my understanding of basic, foundational Christian faith and discipleship—and *The Opening of the Christian Mind* as my understanding of the shape and shaping of truly Christian minds.

Over these fourteen years I gave over five hundred speeches, sermons, seminars and other talks outside of my NCB classes. Our school graduated more than two hundred degree and diploma students and enrolled more than two thousand part time students and conference attendees—too many to count. The full-time and part-time faculty we recruited and empowered contributed great teaching and publication from among the best Christian scholars of our time. The subsequent lives and careers of our graduates (and our part-time students) have made an impact far and wide. My ongoing relationships with many of these NCB students and colleagues have been a huge gift to me. And through it all, Lucia and I created our home on 62nd Street and raised our two kids, sending them off as young adults just as my NCB time ended. All in all, an amazing time, an amazing "channel" for my calling.

NCB POSTSCRIPT A: ESCAPE & FRUSTRATED RECONCILIATION

On the personal level, I could hardly wait to get out the door when I left NCB in June 1990. But I hated to leave with such broken relationships, that is just not my style. So I took the initiative and arranged to meet, first, with a counselor/mediator and Bill Dyrness. I had been deeply disappointed that our veteran Bill had not stepped in to help smooth over the increasingly hostile faculty atmosphere, especially in my final year. I'm sure he had been disappointed in me and my partnership when I was his dean so

I could hardly blame him if he left me to "hang out to dry"—though I can't imagine that was his intention! I probably deserved that. The session went well and I think our relationship was resolved.

Then "Mr. Dean" and I met twice with the mediator. She asked us to speak one at a time (of course) to describe what went wrong in our relationship. Then the other guy was asked to summarize back what had been said. "Did I get that right?" we asked the other guy after giving our summaries. First Mr. Dean had his turn: "David, you were upset with me that I didn't work hard enough." Me: "Mr. Dean, you are saying that I thought you didn't work hard enough." Dean: "Yes." Mediator, "David how do you respond to that?" Me: "Mr. Dean you worked your butt off and I never had anything but compliments for your work as a teacher or on your administrative projects." Mediator "Now you David, what were your issues with Mr. Dean?" Me: "Mr. Dean, over and over you would tell me one thing to my face and then the opposite to board members, faculty, and students, undermining our plans and my leadership. You were lying to me. I talked to you about this, even bringing Bill Dyrness in to hear me describe it to you." Mediator: "Mr. Dean, what did David just say?" Mr. Dean: "David you were upset because I didn't work hard enough." Me (and mediator): "No Mr. Dean, that is not at all what I just said or what the problem was."

And so it went. Over and over, Mr. Dean could never even repeat back to me what I said, much less try to refute it. My only conclusion was that the man was sick, a pathological liar. As we got to the end of the two sessions the mediator turned to me and said: "David, I think the root problem is that you loved this guy, and he betrayed you." Me: "That is exactly right. For me it was a personal and professional betrayal. I was (and still am) more than ready to forgive and be reconciled but he cannot acknowledge what he has done, not once but habitually, over the past four years."

We went out into the night. I later resigned (after twenty years) from being a contributing editor to *Radix Magazine* because my old friend Sharon Gallagher kept this pathological liar on her masthead as a contributing editor with whom I could have no association. Tragic story. Well-meaning people have sometimes thought Mr. Dean and I just had a personality conflict. For me it really boiled down to a conflict of ethics and morality, not personality. He was an impenitent liar and disloyal saboteur I wrongly tolerated for four years.

NCB POSTSCRIPT B: INSTITUTIONAL DEATH AND RESURRECTION

On the institutional level, Richard Benner took over as NCB president for the next three years. Bill Dyrness left in 1990 to become Dean at Fuller Seminary. Bernie Adeney soon left NCB for a long and distinguished career in Indonesia as a university educator and specialist in Christian-Muslim relations. Doug Anderson was off to a long career as Professor of History at Northwestern College in Orange City, Iowa. Frank

Andersen, frequent visiting professor Robert Banks, and Joel Green all ended up at Fuller Seminary with Bill Dyrness. David Batstone came on board after my departure to teach Christian Ethics until he got a great post at USF. Course cross-registration with GTU schools meant that NCB classrooms were sometimes filled with students—but they were paying tuition to their home seminaries, not NCB. Benner was replaced as president after three years by Steve Pattie who heroically presided over the final year before the graduate school doors closed in 1994 with zero money to be seen anywhere.

I left all my notes and administrative records in the president's office when I walked out my last day. I was phoned off and on to provide whatever information and insight I could give on our donor list, but NCB's fund-raising efforts declined to almost nothing. I'm sure many good things happened among faculty and students but "chaos" was the sad refrain I heard from staff members who called me now and then. NCB was able to continue financially only because the board sold our Dwight House student residence and spent all of the $400k equity on operations over the next four years, also draining the $125k I had raised in the endowment account. Every dollar was spent in a futile effort to 'keep on keepin' on" as Mr. Dean and the faculty had insisted.

Can you blame me for my anguish and disappointment as I heard about this from time to time in my office in Chicago? I wondered, did no one think to halt this after, say, two years to save some few shekels for, say, a downsized study center? Imagine if Susan Phillips and Sharon Gallagher could have run the study center out of Dwight House! This galled me especially because I had been ripped at a board meeting in my final semester (by the trustee who soon would sell our Dwight House and drain our endowment fund) for moving $10k from the endowment fund to our operating budget to juggle some urgent bills—for just two weeks before putting it all back. So much for Jay Boone's and my recommendation to move our operation into Dwight House! This could have protected the student residential community and our office operations while eliminating the $40k campus rent at ABSW. I don't question anyone's good intentions—everyone did what they felt was best in service of NCB. But to anyone who took a hard look at NCB's reality it was obviously unwise and bad stewardship.

With no money left, no hope for NCB as a grad school, and talk of closing everything down completely, our long-time adjunct professor Susan Phillips, with her recent PhD in Sociology from Berkeley, and Sharon Gallagher, my long-time friend, colleague, and NCB adjunct professor, wrote up a proposal to take over the NCB "brand," mailing list, and legacy and downsize the school into a "Study Center" offering non-credit short courses, retreats, workshops, and conferences on various topics of interest to layfolk. By this time, I was in Chicago teaching at North Park College. But I, along with Earl Palmer, Laurel Gasque, and former presidents Ward Gasque and Bill Dyrness, wrote the NCB board of trustees to give our strong endorsements of Susan and Sharon's proposal.

The quiet but steady, strong leadership of Susan and Sharon continued for an amazing twenty-seven years. Working out of a modest office in downtown Berkeley, under their leadership NCB solidified a formal affiliation with the GTU as a study center and offered a quality menu of learning opportunities for nearly three decades. NCB is justly admired as one of the oldest and best of the Christian Study Centers, part of a Consortium of now dozens of such centers, most of them located near American and Canadian universities. Earl Palmer has returned every year to lead special weekend courses attended by hundreds of his fans (providing a helpful financial injection in the process). A competent, faithful, and supportive Board of Trustees has been sustained. Susan and Sharon worked sacrificially for minimal, part-time salaries over these years.

Executive Director Susan Phillips became a widely-regarded teacher and writer on friendship, spiritual formation, and related topics. I can't speak highly enough of her leadership, teaching, and scholarship. NCB continued to offer occasional courses or conferences addressing the original NCB target audiences in the academy and marketplace but the spiritual formation side got the greatest emphasis. I always wished they could have sustained those original academy and marketplace emphases to a greater extent—and I wished they could have taken advantage of the opportunities for online, distance learning enabled after 1995 by the emerging internet. But, note well, I have only praise for what they did accomplish, for all the benefits their work has brought to probably thousands of NCB students over these years. My "wishes" are not criticisms, still less demands! Any additional topical focus or technological extension would require money, available teaching resources, and "champions" to drive it forward. As they must, Susan and Sharon have been obedient to their calling—not mine!

NCB POSTSCRIPT C: DISTANCE & DISREGARD

I hesitate to describe how I have experienced (felt, understood) my relationship to the school I served as a leader (not the only one but, on the whole, the primary one) from its inception in 1976 to my departure in 1990. But I am often asked about NCB and about my relationship to it since leaving. This is an important part of my story, even if not actually very important to NCB itself. Many other organizational founders and leaders can probably relate and maybe find solidarity and encouragement here. Founders and long-time leaders (including many former pastors) don't always find it easy. Part of my personal problem is that I am a sentimental, nostalgic guy who hates to let go of the past, especially the people. I stay in touch with scores of former students, colleagues, neighbors, and friends, going back to my youth. I always feel a tug in my heart when I visit or just pass by old places I used to be. I suffer from a deep emotional attachment, a love, for NCB. Not helpful to tell me to just "get over it."

Every year for several years, from the time I left, I phoned the NCB office on April 7 to encourage the staff and remind them of the anniversary. As 1997 approached, I urged Susan and Sharon to schedule a big twentieth anniversary banquet. At my suggestion, all of us former presidents returned to offer one-hour seminars and join in the celebration. I personally raised or donated five or ten thousand dollars to NCB. Five years later, in 2002, I was back in the Bay Area and again supported a big 25th anniversary event, donating or raising five or ten thousand dollars again. At the big banquet, I was asked to offer an opening prayer and my daughter Jodie on piano and five-year old grandson Elijah on violin provided some special music. Three or four other times in the late 1990s or early 2000s, I was invited to teach a couple one-day or short courses for NCB at First Pres or in the basement of my old home church Berkeley Covenant.

In short, for the fifteen years from my departure in 1990 to about 2005 I was not close to NCB's operations (living in Chicago for nine of those fifteen years)—but I was encouraging and supportive, financially and otherwise. When asked to teach a little class, I did. I don't think I ever came back into town without having coffee with my beloved sister and colleague from 1971 onward, Sharon Gallagher.

But around 2005 I suggested that NCB (and *Radix Magazine* and IVCF) consider moving its offices to the newly expanded and renovated Westminster House on the edge of the Cal campus (Bancroft Way at College Avenue). This could put NCB into a fertile, congenial, potentially collaborative, environment, in place of their hard to access second- or third-story downtown office. The new Westminster House had a nice library, a seminar room and lecture hall, and a restaurant. For Westminster House I had designed a potential study program for future Cal undergrad residents we would call the "Westminster Institute."[2] I thought of this as a perfect complement to what NCB had to offer to adult and grad students—but Susan Philips was not interested (too risky? Maybe. It was rejected out of hand, never seriously discussed). The NCB Board chair at this time, an old colleague and friend, took me out to lunch to scold me for even thinking of "starting something that might look like a rival to NCB" (what?). NCB leaders also got First Pres pastor Mark Labberton to speak to me in opposition. I was pretty stunned by this reaction to what I thought would have been a significant benefit to NCB. Beyond that, had NCB somehow acquired veto power over lay education programs serving constituencies and topical arenas well outside of their own? They had no plan to serve residential undergrads like this. So this "What Are You Doing About It?" proposal died before birth—as Westminster House Director Randy Bare also lost interest and the St. Mary's College Graduate School of Business took over my career for the next six years.

That negative experience was followed by another in 2007 when I got an institutional postcard in the mail inviting me to sign up to attend NCB's thirty-year anniversary with Earl Palmer speaking on "The Decalogue in Today's Life and Work" or something to that effect. Sharon Gallagher called me to ask if I would say a prayer at the event. Lucia and I had longstanding plans to visit some old friends in Oregon

---

2. This was to serve as a theological companion to Westminster undergrads' "secular education" at Cal—two hours of class plus two hours of study each week. It is comparable to the Gotham Fellows program at Redeemer Pres in New York City, the Boston Fellows program, and many others that have sprung up in the past two or three decades.

on the now-scheduled NCB anniversary weekend. Unless it was maybe that first big celebration in 1997, NCB leaders never asked me about my schedule availability as they chose their anniversary celebration dates. I was marginalized by a role only as prayer giver, never asked to say a few words, much less be their banquet speaker. And even my old friend Earl Palmer had chosen to give a talk on the topic for which I was best known in both the scholarly and church worlds—applying the Ten Commandments to the workplace. My book on the Decalogue, *Doing Right: Practicing Ethical Principles* had been published in 2004. To say I felt disrespected, marginalized, and insulted by the school I founded and had continued to support all these years is a massive understatement. But No—I did not for a minute think that anyone *intended* to diss me—but their actions did.

As in the case with any relational breakdowns I have ever sensed or experienced, I could not stay in a funk about all of this. At my initiative, I met with Susan, Sharon and the current board chair. I shared how all of this was thoughtless, hurtful, and disrespectful. I followed up by meeting with the board chair, in the presence of a mediator she chose. I got the same message from all three NCB leaders: "David, we are so sorry that you feel hurt and disrespected but we intended no hurt or disrespect." Me: "I am not saying you intended it. Honestly, I don't think any of the three of you are capable of *intending* to hurt me. But you did. I just wish you could see that, accept responsibility for your disrespectful actions, and not do it again." Response: "We are sorry you feel hurt and disrespected—but we did nothing wrong."

I wish I could say that was the end but in 2017, I was asked to record a greeting for the fortieth anniversary NCB banquet (again, scheduled without any concern whether I could make it—I couldn't attend because I had a 50th anniversary trip to Europe with Lucia, departing a day before the banquet). I recorded a glowing, positive greeting and congratulations—but when I viewed the event tape a month or so later, I noticed that they had edited out a minute (just one minute!) of personal remarks I had made about the prehistory of NCB during the year leading up to its founding in April 1977.[3] The message I got was clear again: NCB will take my praise, celebration of them, and donations—but edit me out as an actual person with anything else to say.

Please understand that I am not in need of NCB's or anyone else's praise or gratitude. I have received far more affirmation than I could possibly deserve through my whole career. And I look back at my whole fourteen-year career at NCB with gratitude and (apart from the hard times I have mentioned) contentment. I came to see, soon after leaving in 1990, that God had other adventures for me (described in coming chapters) to which I was called and which shaped and taught me in valuable ways that never could have happened had I stayed at NCB, even under the best circumstances.

---

3. The deleted remarks: "Actually, for me, this is the 41st anniversary of NCB—it was in Spring 1976 that I wrote up a one-page proposal for a new college in Berkeley and sent it to Earl Palmer. He wrote me back enthusiastically and we were off and running." The program editor chopped off this statement. "Too much Gill" I guess.

I did not want to roll back the clock, and had zero interest in leading or even doing more work for NCB, much less competing with it.

Yes, I know NCB lists me as one of its main founders. But given my role in its first fourteen years, given my financial and verbal support from the accession of the Study Center leadership through those big banquets in 1997 and 2002, given my career as a productive writer and leader since 1990 in the faith at work domain, I am baffled and disappointed by the relationship NCB leaders chose to have with me. I could offer a prayer for the food, make and raise donations, and attend banquet celebrations if by chance I was in town. But for thirty-two years, I was never asked my counsel even one time, never invited to share anything about our history and mission with a staff or board meeting, never invited to speak at a banquet or anniversary celebration, never even asked if any of those anniversary banquet dates were free on my calendar. I still find it hard to imagine that NCB's leaders intended to hurt or disrespect me—but they have. That 2017 edit removing my one minute of personal reminiscence was a clear message that NCB didn't want me to have a personal voice, no matter how positive and kind it might be. I don't understand. Disregard and disrespect.

This part of my NCB story is about the anguish and disappointment of a founder and ex-leader. It is an inextricable part of my growth journey—through a valley, not on a mountaintop. I am not looking for sympathy or praise, just telling you my "marginal activist" story. I am hoping that any of my readers who experience similar ups and downs in their active- and then post-leadership lives will at least feel some solidarity—and forge ahead with hope. I got to the point in 2007 (confirmed several times afterward) where I felt God was using NCB's leaders to shout a message at me: "move on, forget it, you have other things to do, they don't want or need you!" It was so different from the love and respect I always got when I returned to University Covenant, North Park, St. Mary's, or my other "channels."

It has often been very painful but that is sometimes going to be the fate of a "What Are You Doing About It" marginal activist. Maybe my rejection came from fear—certainly it came from thoughtlessness. Despite the pain, I would do it all over again—though hopefully with fewer mistakes and less suffering all around.

NCB POSTSCRIPT D: CONTENTMENT & HOPE

I am joining happily and unreservedly in the celebration of Susan Phillips's impressive twenty-seven years of NCB leadership. I am also very excited about the incoming Executive Co-Directors, Tim Tseng and Craig Wong. For the first time in three decades, I was asked for my counsel by some NCB leaders—to have a chat with the Search Committee and with the finalist candidates. And the new Co-Directors have been reaching out with talk about possible partnerships and collaborations. It's been a surprising gift from God after all the years.

18

Pastor, Preacher, Teacher

WELL THAT WAS A surprise ending to my dream! I was now forty-four. What next? My two "almost" calls to the faculties of Regent College and Fuller Seminary in 1989–90 had evaporated. I had always been a ferociously productive writer, including three published books during the 1980s, despite my heavy administrative workload. But my wife Lucia would not hear of it when I suggested spending the coming year as a freelance writer. I had several manuscripts in the works but would not have made any money from them for at least a couple years. We had two kids in college by fall 1990 and no financial savings or margin after giving fourteen years to NCB. My wife had justifiable objections. In any case, just then, in June 1990, I was invited to consider serving as Interim Senior Pastor at University Covenant Church in Davis, seventy miles east of our house. A UCC elder Bill Johnson had been in my NCB classes and brought me to the search committee. Lucia urged me to pursue it and she was right (again!).

Back in 1980, Craig Anderson, pastor of our home church, Berkeley Covenant, and Chair of the NCB Board had (successfully) urged me to apply to the Covenant denomination to be Licensed (not Ordained) as a Covenant Minister, credentialled for pastoral or other Christian ministry. I went through the process, was interviewed by the Covenant Ministerium and approved. I thought it was a good thing to be commissioned like this. I preached all over the place, led communion services, and officiated at weddings, baptisms, and funerals. It was good not just to be a free-lancer but accountable to the Church for my theology and practice. I renewed this status annually until the late 1990s when I joined the First Presbyterian Church in Evanston. The Covenant ministerial license was only available to active members of Covenant Churches.

In this chapter I want to describe (1) my extraordinary, unexpected two-year term (1990–92) as an Interim Senior Pastor, then another one-year interim pastorate, twenty years later (2011–12), (2) my experiences and lessons learned over the years about pastoral care, pastoral search committees, and the interim role, (3) my experiences with adult education in the church setting, and (4) my thinking about church, especially when gathered for worship. My primary calling has always been to the academy and the marketplace. But all my life I was also an active churchman, often serving as an elder, Christian education leader, preacher, pastoral care giver, men's group leader, worship leader, music leader on guitar (until age thirty), and any other way I could help. Lucia was also an active Sunday School teacher, small group host, hospitality leader, Stephen Minister, and sometime elder. We loved church (most of the time!). I often said if I had a second life to live, I would love to be a pastor. I never stopped thinking my primary calling was to be an adult education teacher, academic, and writer, but if I had a second life, it would have been as a pastor. The Plymouth Brethren tradition in which I grew up, had no pastors, just lay leaders, so I never thought to go to seminary or move in that direction. But now after NCB I had the opportunity to experience life as a pastor.

UNIVERSITY COVENANT CHURCH IN DAVIS, CALIFORNIA

I sometimes said to my friends that if I ever was a pastor I would like it to be at a university church like First Pres Berkeley or University Covenant in Davis. And now UCC Davis was calling. UCC had been planted and pastored for its first five years by my friend Randy Klassen. After Randy, the pastor for twenty years was Ron Lagerstrom, who I knew and admired. Ron's son and daughter-in-law, Larry and Lori Lagerstrom, had been wonderful students of mine at NCB and were members of UCC. When Ron retired from UCC in 1990 he left a wonderfully-trained and pastored congregation of three hundred fifty or so, including several UC Davis professors and a large contingent of students. It was a very heathy congregation with a significant band of lay leaders of all ages and gifts.

I signed a contract providing me a modest two-thirds time salary and reimbursement for my travel mileage back and forth from Oakland, seventy miles each way. I should have included a subsidy to help pay for my three speeding tickets on I-80. At that time the national speed limit was just fifty-five miles per hour. Just pacing traffic, I got nailed by airplane surveillance for going too fast. Not just the fines but the rise in my insurance rate for a couple years was painful. My bad. Initially, I would spend my Sundays and two other days each week at the church and one day working on my sermons at home. Four days out of a six-day work week, equaled two-thirds time in my book. Lucia's job at Citibank covered our health care policy at Kaiser-Permanente so UCC didn't have that expense. One year turned into two, four days turned into five or six fairly soon.

When I showed up at UCC in 1990, I was exhausted and beaten up by my years (especially the final one) at NCB. But over the next months I got loved, encouraged, and healed in an incredible way by the UCC congregation. Plus, I got to experience church pastoral leadership from the inside and express my calling through that channel. Thank you Lucia for insisting I consider it and supporting me in it. Lucia stayed active at Berkeley Covenant the next two years but accompanied me to UCC often enough on Sundays to become known and loved there in her own right.

I was not just hired as "pulpit supply" to do the preaching at UCC's two Sunday morning services, but to provide pastoral care and overall leadership. I called a staff meeting for my first day. "What is your usual pattern of staff meetings?" I asked. "Oh, we don't have a regular pattern, Pastor Ron just met with us, mostly individually, as needed," they informed me. "Well, that needs to change," I said, "from now on let's meet together every Tuesday at 11:00 a.m., to discuss our work and pray together—and have lunch together once in a while." Then I asked each staff member to introduce themselves, tell me how long they had worked on staff, and what their job was. Vivian Meyer was the choir and music director. Michelle Berry was the office manager. Woody Underhill was the Associate Pastor. Dave Nystrom was part-time university student pastor while he finished working on his PhD at UC Davis. Pat Pankratz was the pastor's secretary. "Do you have job descriptions?" I asked. Answer, "No." Me: "well your first assignment this week is to write up a job description for yourself and I will be reviewing and formalizing it with you." Over the years, I have been troubled by the lack of job descriptions, staff evaluation and improvement plans, and even regular staff meetings at churches—and appalled by church boards that acquiesce in these failures that so often lead to misunderstandings, poor performance, and staff conflict.

All the UCC staff positions made sense and I hoped they would just carry on, except one. Pastor's secretary Pat Pankratz told me that her main work consisted of setting up appointments, mostly for pastoral visits and care, whenever Pastor Ron requested it. I said "Pat, your job is going to change a bit. I'd like you to play a much more active role. I will do all my study and sermon preparation back home where my library and computer are. I want to make the most of my time so I'd like you to fill up all my hours in Davis on Tuesdays and Wednesdays from 10:00 a.m. to 9:00 p.m.. Could you please schedule weekly meetings with the staff and with worship and music leader Vivian Meyer, and add the hospitalized, shut-ins, and others needing pastoral care. Then add monthly visits with the old guys who live alone. Also schedule me for the Covell Gardens Retirement Home afternoon service once a month."

"Of course," I continued, "I will meet with anyone once—but if someone needs long-term counseling let's connect them with a professional" (we had two excellent therapist/counselors, a man and a woman, in our congregation). "Then Pat, would you call up families and say 'Pastor Gill is in town on Tuesday and Wednesday evenings: would you like to have him over as a guest for dinner?' (Bold, I know). And finally, could you contact any UC Davis students and say 'Pastor Gill would love to meet you on campus for coffee at 8:00 p.m. before he drives home.' And Pat, could you give me a map or directions on how to get to each of these meetings?"

Pat did a fabulous job during my two years at the church. Soon there was actually a waiting list of families wanting to have me over for dinner. Typically, I would just ask my hosts to tell me their stories. The kids would love to show me their rooms and pets and tell me about their schools. Many of these families told me they had never had a pastor in their home, and thanked me for coming. Some marveled that I visited them without needing a crisis intervention to justify it! After a couple months I started figuring out who the "golf widows" were (women whose husbands always skipped church to play golf). I asked Pat to call up these guys and say "Pastor Gill loves golf and would love to play a round with you." So I fairly regularly got on to the country club and public courses—and in time some of these guys even started attending church! One younger guy, a very buff prison guard, worked out at LA Fitness and couldn't believe it that the pastor would go pump iron with him as I did from time to time. Lucia and I brought our bikes up at least once to go cycling with a member who loved it—and who was the guy who wisely got us to wear bike helmets as a safety precaution for the rest of our lives (Lucia and I have been weekly bike riders since 1973 except when prevented by injury or weather).

I kept track of all these visits and blew the elders' minds at our monthly meetings when I handed out reports on my schedule and work over the previous month. Wasn't this what other pastors did, I wondered (both the visitation and the reports to the board)? Apparently not. In doing all of this, I didn't think church was just a "hospital for the sick" but also a "gymnasium for the healthy." Of course, I came alongside the hurting—married couples at each others' throats, the depressed, someone receiving a cancer diagnosis and then walking with them to the very end and leading their memorial service. That was often holy ground. Two different women came to me struggling with histories of sexual abuse—I asked them if they would be interested in a confidential small group with other women coping with these wounds. I was able to connect these two with our female therapist attending UCC. Together they formed an ongoing support group which soon had several other members. By the way, I did not meet with women alone at their homes. When any woman did come to my office, I noticed that Pat always stayed in her adjoining office to prevent even a whiff or appearance of scandal. I loved Pat for her wise concern. I did what I could to encourage our women in leadership. I asked an elderly woman in our congregation, who had been an Assemblies of God pastor in earlier years, to join me in leading communion from time to time.

As I neared the end of my two years, I thought (and said) that if I had continued, I would have begun visiting all my parishioners at their workplaces—something I have advocated to pastors ever since. This kind of pastoral visitation to homes and workplaces does wonders for pastors and congregations. The visits aren't about preaching but about listening, understanding, and caring. My sermons and pastoral prayers got more relevant in their applications—and the people came to church more attentively, knowing their pastor cared about them personally. Even among those who were not personally visited, this practice created a buzz: "our pastor cares about us!" Do they teach and promote this in seminaries—or is pastoral care just about church turf activities except for emergencies? Sad.

PART THREE: CHANNELS (1979–2016)

PREACHER AND TEACHER

My predecessor Ron Lagerstrom was an outstanding pastor, nurturing as fine a group of young and old leaders as I have ever known. I loved these people, loved working with them and seeing their leadership in all phases of church life. But I think the congregation was hungry for the kind of preaching/teaching their interim "professor" brought to them. I have often said that in the academic classroom I was a sort of "preaching teacher"—while at church I was sort of a "teaching preacher." I loved the challenge of preaching to the whole people of God, preparing to go out into their daily lives—not just university and seminary students a step removed from their careers. I loved the challenge of preaching to farmers, blue collar workers, techies, stay-at-home parents, children, retired folk, novice as well as veteran Christians, curious inquirers alongside committed believers. Following Earl Palmer's example, I led a brief monthly "time for young disciples" gathered up on the platform during the big worship services—rather than just delegating that to a youth worker—believing that kids needed to be seen and addressed by the senior pastor.

I preached forty of the fifty-two weeks each year (the rest by David Nystrom or an occasional guest). I did a series of ten on the Decalogue, eight on the Beatitudes, three on the virtues of faith, hope, and love, and so on. Near the end I did a series of ten on the Book of Revelation and I told the congregation I had left my car in the parking lot with the motor running in case I had to quickly flee after stepping on any toes with my interpretation of some of Revelation's controversial prophecies! (I was safe). I put together special series each year for Advent leading up to Christmas. For the seven Sundays of Lent leading up to Easter I did the "Seven Last Words from the Cross" one year and a seven-part series on the Lord's Prayer in year two. I loved planning special services for Labor Day, Thanksgiving, Christmas Eve, Ash Wednesday, Maundy Thursday, and Easter Sunday. We (led by choir director Vivian Meyer and others) celebrated the 25th anniversary of the church over several months during my first year, an amazing time.

My first summer at UCC I was also asked to teach an adult class during the one hour between services. I did a thirteen-week series for a big crowd on "Peter the Rock"—using my 1986 book of that title. After that summer of preaching both services and teaching the adult class in between, I told the elders I couldn't keep up that pace with the middle hour adult class anymore! Instead, in the fall of 1990 I asked Pat to set me up to visit every age group class in the church. First Sunday I visited the nursery, kissed all the babies and thanked the nursery workers. Next Sunday I visited the preschool class, sat on one of their miniscule chairs without breaking it and had a little chat after hearing all the kids say their names. Next week kindergarten. And on up each week from elementary grades through high school, then college, then the various adult classes. Over thirteen weeks I visited every class—not to teach but to meet the people. Just a fifteen or twenty-minute interruption of each class. It doesn't take a seminary degree or special gifts to show interest and make a big impact doing this kind of thing.

I loved meeting with choir and worship leader Vivian Meyer. We worked at picking music and an order of worship that focused on the presence of Christ in our worship, brought the praise and prayer concerns of the people into the temple, and reinforced the Word read and preached with the music sung. I pressed to keep both services inclusive of the whole people of God rather than gearing them to one musical or worship "taste" in each service. I still believe that it is far better to include new and old music in both services. Our worship should gather the whole people of God rather than segregate based on musical taste. Different demographics should learn and hear from each other, not occupy silos.

Every month I handed an activity report to the board of elders. My strong conviction is that pastors, like everyone else on staff or in lay leadership, should be open, accountable, and be evaluated "360" on a regular basis. I told the elders they should also inquire about my marriage and family, my health and fitness, my study and spiritual practice, challenges, and growth if they wanted me to stay balanced and healthy for the longer haul. They should hold me accountable not just for my work but for my rest. I actually suggested that they should tell their pastor that if he or she spent more than three nights a week away from their spouse and family—or failed to work out regularly—they should be fired! It is terrible to allow (or expect) the pastor to be out at church-related meetings night after night. Over and over I have seen failures to do this in churches lead to burn-out, divorce, or health problems.

CHALLENGES

I was very thankful that, during my interim, church attendance and membership held steady and maybe grew slightly—not always the case during an interim phase at a church. I stressed to the church that the "interim" phase was not an "empty" phase but a powerful opportunity for growth and witness. It was actually a small replication of the whole of church history which is an "interim" between the first and second comings of Christ. UCC got it and got busy!

UCC faced two big challenges during my tenure. The first started during my first week on campus when the associate pastor took me to lunch and told me he had just moved out and separated from his wife. I was a bit shocked because I was counting on this veteran to be the primary, full-time, on-campus anchor of our staff and congregation. He insisted it was not a big problem, was a long time coming, and the elders knew about it. I told him I was really concerned and this would now become my number one pastoral concern. I told him that even if the elders knew about it already, he should report this latest development to the elders at our next meeting. At and after that elders meeting we decided to put him on full salary leave for the next six months till the end of the year to work on nothing but restoring his marriage with the help of a marriage counselor. He did not like this but had to agree. In the coming months I met with him and with his wife separately. I then told him I did not see her wanting this separation and that love in word, deed, and attitude could heal the break. They could find and rekindle their first love again. Unfortunately, he did not give himself wholly to the task and we had to end his employment in January (with a generous six-month severance package).

With the budgetary pressure of carrying his salary forward, I felt that we should not hire a replacement but wait for the (presumed) new pastor to begin in the next summer so he or she could pick their own staff associate. I kicked up my time commitment another day each week and our college minister David Nystrom agreed to increase his responsibilities to Associate Pastor. David was a very gifted teacher and pastor and we worked well together for my whole two years a UCC—at the end of which we both moved to Chicago to join the faculty of North Park College. Dave was an excellent preacher and usually preached when I didn't. We were short-staffed but carried on pretty effectively.

SEARCHING FOR MR. (OR MS.) GOODPASTOR

The other, ultimately more important, challenge was the pastoral search process. One thing interim pastors must not do is tamper with the search process. There is a longer horizon of congregational history and a more complex culture that must guide the search process. If the interim pastor is any good at all, some parishioners will suggest that he or she stay on permanently. People don't like uncertainty and just installing the interim can resolve that problem. The interim pastor also has an advantage over other candidates—a sort of "bully pulpit" where his or her views can be preached many times more than any outside candidate coming in and has a familiarity and pastoral care that inclines many to want them. I got asked often by various church members to "please be a candidate" and I always made it clear to them and to the board of elders that I could not.

As far as I could tell the search committee was well composed, but one thing was a red flag: the chair of the elders was also the chair of the search committee. At every elders meeting he called on himself to report on the search progress. The process dragged on until the next May or June when the committee brought their chosen candidate, approved unanimously by the search committee. When David Nystrom and I heard who it was, we were shocked. It was a very nice man, who we both knew, but with a military chaplain background and no experience working in a university context. He was not a very deep theologian or a very good communicator. He was apparently chosen because he checked off all the boxes on the fundamentalist/evangelical doctrines and sexual ethics that were prioritized by the chair.

I did my part and disappeared for ten days so the candidate could preach two Sundays in a row and go through an admirably thorough set of meetings with various parts of the congregation. That process was done well. But when the day arrived for the congregation to vote, the candidate was rejected by a 70% to 30% vote. Nystrom and I had said nothing to anyone to influence this vote. Now in desperation, the elders asked me to stay a second year if I could, and I agreed. However, both David Nystrom and I, about that same time, had agreed to join the North Park faculty in Chicago in 1992, just one year later, so now the pressure was really on to find a good candidate.

At this point I did have a chat with the chair of the board and search committee. I urged him to appoint another search committee chair and replace at least half the committee members. They had unanimously proposed a candidate who was rejected by 70% of the congregation, losing their credibility as judges of acceptable candidates. The congregation deserved a change of committee. The search committee chair needed to be held accountable by the board and its chair—not given a pass by one guy occupying both chairs. The board chair refused and I was not about to get involved in objecting publicly and stirring up any discord. I urged him to at least add a couple new members but again he refused, arguing that his committee now understood what the congregation was looking for. Adding new committee members, he argued, would slow down the process of reconsidering their candidate list. I told him that was exactly what they needed: new questions, new eyes to look at potential pastors. He refused. The chair was a smart guy, a real man of God, well-intentioned—but flawed in his approach. Disaster was ahead.

That fall that same search committee got busy again and by the spring of 1992 was closing in on a finalist list. On a visit I made to North Park, a brilliant young faculty member who had earlier experience working on a Bay Area Covenant church staff, and who was an outstanding communicator, took me aside and asked if I thought he might be a good fit for UCC. Should he throw his hat in the ring? I knew and respected this guy a lot but just to confirm my judgment I called up the senior pastor he had formerly worked for and asked his opinion. "Yes, he could be a great fit" was the answer, so I encouraged him to apply. When I got back to UCC later that week I told the chair that a truly "blue chip" candidate had emerged and it was well worth considering him. The chair declined, saying that they had narrowed the search down to three finalist candidates and they would not consider any others. Within five years, the guy they declined to consider planted a new church which grew to thousands of members and began hiving off several other new church plants (which all became strong in their own right). UCC blew it by not considering him.

Meanwhile the search committee decided on their candidate and brought him in for a thorough candidacy visit at the end of my second year. He was terrible, much worse, less gifted and experienced, than the candidate from the preceding year! Many protested but, with Nystrom and I about to leave, a majority of the exhausted congregation voted to call this man. I tried to cheer everyone up and make a strong finish to my two-year term as interim. I wrote a nice letter of welcome to the pastor-elect and included a detailed report on all my sermon series and other activities. I suggested we get together for a conversation about the church. He never even acknowledged my letter or report or made any effort to get together. Not a good sign. For the next two years after I left, I was often phoned or written in Chicago by UCC members out of their mind over his terrible sermons, leadership, and pastoral care. Something like a third of the members left the church before he was let go two years later. Four or five years of interim pastors followed until my friend Jamie Crook was called to be pastor around 1998. Jamie was a visionary and a great preacher and under his leadership the church grew to several hundred members and built a big new campus in Davis. I preached at his installation.

Part of the problem was that the Evangelical Covenant Church denomination did not, in my view, give much help to church pastoral search committees or guidance to Interim Pastors and their churches. I attended a couple Interim Pastor gatherings at the annual Midwinter Covenant ministers' conference—and was appalled by what I heard (and didn't hear). To be brutally honest, it seemed like these interim guys mostly viewed their task as just holding things together until the "real" pastor arrived. One brilliant exception over the years has been my old Berkeley friend Doug Stevens who has served many Covenant (and other) congregations in their transitional (often tumultuous) phases with wonderful, insightful leadership. But my home church, Berkeley Covenant, had also gone through a three-year period (1983–86) without a senior pastor, the first two years because of a process as inept as the one at UCC 1990–92. We finally pried the search committee leadership away from the board chair in 1985–86 and called Max Lopez-Cepero who then gave most of a decade to good leadership at BCC.

I wrote two essays about what I had learned, "Notes for the Interim" and "Calling Mr. (or Ms.) Goodpastor," but the denominational magazine *The Covenant Companion* declined to publish them and I was never asked to share my experience and ideas at one of the Midwinter Conferences. (Remember the subtitle of this autobiography "Memoir of a Marginal Activist." I have never been invited into the heart of the Covenant denomination. They seem to already have everything figured out).

After I left University Covenant in 1992 to go to Chicago, my heart was often heavy thinking about the suffering friends back at UCC. I tried to encourage them: stay positive, focus on your small group fellowship, volunteer to work in the nursery during worship, listen to recordings and broadcasts of some good teachers. After the bad pastor was let go and other interim pastors came on board, I often guest preached or taught at UCC when I was back in town for a visit. A new and better search committee was still having trouble finding a good candidate.

On one of my visits in the later 1990s some leaders of the search committee took me aside to beseech me to come back as their senior pastor. This time I listened to my heart and really felt the call to come back to these people I loved. But Lucia felt strongly that the time was not right, not least because of her sense of calling and unfinished business at her Citibank post in Chicago. She had already disrupted her

Oakland Citibank job in 1992 to go with me to Chicago. It broke my heart but I agreed and had to decline UCC's invitation. In the next chapter I will describe how her instinct turned out to be right again, for me as well as her own calling. And it was not long before I connected First Pres Evanston's Associate Pastor Jamie Crook with UCC and he went on to lead UCC into a bright new era.

ONE MORE INTERIM: TRINITARIAN CONGREGATIONAL CHURCH

I did not imagine doing another Interim Pastorate but during my second year back in the Boston area at Gordon-Conwell, 2011–12, I agreed to the call at Trinitarian Congregational Church in Wayland. The retiring pastor Jim Pocock had been the first Boston area pastor to welcome me to his pulpit to guest preach. One of the two funders of my chair at Gordon-Conwell was a member of TCC: Tom (and his wife Gert) Phillips. Tom was the long-time CEO of Raytheon, a leader in the faith at work movement in Boston, and a wonderful brother. More on my Gordon-Conwell position in a later chapter. Tom and Gert loved my preaching and sweet Gert always gave me a little hug and a kiss every Sunday. Sometimes I whispered to her after a service, "How'd I do?" (a little joke). She always encouraged me, as did Tom. Jim Pocock was a pastor fully on board when it came to workplace discipleship and the congregation was eager to learn.

I did my (usual, favorite) sermon series on the Decalogue, the Beatitudes, the Pauline Virtues of faith, hope and love, and the Seven Last Words from the Cross (during Lent). There was no let-up from my full-time faculty job at Gordon-Conwell (thirty miles to the north) so my initial job description was just to preach two services each Sunday (plus the preparation and study time, of course). Inevitably though, I was drawn into pastoral leadership tasks as well. I was able to push my workplace discipleship calling into some exciting new territory at TCC. On two successive Saturday mornings I led a six-hour (three hours each week) seminar on the topic for forty attendees representing all manner of workplaces and callings.

COMMISSIONING WORKERS

One of the most exciting things I pioneered at TCC was commissioning different groups of workers during our worship services every two or three months. Let me take a few paragraphs to describe it. Already many churches call forward their mission teams, short-term and otherwise, for commissioning and prayer. We call forward and commission our deacons and elders. Our pastoral installations are powerful occasions of commissioning and joint prayer. Our marriage and baptismal ceremonies include a commissioning, commitment, and prayer. New members get recognized and commissioned. Outside of church, schools ("commencement"), Boy Scouts, service organizations, and fraternities provide other examples. It's a widespread human tradition, sometimes only a forgettable ritual but other times a powerful life passage.

Recognizing and commissioning our parishioners for the work they do during the week is a powerful message that their work matters not just to them but to their brothers and sisters and, above all, to God himself. They are called to serve the Lord in and through their work, to be an ambassador of another way of life and work. It is too easy to slip back into an attitude that our work doesn't really matter except maybe for our paycheck and the tithes to enable God's *real* work. But this is bad, unbiblical theology. Our work does matter to God. It is our arena of service and love to God and our neighbors. It is not just about money.

Recognizing and commissioning our parishioners for their workplace discipleship changes *them* first of all. It is a powerful affirmation from the church leadership and the congregation, hard to forget when they go off to work the next day. It is also a powerful message to our younger people looking on as they are thinking about the meaning and direction of their own education and future work. It can be a powerful message to onlookers in the neighborhood or at work who hear about it: "these people worship a God who cares about their work! What an amazing and unusual thing." Finally, it is a powerful message to pastors and church staffs: we are not the only ones doing God's work full-time.

Introducing this kind of commissioning into our church life and worship is not some kind of "magic bullet" or automatic formula for renewal. But it really can have a renewing effect on congregations and their pastors. My suggestion is that maybe one Sunday worship every three months we carve out ten or fifteen minutes during the congregational prayer time to include this commissioning. At Trinitarian Congregational Church I alerted the congregation two weeks in advance (by newsletter and announcements in the service) that we were going to call our health care workers forward and pray for them during the service. Few if any were surprised then when I walked to the front of our platform during our congregational prayer time on an October morning (repeated in our second service that morning) and began:

"This morning we would like to recognize, commission, and pray for the health care givers in our congregation. Would all of you who work in this field in any capacity, and all of you students preparing for such vocations, would you all come up and stand in front of the congregation this morning so we can pray for you? If you are a doctor or nurse, a chiropractor or massage therapist, dentist, dietician, hospital administrator or orderly, pharmaceutical researcher or manager—if you work in any capacity in health care, would you come up here now? In fact, if you are between jobs but health care is what you believe God has called you to do, you come forward also." *[Thirty people came forward; I had no idea it would be so many].*

"I am going to pass around this portable mike and could you just say quickly your name, where you work, and what you do in health care." *[This took a few minutes but it worked well: "I'm Joe Smith, pediatrician at Mass General." "Eleanor Mays, orderly* at Lahey Clinic." "Joanne Adams, CEO of Cancer Research Pharmaceuticals," "Eddie Ibanez, medical student at Harvard," and so on. What an amazing and diverse group. What a team! (Names and companies changed here)]. I continued:

"This morning my friends we want first of all to thank you: thank you for hearing God's call and being willing to serve our Lord in health care. Thank you for studying and preparing for your work in health care. We are so grateful for your service in the footsteps of Jesus Christ. We all want to remember very clearly that our God is a healer. The mission of our Lord was to heal as well as to proclaim the gospel. The Apostles were sent out to heal as well as preach. Throughout the history of the church our greatest missionaries brought medicine and health care as well as the gospel to the ends of the earth. Health care is at the very heart of the way of Jesus Christ. So thank you for being our health care team out there in a needy world.

"Second we want to challenge and encourage you to carry on, to be the hands of Jesus Christ reaching out with a healing touch to those who suffer. We don't want to do our work just like everyone else but to find the redemptive difference Jesus and Scripture can provide. We want to bring some "salt" and "light" to health care today. We want to challenge you to anchor your health care thinking and practice in the values and insights of Jesus and Scripture.

"So this morning I want to ask if you will pledge, to the best of your ability, to deepen your approach to health care in the perspective of Jesus and Scripture. If you will make that pledge would you say "I will"? *[Health care folk: "I will"]*. And those of you in the congregation, would you pledge to pray for our health care team as God brings them to mind, that God would bless, strengthen, protect, and use them in their work? Could you say "We will"? *[Congregation: "We will"]*.

"And third, we want to join together in prayer for you this morning. I'd like to invite our elders and any others who would like to join them to step up to the front here and lay a hand on one of our health care workers as a sign of solidarity as we pray. *[Dozens of people came forward and surrounded our health care team]*. "Our Father, we thank you for each of these your servants. We pray that you will work your healing and caring purposes through their hands, their minds, their skills, and their efforts, wherever they are working on the health care team. Lord, would you give them strength. Would you protect them from danger and harm. Would you provide for them and supply them with the resources they need for their work. Would you keep them from temptation and discouragement? Work through them O God, just as you worked in Jesus Christ our Lord. Help their colleagues and their patients to see Jesus Christ in them each day. Bless these dear servants of yours, our brothers and sisters, for we pray in Jesus' name, Amen."

One interesting follow-up: a week later two African immigrants working as orderlies in a big hospital came up to me after the service very concerned: "Pastor Gill, we couldn't be here last week because we have to work every other weekend and can't attend church on those days. But we don't want to miss the blessing! Could we have the blessing?" I was only too happy to share the challenge with them and get a nearby elder to join me as we laid hands on these two dear brothers and prayed for them.

Three months later I called up all the financial folk: "This morning I want to invite all of our financial workers to come forward and let us pray for you. If you are a CFO, financial advisor, accountant, or treasurer, if you work at a bank or insurance company, if you are a tax preparer or bookkeeper for a home business—if you work in any way managing money or are studying for one of these professions please come forward. In fact, if you believe this work arena is where God has called you but you are between jobs, you come forward also."

After brief introductions I continued: "First of all, this morning we want to thank you for going into this profession, for studying and learning, for all your hard work in an industry that has been so full of temptation and scandal as well as providing people with such essential service and help. Our Lord had more to say about money, property, and wealth than heaven and hell or most other subjects. He really cared about your field. So this morning we want, secondly, to challenge you to deepen your knowledge and understanding of what Jesus and Scripture have to say about money, debt, loans, and all those related subjects. If you will pledge to do this . . ."

Three months later, again, I called up all the engineers, techies, and builders. "This morning I want to invite all of our engineers and techies and builders to come forward and let us pray for you. If you are in any kind of engineering or technology or work for such a company, if you are an architect, a contractor or builder, if you work in the building trades or are a handyman, if you are an apprentice or hope to get work in this arena, please come forward."

After brief introductions I continued "First of all, this morning we want to thank you for going into this field of work, for all of your study and your hard work. You know the Bible doesn't begin by saying 'In the beginning God preached a sermon!' No, in the beginning God designed and built a beautiful, amazing world. And that's what you do! It is God's work to design, build, and support useful and beautiful things. So thank you for going into this field. There is a lot of corruption, temptation, and challenge— as well as promise and opportunity— in your work area and we are so glad we have you out there to represent the Lord and his way of building something. So this morning in addition to thanking you for going into your line of work we want to challenge you to make a real effort to deepen your understanding of how to honor God and follow Jesus and Scripture in your work so you will be true salt and light. If you are willing to pledge to work on this will you say "I will"?

Three months later I called up all the teachers. You can easily imagine how to affirm teachers (college professors, public and private school teachers, administrators, coaches, home-schoolers, online educators, the whole team!) in light of Jesus' role as a teacher.

I finished off my one-year interim term and the new pastor arrived. I am not sure whether he continued what I started (interim pastors must not meddle!). Had I continued I certainly would have had all the arts folk (painters, singers, poets, thespians, dancers, et al) come forward. I would have loved to call forward the food service folk (grocery store employees, farmers, chefs, waiters, et al). Infant and child care givers and parents could easily have their day (recognizing the true labor of bringing children into the world and caring for them!). Whenever I did these commissionings I tried to be inclusive so students and apprentices and the out-of-work were part of it. It might be good to invite all those who are unemployed or underemployed to come forward for special prayer. I am encouraged to hear that some pastors are doing this kind of thing. My son-in-law, Solano Community Church Pastor Andrew Hoffman, has been exemplary. My friend Pastor Jason McConnell has taken it a step further and brought in members of the local fire and police departments in his small town for prayer and commissioning! It is an opportunity missed by most pastors and churches.

An important follow-up or accompaniment to these vocational commissionings would be the formation (under lay leadership!) of monthly or quarterly "affinity-groups" for these worker groups (health care, engineering/technology, business, child care, etc.)—to provide fellowship, encouragement, support, and learning opportunities related to workplace discipleship. Katherine Leary Alsdorf has had great success creating groups like this at Tim Keller's Redeemer Presbyterian in New York City and I know there are other examples.

PASTORAL STRESS

I guess it is inevitable that a kind of "job creep" happens. I could not long remain "just a preacher." Of course, I worked with a wonderful TCC worship and music team, led by Adam Kurihara, Kristin Neprud and others, on our worship planning and preparation, not least for special Advent and Lenten seasons. I attended elders' meetings every month and often met with chairman Dawson Milne, grappling with various challenges. The youth minister, a very gifted young man, had started (just before I arrived) an independent Sunday evening service appealing to the younger generation (and many of their parents) but his attitude toward the church leadership and Sunday morning services was negative and divisive. Under his leadership the booming youth group never attended the morning services and it seemed to many like he was creating a rival church on site. He was not receptive to my or other's counsel and a couple of his defenders on the elder board were having a divisive, negative impact. When TCC finally called a new pastor (after my interim year), the new pastor had to insist that this youth minister be gone before he would come on board.

Meanwhile, the veteran associate pastor was aggrieved that he had not been appointed interim instead of me—and he insisted that he wanted to be a candidate for the next senior pastor position. That desire met with what might have been a too-rough response from the search committee—which valued his pastoral care work but didn't see the preaching and leadership gifts they were looking for. I wished that they had given him a fuller, more respectful interview to avoid his feelings of rejection and disrespect. I tried hard to honor him and always gave him a central place in our services, welcoming people, leading in the pastoral prayers, doing announcements and occasionally preaching a sermon. But it was never enough to heal his wounds. It bothered me that in his congregational prayers he never prayed for me just before I went up to deliver the sermon. He basically ignored me. My problem was not that I needed more affirmation but I needed prayer and our visitors needed to know who this guy was standing up to preach (yours truly).

One Sunday when the place was packed, I introduced myself as the Interim Pastor and said "You may be wondering what an 'Interim Pastor' is? For the congregation, I am like your boyfriend until you find your new husband." (Big laughter). The associate pastor left in the spring so for my final few months I persuaded my Gordon-Conwell faculty colleagues, Tom and Donna Petter, to come to TCC as part-time pastoral associates. They were spectacular. After I finished my interim year, the Petters stayed on the staff part-time. When the new senior pastor suddenly left for another church after just three or four years, Trinitarian (wisely!) called Tom Petter to be its senior pastor.

When I began at TCC in September 2011, I was feeling as fit and healthy as any time since 1999 when I was in Sweden. But the stress and pressure of TCC, added to my full-time job at Gordon-Conwell thirty miles away, took a big toll on my health. Too busy to work out as much, too many dinner meetings, not enough sleep, and I suffered the first of three TIA mini-strokes in September 2012, just a week after I finished my run at TCC. One evening as I began my class, I found I couldn't speak without slurring my speech. A nurse in my class told me she thought I might be having a stroke—but I insisted on staying and managed to show a video I had planned (Ellul on technology). Thirty minutes later I was okay and finished the three-hour class. The nurse handed me a list of several warning signs she observed as I led the class. When I got home and showed the list to my wife she ordered me into our car and drove me to the hospital where I was admitted and checked out over two or three days and released. Thankfully, there were no lingering effects from this TIA mini-stroke but it was definitely a lesson to me to stop over-committing no matter how much I loved some work opportunity. I suffered another two TIA's in 2014 so, clearly, I didn't learn the lesson!

ADULT EDUCATION INITIATIVES IN BERKELEY, BURLINGAME, AND EVANSTON

One of my major interests has always been to help my churches strengthen their university and adult education programs. During my years at Pasadena Covenant (1975–77) and Berkeley Covenant (1980–90) I was actively involved in Christian education programs, especially for adults. At Berkeley Covenant I also preached fairly frequently and served terms on the board of elders and as men's ministry leader. During one year of BCC's interim phase without a pastor, my wife Lucia and I co-led the year-long confirmation course for our adolescent youth. Responding to requests, we then organized and led a popular adult class we called "Re-Confirmation."

First Pres Berkeley really became my model. They had something like ten adult ed groups with anywhere from twenty to ninety regular attendees. Some were age-related like the "Schooner Club" for retirees, "Mariners" for the next age group, and "On Belay," mostly for younger couples. Other classes were focused strictly on Bible study ("Sunday Morning Study"). These groups functioned a lot like mini-churches, often with singing, sharing, and prayer. They took their own offerings to support class activities and sometimes missionary projects. Several had annual retreats. All were led by groups of lay leaders, not church staff. I probably guest-taught in all of these groups during the 1980s and was retreat speaker for some. They were strongly supported and encouraged by Senior Pastor Earl Palmer and his staff.

During my final few months at New College Berkeley (early 1990) I agreed to get off the road on Sunday and go to Burlingame Presbyterian Church every week to revitalize their adult education program which was limping along with a handful of attendees. Pastor Paul Watermulder was initially thinking I would do this just by teaching a class during each of the two worship hours. I did plenty of teaching but from the start recruited a dozen of the participants and got them enthused about renewing their whole program following the First Pres Berkeley model. One Sunday I got that volunteer leadership group to skip out on Burlingame worship and attend Berkeley Pres. Each of them was to visit a different adult ed group and interview someone they sat by, asking them, "Tell me about this class and why you attend it?" Then I raced back from where I had been at Burlingame in the morning and Lucia and I hosted this research group for Sunday lunch and a sharing and discussion of their experience at First Pres. They were all on fire and over the next months remodeled Burlingame's adult ed program to be like Berkeley's. It was now about lay ownership and initiative, about fellowship as well as learning. It boomed. Adult ed participation doubled or tripled almost overnight.

Just a few years later in 1997, when we joined First Presbyterian Church of Evanston, we inquired during the New Members Class what FPCE had going on in adult education. "Nothing much at the moment," Associate Pastor Jamie Crook told us. First Pres Evanston had a history of some excellent adult ed classes and was the favorite church of Northwestern University's InterVarsity folk. But we responded to Jamie: "Would it be ok if we tried to create something?" "Yes, more power to you," was Jamie's answer—and Senior Pastor David Handley very quickly got behind our initiative. So Lucia and I, with two other couples from that New Members class, designed a new class on the First Pres Berkeley model.

Lucia came up with our name "Open Harbor"—a safe and welcoming gathering at FPCE near the shores of Lake Michigan. The class boomed and soon had forty regular attendees, great teaching and discussion, mutual care and fellowship, good coffee, and a fun class newsletter launched by Lucia. However, at the end of year one, our co-founders Doug Sterne and Terry Neifing moved back to California—and the other couple, Burt and Suzy Petkus, wanted to lead the class in a different style and direction. We set them free to do so, and I organized a second adult ed class called "Sunday Morning Seminary" with North Park professors Don Wagner and Sonia Bodi, Witt Brisky, and Garrett-Evangelical Seminary professor Kenneth Vaux. This class (meeting during the other worship hour, not competing with Open Harbor) soon also had thirty or forty regular attendees.

Berkeley, Burlingame, Evanston: three experiences that convinced me church-based adult ed need not be dead. Of course, there are many other successful examples on other models. Let's never give up. Back in Berkeley, from 2001 to 2006, I regularly taught six-week Sunday morning courses in January and February for First Pres's "Winter Institute" when they suspended regular adult ed courses to offer a menu of electives. I led popular Winter Institute courses on my favorite topics including "The Decalogue," "The Beatitudes," and "Romans 12–13." A big favorite was on "Faith-Jazz"—showing how the basics of jazz—such as knowing your instrument, knowing the standards, improvisation, playing in an ensemble and rotating the lead, expressing the gamut of human emotion and experience—had clear resonance with basic themes in discipleship. The forty or fifty attendees studied the Scriptures, listened to and watched jazz clips, and even moved the chairs and danced a few steps together as part of what may have been my all-time favorite adult ed course! First Pres Pastor Tim Shaw and I experimented twice with mid-week, downtown San Francisco financial district "City Institute" classes for our business members and friends.

Most of my energy over the decades has gone into universities, seminaries, and parachurch educational organizations like the Crucible Study Center, New College Berkeley, Gordon-Conwell Seminary, Fuller Seminary, Regent College, and InterVarsity Christian Fellowship. But I have always believed that the local church should be the primary educator of the people of God. Everything that can be done in the context of a local church, should be done there. I simply do not accept the pessimism about adult education. Every church could and should create the best adult ed program they can. The fight against biblical illiteracy and for truly Christian minds must go on. And while church staff leadership plays a critical role, I think programs often fail if they remain top-down and staff-controlled in content and culture. Set the people free to use their gifts and amazing things can happen. This isn't just my theory, it is my repeated experience.

"IF I WAS YOUR PASTOR"

I have sometimes joked that someday I might write a book called "If I Was Your Pastor," giving all my ideas about how to run a healthy church. "I'm sure that will be a big seller," respond my doubtful colleagues! So instead of that unwritten non-seller, I close this chapter, for what it's worth, with a few reflections on church that come from my experiences. The local church is essential and even central to the Christian life. Christianity is a "team sport," not a solo or individual one, if I may use that metaphor. The primary purpose of the church is to gather together to praise and glorify God. Worship is at the top of our agenda—though pastoral care, education, spiritual growth, evangelism, and community service are all essential as well. The church gathered and the church scattered out into the world are the two realities of the church's existence. Preparation for workplace discipleship must be high on the agenda in all of this. Let's look at several key components in a healthy gathered church.

Call to Worship.

I loved it when Lucia and I worshipped at Oakdale Covenant Church from 1992 to1996 and the service always began promptly at 11:00 (you couldn't get a seat if you were later!) with the mass choir singing majestically and slowly "The Lord is in his holy temple! Let all the earth be silent, be silent before him"—and then out of the silence, the Hammond B-3 started cooking and we stood and rocked the house, singing our hearts out, "We've come to praise the Lord, we've come to magnify his name." Everyone knew without a doubt from this opening why we were gathered. I love it when a worship leader warmly welcomes us into the presence of the Lord, offers a prayer of welcome to our Lord, and expresses heartfelt praise to him. I can't stand "horizontal worship" which ignores the presence of the Lord. Could I also lobby for including children and whole families in our worship services? Kids can learn to be quiet, pay attention, come forward for children's lessons, and sing along with the whole congregation.

Music, Singing, & Style.

When we gather together, we should sing our hearts out in praise to God. We should not segregate our congregations by musical tastes but rather include both the great hymns of the past and the best (and most appropriate) of contemporary Christian music, ranging as wide as the body of Christ for Gospel music, classical, country and other genres. Church is a gathering of the whole people of God—we need to learn to appreciate the diversity of the sounds and voices. We should learn to unite, not separate, in the gathered church. We should choose music with singable tunes, and not use material better suited to performance settings. Our song lyrics should focus on God more than "me"—and more on "we" than "I." We need music and worship leaders who do not perform but lead the congregation. It takes a gift and an attitude. As for the style and format of our worship, we are best when we demonstrate a range from formal to informal, liturgical to spontaneous. As pastor, I might wear a robe one Sunday a month, a suit another time, and casual attire, yet another. We might have a more detailed liturgy one Sunday, more relaxed another. Why? To honor the grand tradition of the church and model and teach inclusion.

Scripture.

We should read something from both the Old and Testaments at every worship service and call these "Lessons" not "texts." Reading, all by itself, already delivers lessons from God's Word—it doesn't just serve up pretexts for a sermon. I love it when we respond to the Scripture lessons with "This is the Word of the Lord. Thanks be to God." Do you think we could have layfolk, including kids, read our lessons? Does that take an MDiv and professional title?

Prayers: Praise, Thanksgiving, Confession, Intercession.

I am anguished when we have services without a pastoral prayer or (better termed) the "prayers of the people." Can't we make sure we begin by praising and thanking God for coming into our midst and for a long list of his blessings? Why do we take God for granted? Do we recognize and welcome visitors into our homes? How about when God enters the house? We also need regular confession and apology—humbly reminding ourselves and acknowledging together before God that we are imperfect. Surely we need to confess our (individual and collective) sins and failures before our righteous, forgiving, gracious God. Not to confess together not only takes God's holiness and forgiveness for granted, it contributes to individual lives devoid of confession and repentance. Following our confession with words of assurance also reinforces a true and holistic theology. Then our "prayers of the people" ask God's help for the hurting and challenged in our congregation, neighborhood, and city. More broadly and less selfishly, we pray for God's help in the face of poverty, homelessness, violence, warfare, addiction, family breakdown, weather disaster, political challenge, international conflict, and so on. God is in his temple, in our midst. Doesn't it make sense to ask for his help and blessing while we are gathered together?

Sermons.

Pastoral training in seminary focuses a lot on preaching (though sometimes too narrow, formal, procedural, and, may I say, white) and on theological doctrines and biblical interpretation. I believe good preaching is grounded in the preacher's (1) intense love for and immersion in Scripture as God's Word, and (2) genuine love for and presence among the people, with practical insight for daily discipleship in the world. The preacher can be ugly and have a terrible voice but if he or she loves God and Scripture and loves the people, we are likely to hear powerful sermons. That takes hours of study of Scripture—and hours of presence in the lives of the people. Congregations need to be given lessons from God's Word they can still remember by the time they get to the parking lot—and when they begin their work the next morning.

Remembering & Offering.

The early church shared in communion, the Lord's Supper, pretty much every week, and I wish we could still do likewise. When we do celebrate the Lord's Supper I wish we could do it in a rich and thoughtful way, not just go through the motions. Church members could also prepare and bring forward the bread and wine we use. Sweet, singable, worship music could be sung during communion. And after remembering with gratitude the sacrifice of Christ, we should present our own sacrificial offerings, not just financial but, when appropriate, in making commitments to service of one kind or another. There is also a place for musical and other artistic offerings in praise of God.

Commissioning, Charge, & Benediction.

In addition to the kind of commissioning of workers, described earlier, and of other servants of Christ, worship services should be brought to a conclusion with a charge ("let's go out of this place changed in the following way") and a benediction ("go out with the blessing and strength of the Father, Son, and Holy Spirit"). Attendance at church should not be a matter of passive, detached observation but a participatory, mobilizing experience.

Beyond Worship in the Sanctuary.

I love how many churches today urge their people into small group, mostly home-based, fellowships—but a strong Christian education program is still important and workable for all ages as I tried to illustrate above. Paul wrote in Romans 12 that we are to "transformed by the renewing of our mind"—not just by the "refreshing of our spirit" or even by "the love of the saints." Our approach to pastoral care and visitation is so essential. I learned so much about that, especially during my interim pastorates. I have also loved the Stephen Ministry, mobilizing lay friendship and counseling that has helped so many. Our churches need to mobilize everyone to be evangelistically loving, wise, and courageous. That is central to the Great Commission for all disciples. Our world, our neighbors, need to hear the Good News. Our presence and activism socially and economically must bring a redemptive and healing presence in our neighborhoods, schools, and workplaces. We are not just called to a holy huddle on church turf.

Yes, it's a big agenda, but I have been around long enough, seen enough, and tried enough to believe our churches can do a lot better. I don't mean just to criticize and lament—a lot of great things are happening in our churches that God is blessing.

My way of doing church is certainly not the only way! My heart is grateful for the glass half-full, not just concerned about the half-empty. Whenever I am tempted to be depressed or too critical, I remind myself that God is gracious in accepting me in my mediocrity—and I should extend the same grace to others and to my church!

SEMINARY AND BIBLE SCHOOL EDUCATION

The weaknesses of our churches have many roots. Our culture presents unprecedented challenges and opposition to the Christian way for congregations as well as individuals. It is all too easy to fall uncritically into (or even invite) the world's thinking, style, and values in our church and individual lives. But we can't blame everything on the world. We have to look at the theological seminaries and Bible Schools we expect to train our pastors. They are pretty much all hugely stressed by finances, bureaucracy, and rapid educational technological changes. But—no excuses—they also must take responsibility for the pastors they are turning out. If, for example, our seminary faculties know or care little or nothing about the rich biblical theology of work—the domain where most of the Christian life takes place—how can we expect our pastors to think and minister any differently? It is just not enough to pay it lip service, it needs to come out of deep conviction and a robust biblical theology.

If pastors don't do better jobs in pastoral staff and financial management, Christian education programing, and gathered church worship—the buck stops where and how they were trained (denominational leadership carries major responsibility also). Looking around us, if all the self-educated, self-credentialled, unaccountable, charismatic-personality, local church planters and leaders continue to be oblivious to our seminaries, it is time for seminaries to reach out to them with programs, study opportunities, and loving community to help them grow. Why are seminary enrollments declining? Lots of reasons but for sure they need new efforts, new strategies, new delivery-methods, to reach out and help all those who could use their resources.

OK, that's it. "If I was Your Pastor" is over and I retreat to my marginal life chair (in prayer and hope). I will always be grateful, and forever changed, by the privilege of serving as a pastor and Christian education leader during my career. And rather than thinking about "If I Was Your Pastor"—I end by thinking about "Since I Am Not Your Pastor." Since I am not, and don't want to be, I accept my role to get busy supporting as well as I can the pastors and church leaders God has called into position at my home church.

19

North Park & Chicago (1992–2001)

THE EVANGELICAL COVENANT CHURCH (ECC) had become my home denomination starting with Pasadena Covenant, then Berkeley Covenant, and then my gig at University Covenant in Davis. I participated in some of the annual Midwinter Ministers' Conferences and one big annual ECC denominational convention. I am proud to have committed the denomination to a million dollar investment in social concerns and programs at one of those annual meetings. The denominational leaders had put together a proposed $19 million campaign to strengthen our churches, missions, and the denominational seminary and college, North Park. Conversing on the sidelines with other socially-concerned Covenanters at the annual meeting, who would be voting on this big proposal, we all agreed: we shouldn't just invest in ourselves. I made a motion from the floor to add $1 million for social concerns, raising the campaign target to $20 million. The amendment passed!

    I am comfortable with the "Covenant Affirmations" about the Bible, Jesus Christ, and basic, historic Christian doctrines and practices. I love the fact that the three big Covenant national churches are in Sweden (the mother church), the USA, and the Congo (where early Covenant missionaries succeeded in planting what became a huge, indigenously-led church). I appreciate the ways predominantly African-American, Hispanic, and Korean Covenant churches have developed over the years. Good friends of mine, theologian Robert K. Johnston and Bonhoeffer-expert Burton Nelson, were on the faculty of North Park College and Seminary and had been visiting professors at New College Berkeley in the 1980s. New Testament professor Klyne Snodgrass had been an academic reviewer approving publication of my book *Peter the Rock*. I raised my family at Berkeley Covenant Church during the 1980s.[1] My paternal

---

    1. The Evangelical Covenant Church was first known as the "Swedish Mission Covenant"—a late 19th century pietist renewal movement in the Swedish state Lutheran Church brought to America by immigrants in the 1880s, with major settlements in Chicago (which became denominational

grandmother (Katie Hallgren) was from a Swedish Baptist family, a denomination (like the Evangelical Free Church), with much in common with the Covenanters.

In 1991, during my first year at University Covenant, I was approached by Rob Johnston and then David Horner, President of North Park College, asking if I might be interested in teaching undergraduates at North Park. They had received a substantial bequest to endow a new position, the Carl I. Lindberg Chair in Applied Ethics. This position would include leading an "ethics-across-the-curriculum" program, working with all faculty at the college. "How did I feel about moving to Chicago and teaching undergraduates?"

It didn't take me long to accept the invitation to be a candidate. I went through the process with the search committee, and was appointed to begin my service in Fall 1992. Our kids were both off at college and independent. When Lucia told her boss that she would be following me and leaving Oakland, she was immediately offered a great job at Citibank in Chicago. We have always loved Oakland, Berkeley, and the San Francisco Bay Area but living in Chicago was very attractive. Most Christian colleges and seminaries abandoned the cities and moved out to suburban or rural areas—where city-boy Gill would have been miserable. North Park, by contrast, was rooted in the city with a fine little campus three miles west of Lake Michigan, three miles north of Wrigley Field, and six miles away from the downtown "Loop." Lucia's new Citibank position would be nine miles west of our house out near O'Hare airport.

We rented out our Oakland home and began paying our long-time next-door neighbors, Ken and Jo Ellis, $100 a month to collect and deposit the rent and keep an eye on the place. We kept our rent the same for the next nine years, which our tenants appreciated (until we told them we were moving back home in 2001—as they always knew would happen some day—and they became aggrieved protestors against their "greedy landlords"). Go figure. Property values in Chicago were about half those in Oakland at the time, so we were able to refinance our Oakland place and buy a small house on St. Louis Avenue, three blocks from campus. We wanted to be close enough to fully participate in campus life, including evening and weekend events. My UCC colleague David Nystrom moved at the same time from Davis to the North Park neighborhood for the same reasons and we were both able to have an impact on the campus culture. Lucia and I loved our little house and neighborhood and our next-door neighbors, the Szurgots and Schillers. I built a twenty-four by twelve-foot redwood deck off the back of our house where we frequently had barbecues and entertained people from North Park and beyond.

Knowing it might be unsettling for our kids (ages twenty and twenty-one) to have their long-time home closed down in Oakland in 1992, I persuaded North Park just to give me the cash equivalent of the lowest of three moving company bids. With that money we rented a big U-Haul van, paid the kids something to be our moving

---

headquarters), Minnesota, and the Midwest. North Park University and Seminary and Swedish Covenant Hospital are in northside Chicago (Foster Avenue and Kedzie).

crew, drove together across the country to Chicago, and set up our furniture in the new house, including rooms they could occupy when they visited. The moving stipend also covered their airfare back to San Diego and Santa Barbara where they were studying. Taking turns driving across the country, we also took turns choosing the music we listened to! We made one detour to visit the house in Omaha where I had lived from birth to age three.

LIFE IN CHICAGOLAND

The weather in Chicago was a new and challenging experience. For six months each year it was often very cold and my breath sometimes froze into little icicles on my mustache when I walked to campus, slipping and sliding on the snow and ice. Lots of snow shoveling on our sidewalk and steps and in the alley behind our garage. The first winter, a water pipe froze and broke. Not until Mother's Day in May was it ever safe to plant flowers outside—and a four-month period of alternating high humidity and nice summer weather began. September and October brought two months of spectacular weather and fabulous fall colors. We actually loved the thunder and lightning and periodic rain storms all summer, after worrisome droughts so often in our California lives.

Regarding this weather, I "fought it" and sometimes grumbled the first year but then learned to "dance with it"—in other words, every nice day we would get outside for a good walk or a bike ride along Lake Michigan or in the nearby forest preserves. We never took a nice day for granted as we did in California. In the summer, on Saturdays, we often rode along the Lake Michigan waterfront bike path from Foster Avenue to Navy Pier, stopping at Oak Street Beach to peel down to our swimming suits for a dip in the lake. I spent the first year pitying myself that golf was only possible during the warm (and mosquito-ridden) half of the year and the green fees were double what I paid at Oakland's Lake Chabot Golf Course. Then I grew up and played weekly during the unfrozen half year, usually with my colleagues Scot McKnight and Jim Nelson.

Lucia and I bought one of those big entertainment coupon books offering two-for-one dinners at hundreds of restaurants and had great times at all manner of ethnic and other Chicago eateries. We solved our coffee needs by regularly mail ordering Peet's French Roast from Berkeley. When a Peet's store finally came to northside Chicago, we wondered if they decided on that location based on the heavy mail order business there!

In 1990, at the end of my often-frantic life at New College Berkeley, I literally changed the dial on my car radio from KRQR (classic rock) to KJAZ (real jazz). Now in Chicago the equivalent was WDCB-jazz as the usual sound track to our lives. My former NCB student and lifetime friend John Ephland worked as a writer and reviewer at Chicago's *Downbeat,* America's premier jazz magazine. I often visited John and his wife Donna, a dancer and dance instructor who had also been an NCB student

(I officiated at their wedding in Berkeley) and was named godfather of their son Sam. John kept me well-supplied with CDs and introduced us to the Jazz Showcase and the Green Mill where we heard all the greats along with many up-and-coming locals: Ray Brown, Bennie Green, Karrin Alison, Eliane Elias, James Moody, Dorothy Donegan, Kurt Elling, Patricia Barber, Marian McPartland, Dave Brubeck, Johnny Frigo, Paul Wertigo . . . an endless list of awesome musicians were part of our life. We loved the three-day annual Ravinia Jazz Festival where greats like Oscar Peterson, Joe Williams, Stefane Grappelli, Marcus Roberts, and other legends played. Chicago was jazz heaven for us. We also took more ballroom dance lessons and loved going out to big band dances as often as we could.

Jazz was our main music but we also had season tickets to the Lyric Opera for a few years and also went to Chicago's many great blues clubs such as Kingston Mines. We followed sensational local blues guitarist Michael Coleman to many of his performances. I have never heard better. We heard lots of great Gospel music, above all at Oakdale Covenant, our home church. We attended plays and visited the Art Institute of Chicago. Chicago is full of great restaurants. One of our favorites was Brasserie Jo. We dined there on a Sunday when France won the World Cup (broadcast on big television screens in the restaurant that day) and loved the party which broke out, with chef Jean Joho leading his crew in spraying champagne all over the place (we drove home soaked!).

From our Chicago base we drove off to explore other midwestern destinations. For our 25th anniversary just after we arrived in Chicago, we drove up to Montreal and Quebec City for a wonderful immersion in Quebecois French.[2] Over time we were able to visit places like Kansas City, Detroit, Minneapolis-St. Paul, Milwaukee, Madison, Dubuque, Champaign-Urbana, South Bend, and Springfield. We really loved our Chicago life and I have often said that if I couldn't live in Oakland/Berkeley (or Bordeaux or Munich), I would choose Chicago (over Boston, and way over Los Angeles). It's the people and culture (blue collar, diverse, the rich music, arts, education, sports, and church scene) first of all, but the location (closer to Europe and the Eastern USA), natural beauty, and wild climate are also drawing cards.

Enrolled in the first class I taught at North Park was Jenny Holmgren, daughter of the Green Bay Packers head coach Mike Holmgren. Mike and Kathy Holmgren had a long association with North Park and the Covenant Church. Mike had been the talented quarterback coach of the 49ers during the Joe Montana and Steve Young era. One Sunday that fall of 1992 I was guest preaching at North Park Covenant Church and saw the Holmgrens all sitting in the congregation. This was the beginning of a lifetime friendship which included tickets to their box at Lambeau Field in Green Bay to watch the Packers destroy my 49ers in a playoff game. Our pregame instructions were to not wear any 49er colors and not root out loud for the 49ers. The Holmgren girls screamed but we weren't even tempted to do so by the 49ers' poor showing! I

---

2. In 1997 we celebrated our 30th anniversary overnight at Chicago's famous Drake Hotel.

eventually got to play golf with Mike in the Santa Cruz area and he provided a generous cover blurb in 2000 for my book *Becoming Good*. Aside from the 49ers, my football loyalty has gone to Mike's teams, the Packers and Seahawks.

CARL I. LINDBERG PROFESSOR OF APPLIED ETHICS

My inaugural address when I was installed as Lindberg Professor was "Feasting On the Fruit of the Ethics Tree." If ethics is about discerning and doing what is good and right, Plan A (in Genesis) was simply to listen for God's voice (the God of all creation not just some tribal or religious god) declaring "this is good" and "this is very good." Plan B was eating from the fruit of the "tree of the knowledge of good and evil," trying to be autonomous, possessing ethical knowledge on our own. The whole history of moral philosophy—and too much moral theology—was a Plan B exercise. Our challenge is to invite Plan A to rule over our Plan B efforts (which, nevertheless, hold some promise; after all God had created that tree!). I was off and running.

With a small grant I was able to run a couple "ethics-across-the-curriculum" faculty worships helping maybe twenty of our professors in all different subject areas to integrate an ethics and values emphasis into their courses. With Professor of Nursing Janet Nelson Wray, I designed and led a course on "Ethics in Health Care" every year for our nursing and pre-med students. Janet was a fabulous co-teacher and colleague. I organized a few interdisciplinary, integrative conferences similar to what I did for NCB in the 1980s. For one on health care, I got as plenary speakers the dean of medical ethicists Dr. Edmund Pellegrino to come from Georgetown and ABC-TV's (and Harvard's) medical and public health expert Dr. Timothy Johnson (who was also a North Park seminary alum). I was primarily based in the philosophy department and taught regular introductory and advanced seminar courses in Ancient and Medieval Philosophy, the Philosophy of Science and Technology, Aesthetics and the Philosophy of Beauty, and Business Ethics (annually with the business department).

I also taught a basic introduction to Christian Ethics course for the Religion department every year, always with big enrollments. This enabled me to keep working on what I thought was a better, more integrally- and organically-biblical approach that eventually I published as two-volume introduction, *Becoming Good: Building Moral Character* and *Doing Right: Practicing Ethical Principles*.[3] My view of the standard or typical approach to Christian ethics (as evidenced in the books, articles, and lectures I had been hearing for years) was that it looked more like the moral philosophy of the European Enlightenment (Kant, Mill, Locke, et al) than the way the Bible itself raised and address matters of good and evil, right and wrong. The applications to specific topics and cases looked to me more like those of the subcultures of the authors than

---

3. David W. Gill, *Becoming Good: Building Moral Character* (Downers Grove, Illinois: InterVarsity, 2000) and *Doing Right: Practicing Ethical Principles* (Downers Grove, Illinois: InterVarsity, 2004).

the "culture" of the kingdom of God presented in Scripture. My quest was for an organically biblical ethics not just in terms of content but its shape and method.

During all my years at New College Berkeley—and now at NPU—I had students write up a description of an ethical dilemma, case, or topic that they personally had confronted or were intensely challenged by. I gathered these cases into a class casebook which we worked our way through in discussions over the course of the academic term. As part of their final take-home exam, students wrote up analyses of their own case and one other they chose from the class casebook. Most other textbooks and courses cherry-picked dramatic and well-known ethics cases which enabled the professor to illustrate his or her point—but which students were unlikely to face in their own lives. Life is not like that. Work is not like that. The reality is sometimes mundane, sometimes exceptional, often grey and imperfect. Learning to cope with that in a biblically-shaped way was my objective.

At NCB and now NPU, I structured my Christian ethics course around Paul's major statement on ethics and discipleship in Romans 12–13. I have not (yet) written a book about Romans 12–13 though I have sketched one out which has the working title "Ethics and Values from Another World, for This World." As Paul put it, Christians are to be not conformed to this world (age, culture) (12:1–2) but rather to the world to come, living "as in the day" not like the "night" around us (13:11–14 which closes the ethics section). The coming (yet already present) kingdom of God is where the will of God, which is "good, and well-pleasing, and perfect/complete" (12:2) is to be found. It is an "eschatological" ethics, leaning toward God's promised future and empowered by the Holy Spirit as the pledge of the future inheritance. And this points us directly to Jesus, who lived as the "Bright and Morning Star," the teacher and exemplar of the will of God and the age to come (13:11–14, "Put on the Lord Jesus Christ"). The teaching of Jesus (Romans 12:9–21) and the Law/Decalogue (13:8–10; fulfilled as love) provide the shape and content of our ethics. Disciples pursue the good with the essential help of the church, the body of Christ (12:3–8), and with awareness and appreciation of God's work through legitimate governing authorities (13:1–7). That is the grand plan of a Christian ethics, organically shaped by Scripture itself. Breath-taking, inspiring, "salt of the earth" and "light of the world" stuff!

Paul and Jesus both drove me to a deeper study of the Law as epitomized and summarized in the double commandment to love God and our neighbor. Inspired by both Jesus and Paul I began teaching and writing about the Decalogue as "ten ways to love God, ten ways to love our neighbors, ten ways of both freedom and justice/righteousness." Jesus, Paul, and the Decalogue all insisted that ethics is a community exercise, not an individualistic one (in the tradition of Modernity and most Postmodern thinking). All biblical ethical thinking also establishes boundaries ("Thou shalt not") and mandates ("Thou shalt"). It is positive, not just negative. The Law is not the enemy of the Gospel but its companion. It is the "form of the Gospel" (dead and deadly if it stands only as a negative) and the Gospel is the "content of the Law" as Karl Barth eloquently stated. While biblical ethics is primarily focused on guiding the life of the community of faith, its values and guidelines still often find resonance even outside that community because all people bear the image of God and have the law "written on their hearts, with their conscience bearing witness" (Romans 1–2).

Meanwhile, I was awakened to the importance and even the priority of the formation of character and community. The principles cannot be followed or practiced by agents and communities that are not "born again" and which have not developed and matured with the virtues, habits, and capabilities essential to enacting those principles. I was deeply influenced in this direction by the philosopher Alasdair MacIntyre (*After Virtue* and *Three Rival Versions of Moral Enquiry*) and by moral theologians Stanley Hauerwas and Peter Kreeft. Even more profoundly, my thinking was inspired by the Sermon on the Mount wherein Jesus first taught the Beatitudes (Matthew 5:1–16; character traits and habits) before moving on to the Gospel fulfillment of the meaning of the Law/Decalogue (5:17–48) and other moral instruction with regard to money, violence and other topics (Matthew 6–7), as well as the famous "Golden Rule" as another summary of the Law and prophets. As with the Decalogue, the primary audience is the faith community, the disciples, but the crowds were themselves paying attention and amazed (Matthew 7:28–29). Paul's ethical teachings made the same move: Spirit-filled individuals and communities characterized by faith, hope, and love are the essential foundation for God honoring ethical behavior and practice. I drank deeply not just from Scripture but from the classic insights of Augustine, Aquinas, Luther, Calvin, Wesley, and the Anabaptist/Free Church tradition. I learned a lot from classical and contemporary Jewish scholarship—and from the history of actual moral practice, not just the ideas of the theorists. With this discovery of the importance and priority of virtue ethics I temporarily set aside my work on *Doing Right* to write what became my book, *Becoming Good: Building Moral Character*.

After just a couple years, the North Park president decided we should convert from the academic quarter system to the semester system. That had been a bad move back at New College Berkeley and, in my view, it was no better at North Park. But in our philosophy department we revamped our freshman level menu to consist of four half-semester courses in Reality (metaphysics and ontology), Truth (epistemology), Goodness (ethics), and Beauty (aesthetics). We typically had forty to sixty students in these courses, not just our philosophy majors but students from across the campus fulfilling one of their breadth requirements. My colleagues Steve Bouma-Prediger, Greg Clark, and I believed that senior professors should teach these intro courses, not just farm them out to our adjunct faculty. I know our students appreciated that.

All of this undergraduate teaching (much of it to freshmen) really made me a better teacher. I think I was already a pretty good and very experienced teacher but my previous graduate students always arrived in class highly motivated and respectful. My big classes of freshman at North Park didn't know me from Adam and were usually enrolled just to fulfill requirements. I had to learn how to get their attention and communicate in ways that they would walk out of class having heard and understood something. I did enjoy some truly great students at North Park, including Karl Soderstrom who went on to get a PhD in philosophy and return as a mainstay in today's NPU philosophy department, Ereena Ayot in business, Osmaan Khawaja, a Muslim philosophy major on the way to medical school, Fadil Lee who is today in business and has eyes on political office, Ishmael McGhee who has had a long career in banking, and Maria Bachova who graduated with honors in philosophy and went on to get her MD and become a cancer researcher. There were many more wonderful students. The time came after several years that I tired of teaching Plato and Aristotle in introductory courses but it was a wonderful learning experience while it lasted.

THE SEMINARY NEXT DOOR

I was disappointed not to be able to work more with North Park Seminary, next door to North Park College. They were a bit stand-offish with regard to their college neighbors with their own calendar, chapel services, and community. I did teach two or three courses in Christian Ethics for the seminary but they had declined to convert to the semester system when the college did, creating schedule difficulties for anyone teaching in both programs. You would have thought that the seminary would embrace the college's programs in sacred classical and (later) Gospel music, but no. You would have thought that a seminary needing bigger enrollments would have tried to include David Nystrom, so well-known around the Covenant denomination, especially for his work with youth and college students, and Scot McKnight, our best and most widely published scholar (in New Testament and theology).

I was hired by the college but I hoped I might be able to help the seminary, especially with my connections to InterVarsity chapters around the country, since 1979. When I moved to Chicago, my old friend and fellow Cal alum, Randy Bare was in Madison leading a booming new IVCF Graduate Student Ministry, in process of growing from zero to fifty chapters in just a few years. Randy wanted me to officially join forces with him. I didn't want to get frantically busy traveling around again like in my NCB days but I wanted to help so I proposed and founded a "National Faculty Advisory Council" for the GSM. My old friend Ward Gasque, now Provost of Eastern College, George Marsden (Notre Dame) Young-il Choo (Yale) and several other well-regarded faculty signed on my committee. We met and strategized with GSM staff at an annual retreat. Our academic profile helped give some credibility to the GSM as it interacted with the universities it approached. It was an exciting initiative, just a shame that our Seminary did not see this as a recruiting opportunity.

I don't mean to pick on the seminary—I'm sure lots of great things happened there. But I was really disappointed about what happened in the mid-1990s, when my son-in-law Andrew Hoffman applied to Chicago, Garrett-Evangelical, Trinity Evangelical Divinity, and North Park seminaries. Our daughter Jodie had been accepted in the Master of Music program at Northwestern University (in nearby Evanston) so Chicago was Andrew's target seminary location. Chicago, Garrett, and Trinity immediately accepted Andrew, the first two with generous financial packages. Early on, I visited the NPTS president and told him my son-in-law was applying and he was a "blue chip candidate" for NPTS and the ECC. "Please encourage him, send him a note, something." But Andrew never heard anything from NPTS; they bungled his application. Andrew went on to graduate from Trinity with both the MDiv and an MA in New Testament and become an outstanding church planter and pastor in the Evangelical Free Church. He was able to fulfil his MDiv requirement in Christian Ethics by studying with me at North Park but what a huge loss to our school and denomination. I need to say that North Park Seminary today is a vastly improved place, for which I am deeply grateful.

LIFE ON THE NORTH PARK FACULTY

When I arrived at North Park in 1992, I found a wonderful, welcoming atmosphere on campus, especially in our Division of Humanities led by Sonia Bodi, our chief librarian. Sonia was a real community builder and a great meeting organizer and chair. She hosted an annual Christmas party at her home. Many of us in her division had our offices on the third floor of old Caroline Hall. Our floor was alive with deep and frequent conversation and great fellowship. Victoria Nelson (communications), Cal Katter (theology), Bob Hostetter (communications and theatre), Steve Bouma-Predigar and then Greg Clark (philosophy), Ron Dooley (English), and Nancy Arneson (English) were a wonderful daily joy to be around. I built a better mailbox and coffee set-up in our little supply room on the third floor. In my own office, I built a new set of bookshelves covering all four walls.

One thing that surprised me was that virtually all the faculty cleared out during the summer and headed off to vacation homes to relax (and work on their boats in some cases!). My understanding of my vocation as professor was that, while some vacation was essential and deserved, summers were mainly for research and writing. I sweltered in my office at our AC-free Caroline Hall during July and August, working on my study projects. I was a pipe-smoker since age twenty-three or so (like C.S. Lewis and Karl Barth) and especially enjoyed it while doing hours of reading and writing. Pipe-smoking had been permitted at Cal, SF State, USC, and in my New College Berkeley office. NPU had a no-smoking rule.

Of course, I agreed that non-smokers should not have to suffer from secondhand smoke—and by the 1990s my wife had banned smoke from our house. But the third floor in Caroline Hall was totally vacant during the summer so I reasoned that if I smoked while alone writing during that vacant-building time I would be preserving the intent and spirit, if not the form and letter, of our rule: (a) I would not impose my smoke on anyone else, (b) I would not set a bad example for any young people, and

(c) I would be careful not to risk any fires in my office.[4] Just like jay-walking to rescue a little child wandering in the street was justified, even ethically mandated, smoking in my office seemed justifiable in my summer context. I would study and write with more insight and productivity and less weight gain from nibbling. (Yes, I know your bs-meter is buzzing now).

Each morning I would bring plenty of coffee to my office and then use masking tape to seal off my doors, and turn on a couple big fans in my office windows to evacuate the smoke. It all went well for weeks. Every afternoon I would wave goodbye to Ann-Helen on the first floor, where behind glass walls and doors she ran the Center for Scandinavian Studies. One day, however, Ann-Helen jumped out from her office and demanded: "David, are you smoking up on the third floor?" I replied evasively, "Ann-Helen I believe I have also smelled some smoke up there" and quickly exited the building. How on earth could she have detected anything, I wondered? I continued but avoided Ann-Helen and was more thorough with my masking tape operation. My writing was going so well! But then I got a message from Vice-President Carl Balsam: "David, there have been reports of smoke on your floor of Caroline Hall. Are you aware of this?" Me: "Well, Carl, all I can say is that yes, there has been smoke up here." Carl: "Well David, I am putting you in charge of finding out the source and getting rid of it." I found the source and it all ended.

During my second year at North Park, my philosophy colleague Steve Bouma-Predigar finished his PhD and announced he would be leaving to take a position at Hope College in Michigan, where he was an alum. What a bummer. But Steve was an alum of Hope College. I knew that one day, I didn't know when, I too would leave to go back home to Oakland. So when we carried out our search for Steve's replacement, the deciding factor among our otherwise equally qualified finalist candidates was that Greg Clark was deeply rooted in nearby Evanston, part of the Reba Place Fellowship. Greg came on board and, with another local, Karl Soderstrom, has provided strong and stable leadership and continuity to the philosophy program for decades. Something to think about when hiring!

When I arrived at NP in 1992, Steve Bouma-Predigar invited me to join him and a couple other faculty in an informal research discussion group. It was great but when I shared about this with a couple other faculty they said they wanted to be part of something like this. At my urging, Steve and I formalized a monthly "Faculty Research Group" and invited the whole faculty. Soon we had twenty or thirty regular participants. We scheduled them to present their research projects and get some cross-disciplinary feedback. Soon we had a waiting list of professors wanting their turn. In time, others organized a "Faculty Teaching Group" where they could share pedagogical concerns about grading, educational technology, and other topics.

Like my colleagues, I found our faculty meetings often a bureaucratic and tedious bore. Much of the agenda consisted of presentations of statistics on our enrollment

---

4. Perhaps a besetting sin of ethicists is the capacity to casuistically rationalize behavior.

and salaries. It was deadly. Some of the veteran faculty griped in the meetings and afterward in hallways and offices about salaries and other administrative moves. They sometimes had reason to gripe but a lot of time and effort was wasted on things they could not control. I often said to these aggrieved colleagues: "This is God's way of telling you to concentrate on your research and teaching! Don't let your energy and attention be consumed by these things you cannot change. Focus on your calling as a professor." Many of them had tenure and were totally inactive as scholars and writers. I'm not sure I had much impact but it was an example of my sense of calling as a senior faculty member to try, informally and without administrative portfolio, to build a healthy faculty community. I loved that role. I could go speak frankly to the president and dean. I had nothing at stake in terms of job security or promotion. In fact, when I was asked about tenure in my initial interview, I told the search committee I didn't care about it and didn't really believe in lifetime faculty job security. "The day that you don't want me here at North Park is the day I don't want to stay any longer."

In an earlier chapter I described how during my second year I started a Black Gospel Choir with several of my Black students, led by Vernard Jones, Fadil Lee, Ishmael McGhee, recent alum Louis Hanserd, and brilliant freshman choir director Michelle Thomas. It grew from twenty to forty through the year and finished the year with a sold-out concert on Mother's Day. I won't repeat the story but it was certainly a highlight of my time at North Park.

CONSULTING BEGINS

Another new experience for me was in organizational ethics consulting. Previously, I had always given time, whenever and wherever asked, to advising other schools, churches, or organizations on their ethical and leadership issues. Now, in my "Health Care Ethics" course, Ed Cucci, President of nearby Swedish Covenant Hospital, was a guest panelist. Afterward he gave me a call asking if I would be willing to help his hospital develop a new, comprehensive Code of Ethics. Swedish Covenant Hospital was, like many independent hospitals at the time, needing to resolve big financial stresses by joining in a partnership with a couple other local hospitals. They had several policy statements on matter like euthanasia, abortion, and assisted reproduction but no comprehensive Code of Ethics. They wanted a clear statement of their standards before joining in a partnership with other hospitals that might not share their values and guidelines.

I agreed to this request and thus began my longer-term work as an organizational ethics consultant. I carefully studied Swedish Covenant Hospital's statements of mission, values, policies, and practices. I collected and studied the codes of ethics of several other hospitals, public, Catholic, and otherwise. I formed an Advisory Group to review and critique my work as it developed. I didn't like most of the Codes I studied which were legalistic in tone, mostly negative ("we don't do x or y"), and detached from the core mission and values of the hospital and of health care in general. The new statement I crafted started with mission, went on to core values, and then specified ethical guidelines for key practice areas. Even these guidelines were distinctively crafted to express, first, the positive "goods" to which the hospital was committed, and only then to the boundary lines they would not cross. Here is an illustration, from the section on the terminally ill (three positives, then one boundary, then freedom and discretion):

Section 4.3.5 *Death and Euthanasia.*

- We affirm life as a sacred gift of God and offer our best efforts to heal and preserve the lives of our patients.
- We provide the best palliative measures we can to relieve the pain, discomfort and suffering of our patients.
- We offer spiritual care and counseling to patients and their families and friends to cope with dying and death.
- We do not act in any way intentionally to cause, assist, or accelerate the death of patients.
- Within this policy we respect the freedom and wishes expressed by patients and their families, personally or by means of Advance Directives (including Living Wills and Durable Power of Attorney for Health Care).

President Ed Cucci and hospital leadership loved it. Covenant denomination president Paul Larsen and his staff were totally positive. In 1997 our statement was cited in an Amicus Brief as part of the Supreme Court's Quill Decision.

DISTINGUISHED GOOD PROFESSOR AT JUNIATA COLLEGE (1994–95)

During the late 1980s when I was still at New College Berkeley, I was nominated and chosen to serve a year at Juniata College as J. Omar Good Distinguished Visiting Professor of Evangelical Christianity. I would be the twentieth "Good" professor, following Merold Westfall, Bruce Reichenbach, Richard Mouw, Mark Noll, George Marsden, Ward Gasque and other luminaries. Juniata was a small liberal arts college in Huntingdon, a town about thirty miles due south of Penn State in State College PA. It was funded and operated by the Church of the Brethren, an Anabaptist, pacifist denomination. After World War II, to take advantage of a broader student application pool funded by the G.I. Bill, Juniata had loosened its faith commitment, first for students, then gradually for the faculty. An alumnus of the school, J. Omar Good, had been alarmed at the erosion of Juniata's faith commitment and decided to generously endow an annual visiting professorship to bring a strong evangelical voice to campus each year. The Good Professor would live in a mini-mansion just off campus and would teach just two or three courses in his or her academic specialty, bringing some

Christian perspective to the subject and to the campus. This one-third teaching load left lots of time for writing. Almost a sabbatical.

When I met with the search committee at North Park I informed them about this commitment, which I didn't want to pass up. North Park agreed, so, after just two years in Chicago, Lucia and I were off to Pennsylvania for a year. We rented our Chicago house to three North Park women students and Lucia's Citibank boss agreed to hold her job for her for a year. We had a wonderful year in Pennsylvania, visiting Penn State and exploring Amish country where we lived. We took the train into New York City for a couple memorable visits and drove to Washington DC three different times to visit the White House, the capitol, and the museums. In the Spring we rode our bikes around the Washington Mall and picnicked under the blooming cherry blossoms by the Jefferson memorial.

We got involved with the monthly Juniata College senior and retired faculty group and even hosted them at our "mansion" for a Lucia-special lunch and a mini-concert with Lucia on clarinet and a wonderful pianist in the group. On Thanksgiving Day, with none of our family around, Lucia and I decided to go to the local Senior Center and help serve several dozen community guests who would otherwise have been alone. Suddenly a cry went up from the organizers that they had forgotten to order the pumpkin pies for dessert! Incredibly, Lucia had stowed several pie crusts and cans of pumpkin back in our refrigerator, in anticipation of hosting guests to come. We jumped in the car and raced home where over the next hour Lucia made and baked enough (eight or ten) pies to provide every diner with a piece that day. I have always said that these people must have reminisced for years afterward about the year God sent an angel to their Thanksgiving feast!

I had a great year teaching at Juniata. The faculty's typical attitude was "who do we have to have as Good professor this year?" (Though I can't imagine they thought that about Marsden, Noll, or Mouw!). There was a lot of (mostly unjustified) theological snobbery and cynicism about evangelical religion, even then (before its popular capture by Trumpism). I remember sitting among the robed faculty at an academic convocation and hearing our theologically-unanchored chaplain lead a prayer to some vague "spirit of learning, wind in the trees"—at which point a colleague whispered to me "why do we have to have all this religion and faith stuff?" But I enjoyed my colleagues and students, and the president was very gratified by the faith perspective I brought, including my final baccalaureate address.

During my time at Juniata I guest preached for several Church of the Brethren congregations, including the late J. Omar Good's church in Philadelphia. I joined the Institutional Review Board at the local hospital and helped them develop their policy on the use of patient restraints. A nearby Retirement Village hired me to create a code of ethics, after they learned of my work with Swedish Covenant Hospital. I rough-drafted the manuscript that eventually was published in 2000 as *Becoming Good*. As my term neared the end, Earl and Harriet Kaylor and Clem Rosenberger, leaders of the Good Professorship endowment committee, mused to me how sad they were that the Good Professors came and went, leaving a legacy only in the memory.

I proposed (remember: "What Are You Doing About It?") recruiting and editing a volume of essays from as many of the now-twenty former Good professors as possible. All of my predecessors agreed except one or two. The volume was appropriately entitled *Should God Get Tenure: Essays on Religion and Higher Education*.[5] I wrote the introduction and a chapter "Ethics With and Without God"—interacting with atheist philosopher Kai Nielsen's influential *Ethics Without God* and sociologists like Jacques Ellul and Robert Bellah—who showed that something always served as a "god" at the foundation of morality and ethics, even if it was not a traditional deity. I later returned to Juniata in 1997 to present the book to the Juniata faculty and the Good committee.

BACK TO NPU (1995-99)

At the end of our year in Pennsylvania Lucia and I spent a month in summer 1995 working on our German in Munich, a week in Paris, and another month in Bordeaux working on our French and meeting with the Ellul family and Ellul scholars and friends, still reeling a bit from Ellul's death in 1994. When I returned to North Park in the fall, the Gospel Choir was in the firm hands of someone else. I hit the ground running again with my course teaching and conference organizing. With my efforts to launch a new faculty committee on "Minority Student and Faculty Recruitment and Retention" rejected once again, I signed up to be a member of my beloved colleague Janet Nelson Wray's "Faculty Development Committee."

The Faculty Development Committee had a small budget for Computer and Research grants, to which faculty members could apply. Faster personal computers, in-house networks, email communications, and internet research were on the way to becoming standard, expected tools of the trade. The research grants typically paid the cost of an adjunct prof to free a professor from one course to find time for some project our committee approved. Often the same few faculty members repeatedly applied for the research grants. Then Janet got pregnant and decided to take a leave for the Spring of 1996. She asked me to step in as chair of her committee. That was the beginning of my three-and-a-half—year tenure as chair of Faculty Development. I have sometimes said that it was like having most of the fun side of being dean without all the hard stuff.

The first thing I did was simplify the application forms and process so it was easier to apply and more straightforward for our committee to decide on the computer and research grants. Our committee meetings became more efficient and ended on time. Then I got very proactive in reaching out to several of my colleagues struggling to finish their doctoral dissertations. It was an old story of people getting hired when

---

5. David W. Gill, editor, *Should God Get Tenure: Essays on Religion and Higher Education* (Grand Rapids: Eerdmans, 1997)

they became PhD candidates and then being distracted by teaching and academic tasks, adding stress, and delaying the PhD finish for sometimes years. I got several of these colleagues the grants and spent time encouraging and sometimes coaching them across their PhD finish lines over the next years.

Next, our committee was in charge of an annual Spring Faculty Banquet downtown at the prestigious University Club. This was a gala event with a lovely banquet, but consistently boring (I am telling you how I felt—but also what filled my ears constantly) and expensive with guest speakers (maybe $2000 a pop) on topics like educational "assessment." I changed the approach. Now we invited Mark Noll (from Wheaton), George Marsden (Notre Dame), Susan Gallagher (English prof at Seattle Pacific), and my Ellulian friend Langdon Winner (Rennsalear Polytechnic Institute). I promised them travel expenses plus (only) a $500 honorarium—and our love and appreciation forever. I also guaranteed them a good time while among us—sometimes with a special dinner gathering at my house with a few colleagues in their field. Langdon Winner gave a brilliant, funny presentation on educational technology called "The Automatic Professor Machine." His special, auxiliary interest was to go to a Cubs game and see slugger Sammy Sosa, which we did. The University Club cost a fortune so I took my Faculty Development Committee to have lunches at restaurants near North Park to test the facilities and cuisine for sites for our banquet. With a possible contract for one hundred banquet guests on the line, several of these restaurants gave us a delightful free lunch! Word spread and it wasn't long before many faculty wished they were on our committee.

Finally, our committee was responsible for our annual January faculty retreat up at Lake Geneva. Attendance was poor (60–70%?) and programming was expensive and boring (same old lineup of supposed experts from outside, on "the psychology of undergraduate learning," etc.). The only fun times, waiting for which we tapped our toes, were later after the evening session when half of us walked through the snow into town to the local bar and lounge and had hours of conversation over beverages. Sonia Bodi led those interested in smoking stogies on the walk over from our retreat center. We joked to the bar tender that we were the Wheaton faculty (notorious teetotalers) on a retreat. We completely shifted the programming to focus on our own faculty, with panel discussions on grade inflation, educational technology, maintaining life balance and fitness, finding time for reading, research and writing, and other topics of real interest and concern. We started recruiting more actively and winsomely and soon had more than 90% attendance. Faculty morale was way up. Costs to North Park were way down. I don't remember the administration ever thanking me for my Faculty Development leadership but plenty on the faculty did.

PROVOST?

A friend at First Presbyterian Church of Evanston was Richard Osgood, a consultant working for Arthur Andersen. Dick recommended me as a Subject Matter Expert/

Consultant/Curriculum Writer for a well-funded new online MBA program called UNext.com, Cardean University. I worked quite a few hours for them developing a curriculum based on the 1990s business best-seller *Built to Last* by Jim Collins and Jerry Porras. Collins and Porras studied long-term successful companies and stressed the importance of a strong core mission and purpose, expressed in attempting "Big Hairy Audacious Goals," and "Trying a Lot of Stuff and Keeping What Works" while building "Cult-like Cultures."[6] It was all music to my ears when I first read the book, after I had come to see earlier that biblical ethics proceeded from mission to values to practices in a strong community. The UNext.com experience contributed to my own developing expertise as an organizational consultant.

I gave copies of *Built to Last* to our North Park president and dean, urging them to read it and think about what these ideas might imply for North Park. The president told me he knew the book and had even taught seminars on it. He had a PhD from Stanford and was a very bright, articulate guy. I had talked with him from time to time about the restlessness and discontent I observed on the faculty. I advised him to stop burying us at faculty meetings in statistics about enrollments, salaries, and data comparisons with similar colleges. "We didn't go to graduate school in order to compete with Wheaton or Central College on data comparisons. Yes, we are concerned about our salaries, teaching loads, and student quality—but we came to this profession because we love ideas and the mission of serving and educating our students. Talk to us about that mission. Give us examples, including from our own faculty, of excellence in reaching out, lifting up people, honoring God, and loving our students." The president just didn't get it. He was a great platform speaker at big events, great at fund-raising, but not so great in smaller meetings, community-building, and teamwork.

During 1998–99, our president was thinking bigger. A couple years earlier he had pushed through the change of our name from college to university. I protested mildly against this trend toward "name inflation" in which little colleges declared themselves universities despite no actual change of academic substance. When our tiny competitor Trinity College (in Deerfield, Illinois) rebranded itself as "Trinity International University," I jested that for competitive purposes we should rebrand ourselves as "North Park Intergalactic University." (This was a joke of course!).

Our president did have ambitions in a university direction with projected growth of professional and pre-professional programs. Along with that he proposed that we should have a chief academic officer to be called the Provost. (North Park had had a provost before the time I arrived but none now for a few years). With that announcement, I was besieged by faculty colleagues urging me to be the candidate. Honestly, I think I was "the peoples' choice" and I began to seriously consider it. The political progressives on the Left liked me and trusted me—but conservatives, like political science professor Warren Wade, also liked me because I was anchored to classic, core

---

6. Jim Collins and Jerry Porras, *Built To Last: Successful Habits of Visionary Companies* (San Francisco: Harper Business, 1994).

Christian values. The more Fundamentalistic Christians liked me because they knew I was hard core biblical—the more liberal academics admired the way I hung out in major academic venues and published more than any of them. The old Covenantors liked the fact that I was in the Covenant and had served as a Covenant pastor—the non-Covenant Catholics and others liked my being an outsider from Berkeley with Anabaptist theological roots. The music and arts traditionalists knew my daughter was a classical pianist and we went to the Lyric Opera—the jazz and blues folks heard the music in my office and knew who I was. And so it went.

SWEDEN & BORDEAUX 1999–2000

Time flies and 1998–99 was my sixth full year at North Park. I earned a sabbatical for 1999–2000 at full pay for a half year or half pay for a full year. North Park's Swedish roots meant that we had an academic partnership with a community college, Södra Vätterbygdens Folkhögskola, in Jönköping in central Sweden. Every fall NPU sent one of its professors there to teach their English language program cohort two courses, one in American history and culture the other in the professor's specialty. One of the objectives was to habituate the Swedes to hearing lectures in English in preparation for their Spring semester on campus in Chicago. (Lucky me to be in Sweden in the fall, poor them to be in Chicago only January to May!). I was selected by the two schools to be the visiting prof in Fall 1999—after which I would be on sabbatical in Bordeaux January to June 2000.

None of my predecessors from NPU had apparently thought to do this but Lucia and I sold our Toyota Camry with 100,000 plus miles on the odometer and purchased a beautiful new Volvo S80 to pick up in Gothenberg in early June 1999. We drove it all year in Europe and then gave it back to Volvo to ship to Chicago where we retrieved it and used it for several years. We got to Sweden early enough to visit the Midsummer Festival in June, the summer solstice with the raising of the Maypole, folk music and dancing around the pole. We bought a small tent, sleeping bags, and lawn chairs and took some two-week road trips, camping all over Sweden, Norway (fjords and all), and Denmark. In addition to our trusty Michelin Green Guide we both read Vilhelm Moberg's historical fiction about the *Immigrants*, Karl Oskar and Kristina. In between camping trips we got used to our modest visiting professor's digs in Jönköping. We got lots of exercise at our local gym Mo Bättre and discovered great music and dance venues. I lost thirty pounds and got back to a great fitness level, working out mostly with Muslim taxi driver Habib. Funny story: I tried to say "Hej" (hi) and "tak" (thank you) like a native but one time entering our gym I said "hej" (pronounced "hey") to the front desk and someone responded "I love your American accent!" Really?

We got over to Stockholm several times during the year, also Gothenburg, Malmo, Upsala, Dalarna, Fjällbacka, and beyond. We visited Vadstena where my great-grandpa Gustav Hallgren came from in the 1880s. We visited Åmål and Halden where

Lucia's Paulson ancestors hailed from, even visiting one of the houses they lived in. We enjoyed visiting Liseberg, the wonderful amusement park in Gothenburg, and Tivoli in Copenhagen which inspired Walt Disney. When Lucia had a bad fall on a slippery floor one weekend, her shattered arm was soon repaired by a team of skillful doctors and in a cast. We were charged $130 for the emergency hospital visit on a late Saturday night (same as the $130 later just to remove the cast!). I preached and led a retreat for the International Covenant Church in Stockholm, pastored by our friend, former NPU chaplain, Jodi Mullen Fondell. I also spoke to a local business group about building ethically healthy organizations. The SVF program director Hans Neilson was a great friend and host.

I had twenty or so great Swedish students and taught them courses on "Business Ethics" and on "Immigrant and Minority Groups in U.S. History." The course included films like Spike Lee's "Do the Right Thing," the Italian "Godfather," and the Chinese "Joy Luck Club"—to bring up not just issues of history and justice but ethnic stereotypes. In the middle of the fall semester, we were able to participate in a two-week study tour of Greece: Athens, Corinth, and one of the islands. That fall I also worked through the final edits of *Becoming Good: Building Moral Character* and began drafting *Doing Right: Practicing Ethical Principles.*

We loved the Swedish traditions, such as the St. Lucia Day festival on December 13, when five or six of my female students woke us up at 5:00 a.m. in white gowns and with crowns of burning candles on their heads, breakfast delights and some beautiful singing—just the way we had heard traditional Swedish families did it. Of course, my own Lucia was recognized for the saint she was. We spent one summer night on a sailboat in Oslo fjord owned by our old friends and Berkeley neighbors Oivind and Elin Kure, who we got to know when they were both doing PhDs at Berkeley. Oivind was now a major executive with Norwegian Telecom.

DOWN TO BORDEAUX

We flew back from Sweden to California for Christmas. One of my worries was driving our new Volvo in France after the first six months in Sweden. The rules had changed since we had purchased a vehicle and driven it all year in 1984–85. Back then the temporary European license for foreigners was valid for twelve months—saving USA buyers the stiff European taxes on a new car—and saving us California taxes when the car came in as a "used" vehicle. Sweet deal. But alas, in Sweden in 1999 I discovered that they only allowed a six-month stay, after which you had to pay those European sales taxes or send the car home. But I found in the fine print that you could keep your car in Europe a whole year if it had plates from an American state. Here is the amazing story: when we flew from California to Pennsylvania between Christmas and New Year's, we had a change of planes in Chicago with a one-hour layover. I had brought all the Volvo paperwork with me and we decided to grab a taxi and speed to the Motor Vehicle department to register our Volvo and get Illinois plates. We knew we would miss our connecting flight but we couldn't risk driving our car without plates in France for six months. As our taxi headed to the RMV, a huge snow storm hit, delaying our flight a couple hours and we managed to get back to O'Hare in time to catch our scheduled flight. Thank you Lord.

In January 2000, suffering no effects from the much-discussed Y2K calendar transition, we moved from Sweden down to Bordeaux, where we had a great reunion with our neighbors (we rented our same old flat at 6, rue St. Joseph), and with the Ellul family and scholars. Patrick Chastenet and I plotted out the formation of the sister fellowships—the International Jacques Ellul Society and the Association Internationale Jacques Ellul—which were officially founded, with the blessing of the Ellul family, in fall 2000. I continued working on *Doing Right*, the second volume of my major work on Christian ethics. Lucia and I took major road trips through Spain to Gibralter and back up through Portugal, to Lyon, and to other favorite places in France. We regularly visited the Medoc and St. Emilion wine regions.

I loved living in Bordeaux. My French was now good enough to preach one Sunday at the L'Oasis church out near the University of Bordeaux. I spoke on my favorite text, Romans 14:17, "the kingdom of God is righteousness, peace, and joy" ("Les Trois Choses les Plus Importantes"). I made minor pronunciation gaffs when I spoke about the purpose and goal of life using the French word "but" (meaning goal, as in soccer) but it sounded like a word for "bits of dust" and when I said "paix (for peace) it sounded to the audience like "pays" ("country"—certainly not the second most important thing in the Romans text or the mind of Gill). The gracious congregation chuckled but knew what I was trying to say. Humbling but a great honor and joy for me.

My one real crisis in December-January was that I had heard nothing from the NPU provost search committee for months. Finally, I got an email informing me that I was one of eight finalists and asking me to fly back to Chicago for a one-hour interview (over the same two days they would give an hour to each of the other candidates). I spent a sleepless night before writing back to withdraw from the search. All night I wrestled with two facts: (1) the President had expressed no real encouragement to me when I had told him I was a candidate—and I reflected on the fact that every strong leader type (like my old friend Rob Johnston) who had worked for this president had quickly left or been pushed out. I realized that (unlike Ward Gasque, my boss at New College Berkeley), I would not thrive or be a good fit with a boss like that. The only ideas this president liked, were his own, as I thought about the past six years. (2) Almost as important, I felt that if the search committee thought they had seven other candidates competitive with me (each deserving to get a one hour of attention just like me), I must have overestimated my strength and that of my faculty support. When I withdrew, I never heard a word from either the president or search committee. I was not playing any games or trying to manipulate the committee but if any of them had just written a note urging me to stay in the search I might have continued. In my own experience of recruiting others, I never took the first "No" for the final answer. I think I could have been a great provost for North Park. When I left for my sabbatical I was really feeling the call from God and my colleagues—but it all evaporated over the next six months.

TIME TO GO HOME, 2001

When I returned to North Park it was clear to me that it was time to move home to Oakland. I had arrived at a time when it was sort of "up or out" at NPU. By 2000–2001 I had given my all. I did not want to remain on the faculty as an influential veteran fielding complaints and grievances or listening to colleagues telling me they wished I was their leader! Time to move on and make space for someone else. Another huge factor was that our family was eager to get back together in the same town, or at least the same state. Jodie and Andrew and their two kids were living in Hershey, Pennsylvania, with pressure on Andrew to commit long term to the huge Hershey Free Church. Jonathan and Carrie were now deeply rooted in San Diego with their first son. Two other grandchildren would be born in August 2001. We couldn't move to Hershey or San Diego but we and the Hoffmans could return to Oakland. The planning began.

Meanwhile the project Al Erisman and I had launched in 1998—the Institute for Business, Technology, and Ethics, with its *Ethix Magazine*—was getting way too much for us to handle in our spare time. Al decided to take early retirement from Boeing and we decided that I would be employed by IBTE, working from my Oakland base near Silicon Valley and the San Francisco business district. Departures are often sad, and it certainly hurt to leave my colleagues and our Chicago friends and neighbors. But it was time. Lucia broke her boss's heart for the third time (1994, 1999, and now 2001), this time for good. My friend and faculty colleague Victoria Nelson organized and hosted a wonderful evening farewell gathering at her place. The NPU president did not bother to attend or even say good-bye, much less say or write a "thank-you" for my nine years of work. What a guy.

Knowing when to stay and when to go is a difficult challenge I have found. I didn't feel like I had any unfinished business in Chicago or at North Park. I felt I had given my all. The Gospel Choir, my favorite accomplishment in nine years, was in the brilliant hands of Professor Rollo Dilworth. The incoming provost had lots of ideas and she didn't need mine! I just wasn't feeling the call to stay on. Meanwhile regathering our family was a huge draw. Even our long-time neighbors on 62nd Street were eager for our return. Our Institute for Business, Technology, and Ethics, founded in 1998, was starting to boom and seemed to have unlimited potential.

Apart from my uncomfortable provost job flirtation at the end, my nine years on the faculty at North Park —and living in Chicago—were pretty much an unmitigated joy. Lucia also had a wonderful experience working for a great boss at Citibank. It was clearly time to go back home but I was very sad to be leaving dear friends and such a fulfilling work experience.

THE HARRIS WAY

Mission, Vision, Core Values, and Ethical Guidelines

 Harris & Associates.

20

IBTE & EthixBiz Consulting (1998–2011)

In summer 2001 we sold our Chicago house and moved back home to Oakland. In all of our many previous residential moves we had rented a U-Haul truck and done the work ourselves. This time we decided to hire a moving company. The internet was still fairly new but we did some research and found the best price was from "America's Best Movers" so we signed a contract and gave them a substantial down payment. Bad move! They failed to show up on the day they promised and we left to drive back to California with a real estate friend agreeing to oversee the load and leave process, delayed yet another day. About the time we arrived halfway across the country we got a phone call from the company saying our load was much bigger and heavier than they expected and the price would now be thirty percent higher. Half of our stuff was now in their van but they wouldn't finish the job unless we agreed to the higher price. Furious at their breech of contract (we had very carefully told them the dimensions of our load), but over a barrel, we had no option but to agree. When they delivered (late) our stuff to our house in Oakland, a few items were missing, and a couple valuable things were broken. They delivered the wrong mattress and also some wedding pictures belonging to some other customer. I called the police, we made reports, and filed claims but never got any satisfaction. Later, we did another internet search and found plenty of warnings about this company when we searched "moving company scams." Live and learn.

Our Chicago house had increased in value over our nine years there and we plowed these "profits" into an upgrade of our old 62nd Street house in Oakland. This included earthquake retrofitting (sheer wall, foundation work, etc.), upgrading the water, gas, and electric, expanding our upstairs, remodeling our kitchen, repaving our driveway, building a carport and bike shed, and upgrading the patios and gardens in front and back. Our son-in-law Andrew Hoffman's brother, Mike Hoffman, was our contractor and overseer of the whole project from design to completion, a beautiful and brilliant job.

Part Three: Channels (1979–2016)

We suffered for a couple years after we got back, with a nasty, toxic next-door neighbor but survived until she finally was kicked out by the owners and everything got better overnight. Lucia and I got involved again in our block leadership and the 62nd Street culture was soon beautiful again (it certainly wasn't just our doing but we did help mobilize teamwork and leadership). We had a great time back in the Bay Area reconnecting with favorite old wineries like Rosenblum and A. Rafanelli (the zindandel maker on West Dry Creek Road near Healdsburg), hearing great jazz at Yoshi's, walking around Lake Merritt, biking around Alameda, enjoying Stern Grove summer concerts, strolling along our College Avenue, and dining at Skate's, the Dead Fish, King Yen, and Sam's Anchor Café. For our thirty-fifth anniversary in September 2002, we had a spectacular week at Lake Maggiore in northern Italy, with another few days in Venice and Florence. For our fortieth anniversary in September 2007, we had a fabulous week at Lake Como and then a week at Santa Margarita di Liguria, Portofino, and the Cinque Terre—best vacation ever!

From 1997 to 2001, we had been members of First Presbyterian Church of Evanston and when we got home we joined First Pres Berkeley where we had many old friends. Pastor Earl Palmer had left in 1990 but we still really enjoyed the church. I preached a couple times and Lucia and I enjoyed a wonderful small fellowship group with Art and Marilyn Amman, Larry and Arlene Hatfield, and David and Anne Lyons. Associate Pastor Tim Shaw got me regularly involved in leading the First Pres Men's Fellowship and I led one men's retreat on the Old Testament David. For several years I taught a six-week Sunday morning adult course in the January-February "Winter Institute" to eager groups of thirty or forty people. Tim and I also ran a couple experimental "City Institute" courses in the downtown San Francisco business district.

Tim Shaw came up to Regent College to enroll in my course on the Decalogue in summer 2004. This Regent visit had its own memorable drama. On the Friday before the class was to begin in Vancouver, I obliterated my left arm on my driveway when my old wooden step ladder broke while I was standing near the top reaching up to trim branches off my toxic neighbor's messy plum tree. I fell six feet onto the concrete driveway and trashed my arm. In getting up and staggering to ask my neighbor for a ride to the hospital I fell and hit my head on a corner of my house, knocking myself out cold. When an ER guy got to me, he woke me up and asked, "Who is the president of the United States?" Woozy still, but coherent, I said "George Bush, unfortunately." The ER guy called out, "He's okay!" It was off to the emergency room to screw and sew my arm back together and put it in a big cast, and staple my forehead together. My mother, wife, and daughter greeted me when I woke up from surgery. The doctor instructed me to take it easy for a week or two but I said "No way, I'm flying to Regent in two days. I've been waiting forever to get to teach the Decalogue up there!" I did fly up and teach the course, looking like Frankenstein's monster, and in continual pain, mostly from my bruised ribs. But I got it done and loved my class.

A year after Lucia and I moved home in 2001, our daughter Jodie, husband Andrew Hoffman, and their kids moved back to Oakland where Andrew took a post as associate pastor at Oakland's First Evangelical Free Church. After two years of membership growth at that church, Andrew and a dozen church members were sent out in 2004 to plant a new congregation, Solano Community Church. They chose Albany, just north of Berkeley, because it was statistically the most unchurched town in the area. Growth was slow the first few years but it grew to five hundred members or so by the 2010s. Andrew is a terrific pastor and leader, an excellent preacher and worship leader, and has mentored a wonderful team of lay and staff leaders. Our daughter Jodie has been a magnet for young mothers and young people. From their founding until 2010 when we moved to Boston, Lucia and I usually attended both First Pres and Solano Community Church, and most of our church tithes from 2004 to 2016 went to support SCC. I preached occasionally and did what I could for adult education but never felt fully at home, partly because of congregational demographics and partly because of some disagreements with Evangelical Free Church theology and policy. SCC got bigger and stronger and I wasn't involved after I moved to Boston in 2010—though to this day I love and admire the church and its leadership, and enjoy attending worship when I can.

INSTITUTE FOR BUSINESS, TECHNOLOGY, & ETHICS (IBTE) (1998–2003)

Meanwhile, I made a big career move in 2001, from university professor to business consultant. In an earlier chapter I described how I started doing some ethics consulting while at North Park—helping a hospital and a retirement home create their ethics policies and statements, developing curricula for an online MBA program, and serving on ethics and institutional review boards. A huge step forward for me had its roots earlier in 1993, when I was invited to teach a course on "Jacques Ellul and the Age of Technology" for the Regent College summer school in Vancouver. During all my years at New College Berkeley in the 1980s, I could never teach up at Regent because I was either running our own NCB summer schools or on a study visit to Bordeaux. On my way from Chicago to Vancouver in 1993, I stopped in Seattle for a night with my old friends Al and Nancy Erisman. Al and I had been friends since the late 1960s, when, you might remember, Al, his brother John, and I tried to start a magazine for young people in our Plymouth Brethren denomination (and were shut down by the elders before we got it going). We kept in touch over the years and always shared a strong interest in developing a Christian mind.

Visiting with Al on that 1993 visit, I became aware that he was not just an engineer and mathematician at Boeing but was now the Director of Technology Research and Development, managing a group of Boeing's top three hundred or so researchers. I immediately thought, "I should have Al co-teaching this class with me at Regent!"

When I showed him a one-hour film of Jacques Ellul talking about (and critiquing) technology, I asked Al what he thought. "He doesn't understand how we view and approach technology," Al said. I was a technology critic and Al was a technology builder. I participated in conferences of tech critics—Al did the same with technology builders. Both communities thought technology was the most important driver of change in the (business) world—but the two world's never interacted and hardly knew of each other's existence. Al and I decided we should try to create a conversation and find some common conversation if not common ground. We two operated from a shared set of Christian values. Maybe we could bring our worlds together. We decided we should try to write a book together.

We were both super busy and made little progress on our writing project over the next couple years so I asked Al if he could get free to co-teach a course with me at Regent in summer 1996 on "Business, Technology, and Christian Ethics." He could. Regent jumped at the chance. We had thirty or more students—techies from Microsoft and other companies, business leaders, academics, and pastors or church leaders. We designed a curriculum and on each of the ten class days one of us would give a lecture, followed by the other guy's response, e.g., "Al, I understand what you are saying but I think what you are missing is this." Al responded to my lectures the same way. Then we opened up the class to an exciting discussion. Our interactions and differences of opinion liberated our whole class to jump in and give their opinions and perspectives, no holds barred.

There was a strong buzz around the Regent campus during our two-week class. Regent president Walt Wright was totally excited and said "We have to keep this going. This is exactly what Regent is about!" Walt flew us with him down to Seattle one evening to meet with two Regent board members and brainstorm the possibilities. Regent made available to us a small grant to explore the possibilities for some kind of ongoing program. Over the next two years Al and I visited Penn State's Science, Technology, and Society program, the Hastings Center for Ethics in New York, the University of Washington School of Business, and several other schools, think tanks, and study centers. We usually gave tag-team lectures in these places and found enthusiastic responses.

Also in fall 1996, the Seattle Pacific University School of Business began a search for a professor of business ethics—and told me that I was going to be the only candidate they would be considering! I was interviewed by the faculty and the message that I was "the one" was repeated by the dean. Lucia and I looked at houses for sale around Green Lake. Months passed but in December the dean called to tell me, on "the most painful call I have ever had to make," that they had decided to hire another guy (a University of Washington alum with an MBA, a business ethics textbook coming out, a PhD from the same USC program as me—and a non-Caucasian, adding some needed diversity). Yes, Al and I were disappointed, but forged ahead on our research for a Regent College-based initiative.

After our two-year study we proposed that Regent College start a "Regent Institute" at the University of Washington in Seattle. I would leave North Park, move to Seattle and provide leadership with Al. We would put on short courses, conferences, and other programs on business, technology, and ethics and we could also host Regent extension courses. I would commute up to Vancouver one day a week to stay tightly connected to the mother ship and do some teaching there. It was a great plan but the Regent board decided not to approve it. They did not want to risk their "brand" or lose any control. We understood but were disappointed.

When Regent (and SPU) dropped out, we gathered a half-dozen of Al's local Seattle Christian business friends and together decided to found an independent, non-profit 501(c)3 "Institute for Business, Technology, and Ethics" (IBTE) in 1998. Al and I continued to give some co-lectures but mainly focused on creating a bimonthly magazine/journal soon called *Ethix* (our friend Mark Neuenschwander came up with this great name). We archived our issues at a new web site www.ethix.org. In every issue Al wrote a column called "Technology Watch," I wrote a column called "Benchmark Ethics," we both contributed brief book reviews, and did a joint interview of some business, technology, or ethics leader. Cinda Peters did our monthly design and production and we began building a mailing list which grew to over a thousand. While our board and Al and I all shared a common faith foundation, IBTE and *Ethix* were addressed to the broader marketplace, not just to Christians. We were in search of truth and insight not just for the church but for the marketplace. Our interest was any place business, technology, and ethics—all three—intersected.

By 2000, two years later, Al and I were having a big challenge managing our growing IBTE "side gig." We either needed to hire some help or get much more involved ourselves. As I described in the previous chapter, I was feeling in 2000 that my time was up at North Park so I gave notice and the IBTE board hired me full-time beginning in fall 2001. I would work mainly from the Bay Area, trying to connect with Silicon Valley's robust technology and business world. Al decided to take early retirement from Boeing after thirty-two years and he would be a volunteer, full-time worker. We found financial commitments for the IBTE from several successful business friends. It looked like a period of vigorous growth was in front of us.

Unfortunately, just as we launched our full-time efforts, the fall of 2001 saw not only the horrors of the 9/11 terrorist attack, but the massive business ethics scandals that brought down Enron, Arthur Andersen, and other companies, and the bursting of the financial bubble in Silicon Valley. Several of those who promised (in good faith!) to help fund IBTE had to cut back or even withdraw from their financial pledges. Al and I busted our tails for that next year 2001–02, but our start-up funds were running out. We had hoped, in addition to our *Ethix Magazine,* to develop an IBTE consulting business but after the 2001 economic downturn, ethics consulting seemed like an unaffordable luxury to companies feeling they mostly needed marketing help. I cut back to a half-time salary in 2002–03 and made up for my reduced income by taking on several adjunct teaching commitments (see next chapter).

With growing stress and pressure on us, Al and I disagreed on strategy. I was always a grass roots organizer and wanted us to double the size of our board and get stronger board leadership. I was also feeling increasingly detached by my residence in the Bay Area instead of Seattle where all of our board members lived. Believing we couldn't maintain my salary or get out of this situation anytime soon, I resigned from IBTE in 2003 after five years. Al soldiered on for fifteen years putting out *Ethix* and building the web site until it became a first-class resource. He continued to do brilliant interviews with all manner of business, technology, and political leaders. My abrupt departure was very painful and I wish it could have been smoother, and easier on Al. I was getting desperate though and I still think it was a necessary decision.

Over the ten years we had worked and debated together since 1993, Al and I had not persuaded each other to embrace the other guy's perspectives on technology—but we both learned a lot from each other. "Iron sharpened iron" and we almost always enjoyed working and teaching together. Our students and audiences certainly seemed to love it. I learned a lot about business and technology from him—his ideas, experiences, network, and endless book recommendations. On the ethics side, my work on the Decalogue, Beatitudes, mission, values, and organizational consulting was sharpening up every year. Al often adopted (and revised on occasion) my approach to translating biblical ethics for the business world. But I felt a "territorial" need to work on my own for a while to get it to the level I was seeking. I wasn't quite ready to accommodate to a fully shared approach.[1] Over the next eight years I found the growth opportunity and experience I needed for my consulting and MBA teaching—and in 2011 Al and I came back together, stronger than ever, to co-teach courses at Gordon-Conwell and impact together the broader faith, work, and technology movement. Next to Jacques Ellul, Al is by far the most important influence on my work and I treasure his friendship and collegiality. I dedicated my 2020 book *Workplace Discipleship 101* to him and Nancy (and to his brother John Erisman and wife Marj).[2]

ETHIXBIZ CONSULTING, 2003–2011

After I left IBTE and *Ethix* Magazine in 2003 I needed my own flag to fly and started my own consulting business called "EthixBiz." I created a web site at ethixbiz.com and, from 2007 to 2010, published a monthly online "EthixBizine" with a regular

---

1. I have a long track record of choosing to lead with a "co-editor," "co-director," etc.—and an even longer record of initiating "co-teaching." I have not liked "co-authoring" however. The difference? Co-authoring requires a homogenized, single voice. In co-teaching or co-directing I keep my own voice but exercise it in a dialectical, yin and yang, dance that I think brings strength—more strength than you get from a homogenized voice or mind.

2. David W. Gill, *Workplace Discipleship 101: A Primer* (Peabody, Massachusetts: Hendrickson, 2020)

column, book reviews, and "Ask Dr. EthixBiz" business case analyses. Before long I had seventeen hundred (free) subscribers. When I moved to Boston in 2010, I gave my subscription list to be added to the IBTE *Ethix* list. There was some small degree of overlap of our mailing lists but not much.

During this first decade of the 2000s, I got hired as an ethics consultant and trainer for shorter or longer gigs at the Santa Clara Water District, Nikon Precision (Belmont, California), the East Bay Municipal Utility District (EBMUD, our big water district), and Kaiser-Permanente Health Care. I did an extended project for my friend David Gilmour and his Corte Madera grocery store, Paradise Foods, helping them articulate their mission, values, and ethical guidelines. David Gilmour and I had often worked together over the years on his projects like the San Francisco Prayer Breakfast, a new radio station based in Santa Rosa, the Marin Leadership Foundation, and Paradise Foods—and he was always a big support to my projects New College Berkeley, the Institute for Business, Technology, and Ethics, and Westminster House.

I was very busy giving lectures and presentations on business ethics topics out in the business community. The most distinguished of these were two different visits to the Commonwealth Club, San Francisco's historic public affairs organization. In October of 2003 I spoke on "Ten Critical Reasons to Run A Business in an Ethical Manner." In August 2008. I was invited to return to speak on "Building Ethically Healthy Organizations." For the big Contra Costa Business Council I did a plenary talk on "Trust Needs Trustworthy." I know I was nobody's big drawing card but it did shock me just a bit when I heard they paid Larry King $50,000 and Robert Kennedy, Jr., $10,000, for their plenary addresses at dinner and lunch. A panel of California political leaders—and then yours truly—provided the morning plenaries for nothing but free display table space! Of course, we had hundreds, not a thousand, attending our talks, but still . . .

I also gave talks for groups like the Society of Human Resource Professionals, the American Marketing Association, the Beta Gamma Sigma business honor society, the American Association of Healthcare Administrative Management, the Silicon Valley Public Relations Society, the Tri-Valley Human Resources Commission, Rotary Clubs in Alameda and Richmond, Chambers of Commerce in Lafayette and elsewhere, the Rutland Institute for Ethics at Clemson University, the Sandberg Leadership Center at Ashland (Ohio) University, the Project Management Institute, the Association for Practical and Professional Ethics, the business schools at USC, the University of Wisconsin, and elsewhere.

It was all a terrific opportunity for me to sharpen up my thinking and my communication skills to general business audiences—and to share my biblically-grounded values and insights, not in "Bible-speak" but "business-speak." And it wasn't just Bible study that fed my approach, it was classroom teaching and discussion with MBA students and colleagues (see next chapter), a ton of reading the important books and articles, and all those hours of "in the trenches" ethics consulting experience. Two consulting projects that loomed especially large for me were for Berkeley student residence Westminster House (2003–06) and Harris and Associates, a construction and project management firm (2005–11).

WESTMINSTER HOUSE & INSTITUTE

Westminster House (WH) was a historic, Presbyterian-owned, student residence on the corner of College and Bancroft on the edge of the Cal campus. Director Randy Bare had taken this position with my encouragement when he was leading IVCF's Graduate Student Ministry from Madison and Minneapolis. Before he returned to Berkeley, Randy and I had chatted about working together on some kind of "Westminster Institute" study program for resident undergrads attending Cal Berkeley. He was a very bold and creative thinker who woke Westminster up from its decades of slumber, with a proposal to rehab its classic but neglected old building and construct a big new residence and meeting faculty next to it. Over two or three years, a gorgeous architectural project was completed, funded by cheap loans in a rapidly ballooning real estate market. But WH had persistent problems in controlling expenses, raising money, recruiting residents, and managing its programs.

In 2003, Randy invited me to help out. I personally raised $20,000 to enable WH to pay me $50/hour for my consulting project (I never took more than half of it and left the rest for their operations). With almost constant worries about the finances, WH refinanced their building project for more money and signed on to eventual balloon payments. Construction project costs grew to double the original estimate. I often offered to go with Randy or even by myself to make the "ask" for donations; "just get the list together and let's go do it," I implored them. They never took me up on my offer. Everything was funded by a skyrocketing real estate bubble that would eventually kill the whole project.

By March 2006 I designed and submitted a "Westminster Institute" proposal that I think would have not just saved WH but enabled it to fulfill its century-old promise. Here were the basics: First, we needed a much bigger, more talented and active board of directors, not just friends led by Randy. Second, we would recruit New College Berkeley, Radix, IVCF, and perhaps other campus-oriented ministries to rent the offices ringing the big interior patio to facilitate collaborations (NCB declined an invitation to discuss it, thinking a WI would be competition, and stayed put in their downtown, upper floor office). Third, we would invite two distinguished visiting scholars to live for periods up to a year in the classy suites of our older building. We would give them free rent and they would lead periodic discussions and be part of a lively community. Next to Cal, one of the world's greatest universities, scholars would line up for the privilege of being one of our resident scholars. Fourth, we would require our resident students to participate in a four-hour-per-week, non-credit "Westminster Institute" study program in basic Bible, theology, history, ethics, and developing an integrated Christian mind (two hours in class plus two hours of study each week for nine months).

Fifth, we would advertise in the *Cal Monthly* alumni magazine (and the *Daily Californian* newspaper) to build a supportive constituency among current and former Cal Christians. Sixth, we would seek donations and endowments to cover specific construction and operating costs, room-by-room, for the whole building. I thought we could promote our diversity by funding individual residential suites honoring African, Chinese, Latin American, French, African-American and other national and international students—and fields like Technology, Science, and the Arts—not that our residents would be sorted out that way but to highlight our commitment to diversity, learning from and serving all people in all fields.

I vetted this big proposal to twenty or thirty leading scholars and educators across the USA and beyond—and they all were very enthusiastic. After all this careful planning and research, I submitted the final proposal and told Randy the ball was now in his court to approach his board. I never heard a word back, never was called into a board meeting. I really doubt the WH board ever got to see or consider my proposal. Randy had lost interest. He moved his own office to the rooftop of the building, he told me, to avoid interruption by the student residents. I urged him, to the contrary, that he (and I) should have offices right in the middle of our students and staff to build community! Randy became more interested in traveling the country to talk to other university study centers about aggressive building programs exploiting the real estate bubble. Cheap loans turned out not to be enough. To cover the rising costs, WH residential suites and the originally-designated offices were soon overcrowded, jammed with anyone who would pay some rent. There was zero reason why any Christian student would choose to live at a building with nothing going for it except expensive, crowded rooms on the edge of the campus. Desperately need renters had to be recruited without regard to any interest in Christianity. After 2008 the real estate and mortgage banking bubble burst in a huge national scandal. WH defaulted on its overextended loans and the building was lost forever. Like NCB's Dwight House in 1992, another strategic, incredibly valuable, piece of property in the university neighborhood was squandered.[3]

How could this saga have ended better? I still think my plan was sound, even inspiring—but it was too bad that I didn't find a couple Westminster House board members to work with me as I developed the plan. That would have built a communication and leadership bridge to the board—rather than having a bottle-neck created by the director. I also have to say that this is another illustration of the critical importance of having a strong board which pays close attention to financial management and managerial performance. The Westminster board was derelict in their duties.

---

3. The Westminster Institute was another of my "What Are You Doing About It?" initiatives that never got off the ground despite a lot of effort. Killed before being given even the most basic consideration.

PART THREE: CHANNELS (1979–2016)

HARRIS & ASSOCIATES (2005–11)

In 2004 I was contacted by Vern Phillips about his company Harris and Associates, based in Concord. Harris was nearing thirty years old and was a very healthy five hundred-employee construction and project management company, a regional player in the field Bechtel and Halliburton dominated internationally. Vice-president Vern had shared with his wife Pat that his company was starting to think about formulating some kind of code of ethics for the first time. Pat had been a student in my 2002 Fuller Seminary course on Christian Ethics and remembered my talking about my work in business ethics. She urged Vern to contact me.

After some weeks Vern brought me out to Harris headquarters to meet with company founder and board chair Carl Harris and president Guy Erickson. They explained what they were thinking to me. The founding generation, including themselves, was nearing retirement age, and a company that had once been gathered mostly in the Concord headquarters and one satellite office in Orange Country now had ten branch offices around the western USA. The workforce had grown to include some five hundred employees—all of whom were carefully interviewed but inevitably brought with them values and approaches from previous employers. In this context, how could Harris solidify and perpetuate their own ethical way of working and their strong community? Until now, Carl Harris and Guy Erickson could be the ever-present, walking embodiment of the "Harris Way." How could that be guaranteed for the future as the leadership changed and the workplace spread out? One could easily imagine someone, somewhere responding to a challenge by saying "Well, when I worked at Haliburton, this is how we did it." The challenge the company was facing now was how to perpetuate the Harris Way.

Harris was a highly ethical, respected industry leader. They focused on managing public works projects like hospital buildings, freeways and interchanges, bike paths, school buildings, and government projects, managing them for excellence and budgetary fiduciary responsibility. For their employees, Harris paid well and made possible employee stock purchases so all could share in company growth and profit. The Harris headquarters was in a warehouse with offices around the outer ring and a shared lunch room and meeting spaces in the middle. Even their office layout signaled fairness, functionality, respect, and an open-door atmosphere. One of the most extraordinary things I learned was that in the earliest years, Carl Harris had made his Hawaii vacation home available to other employees for vacation stays during the year when he was not using it. Over time, the company acquired ten more vacation homes in Hawaii, at Lake Tahoe, Mammoth, and other great vacation spots so that every employee in the company, at all levels and no matter how new, could get a free week-long vacation stay at one of the company homes (priority of choice to longer term employees, but everyone did get the perk). I was amazed.

Initially, the leaders imagined that I would just research and compose a good code of ethics for the company. I told them I could do it but that that should be Plan B. Plan A, which I strongly recommended, would be to take a bigger perspective and basically mobilize the whole company to clarify its mission, vision, and core values and only then spell out their code, their practice guidelines. I argued that we should first *Identify* and articulate these things, then figure out how to effectively *Educate* everyone year by year, then be sure we *Implement* our Harris Way (not just leave it as a theory, even one we all knew), and finally set up ways to *Evaluate* our performance. "Identify, Educate, Implement, and Evaluate"—that was my proposal. I argued that this would be the best way to assure the perpetuation of Harris ethics and culture. I suggested they contract with me for the first "Identify" phase, then extend me for the other three phases if they thought things were going well.

I left the executive meeting and didn't hear back for a few months, though Vern assured me now and then that the proposal was being mulled over while they attended to some other pressing concerns. Finally, in July 2005, Board Chair Carl Harris, President Guy Erickson, and Senior Vice President Vern Phillips met with me and agreed on a five-month project to guide the company through a process to identify and articulate the Harris & Associates mission, vision, core values, and code of ethics. We designated an ethics project group (the "EPG") composed of the senior executive leadership of the company plus Corporate Marketing Manager Tanya Wollman. Let me take some space to describe the process I designed and implemented at Harris and Associates. A much more detailed account is given in my book, *It's About Excellence: Building Ethically-Healthy Organizations* (2008). This is the approach I have taught to MBA students for many years, and what I promote in my speeches and consultations. I think it applies to schools, churches, and non-profits as much as to for-profit businesses, and to big as well as small organizations.

PHASE ONE: IDENTIFY (FIGURE OUT) THE ORGANIZATIONAL MISSION/PURPOSE AND VALUES[4]

First: Get the Mission Straight.

During the first three weeks of August 2005, the initial goal was to figure out and articulate the mission and vision of Harris & Associates. Like Jim Collins and Jerry Porras (*Built to Last*) I believe that purpose (mission) is the key to good business. Like Aristotle, I believe "the good is that which everything aims"—our chosen "End" drives our ethics. If our purpose is just to "move money from other peoples' pockets into

---

4. Unfortunately, many organizations invent a "mission statement" that may sound nice but has little or nothing to do with the real, operative purposes pursued by the company. Their "values" statements, similarly, may look nice but they are disconnected from the mission as well as from the reality of their culture. At best these statements are aspirational. At worst they are hypocritical public relations. The employees treat it all accordingly.

our own," watch out! Ugly behavior is ahead. On both a personal and organizational level having a good, inspiring purpose leverages good behavior. The goal of organizational ethics and values for Harris was not just "staying out of court and out of jail" (a minimalist, damage-control approach). Rather, the point of Harris ethics would be to provide guidance on "what kind of company we want and need to be" and "how we need to treat one another—and all of our stakeholders—in order to excel and succeed in accomplishing our mission and achieving our vision."

As we began, Carl Harris explained that "Unlike many other companies, our 'bottom line' is not our 'bottom line.' Our company wants to be financially successful and we have been. But our focus is not merely on our financial return but on people—on our employees, clients, and communities. The irony is that focusing on people *is* good for business. Something like 70% of our business is repeat business, so in the end it makes good business sense to invest in our ethics."[5]

Intensive study of Harris's internal publications, external marketing and advertising presentations, interviews of Carl Harris and other old-timers and current leaders, and comparative study of mission and vision statements from industry competitors provided the initial ideas and concepts. Vigorous round table debate in the EPG distilled a brief statement describing the core business of Harris & Associates. What, in a nutshell, did Harris do for its clients and other key stakeholders (the mission)? What, in a nutshell, did Harris envision becoming as a company (the vision)? What key words would make clear Harris's products and services (in contrast to a generic business statement)? What key words would differentiate Harris from its competitors in the same industry? What was it that Harris delivered to its clients (what product, service, change) in light of which clients would pay its invoices?

After three weeks of research, discussion, and frequent reiteration of the core ideas and terminology a consensus emerged that the Harris mission was simply to "help our clients succeed." Harris people are consulting engineers and project managers for hire. And how do they help their clients succeed? Through "industry-leading management and consulting services." Harris's vision for its company was not to be the biggest "gorilla" in the industry but to be "the excellence and integrity leader" in the arenas where it operated. Carl Harris also insisted that the company didn't just help its *clients* succeed—it also helped its *employees* and *communities* succeed. These two latter groups also had to be named in the mission statement. In summary, then, the mission was to "help clients, employees, and communities succeed through industry-leading management and consulting services." Everyone agreed, "Yes, this is Harris. This is what we are all about."

Because it was their job to be concerned with every aspect of the entire company, the primary creators and guardians of the mission and vision were, of necessity, the top executives and the board of directors. Yet it would have violated the Harris culture for the mission and vision statement to be imposed by a simple edict from the top.

5. All quotations from Harris leaders are from my interviews or statements in company publications.

Thus, the statements were viewed and described as provisional, until all managers and employees in the company had an opportunity to examine and comment on them.

Second: Identify Core Values to Embed in the Corporate Culture.

With a provisional statement of the Harris & Associates mission and vision in hand, the project turned to the broader question of the company culture. The mission and vision were dependent not just on compliance with ethical rules but on building and nurturing an organizational culture that aligned with and empowered that mission and vision. What had been the chief characteristics of Harris's culture that had produced the successful company of today? What characteristics were critical to maintaining excellence and success into the future as the leadership transitioned and the company expanded? These were questions about "core values." Since "culture" is not just a vague reference to the company as a whole entity but gets real in the concrete experience of working groups and branch offices, the managers of those micro-cultures needed to play a central role in defining the core values for Harris & Associates. Fortunately, seventy company leaders were already scheduled for a management retreat in late August at the Tenaya Lodge in Yosemite National Park. This was the perfect group to mobilize on the core cultural values part of the project.

On Friday, August 26, 2005, President Guy Erickson rolled out the provisional statement of Harris's Mission and Vision before the Tenaya management group, explaining how and why it had been generated over the past month. Erickson then introduced me as the ethics consultant who would explain the culture and core values part of the project, why it was important, and how Harris managers were going to attack it. The seventy Harris managers were given a one-page worksheet to fill out on their own in twenty minutes or so. Then they were asked to form breakout groups with three or four others and brainstorm together for twenty or thirty minutes the critical, core values and characteristics of Harris & Associates. After this individual reflection and group consensus building, one person from each group took a few minutes to rise and summarize their breakout group consensus and the highlights of their discussion. I collected the worksheets, drove home, and then analyzed and distilled the findings into a working "core values 1.0" statement which was then circulated and discussed by our EPG.

The goal of the core values phase of the project was to identify the five or six central, recurring concepts in the managerial feedback and figure out the one best, most helpful, single term to use for each headline "value." Then an effort was made to be as inclusive as possible by utilizing much of the other terminology proposed by the managers in the brief explanatory elaborations under each core value headline term. In this way the core values, accompanied by their subheadings, provide a rich, "thick" meaning and message. The participating managers were more likely to "own" the values statement on seeing their language and nuance included in the larger statement.

I served as editor and "wordsmith" but with regular and intense back-and-forth conversations in the EPG. I contributed some brief "slogans" to define each headline value term, e.g., "Integrity: Doing the Right Thing," "Teamwork: Working Better Together."

A "version 2.0" was then e-mailed to all seventy of the managers who had participated in the Tenaya Lodge meeting. "Is this what we were seeing and describing at Tenaya? Is this who we are and need to be as a company? Are these really our defining characteristics, the habits and attributes that matter most now and in the future? Take a careful, critical look and get back to us within the next two weeks with your affirmations, criticisms, or suggested changes." The e-mail response from the managers was massively in favor of the emerging statement. A dozen questions, critiques, and suggested modifications were followed up with emails and telephone calls to try to understand the issues and concerns better. A few minor tweaks were made as a result and version 3.0 was ready to roll out to the whole company—though not yet to the public. Here are the six core values and the way we framed them:

Harris Values

In carrying out our mission and pursuing our vision, we are shaped and guided by six core values:

- Integrity: "doing the right thing"

We are about honesty, fairness, and responsibility, about consistently living out our values and principles with uncompromising integrity and ethics.

- Quality: "doing things right"

We have a passion for excellence and high standards, for industry-leading innovation, expertise, and effective performance.

- Reliability: "you can count on us"

We do what we say—and we stand behind what we do—with accountability, responsiveness, and follow-through, from project start to project finish.

- Respect: "everyone is important"

We value and respect every member of our team—whatever their role—and each of our clients, business partners, and communities.

- Teamwork: "working better together"

We team with each other and our clients to meet challenges and then share the success. It's about collaboration, approachability, good listening, and sharing ideas.

- Fun: "more than just a job"

We enjoy our work and our fellow workers, experiencing personal freedom, creativity, and growth in a "family" atmosphere of mutual support and celebration.

Third: Create A Helpful, Expert Code of Ethical Guidelines.

Five weeks after the Tenaya management retreat, the company had its biennial "HarrisFest"—a two-day gathering of as many Harris employees as possible for team and culture building, knowledge sharing and networking, celebration and orientation. Upwards of three-quarters of the Harris workforce was able to come together for these festive events. We were now going to turn the spotlight on the creation of a code of ethics and who better to take the lead than the employees themselves?

If the board of directors and top-level executives were, and had to be, the mission and vision guardians and champions . . . if the working group, departmental, and branch office managers were, and had to be, the primary hands-on culture builders and tenders of the core values . . . it would now fall to the rank-and-file in Harris's business trenches to play the major role in creating and implementing ethical guidelines for the day-to-day business practices of the company. As Guy Erickson described it, "It was a natural extension of our culture of respecting all of our employees to ask their participation in creating our code of ethics. I had never thought of writing a code of ethics this way but it made perfect sense to all of us."

The objective in mobilizing the rank-and-file to write the code of ethics was twofold: first, to gain their expertise. After all, who knows the temptations, challenges, and positive opportunities in marketing practice as well as a marketing person? Who knows the temptations, challenges, and positive opportunities in building inspection practice as well as a building inspector? Those who know the practices and problems best and most intimately are the practitioners themselves. The second objective was "ownership." A code written by the people would likely be owned in a way that a code from an external, outside expert, or from upper management, could never achieve.

On Saturday morning, October 1, 2005, in the Oakland Airport Hilton Grand Ballroom, Harris President Guy Erickson took the stage to roll out the new, provisional, mission and vision statements along with the new core values statement. I followed the president by describing the code of ethics project and explaining why the people's expertise, leadership, and ownership was essential to its success. I called attention to the popular web site Wikipedia and the amazing degree of accuracy that fact-checking organizations had found there despite (or "because of") its open, mass collaborative authorship. "Think of this exercise as writing guidelines for new employees in your work area," I said. "What are the most important working guidelines you would give them if you were mentoring them one-on-one in person? As we expand, not all people coming into our work areas can have your personal mentoring close at hand every moment, so our backup plan is crucial: to provide a set of written guidelines."

The three hundred or so attendees, sitting around tables of eight, took out a one-page code of ethics questionnaire that asked them five questions: (1) what are the basic tasks that make up your work days?; (2) what basic, written guidelines should be given to a new (or uncertain) employee for each of those basic work practices, both to avoid getting into trouble and to ensure excellence and ethics in the task?; (3) what are the most significant temptations and problems that can arise in your work area?; (4) what written guidelines would help new or uncertain employees avoid trouble or ethical missteps when faced by each of these challenges?; and (5) can you suggest any other important rules or guidelines that should be part of our code of ethics, guiding all of us, all the time, at Harris & Associates?

After about twenty minutes of individual work on the survey forms, the participants were asked to huddle with three or four others at their table and take turns sharing what each of them had highlighted, discussing and clarifying things where needed. After about thirty minutes of breakout discussion the forms were collected in an envelope on each table. Participants were invited but not required to put their names and contact information on the forms to enable follow-up discussion if something they wrote wasn't clear. Most did identify themselves.

Over the next three weeks, I painstakingly analyzed, summarized, and organized the information on the three hundred forms. A rudimentary version 1.0 of the emerging Code of Ethics was reviewed and discussed by the EPG. None of the dozen primary competitors of Harris & Associates had been willing (or able) to share their code of ethics with Harris for comparative purposes but Bechtel's code was publicly available and, along with a few other professional codes (such as that of the Association of Civil Engineers), served as a helpful comparison. We decided to "front-load" the code by making as much of the guidance as possible apply to everyone in the company. The opening section summarized twelve general principles. Following the twelve general principles and their bullet-point elaborations came three brief sections addressing relations with clients, with business partners and sub-contractors, and with fellow-employees.

Once we felt that we had a reasonable "version 2.0" that was ready to be critiqued by the whole Harris workforce, it was e-mailed to everyone with a request for a careful reading and an e-mail response affirming, questioning, and improving the product— the mission, vision, and core values material as well as the ethical guidelines themselves. Roughly one-third of the workforce sent back a one-line message affirming the code as it was, one-third did not respond at all, and one-third sent back (mostly minor but a few major) suggestions for changes and improvements. Every suggestion and question was taken seriously and followed up by e-mails or, in some cases, phone conversations to be sure the point was heard and understood. By mid-December the major work was done: a holistic, comprehensive, aligned, account of the "Harris Way"—the mission, vision, core values, and ethical guidelines of the company—had been identified and articulated with the broad participation of virtually the whole Harris & Associates workforce. They built it, they owned it now.

Fourth: Outline a Reporting and Trouble Shooting Process for Ethical Problems.

With the values and guidelines now identified, the final question was what employees should do if they encountered a problem or had a serious question about ethics? A section was thus added at the end of the Harris Way on "What to do if you have an ethics question—or need to report a possible violation." The wording of the section title was very deliberate: "if you have a question" . . . "report a possible violation." Harris employees must not be afraid to raise questions. The process should not be worded in such a way that employees would be fearful that raising a question was equivalent to a formal accusation, with all that might entail. Three subsections followed.

First was a checklist to help employees and managers reflect on whether a particular concern was important enough to take action.

- Is it illegal?
- Does it violate our company values and ethical guidelines?
- Does it violate the Golden Rule or our internal sense of right and wrong?
- Would we be doing this if it was the lead story in the news?
- Could someone be seriously and irresponsibly harmed?

Warning lights or red flags on any of these tests meant that Harris employees should report the question or concern.

Where and how should they report their questions and concerns? Harris did not like the concept of immediately and automatically escalating every problem by filing a report—whether on a hotline or with upper management. After all, the EPG reasoned, how would we like to be treated? Answer: if we make a mistake or a bad decision, we would prefer that our colleagues come to us and ask us or even confront us about it. Harris wanted to maintain a culture of openness, respect, and candor. "If possible," the Harris Way thus advised, "speak to the offender(s)." Or "ask a trusted colleague for advice and help." Failing that, "report it to your supervisor," or "report it to any supervisor or manager with whom you feel comfortable." And finally, as a last resort, "report it to the HR Manager" or even "Report it to the President" if you wish. "You may submit your question or report anonymously if you feel it necessary," the Harris Way counseled. Of course, if the recommended initial steps "seem dangerous, unwise, or unproductive," employees should not hesitate to take the later steps. Harris certainly did not want to put anyone in danger—but many, if not most, problems are best dealt with immediately by colleagues closest to the situation.

Finally, the Harris Way process raised and answered the question "What happens to your ethics questions and reports?" Harris employees were assured that all questions and reports would be taken seriously, that retaliation was never allowed, and that, unless anonymous, inquirers and reporters would be acknowledged and informed on the case or question they submitted. If a supervisor could not resolve a case to everyone's satisfaction, it could be reviewed (and appealed) all the way up to the board of directors level for a final decision. Harris did not want a situation where ethics questions and problems disappeared into a black hole. Employees should know what happened to the questions they raised.

In January of 2006 a beautiful, spiral-bound, twenty-three-page copy of "The Harris Way" was given to all five hundred current employees of Harris & Associates. Introductory statements from Carl Harris and Guy Erickson on the importance of Harris's ethics and values led off the document. The leadership along with the rank-and-file employees of Harris & Associates took a lot of pride in this collective effort. The ethics and values heritage of Harris & Associates certainly seemed now to be well-defined and articulated. Now, it seemed, there could be no excuses on the part of new or old, near or distant, Harris people, when it came to the ethics and values at the heart of the Harris Way. It was easily available in print and online, in clear and understandable language. When a business strategy consulting group did a survey of Harris employees later in 2006, the "Harris Way" was cited as the strongest asset of the company by about eighty percent of the people, more than double whatever was in second place.

PHASE TWO: EDUCATE: MAKE SURE EVERYONE KNOWS AND UNDERSTANDS.

Harris had made a major stride forward in carefully identifying and articulating its values and ethics but it would all be a waste of time if they did not make the right moves going forward on the communication and training tasks. At this point, I suggested Harris could either take it forward on its own—or hire me for (say) ten hours per month to help them educate, implement, and evaluate the company's commitment to the Harris Way. The decision was made to keep me on board, and I served for the next five years until I moved three thousand miles away to Boston.

The "phase two" challenge was to design a program to communicate the content and the meaning, nuance, and application of the Harris Way to specific concrete circumstances. After its initial distribution to all current employees, the Harris Way booklet became part of all new employee recruitment and orientation from 2006 onward. Some companies were secretive about their ethics and values but others were forthcoming and transparent about what they stood for. From Harris & Associates' point of view, what could possibly be lost by making public one's company ethics and values? As President Guy Erickson put it, "All stakeholders affected by our company should know where we stand: clients, business partners, subcontractors, political and community leaders, journalists, and even competitors. Making our values and ethics public sends a clear message about who we are and how we intend to relate to anyone with whom we do business." Publicizing company values and ethics was, for Harris, a way of accepting responsibility and inviting accountability. It was also a way to set an example and send a message to the construction and project management industry—and even beyond.

Visual Working Environment Messages.

A booklet like the Harris Way, even if it was lying on a table, might be ignored. Harris took steps to place visual reminders of its ethics and values on display everywhere. A wall poster of the mission, vision, and core values was prominently placed on a wall of every branch office and often in conference rooms. A large wall just inside the entry to Harris headquarters interspersed plaques quoting parts of the Harris mission, vision, and core values among photos of hundreds of the people of Harris. The message was clear: the Harris Way is embedded in the people—our people carry and exhibit the Harris Way. The six core values were also printed on a Harris coffee cup which found its way throughout the organization, sitting on desks and quietly reminding everyone of the six core values. (The cup also had the company name and web site address for the benefit of any non-employees to whom the cups might be given). Participants in ethics workshops were given a Harris coffee cup, a desk clock picture frame, a flash drive (memory stick, thumb drive), a key chain, an umbrella, a mouse pad, or other "tchotchke"—all inscribed to keep the core values in the visual working environment.

Company Presentations & Newsletter Articles.

President Guy Erickson included ethics and values reminders in his twice-yearly webcasts on the state of the company. The monthly company newsletter became the most regular communication channel for the Harris Way. "Harris Highlights" was a print (and soon electronic) publication about sixteen pages long, filled with project and personnel news around the company, birthday and anniversary news, photos of work projects and branch office celebrations, job postings, and calendar items. With all of its people names and news, Harris Highlights was avidly read by most company employees. Page three of Harris Highlights, the first thing a reader saw on opening the publication, was (on my recommendation) dedicated to a brief essay about some aspect of the Harris Way. I contributed as researcher and partial "ghost writer" for president Erickson, under whose byline the essays appeared. I provided definitions, explanations, business quotations, and illustrations for each of the topics treated in the newsletter. Erickson quoted or rewrote what he found useful in my work but always added his own take on each topic and some concrete illustrations of the particular value or guideline in the lives of Harris employees. For example, a column on the core value of Teamwork would draw on my research but culminate in stories from

Erickson about exemplary teamwork in the company. The same pattern was followed every month: every concept was illustrated from the Harris "trenches," with names, dates, and facts accounted for.

Ethics & Values Workshops.

Harris leaders had noted even before beginning their own ethics and values project that some companies, including many of their competitors, required no ongoing ethics and values training. Many others, however, especially larger companies, relied on annual (sometimes even quarterly or semi-annual) ethics training, usually in the form of an on-line module to be completed by each employee. Participants were instructed to click the correct answer from among multiple choices in order to advance the program slides to the completion of the training program. Harris's choice, however, was to strongly urge, if not quite "require," all of its employees to participate in one face-to-face, two-hour, ethics and values workshop per year.

These workshops were usually scheduled at the start or end of the work day. Each workshop would have fifteen to twenty-five Harris employees led by two executives or managers. The workshop sessions began with a welcome and with participants introducing themselves. The workshop leader reminded everyone of the basic mission and vision of Harris & Associates and explained that ethics and values were intended to help the company achieve success and excellence in those purposes and goals. Each year the workshop content focused on two of the six core values of the company. The core value definitions from The Harris Way were displayed on the screen. For example, "*Respect: everyone is important. We value and respect every member of our team—whatever their role—and each of our clients, business partners, and communities.*"

Workshop participants were then asked to describe experiences where they saw respect lived out and practiced in the company. The second discussion question was "What, in your opinion, are the obstacles or challenges we sometimes face in living out our value of respect?" Following the opening forty-five minutes which wove together the mission, vision, and the two core values of that year's training, the workshop agenda moved to a brief review of the ethical guidelines and the recommended reporting and trouble-shooting method of The Harris Way. Two or three specific ethics problem cases were written up for each of the two core values being emphasized that year. One case might describe a situation where a supervisor was disrespecting an employee, perhaps not taking their expertise seriously in a dangerous, high stakes project. Another might concern how to respond when a client disrespects and insults a colleague or business partner. Workshop participants were divided into smaller four- or five-person breakout groups to discuss a "respect case" and then reassemble to share "takeaway insights" with the whole group. The process would be repeated with sample cases related to the second value (e.g., teamwork, integrity, quality, etc.).

One lesson intended by the Harris ethics workshop format was about the integration and alignment of mission, vision, core values, with the ethics code, problem case analysis, and decision-making. Ethics, at Harris, was not a narrow, reactive, defensive, legalistic exercise but a holistic organizational health issue. Second, ethics at Harris was a "team" effort. Sitting by yourself in front of a computer screen communicates a message that ethics is an individualistic activity. Third, the Harris workshops inevitably would show the ambiguity and complexity of ethical issues as different people expressed their viewpoints and this quality reflected the reality of ethics in the business trenches. The artificial neatness built into computer training programs could not capture the human complexity in real-life ethical drama.

A simplified, online version of the workshop content was created so that anyone who had been unable to attend a workshop in person earlier in the year could get much of the content online. This was viewed as "Plan B" ethics and values training, not Plan A at Harris. Nevertheless, it did have real value and was much better than no training at all. Despite busy travel and work schedule conflicts, fewer than half as many employees opted for the online ethics and values program as for the in-person workshops. Managers were instructed to make time for themselves and their direct reports to attend the training. The workshop atmosphere was congenial and good food and beverages were always provided. A small tchotchke (coffee cup, clock, flash drive) was given to the participants.

PHASE THREE: IMPLEMENTING THE HARRIS WAY THROUGHOUT THE COMPANY.

For Harris & Associates, the goal was not just communicating but *implementing* its mission, vision, core values, and ethical guidelines. Harris didn't just want to "talk a good line" in ethics—it was determined to "walk the talk." How would the company "walk" or implement its mission? First of all, the mission was, in effect, the ultimate "boss" of company strategy. The mission said "No" as well as "Yes." The mission *excluded* possible projects, directions, and activities if they did not clearly fall within its range of purpose. Positively, the mission stimulated and generated business development: what projects, what "big, hairy, audacious goals" would give substance to the espoused mission?

Harris's way of looking at core values and cultural implementation was to see the culture (like a cultural anthropologist) as having four levels: (1) the physical infrastructure (buildings, offices, computer equipment, transportation fleet, etc.), (2) organizational systems, policies, and procedures (compensation, communication, meeting, promotion, evaluation, etc.), (3) personnel (skills, experiences, abilities, character, etc.), and (4) informal culture (atmosphere, rituals, habits, styles, etc.). To fully implement its core values Harris had to examine continually whether and how each of its six core values was embedded and exhibited (or contradicted and undermined) at each of those four levels.

For the core value of "teamwork," for example, implementation meant that the physical infrastructure didn't isolate workers or impede teamwork. Each employee is provided with what they need to do their job in collaboration with others. In the organization and policy arena, having teamwork as a core value meant that compensation should be given to effective teams, not just to high performing individuals.[6] "Respect means rewarding employees who show respect for others (and sanctioning or penalizing those who don't). The Employee Stock Ownership Plan and the one-week-per-employee vacation home benefit were also examples of implementation policies that showed respect for all employees and all jobs in the company. On the personnel level of the culture, the core value of respect meant hiring and promoting people who have respect for others as a character trait. On the informal, ritual level of the culture, respect should always be shown in the way we listen and talk to (and about) each other, and in making inclusion important.

What was important about implementing and living by the mission, vision, and core values was also true of the ethical guidelines. Implementation meant applying and enforcing the standards, not just talking about them. "Complying with applicable law" meant knowing the relevant laws and regulations and acting accordingly. "Protecting life, health, and safety" meant avoiding danger and risk and actively pursuing and promoting health and safety. The ethical guidelines were established to guide company business practices, not just company thinking.

PHASE FOUR: EVALUATION: ASSESSING COMPANY ETHICAL HEALTH.

Finally, nothing can just be taken for granted when it comes to ethical health. I met monthly with President Erickson, and HR Director Marie Shockley through my six years as their ethics consultant, reviewing our progress and performance. Larger executive team meetings would often bring up Harris Way matters and performance. Employee evaluations would include ethics performance questions and comments from both supervisor and employee as appropriate. All ethics training sessions requested evaluation of company performance and suggestions for improvement. Anecdotal

---

6. During this time period I was called in by the manager of a downtown San Francisco office space rental agency. He had been unsuccessful at getting his individual agents to work together. If a corporate client could not find the office space they wanted in the quadrant represented by one agent, the client was often lost. But couldn't the agent hand the client to a colleague in the office managing a neighboring quadrant? Pep talks from the manager to the staff were not getting the job done. The Gill recommendation: (1) require all the agents in the office to use a computer program facilitating information sharing (they each were attached to their own pet, idiosyncratic programs) and (2) tie compensation not just to individual sales commissions but to collaborative, team or partner successes. The agents heard the case, but dug in their feet, and continued to lose business.

and informal feedback had been very positive but it was also important to create an audit and assessment program that would reveal the company's ethical health.

For my final ethics and values session with the larger management team in 2011, I created an evaluation sheet which focused attention first on our mission and asked for concrete and specific evidence of its implementation. Then another sheet listed the six-core values across the top and the four levels of our culture down the left-hand side. We asked all managers to assigned a letter grade—A, B, C, D, or F—to company performance—for example on "Teamwork" in terms of our physical infrastructure (offices, equipment, etc.), then our policies and organizational structures, then our personnel, and then our informal atmosphere. Give a grade and make a couple notes "why this grade?" Then the same rubric for "Respect, "Fun" and so on. We had a terrific discussion. I was only surprised at how tough many were in grading the company (themselves as leaders). Harris & Associates was totally committed to making its Harris Way real.

MR. ORGANIZATIONAL ETHICS CONSULTANT

In fall 2010 I moved back to Boston to take a new faculty post at Gordon-Conwell seminary. Carl Harris was living out of state and no longer involved in day-to-day operations of the company he started. President Guy Erickson retired just as I finished my own time. Working with HR Director Marie Shockley, President Erickson, and Chairman Harris was one of the best experiences of my life. Leaving Harris & Associates after this six-year experience was both sad and satisfying. Sad because I really loved this company and its people, satisfying because I left them stronger than when I arrived. They were strong already but I helped them put in place the means to stay strong. I have always felt that the role of a business consultant is not to create dependence (on the consultant) but independence. I coached president Guy Erickson, did a little ghost-writing for him, and each month brought him recommended readings for what I called the "Guybrary." When I led working sessions it was usually as part of a process to hand off up-front leadership to others. I did not lead the annual ethics workshops but oriented and coached others to lead. I wanted the Harris Way to be owned and led by Harris people, not an outsider like me. I viewed it as a victory to work myself out of the job.

Harris & Associates was, in an important and decisive way, my own organizational ethics laboratory. I worked hard for Harris and Associates. After an initial eighty hours to help create the Harris Way in Fall 2005, I usually worked ten hours per month (and gave them a fifteen percent discount on my monthly hours). What I learned or refined at Harris were things I often shared in my various business group lectures and sessions and describe in detail in my *It's About Excellence: Building Ethically Healthy Organizations*.[7] My teaching and writing as a Professor of Business and

---

7. David W. Gill, *It's about Excellence: Building Ethically Healthy Organizations* (Eugene, Oregon: Wipf & Stock, 2008/2011).

Part Three: Channels (1979–2016)

Workplace Ethics were immeasurably strengthened and enriched by my early factory and other labor experiences and by my immersion as a long-term consultant in the business trenches, especially at Harris & Associates. In the trenches experiences are so important to teachers and writers. We must get out of our ivory towers! It was an exact parallel for my teaching and writing as a Professor of Christian Ethics—immeasurably strengthened and enriched by my interim pastorates and other in-the-trenches experiences among the people in churches.

21

St. Mary's & Adjunct Professor Life (2002–10)

Soon after I got back to Oakland in 2001, I was invited by some local schools to teach for them as a part-time "adjunct" professor in one of my ethics fields, business or theology. My full-time job and career plan at that point was all about the Institute for Business, Technology, and Ethics (IBTE), business consulting, and writing. Still, I had always enjoyed teaching and was not opposed to keeping one foot in the classroom. Adjunct professors get vetted and interviewed to make sure their credentials, skills, and teaching ability meet at least some minimal standard. Usually adjuncts are free of faculty meetings and other academic distractions. It can be a good gig as long as one has income from other sources. All too often, though, adjunct faculty have the qualifications and desire to be full-time professors but the jobs are just not there. PhD students need to carry out their studies aware of the possibility they will never find the position they wish and have worked for.

The typical teaching load for a university or seminary professor (without an administrative post like Dean or Center Director) is two or three courses per term, six to eight per year, depending on the hours and length of the academic term. Additional credit (or remuneration) is given for supervising individual projects, theses, and dissertations. Normally a professor is expected to do research and writing, counsel students, work on academic committees, and do some limited sort of community service. Salaries are accompanied by benefits like health care and retirement, possible sabbatical study leaves, computer equipment, an office, and other help. Adjunct professors, by contrast, get almost nothing except a small stipend for teaching and maybe some transportation expense help. Not all adjunct professors take their work seriously or give more than the minimum, though many do. Employing schools get to save lots of money. Accreditation agencies do not like it when schools depend too much on part-time adjuncts. Neither do students! Still, I was happy to do some of this adjunct teaching.

REGENT COLLEGE.

From 1993 to 2018 I taught (or co-taught) ten different one- or two-week Regent College Summer courses in Vancouver, British Columbia. Regent was always very fair in what they paid their visiting faculty and they had a great international student body. I loved guest teaching there. Our New College Berkeley had been modeled on Regent. Regent had designed its campus building with offices, classrooms, and the book store around the sides, all opening up into a large, congenial lounge, coffee shop, and seating area in the middle, under a glass roof. Regent values community and designed a building to promote it. Architecture is embedded with values! Although Regent had added an MDiv program to train pastors, they continued to have a major focus on educating lay folk to develop biblical Christian minds integrating faith, life, and work. My friend, professor Paul Stevens, was a pioneer and leader in the faith at work movement, writing many classic books. NT professor Ward Gasque had been our first president and Laurel Gasque our professor of Christianity and Art at NCB. All my visits to teach at Regent were an unqualified joy. Previous presidents Carl Armerding and Walt Wright were always great encouragers of my work over the years. Current president Jeff Greenman has also been a long-time colleague in the International Jacques Ellul Society.

SEATTLE PACIFIC UNIVERSITY SCHOOL OF BUSINESS.

I also enjoyed teaching a core MBA ethics course for Seattle Pacific University seven times from 2003 and 2009. Next to Regent and New College Berkeley, SPU's School of Business was the most committed to faith, learning, and work integration of any place I knew. At one point in 1996 I thought I might be called to the SPU faculty but that didn't work out. My annual visits (one course taught over three weekends) were a great joy. Dean Jeff Van Duzer was always a welcoming and encouraging leader.

SAN JOSE STATE.

Between 2003 and 2007 I taught ten continuing education courses in business ethics for San Jose State University's Silicon Valley Professional Development Center. I loved working with program director Judith Kaiser. Most of my students were from Silicon Valley tech companies. San Jose State also sent me down to El Salvador to lead a weekend ethics workshop for fifty human resource managers of leading Central American companies—from the biggest chicken producer to major oil producers and cigar makers. What an experience that was. I didn't speak Spanish (one of my big regrets in life) so my sessions were simultaneously translated by a talented woman. I heard the HR executives' questions in my headphones in English as they spoke in Spanish; they heard me through their headphones in Spanish as I spoke in English.

All simultaneously. I asked the translator in wonder, how she did it! She said "Well I have three children talking to me at the same time and I have to answer 'Yes,' 'No,' and 'Maybe' at the same time."

UNIVERSITY OF SAN FRANCISCO.

My friend Marvin Brown, a professor at the University of San Francisco's Graduate School of Business, connected me to USF where I taught two MBA ethics courses in 2006 and 2007. Like St. Mary's College and the University of Santa Clara, USF was one of the Bay Area's thriving Catholic colleges.

GOLDEN GATE BAPTIST SEMINARY.

My friend professor John Shouse got me invited to teach the basic Christian Ethics course at the Southern Baptist seminary in Mill Valley.[1] Everything went well except for the time when I was explaining the difference between taking the name of the Lord in vain (profanity) and some other objectionable (but not commandment-violating) terminology like vulgarity. My quotations of some of these words offended a couple students who complained to the dean, who asked that I not again write these words on the board! I agreed of course but argued that these distinctions were important for pastors in their guidance and shepherding of today's young people living in our world of profanity, cursing, and vulgarity. Taking the name of the Lord in vain—and casually using euphemisms for sex to refer to violence—are the major issue. Oh well. Guess I wasn't cut out for Southern Baptist circles.

FULLER THEOLOGICAL SEMINARY.

You will recall from earlier chapters that my first teaching experience with graduate students was at Fuller Seminary in Pasadena—a course on Jacques Ellul in Fall 1976. Professor Lew Smedes was a leading evangelical voice in ethics at the time and wanted Fuller to hear more about Ellul. At the same time my friendship with Bill Pannell was flourishing both at Fuller and on the golf course. Homer Goddard had been so supportive of the foundation of New College Berkeley in 1977. And in 1990 Richard Mouw had urged me to apply for Fuller's ethics post. I have a long history of great admiration for Fuller's history and massive contribution bringing so many out of a reactive Fundamentalism into a positive new Evangelicalism. I loved George Ladd's NT theology and G.W. Bromiley's massive efforts to translate both Karl Barth and Jacques Ellul. My old friend Tony Petrotta was a Fuller grad (before going on to his PhD in OT

---

1. Have you noticed that often it was because of a "friend" that I got these invitations? Lesson: along with building up your portfolio with teaching experience and publications, build your network of friends and keep them posted on your interest and availability.

in England) and had been a student in the 1976 course on Ellul. When I returned from Chicago to the Bay Area in 2001, I found Tony teaching several courses each year for Fuller extension—and urging me to get involved in the program.

From 2002 to 2006 I taught ten quarter-length (ten-session) courses in Christian Ethics for Fuller Seminary's extension programs in Northern California and Phoenix, Arizona. Fuller's northern California extension program had a bigger enrollment than most of the dozen full-time resident seminaries in the region. Phoenix also had a thriving Fuller extension program which I enjoyed for three straight summers (loved the students, hated the one hundred degree plus temperatures!). My first class in 2002 (in Menlo Park) had about forty students, including Sheila Robinson, Pat Phillips, Kim Daus, and Andrew Braine (son of my 7th grade teacher who I described in my chapter on my youth). On the night I taught the Beatitudes, this class surprised me by bursting into applause at the end (not because I was finished but because the Beatitudes were so inspiring, I should add!). I had so many other great students like Gina Casey in Phoenix and Susan Cosio in Sacramento. I'm still friends with many of my Fuller students.

I loved teaching these ten courses but was disappointed by the way Fuller treated us adjuncts. The first problem was the pay. My first class of forty (most of my Fuller courses enrolled fifteen to thirty students) was paying Fuller about $40,000 in tuition—but paying me only $3000 for teaching the class. Adjunct professors like Tony Petrotta and I were not just "drop-in" lecturers but busy, caring counselors and guides for our Fuller master's degree students. Fuller reimbursed me fifty cents per mile for my travel to classes (and my airfare costs for Phoenix visits), but nothing for the computer equipment and internet access I used all the time for them, nothing for my office at home, or for professional books and journals, nothing for my many hours driving back and forth to Menlo Park or Sacramento, nothing for my time flying to Phoenix, nothing to help me attend the Society of Christian Ethics as I did. My teaching ten courses for them cost them no more than a total of $40,000, including my travel. A regular Fuller professor teaching the usual six courses per year would cost them at least $90,000 for salary and perks. At that rate it would have cost them $150,000 to cover my ten courses using "regular" faculty—for which I was compensated $40,000 (travel included). My wife was upset enough by it to insist that I stop letting them exploit me.

The other problem was that the ethics faculty at Fuller's Pasadena home campus also imposed their curricular ideas and requirements on me—and never thought to invite my input or bring me down to their campus, even though I had published more than most of them in the field and had decades of experience. It felt like disrespect and exploitation.

I proposed that Fuller should create another category for those of us who taught two or three (or more) courses year-after-year. Call us "Teaching Fellows," pay us $5000 per course instead of $3000, provide us with a $1000 budget per year for books, computer expenses, and travel to professional conferences. Invite us to the Pasadena campus once per year to discuss our teaching areas with our counterparts. Mobilize those of us in the Bay Area to help recruit as well as care for our extension population. There was not a hint of interest. I still appreciate what Fuller has done over the years but their treatment of adjunct faculty like me was a shame and disgrace. No wonder eventually they had to close down all their extension programs. The regular, core local adjuncts (and alumni) could have led them to a different result, I am convinced. I continue to have great respect for Fuller Seminary and I assume their treatment of adjunct faculty does not represent the values of the institution or its faculty (or its leadership). But someone once said "show me your budget and I will tell you your values."

When I speak up about the mistreatment of students, faculty, staff, or alumni at Fuller or anywhere else it is rarely for reasons of self. My kids were raised, my house nearly paid off, my wife salaried . . . and I am a glutton for meaningful work. I can't recall ever asking "how much do you pay?" when invited to teach or preach anywhere (I do often ask if my transportation costs will be covered. And if pushed, I will usually say "just pay me what you paid your last guest speaker/teacher"). But who will speak up for underpaid or disrespected staff workers? For professors and lecturers without tenure and low on the pecking order? For mistreated women and minorities in our communities? Will no senior professors stand up? This habit of mine probably helps explain my memoir of "a *marginal* activist." Mainstreams don't much like being challenged and called out. On the other hand, I also tried to explain administrative roles and actions to faculties, staffs, and student bodies when that seemed necessary. I have tried to be both a "righteousness" and "peace" Christian faculty presence (Romans 14:17)—with some "joy" added.

ST MARY'S COLLEGE MBA PROGRAM (2004–2010)

My real break came when I was contacted in early 2004 by our local St. Mary's College (SMC) Graduate School of Economics and Business Administration in Moraga, California, ten miles to the east of my house on the other side of the Oakland hills. SMC was a small, Catholic liberal arts college with a beautiful campus (and a championship basketball team). In the 1970s they (along with Golden Gate University in San Francisco) had pioneered the Executive MBA program offering. SMC offered a traditional MBA for full-time students but their excellent Executive MBA (EMBA) put them on the map. These days just about every business school offers such a program but in the first decades it was just St. Mary's and Golden Gate. The EMBA has the traditional admission standards and academic requirements but schedules classes during evenings and on Saturdays so students can keep their day jobs at Chevron, Hewlett-Packard, AT&T, Kaiser-Permanente, or any other business, large or small. By going year-round, students can finish a normal two-year program in about eighteen months. It is grueling but effective. And popular.

St. Mary's admitted two or three new twenty-member cohorts of MBA students every academic quarter. These cohorts studied together through the whole program, with two eleven-week, four-hour classes on Monday and Wednesday evenings or Tuesday and Thursday, or Saturday morning and afternoon. Most cohorts met on the Moraga campus but others met in Santa Clara, Sacramento, and San Ramon. Another degree program leading to the MS in Financial Analysis and Investment Management (MS-FAIM) degree followed the same kind of intensive schedule in downtown San Francisco. A separate Global MBA program met one intensive weekend per month in San Ramon. A hybrid MBA cohort met half of its hours in person and half online.[2]

All EMBA and MS-FAIM students were required to take half-term (five-and-a-half week) courses in Business Ethics and Business Law. That meant that we Business Ethics and Business Law professors taught ten or twelve of these half-term courses each year—plus one or two full-quarter-length, day-time, business ethics courses to traditional MBAs on campus. I actually loved repeatedly teaching the same courses. That allowed constant improvement and research—and a new group of students always brought lots of variety! Never boring.

The long-time SMC business ethics professor Jim Hawley contacted me to see if there was any possibility I could replace him for the 2004–05 academic year when he hoped to go on sabbatical. After coming to campus and visiting with the dean, I agreed. I was free to organize and teach the content I thought was best. (I had investigated adjunct MBA teaching possibilities at Cal's famous Haas Business School but was turned off by their rigid curriculum and the fact that they had sixty (not twenty) students in each class). I started at SMC in fall 2004. I was immediately struck by how tight the culture was in each cohort. I was walking in on a group that all knew each other well after a year together (and laughed as I mispronounced some challenging student names). The business ethics course always came in the fifth of any cohort's six terms. Students were outspoken and challenging (perhaps especially with a "rookie" in front of them my first quarter). But after that 2004 maiden voyage things went from well to very well for me as an MBA ethics teacher.

In my courses I began with the usual definitional and theoretical foundations in business ethics, then asked each of them to write up a description of an ethical issue or challenge they had personally faced or been close to in their business experience. I assembled these into the class "casebook" which we then worked our way through in class discussions over the coming weeks (this was the same as my practice in most other ethics courses I taught over the years). So many business ethics textbooks (and courses) hand-picked a few famous cases (like the wreck of the Exxon Valdez, the deadly roll-overs of Ford Explorers, the fall of Enron) which easily illustrated their

---

2. I really admire the SMC business faculty and deans for their uncomplaining willingness to create and teach courses at convenient times and locations for students—something resisted by so many other faculties I have seen.

points. But that approach is artificial—I wanted in-the-trenches reality for our discussions and test cases.

But I also went beyond the "ethics of decision-making about bad cases" to work at constructively building ethically healthy companies (the "mission plus cultural values plus principles/guidelines" approach). I wanted my students not just to treat "disease and injury" but build business "health" in a positive way (not "damage control" but "mission control" ethics). How could we help that happen where we work? I often had guest presenters visit my class such as Guy Erickson (President) and Marie Shockley (HR) of Harris & Associates, Doug Sterne (Pandora), Kim Flom (Safeway), and Dave Stewart (State Farm). Gael MBA alumni Beth Boyle (Protiviti) gave guest lectures on corruption in international business and Syed Mubeen Saifullah on doing business in Muslim contexts.

The capstone project for my MBA students was a three or four-member team analysis of the ethics and values (both espoused and practiced) of a specific company they chose. These were terrific projects, presented brilliantly during our final class session. We schlepped in great food and adult beverages to accompany this final class session, like we imagined an ancient Greek symposium. One thing I especially loved about teaching Executive MBAs (ranging in age from 25 to 65) was their rich work and leadership experience, not just in the past but during the very weeks I was teaching them. They didn't check my teaching against textbook theories but against their daily management realities. They were fearless in disagreeing with each other—and with their professor. They thrived on honesty, openness, respect, and our shared quest for the keys to ethics and excellence. In 2008, my own book came out, *It's About Excellence: Building Ethically Healthy Organizations,* and served all my students from that time forward. Part of why I created my EthixBiz web site and monthly "EthixBizine" online newsletter was to serve my SMC students and graduates—not just my consulting clients at Harris & Associates and elsewhere.

At the end of each MBA cohort study experience, the Grad School of Business Dean hosted a dinner party for the cohort members and their spouse/partners. What a generous and lovely gift to these hard-working MBA achievers. I was always one of the two or three professors (out of the thirteen these students had studied with during their program) who chose to participate in these dinners. For most of my years at SMC my dean was Guido Krickx, a well-organized visionary and community builder. Guido brought in Shyam Kamath to create our Global MBA track. Roy Allen provided great overall leadership of our School of Business and Economics. When Roy retired, we got to have Larisa Genin as our interim dean, maybe the best of all the deans I ever worked for during my forty years as a professor.

My first year at St. Mary's I took on a full-time load as Jim Hawley's one-year sabbatical replacement. In the fall of 2005, my second year, I was cut back to a course or two because Jim was back. When Jim caught me in the hallway at the beginning of the fall term, he pulled me aside and quietly said "Don't go anywhere, David. I am about to resign and they will be needing you." It turned out some of his relatives had passed on and left him with the resources to pursue his special interests in sustainability. So, the dean soon signed me up for another full-time load for year two. From then on, there was occasional talk of opening an official search for a tenure-track business ethics prof—but nothing happened until I left a few years later. In the meantime, I was at SMC on a year-to-year "visiting" basis. I had no security. To protect myself I continued for two years to adjunct teach for Fuller, USF, San Jose State, and Seattle Pacific along with the full-time load at St.Mary's. I was thus teaching double the course load a full-time prof would handle. As my third year began, I begged Dean Allen to give me a two-year contract and some longer-term assurance—which he did, and which enabled me to focus on St. Mary's and phase out the other schools. Over time I earned a lot of respect and even gratitude from my colleagues at SMC, but I was always conscious of having coming in through the "back door" rather than as the result of an official search. I sort of worked myself into a job at the core of the MBA faculty. There's a lesson there. Work yourself into a job where you are functionally irreplaceable if you can.

ORGANIZING THE GRADUATE BUSINESS ALUMNI: NETWORK, LEARN, AND SERVE

The SMC programs in graduate business held two graduation academic convocations per year at which about a hundred grads received their degrees each time. Faculty and students marched in their robes, an excellent speaker delivered a commencement address, degrees were awarded, students were recognized, grads, families, and friends packed the SMC Chapel, and then celebrated at a nice reception. At each of these ceremonies, someone made an announcement inviting participation in an SMC "MBA Alumni" group. At the September 2007 graduation, I introduced myself to this representative, Mike Clothier, and asked what the alumni group actually did. "Not much" was his answer. "We can't seem to get enough of our alumni to help us lead and, aside from the annual MBA alumni golf tournament, we don't sponsor any regular activities." Actually, even the annual golf tournament was poorly-attended and faculty were urged to participate for free to fill up the otherwise unused tee times.

SMC had more than seven thousand MBA alumni, mostly still in Northern California. Already by the end of my third year I had taught ethics to five or six hundred SMC MBAs. I was proud of them and sad to say good-bye—as they were to their fellow-cohort members after an intense eighteen months together. Too bad, I thought, that there wasn't a strong alumni association. St. Mary's undergrads were a feisty, loyal group, with a large and active alumni program. Graduate students, like MBAs, however, tend to have a less visceral and more utilitarian connection to their grad institutions—but not to their closest fellow students and professors. I arranged to meet Mike Clothier and two other members of his alumni leadership group for dinner to find out more. I offered to help out if I could. Mike and the others were happy to hear that. So I met with our Dean Guido Krickx and requested that he relieve me of any other faculty committees and let me work as "Faculty/Alumni Liaison"—a new role I would create. Guido agreed.

That fall of 2007 I met with Mike Clothier and Guido Krickx to discuss the history and possible goals and strategy for a renewed alumni initiative. In December, Mike and I convened a group of four alumni in Santa Clara to discuss a South Bay Chapter and then ten in Oakland to discuss an East Bay Chapter. What should be the mission, the purpose of such a group? Everyone shared their ideas and we distilled it into three goals: Network, Learn, and Serve. First of all, we wanted to help our alumni (a) sustain their existing network of relations with their cohort colleagues and (b) expand their network to other alumni and guests at our events. Second, we believed in lifelong learning beyond the MBA classroom from (a) each other, alumni sharing their knowledge and experience with each other as well as (b) hosting guest speakers at our events. Third, we committed to serve, (a) helping each other as appropriate, (b) tutoring grad and undergrad business students at SMC when they needed special help with English (as a second language), business mathematics, or other topics, and (c) doing some pro bono consulting to assist struggling small businesses in the region. From day one this was an inspiring three-fold mission. We had a lot of success on the Network and Learn missions and were making some first steps on the Serve side by the time I left three years later.

It was totally impractical to expect all alumni to return to the Moraga East Bay campus for events so we launched separate East Bay and South Bay Chapters in January of 2008 and added chapters in Sacramento and San Francisco in January of 2009. Our idea was not to have Moraga administrative staff plan and control meetings and activities but to build alumni councils to take the initiative. So often central administrative staff, usually from the fund-raising "Development" department, plan events which do not really meet the needs and interests of the target audience—and their not-so-hidden point is to solicit donations. I protected our alumni groups from any financial pitches, arguing that these alumni had already forked over a tidy sum just for tuition and we should try to give back to them. Later on there would be plenty of opportunity to raise money if it was for projects on which they had input and some ownership (a new business school and conference center building would surely have resonated—and was badly needed!).

To plan our activities, the East Bay and South Bay Councils began meeting roughly every other month for two hours on a midweek evening, 6:00–8:00. Once in a while we met in restaurants (and at my home around Christmas!) but more likely in a business office loaned by one of our alumni. We always had great beverages and usually someone contributed some tasty appetizers. We would first go around the room for introductions and a couple lines about what was going on with each of us. By itself this was community-building. More than once someone shared a job loss or transition and someone else followed up to help with a link to a new job. Then we got into our brainstorming future events and evaluation of recent ones. We always finished our agenda, got our tasks assigned, and adjourned by 8:00 so people could get home and on with their evening.

I am a driver and organizer but I was joined in March 2008 by Jackie Yang Williams who was hired to work as Director of Corporate Relations and Alumni Development. The Dean invited me to sit in with the search committee when they interviewed their four finalist candidates for the position. Each of the candidates came into the room and talked for thirty minutes. Then the Dean had all eight of us sitting around the table give our recommendations. I was last. One after another the committee members named one of the candidates who had applied from somewhere else on campus; they were all in-house friends from SMC. They were all nice and must have been competent in their own ways. But, speaking last, I said "Just imagine each of these candidates going in to speak to the CEO of Chevron or Kaiser-Permanente on our behalf. There is one candidate who stands out for being especially professional in demeanor, confident, and knowledgeable. Jackie Yang Williams is the best fit by far for this position." Everyone was convinced, changed their vote immediately, and Jackie was hired. She was a graduate of USC (so we bonded over our Trojan roots) with a great track record of leadership and management. For the next three years, teaming with Jackie on all of our alumni initiatives was, honestly, the best working experience I have ever had. She was The Best.

Both Jackie and I were detail-fanatics, making sure everything got done, well, and on time. We could always totally count on each other. She navigated the internal administrative and bureaucratic challenges better than I could. She brought unfailing wisdom and good judgment to our team. She had loads of good ideas at every turn. We tag-teamed the leadership of our council meetings so we got lots of travel and conversation time together driving to Santa Clara, San Francisco, and Sacramento. Leading any meeting she was always professional and prepared. People loved her. She also was always my advocate and made sure the SMC and business school administration knew what I was doing and got some credit—since most of what I did was out of their sight.

The biggest challenge (after getting that inspiring, compelling three-fold mission articulated) was recruiting our four alumni councils. This is where my "Faculty/Alumni Liaison" role came into play. When Mike Clothier mourned about not being able to find willing alumni I told him, "Mike I already know twenty great prospects who I am sure will join us!" I reviewed my class lists and picked out twenty men and women who I knew would join us if they could and would be talented and capable leaders. Half on my list were available and joined us. And so it went from then on. I continued to recruit leaders to join our councils in all four regions. We soon had eight to twenty members on each of our four councils. The council experience was gratifying and contagious. After a while we had people volunteering to join us. Council members were not there to rubber-stamp somebody else's ideas but to come up with their own.

The next step was to create some social gatherings in each of the four regions. In the East Bay this became "Third Fridays," usually out at the lounge in Bing Crosby's Restaurant in Walnut Creek, and "First Fridays" in the SF financial district. The South Bay and Sacramento chapters had social gatherings more on a quarterly basis. I attended most of these social gatherings (Jackie had to get home to her kids most of the time!). Our South Bay and East Bay Councils sponsored some Alumni Family picnics bringing not just MBAs but whole families together. The annual MBA Alumni Golf Tournament had limped along for a few years so when the date was announced for fall 2008, I invited its chairman Joe Buenavista to an East Bay Council meeting. Joe had participated in Mike Clothier's earlier leadership group but not joined us in the revitalized group yet. He was clearly impressed, even taken aback by the twenty alumni council members he encountered when he arrived. He described the basics of the tournament plan but mentioned the low, fifty-plus-or-minus traditional attendance.

At this point I asked him how many golfers the course could actually accommodate for a shot-gun start? "A hundred-and-twenty" was his answer, if I recall. So I said, "Joe, let's aim for a new record, one hundred, this year. But instead of recruiting one hundred, let's aim for twenty-five—twenty-five 'captains' who each agree to recruit a foursome. How many of us around the table will commit to a foursome?" I asked, and put my own hand up. Eight other hands shot up. "So we already have thirty-six players and when I challenge our South Bay Council I'm sure we'll get six more, meaning we'll be up to sixty total, a new record! And I am sure we can find the rest." We did and set a record with one hundred seven golfers—plus another twenty alumni volunteers helping run the golf tournament along with a bocce ball tournament, a putting contest, long drive contest, and fun banquet, to which even more alumni came. Jackie Yang Williams's incredible organizational and leadership touch was all over this event from 2008 onward.

A huge addition to our alumni association leadership was Mike Leary, a brilliant teacher of Business Communication, who was magic in our East Bay and South Bay councils and a rock at their social gatherings. Long after I left for Boston in 2010, Mike kept these Happy Hour meetings going. He also initiated a "Serve" activity that brought together many of our alumni to help in a food distribution program. Mike was a wonderful partner to Jackie, me, and our active alumni but his contact with current students was limited by only teaching two or three cohorts per year as an adjunct, picking up classes that couldn't be covered by the full-time guy. My contact with ten cohorts, two hundred students, year-after-year was key to our growth. I have recommended this "Faculty/Alumni Liaison" strategy to other schools (including Gordon-Conwell when I got there) but had no takers. The SMC program faltered in the absence of a replacement liaison (volunteer or assigned) after I left, and really declined when Jackie left a few years later. By 2017 or so, the SMC development office took it all over again and you can imagine the result.

ALUMNI LIFELONG LEARNING

After the regional councils and the social gatherings, it was time to launch a series of professional development "Learning" events. Our format was always to begin with a Happy Hour" networking time and then have a bang-up one-hour presentation and discussion. We urged attendees to bring their business cards and meet some new friends. The councils decided on the event topics and played host to the people who attended—mostly our alumni but also friends from the business community. We charged only a nominal registration fee to cover our food and room rental expenses. Our speakers were volunteers, donating their expertise. We created flyers advertising the events and sent them to our alumni list and to my *EthixBizine* subscribers (one thousand and growing), and distributed them to current MBA students, including, of course, those in my current classes. My argument to our councils was that we should never plan an event that we were not personally eager to attend—that would guarantee at least a small but enthusiastic crowd. But if we were enthusiastic, others probably would be also. They were.

Our maiden voyage was February 2008 in Santa Clara, repeated a couple days later in Moraga, on "Beyond Damage Control: Ethics 2.0"—with a couple business leaders responding to my plenary presentation of my just-published, *It's About Excellence: Building Ethically Healthy Organizations*. We used me for the first program as a guinea pig since we didn't know how well we would do. Things went great with a good crowd in both locations so we were bold to forge ahead with program topics like the following.

"A Conversation on Entrepreneurship" (with Barbara Carey, Peter Jackson, and Song Woo)

"A Conversation on Venture Capital" (with Mark Kvamme, Sequoyah, and Rich Ferrari, DeNovo)

"Brand Yourself" workshop

"Economic Forecast Panel"

"How to Network Effectively" workshop

"Start Something!" on entrepreneurship (with Guy Kawasaki)

"Starting & Growing Your Own Consulting Business" (with a panel of four veterans)

"CEO & Senior Executive Roundtable: Surviving the Upturn"

"Leveraging Facebook and LinkedIn for Business Success"

"Who's Getting Hired?"

"Jump Start Your Career" workshop

"Business Faces the Healthcare Challenge" (with Safeway & Oracle executives)

"Green to Gold: Get On Board the Cleantech/Green Business Revolution"

"Electrifying Transportation: Foreign Oil to Domestic Electrons" (with several display models)

Maybe our biggest success was organizing the January 2010 program "Bank Lending on the Hot Seat: What Lies Ahead" with Steve Buster (CEO of Mechanics Bank), Perry Pelos (Wells Fargo Executive Vice President), and Michael Walker (U.S. Bank President) at San Francisco's historic Commonwealth Club. A sold-out crowd was treated to insightful, responsible bankers' insights on the bank meltdown of 2008 and its aftermath. We followed up in the fall of 2010 with a similarly great program at the Foreign Affairs Council in San Francisco on "The Decline of The West and The Rise of the Rest? The Changing World Order After the Financial Crisis"—with Bank of the West CFO Duke Dayal (Lucia's boss earlier at Citibank) and others.

Where did we get these speakers and topical ideas? Many of the speakers were part of my network from years of teaching, lecturing, and networking. Friendship made it happen and they donated their services. St. Mary's, especially its MBA program, was highly respected. Prospective speakers knew about our program. Our alumni council members soon got the idea and reached out to their own networks and built new ones. We never let the fact that we didn't know someone personally deter us from trying to recruit them! Our alumni council members' program ideas were spot on to what our alumni (and many in the business community) needed and were interested in. Our speakers (and attendees) always felt warmly welcomed and genuinely appreciated. Nobody was taken for granted. The Happy Hours were truly happy networking and reunion gatherings.

Around the time I started working on the alumni project a self-study linked to our quest for (re-) accreditation by the Association of Business Schools tagged SMC's alumni program as a serious weakness. Two years later, it was noted as one of our greatest strengths! During the first year, we rarely succeeded in getting our MBA faculty members or deans to attend our activities. But over time the word spread and our leaders like Guido Krickx, Shyam Kamath, and Larisa Genin were more and more frequently present. I made sure to get them on the platform to welcome audiences. We used four or five of our faculty on our program panels. Professor Tom Cleveland from the undergraduate business faculty became an enthusiastic and regular part of our East Bay and San Francisco alumni activities. When our deans or professors visited our council meetings or attended our events they had trouble believing their eyes.

In 2010, Dean Larisa Genin surprised me with a beautiful plaque to honor my service to the alumni and the business school and called me up in a faculty meeting to confer it. With my consulting work at Harris & Associates humming along successfully, my classroom teaching going well, my new book out, and with a steady stream of requests to speak at Rotary Clubs, professional groups, and the like—and with my all-time favorite colleague to work with, Jackie Yang Williams—I was a happy and fulfilled man. All of my life I had been trying to explore the ethical insights of Jesus and Scripture—and those of great business writers and leaders—to find concrete, positive ways those insights could "salt" and "light" ethics in a challenging, diverse marketplace—and I had found the language and channel to do so.

I was "happy as a clam" at St. Mary's and had every expectation of continuing there for another six years till I turned seventy. So I was a bit shocked when I got an e-mail out of the blue from Boston, with a job offer I couldn't refuse. The St. Mary's business deans tried their best to counter the offer and get me to stay on. I have never had such a wrenching, sad departure from a job. I had invested my heart and soul, not just my mind and physical energy in St. Mary's. Jackie Williams organized an amazing farewell party for me as I left.

I still feel the emotional tug and some pain when I think about my time and the people who were there. I remain connected to many of my former MBA students to this day. Whenever I was back in town from Boston over the next few years, I tried to attend any alumni event happening during my visit—and was there at the final gathering in 2017 when the SMC Development office killed our alumni-led program and took over. Mike Leary, Jackie Williams, and several of our key alumni leaders mourned the loss with me, even while we celebrated an incredible ten years.

22

Gordon-Conwell & New England (2010–16)

IN SPRING 2009, LUCIA and I flew back to Boston for a ten-day vacation. We had often picked our vacation destinations based on where Southwest Airlines flew—so we could take advantage of our frequent flyer awards. This had meant a couple vacations in Florida, another in Savannah and Charleston, one in New York City, and now one in the Boston area. We drive out to Provincetown on Cape Cod, out to the Berkshires in the other direction, and up the New Hampshire and Maine Coast—and then took long walks in Boston neighborhoods. I vividly remember standing by the statue of Paul Revere on the Freedom Trail in the North End and saying to Lucia "Wouldn't it have been great if we could have lived back here for a while?" If you like San Francisco you almost certainly like Boston.

So what a surprise when just a few months later I received an e-mail from Dennis Hollinger, the president of Gordon-Conwell Theological Seminary in South Hamilton, just north of Boston, asking me about a new faculty position they were trying to fill. He asked if I personally might be interested and, if not, did I have any candidates to recommend. The job description for a new "Mockler-Phillips Professor of Workplace Theology and Business Ethics" was attached. The e-mail came in during the first half of my MBA ethics class so during the break I read it along with the job description. "Dennis, you just messed up my life," I joked in an email back to him before resuming my class (meaning: you just disrupted my plans). "Yes, I would like to discuss it with you."

Gordon-Conwell was a non-denominational, evangelical (not fundamentalist/separatist) theological school, one of the five biggest in the USA. I knew several of their faculty by reputation and from their writings, if not personally. I had been a friend and admirer of Stephen Mott, a social ethicist, and former member of their faculty. Their main campus (which I had never visited) was a beautiful sprawling green space with classic old brick buildings. Their student body was interdenominational, international, and had a large percentage of women (as did the faculty). Critically important to me, they had a downtown Roxbury branch known as CUME (the Center for Urban Ministerial Education). I would insist on teaching some of my courses there every year.

Two major business executive couples had donated a couple million dollars to endow a new faculty post: "Mockler-Phillips Professor of Workplace Theology and Business Ethics." This professor would also be Director of the already-existing "Mockler Center for Faith and Ethics in the Workplace." Colman Mockler had been the long-time CEO of the Gillette Corporation and was held up by Jim Collins in his best-selling *Good to Great* as the exemplar of "Level Five" leadership—humble, teachable, mission-driven, excellence-oriented. Colman had sometimes said to his wife Joanna that in all his decades of attending church he had never heard a pastor show interest in what he did for work, much less pray for or commend it. The church got interested only at fund-raising time! Colman dropped dead of a heart attack on the day he retired but his widow Joanna generously committed to supporting both the Mockler Center and now the Mockler-Phillips Chair to try to have an impact on future generations of pastors.

Tom Phillips, the other major donor to endow my Chair, was the long-time CEO of Raytheon, a major defense contractor. Tom was all about peace through deterrence and ran one of the most ethical businesses around. I did not know him personally but I had used the Raytheon code of ethics in my MBA classes as a best practice example. I found out that it was Tom who led Chuck Colson to being "Born Again"—as Chuck's autobiography called it—on his driveway when they met after Colson's imprisonment for the Watergate disaster. Chuck, now leader of Prison Fellowship, wrote me to say how pleased he was that I came to Gordon-Conwell (remember my meeting with him in the late 1970s to discuss Jacques Ellul at his request). After I arrived at Gordon-Conwell I became a regular attendee and sometime speaker at Tom's longstanding "First Tuesday" executive breakfast (and as I described in an earlier chapter, the Interim Pastor of his home church in 2011–12). Partly through his collaboration with Will Messenger, my predecessor as Director of the Mockler Center, Tom had a robust, articulate theology of work. He and his wife Gert became dear friends, as did Joanna Mockler.

Gordon-Conwell was looking for exactly the combination represented by my career to that point. They wanted someone with both scholarly credibility (PhD and publications) and practical experience (my work as a pastor as well as working with businesses like Harris & Associates). They wanted someone with credibility and experience on both the theological and business sides of the street. They wanted a classroom teacher and a creative, people-loving organizer with an entrepreneurial streak. I may not have been a star at any one of those things but I checked all of those boxes and got the call. Funny side story: When I told an old colleague from North Park about this move, he asked me, "Do they know how old you are?" Hah! I was sixty-four, not a spring chicken, but still healthy and full of energy. I told Gordon-Conwell I would come for at least three years and ended up staying for six, until I retired at age seventy.

Lucia had been laid off from Citibank in 2008 after the mortgage industry meltdown killed her finance office in San Francisco. So she was free to move. It was easy to rent out our Oakland house again, and refinance it for enough money to buy a condo overlooking the harbor in Gloucester, the oldest fishing town in New England, site of the film "The Perfect Storm," and ten light-traffic miles from the Hamilton campus of Gordon-Conwell. We had a wonderful four years based in Gloucester (after which I commuted two more years from California and lived in a GCTS campus apartment), walking the shoreline and the town, exploring Boston, Cape Cod, Nantucket and Martha's Vineyard, Connecticut, Rhode Island, New Hampshire, Vermont, Maine, and eastern Massachusetts. We enjoyed the Boston Ballet, the Boston Pops in their summer digs out in Tanglewood, visiting the great museums and historic sights, Saturday bike rides along the Charles River and the Minuteman Bike Trail, great jazz at Sculler's and other venues, and three visits to the Newport Jazz Festival in the summer. It was just a short jump down to New York City, up to Montreal and Quebec, and across the Atlantic to London. We loved the fall colors and the change of seasons. That dream about living in New England? It came true.

It was painful for me to leave St. Mary's College, and painful for both of us to leave our neighborhood and family again. But my closest colleagues at St. Mary's, like Jackie Yang Williams, and our daughter Jodie (with tears) said "You have to go David/Dad . . . this job has your name written all over it. You are the one." As soon as I knew I would be teaching for the first time as a full-time faculty member at a theological seminary training pastors, I approached my old mentor and friend Dr. J. Alfred Smith, Sr., pastor of Allen Temple Baptist Church in Oakland to ask if I could go through their process and be ordained by Allen Temple. Gordon-Conwell did not ask this of me but I wanted to be ordained and sent by the church in Oakland, not just go as a free-lance, independent scholar. Allen Temple was part of the Progressive National Baptist Convention, which J. Alfred Smith had helped found with Martin Luther King Jr.. It represented my theology, ethics, and ecclesiology better than any other denomination (I hadn't been a member of an Evangelical Covenant Church since 1997 so Covenant ordination or licensure was out of the question). One of the greatest days of my life was May 9, 2010, when I knelt to be ordained by Allen Temple with J. Alfred Smith Sr., and my friends Sheila Robinson and Randy Roth joining in.

My candidacy lecture to the Gordon-Conwell faculty was on a biblical theology of work. I think they were delighted as I probed the ways creation, providence, and redemption informed my business consulting at Harris & Associates and elsewhere. I remember afterwards our distinguished historian Garth Rosell telling me with a tear in his eye how he wished his father had been able to hear my talk, a hard-working Christian man who never felt that his work mattered to God. When I got moved back to Gloucester and showed up on campus the first day, I will not forget the warm welcome in the parking lot from Old Testament Professor Donna Petter and then in the hallway leading to my office from Theology and Ethics Professor Patrick Smith. The whole faculty was welcoming and a joy to work with for the next six years. My installation address (from Genesis 11–12) was on "Two Ways to Build Something: The Tower of Babel and Abraham's Altars."

Donna Petter and her Swiss-born husband Tom (both professors of Old Testament) were French speakers, as were Karen Mason and Paul Martindale on the GCTS faculty. Throughout our time there, Lucia and I joined with them in delightful French language, food, and beverage soirees. I was able to bring Tom and Donna over to Trinitarian Congregational Church during the final months of my Interim Pastorate when I badly needed some pastoral assistance after the associate left the staff. Wonderful team—and today Tom is the permanent Senior Pastor of TCC. What an honor and joy it was to be part of a faculty with all of the aforementioned plus David Wells, Peter Kuzmich, Gwenfair Adams, Todd Johnson, Dennis Hollinger, Rick Lints, Bill and Aida Spencer, Al Padilla, Patrick Smith, Haddon Robinson, Ed Keazirian, Dean Borgman, Scott and Rhonda Gibson, Gordy Isaac, Peter Anders, Doug Stewart, Pablo Polischuk, XiYi Yau, and Mark Harden . . . and I know I have forgotten some names. I loved being part of this faculty community.

I was in the Theology Division of the faculty ably led by professor Jack Davis. Jack was exactly one day younger than me and I sometimes joked that I expected him to treat me with extra respect as his elder. Jack and his wife Robin hosted a monthly breakfast and discussion for our division at their home. Community builders! I was also welcomed by David Horn into his Ockenga Institute leadership team composed of the heads of seven different centers, including Mockler. Both Jack Davis and David Horn were leaders of the caliber of Jack Sparks (CWLF), Ward Gasque (NCB), Sonia Bodi (NPU), Guy Erickson and Carl Harris (Harris & Associates), Guido Krickx and Larisa Genin (St. Mary's)—visionaries, team builders, and empowerers of those who worked for and with them.

MOCKLER CENTER FOR FAITH & ETHICS IN THE WORKPLACE

The Mockler Center had done some good work in the decade before I arrived and my predecessor Will Messenger went on to found and lead the Theology of Work Project, producing a massive team-driven commentary on the workplace lessons from every book of the Bible, a valuable resource for preachers and workers alike (www.theologyofwork.org). But for the new faculty professorship, the seminary needed a PhD-type scholar and it made sense to have this same person also direct the Mockler Center. It was also time for a fresh infusion of energy and vision. I did my best to recognize and honor Will for his pioneering efforts over several years.

When I got busy in the fall of 2010 I first reviewed (and reorganized) all the old files and records from the Mockler Center: order from chaos! I had a mandate to promote a theology and work integration on campus but soon realized that very few of our hundreds of students (and dozens of faculty) would be able to enroll in the courses

I would teach. They were almost totally "booked" into the classical, traditional courses on Bible, theology, preaching, pastoral care and the like. I wished that all seminary students would have at least a short course on Vocation and Work but curricular space was just not going to be made available. I volunteered to give a guest lecture or two—say on "Decalogue Implications for Ethics and Work" in the OT courses—but had no takers; course syllabi were already jammed with other things.

In my second year at Gordon-Conwell, I ran a search to find a student assistant for my work with the Mockler Center. Several talented men and women applied but one of them knocked me out. Yuna Oh's professional appearance and demeanor (important in representing us in the business community), her passionate faith and commitment to faith and work, her technical and design skills, and her typing speed (well above one hundred words per minute) made me feel dizzy! God sent an angel to help me! For three-and-a-half years Yuna was my assistant, putting in one day per week, organizing events, helping me lead study groups on campus, around Boston, and in New York, Seattle, and Honduras. She was so good I had to back off sometimes from expecting things from her so she could attend to her own class work. Together we created a Mockler web site and put out a quarterly "Mockler Memo" newsletter. I was the envy of many other leaders on campus (and she said she was the envy of the other student workers!). One of my most precious times each week was meeting with Yuna to review our projects and then pray together. With my assistant Yuna, I created a small local advisory council to help guide our work. With the support and encouragement of my bosses David Horn and Jack Davis, I was a lucky and blessed man.

My strategy would need to focus on special lectures, workshops, and conferences. Maybe, I hoped, alumni pastors could also be lured back to campus for such events, since their seminary educations had not touched on the subject. I kept up a pretty active pace of outside sermons, lectures, and seminars for local churches and various business and study groups, but what could I do on campus? There I had a serious scheduling problem. The daily lunch break was only sixty minutes, hardly enough time to get food and attend a meaningful event. So I carefully studied the daily and weekly class schedule which had been in operation for decades and came up with a radical proposal. Chapel had been sandwiched between classes in mid-morning a couple days each week. My proposal was to have a dedicated three-hour block of time every morning, Monday to Friday, from 8:00–11:00 for classes, then preserve the 11:00–12:00 hour for (a) clubs, associations, and denominations on Mondays, (b) all-campus Chapel on Tuesdays and Wednesdays and (c) guest lectures and events on Thursdays and Fridays. The next hour, 12:00–1:00, would be kept free for lunch, enabling the Monday clubs and groups and the Thursday-Friday guest lectures and events to have two hours 11:00–1:00 for a longer lunch gatherings. I proposed that afternoon classes should meet from 1:15–4:15.

On the Tuesday and Wednesday "chapel days" I urged faculty to very intentionally go have lunch after chapel with students and build our community. I also urged our poorly-attended chapel services to reach out to draw in not only more of our students but their families and even local friends of the seminary. As a seminary, I thought our chapel services should be "best practice" examples of worship and learning, led by a committee of faculty and students representing the diversity of both the seminary and the church. We had modest success on the "lunch with students" front but our chapel services never escaped the "one-guy-leads" default approach. I was never asked to preach in six years of attending GCTS chapel and adding liturgical and musical variety never much happened. Had I stayed on, I would love to have served a term as Dean of the Chapel.

I floated my schedule reorganization proposal to lots of individual faculty members with unanimous enthusiasm, and even attended the other divisional faculty meetings to present the idea and get feedback. When it finally got on the agenda at a faculty meeting there was strong support—but the president suggested we delay consideration till the following year. The registrar also worried—unnecessarily—about the transition. But almost as one, the faculty rose up and demanded we change the very next semester! It was a huge improvement in all directions when it happened. The dean then arbitrarily changed the afternoon class starting time (from my proposed 1:15) to 2:00, creating a three-hour break between morning and afternoon classes. I thought this was unwise because creating a too-long break might incentivize some local students just to leave campus for three hours. (I turned out to be right; you have to think all these things through carefully!). Faculty were told not to schedule class activities in these 11:00–1:15 (now 11:00–2:00) hours but leave them free for these co-curricular activities. Most of us complied but the dean did not come down on the malefactors—a special regret for me when a popular professor scheduled a required class session in conflict with my final Mockler Seminar before I retired—preventing some of my closest students from joining me. I think the schedule restructuring was one of my best contributions to Gordon-Conwell.

Everything I did was not about Mockler-theme events. I organized a couple faculty forums on "Should I Stay or Should I Go?" (when our church or denomination gets off track) and "How I Make Decisions on Politics and Elections" (not "who I vote for" but "how I decide as a thoughtful Christian"). These first two events drew big crowds on campus. But the Dean (same guy who arbitrarily changed afternoon class starting times to a less strategic time) decided on his own to take our forums over and re-brand them as "Dean's Forums." My proposal had been to have a rotating group of faculty from our various departments design and run these forums. Top-down imperialism rarely works.

With my administrative assistant Yuna Oh and my student assistants Andrew James and Mike Garry, I made the most of the new schedule opportunities on Thursday or Friday, with Mockler events (averaging six per year) on topics including the following:

- "Salting Today's Workplace" with ServiceMaster's Bill Pollard and five business leaders
- "The Role of the Arts" with British actor Nigel Goodwin
- "The Theology of Sports" with Australian Rules footballer Paul Kupke and golfer Rob Copeland
- "Sent Out to Heal: The Church's Role" with Drs. Timothy Johnson, Ray Hammond, Stephen Ko, and Endo Mondesir
- "Faith In the Halls of Business Power" with Michael Lindsay, Ralph Larsen, and Deborah Dunsire.
- "Biohealth" with Kenyan physician and author Dr. Ray Downing
- "The Arts Minister" and "The Beauty of Church" with David Taylor, Bruce Herman and local artists, co-sponsored with CIVA and Gordon College
- "The Theology of Work Project" with Will Messenger, Randy Kilgore, and Sean McDonough
- "Christianity in the Chinese Workplace" with Chinese economist Zhao Xiao
- "Leadership in Churchplace & Workplace" with Gina Casey, Catherine Blake, Sharon Harden, and Jewel Hyun
- "What the Church Can Learn from Business" with Bill Burke and Lee Truax
- "Technology" with the Ockenga Institute
- "Workplace Evangelism" with CBMC leader Andrew James
- "The Movies and America" with film critic Drew Trotter
- "Work Matters" with Tom Nelson and Steve Garber of Made To Flourish
- "Start Something: Entrepreneurship in Church & Community with Carter Crockett and Larry Ward
- "Dance as Profession, Art, & Ministry" with Ravenna Tucker, Helena Froelich, and Ed Keazirian
- "Islamic & Christian Ethics" with Bernard Adeney and Paul Martindale
- "Loving The City, Loving the Workplace" (in Berkeley) with Rev. Dr. J. Alfred Smith, Sr..

One of our most ambitious and exciting programs was on "Religion & Work: Constructive Insights from the World's Religions." This was a six-hour Saturday event with speakers representing Judaism, Islam, Sikhism, Catholicism, Orthodoxy, and Protestantism. I insisted to these speakers that they focus their twenty-minute "TED-Talk" on ideas about good work that come from their religion, not on other topics in comparative religion. It was superb and all the speakers told me they felt respected and heard—"the best interfaith conference ever" they said. I spoke last as the "protestant" and reflected on how each of my preceding speakers had given some version of "at the end of my life God will accept me based on how just and ethical my work has been." "We Protestants," I commented, "believe that we are saved not by our good works but by God's grace and forgiveness in Jesus Christ—so where does our motivation for good, ethical work come from?" "Yes, we feel an obligation and accountability but it ultimately comes out of gratitude and grace," I was able to share.

It was a demonstration to our seminary and pastoral attendees that an open and respectful interfaith conversation, far from a threat, is an opportunity to learn and to share the Christian Gospel. I arranged a panel of business folk to respond on "where do we go from here in our business environment?" The room was abuzz with great one-on-one conversations all afternoon. My only regret was that our GCTS world religions professors and students (and our administrators) didn't make time to participate. Here the world's religions were on our campus, and they missed out. "Marginal Gill" remember.

One day Greg Forster and another representative of the Kern Family Foundation showed up in my office to find out more about the programs we were running and offer their financial support. "What would I like to do if they could provide some funds?" Gratefully, I suggested they fund a series of small group lunches I could host with faculty and with students—how about twenty of them with ten people at a time? Maybe fund them at $10 per person for a $2000 total? OK, they said, but think bigger! So, I said, here are two big ideas. First, how about supporting a major "Faith at Work Summit Conference" drawing together faith at work business and organizational leaders from across the continent? The movement is growing and we could all benefit from coming together for networking, sharing ideas, praying and encouraging one another. Second, how about supporting an "Entrepreneurship in Church and Community" program to mobilize churches to assist those in need of work—a hidden and neglected population in the faith at work movement almost everywhere?

THE FAITH AT WORK SUMMIT CONFERENCE

As much as I am an entrepreneur and driver, I rarely work without a team. So my first move toward the Faith at Work Summit was to recruit two co-leaders, Al Erisman and Bill Peel. Al was my long-time colleague, co-leader of the Institute for Business, Technology, and Ethics (1998–2003), and co-teacher at Regent College and now at Gordon-Conwell in the Doctor of Ministry track on Workplace Theology, Ethics, and Leadership (more on that below). Al was part of the business faculty at Seattle Pacific University. Bill Peel was a DMin student in our program but also the author of *Workplace Grace,* the best book on workplace evangelism, and Director of the Center for Faith and Work at LeTourneau University in Texas, an engineering school. Beyond their superb talents as individuals, beyond our friendship, this meant that our summit was co-sponsored by a theological school, an engineering school, and a business school, located in Massachusetts, Texas, and Washington: a broad base for a summit conference. We picked a weekend in October 2014, about eighteen months out. I was in the position to captain this project and deal with most of the details with Yuna, but Al's and Bill's wisdom, connections, and targeted tasks were essential to our success. Standing just outside this triumvirate and crucial to our success was Greg Forster from the Kern Family Foundation.

From the start, the Kern Foundation put up $30,000 (and later doubled it to fund the production of conference recordings and some other expenses). The Mockler Center, LeTourneau Center, and SPU each committed $10,000 so we had a good foundation. I recruited ten other faith and work organization as co-sponsors donating $1000 each to the cause. All of us were already salaried (with offices) from our home institutions. In addition to my assistant, Yuna Oh, Bill Peel's assistant in Texas, Amanda Battaglia, played a key role as things developed, and David Horn's Okenga Institute staff stepped in big time during the conference itself.

Yuna and I found a hotel next to Boston's Logan Airport that could accommodate a conference of up to two hundred fifty participants and we boldly signed the contract for meeting space and the lunch and dinner events. We were operating on faith that people would come but no one had ever tried a national faith at work summit like this before so would we be happy if only one hundred fifty people came? We just didn't know. In the end we crammed two hundred eighty people into our conference and turned another fifty away.

We decided that our Summit Conference theme would be "Where Are We? And What Still Needs to Get Done?" We decided to invite speakers representing business (small and large, agriculture, manufacturing, service, and other fields), the professions, the academy (theology, business, engineering), the church, and parachurch faith at work ministries. We wanted to be inclusive and have both old and young, women and men, and various ethnic groups on our platform and among our attendees. We decided to go with a "TEDTalk" format, giving each of our speakers a seventeen-minute slot (a clock would be counting down in front of the speaker podium), followed by a two-minute response and a question from a designated respondent. It worked like charm and many attendees marveled to me "how did you get these speakers to be disciplined like this when most of them would normally take forty to sixty minutes to say the same thing?"

We asked our speakers to donate their time but offered to pay their transportation and hotel costs. One afternoon in my office a young man who was enrolled at Asbury Seminary visited me to discuss his interest in faith at work. In the course of conversation, I found out that he had some good experience in conference organization. I had been worrying about how I could be ushering speakers on and off stage during our conference when I had to be managing the event from near the front of the stage. By the time Devin Marks left my office he had signed on to manage that speaker dance back stage. In addition, Devin offered to coach our speakers on delivering an effective TED Talk. Devin did such an outstanding job that after the Summit he was hired by some of the attendees to do more personal communication coaching and conference support. He turned this into a career ever since. Devin was another gift of God into my life and work. Also on a more immediate-need level, Gordon-Conwell student Bobby Durning offered to be our head usher during the Summit conference, moving the crowd through tight spaces in and out of the assembly hall into the dining area. A team of volunteers helped Bobby get the job done. Meanwhile Yuna was managing the front end registration and back end display areas where various organizations had their literature. With Devin's help we hired lighting, sound, and recording crews to execute the event. Bill Peel's crew managed the post-summit process to turn the recordings into viewable short films and Al Erisman wrote a study guide for groups to use with the film series.

Our plenary TEDTalk speakers from all parts of the movement covered most of the key topics:

- Why Faith at Work Is Important: The Case (Katherine Leary Alsdorf)
- Biblical Foundations: The Big Picture, God's Word on Work (Will Messenger)
- Stewardship Economics: Work in the Larger Economic Frame (Greg Forster)
- Economics & Work On the Margins: Remembering the Poor & Powerless (Julius Walls Jr)
- Godly Globalization: Work & Workplaces in a Global, Diverse, Connected Reality (Tim Liu)
- Technology: Transformation & Challenge for Workers & Workplaces (John Dyer)
- Workplace Ethics: From Damage Control to Mission Control (David Gill)
- Workplace Evangelism: Sharing Our Personal Faith (Bill Peel)
- Workplace Discipleship: Presence, Growth, & Impact (Randy Kilgore)
- Shaping Workers: Calling, Valuing, Training, & Empowering (Cheryl Broetje)
- Creating Jobs: Entrepreneurship & Community Economic Development (Larry Ward)
- Shaping a Company: Leadership & Executive Impact (Don Flow)
- Salting a Corporation: Faithful, impact In A Larger Organization (Gloria Nelund)
- Marketplace Groups: Discipleship, Fellowship, & Support (Eric Welch)
- Seminary Education: Rethinking What's Important (Gideon Strauss)
- B-School Education: Rethinking What's Important (Al Erisman)

- University Student Groups: Coming Alongside the Next Generation (Mark Washington)
- William Wilberforce Yesterday & the Film Industry Today (Micheal Flaherty)
- Faith at Work in the Suburban Church (Tom Nelson)
- Faith at Work in the Urban Church (Ray Hammond)
- Learning from our History, Leaning Toward Our Future (David Miller)
- The Soul of the Movement (Bill Pollard)

On Day Two we broke up into five Workplace/Marketplace Arena Discussion Groups

- Churches & Congregations: pastors and church leaders (Tom Nelson)
- Workplace Disciples: individual workers in various vocations (Andy Mills)
- Marketplace Fellowships: workplace ministries and initiatives (Eric Welch)
- Seminaries & Bible Schools: faculty, students, administrators, alumni (Scott Rae)
- Colleges, Universities, & B-Schools: faculty, students, administrators (Leigh Anne Walker)

Each day we began with a powerful Devotional Reflection & Challenge from Mark Roberts (Friday) and Gina Casey (Saturday). At various points through our program we recognized "pioneers" in the faith at work movement: Tom Phillips (presented by Andy Mills), Howard Butt (Mark Roberts) Wayne Alderson (Al Erisman), R. G. LeTourneau (Bill Peel), and Pete Hammond (John Terrill). Only Tom Phillips was alive to be present of course. This pioneer recognition was important as a reminder that we were not the first—we stood on the shoulders of others.

This initial Faith at Work Summit was an awesome event and experience. God was with us and blessing us. We pulled it off for about $100,000 which was astonishing in its own right. Two years later, Bill Peel led a team that put on a second Faith at Work Summit in Dallas, this time with four hundred or so attendees. In my plenary talk to kick it off, I chided the movement for being "too pale and too male." I hope I said more than that but that was the phrase that got quoted again and again. And in 2018 Greg Forster led the organization of a third Faith at Work Summit in Chicago, another great event with four hundred or so attendees. Our hopes for a 2020 Summit failed for lack of a sponsoring institution and leadership—and, as it turned out, the Covid-19 pandemic. Al, Bill, Greg, and I did not feel called or institutionally-positioned to organize another big Summit conference, though we saw its value and wished for others to do so. We have thought that regional or local "summits" may be a more likely and even beneficial future but it remains something up in the air. It is a good thing to gather together to network, collaborate, learn, and celebrate a movement that is growing and only God can be said to be in charge!

PART THREE: CHANNELS (1979–2016)

PROFESSOR OF WORKPLACE THEOLOGY & BUSINESS ETHICS

Directing the Mockler Center was defined as one-third of my job. The other two-thirds was teaching classes and that had its own exciting adventure (of course I was also expected to be a working, publishing scholar, and a contributor to campus and community life). I taught regular seminary courses every year on Christian ethics, workplace and business ethics, and the theology of work. I enjoyed teaching one of these courses every year downtown in Roxbury at our urban campus. Actually, on my first visit to the downtown CUME campus I participated in my academic robe in the fall opening convocation. For some reason the dean didn't show up and when they got to the place in the program for greetings from the dean I was surprised to be called up to the stage to speak for the Hamilton main campus! Good thing I was raised in those Plymouth Brethren circles where everyone had to be ready on a split-second notice to give a talk! (What happened to you Mr. Dean?).

In my first week on campus I was informed that I would be needed as the second reader for two Doctor of Ministry (DMin) thesis examinations. I speed-read the two theses and was shocked by their abysmal quality. I have never been a hard grader but I wouldn't have passed them as undergraduate term papers, much less doctoral work. I wrote up my critique as gently as I could, mostly in the form of "if you want to take this to the next level, here is what I would suggest." The chair of this DMin thesis committee had only one basic question, "Tell me Joe (name changed), what did ya learn from your thesis work?" Then he kicked it over to me for questioning. I delivered (gently) my comments and suggestions which were received with no push back. Then I asked each student during their exam, "Tell me Joe, how many times did you meet with your thesis director between the start of your thesis work and your defense today?" Answer from both candidates, "Zero." Though this was really educational malpractice, I signed off to approve the two theses because they had been promised (though betrayed) by the system.

My Gordon-Conwell colleague Professor David Wells once published an essay called "The DMin-ization of Seminary Education" criticizing the quality of the typical Doctor of Ministry programs and the embarrassment of binding and shelving most DMin theses in our libraries. But DMin programs are a cash cow at Gordon-Conwell and elsewhere and making them more academically rigorous would be bad for business. I actually think there is a legitimate place for a good DMin program but not the usual way I have seen them operated. At any rate, I found myself now put in charge of the Gordon-Conwell DMin program track called "Christianity in the Marketplace" or words to that effect. This had not been mentioned to me during any part of my application process. But ok.

I studied the DMin curricula that had been offered four or five times before I got to GCTS. They all seemed extraordinarily weak. During the first go-round of the workplace/marketplace track a few years earlier, one of the two instructors was also enrolled as a student and earned his DMin that way. If that wouldn't be enough to cost GCTS its accreditation I don't know what would (and you would think the student would die from embarrassment were it well known how he "earned" his doctorate). Oh well. Bygones. Turn the page. "So what are the sacred cows here?" I asked the DMin program director and seminary dean. How free a hand can I have to redesign the program? Almost total freedom, was the answer.

My first move was to recruit my old colleague and collaborator Dr. (PhD!) Al Erisman to be my co-teacher. I learned that other DMin tracks had co-teachers—but they usually divided up the teaching duties and didn't show up when the other guy taught. They were also only too happy to leave all the advising and program guidance to the DMin office, most of which fell to a sullen office worker who knew their rules but next to nothing about theological education (sorry, but true). I came from a completely different tradition of graduate education where professors take responsibility for their students from admission to graduation, mentoring and caring for them. Al and I changed the program title to "Workplace Theology, Ethics, and Leadership" (WTEL). Like other DMin programs we would have six intensive weeks in residence with our student cohort, spaced over eighteen months, followed by anywhere from six months to two years for the completion of a final thesis project. Unlike most other DMin tracks we scheduled forty-five contact hours together during each of those six weeks, not thirty to thirty-five like the typical track. Less than forty-five hours seemed to me undeserving of the unit/credit hours advertised. Half of our cohort of fifteen would be pastor types, the other half business or parachurch types. No auditors were allowed by DMin office.

I raised enough outside money to be able to pay my co-teacher the equivalent of adjunct course pay (the DMin office wanted to split one pathetic adjunct stipend between the two of us! Al was flying out to Boston from Seattle and would also be rooming with me to save money). It was embarrassing to me, but Al was a generous man, not doing it for the money anyway. I went to work recruiting some great students. We ended up with five Black students in a cohort of fifteen which surprised and pleased all of us involved. One student I recruited was Pastor of an AME Zion Church in Boston and had been my student in a Fuller Seminary ethics class a few years earlier. The DMin office bureaucrats told her she needed three or four classes in pastoral counseling or preaching because her Fuller master's degree had not included those courses. She had been an outstanding pastor and preacher for more than fifteen years—but their bureaucratic system wouldn't budge. I was furious that they didn't even consult me, the subject matter expert, before imposing this ham-fisted, irrelevant requirement. She was a saint and jumped through their hoops. It was ridiculous.

Later on in our program one of our students (from Taiwan) decided he should not go with our class to Honduras out of fear his expiring Taiwan visa might create problems getting back into the USA. He was completely legal but you know the warnings about paying attention to when your passport expires. So Al and I devised a make-up plan where a few months later James (new visa in hand) would accompany Al to a faith at work conference in Kuala Lumpur. No, that wasn't acceptable and the DMin Director assigned James to accompany another DMin cohort to some other global site, costing double the money and time and focused on a topic utterly irrelevant to our WTEL. I protested to the GCTS President and Dean but they decided that, despite the educational and ethical merits of my case, they would uphold the DMin Director's authority. It was the worst case of educational malpractice in my forty years as a professor. The worst! Our first cohort was in residence with Al and me in 2011–13. When our second cohort ran from 2014–16, I detached it from the DMin office and ran it as a Masters level program for reasons of both educational quality and academic freedom. I felt sorry for all the applicants who wanted to do the DMin with us but we had a great cohort of Masters level students the second time around, completely free of DMin mis-education controls. It really was a shame.

Al and I designed a six-part curriculum in which Week One was about "Workplace Theology"—what is the truth and reality of work, especially from God's perspective in Scripture? Week Two was on "Workplace Ethics"—what is the right thing to do in light of that truth and reality about work? Week Six, at the end, was about "Workplace Leadership"—how can we influence people and organizations to see that truth and reality and do that right thing in the workplace? For Weeks Three, Four, and Five we focused on what we viewed as the three main drivers in the contemporary workplace: finance, technology, and globalization. For finance week we went to New York City where I found us cheap housing on the Upper West Side at Hephzibah House. In addition to our readings (secular and Christian), lectures (often by guests from Wall Street, Redeemer Pres, Reuters, etc.), and discussions, we went on field trips to the Stock Exchange and to Abyssinian Baptist in Harlem. For technology we spent a week in Seattle, housed in SPU dorms, with field trips to Boeing and to Steve Bell's cabinetry factory, and guest presentations from Amazon, Microsoft, and other techie folk.

For globalization we spent a week in Tegucigalpa, Honduras—we wanted to do our study in a "developing" economy and Honduras was close and inexpensive enough to meet the need. There we visited the TEGU Toy manufacturing business, a big Pepsi bottling factory (to view a multinational up close), and the city dump with its impoverished scavenger population, and with guest lectures from World Vision, the Association for a More Just Society, and some local business folk. My San Leandro High School classmate Kendall Mau invited us to a presentation and then a barbecue at the offices of his microfinance bank.

In between our weeklong intensive experiences there were books to review and papers to write. Al and I were always contactable by our students and held online class sessions about every six or eight weeks. Al and I divided up the responsibilities for thesis supervision of those doing the DMin so they all got lots of attention, guidance, and support. They all finished by 2016, my last commencement ceremony at GCTS. After I left GCTS in 2016, I organized a couple WTEL zoom reunions and one in-person New York City reunion for all who could make it from both cohorts. We had outstanding students in both cohorts, most of whom would say—as would I and Al—this was the best study program, the best educational experience of our lives.

One other exciting teaching experience I had was working with David Horn on a two-year continuing education program for young pastors in New England. Every two months, fifteen younger pastors selected for the program met on the GCTS campus for a 30-hour intensive "retreat" on some major topic that would strengthen their understanding and capacity to communicate with contemporary culture. I participated in all eight of the retreats and was the chief organizer for the retreats on health care, business, and technology—for which I set up visits to MIT and Harvard Business School and panel discussions with veterans and leading-edge thinkers in all three fields. The retreat on global mission was a ten-day visit to mainland China, my first ever, in summer 2015. I was delighted to get to tour Beijing, Xi'an, and Shanghai (the Great Wall, the Forbidden City, the terra cotta warriors, etc.) and listen in on meetings with Christians in the house church movement (several of them GCTS grads) and the Three Self official church. It was just mind-boggling, both the ancient and modern sides of China. The vitality and explosive growth of Christianity were unforgettable.

When word of my upcoming PRC visit spread among some Chinese students (now back in the PRC) I had taught at GCTS and a group of touring PRC Christian business leaders to whom I had spoken about business ethics, I was invited to come to China a week early and give a series of talks to both Christian and mixed groups of business folk in Beijing, Xi'an, and Shanghai. My current student at GCTS, Choe Wu, told me she would be in Beijing that summer when I would be there. And out of the blue a GCTS student from China I had not met before, Ruqiong Tang, showed up in my office to volunteer to help me with translation of my slides and materials in preparation for my lectures in China—a huge task. She also said she would be in Beijing during my upcoming visit and would translate for me if I wished. "Yes" I said. "Maybe you and Chloe can take turns since it will be several hours over several days."

And so they did. What an incredible team they were. GCTS professor Xiyi Yau and GCTS-friend and Chinese-American business entrepreneur Chikong Shue also accompanied the tour and helped with logistics and translation when Ruqiong and Chloe were not with me. (Chikong, by the way, also joined our WTEL cohort in Tegucigalpa, Honduras, not long after the China tour, adding his rich perspective on globalization to our cohort). I loved the China tour, the Chinese people and culture (Ruqiong taught me the Chinese Tea Ceremony, or as much as an old professor could take in on a first exposure; it was beauty and poetry), and the Chinese Christian folk, mostly young business and professional types.

When I got back to GCTS to begin my final year, I was bummed that Yuna had graduated and moved back to New York. What was I going to do for a Mockler Center assistant? I advertised and interviewed some talented applicants. But then Ruqiong and Chloe walked in and asked if they could share the position. They didn't have all the technical skills Yuna had (who did?) and I worried a bit. But my colleague David Horn reminded me how much more important trust and chemistry are than skills per se—and I made the deal with Ruqiong and Chloe. What a total joy to have them by my side every step of the way in the final year of my career as a professor. They are my lifetime friends and sisters. Ruqiong began to call me "Godfather" which I loved and to this day she really is the goddaughter who Lucia and I treasure as our own. I told both Ruqiong and Chloe that I wanted to vet any guys pursuing them to make sure they were good enough for them! When Ruqiong surprised us with her engagement to a fine young Texas brother Steven Walter, I walked her down the aisle. When Chloe got engaged in Beijing, she made sure we met her fiancé and later participated in her wedding on zoom. Precious.

ENTREPRENEURSHIP IN CHURCH AND COMMUNITY

I have spent a lot of my life trying to help people take their faith to work. But I have always been concerned about those who could say to me "David, I would love to do that but I have no work to take my faith to." Most faith at work organizations like to focus on business and professional workers, "white collar" folk. Blue collar folk in manufacturing, service jobs, volunteer or unsalaried work (like parenting!)—these workers don't get nearly as much attention. And least of all are those without work or in between jobs. This is maybe the hardest work of all: looking for work! Stressful, discouraging, disappointing. Some workers have jobs that are terrible but they are stuck.

Despite the harsh and sweeping judgments made by some, the unemployed are rarely lazy and never without some kind of work skill at some level. Many in our churches and neighborhoods want to work but don't know how to find a job or turn their skills into paid work. But our churches are full of other folk who do know how to train workers and how to turn skills into a small business. What a ministry, what a mission this could be—to help the unemployed and underemployed find decent work. Following Jesus doesn't just mean helping the rich and successful to do better, it is also (and I think mostly) about helping the downtrodden get on their feet, not just spiritually but economically. Christians, tragically, are every bit as partisan and divided when it comes to politics as the world around us. But when it comes to work and jobs, conservative, liberal, and nonpolitical Christians all agree that jobs and work are important, even a commission from God. I wish we Christians could talk much less about politics and instead join together to help create good work in our communities.

When I arrived at Gordon-Conwell in fall 2010 I was already thinking about trying to do something about small business entrepreneurship. Within a month I found myself sitting next to Larry Ward, pastor of Abundant Life Church in Cambridge, Massachusetts, at an advisory council meeting for our urban campus in Roxbury. As we went around the room and introduced ourselves, Larry mentioned his work mentoring young men and teaching them basic entrepreneurship so they would imagine and pursue something more constructive than selling drugs on the street corner. After the meeting we began our lifetime friendship and partnership. The Kern Family Foundation provided us a grant to pay (1) tuition for fifteen students enrolled in our new co-taught GCTS course "Entrepreneurship in Church and Community," (2) a modest stipend for Larry's co-teaching with me, (3) business start-up grants of $500 for each of our fifteen wannabe entrepreneurs, and (4) a celebratory lunch together for the thirty-two participants (mentors plus entrepreneurs and professors) at the end of the course. Our funding was renewable for three years. Gordon-Conwell approved our course proposal.

The first thing we did was recruit our fifteen students—some came from the current GCTS urban student body but others were local pastors and lay leaders. All of them were going to learn how to coach a wannabe entrepreneur from their congregation or surrounding community. Their first assignment was to find a good prospect and get them to accompany them to our Saturday morning class for the next nine weeks. We created a simple application form they could use for their prospects and a list of "Characteristics of High Potential Entrepreneurs." From week two onward we had thirty people in class each week—fifteen coach/entrepreneur pairs. Larry and I always began with a workplace-oriented devotional out of Scripture and then a prayer. Then over the next weeks we taught the basics of starting a small business, always with an exciting biblical/theological foundation. Honestly, it often felt like church. Many of our entrepreneurs had never been around people who believed in them and their potential before. Starting a business with a coach/mentor/partner is infinitely better and more promising than doing it all alone. Being part of a cohort of fellow entrepreneurs once a week is hugely encouraging. Praying together and not just going for it 'secular-style" makes a big difference.

We had our students read *The $100 Startup: Reinvent the Way You Make A Living, Do What You Love, and Create a New Future* (New York: Crown, 2012) by Chris Guillebeau, a secular best-seller but in harmony with biblical values and full of amazing true stories. I pointed out to our entrepreneurs that they "won the lottery" because they would get a grant of $500, not just $100. Larry and I created our own material rather than rely on one of the "Start Your Own Business" manuals available in bookstores. We also had several guest speakers who were experts in setting up good financial systems (Jackie Cooper), marketing (Catherine Blake), legal matters and permits (Betsy Cowan), e-mail and web sites, and other aspects of small business.

Once we had our mentors and prospects in class the first big topic was "what business should I start?" We taught them to find the intersection of (1) their own skills and abilities, (2) where there was or could be a market, and (3) God's mission and values. Lots of businesses could be imagined that only satisfied one or two of those criteria but we insisted on all three and helped them learn how to figure out each of the three. The next big step was to draft an overall start-up business plan for the first six months or so. What's the name of the business, specific tasks, equipment needed, advertising, due dates, costs . . . all the basics but on two pages or so.

Third, a bank account and accounting system needed to be put in place. We insisted that when we gave them the grant they had to have a dedicated business bank account and couldn't just mix business and personal funds. My brilliant GCTS student Devon McCarley already had an MBA and worked part-time for a local bank. She got her bank to agree to open accounts for each of our entrepreneurs and she personally helped each one do it. Fourth, everyone needed a marketing plan, advertising, and a mailing/distribution list of potential customers. Fifth, everyone needed a web site and the ability create newsletters, posters, and business communications. Sixth, everyone needed help with any permits or business licenses required by the city and the particular industry. Finally, we helped our entrepreneurs plan out their approach to personnel: things like an advisory council, board of directors, job descriptions, and worker evaluations if and when any of these became appropriate. The entrepreneurs had to meet with their coaches outside of class each week and prepare some short reports on all of these topics.

When the business plan and budget were tweaked, strengthened, and approved by Larry or me, we transferred the $500 grant to their business bank account. After a two-week break for them to work on their business we schedule two Saturdays of "Launch Day"—complete with room decorations and refreshments. Each entrepreneur (not their coach) had twelve minutes to present and promote their new business to the rest of the class—and all the other invited guests they wished—as though we were prospective customers they were selling. Even if, for example, it was a women's hair or cosmetics business or a music studio, sell us, we said, on sending our women friends or musician friends their way. Many of our entrepreneurs had never before in their life stood up in front of a group and spoken. They answered a few questions from the "prospective customers" and received rousing applause at the end. It was incredible. We ran the course on Saturday mornings in the Spring Quarter after Easter so the weather was good and they could launch at the beginning of summer. Three months later we reconvened over lunch and Larry and I gave out two $500 awards to the (at that point) most successful start-ups.

Larry and I ran the course three years in a row from 2013–2015. Seven years out now, of our forty-five start-ups, my rough estimate is that ten developed into durable, successful businesses, twenty are functioning but are not yet strong enough to support the entrepreneur full-time, ten of the start-ups are on hold or life support for various reasons, and about five died fairly quickly because of business permit problems (usually food related) or overly ambitious and then costly challenges. Here are twenty-three of the forty-five start-ups to give you an idea of what was accomplished:

- Devin Marks's speaker coaching business is thriving (remember how the seeds were sown at the Faith at Work Summit).
- Christine Paige's "Bliss Salon" (hair) in Providence, Rhode Island, is booming and expanding with several employees.

- Julie Phillips's "Jesignz Graphix" graphic design business is booming.
- Victor Cubi turned his odd job career into a more organized, formal, profitable "Victor for Hire" landscaping and handyman business, now including some hired hands.
- Izetta Jackson, a minimum wage staff hotel worker often forced to work on Sundays and miss church, launched her own "Mama Boney by Faith Cleaning Service" where she earns a fairer wage and can control her working hours and get to church regularly.
- Eva Clark, founded "L.A.S.T." (Love All Skin Tones) a cosmetic business about rejecting tanning and bleaching and learning to love the colors God made us in a healthy way.
- Jennifer Dhanjee developed a vocal training school, "Lift Up Your Voice."
- Derek Canton launched "G1G" ("God is Good") a branded/message line of clothing and wearables which won some start-up business awards.
- Daryl Best founded "Best Media," a producer and vendor of a new photo-sharing app.
- Pamela Cazeau launched an event planning business "Expressions of You."
- Michelle Lagene developed "Michelle Clothing and Accessories," a Haitian import business.
- Huegens Alexis, started "1sq Inch Custom Storage Solutions," custom cabinetry and remodeling.
- Veronique Francois turned her cooking skills into "Anointed Catering Services."
- Walesk Dube, turned his photography talents into "M.A.D. Productions."
- Jinie Yang, founded "Olivewood Design," a graphic design and branding business.
- Nyjah Wyche-Alexis founded "Spa Kitchen," non-toxic, healthy, custom-made cosmetics.
- Neal Samudre created "JesusHacks" an online discipleship training program.
- Chad Ryan started "Make It Interactive," a board game.
- Annie Quinones founded "Real Victory Estate" to focus on university housing rentals.
- Leslie Moore created "GeoForts," an educational game/toy.
- Ronia Stewart started "Garden of Eden" leadership and empowerment training.
- Shannon Lankford turned her hobby into "Real Life Photography."
- Sokhan Prak entrepreneured "Straight Ahead Silkscreen" (tee shirts).

One thing was abundantly clear: our churches could (if they so decided), individually or in church-partnerships, run programs like this and have a huge grass roots impact on communities in need of good jobs. What a witness to the Gospel this would be. Any takers reading this?

LAST DAYS

After four years in Gloucester, we decided to move our base back home to Oakland. It was time for grandma to get back to the grandkids (grandpa also). We sold our condo for a slight loss after four years. Our property had been redesignated as a flood plain, scaring away some would be purchasers. Sea levels are rising! I was not done yet at GCTS however so I rented a small apartment on campus so I could run our Mockler Center and continue my teaching. For the next two years I returned to Oakland every school break and also for long weekends every three weeks or so during the academic terms. The big Faith at Work Summit was in October of my fourth year, the China trip was during my fifth summer at GCTS. The second WTEL cohort ran from 2014–16.

Going back to one week into the fall term 2012, after the end of my interim pastorate at Trinitarian Congregational Church (2011–12), I suddenly couldn't talk without slurring my speech in class. This activistic "What Are You Doing About it" man was having a TIA, mini-stroke in class. I was hospitalized for two or three days and thoroughly checked out. No permanent damage but a warning sign about my stress-filled (by choice!) life. I wised up for a while, cut back a bit, but in the fall of 2014 I had another TIA, also just as I tried to call my class to order. I couldn't remember my password to open my laptop. When asked what year it was, I answered that I knew we were in the 2000s but that was as precise as I could get. I couldn't remember the name of our hospital (Lahey!) when the ambulance came to get me. This time it was the combined stress of the huge 2014 Faith at Work Summit and the very same month dealing with my elderly aunt's stroke, death, memorial service, and closing affairs in Seattle. It was time to start wrapping things up and go home. I decided that should happen in June 2016 after my last group of WTEL students was finished. I turned 70 in February of 2016. I was about done with the full-time professor life after forty years (and fifty as a teacher).

During my final year at GCTS, the dean decided (after a number of faculty suggestions) to appoint me and two or three other professors to organize and chair our remaining faculty meetings. I proposed that at each faculty meeting we bring in two campus staff members to briefly interview them, thank them, give them a small gift like a book, and pray for them. Our whole staff felt demoralized, underpaid, and above all, unseen and unappreciated. The head of our kitchen and food services, the registrar, the groundskeeper, the head of campus security, and others were deeply touched by this new "tradition." I suggested we sing a hymn at each meeting which was also a huge hit. And I insisted that after almost every report, someone say a prayer for that leader. I had been depressed for years by the failure to do this—our president might stand up and share some giant fund-raising burden or initiative, sit down, and the agenda moved on; a professor might share that his adult kid was back on drugs; silence. I sometimes called out in those meetings "Pray for him!" And then the dean would awkwardly say "Oh yes, David would you pray for him." When it was my turn to chair the faculty meeting on February 24, 2016, our guest for that meeting was Ann McClenahan, the incoming president of the Boston Theological Institute (the consortium of Harvard, GCTS, Boston College, Andover-Newton and other theological Schools). As one of the agenda items, I called on her to share her BTI vision. After that meeting, she said to me that none of the BTI schools had anything like the healthy camaraderie or sense of mission she felt at GCTS. At that moment we all felt it. It didn't last long.

It should have been for me a smooth and sweet sail off west into the sunset but the president dropped a bomb on the school later that Spring 2016. My friend and Ockenga Institute boss David Horn was summarily fired with no warning, at age sixty-four, after twenty years of what all of us who worked for him would call great leadership. My friend Alvin Padilla, a legendary leader of GCTS's hispanic and urban ministries was also pushed out, along with a few other faculty and staff. This was all because of what were deemed unmanageable financial pressures. Several other steps would be taken including closing down the Ockenga Institute and the dining commons.

I was both saddened and outraged, as were most of my faculty colleagues. But I was a senior professor on the way out the door, and not, like them, intimidated by any fear of being next to be let go! So I spoke up in vigorous protest and circulated my protest letter to the whole faculty—making me appreciated by the faculty but persona non grata to the administration and board (doing something that immediately guaranteed I would be only marginal to Gordon-Conwell in the future!). I protested against the cruelty and injustice of firing Horn. He deserved notice and an opportunity to resolve any financial shortfalls in the Ockenga Institute and its seven member centers. If he had known and shared with the seven center directors that we were running, say, $300,000 short each year, we would have rolled up our sleeves and raised the money. We would have all taken pay cuts or made budget cuts to keep him on board. We never even had the chance. We loved and valued this guy.

Furthermore, it just seemed wrong-headed to eliminate our dining commons when we had hundreds of residents on campus. Why not raise the prices a bit and market the food service to our nearby alumni and neighbors? Eating together was absolutely crucial to our being a residential community. The Hispanic program was well-attended and had a huge upside growth potential. Cutting Al Padilla and his colleagues was a very shortsighted saving that promised only shrinkage and loss—as well as contradicting our espoused comitment to diversity and inclusion, Jesus-style. GCTS, I argued, in summary, was never going to cut its way out of its financial hole, it needed to grow its way out. It could but it didn't. If there was one promising link to new students it was David Horn's Ockenga Institute which was connected to hundreds of churches and pastors, and to thousands of GCTS alumni. Our traditional, residential seminary degree program might be fated to have declining enrollment—but even there it seemed to many of us that our advertising approach was terrible and our recruiting neglected many potential sources of new students.

In any case, there were more than enough potential students "out there" for innovative continuing, extension, customized, and online options. A muscled-up GCTS alumni association (like we developed at St. Mary's) could have played a huge role—but GCTS could never get past the old-school alumni approach consisting of an occasional presidential visit to raise money and encourage the troops. David Horn and the Ockenga Institute could and should have been unleashed as the primary interface with churches and Christian workers. The Mockler-Phillips workplace initiative—that had distinguished GCTS from every other seminary and which had incredible potential—was, during my six years, admired and encouraged but always kept in a "silo" alongside the "real" seminary program. Its potential was never fully grasped. (The final bummer, a couple years after I left GCTS, was the renaming and refocusing of the Mockler Center from "the Workplace" to "the Public Square"—a popular but generic and meaninglessly general target indistinguishable from such centers at competitor schools.

Another GCTS veteran in the neighborhood, Doug Birdsall, wrote an even more powerful public letter of concern, opposition, and rebuke to the "midnight massacre" we had just experienced. In the end, nothing was changed and the diminished GCTS carried on as I left. I felt terrible for our beleaguered president, but it was his choice to go this route. Losing my relationship with him and a couple other administrators was the cost of my speaking up. But I just couldn't remain silent in the face of this cruel injustice and this undermining of the GCTS heritage, mission, and vision.

On April 22, 2016, I led (solo) a Mockler Seminar for the first time, speaking on "Fifty Years, Twenty-four Lessons"—some of the core beliefs, discoveries, themes, and commitments of my life and work. The next day, Ruqiong Tang organized a wonderful farewell party for me in Alumni Hall. At the baccalaureate service, May 6, 2016, the night before graduation exercises, I gave a sermon to graduates, faculty, family, and friends on "Light A Candle (Don't Just Curse the Darkness)" based on Titus 2:14–17. It expressed the heart of what I have long believed. We live between the two appearings of our Lord and it is dark outside. We must learn to say No to what is evil—but not stop there and just be the denouncers of what is bad, a "religion of No." We must also be shaped by the "Yes" of the "blessed hope"—and have our lives positively shaped by the coming day. I gave lots of examples. For example, the day is coming when our "swords will be beaten into ploughshares"—so let's do it now to the extent possible, replacing violence in our society with meaningful work. The day is coming when "every tear will be wiped away"—so let's do it now, coming alongside the hurting to comfort them. The day is coming when "people will come from east and west, north and south and sit at table in the kingdom of God"—let's do it now, bringing stranger and friend from this diverse, divided planet to our tables. And so on.

Thus, my formal career as an academic (and pastor and organizer) came to its end. More than enough pain and mistakes, but for sure I had tried hard to answer my dad's challenge "What Are You Doing About It?" My impact was marginal but I had been an activist, not a griper on the sidelines.

23

Postscript: Fourth Quarter (2016-)

ON GROUND HOG DAY in 2016 I turned seventy years old. It was my sixth year on the faculty of Gordon-Conwell in the Boston area, my fortieth year as a university or seminary professor, my fiftieth year as a regular teacher (and often organizer, pastor and preacher over those years). It was time to go home to Oakland, time for a big transition and a different rhythm to my life and work. I didn't (and don't) believe in "retirement" in the sense of a "post-work" life. Everyone is made to work six days and rest a seventh throughout their days. But now, by the grace of God and my wife's wise input on our planning (Live within your means! Build up some savings!), I did not need to work for financial compensation. Our great old house (purchased in 1972) on 62nd Street in the ("Lower"!) Rockridge neighborhood of Oakland was waiting for us.

The words of "Moses the man of God" in Psalm 90 were on my mind as I got closer to seventy: "The days of our life are seventy years, or perhaps eighty, if we are strong; even then their span is only toil and trouble; they are soon gone, and we fly away . . . So teach us to count our days that we may gain a wise heart . . . Satisfy us in the morning with your steadfast love, so that we may rejoice and be glad all our days . . . Let your work be manifest to your servants, and your glorious power to their children . . . Let the favor of the Lord our God be upon us, and prosper for us the work of our hands—O prosper the work of our hands!" (vv. 10, 12, 14, 16, 17).

The irony of these words coming from a man whose greatest days of leadership were from age eighty to one hundred twenty, was not lost on me. I remember joking with my dad on his 80th birthday that everything to that point in his life was preparation for the great things we now expected of him! My dad lived to age ninety-one and my mom to age eighty-nine—and neither of them was ever as healthy and athletic as I had been for seven decades. But there are no guarantees in these matters. In my youth I often had a foreboding that I would die by age thirty-three as my Lord had done. That foreboding strangely disappeared at age twenty-five when our first child was born! As I wrote in an earlier chapter, I experienced a kind of life and work catharsis at age forty-two in 1988 when my ambition was dialed back, as my kids were about to leave the nest, and as the biggest, most ambitious project of my life (New College Berkeley) was clearly faltering. And in 2001, at age fifty-five, I "gave up" some more of my dreams, hopes, and expectations and decided to practice contentment and gratitude as much as I could, with God's help, for the rest of my life. Outwardly, I was still the same activistic "what are you doing about it" guy right up to 2016, but my spirit and attitude were changed 1988, 2001, and 2016.

It was a little bit painful to close off my formal career and hang up my doctoral robe and academic regalia, this time deep in my closet. Literally! I bought my robe for $600 in 1979 for my graduation at USC. I wondered at the time if that would be a good investment. It was. I never had to rent one. It was black so I could use it when needed for church, weddings, etc.. And I wore it well over a hundred times for academic convocations. I feel the absence of colleagues and students who I almost always loved. I miss the daily interaction, the vigorous exchange of ideas, the up-close observation of learning and growth, the deep satisfaction and "high" of a successful program or project completed. But I knew it was time to go. My TIA "mini-strokes" in 2012 and 2014 were a clear signal that my life- and work-style could not be sustained much longer. I also had the feeling that I had given all I had to give to Gordon-Conwell and more generally to the "professoriate." My life "calling" remained the same but what would be the new channels through which it should be expressed?

A YEAR OF QUIET AND REFLECTION

I decided to devote the first year of my "retirement" to listening, reading, prayer, and reflection—seeking to hear God's calling for whatever years I had left. Aside from one last speech at the fall 2016 Faith at Work Summit Conference in Dallas, I declined to speak, lecture, or preach for the whole year. I told myself I had been "running my mouth" for fifty years (except for three sabbatical years over that time period when I had a greatly reduced speaking schedule)—and now was a time for silence. Twelve months passed and I had no answer. Twelve months stretched into eighteen! Patience.

Then in early 2018, we attended worship at First Covenant Church in Oakland. My old friends Kurt and Karen Morrill were visiting the church to give a report on their work at the University of Strasbourg in France. For us, it was a reunion with a couple that had been part of francophone soirees in our home in years past. It was great to see and hear the Morrills but what "blew me away" was the congregation itself. The ethnic, age, and vocational diversity looked like Oakland, the home town I loved—and like the kingdom of God, present and coming. The love and spirit felt to me like I was home. We were welcomed into the family and committed ourselves.

This was the completion of a circle that began at Pasadena Covenant Church in 1975 during my graduate school days at USC, then raising our family at Berkeley

Covenant Church through the 1980s, then my two-year Interim Pastorate at University Covenant Church in Davis (1990–92), and then my nine years at North Park, the Covenant Church's university in Chicago (1992–2001), I had found a theological and ecclesiastical home. From 2001 to 2017, my work, teaching, and relational commitments found me in Presbyterian, Free Church, and Congregational fellowships—but I was never fully at home theologically or ecclesiastically. Attending the big annual Covenant Ministers' Midwinter Conferences in 2019 and 2020 was for me a powerful and even surprising affirmation that I was home. The leadership and the voices of our Black, Hispanic, Korean and other ethnic ministers were powerful and inspiring, a huge stride forward from what I experienced back in the 1980s and 1990s.

Lucia and I followed our practices of the past fifty years and began inviting people from the church into our home, often six at a time for Sunday dinner after church once a month. Good food, good fellowship and conversation, people from east and west, north and south, all sitting at table in a foretaste of heaven. In my view, this is our main ministry, our main contribution to the church—and what a gift it is back to us. I have been preaching at FCC or elsewhere maybe three or four times each year—just the right amount for this "retired" veteran. I have led a few adult education sessions at FCC and other churches. I have enjoyed setting up tables and chairs and washing some dishes at special senior events.

WORKPLACE DISCIPLESHIP

During the fall of 2018, I offered a six-hour seminar at FCC that I called "Workplace Discipleship 101"—the most basic teaching on the biblical meaning and guidance for our work. I prefer the term "workplace" to "marketplace" because the latter puts the focus on the exchange of goods and services, not their production and delivery, which may or not be "marketed" or financially compensated. I prefer the term "discipleship" to "faith at work" because it is a broader, more holistic reference to the Christian life. My interest is in what it means to be a follower (disciple) of Jesus Christ in our work, whatever and wherever that may be. I repeated this seminar three more times until the Covid pandemic ended our in-person gatherings. But really, if there is one supreme and constant focus of my life calling, it is this: workplace discipleship.

By the end of 2016 I had rough drafted a manuscript called "The God of Good Work" (a biblical theology/philosophy of work) but I decided to put that aside in favor of a more practical, in-the-trenches introduction following the outline of my FCC seminars. This was published (print, e-book, and audiobook formats) as my ninth book in fall 2020: *Workplace Discipleship 101: A Primer*.[1] Part One contains five chapters about "Preparation" for workplace discipleship: Commit, Pray, Listen (to Scripture), Partner, and Learn (continuing education, lifelong learning). Part Two is about

---

1. David W. Gill, *Workplace Discipleship 101: A Primer* (Peabody, Massachusetts: Hendrickson, 2020).

five aspects of "Presence" in the workplace: Align (your work with God's), Model (good character and workplace habits), Light (bring biblical insights about work to our workplace), Share (appropriate and effective evangelism), and Overcome (conflict and wrong-doing). Part Three is about "Post-Workplace" life: Contribute (to church and community) and Rest (no good work without good rest). I added a "Postscript for Pastors" on six ways pastors can improve their ministry to their workplace disciples. This book is in many ways a summary of my life calling and message. It is an inexpensive paperback that includes questions for personal reflection and group discussion. My hope is that it is helpful wherever individuals, churches, and study groups have an interest. In the first year after its release I did something like thirty or forty radio and video interviews and online presentations to study groups from Seattle to Boston, even a couple for Mongolia and China. Wherever there is an interested audience I hope to spread the message.

I am appalled by the political division and folly in today's churches—and equally troubled by the way our churches fail to support the work lives of our people. Bring up your political views and get ready to be attacked. But virtually all Christians agree that people need to work—to survive but also to thrive. Having a decent job is also about our dignity, made in the image and likeness of a working (creating, sustaining, redeeming) God. We can all work together to help people find or create work, and lift up our workplaces toward God's standards of ethics and excellence. If our churches would only wake up to this biblical mandate!

WORKPLACE 313

I wondered what I could do to help our workplace disciples beyond the "101" introductory level. From the day I launched my 101 seminars, I began brainstorming with my old friend, artist and website designer Keith Criss. Keith and I went all the way back fifty years to the Christian World Liberation Front, *Radix Magazine* and New College Berkeley. In September 2019 we decided to form a non-profit organization called "Workplace 313." The "313" is a reference to the three hundred thirteen days of the year that are not the fifty-two Sundays. Of course, we want to support the fifty-two Sunday discipleship experience, largely focused on the "gathered church"—but our target is those three hundred thirteen days, Monday to Saturday, when we are the "scattered church" out in our workplaces of all kinds, from the home to the art studio, factory, office building, hospital, or wherever. Keith and I were soon joined by FCC members Kelly Bresso, and Art Hom, and by Gina Casey (AME Zion), Sid Smith III (Third Baptist, San Francisco), Al Kropp (Berkeley Covenant), Marda Quon Stothers (College Avenue Presbyterian, Oakland), Tom Cowley (Tiburon Baptist), Vent Traylor (First Presbyterian, Berkeley), and Susan Cosio (University Covenant, Davis) on our Board of Directors. WP313 serves and belongs to the whole church.

Our Workplace 313 mission and purpose is to explore and promote workplace discipleship wherever there is interest but especially in Oakland and Northern California. We are building a helpful resource at our web site www.wp313.org. We produce a free e-zine, "The 313," now sent to over a thousand subscribers—containing brief essays, book and media reviews, and introductions to other organizations and web sites addressing aspects of workplace discipleship. We host frequent online "WP313 Forums" on various aspects of workplace discipleship such as law, health care, manufacturing, evangelism, technology, engineering, plumbing, art, racial relations, leadership, and chaplaincy. This is all in addition to our in-person and online presentations on the basics: workplace discipleship 101.

Our team is composed of volunteers, our services are free of charge, and our expenses are paid by charitable donations from our board members and friends. Our biggest challenges going forward are (1) to impact the early career age group and (2) to come alongside the unemployed and underemployed with job-finding and job-creating assistance. As you can imagine, this project keeps me as busy as my time and energy allow! WP313 believes in collaboration with other kindred spirits and organizations as much as possible, so we are in no way "going it alone." Of course, I am always cognizant of my advancing age, so WP313 is exploring possible collaborations and mergers going forward.

OVERTIME

I call this "postscript" my "Fourth Quarter" as a reference to the final period in a football game. I don't call it "Two Minute Warning" or "My Final Hours" or "Last Ditch Efforts"—though if "threescore and ten" is the standard for human life, maybe this is actually "Overtime" or "Extra Innings." My life- and work-style has changed since 2016 (though I find myself still struggling with overcommitment). Now that we don't have to run off to offices somewhere every day, Lucia and I love to get up each morning, make a great mug of Peet's French Roast and listen to some classical chamber music or Oscar Peterson while we read the (old school print edition) *San Francisco Chronicle* and *New York Times*. We review our calendars, read a chapter together out loud from our French Bibles (often listening to it in French first to sharpen up our pronunciation!), and pray together with plenty of thanksgiving for our many blessings and then a long list of health and other challenges faced by our family, friends, church, neighborhood, city and world. Then we go for an hourlong walk on one of our favorite routes near our house. A couple times each week I go work out at my gym (and Lucia might swim). Once a week I play a round of golf at the crack of dawn, usually at Oakland's municipal Lake Chabot Golf Course which I have frequented since my early twenties (now happy to score in the 90s, but dreaming of the 80s when I was younger).

Most Saturday mornings Lucia and I do a one-hour bike ride in Alameda along San Francisco Bay. We try to go off in our car on Thursdays for a longer drive (often including that hour-long walk) in San Francisco, Half Moon Bay, Sausalito, Danville, Santa Cruz, Benicia, or up to the Sonoma or Napa Valley wine country (with appropriate beverage tastings). We never cease to praise God for the beautiful area we live in. Once in a while we do a longer, overnight trip to Monterey and Carmel, Yosemite or King's Canyon/Sequoia National Parks. Once or twice a year we drive down to San Diego to visit our son and grandsons in San Diego, with overnight stops in San Luis Obispo, Santa Barbara, and Santa Monica on the way down or back. We both spend time on e-mails, text messages, FaceBook, and zoom meetings with family and friends. Once a month we have a zoom conversation with my three sisters. Once a month we meet with three other neighborhood couples in our "Oenology" (wine tasting) group at one of our houses or gardens. Our kids and grands and friends sometimes come over to spend a couple hours with us in our front garden. Once a month we host a "big family" dinner. Lucia and I do our household and garden chores every week and love the look when we finish. We each cook about half the evenings and watch the PBS Newshour and Jeopardy regularly. We watch a lot of PBS series like Vera, Morse, Lewis, and Endeavor. We get out to live music at Yoshi's, the Sound Room, and Freight and Salvage when we can see and hear a great musical group.

My own work with Workplace 313 and the International Jacques Ellul Society continues and I do some informal consulting and reviewing for individuals and publications who track me down. I read a lot—and more widely than when I was preparing for specific teaching assignments. I still write a lot, every month for our "313" e-zine, sometimes for the *Ellul Forum* and IJES Conferences, but mostly on book projects. I hope to go back and edit my rough draft on *The God of Good Work*. I would like to gather about twenty of my best sermons into a book on the Christian life and my many essays on Jacques Ellul into an anthology on the *Prophet in the Technological Wilderness*. Many of my students and friends have urged me to write a little book on Paul's Romans 12–13 text which I have called *Ethics and Values from Another World— for This World*. Hoping I don't run out of time on that. I have never written out of duty but out of passion and (I hope) inspiration. I write about what I teach and feel like I have to get it out in written form.

FAITHJAZZ

Sometime back in the 1980s and 1990s, as I got deeper into my love and appreciation for jazz music, I was struck by the parallels between jazz and the Christian life. Jazz connects with my soul—and so does Christian discipleship, following Jesus Christ. Attending the Sun Valley Jazz Festival together years ago, my old friend John Erisman encouraged me that I was really on to something and should write about it. My other jazz friends like Gina Casey have said the same over the years. I developed it into a six-week adult education course at First Presbyterian Church of Berkeley around 2006 and was amazed at the turnout and excitement. I organized it into a graduate level elective course during the Summer of 2011 at Regent College and invited Bill Edgar (theology professor and jazz pianist) to co-teach it with me.

"FaithJazz" is an apt metaphor for my whole marginal life and my work. Let me explain. Jazz depends, first, on the players finding, developing, and perfecting their play on their own instrument. So too, that's what all of us Christians need to do— identify and develop the gifts and callings God has given us. We are not all the same. A rare few are multi-instrumentalists. The process continues throughout our "career" but at some moment we begin "performing" in public. In my earlier Parts One and Two I described my own discovery of my calling and voice, especially from age eighteen to thirty-three.

Secondly, good jazz depends a lot on "knowing the standards." Jazz performers need to know Caravan, Take the A-Train, Autumn Leaves, Body and Soul, Billie's Bounce, It Could Happen to You, Misty, My Funny Valentine, Green Dolphin Street, Night and Day, The Girl from Ipanema, I'll Be Seeing You . . . and others. The catalog is not fixed and it can vary from one genre of jazz to another. But I will never forget a great night at Oakland's Yoshi's Jazz Club when we were to hear Hammond B-3 ace Joey DeFrancesco play with (I think it was) French gypsy-jazz guitarist Bireli Lagrene. This promised to be an awesome combination. But a couple days before the concert we heard that visa issues forced Lagrene to withdraw. No problem, Yoshi's announced, the legendary Kenny Burrell would replace him. But when we arrived for the concert it was announced that Burrell had taken ill and would not be appearing after all. Instead, local guitarist Mimi Fox would sit in. When Joey led off with Caravan I wondered how it would go. Then Joey kicked the solo over to Mimi and she absolutely tore the house down with some inspired playing. At the ecstatic finish, Joey, who had never met Mimi before that very moment, just shook his head in amazement and said to the audience "How can this happen? It's the standards." Knowing her instrument as she did and knowing the basic structure of the standard tune, made this incendiary performance possible.

And so it is in the Christian life: we need to know our "standards." That means knowing the life and teaching of Jesus, knowing the Bible, especially its classic texts like the Decalogue, Psalm 23, the Sermon on the Mount, the Lord's Prayer, the Love Chapter (I Corinthians 13), the Faith Chapter (Hebrews 11), and so on. And shouldn't we also know the Apostles Creed and the hymn Amazing Grace? These are our standards, the truth and the anchor of our Christian faith. This is why I have spent so much of my life reading and studying the Bible. I have always wanted to understand and communicate an ethics that is deeply, organically, and integrally biblical. That is where the power and insight will come from. Biblical illiteracy is a scourge on the Christian community.

Third, jazz depends on improvisation. Improvisation is about making the tune your own, freely expressing it in your own way for this moment. Composition has its place but jazz is fundamentally about improvisation on an already existing theme.

Jazz is not about "woodenly" sticking to repetition of an exact script but about playing with it, teasing out its possibilities, finding new ways of bringing meaning to it. And isn't that true of the Christian faith? Christianity is not about wooden repetition—nor about writing our own standards. It is about personalizing and contextualizing the standard God has composed into a living reality. This has been my goal: to find new and dynamic ways of interpreting and applying biblical truth for contemporary discipleship, not just in the church but in politics and the workplace.

Fourth, while a jazz solo performance can be wonderful, it is the jazz ensemble which is for me the great metaphor for the Christian life. Unlike some other musical forms that keep the spotlight on the megastar leader, jazz ensembles "pass the lead" from one player to another. The big name might be Oscar Peterson or Dave Brubeck but in performance, Oscar or Dave will play the lead role for a while, then back off and the guitarist will "solo" or play the lead while Oscar plays softly and supportively underneath, then it is over to the bass, then to the drummer—each time the other players are providing a supportive background, until it all circles back to a rousing finish together. Sometimes one or another of the players is new on the scene but they get the same kind of support. Isn't this a beautiful metaphor, "the way it should be," in what we call "the body of Christ and its members"? Christianity is about playing together as an ensemble, not about megastars but about each of us contributing our bit when it is our turn. I have always tried to build teams in my life and work, help the members develop, give them space to grow and contribute, and lead the cheers for their solos. It's about church as a jazz ensemble.

Fifth, jazz ensembles interact with their audiences—sometimes even inviting their participation, singing and clapping along. Unlike classical performers, jazz musicians actually and intentionally interact with the audience. Audiences usually clap in the middle of a tune for each of the solos and sometimes call out or groan or cheer in various ways. As Christians we are "performing" for God as our audience above all. But shouldn't we also be paying attention to those who are watching and listening, to our "audience"? Are they with us, are we communicating with them—our neighbors, family members, friends? Or are we oblivious and uncaring, lost in our own little pious world? To me this has been critical. It's why I didn't just teach in a seminary, I worked with people of all types in the church. It's why I didn't just teach in the MBA classroom but got out and worked in the trenches with businesses of all types. I want to know and connect with the audience.

Sixth, I love how "universal" jazz is. What I mean is that you can find jazz played by all nationalities, all age groups, and on all instruments around the world. Jazz grew out of the American Black experience, which must be honored and for which we thank God. But jazz audiences as well as performers are the most ethnically-integrated of all musical genres. Part of the joy of being a jazz fan is hanging out in such a gloriously, joyously diverse crowd. Isn't that what God intends for Christianity? "Many will come from east and west, north and south . . ." In the New Jerusalem "they will bring the glory of the nations into it" (Revelation 21:24–26). Jazz is not owned by just one people, one nationality—it is loved and played around the world among virtually all nations who each put their special stamp on it. So too, even though we honor its Jewish roots, Christianity is not an Israeli or a western religion but a crossroads, universal faith around the globe. We worship the God who created everybody in his own image and likeness (but each with their own unique character and value), a Savior who died for the sins of the whole world, who loves and wishes to set free every man, woman, and child.

And, seventh, jazz speaks to every possible emotion and experience of life. There is jazz for romance, for melancholy, for lament, for dancing, for the blues—it is all represented and expressed. And I love that about Christianity. We follow a Lord who has endured all the temptations and trials of life. Christianity is about mountaintop experiences of joy and about walking through the valley of the shadow of death. It is a faith for everyone and every experience of life. So my faith is a kind of "faithjazz." The analogy and metaphor are imperfect. My performance has been imperfect. But I'll keep on playing.

MARGINAL ACTIVIST

So the end is near (of my memoir). Again, my reason for writing this is first of all personal: I wanted to look back and reflect on "all the way the Lord our God led me," tested and tried me, blessed me and protected me. My feeling is one of gratitude for the whole story. I love the old Gospel song "We've come this far by faith, leaning on the Lord, trusting in his holy Word. He's never failed me yet."

I also wanted to tell the story to my kids and my six grandkids: "This story is about part of your roots. I hope you will all come to love the Lord our God with all your heart, soul, mind, and strength, and your neighbor as yourself, like your grandpa and grandma tried to do. I expect you will follow other paths and find other callings than mine but I hope and pray you follow the same Lord and experience the same blessings."

For my students, colleagues, neighbors, and friends—as well as strangers I have never met—maybe this will explain some of what you experienced or heard about me or about the events and movements I describe. For every reader, I hope my story will encourage you. When you see a challenge or problem or opportunity, I hope you will not just stand there looking, but get up and do something about it with God's help.

I know well the reminder that we are "human beings" not "human doings." Cute phrase. I get it and agree that character is more fundamental than behavior. I have often enough preached on Psalm 23 and pointed out that the opening declaration "The Lord is my Shepherd, I shall not want (lack anything)" is immediately followed by "He makes me lie down in green pastures . . . he leads me by quiet waters . . . he restores my soul." Only with that sort of contemplative, soul-shaping foundation are we ready for the next challenge in the Psalm—"He leads me in paths of righteousness/justice."

Yes, with my personality, I probably would have skipped right over the green pastures and quiet waters to that active life of pursuing righteousness and justice—and I would have been terribly wrong. We can't truly see, much less achieve, justice (good ethics!) if we don't begin in a quiet, humble, centering of ourselves under God's care.

Still, as Jesus said, "by their fruits you shall know them." "Why do you call me Lord, Lord, and do not do what I say?" James says that "faith without works is dead." So "being" is critical and foundational to "doing" but it is not either/or. I often told my classes that ethics is "Do-Be-Do-Be-Do"—see, it is about faith jazz! Yes, my dad's challenge was "What Are You Doing About It?"—not "How Are You Being today?" But my dad also taught (and modeled) the importance of quiet time, character, and one's walk and talk with God. Without that I knew I would go wrong or run out of gas or both. My friend Bernie Adeney recently told me he felt he had been "striving" all his life and it was time to stop. I think there is a lot of wisdom there. "Doing" with less "striving" and "stress"? Can I manage that?

I feel a little exhausted after writing this review of my life. I have worked so hard and done so much. It is very humbling to look back and realize that, while a few of my dozens of initiatives endure, a lot more lasted for a while but came to an end at some point. Other ideas and initiatives of mine never got off the ground because of bad timing, resistant leadership, lack of funding, or my mistakes. Some were sabotaged or failed by others, usually from ignorance and fear. You have heard the joke that the "Seven Last Words of the Church" are "We Never Did It That Way Before." Truth. Of course, some of my ideas and proposals were unrealistic or otherwise inadequate (though this is still hard for me to accept—usually!).

In the end, only God will be the judge of what in my life is "wood, hay, and stubble" needing to be incinerated, and what might be more like "gold and silver" worth keeping. Long ago I chose to live in accountability to God rather than to any other authorities or powers trying to take God's place in my life. I look back and see lots of mistakes and some failures and I regret the pain I have caused anyone, especially my wife and family. I am proud and thankful for the good things I was part of, the answers to questions, the help to the hurting, the responses to need and opportunity. The best and most enduring result of all is in the people I have known and helped—and been helped and loved by in return.

In looking back and even around me now, I see myself and my work as "marginal," not mainstream, not path-breaking, not major, maybe not often enduring. But it was to the margins of society, church, marketplace, and academy that I was called to serve and for which I was equipped. There I discovered and raised my voice. There I didn't just stand and watch but got busy. There I spent my life as an irrepressible activist, never forgetting my dad's challenge "What Are You Doing About It?"

Curriculum Vita

PERSONAL INFORMATION

Born: 2 February 1946 (Omaha, Nebraska)

Married: 9 September 1967 to Lucia Lynn Paulson

Two Children, Six Grandchildren

Hometown: Oakland, California

Web site: www.DavidWGill.org

FORMAL EDUCATION

1964 Diploma, San Leandro (California) High School

1968 BA (History), University of California, Berkeley

1969 Standard Secondary Teaching Credential, UC Berkeley School of Education

1971 MA (History), San Francisco State University

1979 PhD (Religion/Social Ethics), University of Southern California

PROFESSIONAL EXPERIENCE (REVERSE ORDER)

Current: Writer/speaker on (1) Christian ethics and (2) workplace ethics in a diverse world. Executive Director, Workplace 313 (www.wp313.org) (Oakland, California)

2010–16 Mockler-Phillips Professor of Workplace Theology & Ethics; Director, Mockler Center for Faith & Ethics in the Workplace, Gordon-Conwell Theological Seminary (South Hamilton & Boston, Massachusetts)

2011–12 Interim Pastor, Trinitarian Congregational Church (Wayland, Massachusetts)

2003–11 Organizational ethics consultant and trainer (www.EthixBix.com); Clients: Harris & Associates (Concord, California), Nikon Precision, Paradise Foods, East Bay Municipal Utility District, Marin Leadership Foundation, Westminster House, Santa Clara Water District, Kaiser-Permanente

2001–11 Lecturer/program leader: Commonwealth Club, Society of Human Resource Professionals, American Marketing Association, Beta Gamma Sigma, American Association of Healthcare Administrative Management, Silicon Valley Public Relations Society, Contra Costa Council, Tri-Valley Human Resources Commission, Rotary Clubs in Alameda & Richmond; Chamber of Commerce in Lafayette, others. Multiple business schools

2004–10 Visiting Professor of Business Ethics, Faculty/Alumni Liaison, MBA Alumni Association, St. Mary's College Graduate School of Business (Moraga, California)

2002–07 Visiting/Adjunct Professor of Ethics. Seattle Pacific University Graduate School of Business, University of San Francisco Graduate School of Business, San Jose State University, Fuller Theological Seminary

1998–2003 Co-founder & Co-Director, Institute for Business, Technology, & Ethics; Co-editor and columnist, *Ethix* magazine (www.ethix.org) (Seattle, Washington)

1992–2001 Carl I. Lindberg Professor of Applied Ethics, Director, Ethics-Across-the-Curriculum, North Park University (Chicago, Illinois)

1999 (fall) Visiting Professor, Södra Vätterbygdens Folkhögskola (Jönköping, Sweden)

1994–95 J. Omar Good Distinguished Visiting Professor, Juniata College (Huntingdon, Pennsylvania)

1990–92 Interim Senior Pastor, University Covenant Church (Davis, California)

1977–90 Founding Project Director, Board Chairman, & Instructor in Ethics, 1977–79; Dean & Assistant Professor of Christian Ethics, 1979–82; Dean & Associate Professor, 1982–86; President & Professor, 1986–90. New College for Advanced Christian Studies (Berkeley, California)

1973–75 Instructor in Christian Ethics & Church History, Culver City Bible School (Culver City, California)

1971–73 Co-editor, *Right On/Radix Magazine*; Founding Director & Instructor in History & Ethics, The Crucible: A Center for Radical Christian Studies. Christian World Liberation Front (Berkeley, California)

1969–72 Social Studies & Math teacher, John Muir Junior High School (San Leandro, California)

1964–68 Factory laborer (part-time), Crown Zellarbach Flexible Packaging Factory (San Leandro, California).

SELECTED PUBLICATIONS

Note: *This section excludes most book reviews, many smaller notes and articles, most translations of my work, and six extended writing/editing projects (in chronological order):*

1. *Straight to You* (1967–71), editor, author of short essays, forty-four issues of mimeographed publication for Alameda County Juvenile Hall inmates

2. *Right On/Radix.* Co-editor (1971–73), Contributing Editor (1973–90). Fifty "Radical Christian" columns (1972–79), many reviews, essays, interviews

3. *The Ellul Forum for the Critique of Technological Civilization* (semi-annual journal of International Jacques Ellul Society) (1988–present), contributor and editorial board member; (2003–present), publisher and frequent essayist and reviewer (www.ellul.org)

4. *Ethix Magazine.* (bimonthly bulletin of the Institute for Business, Technology, and Ethics), co-founder, co-editor, thirty "Benchmark Ethics" columns; book reviewer, interviewer (1998–2003), (www.ethix,org)

5. *EthixBizine Monthly.* (2007–10) editor/writer, thirty issues of monthly e-zine sent to 1700 business leaders; with Benchmark Ethics columns, reviews, "Ask Dr. EthixBiz" business ethics case analyses www.ethixbiz.com.

6. *The 313.* (2020–present). Editor/writer for monthly/bimonthly e-zine sent to 1200 readers interested in faith at work; essays, reviews, resources (www.wp313.org)

BOOKS (IN REVERSE CHRONOLOGICAL ORDER)

What Are You Doing About It? The Memoir of A Marginal Activist (Eugene, Oregon: Wipf & Stock, 2022)
Workplace Discipleship 101: A Primer (Peabody, Massachusetts: Hendrickson, 2020)
Political Illusion & Reality: Engaging the Prophet Insights of Jacques Ellul. Edited with David Lovekin (Eugene, Oregon: Wipf & Stock, 2018)
It's About Excellence: Building Ethically Healthy Organizations (Eugene, Oregon: Wipf & Stock, 2008/2011)
Doing Right: Practicing Ethical Principles (Downers Grove, Illinois: InterVarsity, 2004; Eugene, Oregon: Wipf & Stock, 2022)
Becoming Good: Building Moral Character (Downers Grove, Illinois: InterVarsity, 2000; Eugene, Oregon: Wipf & Stock, 2022)
Should God Get Tenure? Essays on Religion & Higher Education, editor (Grand Rapids: Eerdmans, 1997; Eugene, Oregon: Wipf & Stock, 2020)
The Opening of the Christian Mind (Downers Grove, Illinois: InterVarsity, 1989; Eugene, Oregon: Wipf & Stock, 2022).
Peter The Rock: Extraordinary Insights from an Ordinary Man (Downers Grove, Illinois: InterVarsity, 1986; Eugene, Oregon: Wipf & Stock, 2019)

The Word of God in the Ethics of Jacques Ellul (Metuchen, New Jersey: Scarecrow Press, 1984; Eugene, Oregon: Wipf & Stock, 2022)

SELECTED ESSAYS, CHAPTERS, INTRODUCTIONS (IN REVERSE CHRONOLOGICAL ORDER)

"Jacques Ellul's View of Scripture," in Jacob Marques Rollison, ed., *Jacques Ellul and the Bible: Toward A Hermeneutic of Freedom* (Eugene, Oregon: Wipf & Stock, 2020), 17–28.

"The Political Theology of Jacques Ellul," in David Gill & David Lovekin, eds., *Political Illusion & Reality: Engaging the Prophetic Insights of Jacques Ellul* (Eugene, Oregon: Wipf & Stock, 2018), 67–88.

"Introduction to Jacques Ellul's Life & Thought," in Jacques Ellul, *Presence in the Modern World* (Eugene, Oregon: Wipf & Stock, 2016), 107–112.

"The First Word on Business," with Al Erisman in *Christian Business Review* (Issue 5, Fall 2016), 22–31.

"Foreword," to Jacques Ellul, *Islam & Judeo-Christianity: A Critique of their Commonality* (Eugene, Oregon: Wipf &Stock, 2015), vii-xi.

"Foreword," to Jacques Ellul, *If You Are the Son of God: The Suffering & Temptations of Jesus* (Eugene, Oregon: Wipf & Stock, 2014), vii-viii.

"Who Then is the Faithful & Wise Leader?" in Susan S. Phillips & Soo-inn Tan, eds., *Serving God's Community* (Singapore: Graceworks, 2014), 67–84.

"L'Importance durable de Jacques Ellul pour l'éthique des affaires" in Patrick Troude-Chastenet, ed., *Comment peut-on (encore) etre ellulien au xxi siècle* (Paris: La Table Ronde, 2014), 113–132.

"The Enduring Importance of Jacques Ellul for Business Ethics," *Ellul Forum* Issue 52 (July 2013).

"Eight Traits of an Ethically Healthy Culture: Insights from the Beatitudes." *Journal of Markets & Morality*, Volume 16, Number 2 (Fall 2013): 615–633.

"A Theology of Care for the Vulnerable" chapter in Arthur Ammann, ed., *Women, HIV, and the Church* (Eugene, Oregon: Wipf & Stock, 2012), 62–80.

"Jacques Ellul & Technology's Trade-off," *Comment Magazine* (Spring 2012), 51–58.

"A Fourth Use of the Law? The Decalogue in the Workplace," *The Journal of Religion and Business Ethics,* Journal 2, Issue 2 (September 2011), 1–18.

"Ethics in the Workplace," *Contact Magazine* (November 2010), 14–16.

"Upgrading the Ethical Decision-Making Model for Business," *Business & Professional Ethics Journal* 23.4 (2005).

"Business Ethics," *Encyclopedia of Science, Technology, and Ethics* (Macmillan Reference, 2005), Vol 1, 272–281.

"Jacques Ellul's Ethics: Legacy and Promise," in Patrick Troude-Chastenet, *Jacques Ellul: Penseur sans frontières* (Le Bouscat, France: L'Esprit du temps, 2005), 61–77.

"Finding Common Moral Ground in An Age of Diversity & Conflict," *Radix Magazine (May 2005)*

"Misleadership on Business Ethics: John Maxwell," *Books and Culture* (March-April 2004).

"Modern Technology: Servant and Master," *Radix Magazine* 30.2 (2003): 4–7, 22–24.

"Ten Principles of Highly Ethical People," *Radix Magazine* 29 (2002).

"Managing Corporate Knowledge," *Bridges: An Interdisciplinary Journal of Theology, Philosophy, History, and Science* 9:3/4 (Fall/Winter 2001). Co-author with Albert Erisman.

"The Technological Blind Spot in Business Ethics," *Bulletin of Science, Technology & Society,* 19.3 (June 1999):190–98.

"Prolegomena for a Theology of Technology," *Bridges: An Interdisciplinary Journal of Theology, Philosophy, History, & Science,* 5.3/4 (Fall/Winter 1998): 155–173.

"Ethics With and Without God" in David W. Gill, editor, *Should God Get Tenure? Essays on Religion & Higher Education* (Eerdmans, 1997; Wipf & Stock, 2020), 129–146.

"Educating for Meaning & Morality: The Contribution of Technology" *Bulletin of Science, Technology, and Society* 17.5–6 (1997): 249–260.

Articles in *The Complete Book of Everyday Christianity*, R. Banks & P. Stevens, eds. (InterVarsity, 1997) "Power/Workplace" (781–783), "System" (997–999), "Technology" (1011–1019).

Articles in the *New Dictionary of Christian Ethics & Pastoral Theology*, edited by David Atkinson and David Field (InterVarsity, 1995), «Ellul» (337–38), «Fraud,» (392–93), «Hope,» (455–57), «Violence,» (875–79).

"The Moral Character of Means and Ends," *The Real Issue,* 14.2 (Nov-Dec 1995), 4–7.

"My Journey with Ellul," *The Ellul Forum,* No. 13 (Jul 1994), 7–8.

"Interview with Jacques Ellul on Vocation & the Ethics of the Workplace," *Radix Magazine,* 22.4 (Summer 94): 10–13, 28–29.

"Whatever Happened to Karl Marx?" *Radix Magazine,* 21.1 (1992): 8–9, 26.

"Jacques Ellul," in J.D. Douglas, ed., *New 20th Century Encyclopedia of Religious Knowledge*. 2nd ed. (Baker, 1991) 294–295.

Interviewed by Jeff Dietrich, "Engaging the Technological Phenomena," *Catholic Agitator,* 20.5 (Jun 1990): 4–5.

"Foreword," to Daniel B. Clendenin, *Theological Method in Jacques Ellul* (University Press, 1987), xiii-xiv.

"Why Isn't Christendom More Christian?" (review essay on Jacques Ellul, *La Subversion du christianisme*, l984), *Fides et Historia* 17.2 (Spr-Sum 85):70–77.

"Foreword," to Jacques Ellul, *Money and Power* (InterVarsity, 1984), 5–8.

"Interview with Jacques Ellul," (1982 interviews in Bordeaux), *Radix Magazine,* 15.4 (Jan-Feb 84): 4–7, 28.

"Jacques Ellul: Answers from a Man who asks Hard Questions. An Interview with Jacques Ellul" (l982 interviews in Bordeaux), *Christianity Today* 28.7 (Apr 20, 1984): 16–21.

"Introduction," to Jacques Ellul, *Living Faith* (Harper & Row, 1983), xi.-xvi.

"Violence and the Spirit of Technology," *Radix Magazine* 14.5 (Mar-Apr 83): 3–5.

"Introduction" to Jacques Ellul, *In Season, Out of Season* (Harper & Row, 1982), v.-xiii.

"Jacques Ellul's View of Scripture," *Journal of the Evangelical Theological Society,* 25.4 (Dec 82): 467–478.

"Bibliography: The Works of Jacques Ellul," in Clifford Christians and Jay Van Hook, editors, *Jacques Ellul: Interpretive Essays* (Champaign: University of Illinois Press, 1981), 309–328.

"Jacques Ellul and Francis Schaeffer: Two Views of Western Civilization," *Fides et Historia,* 13.2 (Spr-Sum 81):23–37.

"Jacques Ellul: The Prophet as Theologian," *Themelios* (London) 7.l (Sep 81): 4–14.

"Eros and Narcissus on Trial" (review essay on *The Betrayal of the West* by Jacques Ellul & *The Culture of Narcissism* by Christopher Lasch), *Reformed Journal,* 30.9 (Sep 80): 26–29.

MAJOR LECTURES & PRESENTATIONS

Note: *This section excludes hundreds of interviews, sermons, conference, retreat and chapel talks, and in-house presentations for my educational and business employers.*

"Scripture & Word in Jacques Ellul's Writings," plenary address, IJES Biennial Conference, Regent College, 28 June 2018.

"From Faith at Work 101 to 201," plenary address, Faith@Work Summit II, Dallas, October 2016

"The Political Theology of Jacques Ellul," plenary address, IJES Biennial Conference, Berkeley, 6 July 2016

"Light A Candle," Baccalaureate Address, Gordon-Conwell Seminary, 6 May 2016.

"Ten Good Reasons to Manage A Project in an Ethical Manner," Project Management Association, Charlotte, North Caolina, 26 September 2015

"Business Ethics: From Damage Control to Mission Control?" plenary address, Faith@Work Summit I, Boston, 12 October 2014

"On Educating & Being Educated: Technique, Technology, Trade-offs, & Tactics," plenary address, IJES Biennial Conf, Ottawa, 14 July 2014

"Eight Traits of an Ethically Healthy Culture: Insights from the Beatitudes" Evangelical Theological Society Annual Meeting, Milwaukee, 14 November 2012

"The Enduring Importance of Jacques Ellul's Thought for Business Ethics," plenary address, IJES Biennial Conf, Wheaton, 9 July 2012

"L'Importance durable de la pensée de Jacques Ellul pour l'éthique des affaires," Bordeaux, 7 June 2012

"Public Company Transparency: What Light is Shed by the 9th Command?" with John Mesher, Center for Christian Business Ethics Today, Annual Conference. Philadelphia, 1 June 2012

"Jacques Ellul on Violence and Revolution" Society of Christian Ethics Annual Meeting, Washington DC, 7 Jan 2012

"Business Ethics 2.0," Point Loma Nazarene Business Center Lecture, 29 June 2010

"Decalogue & Christian Ethics," Koinos Seminar, Vancouver BC, 12 June 2010

"Does Ethics Pay?" Kiros Business Fellowship, Seattle, 30 April 2010

"Integrity in Business" Sandberg Leadership Center, Ashland (Ohio) University, 9 April 2010

"Business Ethics," USC Marshall School of Business (3 lectures), 6 April 2010

"Business Ethics 2.0," Alameda California Rotary Club, 23 March 2010

"Outlines for a Workplace Theology" Gordon-Conwell Faculty Lecture, 3 March 2010

"Accounting Ethics," Institute for Managerial Accounting, Walnut Creek, Caifornia, 23 Feb 2010

"Business Ethics 2.0," Richmond, California, Rotary Club, 19 Feb 2010

"Christian Ethics for Marketplace Disciples," Olivet College, San Francisco, 16 Feb 2010

"A Fourth Use of the Decalogue?" Society of Christian Ethics, Pacific Region, 12 Feb 2010

"God Created Sex," Patten College, Oakland, 9 February 2010

"Recruiting for Character," Marin HR Forum, 16 June 2009

"Six Essentials in Ethical Organizations," Rutland Institute of Ethics, Clemson University, 20 April 2009

"Grounding Business Ethics in Faith & Philosophy," North Park University Annual Lectures, 17 Apr 2009

"Is Ethics A Luxury During An Economic Downturn?" North Park Business Honors Banquet, 16 Apr 2009

"Harris & Associates Business Ethics Case," Western Casewriters Association, Utah, 19 March 2009

"Mission-Controlled Organizational Ethics," Kiros, Bellevue, Washington, 13 Feb 2009

"Is Ethics A Luxury During An Economic Downturn?" Seattle Pacific University, Business Alumni annual reunion, 31 Jan 2009

"Integrity & Ethics," Sandberg Leadership Center, Ashland University, Ashland, Ohio, 16 Jan 2009

"Building Ethically Healthy Organizations," American Association of Hospital Administrative. Management, 7 Nov 2008

"Ethics & Excellence," Project Management Institute plenary lecture, Stanford University, 3 Sept 2008

"Building Ethically Healthy Organizations," Commonwealth Club of California, 6 Aug 2008

"Three Organizational Ethics Lessons" Contra Costa Council Small Business Awards Banquet, 9 May 2008

"Excellence, not Jail Avoidance," Marin HR Forum, 19 Feb 2008.

"Ethical Choices for Today's Business Leaders, plenary lecturer, Sandberg Leadership Center, Ashland University, 2–3 Nov 2006

"Ten Good Reasons to Run a Business in an Ethical Manner," University of Wisconsin Grad School of Business, 6 Oct 2005

"Moral Values in An Age of Diversity & Conflict," Regent College, 3 Mar 2005

"Ethics for Human Resource Directors," two-day workshop for HR directors of El Salvadoran companies, San Salvador, co-sponsored by FEPADE & San Jose State University, 21–22 Jan 2005

"L'Ethique de Jacques Ellul: Heritage et Defi," Colloque internationale, Universite de Poitiers, 21 Oct 2004

"The Role of Character in Corporate Decision-making," plenary address, Wheaton College, 18 Mar 2004

"Rx for Corporate Health," San Jose State University Professional Development Center, 3 Mar 2004

"Six Critical Components of a Healthy Organizational Ethics," American Association of Healthcare Administrative Management, 20 Feb 2004

"Marketing Ethics" Silicon Valley Marketing Association, 12 Nov 2003

"Ten Critical Reasons to Run a Business in An Ethical Manner," Commonwealth Club of California, 30 Oct 2003

"Ethical PR: Non-negotiable for 21st C. Business Success," Silicon Valley Public Relations Society, 10 Sept 2003

"Trust Needs Trustworthy," Contra Costa Council (plenary speech), 23 Jan 2003

"Ten Good Reasons to Run a Business in An Ethical Manner," Tri-Valley Human Resources Commission, 15 Apr 2003; Beta Gamma Sigma Business Honor Society, 15 May 2003

"Rebuilding Corporate Ethics" Small Business Task Force, Contra Costa Council, 23 June 2003

"The Firestone Recall," Association for Practical & Professional Ethics annual meeting (Cincinnati) 2 Mar 2001

"Character as Leadership," (plenary lecture) Skirball Institute annual conference (Los Angeles) 22 May 2001

"Ethics in Business," seminar for small business owners, (Jönköping, Sweden) Nov 1999.

"Mission or Damage Control in Technological Ethics," National Association for Science, Technology, and Society (Baltimore), 5 March 1999

"Teaching Ethics with and without Religion," plenary speaker, Association for the Development of Philosophy Teaching, annual meeting, Benedictine University, 9 April 1999

"The Technological Blindspot in Business Ethics," Fifth Annual International Conference Promoting Business Ethics, DePaul University, 30 October 1998

"Ethical Perspectives on the Technologizing of Business," plenary address, symposium on Technology and Business, Univ. of Washington Graduate School of Business, 24 Oct 1997

"Feasting on the Fruit of the Ethics Tree," Inaugural Lecture, Carl I. Lindberg Chair in Applied Ethics. North Park University, 27 Oct 97

"Educating for Meaning and Morality: The Contribution of Technology," plenary address, international symposium on Education & Technology, Penn State University, 19 Sept. 97

"Five Principles of Ethical Management," New College Berkeley, Saturday Conference, 12 July 97

"The Autonomy of Technology," Penn State University, Science, Technology, & Society program, 18 Nov 1996

"Ethics & Information Technology," Argonne (IL) National Laboratory, 15 Oct 1996

"Justice in Health Care," Swedish Covenant Hospital Ethics Conference, Sept 1995

"Academic Ethics," (2 plenary lectures), University of Pennsylvania, 18 Nov 1995

"The Ethics of the Human Genome Project." plenary lecture, Institute for Advanced Christian Studies Conference, Mundelein, 26 Mar 1995

"Modern Technology: Our Servant or Our Master?" public lecture, Juniata College, 7 Dec 1994

"Ethics Isn't Pretty," public lecture, Oregon State University, 22 Feb 1993

"Approaching Our Disciplines Ethically," (2 lectures) Faculty Conference, Univ. of Illinois, 30 Oct 1993

"Technology, Creativity & Fidelity," C.S. Lewis Summer Institute, Oxford University (UK), 9 Jul 1991

"Is There a place for Christianity in a University Pledged to Pluralism," and "The Burden of Jacques Ellul, University of Wisconsin Ecumenical Lectureship, Madison, 15–16 Apr 1988

"Three Temptations in Today's Business World," Christian Business Leaders' Conference, St. Mary's College, Moraga California, 17 Sep 1988

"The Dialectic of Sociology & Theology in Jacques Ellul's Work," American Academy of Religion Annual Meeting, Chicago, 21 Nov 1988

"Religion in a Post-Modern Era," Religious Studies Colloquium, San Jose State University, 8 Apr 1987

"Information Ethics," American Library Association (FOCLIS), San Francisco, 30 Jun 1987

"Jacques Ellul & the Technological Challenge," American Scientific Affiliation, Santa Barbara, 14 Nov 1987

"Ethics in Business" Visiting Lecturer, St. Mary's College, 13 Feb 1987

"Ethics of Confidentiality," Plenary Lecture, San Jose Christian Counseling Group conference, 8 Apr 1984

"Religious Values and Business Ethics" Plenary Lecture, Marketing Research Association, SF, 16 Feb 1984

"Religious Values in the Secular University" Arizona State University, Sociology Dept. Colloquium, 25 Feb 1983

"Violence and the Spirit of Technology," Sonoma State University Peacemaking Conference, 16 Apr 1983

"War & Peace in the Atomic Age: A Religious Issue," University of California, Davis, 13 Jan 1982

"Technological Ethics & Christian Ethics" Plenary Lecture, American Scientific Affiliation, Berkeley, 20 Feb 1982

"Sociology & Ethics of Jacques Ellul" (3 lectures), Mennonite Brethren Seminary, Fresno, 22–23 Feb 1982

"Comparative Religious Ethics: Preliminary Notes on its Importance for Normative Christian Ethics" Plenary Lecture, Pacific Coast Theological Society, Berkeley, 2 Apr 1982

"Technology & Social Change," California State University, Hayward, Interfaith Conference, 17 Nov 1982

"The Political Theology of Jacques Ellul" and "Institutional Obstetrics: The Birth of New College Berkeley" American Academy of Religion, Western Regional meeting, Berkeley, 28–29 Mar 1980

"Ellul as Prophet" Visiting Lecturer, Trinity Episcopal School, Ambridge, PA, 12 Nov 1979

"Two Views of the West: Ellul & Schaeffer," American Historical Association, San Francisco, 29 Dec 1978

COMMUNITY SERVICE

62nd St (Oakland CA) block association co-leader (2002–2010; 2016 ff)

The International Jacques Ellul Society (Founding President, 2000-)

Swedish Covenant Hospital (Institutional Review Board, 1993–96)

Huntingdon (PA) General Hospital (Medical ethics committee, 1994–95)

Consultant (pro bono) for non-profit educational and social action groups and programs

UNIVERSITY & SEMINARY SERVICE

Gordon-Conwell Theological Seminary (2010–16): Director, Mockler Center for Faith & Ethics in the Workplace

St. Mary's College (2004–2010): Graduate Business Faculty/Alumni liaison (primary strategist and entrepreneur of reborn Graduate Business Alumni Chapters in East Bay, South Bay, San Francisco, and Sacramento; alumni program organizer); frequent guest speaker for Graduate School of Business recruiting, orientation events

North Park University (1992-2001): Director, Ethics-Across-the-Curriculum project; Chair, Faculty Development Committee ; Organizer, Symposium on The Goals of Education at North Park; Bioethics Lectures steering committee; Faculty Research Group committee; Advisory Council, Occupational Therapy Program; Faculty Compensation Committee; Honorary Degrees Committee; founding faculty sponsor, North Park Gospel Choir

New College Berkeley (1976-90): Instigator/catalyst/theoretician/organizer:1976-77; Author/editor of original Articles, Bylaws; Board of Trustees: member, 1977-82, l986-90; Founding Chair, 1977; Member and/or Chair of Executive, Academic Affairs, Personnel, Long Range Planning, Finance committees; Administration: Project Director (1977-79), Dean (1979-86, 88-89), President (1986-90); Academic affairs: curriculum design, faculty recruitment, conference organizer; Author/editor of Faculty & Staff Handbooks, Catalog, brochures, policy statements, space/display ads; Author/coordinator of projects for California State Degree Approval (1982) and WASC self-study eligibility (1984); Financial affairs: Fund-raising, budget formation, financial management, contract negotiations, etc.

Acknowledgments

I THINK I HAVE already made pretty clear my grateful acknowledgement of God's help throughout my life in all of the preceding chapters—living them, and now remembering and writing about them. For their help with this memoir, I want to thank, first and specifically, my wife Lucia who has not only read every page, lived most of them with me, and given me good advice on the memoir (much of which I have followed). Debbie Braithwaite Anderson, Sonia Bodi, Daniel Cerezuelle, Patrick Chastenet, Liz Lismer, Vern Phillips, Scott Thomas, Drew Trotter, Ruqiong Tang Walter, and my three sisters, Dorothy Weise, Kit Faria, and Elizabeth Gill, all read parts of my memoir and gave me helpful corrections where I needed them. Thanks to Keith Criss and Stephen Sparks for help on the photographs and to Keith for the cover art. I owe special thanks to Bernie Adeney for reading it cover to cover and helping me see the larger contours more clearly. Above all, I want to thank Al Erisman for reading it all carefully and really pushing me to the wall on several sections, helping me see things about my life, work, and times that I would otherwise have missed. Finally, I thank all of you who urged me to write this story—and thank you to anybody who reads it. Happy to hear your own stories and thoughts! dwg@davidwgill.org.

"What do workers gain from their toil? I have seen the burden God has laid on the human race. He has made everything beautiful in its time. He has also set eternity in the human heart; yet no one can fathom what God has done from beginning to end. I know that there is nothing better for people than to be happy and to do good while they live. That each of them may eat and drink, and find satisfaction in their work—this is the gift of God. I know that everything God does will endure forever, nothing can be added to it, and nothing taken away."

ECCLESIASTES 3:9–14

Bibliography

Baylis, Robert. *My People: The History of those Christians Sometimes Called Plymouth Brethren*. Wheaton, Ilinois: Harold Shaw, 1995.
Christians, Clifford and Jay Van Hook, editors. *Jacques Ellul: Interpretative Essays*. Champaign: University of Illinois, 1981.
Coad, Roy. *A History of the Brethren Movement*. Grand Rapids: Eerdmans, 1968.
Collins, Jim and Jerry Porras. *Built To Last: Successful Habits of Visionary Companies*. San Francisco: Harper Business, 1994.
Cotherman, Charles E.. *To Think Christianly: A History of L'Abri, Regent College, and the Christian Study Center Movement*. Downers Grove, Illinois: InterVarsity, 2020.
Durnbaugh, Donald F.. *The Believers' Church: The History and Character of Radical Protestantism*. New York: Macmillan, 1968.
Ellul, Jacques. *The Ethics of Freedom*. Grand Rapids: Eerdmans, 1976.
———. *False Presence of the Kingdom*. New York: Seabury, 1972.
———. *The Humiliation of the Word*. Grand Rapids: Eerdmans, 1985.
———. *In Season, Out of Season. Interviews with Madeleine Garrigou-LaGrange*. San Francisco: Harper & Row, 1982.
———. *Jacques Ellul on Politics, Technology, and Christianity: Conversations with Patrick Troude-Chastenet*. Eugene, Oregon: Wipf & Stock, 2005.
———. *The Meaning of the City*. Grand Rapids: Eerdmans, 1970.
———. *The New Demons*. New York: Seabury, 1975.
———. *The Political Illusion*. New York: Knopf, 1967.
———. *The Politics of God and the Politics of Man*. Grand Rapids: Eerdmans, 1972.
———. *Presence in the Modern World*. Eugene: Wipf & Stock, 2016. Previously published as *The Presence of the Kingdom*. New York: Seabury, 1967.
———. *Propaganda: The Formation of Men's Attitudes*. New York: Knopf, 1965.
———. *The Technological Society*. New York: Knopf, 1964.
———. *To Will and To Do: An Ethical Research for Christians*. Philadelphia: Pilgrim, 1969.
———. *What I Believe*. Grand Rapids: Eerdmans, 1989.
Ellwood, Robert S., Jr.. *One Way: The Jesus Movement and Its Meaning*. Englewood Cliffs, New Jersey: Prentice-Hall, 1973.
Enroth, Ronald M., Edward E. Ericson, Jr., and C. Breckenridge Peters. *The Jesus People: Old Time Religion in the Age of Aquarius*. Grand Rapids: Eerdmans, 1972.
Eskridge, Larry. *God's Forever Family: The Jesus People Movement in America*. New York: Oxford, 2013.
Gill, David W. *Becoming Good: Building Moral Character*. Downers Grove, Illinois: InterVarsity, 2000; Eugene, Oregon: Wipf & Stock, 2022

Bibliography

———. *Doing Right: Practicing Ethical Principles*. Downers Grove, Illinois: InterVarsity, 2004; Eugene, Oregon: Wipf & Stock, 2022.

———. *It's about Excellence: Building Ethically Healthy Organizations*. Eugene, Oregon: Wipf & Stock, 2008/2011.

———. "Jacques Ellul: The Prophet as Theologian" in *Themelios* (7.1 September 1981) 4–14.

———. *The Opening of the Christian Mind*. Downers Grove, Illinois: InterVarsity, 1989; Eugene, Oregon: Wipf & Stock, 2022.

———. *Peter The Rock: Extraordinary Insights from an Ordinary Man*. Downers Grove, Illinois: InterVarsity, 1986; Eugene, Oregon: Wipf & Stock, 2019.

———. editor. *Should God Get Tenure? Essays on Religion & Higher Education*. Grand Rapids: Eerdmans, 1997; Eugene, Oregon: Wipf & Stock, 2020.

———. *The Word of God in the Ethics of Jacques Ellul*. Metuchen, New Jersey: Scarecrow Press, 1984; Eugene, Oregon: Wipf & Stock, 2022.

———. *Workplace Discipleship 101: A Primer*. Peabody, Massachusetts: Hendrickson, 2020.

Gill, David W. and David Lovekin, editors, *Political Illusion and Reality: Engaging the Prophetic Insights of Jacques Ellul*. Eugene, Oregon: Wipf & Stock, 2018.

Gitlin, Todd. *The Sixties: Years of Hope, Days of Rage*. New York: Bantam, 1987.

Hearn, Virginia, editor. *What They Did Right: Reflections on Parents by Their Children*. Wheaton, Illinois: Tyndale House, 1974.

Keillor, Garrison. *Lake Wobegon Days*. New York: Penguin, 1985.

Keller, Timothy. *The Reason for God: Belief in an Age of Scepticism*. New York: Penguin, 2008.

Kuhn, Thomas. *The Structure of Scientific Revolutions*. University of Chicago, 1962.

Kurlansky, Mark. *1968: The Year That Rocked the World*. New York: Random House, 2004.

MacIntyre, Alasdair. *After Virtue*. Second edition. University of Notre Dame, 1984.

———. *Three Rival Versions of Moral Enquiry*. University of Notre Dame, 1990.

Malcolm X. *The Autobiography of Malcom X*. New York: Grove, 1964.

Moberg, Vilhelm. *The Emigrants*. Four volumes. St. Paul, Minnesota: Borealis, 1949–1959.

Newbegin, Leslie. *Foolishness to the Greeks: The Gospel and Western Culture*. Grand Rapids: Eerdmans, 1986.

———. *The Gospel in a Pluralist Society*. Grand Rapids: Eerdmans, 1989.

Pinnock, Clark. *Set Forth Your Case: An Examination of Christianity's Credentials*. Chicago: Moody, 1971.

Quebedeaux, Richard. *The Young Evangelicals*. San Francisco: Harper & Row, 1974.

Rollison, Jacob Marques, editor, *Jacques Ellul and the Bible: Towards a Hermeneutic of Freedom*. Eugene, Oregon: Wipf & Stock, 2020.

Roszak, Theodore. *The Making of a Counterculture: Reflections on the Technocratic Society and Its Youthful Opposition*. Garden City, New York: Anchor, 1969.

Schaeffer, Francis A.. *The God Who Is There: Speaking Historic Christianity into the Twentieth Century*. Downers Grove, Illinois: InterVarsity, 1968.

Sparks, Jack. *God's Forever Family*. Grand Rapids: Zondervan, 1975.

Strobel, Lee. *The Case for Christ: A Journalist's Personal Investigation of the Evidence for Jesus*. Grand Rapids: Zondervan, 1998.

Swartz, David R.. *Moral Minority: The Evangelical Left in an Age of Conservatism*. University of Pennsylvania, 2012.

Wangerin, Walter. *As For Me and My House: Crafting Your Marriage to Last*. Nashville: Thomas Nelson, 1990.

www.ingramcontent.com/pod-product-compliance
Lightning Source LLC
Chambersburg PA
CBHW080722300426
44114CB00019B/2458